# HOME RULE

# HOME RULE

## AN IRISH HISTORY, 1800–2000

ALVIN JACKSON

Weidenfeld & Nicolson
LONDON

First published in Great Britain in 2003
by Weidenfeld & Nicolson

A CIP catalogue record for this book
is available from the British Library.

ISBN 0 184212 724 1

Typeset by Selwood Systems, Midsomer Norton

Printed in Great Britain by Butler & Tanner Ltd,
Frome and London


Weidenfeld & Nicolson

The Orion Publishing Group Ltd
Orion House
5 Upper Saint Martin's Lane
London, WC2H 9EA

# CONTENTS

## AUTHOR'S NOTE

Names are contentious, and a short note on nomenclature is clearly necessary in a work of this kind. Generally I have called places, parties and churches by the names that are in popular usage. I have used 'Derry' for the city, where there has for long been a predominantly Catholic population which favours this name: I have used 'Londonderry' for the county, where there is a Unionist majority which (equally) prefers this version. I have often deployed 'Stormont' as a general label for the devolved government which ruled Northern Ireland between 1921 and 1972, even though the parliament buildings on the Stormont estate were opened only in 1932. I have used 'Belfast Agreement' and 'Good Friday Agreement' interchangeably, in referring to the arrangements struck in 1998.

# ABBREVIATIONS

| | |
|---|---|
| AIA | Anglo-Irish Agreement |
| BIC | British-Irish Council |
| DUP | Democratic Unionist Party |
| GAA | Gaelic Athletic Association |
| GLC | Greater London Council |
| GOC | General Officer Commanding |
| HRL | Home Rule League |
| IFS | Irish Free State |
| INLA | Irish National Liberation Army |
| IPP | Irish Parliamentary Party |
| IRA | Irish Republican Army |
| LVF | Loyalist Volunteer Force |
| NI | Northern Ireland |
| NIO | Northern Ireland Office |
| NSMC | North-South Ministerial Council |
| PIRA | Provisional Irish Republican Army |
| PR | Proportional Representation |
| PRONI | Public Record Office of Northern Ireland |
| ROI | Republic of Ireland |
| RTE | Radio Telefís Éireann |
| RUC | Royal Ulster Constabulary |
| SDLP | Social Democratic and Labour Party |
| UDA | Ulster Defence Association |
| UFF | Ulster Freedom Fighters |
| UIL | United Irish League |
| UUC | Ulster Unionist Council |
| UUUC | United Ulster Unionist Council |
| UVF | Ulster Volunteer Force |
| UWC | Ulster Workers' Council |

For Olivia

# ACKNOWLEDGEMENTS

I have accumulated many scholarly debts in working on this volume, and I am glad at last to acknowledge the help, patience and kindness which I have been shown. A number of friends read through a draft of the work, and offered their reflections and criticism: Seán Connolly, Peter Jupp, and Patrick Maume. Jon Jackson and Georgina Capel have been consistently supportive and helpful. I am grateful for the support of colleagues in the School of History and Faculty of Arts at Queen's University Belfast: I cannot fail to mention Ian Green who, as head of department between 1998 and 2001, offered great encouragement. Some early work on the project was undertaken during a year spent as Burns Visiting Professor at Boston College: I am grateful to Kevin O'Neill and Bob O'Neill for their invitation, and to Rob Savage and many other Bostonian friends for support. I remember with affection Adele Dalsimer, whose passing remains a matter of great sadness for all in the Irish Studies community.

I have undertaken work for this volume in a number of libraries and archives. I am grateful for the patience of archivists at the Bodleian Library, the Burns Library of Boston College, the Library of Trinity College Dublin, the Linenhall Library, Belfast, the National Library of Ireland, the Public Record Office at Kew, the Public Record Office of Northern Ireland.

I am grateful to numerous individuals and institutions for access to manuscript materials, and for permission to quote relevant passages: the Bonham-Carter Trustees and the Bodleian Library, the Clerk of the Records, the House of Lord Record Office, acting on behalf of the Beaverbrook Foundation Trust, the Deputy Keeper, Public Record Office of Northern Ireland, and the Librarian of *The Spectator*. To owners of manuscripts or copyright whom I have been unable to locate, or whom I have omitted through oversight, I offer my apologies.

The British Academy has supported my work since my days as a research student. In 2000 the Academy awarded me a Research Readership in the Humanities, which brought two years of liberation from teaching and administration. Without this backing, much of the research which underpins the middle and later sections of the volume would not have been undertaken. I am grateful to those responsible for the Research Reader competition: I am grateful, in particular, to Ken Emond, for his unremitting good humour and encouragement. This book is part of a larger project on modern Irish political history: I hope that (whatever its failings) the work will prove to be an acceptable initial return on the confidence which has been invested.

The work is dedicated to Olivia, and to the grandmother who loved her.

AJ

# CHAPTER 1

# SHARED HISTORIES

Barricaded in his Georgian town house, a 65-year-old depressive watched anxiously from his windows as the ripples from nearby street-fighting lapped up against his doorstep. Normally proactive, he was compelled to spectate; normally punctilious, he lost track of time. The crack of rifle fire, and the pounding of field guns, meant that sleep was impossible: the barriers between night and day were breached. Food was in short supply, and the carefully observed rituals of dining broke down. Whispered rumours hinted at obscene murders and a countryside in revolt: lies and hyperbole governed in the place of truth. Apparently fixed landmarks were obliterated in the fighting. The social order tottered: familiar figures in society had had their brains blown out, and streams of looters carried off their plunder with a brazen confidence.[1]

John Dillon, the deputy leader of the Irish Home Rule movement, was the spectator here, and this was the outlook from his home in North Great George's Street, Dublin, during the Easter Rising of April 1916. Since the 1870s Dillon had helped to lead the struggle for Home Rule, and for at least the four years since 1912 he had been treated as a key figure within the impending devolved administration. But Home Rule was a promise that was never realised, and Dillon, who had teetered on the threshold of ministerial grandeur, was pulled back into the margins by a new generation of militants. His plight might serve as a metaphor for the broader condition of the political cause that he had helped to lead. Home Rule retained a rasping hold on electoral life after the Easter Rising, but to all intents and purposes the cause was corralled into a metaphorical Great George's Street while the real action was played out elsewhere.

Fifty-six years later and a hundred miles to the north, dejected men in grey suits politely jostled for position as they shuffled out on to a high balcony and into the view of their fellow citizens. A short, dapper figure with a crooked smile and an unconvincing manner clutched a micro-phone and read to the crowd from a crumpled sheet of paper. Flanking

1

him was an ashen-faced 35-year-old, bearing the scars of recent bullet wounds to his cheeks and jaw: to his left stood a tall detached-looking figure, who had dreamt of power and military action, and who dreamt still. Beneath them were arrayed perhaps 100,000 of the confused and dejected, some straining desperately in the hope of being called to the barricades.[2]

On this day, 28 March 1972, the members of the Northern Ireland cabinet, led by the Prime Minister, Brian Faulkner, John Taylor (the victim of an assassination bid by the IRA) and the militant Bill Craig, appeared on the balcony at the Stormont parliament building, Belfast, and addressed a huge gathering of angry loyalists. The occasion was Edward Heath's prorogation of the Northern Irish government and parliament; and though the event was designed to present a united protest to the British, in fact (with the benefit of hindsight) it can be seen as a funeral rite rather than an act of defiance. These were the obsequies of the Unionist state: the men in dark suits and dark ties on the balcony were the chief mourners at the burial of a fifty-year-old experiment in provincial Home Rule. The massive and well-regimented crowd had been brought together in one of the first of numerous acts of loyalist catharsis, occasions characterised by soothing and empathic rhetoric and by the comfort of numbers. But these efforts to preserve the familiar were intrinsically self-defeating; and the true focus of political dynamism within the community lay beyond the straggling ranks of the bewildered. The speakers offered them the hope of a political resurrection and the mystery of the loyalist faith, but in fact Unionist Home Rule remained in the tomb.

At one level the history of Home Rule on the island of Ireland is a history of failure, of high ideals and ambitions together with crushing humiliation and disappointment. Disappointment, perhaps, was inherent in the very concept of Home Rule, for the notion of 'Home Government' or 'Home Rule' was a superb manifestation of Victorian marketing skills, parcelling some negative or ambiguous connotations within a formula redolent of family values and fireside comfort. 'Home Rule' was about mobilising patriotic support in nineteenth-century Ireland for a repeal of the Union with Great Britain. Home Rule was about channelling the varieties of Irish nationalism into a call for the restoration of a limited, devolved legislature in Dublin. Home Rule involved an acceptance (however conditional) by the Irish that Westminster was the supreme or sovereign parliament. In a sense, then, Home Rule was always a triumph of image over substance.

Yet, Home Rule was more than simply an antique propaganda coup or a Victorian political cul-de-sac. Instead it has had a protracted history and a sustained influence within modern Irish and British politics. The

2

Home Rule movement drew upon a legacy of patriotic thought that dated back at least to the late seventeenth century, and which continued to mourn the loss of Ireland's legislative independence through the Act of Union. At the end of the nineteenth century Home Rulers borrowed from, modified and exploited the achievement of earlier Irish constitutional leaders like Daniel O'Connell, who won 'emancipation' for Irish (and British) Catholics in 1829. Home Rule harnessed the energies of a more recent tradition of militant nationalist endeavour, attracting into its ranks those who had fought British rule in the rebellions of 1848 and 1867. The strength of Home Rule, certainly in the 1880s, rested in the fact that it simultaneously provided an alternative to militancy and a refuge for militants.

Home Rule reflected changes in the nature of Irish Catholic society and drew upon them. It provided a political vehicle for propertied Catholic farmers and rural businessmen, whose position had improved relatively in the aftermath of the Great Irish Famine of 1845–51, when smallholders and labourers had been racked by starvation and disease, or driven by despair into the emigrant boats. Home Rule also represented an opportunity for Catholic professionals, whether long-established classes such as doctors and lawyers, or relatively new interest groups such as journalists. Above all Home Rule held out the promise of a new order, when increasingly influential groups such as these would no longer be held back by the constraints of British rule and Protestant predominance.

For almost half a century – from the early 1870s to the end of the Great War – Home Rule was both the single most important feature of Irish political life and a major influence within British politics. Between the elections of 1874 and 1918 Home Rule dominated Irish parliamentary representation, peaking in 1885 with Home Rulers winning 85 of the total of 103 Irish seats. The leaders of the Irish parliamentary party at Westminster were, by definition, the leaders of the Irish people; and when, as in 1912–14, Home Rule seemed to be on the verge of enactment, these men were treated as the emerging rulers of the new Ireland. There were certainly divisions: the party was split between 1891 and 1900, and thereafter faced electoral threats from influential mavericks such as Tim Healy and (particularly) William O'Brien. There was also the challenge of 'new' nationalism, created by those who laid a greater emphasis upon Gaelic culture and political separatism than the Home Rulers. But, while the Home Rule movement was unquestionably characterised by weaknesses and misjudgements, it continued to dominate mainstream Irish politics until 1916–17.

Home Rule was important because it united Irish and British statesmen: its politics reveal much about the thought and priorities of British leaders in the late nineteenth and early twentieth centuries. For some English sympathisers, like W. E. Gladstone, Home Rule was about the reconciliation of Irish nationalism to the British state. For others, it was an adaptable political formula that might be applied to Ireland, but which could also be melded within a wider constitutional reform of the United Kingdom. For yet other English politicians, the Conservatives and Unionists, Home Rule presented such a threatening and fearful spectacle that for a time (during 1912–14) it seemed that they might wholly set aside constitutional action. There is now a stronger than ever case for believing that the Conservative leadership was implicated in the most extreme forms of Ulster Unionist resistance to the challenge of Home Rule. It has long been known that front-bench Tories were close to the loyalist gun-runners of 1913–14. But it now seems possible that even the Tory leader of the time, Andrew Bonar Law, met and blessed these militants.

The battle over Home Rule became so impassioned that it threatened both the institutions of parliament and indeed the very existence of the British state. In the late 1870s Home Rule MPs made their case by filibustering in the House of Commons, and obstructing parliamentary procedures. Thereafter the energy of these MPs, together with the often disturbed condition of Ireland, meant that the normal timetable at Westminster was overburdened with Irish business. By the time of the third Home Rule crisis, in 1912–14, the ferocity of political emotions was such that the norms of British parliamentary culture were beginning to fracture: party opponents, who normally set aside their differences beyond the hustings and the debating chamber, refused to dine with one another. Angry partisans histrionically flounced out of the Commons in gestures of contempt. At a more fundamental level, the opponents of Home Rule sought to subvert the conventions of parliamentary business: in 1914 there was a Tory conspiracy to vote down the Army Annual Bill, the measure that provided the basis for military discipline and which was normally passed every year as a matter of course. By the summer of 1914 the deadlock within British politics over Home Rule, and in particular over Ulster's opposition to it, was so complete that a civil war seemed to offer the only path towards a resolution.

Yet the enduring paradox of modern Irish politics has been that Home Rule, which fell out of favour in nationalist Ireland after 1917, had an after-life within Ulster itself, where Unionists exercised political dominance through their devolved administration at Stormont. This irony is all the more compelling, given that many of the legal restrictions that were applied by the British to Stormont were the indirect by-product of the Unionist campaign against Home Rule for all of Ireland. Indeed, the irony lives on – in so far as a form of 'Home Rule' government has now been reinvented in Northern Ireland under the terms of the Belfast Agreement of 1998.

Home Rule, then, unites the story of Irish Catholics and Protestants, nationalists and Unionists, even though their histories and experiences are often treated as separate or mutually exclusive. For a time – in the early 1870s – Home Rule bound some Irish Catholics and Protestants in a shared, moderate, secular and conservative vision of a semi-independent Ireland. This bond was ephemeral, and was superseded by the increasing sectarian polarisation of Irish politics in the later 1870s and after. But the history of Home Rule is also, indirectly, the story of its opponents, the Unionists, whose organisation evolved in Ireland in the early and mid-1880s; and any narrative of this kind must inevitably illuminate the relationship between the two movements. This is all the more clear, given that it was the Unionists who eventually inherited a corrupted version of Gladstonian Home Rule in the shape of the Northern Ireland government and parliament.

The importance of Home Rule rests, too, in its continuing emotional hold over the Irish and British people. Some Home Rulers have been incorporated into the prehistory of the Irish state. The darkly charismatic Charles Stewart Parnell, the leader of the Home Rule movement in the 1880s, remains an iconic figure for the Irish people. Parnell's illicit love for Mrs Katherine O'Shea, the wife of one of his parliamentary colleagues, has invested the constitutional politics of the time with a frisson of romance, and his death at the age of forty-five has tinctured this romance with high tragedy. If Parnell has simultaneously commanded and troubled the Irish people, Edward Carson has stimulated a similarly complex array of emotions among Irish Unionists. Carson's career at the Bar involved some of the highly charged cases of the era, and brought him into conflict with Oscar Wilde during the trial of Lord Queensberry in 1895, and with the Admiralty in 1910 during his defence of the original 'Winslow Boy', George Archer Shee. Carson, like Parnell, has been widely featured in literature and on film; each has been commemorated by significant memorials in Belfast and Dublin respectively. The lives of each illustrate that, despite the complexities of their political legacies, the romance of the Home Rule era still exercises a very powerful and ongoing sway. Each continues to supply a point of reference and a source of legitimisation for contemporary politicians.

But even within British politics Home Rule, and the personalities associated with it, still exercise a fascination and an influence. The British father of Home Rule, Gladstone, continues to arouse passionate debate, at least partly because parallels have been drawn between the style and substance of his politics and those of Tony Blair. Gladstone's historical reputation remains largely unresolved, wavering between an image of intense spirituality, integrity and profundity, and an alternative portrayal of hypocrisy, self-delusion and misjudgement. For the Liberals as a whole, Home Rule bestowed a complex legacy of moral vindication, combined with division and defeat. The party may have been morally and strategically right in supporting the demand of the Irish people for Home Rule, but Ireland divided Liberals and may in the end have represented a damaging electoral distraction. For their part, the Tories (despite some spirited arguments for the defence) remain embarrassed by the rhetoric and actions of their leaders during the Home Rule era. The genially outrageous loyalist oratory of Lord Salisbury in 1885–6 and the political brinkmanship of Andrew Bonar Law in 1912–14 continue to unsettle and divide even convinced Tory partisans. The sanction bestowed by the Tory leaders upon the most extreme forms of Ulster Unionism during the third Home Rule crisis has burdened the party with an extremely awkward political legacy. For both Tories and liberals, Britons and Irish people, Home Rule lives on.

It is in these synergies that the fundamental significance of Home Rule lies. Home Rule united the Irish past with the present, and bound militants with constitutionalists, and Irish with British politicians. It was an essential mechanism in the sculpting and unification of the Irish nation, providing an alluring and helpfully ambiguous war-cry to a people who had been decimated by famine and emigration in the nineteenth century, and whose political culture was otherwise splintered and particularist. It also became an essential tenet of late Victorian and Edwardian liberalism, and a central point of differentiation between British Liberals and Conservatives. The history of Home Rule binds the stories both of Irish nationalists and Irish Unionists, and of those who sought to mediate between them.

This book is concerned, therefore, with a crucial and extended motif in modern Irish and British history. The focus of the work is on the political leaders and thinkers who sought to revise the Union in a manner that met Irish aspirations and which nevertheless preserved a significant constitutional link between Ireland and Great Britain. It is concerned with those, Britons and Irish people, nationalists and Unionists, who have been content to keep Ireland, or part of Ireland, within the framework of a 'renegotiated' Union (to borrow an expression from Gerry Adams). It is concerned, however indirectly, with what might be dubbed the centrist tradition in Irish politics from the late nineteenth century onwards – with the efforts of those who have sought a friendly accommodation between Irish nationalism and the British state, and who have sought to reconcile Irish nationalism and Irish Unionism within the structures of a devolved government, whether in Dublin or Belfast. It is the first work of its kind to trace the theme of Home Rule from its origins through its corrupted reinvention in the Stormont years into its contemporary efflorescence within the Belfast Agreement.[3]

Using both original research and secondary sources, the book examines the personalities, strategies and measures connected with the Home Rule movement both in its classic phase (from c.1880 through to 1916) and in its partitionist after-life (from 1920 to the present day). New historical evidence from numerous archives has provided fresh insights and revelations. This book documents for the first time the full extent of Tory involvement in militant resistance to Home Rule in 1912–14. It offers a re-reading of the strategies of Prime Minister H. H. Asquith over Home Rule, deciphering his goals and the extent to which he created trouble for his Unionist opponents. It offers new insights into the careers and thought of Northern politicians such as Terence O'Neill, Brian Faulkner and David Trimble. It harnesses newly released documentation on British policy towards Northern Ireland in the crucial early years of the 'Troubles'.

The work may also be regarded as a political and intellectual pre-history of the Belfast Agreement – given that many of the ideas and models that surfaced in 1998 have lurked in the lagoon of Irish politics since the end of the nineteenth century.[4] For, although the novelty and the immediate origins of the agreement are often stressed, it is also the product of a constitutional evolution that began not simply with the creation of Northern Ireland and Unionist 'Home Rule' in 1920, but with the political movements of the 1870s and 1880s. Indeed, the book contains a form of historical and constitutional symmetry, in so far as Home Rule, imagined by Gladstone as a means of kick-starting the Union, was reinvented in 1998 for much the same purpose.

But historicism is the besetting sin of Irish history and politics, and it would be ironic if this book, which seeks to illuminate some historicist influences within the story of Home Rule, were to become part of the argument that it is purporting to document. Irish history and the history of Home Rule are, of course, infinitely more than the context or prelude to the agreement of 1998. While it might be tempting to provide a Whiggish narrative of constitutional struggle, progress and (in 1998) triumph, the condition of Ireland remains too uncertain for any such bullishness. Home Rule failed to keep Ireland within the British connection, but, rebooted through the partition settlement of 1920, it helped to preserve the connection between Britain and the six counties of Northern Ireland. Now, with even this diminished Union in apparently irreversible decline, a new form of Home Rule has been honed for a familiar purpose. It remains to be seen just how far the symmetry between the early twentieth century and the early twenty-first holds true; and whether the vestigial Union will miraculously discover a second wind or quietly subside into oblivion – or whether its collapse will be bloody and complete.

# CHAPTER 2

# THE EVOLUTION OF AN IDEA

Home Rule dominated Irish politics in the half-century preceding independence, from its first coherent formulation as a policy in 1870 through to the supersession of the Home Rule party in 1918: the legacy of these bitter but fertile years is with us still. Home Rule, its advocates and opponents, dominated parliamentary politics in this period, and the controversies played out in the Edwardian House of Commons continue to resonate in British politics. Yet Home Rule, as defined by its principal British sponsor, W. E. Gladstone, amounted to a painfully modest grant of legislative autonomy to the Irish. Moreover, the Home Rulers, though led by men of (for the most part) transcendent ability, were often political nonentities: there was no martial glamour in their oratory, no patriotic charisma in their committee work, no revolutionary asceticism in their sometimes boozy and self-pitying exile in London.[1] From this perspective, therefore, it is hard to see quite how the political ascendancy of the Home Rule idea should have been achieved and, still less, sustained.

Home Rule was indeed a recent demand for limited self-government; it was pursued by some gauche or tongue-tied Irish parliamentary performers as well as the icily charismatic Charles Stewart Parnell, the brilliant but caustic Tim Healy and the sonorous John Redmond. But Home Rule was not so much a newly sprung, single political stream as the confluence of numerous tributary political traditions and causes. Here rested its significance. The Home Rule movement articulated a longstanding Irish desire for the repeal of the Act of Union of 1801; it was an expression, in the view of some nineteenth-century authorities, of the political discontents of an ancient nationality. Home Rule harnessed the immediate social and political aspirations of Catholic Ireland. For some, it was an extension of the Irish land question; for others, town-dwellers, it promised liberation from the economic restraints imposed by the old regime. Home Rule united constitutional politicians with those whose faith lay in violence, but who were willing to suspend their disbelief in the efficacy of parliament. Less obviously, it also drew upon a tradition of Irish Tory patriotism dating to the 1830s and (certainly in the estimation of the Tory patriots themselves) earlier.[2] Home Rule was each and all of these traditions or aspirations, and in the diversity of the cause lay both its strength and its fragility.

Each aspect of the movement's origins – its ideological roots, institutional precedents and wider social and economic context – requires some investigation. The demand for Home Rule in late-nineteenth-century Ireland was sometimes expressed as a call for the restoration of the Irish parliament that had been abolished in 1800 by the Act of Union. The old Irish legislature was landed and exclusively Protestant, while the Home Rule movement recruited Catholic farmers and professionals. Yet Home Rulers embraced these eighteenth-century parliamentarians as honoured ancestors, and adapted their patriotic arguments to the demands of late-nineteenth-century political debate.

This, subordinate, Irish parliament had been in intermittent conflict with Westminster from the 'Glorious Revolution' through to the 1780s and 1790s, by which time a form of legislative independence had been wrested from London. These contests were generally over political autonomy, and they were accompanied by an increasingly assertive, if not always coherent, elaboration of the Irish viewpoint. The Irish melded notions of natural right with legal and constitutional arguments centring on the incomplete nature of the Anglo-Norman conquest of Ireland, the sovereign state of the kingdom of Ireland and the English origins of the predominant, Protestant, section of the Irish people. Their arguments had a lasting impact. The most celebrated ideologue of this 'patriot' school was William Molyneux, whose *Case of Ireland Stated* (1698) was wielded throughout the eighteenth century in defence of the claims of the Irish parliament. Charles Lucas, the key patriot leader of the mid-eighteenth century, was a devotee of Molyneux, as was Henry Grattan, the father of the constitutional settlement of 1782–3. In fact Molyneux was also prepared, in a throw-away line, to argue that a union would be an equally satisfactory means of representing the interests of the Irish nation. But this did not, of course, feature in later patriotic glosses.[3]

Many of Molyneux's arguments were resurrected in the late 1770s and early 1780s when, in the context of Britain's engagement in the American War of Independence, there was an efflorescence of Irish patriotic anger. At first this assumed an economic form, and highlighted the remaining British restrictions on Irish manufacturing and trade. But after the lifting of some of these economic constraints in 1779, the patriots' campaign took on a more explicitly political and constitutional colouring. Their agitation eventually bore fruit in 1782–3 in a series of British concessions that were hailed in Ireland as a discrete 'constitution' and as 'legislative independence', but which in fact fell miserably short of each claim. Yet for the Home Rule movement this victory was an ongoing inspiration. The emergent settlement was dubbed 'Grattan's parliament' (after Henry Grattan, the leading patriot of the era), and was seen as the bedrock of a political and economic golden age. In reality, many patriots continued to harbour a chilly attitude towards the majority Catholic interest, and 'Grattan's parliament' was never able (at least without outside stimulus) to produce a thorough-going reform of Catholic civil rights.

The demand for Home Rule reflected not just the political legacy of the patriots, but also a related scholarly view of the Irish as a coherent ancient nationality whose political rights had been cruelly suppressed by the Saxon conqueror. The Home Rule movement had been preceded by a century and more of polemical and indeed reasoned historical scholarship that had investigated the lineage of the Irish nation and the history of its political expression.[4] Home Rule politics fed off these interpretations of the 'story of Ireland' and looked to a history of parliamentary representation on the island which dated back to 1264, and which had continued to its final flowering in the late eighteenth century. Home Rule polemicists looked bleakly at those who, wallowing in corruption, had helped to overturn the parliament at the time of the Act of Union, in 1800. From this perspective, Home Rule was not simply a modish aspiration, but rather the normal condition of Irish political life. It was not a new protest, or a call for concessions, but rather a demand for the restoration of the political rights of an ancient nation.

The Home Rule idea, then, drew upon an enlivened and newly documented popular interest in the history of the Irish nation and of its political institutions. But this raises other questions. The investigation, sometimes the invention, of the 'story of Ireland' in the early and mid-nineteenth century was fired by the recovery of Catholic Ireland from the penal era – a period of religious suppression and expropriation covering much of the late seventeenth and eighteenth centuries. The 'penal laws', beginning with statutes enacted in 1695, targeted Catholic landholding and further reduced the Catholic aristocracy and gentry. But other classes, while touched by this legislation, possessed a greater degree of latitude. The booming of Irish agriculture after c.1740 resonated through almost every aspect of the economy and benefited Catholic manufacturers and merchants. A substantial Catholic farming interest emerged in the eighteenth century, despite the concern of the legislators for Catholic landed property. The penal laws were slowly repealed in the last quarter of the eighteenth century, but a final grant of civil equality, or 'emancipation', came only in 1829. Ireland in the early nineteenth century thus had a propertied Catholic interest which was virtually excluded from the politics and government of the country.

But not all Catholics were driven by these injustices into radical politics.[5] Many, following the lead of the Church hierarchy in the late eighteenth and early nineteenth century remained overtly faithful to the Hanoverian dynasty, and there was even some nominal loyalism among mid-eighteenth-century rural secret societies. There were certainly profound social fractures: the intersection of mounting Catholic prosperity with the painfully timid progress of Catholic relief opened up some deep resentments. In addition the revolutions in America and France provided inspiration and political ideas to Irish Catholic (and Presbyterian) radicals in the 1790s, and these fed into the popular rising of 1798. Perhaps 30,000 people, mostly insurgents, died in this bloody attempt to overthrow British rule and to establish an Irish republic. But it is important not to equate the social and political ideals of the insurgents with the whole of Catholic Ireland. Catholics were well represented in Crown forces, such as the militia, who were active in suppressing the rebels, and the Church was, of course, hostile to the rising.

William Pitt, the Prime Minister, used the opportunity created by the rising to force through a measure of union between the British and Irish parliaments. Here, again, a number of key elements within Catholic Ireland were prepared to acquiesce in the policies of the Crown. Pitt had originally planned to abolish the Irish parliament and at the same time to equalise Catholic civil rights. But while part of his strategy was realised – the Dublin parliamentarians obligingly voted themselves into oblivion – Protestant interests in Britain soon scuppered any thoughts of Catholic relief, and the newly propertied and powerful Catholic interests remained unaccommodated. It is possible that the British state, suitably reformed, might have lastingly embraced these interests; but reform was too late in coming and too dilatory in its impact to attain this end. It is not too fanciful to see the different Catholic protest movements of the nineteenth century, which culminated in Home Rule, as being rooted in this lasting disparity between wealth and representation. Nor is it overly fanciful to see Home Rule as being partly rooted in Pitt's failure to replace an Irish parliament founded on Protestant privilege with a United Kingdom parliament accessible to all.[6]

There was, indeed, a history of popular agitation before the demand for Home Rule was formulated, and which served to bring this demand about. The economic rise of Catholic Ireland, the popularisation of democratic and libertarian ideas through the revolutions in America and France, and the frustratingly slow demolition of the penal laws all fed into a popular movement for full 'emancipation' from religious disabilities. The commander of this political enterprise was Daniel O'Connell, a Catholic lawyer and landowner from County Kerry. In 1823 he created the Catholic Association which served as the driving force for reform.[7]

O'Connell was a vibrant, eloquent and histrionic figure whose personality and achievements made a lasting impression on Catholic Ireland, and indeed more widely on Catholic Europe. He emerged as a master of theatricality, whether in terms of his dress, his speech or his manner. O'Connell's public appearences in the 1820s and after came to be carefully stage-managed: he was regularly decked out in his trademark emerald green suit, and installed in magnificent carriages or on elaborate platforms. His concern for public presentation stretched in the end to a wig, which gives an eerie and unconvincing impression of youthfulness to his later portraits. All Ireland knew of his ferocious political energy: all Ireland knew of, or believed in, his epic prodigality and promiscuity.[8] In almost every sense he was (or was thought to be) larger than life: more eloquent, more sarcastic, more sentimental, more loving, more rebarbative, more pious and more wayward than his contemporaries. His extraordinary personality seized Catholic Ireland in the 1820s, and its hold has never been completely relaxed. Later generations borrowed much from his organisational achievement, but he also bequeathed a sense of political style and theatre to some unlikely heirs in the Irish national tradition, such as Charles Stewart Parnell and Eamon de Valera.

The campaign for emancipation is important to the consideration of Home Rule, for O'Connell created strategies and institutions to which later Home Rulers would turn, and defined a popular constituency upon which the Home Rule movement would, in part, rest. He sought a mass membership for the Catholic Association and bound it closely with the Catholic clergy. In rousing his subject people, he used rhetoric larded with a coherent vision of Irish Catholic history and used language burning with anglophobic and anti-Orange zeal. He devised a strategy of direct political combat with the Protestant ascendancy, taking them on at the general election of 1826, and seizing a number of parliamentary seats for the Catholic cause: he was himself returned (for County Clare) in 1828. His crowning achievement was the great relief measure of 1829, which granted Catholics access to parliament and public office. This 'emancipation' of Irish and British Catholics secured for O'Connell the popular title of 'Liberator'.

Given that the Home Rule movement of the 1880s continued to address issues of social justice for Catholics, and given that mass organisation and an electoral strategy were central to its concerns, the precedents supplied by the campaign of the 1820s were of lasting importance.

It would be quite wrong to forget the mass politicisation and mobilisation of Irish people in the 1790s, culminating in the rebellion of 1798. But O'Connell, who was an opponent of the rising, defined an even wider constituency than this, and kept it within broadly constitutional parameters. Here, too, was a legacy that the Home Rulers were to enjoy.

Daniel O'Connell popularised, if he did not invent, a form of intense Irish patriotism that was compatible with some of the central institutions of the British state and of the British empire. He learned from the theory and practice of British radical politics in the 1820s and 1830s, but he also looked back to the restrained, genteel and loyal Catholic reformers of the late eighteenth century. In this way he supplied a highly complex legacy to the Home Rule movement, a legacy which of course included patriotism and bitterly partisan action and expression, but which also embraced a possible sympathy for the monarchy and the idea of Irish Catholic involvement in the institutions of empire.

But O'Connell also fathered Home Rule in a more obvious way, for in the late 1830s he rejuvenated the emancipation movement as a campaign for the repeal of the Act of Union. His lasting commitment to the overthrow of the Union settlement need not be doubted: as early as 1810 he had proclaimed in characteristically shocking language that, were the Prime Minister 'to offer me the Repeal of the Union upon the terms of re-enacting the entire penal code, I declare it from my heart and in the presence of my God that I would most cheerfully embrace his offer'.[9] But as always with O'Connell, principles might be relegated or advanced according to broader pragmatic concerns. Through most of the 1830s he used the issue of repeal both as an offensive weapon and as a defensive position: repeal was used as a threat through which other concessions might be levered from successive British Whig governments, but it was also valuable as a popular fall-back if all else failed. In 1835, in the wake of the Lichfield House Compact, an informal agreement reached with the Whigs, he agreed to suspend his call for repeal provided that Ireland was granted parliamentary and municipal reform, as well as a reform of the tithe, the controversial tax levied on agricultural income for the support of the Established (Protestant) Church. But by 1838, despite a succession of minor reforms, he remained disappointed and moved to renew British apprehensions concerning repeal by founding the Precursor Society, a body that he pointedly claimed was designed not to mobilise support for repeal, but rather 'to prevent [its] necessity'.[10] This shrewd teasing of the British establishment continued into 1840, when O'Connell launched his National Association for Full and Prompt Justice or Repeal. But with legislative concessions in short supply, and with the threat of a Tory election victory looming (the Tories under Peel were returned in 1841), he reverted to a more simple and direct anti-Union strategy.

For most of the 1830s O'Connell had sought to entice the British, and in particular British Whigs, into promising more reform in Ireland. It would be tempting, but possibly a little over-imaginative, to see O'Connell not simply as the father of Home Rule, but also – given his strategies and goals in this decade – as the father of constructive Unionism. This was the reform policy designed to avert the 'necessity' of Home Rule, which was pursued by Conservative administrations in the late nineteenth century, and which focused (like O'Connell, for part of the 1830s) on land and local government reform. It is certainly the case that O'Connell highlighted the ways in which a controversial Irish national demand could be used to extract concessions from the British government. And it is also true that O'Connell in the 1830s founded the first recognisably popular Irish parliamentary party, and deployed it at Westminster in the cause of reform. Both achievements were premonitions of the Home Rule era.

It was only after 1840 that O'Connell's commitment to the repeal of the Act of Union emerged untrammelled by the compromises of the Whig alliance. Agitation at Westminster had failed to produce results that met the high expectations of 1835, and O'Connell turned to the mobilisation of his forces in Ireland. Some of the strategies of the 1820s were revived: the Catholic Association was reborn as the Loyal National Repeal Association (1840), while the electoral thrust of 1826 was replayed in 1841 and after. Mass demonstrations, important in the fight for 'emancipation', assumed a greater significance in the struggle for repeal: between March and September 1843 an unprecedented series of 'monster' meetings was held, several of which attracted audiences estimated at around half a million people, and peaking at Tara, County Meath, in August where perhaps 750,000 gathered to hear the repeal message expounded. The evocation of history and of ancient wrongs at the meetings was uncompromising; the language was provocative, sometimes – as at Mallow, County Cork, in June – threatening and defiant.[11] But there were fatal ambiguities in both the repeal message and in the strategies by which it was promulgated, and these would help ultimately to undo the movement as well as bequeath a set of problems that the Home Rule movement never adequately resolved.

Repeal and, later, Home Rule were simultaneously constructive and destructive concepts. Repeal was a movement of opposition to the Union but also a call for the restoration of the historic Irish parliament. But the positive aspect of the message was left in only the loosest formulation. O'Connell proclaimed that he wanted the 'independence of Ireland' but defined this as the creation of an assembly charged with the control of internal Irish affairs together with an exclusively Irish judicial system. However, in the 1830s, given his gradualist strategies, he appeared to be arguing that the 'independence of Ireland' was negotiable; and aside from this occasional willingness to trade repeal for social reform, he was willing to countenance other forms of constitutional experimentation. Through the controversial 'Derrynane manifesto' of October 1844 he announced 'his preference for the federative plan', an allusion to the American-style federalist principles enunciated at this time by such Irish political sages as William Sharman Crawford and J. G. V. Porter, both from Ulster.[12] The subsequent outcry among his supporters (and indeed the federalists) led O'Connell within a few months to seek cover in the original notion of 'simple repeal'. The vagueness of 'repeal' had been a source of strength, given the extent and diversity of the popular movement, but the 'Derrynane manifesto' also highlighted the dangers involved when a leader sought to exchange the generous ambiguities of the national cause for a more specific programme. Here, again, O'Connell charted a path that the commanders of the Home Rule movement would follow – indeed, as will become clear, there are parallels between O'Connell's flirtation with federalism, and the interest of some Home Rulers in the devolution proposals of the Edwardian period.

But repeal did not founder solely because of the divisions over its definition. There were also, for example, tensions within the movement on the question of political violence. The repeal movement, like its Home Rule offspring, embraced a wide variety of forces in Irish politics; amongst whom was a group of cultural nationalists, the Young Irelanders, associated with the newspaper, the *Nation* (1842).[13] While O'Connell exploited, but did not further, Irish national culture, the Young Irelanders were much more proactive, taking steps to promote a national literature and to resuscitate the Irish language. The Home Rule movement of the late Victorian era would inherit O'Connell's friendly but largely passive approach to Gaelic culture. O'Connell, like these Home Rulers, took an at best ambiguous attitude towards the dominant Protestant minority, veering from occasional conciliatory efforts towards righteous anger. In contrast the Young Irelanders, drawing on the enlightened republicanism of the 1790s, had a more inclusive definition of the nation. O'Connell proclaimed that the restoration of an Irish parliament was the lodestone of his political career, but, as has been seen, he had been prepared to meander off course in the apparent interests of securing his ultimate goal. The Young Irelanders, however, saw repeal as embodying their minimum terms, and some, such as John Mitchel, veered into full-blooded revolutionary republicanism. O'Connell, like later Home Rulers, was not above raising the threat of violence in his orations, but was otherwise a strict constitutionalist. For example, he called off a 'monster' meeting planned for Clontarf in October 1843, which had been banned by the government. But the Young Irelanders, unlike their master, were not prepared to exclude the possibility of force from their strategies. This divergent thinking brought a split in the repeal movement in July 1846. Divisions on force and federalism, the onset of famine in Ireland, and the death of O'Connell in January 1847 served to beach a movement that had in fact been drifting since the Clontarf débâcle.

The ideals and achievements of O'Connell's repeal movement were mediated to the Home Rule generation in the 1870s and after by various means. Some survivors from O'Connell's great campaigns for emancipation and repeal exercised an influence over the early Home Rule movement. For instance, Charles Mahon, known as 'The O'Gorman Mahon', was an influential supporter of O'Connell in the late 1820s, and survived until 1891, when – at the age of 91 – he was still sitting as Home Rule MP for Carlow; W. J. O'Neill Daunt was elected as a repeal MP for Mallow in 1832, served as secretary of the Home Government Association in 1873–4 and died at the age of eighty-seven in 1894. But there were other agencies. A parliamentary alliance of dissident Catholic Liberals and proponents of tenant right was forged in the early 1850s and, operating as the Independent Opposition Party, or Independent Irish Party, wielded an influence.[14] This body clung on to life into the mid-1860s, and in some ways it represented a resurrection of O'Connell's strategies of the 1830s – the idea of such a party had been broached in the O'Connell era, while the emphasis of the Independent Oppositionists on specifically Catholic interests evoked the preoccupations of the O'Connellites. Parnell, the great Home Rule parliamentarian, acknowledged his strategic debt to the Independents of the 1850s.

It should not be assumed, however, that Young Ireland was irrelevant to the story of the emergent Home Rule cause. The Young Irelanders were cultural ideologues and militants in the manner of contemporary European romantic nationalism. While their concerns were distinct from those of O'Connell, for a time they united in his project, and they interpreted his legacy in crucial ways to later generations of Home Rulers. Following the French revolution of February 1848, the Young Irelanders rose in rebellion against British authority, thereby aligning themselves with the insurgents of 1798 and apparently distancing themselves from the mainstream, pacific, O'Connellite tradition. Yet on the eve of the rebellion there had been a *rapprochement* between the Young Ireland militants and the more moderate followers of O'Connell. The Young Ireland movement foundered after their abortive uprising of July 1848, but

17

members of the movement contributed to the foundation of a revolutionary secret society, the Irish Republican Brotherhood or Fenian movement (1858), which sustained the tradition of armed insurrection through another failed revolt in 1867. These Fenian militants indirectly facilitated the creation of the constitutional Home Rule movement after 1870 by supplying martyrs to the Irish national cause. Three Fenians – the 'Manchester Martyrs' – were hanged in November 1867 having been convicted of the murder of a policeman. In addition many Fenians were imprisoned at this time, and the campaigns in 1869–70 to secure their release trained leaders and mobilised public opinion in ways that the Home Rulers of the 1870s were able to exploit. The Fenian movement supplied additional help in so far as its leaders were prepared to unite with constitutional nationalists at critical junctures, such as the early 1870s and in 1879.

In the last decades of the nineteenth century there were undoubted tensions between militants and constitutionalists, but the national movement in Ireland should be seen as a spectrum of opinion rather than as a rigid polarity. The tradition of militant separatism was a practical influence on the strategies of Home Rule and constitutional nationalism. The militants helped decisively to launch the Home Rule movement in 1870, and to relaunch it in 1879, while Parnell cultivated Fenian connections and was perhaps himself a member of the Irish Republican Brotherhood.[15] Constitutionalists and militants always grasped the importance of national unity, and constitutionalists often turned to the militants in order to prop the parliamentary struggle. Some constitutional leaders, such as Joseph Biggar and perhaps Parnell, were secretly members of the Fenian conspiracy, while some Fenian leaders were essentially pacific and pragmatic in their outlook. There were certainly years when the constitutionalists' ties with the Fenian tradition grew strained, or when the Fenian movement itself was in disarray; but these were – by definition – periods when the national movement was threatened with division and disintegration.

The Young Irelanders and Fenians were therefore important to the emergent Home Rule movement. There were dynastic bonds tying the Young Irelanders to the Home Rule party of the late nineteenth century. Perhaps the most important of these linked John Blake Dillon, one of the circle of *Nation* intellectuals, with his son, John Dillon, the Irish Parliamentary Party commander of the 1890s and after.[16] Some Young Irelanders, blessed by longevity, themselves survived the battles of the 1840s to participate in the Home Rule campaigns of the 1870s and 1880s. John Martin, a Young Ireland activist, was a founder of the Home Rule movement, and sat as MP for Meath between 1871 and 1875. John

Mitchel was elected as Home Rule MP for Tipperary shortly before his death in 1875. Charles Gavan Duffy, editor of the *Nation*, was an influential supporter of the Home Rule movement in the years before his death in 1903. Duffy, an historian and biographer as well as a politician, sought through his voluminous writings to inculcate the Young Ireland ideal into the Home Rule generation. Young Ireland helped to create Fenianism, which in turn often served as a valuable adjunct to the constitutional Home Rule movement.

But the Home Rule movement was not simply a union of Catholic Liberalism with secular republicanism. The roots of Home Rule can be followed down another, perhaps less obvious, genealogical line: that connecting Home Rule with Tory patriotism. There are dangers in exaggerating the distinctions between constitutional and militant traditions in nineteenth century Irish politics: the personalities, institutions and ideas of both the repeal and the Fenian movements fed into the Home Rule cause. But there are also dangers in exaggerating the distinctions between Catholic and Protestant politics. Here again, as with constitutional and militant nationalism, political diversity is perhaps best described as a spectrum of opinion rather than as a neat polarity. It would of course be absurd to minimise the bloody sectarian and national divisions of modern Ireland, but 'centrist' politics have also had a significant, if battered, role in Irish history. In addition, there has been a cross-fertilisation of ideas and strategies between the two seemingly discrete traditions, Tory and national, Orange and Green.

Patriotic Toryism contributed vitally to the emergence of Home Rule. Irish Toryism has been, until recently, one of the great neglected themes of nineteenth-century Irish political historiography. Yet its significance, whether in terms of seats won (it was the biggest Irish parliamentary grouping as late as 1859), or in terms of its organisational and intellectual vitality, seems hard to miss.[17] It would be wrong to see Irish Toryism, any more than the repeal or Home Rule movements, as homogeneous; and it would be wrong to suggest that the ferociously anti-Catholic popular Toryism of parts of Ulster had any direct or meaningful influence over the emergent Home Rule movement. Still, the defensive and sectarian loyalism of, say, working-class Belfast was only part of a complex wider picture, and the intellectual leadership of the Dublin Tory Party in the 1830s and 1840s, represented by a group of Trinity College graduates associated with the *Dublin University Magazine*, had perhaps more to offer to Home Rule.

The apparently paradoxical role of patriotic Toryism in the emergence of Home Rule becomes easier to comprehend when it is recalled both that Tories were essentially the advocates of the Protestant interest, and that the Irish parliament that had flourished before the Union (1800) had been an exclusively Protestant institution. Many Dublin Protestants had been enthusiastic Irish patriots in so far as the representative institutions of the Irish nation had been dominated by their own co-religionists; and it had been Protestant patriots who, throughout the seventeenth and eighteenth centuries, had been first in defending the rights of the Irish (Protestant) parliament against English legislative incursion. These Dublin Protestants had, of course, been opponents of the Union, on the grounds both of patriotic principle and of immediate economic interest, since the end of the Irish parliament brought a severe blow to the many trades that had enjoyed the patronage of rich Irish peers and MPs. Though many were ultimately scared away from the repeal movement by the ambition and confessional thrust of O'Connell, it is clear that they came 'to unionism reluctantly and late, and their support was never to be unconditional'.[18]

The key thinkers within Irish Toryism in the 1830s were two luminaries of Trinity College Dublin: the Revd Charles Boyton, a Church of Ireland clergyman, and his protégé, Isaac Butt, a Donegal man who was himself a son of the manse. Both these men rejected O'Connellite repeal, but each did so in cautious and patriotically charged language. The *Dublin University Magazine*, launched by Butt and his circle in 1833, thought repeal 'a senseless but not uncaptivating cry' while the main organ of the Dublin Tories in the 1830s – the Irish Metropolitan Conservative Society (1836) – held a debate on the issue in 1840 during which 'some spoke most vehemently in favour of an open declaration for repeal and none spoke directly against it'.[19] Butt's support for the Union at this time was expressed not as a reflection of sentimental or deep-seated regard for the British connection, but rather in hesitant and deeply patriotic terms: the Union was an experiment that for the moment permitted Ireland a say in the government of a great empire. Repeal, as defined by O'Connell, was an illogical patriotic expression because it represented a return to the constitution of 1782, which had been grudgingly conceded, not as an expression of intrinsic Irish rights, but rather as a reflection of transient English weakness at the time of the American War of Independence. In any event, the legislative independence of 1782 was heavily circumscribed by the English parliament. Butt, like some later Irish Unionists, claimed that he could appreciate the separatist demand more readily than that of the repealers: some Irish Unionists would claim to understand the Sinn Féin programme more readily than the milk-and-water Home Rule agenda of the Irish Parliamentary Party.[20]

These patriotic Tories of the 1830s and 1840s were important partly because they defined a hesitant Unionism in highly patriotic language.

Their ideas and arguments have a relevance both for the later history of organised Irish Unionism, which was an obvious lineal descendant, and for understanding the emergence of the Home Rule cause. Butt, seeing the Union as experimental, and rooted in the Protestant patriotism of the eighteenth century, was opposed not so much to the principle of repeal as to its O'Connellite definition. With the death of O'Connell in 1847 and the flourishing of apparently more inclusive national movements, Young Ireland and the Fenians, Butt could relocate himself within a more popular national context than that supplied by the Tory Party. He defended Young Ireland and Fenian prisoners, and in 1870 he emerged (with other Tories and ex-Tories) as a founder of the Home Government Association, an immediate precursor to the Home Rule movement.[21] The Dublin Tories of the O'Connell era, patriotic, socially aware and self-critical, may in this way be seen as architects both of the early Home Rule movement and indeed of the inclusive Unionism that was briefly envisioned in the 1880s and occasionally thereafter.[22]

The Home Rule movement was simultaneously an expression of an empowered and politicised Catholic Ireland and of Protestant Tory patriotism and disorientation. The rise of Catholic Ireland continued in the nineteenth century, aided by emancipation in 1829, and by agricultural growth in the aftermath of the potato famine of 1845–51. The Great Famine devastated the poorest section of rural Ireland, the landless labourers or cottiers, bringing the death of perhaps a million people through starvation and disease. It wrought economic havoc on the native landlord class, upon whom fell much of the burden of poor relief. The smaller, comparatively more wealthy rural population that emerged from the famine years was dominated by a prosperous class of farmers whose political needs were met first through the Independent Opposition Party and later, as land reform and the demand for devolution were skilfully linked, through the Home Rule movement. Home Rule promised to represent the needs of this dominant farming caste, but it also reflected the aspirations of other sections of Catholic society. The growth of an educated urban elite in the nineteenth century created a crisis of bourgeois expectations. The newly strengthened Catholic middle class had aspirations, but its upward mobility was checked by the domination of the higher ranks of the professions and public service by the residual Irish Protestant elite or (still worse) by Englishmen. Home Rule promised these thwarted Catholics a further social and economic liberation – a removal of the glass ceiling that, under the old system, appeared to curtail their advancement.[23]

On the other hand, the consolidation of the Catholic farming interest in the nineteenth century was complemented by the uneven but relentless retreat of the Irish gentry. In part the beginnings of this relative decline may be located in the masochistic leasing policies of the gentry at the time of the eighteenth-century agrarian boom. The famine desta-bilised the existing landed classes, but successive government reforms threatened either the economic interest of Protestant landlords, or their cherished institutions, or their political rights. Land reform, beginning tentatively in 1870, favoured the tenant interest with an increasingly uncomplicated directness. The disestablishment of the Church of Ireland, under legislation passed in 1869, represented the humiliation of the central institution of the Protestant ascendancy class. Electoral reform through the Irish Franchise Act (1850), the Irish Reform Act (1868) and the Ballot Act (1872) appeared to gnaw further at the gentry's already shaky political authority. Indeed, the Act of 1850 has been seen as a key-stone of the early Home Rule movement, in so far as it created a still small but discrete and accessible electorate.[24] Other, less tangible expres-sions of landed ascendancy, such as overt social deference, had long been under threat, pummelled by O'Connell, the Fenians and other iconoclas-tic leaders. Given these contexts, and given a patriot lineage, it need come as no surprise that some disillusioned Protestant Tories should have looked, however briefly, at the possibilities offered by Home Rule in 1870.

Home Rule was made possible both by these social changes and by other cultural, economic and technological shifts. The Home Rule move-ment was by no means the first popular mobilisation in Irish political history: the emancipation and repeal campaigns supplied valuable prece-dents. Nineteenth-century cultural and technological developments greatly helped in the creation of the Home Rule movement. The spread of accessible education with the creation of the national schools (1831) and the endowment of intermediate schools (in 1878) meant, in turn, ever higher levels of literacy and, arguably, political awareness. It is important not to push this point too far, as the reading of news sheets and pamphlets had been popular in the 1790s, and had helped to politi-cise those with poor standards of literacy. But heightened levels of litera-cy in the mid and late nineteenth century, combined with the abolition of the stamp duty and taxes on paper, gave a spur to the newspaper industry, which in turn often acted as an evangelist for Home Rule. In particular, the luxuriant spread of the Irish provincial press was an important resource for the national cause. Moreover, numerous leaders of the Home Rule movement were either themselves grounded in the news-paper trade (Tim Healy, William O'Brien, T. P. O'Connor) or adept at the manipulation of the press (C. S. Parnell).[25]

The spread of the electric telegraph and the growth of the railway network assisted the newspaper industry in terms of garnering stories and distributing copies, but each also possessed a wider political significance. O'Connell had not needed railways in arranging his campaigns and mass meetings in the 1820s, although his repeal effort in the early and mid-1840s had benefited from the nascent rail system. The efficient Bianconi coach business served the politicians of the early nineteenth century, as so many others, and Charles Bianconi was in fact a great friend of O'Connell. However, the Home Rule movement coincided with the golden age of the Irish rail network, which cut down the time and expense of travel and opened up hitherto relatively inaccessible parts of the country. Parnell himself acknowledged his debt to trains by arguing that if the Young Irelanders had possessed similar resources in the 1840s, they might have built up an effective national organisation thirty years in advance of his own.[26] It is scarcely an exaggeration to suggest that the railways, like the electric telegraph, made possible the emergence of a tightly disciplined, hierarchical and coherent Home Rule movement. These technological advances were not essential to a mass mobilisation, but they made it easier to achieve than would otherwise have been the case. And, while technological innovation did not create the Home Rule movement, it is possible that it did help to determine the shape of the movement.

Home Rule, then, was a demand for limited legislative autonomy pursued by a handful of gifted Irish leaders in collaboration with many less distinguished colleagues. But it was a demand that captivated the majority of Irish people for almost half a century. It was a demand rooted not simply in the lacklustre Gladstonian definition of legislative independence, but rather in earlier patriot ideology and history, in earlier popular political movements, and in some of the fundamental social, economic and technological changes affecting nineteenth-century Ireland. Home Rule was important and successful in spite of the Home Rule bills and in spite of some of the Home Rulers. Both the legislation and its advocates symbolised a glorious patriotic past: both were shaped and streamlined by the shifting pressures of the present day.

# CHAPTER 3

# ALL BUT A NATION:
# HOME RULE, 1870-79

From a corner of the room a little boy looked up at the rubicund and portly figure who was conversing with his father. The colouring and build of this stranger brought to the child's mind the lurid images of John Bull, which were prevalent in the nationalist literature of the time. Indeed, the boy's father, the distinguished Irish journalist and newspaper proprietor A. M. Sullivan, both bought and propagated such images. Sullivan invited his son to shake hands with the visitor, but the boy – thinking that he was being tempted to be civil to the very personification of the Saxon oppressor – demurred: 'I will not shake hands with this Englishman.'

The 'Englishman' was in fact Isaac Butt, the Donegal Protestant who had founded and led the Home Rule movement of the 1870s, and who was now, at the time of this exchange, approaching the close of his life. His achievement was already being challenged by a younger, more radical and embittered type of activist such as Charles Stewart Parnell; and though Sullivan was one of the most loyal of his supporters, the child's remarks seemed to imply that even here treachery was being whispered. 'So the wind blows that way in this house now, A.M.', Butt remarked. An embarrassed Sullivan dismissed the notion, yet the damage was done, and Butt never again deigned to visit. In the end the embattled Butt saw himself as a failure, haunted by betrayal, with even little children damning him as an 'Englishman'.[1]

Butt founded the Home Rule movement and popularised the concept of Home Rule, yet his achievement remains in the shadow of that of his successor, Parnell. It was Butt, however, who not only launched the idea of Home Rule, but also laid down strategies and institutions which in essence remained in place virtually until the demise of the movement after the First World War. Butt was perhaps a more fundamental influence on Parnell than that somewhat dismissive and self-contained commander was ever prepared to acknowledge. Parnell admitted a debt to the safely lacklustre and incoherent Independent Opposition Party of the

1850s, but was rather slower to acknowledge obligations to those who might – however weakly – eclipse his reputation or influence.[2] The chemistry of Butt's political successes was in certain respects successfully duplicated by Parnell, while his ultimate demise might well have provided a warning to later Home Rule leaders, had his achievement been treated with the seriousness that was in fact its due.

In May 1870 Butt founded the Home Government Association, a body that was succeeded in November 1873 by the Home Rule League.[3] These were effectively the first agencies for the new cause, and they were launched in complex but propitious circumstances by a highly sophisticated political intelligence. Butt was originally an Orange Tory, and was associated with the effort in the 1830s to create an Irish Conservative Party distinguished by a greater social and strategic awareness. He was a founder both of the cerebral *Dublin University Magazine*, the manual of sophisticated metropolitan Toryism, and of the *Protestant Guardian*, a somewhat more emphatic and straightforwardly tribal organ. Patriotism and Protestantism were the two consistent themes of Butt's long political career; while this is evident from his Orange activism in the 1830s, it is also true, though less obviously so, of his later position as a national leader. Butt expressed his Toryism in the language of patriotism, and defended the Protestant interest in similar terms. Although he was perhaps the most thoughtful opponent of repeal, O'Connell himself famously admitted that Butt was 'in his inmost soul an Irishman, and that we will have him struggling with us for Ireland yet'.[4] Butt, the ardent Protestant, never reconciled himself to the Catholic thrusts of O'Connell's campaigning, but as a Tory patriot and as a luminary of Trinity College Dublin, he moved freely and intimately with a number of the youthful intellectuals who formed the Young Ireland grouping. Even in his later reformulation as Home Ruler leader, Butt preserved an interest in the Protestant landed elite, a respect for the institutions of the British state and a hostility towards Liberalism that were all consonant with his earlier Tory career.

The horrors of the Great Irish Famine of 1845–51, combined with the tardiness of British relief policy, have traditionally been defined as a turning point in Butt's political evolution.[5] And, indeed, in 1848, at the height of the famine, when the Young Irelanders rose unsuccessfully against British rule, Butt took on the legal defence of some of the rebel leadership. Viewed from a narrowly Orange Tory perspective this was perhaps a rather strange proceeding, yet Butt the Protestant patriot and social conservative was fighting for a sober Protestant patriot and social conservative like William Smith O'Brien, an ex-Tory and the generalissimo of the abortive revolt. Twenty years later, Butt defended the leaders of the Fenian (or Irish Republican Brotherhood) revolt of 1867, in some ways a more shocking brief than that supplied by the Young Irelanders. Yet here again were insurgents who proclaimed a secular and inclusivist nationalism, and who, despite the presence of some social radicals, were often nostalgic conservatives with a practical concern for property. Seen in these lights, the distance between Butt the Orangeman and Butt the Home Rule leader was perhaps not so very great.

The unsuccessful Fenian rising and its immediate aftermath were crucial to the early success of the Home Rule movement. The rising was a failure, perhaps even a fiasco, but it was not a joke, as the 1848 rebellion had threatened to become. It supplied much-needed martyrs to the national cause in the form of Allen, Larkin and O'Brien, three Fenians executed in Manchester in November 1867 for the killing of Police Sergeant Brett. The rising certainly sustained the patriotic tradition of heroic failure: militancy was simultaneously popularised and, because the Fenians had shot their bolt, defused. Public outrage in Ireland over the deaths of the Manchester Martyrs fed into a wave of sympathy for the Fenian movement; but despite its origins, this was essentially a pacific reaction, and it came to be led by Butt, the leading constitutional apologist for the Fenian cause.

The campaigns to commemorate the martyrs and to secure the release of their imprisoned Fenian colleagues were directed firstly by the Irish Liberation Society and then, after June 1869, by the Amnesty Association whose president was Isaac Butt. These campaigns have been seen both as a crucial revival of national politics after an era dominated by essentially local concerns and as bringing about a decisive politicisation (perhaps repoliticisation) of the Irish countryside after the trauma of the famine years.[6] Farmers and indeed the Catholic clergy had originally been perturbed by the apparent social radicalism of some Fenians and of the Fenian newspaper, the *Irish People*. But there was a swift realignment of these key social forces in the months after Allen, Larkin and O'Brien went to the scaffold. Moreover, while W. E. Gladstone, the Prime Minister, and the Liberal government sought to disrupt this emergent alliance, their weapons were only partly effective. The disestablishment of the Church of Ireland in 1869 satisfied a long-standing Catholic grievance, but the timid Land Act of 1870 was a profound disappointment to the farming classes. Gladstone's later failure to address Catholic demands in the realm of higher education served to damage further his popular standing in Ireland.

A fresh political alignment was clearly emerging after 1867–8. The rising and the amnesty campaign had created a new patriotic coalition that embraced not only the artisans and labourers who had originally been attracted to Fenianism, but also priests and farmers who had remained aloof. Gladstone's efforts to break this coalition had simultaneously failed to impress Catholics who might in different circumstances have supported the Liberal Party and also profoundly rocked key elements within the Irish Protestant establishment. The popular anger released by these political quakes could not be directed into physical force nationalism, since this, though now immensely revered, had so recently and comprehensively failed. A resurgent patriotism now co-existed alongside a hungry but disappointed Catholicism, a hungry but disappointed farmer class and a respected but broken revolutionary movement. In this configuration lay Butt's political opportunity.

Butt had successfully identified himself with advanced nationalism through his defence of the Fenian prisoners and his presidency of the Amnesty Association. He had written on, and championed, the cause of moderate agrarian reform.[7] He also remained accessible to the Protestant and Tory elite: the Ulster Liberal editor, Thomas Macknight, a cool and shrewd observer of Irish politics, affirmed that 'Isaac Butt was always at heart a Conservative. He was never a Whig, never in the ordinary party sense a Liberal'.[8] Butt drew some of these disparate forces together in launching the Home Government Association at Bilton's Hotel, Dublin, on 19 May 1870. The immediate political opening was provided by the cool popular reception accorded to Gladstone's land bill and by Tory outrage at the disestablishment of the Church of Ireland. David Thornley's classic study of the composition of the Bilton's meeting has revealed that, of the sixty-one people either present or offering support, there were thirty-three Liberals or nationalists and twenty-eight Conservatives, or – using religion as the yardstick – thirty-five Protestants and twenty-five Catholics.[9] Six Fenians, or associates of Fenianism, were among these sixty-one patriarchs of the Home Rule movement; and indeed it seems clear that Butt had consulted with the Fenian leadership, in the form of the Supreme Council of the Irish Republican Brotherhood, before launching his initiative. An additional list of 359 supporters was published in August 1870 which included twenty-one Church of Ireland ministers, twelve Catholic priests and an over-representation of the disproportionately propertied and Protestant Dublin middle classes.

Later commentators have concentrated on the limitations of this grouping, and on Butt's desperate efforts to keep the Tories on board at the expense of some essential Catholic support.[10] But here, surely, was a startling conjunction of Toryism and Fenianism – an ill-starred union, perhaps, and a union marred by the relatively few farmers and priests present at its celebration. Yet for a brief moment it seemed as if Butt had succeeded in uniting the propertied elite of the country with the forces of advanced nationalism. And, even if this compound would shortly prove to be unstable, its transient existence was in itself remarkable and suggestive – and all the more so given the subsequent violent political chemistry of the island.

What were the demands of the Home Government Association, and its successor organisation, the Home Rule League, founded in 1873? The Home Government Association was launched in the aftermath of the reconstruction of the federal government in the United States (in the late 1860s), and the birth of a new federal constitution in Canada (1867). These precedents seem to have influenced Butt and the Home Rulers of 1870, who called both for an Irish parliament with domestic autonomy, and for a federated United Kingdom that would respect local needs while preserving the 'one great Imperial State'. Butt fleshed out his own ideas in the pamphlet *Home Government for Ireland* (1870) where he proposed Canada as a model for the constitutional relationship between Britain and Ireland, and thereby anticipated the treaty negotiators of 1921 who were much taken with the same analogy.[11] Ireland under such an arrangement would have been able to enjoy self-government and a distinctive 'national life' while fully participating in the government of the wider empire. Butt envisioned an imperial parliament in London that would retain English, Scottish and Irish MPs and which would continue to legislate on military matters, and foreign and imperial affairs (the latter to include relevant taxation). The Irish parliament, on the other hand, was to have complete control over Irish matters and was to comprise a House of Commons with some 250 members and also a House of Lords (here, too, perhaps, was a vestige of Butt's Toryism).[12]

Butt was wary of supplying too much detail for fear of diverting criticism into the minutiae and away from the main thrust of his scheme; and there are many aspects of his federal vision that are at best hazy. John Kendle, the scholar of the federal idea in late-nineteenth-century Britain and Ireland, has observed that Butt did not tightly define the relationship between the proposed imperial and Irish parliaments, and he did not trouble to enlarge upon the crucial issue of customs and excise. His scheme did not, therefore, make clear whether the federal United Kingdom would have been a customs union or a more disparate trading community.[13] In so far as Butt seems to have had in mind a division of sovereignty between the two assemblies, Irish and imperial, and in so far as the Irish parliament was to have had 'supreme control' over Irish affairs unless 'specifically reserved' to London, it seems possible that (like the Home Rulers of 1917–18) he favoured local control of customs, and thus a loose federation. But the evidence is ultimately unclear – in part because it was left that way.

This scheme was, at least nominally, the charter of the Home Rule movement from its foundation in 1870 through to the death of Butt in 1879. The Home Government Association promoted the federalist agenda, and its successor the Irish Home Rule League, formed after a conference at the Rotunda in Dublin in November 1873, did likewise. It is difficult to gauge the intrinsic appeal of federalism. The Home Rulers contested by-elections from May 1870, when Major Laurence Knox stood unsuccessfully for Mallow, County Cork. The first Home Rule victory was secured in January 1871 in County Meath with the return of the veteran Young Irelander John Martin. A wave of similar by-election successes followed in 1871–2: Galway, Westmeath, Limerick City (where Butt himself was returned), Kerry, Wexford and Cork City all fell to advocates of the cause. Within three years, by the general election of February 1874, fifty-nine supporters (or, in many cases, nominal supporters) had been returned under the federalist banner. The evidence suggesting widespread support for Butt's sophisticated constitutional engineering is therefore superficially impressive.[14]

But in truth, Butt's achievement lay not so much in winning converts to federalism as in winning support for the Home Rule movement, which was quite a different matter. The Irish Republican Brotherhood, which was in some disarray in the early and mid-1870s, was not seriously diverted from its militant republican ideals. The Fenian leadership was prepared to give the federal idea and the constitutional strategy a three-year trial, beginning in 1873, but under pressure from its hardline American sister organisation, Clan na Gael, there was a rapid retreat even from these nervously pacific gestures. The Catholic Church, on the other hand, was initially suspicious of what seemed like a Tory Protestant ruse, and sought to counter Home Rule with the creation in November 1872 of the Catholic Union. This was yet another organisational initiative arising from the fertile political intelligence of the primate, Cardinal Paul Cullen.[15] In addition patriotic farmers in the early 1870s were interested, as always, in tenant right and only secondarily, if at all, in the federal ideal.

It would have been astonishing if there had been a popular political realignment behind Butt's scheme, bound up as it was with loyalty to the British Crown and the empire; and in fact no such shift occurred. Enthusiasm for the Home Rule cause came not from its federalist appeal, but rather because of a range of external forces. Militants, for example, had little to offer after the failure of the 1867 rising, and even the amnesty movement had withered by 1871 as the British obligingly released some Fenian prisoners. On the other hand, the Catholic Church, and with it many of the laity, were angered by Gladstone's failure to devise a satisfactory university scheme. They were also progressively more interested in the Home Rule party as, in 1872–3, it rapidly lost its original pungent Tory flavour. Liberalism, the chief Catholic alternative to Home Rule, was finally damned in the eyes of the hierarchy when, in 1874, Gladstone unburdened himself of much Anglican fury at the Vatican decrees and the pretensions of Pope Pius IX. Home Rule worked in the early 1870s not because Irish voters were enthused by the federal proposal, but because Home Rule candidates specifically endorsed the Catholic and tenant right (as distinct from the federalist) cause. Vincent Comerford has argued emphatically that 'in the early 1870s, as for long before and long after, popular Irish nationalism was a matter of the self-assertiveness of the Catholic community and of a search for material benefits rather than a question of yearning for constitutional forms'.[16] Certainly there is not much evidence to affirm that the byzantine constitutional architecture devised by Butt was the object of much passionate yearning.

Nor did the electoral success of the early Home Rule movement hinge upon the possession of an efficient, mass organisation. Here again was evidence of Butt's roots as a Tory and an opponent of O'Connellite popular mobilisation. Butt, the defender of the Fenians, had been swept into the popular amnesty movement, but he had not been the originator of this campaign (these laurels fell to John McCorry, the founder of the Irish Liberation Society) and he had been a reluctant, if admittedly eloquent, populist in 1869–70. The Home Government Association was designed not as a popular movement, but rather as a political club, and in the first months of its existence it was so far from being a magnet for Catholic opinion that it harboured strong Tory sentiments. It has even been said that the Association 'was divorced from the main sources of Irish political energy'.[17]

There was a marked shift in the Association's membership in 1871–2, and a movement away from a Protestant Tory towards a Catholic Liberal character. This culminated in the useful appointment of W. J. O'Neill Daunt, a Catholic convert and veteran repealer, as the Secretary of the Association in January 1873. But even the Association's successor, the Home Rule League, for long lacked a strong organisational base; Butt believed that for legal reasons the League could not construct a local network, and that any initiative had therefore to come from below. Moreover, the League was perpetually broke, and it entered the general election of February 1874 with only the scantiest infrastructure.[18] It was ironic, but not surprising – given Butt's nervousness – that the Home Rule Confederation of Great Britain, which depended on the initiative and energies of the Irish immigrants, should have been a much more radical and elaborate machine.

The same lack of cohesion existed at the level of the House of Commons. The fifty-nine Home Rule MPs did not constitute a 'party' in any formal sense, and – even allowing for the more relaxed parliamentary discipline of the 1870s – they were remarkable for their lack of direction. The reasons for this are not hard to find. The general election of 1874 was sprung on the nascent Home Rule League and permitted its leaders little time to vet and nominate appropriate parliamentary candidates: 'more than from any other single cause', it has been remarked, 'the futility of the first Home Rule party stemmed from the haste and disorganisation of those three hectic weeks [before the election]'.[19] The result was that many of those returned as Home Rulers were former Liberals (and others) who, at best, demonstrated no visceral loyalty to Butt's federalist notions. One unusually candid patriot explained to a Liberal minister that his new-found separatist enthusiasm was his 'only chance [of election]. I do not think anyone can make much of my Home Rule'.[20] When a conference of the new Home Rule 'party' was held in Dublin after the election, in March 1874, only forty-six of the fifty-nine MPs managed to attend, and they affected to believe that a meaningful struggle for the federalist cause could be sustained by 'taking counsel together, making all reasonable concessions to the opinions of each other, by avoiding as far as possible isolated action'.[21] In truth, even these highly modest hopes were disappointed, for the Home Rulers rarely acted as a unified bloc, and were distinguished instead by divisions and absenteeism.

This partly reflected the diverse nature of the Home Rule group, and also perhaps some abstentionist sympathies among the more 'advanced', or extreme, Home Rule MPs such as John Martin; but the personal impact of Butt is also to be observed.[22] Butt's character and political vision were marked by writhing contradictions. His life and career teetered for years on the brink of ruin, as he amassed debts, pursued romance and accumulated illegitimate children; it was said that at meetings he was occasionally heckled by mothers whose offspring he had fathered.[23] On the other hand, he was a son of a Church of Ireland minister, and seems to have retained a High Church religiosity throughout his life. Tim Healy, a sharp observer of religious affinities, noted Butt's devotion to the Virgin Mary, and was pleased to report that – though a Protestant – Butt had prepared for a particularly important court-room appearence by reciting the rosary.[24] The influential Home Rule journalist and politician, T. P. O'Connor, recalled that Butt, in gaol for debt, had asked for the loan of a large-print Bible because his own could not be read in the gloom of the cell.[25] Andrew J. Kettle reported to Parnell 'a very serious conversation with poor Butt a short time before he died, and he [Butt] seemed to have a decided leaning towards the Catholic religion'.[26] Kettle may well have mistaken interest and respectfulness for an embyronic conversion, but anecdotes such as this serve to underline the undoubted seriousness with which Butt nurtured his religious convictions.

Despite his financial and amatory problems, it is Butt's moral vision that shines through his federalist convictions, and through his definition of the parliamentary role of the Home Rule movement. Butt defined the MP as being a representative, rather than a delegate, and he earnestly resisted efforts (formulated by the likes of J. G. Biggar, MP for Cavan) to foist a more rigorous discipline on the Home Rule 'party'; 'the only way to get home rule from the English parliament', Biggar claimed, 'was for the Irish members to keep honestly and compactly together'.[27] Despite the chaotic condition of his party, Butt had no wish to manage the sort of political machine that C. S. Parnell came to favour.

It would doubtless be unduly cynical to add that Butt's principled vision of his 'party' also suited his personal needs, preoccupied, as he was, by his debts and by the need to pursue a career in the courts in order to keep his creditors at bay. It might also be misguided to relate Butt's vision of the Home Rule grouping to some stray remarks that he offered in the autumn of 1870 concerning Westminster. Visiting Belfast, Butt told Thomas Macknight that 'I shall never sit in Parliament until we have one in College Green.' Questioned by Macknight, Butt replied that he was 'quite sure' of this.[28] It is just possible, however, that underlying Butt's polite and generous view of Home Rule at Westminster was a sense of detachment, and some unresolved sympathy with the view that Irish politicians should stay clear of the British parliament.

Butt certainly sought to impress the House of Commons by the dignity of the Irish cause, and by a patient though consistent exposition of the federalist creed. He also seems to have been prepared to seek gradual change in the manner of O'Connell, pursuing practical reform matters while retaining a passive commitment to the idea of an Irish parliament. Just as O'Connell had pressed for the consideration of repeal in the early 1830s, and then reverted to seeking 'justice for Ireland' in the shape of tithe, local government and other measures, so Butt moved in March 1874 to get the House of Commons to consider the issue of Home Rule; and when his motion inevitably failed, he sought minor reform in alternative areas. All this is not to say that Butt altogether gave up the demand for Home Rule: he broached the issue before the Commons once again, in June 1876. But it is to suggest that Butt was content to see Home Rule as a very long-term objective, and it is also to affirm that he sought in the meantime to accustom English parliamentarians to the federalist idea, and to sustain support at home through minor legislative victories.

Others within the Home Rule League were also keen to align

themselves with the O'Connellite tradition. It is surely telling that in August 1875 the League seems to have been able effectively to harness the centenary celebrations for O'Connell's birth. Indeed the zenith of Butt's influence has been linked to the expressions of popularity with which he was greeted at demonstrations and dinners marking the centenary, as well as to the manner in which the Home Rulers were able to marginalise Irish Liberals during these proceedings.[29] At this time Dr J. A. Galbraith, a Fellow of Trinity College Dublin and one of Butt's lieutenants, related Butt's strategy to an O'Connellite template, and lamented that the 'mad precipitancy' of Feargus O'Connor in the 1830s had come close to wrecking O'Connell's strategic design (O'Connor, nominally one of O'Connell's followers in the Commons, had defied the Liberator by recklessly trying to force a speedier progress towards repeal). This 'mad precipitancy' was not, in Galbraith's argument, to be repeated over Home Rule.[30]

Butt's difficulty, not unlike that of a later Home Rule leader, Redmond, during the First World War, was that he was sandwiched between, on the one hand, a British government uninterested in Irish reform and diverted by foreign wars and, on the other hand, advanced Nationalists who were becoming ever more hungry for results. O'Connell had had an informal alliance with the Whigs, in the shape of the Lichfield House Compact of 1835, and had thereby secured some important legislative and administrative reforms. Butt, on the other hand, faced a Conservative administration that was much more concerned with the Eastern Question and with pursuing wars in South Africa and Afghanistan than with the apparently eccentric demand for Home Rule. Moreover, O'Connell, the great emancipator, had a much more secure position as a national leader than Butt, even though the two men enjoyed – or were damned by – a similar reputation as free-spending and amorous. O'Connell exercised an untrammelled national authority for much longer than Butt, and only began to experience significant opposition after 1843 and the Clontarf débâcle. Butt, on the other hand, was given three years by the hardliners to deliver a triumph.

It has sometimes been said that Butt missed a historic opportunity by resisting those within his party who wanted a more radical approach, but to envision him in charge of the young turks is to conjure up a figure divested both of his innate social conservatism and of his concern for parliamentary procedure.[31] It is doubtful whether Butt, who was much loved, could have secured the lasting respect of the younger Home Rulers. His enforced absences from the Commons, his record as an imprisoned debtor and his personal niceness all militated against any firm authority. Critics complained that he lacked 'exasperation'. Healy, offering a summary but not unfriendly judgement, argued that 'Butt is no man to lead. He is too soft and easily gammoned. He is clever, plausible, statesmanlike and eloquent, but he is *not* a leader of men'.[32]

The impatient youngsters of the Home Rule party included J. G. Biggar (MP for Cavan from 1874), Edmund Dwyer Gray (MP for Tipperary from 1877), F. H. O'Donnell (returned for Dungarvan in 1877), Charles Stewart Parnell (returned for Meath in 1875) and John O'Connor Power (MP for Mayo from 1874). It is important, however, not to exaggerate the differences initially dividing these men and their followers from Butt. The young turks had close connections with the Fenian movement (Biggar, O'Donnell and O'Connor Power were all initiates); they had equally good links with the trenchantly patriotic Irish communities in Britain and the United States. In parliament they sought to break British opposition, not through the charm offensive favoured by their party leader, but rather through a more direct and brutal tactic: obstructing government business.

Yet in all of of this there was no great difference in principle separating the radicals from Butt. Butt had made himself the hero of Fenianism through his court-room efforts on their behalf, and he pioneered the effort to 'constitutionalise' the Brotherhood. His truce with the Fenians in 1873 bears a resemblance to the 'New Departure' of 1878–9, through which Parnell and the militants loosely accepted a shared strategy of agrarian agitation together with the goal of self-government. It has indeed been said that a form of New Departure was charted as early as 1868–9, when Butt's Fenian ally, John O'Connor Power, met with George Henry Moore and others in an effort to unite militant and constitutionalist endeavours.[33] Butt for long enjoyed the support of many ex-Fenians in Ireland and also 'a few active Fenians, mostly in the North of England'.[34] He lived long enough to witness the evolving New Departure of 1878–9; and though he was opposed to this, he was sufficiently in tune with its architects to understand its radical significance. John Devoy, one of the key ideologues of the New Departure, wrote that 'Butt from the first understood [its] revolutionary purpose...better than many of its Fenian critics'.[35]

Nor was Butt opposed in theory to the filibustering tactics of the obstructionists. In November 1873, at the conference which saw the launching of the Home Rule League, he conceded that 'extreme cases might justify a policy of obstruction', and he was soon prepared to give effect to these threats.[36] Butt led a campaign of moderate obstruction to the Conservative government's Expiring Laws Continuance Bill of 1874 and to its Peace Preservation (Ireland) Bill of 1875, when he promised that 'the Irish party will...exhaust all the forms of the House to attain their just and righteous object'.[37] F. H. O'Donnell, who became an extremely bitter critic of Parnell, argued that it was Butt and his lieutenant, A. M. Sullivan, rather than Parnell and Biggar, who in 1875 effectively pioneered the policy of obstruction.[38]

Although Butt was prepared to sully his reputation for constitutional activity and lawfulness with obstructive tactics in parliament and support for the Fenians, there were nevertheless marked differences in emphasis and temperament between him and his radicals. Butt's moderate obstructionism was an expression of his rationalist approach to politics: he sought, through 'a policy of argument', to urge his own case, and to interrogate that of his opponents with unrelenting vigour. The radicals, however, were much less interested in rational argument than in emotional calculation. While Butt sought to convince the British by elaborate and unrelenting advocacy, they sought to break British willpower by elaborate and unrelenting mischief. And in truth Butt's rational and moral approach was no match for the emotional shrewdness of his young turks.

Beyond this, however, it is clear that there were important personal issues. Butt, his patriotic lineage notwithstanding, never truly persuaded others of his ability to command. At the same time, the ambitions of the youngsters in the party were stimulated by the smell of decay and weakness emanating from the leadership. After the election success of 1874, Butt delivered no victories to his supporters.[39] Some continued to be persuaded by Butt's political versatility, and dubbed him 'All Butt'. As early as 1874, however, the sceptical John Mitchel was suggesting an alternative title, 'Anything Butt'.[40] While even an unforgiving judge like Healy was impressed by the intellectual quality and fine style of Butt's parliamentary performances, the Home Rule motions of 1874 and 1876 were easily defeated in the Commons. Indeed, it was not altogether clear whether the Home Rulers themselves were agreed on the precise definition of their ultimate purpose. Butt's land bill of 1876 suffered an ignominious rejection, with forty-five of his so-called Home Rule colleagues helping to vote it down. Crucial elements elsewhere in his support were also weakenening or deserting: he was unable, for example, to devise a university settlement that satisfied the Catholic bishops. At the opposite end of the patriotic spectrum, his alleged truce with the Fenians seems to have expired in unhappy circumstances in 1876-7. Those members of the Supreme Council of the movement who, like Biggar or O'Connor Power, were also Home Rule MPs suffered expulsion in 1876. The Fenian-infiltrated Home Rule Confederation of Great Britain grew restive, while the activists of Clan na Gael pressed for an ever more hardline stand, and encouraged a purge of the moderates from their Irish sister organisation.

Butt's definition of the Home Rule cause, Whiggish and rational, held sway until 1876; thereafter the tensions between him and the radicals became increasingly overt and bitter. By 1877 the obstructionists had abandoned the caution of their leaders and were engaged in an increasingly aggressive struggle with the British government, and with the procedures of the House of Commons. Three episodes in particular illustrated the growing rift within the ranks of the party, and the developing anger with Butt: Butt's exchange with Parnell in April 1877, the obstructionists' assault on the South Africa Bill in July–August 1877, and the removal of Butt from the presidency of the Home Rule Confederation of Great Britain in August 1877. First, Butt offered a public rebuke to Parnell which badly backfired. It was, after all, an 'unforgiveable sin for an Irish nationalist – to condemn a fellow countryman in a foreign assembly', as F. S. L. Lyons has observed.[41] Second, the guerrilla war against parliamentary procedure came to a climax at the end of July 1877, when the government was trying to secure the passage of the South Africa Bill: Parnell and Biggar forced an all-night sitting of the House of Commons on 31 July–1 August while an appalled Butt, who was mutedly sympathetic to British imperial policy, watched on. His attempt to reassert his authority after this well-publicised and (in Ireland) popular assault on the British constitution only underlined the divisions within the Home Rule party and the mounting opposition to his own leadership. If this required further demonstration, then it came at the end of August when, at a meeting in Liverpool, Butt was ousted from the presidency of the Home Rule Confederation of Great Britain: his successor was Parnell, who was reaffirmed in office in 1878.[42] A similar assault against Butt in February 1879, this time on home territory, failed but landed a damaging blow nonetheless: the youthful John Dillon, a future leader of the Irish Parliamentary Party, tried to carry a vote of no-confidence in Butt's leadership at a meeting of the Home Rule League in Dublin.

At the end Butt was ailing and defensive. When he was deposed at Liverpool, he was reported to have been in tears. The anecdote concerning A. M. Sullivan and his son, recounted at the beginning of this chapter, dates from this time, and conveys the tautness of his political nerves.[43] As Butt was losing allies, or (as in this case) threatening to lose allies, so Parnell and the obstructionists were gaining support. In early 1878 Parnell met an emissary of Clan na Gael, William Carroll, and by October of that year he had been offered the conditional support of the American militants. These conditions, devised by the leading American hardliner, John Devoy, amounted to a redefinition of the relationship between the parliamentary movement and the militants, with a new emphasis on the land question in Ireland. Devoy's bargain involved, too, a more direct abandonment of Butt's approach, in so far as the American wanted an end to the federalist programme and a more aggressive parliamentary policy. Parnell, increasingly celebrated for his plucky stand against the stuffed shirts of the British parliament, could afford to resist this salesmanship, and in spring 1879 Devoy offered a reformulated deal which has become known as the 'New Departure'. On 1 June 1879 Parnell and the American Fenians fudged an understanding of sorts which bound them to mutual support and a shared political agenda.[44]

Isaac Butt had died in the previous month, May 1879. The 'New Departure' apparently signalled the end of his political creed. But here, as ever, it is important to recognise Butt's achievement and his relevance to the parliamentarians of later generations. The 'New Departure' was anticipated by Butt's earnest efforts ten years before to win the acceptance, or at least the silence, of the Fenian movement when launching the Home Rule initiative.

Devoy's emphasis on the land question was neither startlingly new nor, as was sometimes said, a straightforward return to the radical philosophising of James Fintan Lalor, the agrarian sage of the Young Ireland movement. Parnell, though the generalissimo of the ensuing Land War, was neither a great thinker on the subject nor indeed a great innovator. The obstructionists were in fact distinguished not by any sustained thought on landed matters, but rather the reverse. Devoy and Michael Davitt, a Fenian ex-prisoner and social radical, recognised much more quickly than Parnell and his parliamentary allies the potential of agrarian radicalism.

And yet Isaac Butt, the political relic from the 1830s, saw the need to address land reform even in the relatively comfortable years after the devastation of the famine. Butt, who was profoundly moved both emotionally and intellectually by the famine, was a learned advocate of tenurial reform and published lengthily on the subject. He was aware of the importance of farmer support for his Home Rule movement, and exploited the opportunities presented by the failure of Gladstone's land measure. More than his successors, Butt was an informed proponent of reform, and the architect in 1876 of a major land bill. For better or worse, his parliamentary style prefigured the heyday of the Home Rule movement much more directly than that of his young turk critics. Certainly the leading militant, Colonel Arthur Lynch, complained in March 1909 that 'we have now reached the conditions that prevailed in the days of Isaac Butt, before Parnell put some life into the Party'.[45] Here, as elsewhere, Butt pointed the way in both strategic and ideological terms for the generations that lay ahead.

# CHAPTER 4

# FORSTER'S SOFA:
# THE ADVANCE OF PARNELL
# 1879–86

Forster's sofa might serve as an emblem for the achievement of the Home Rulers through the early and mid-1880s. At half past ten on the evening of 5 April 1886 the septuagenarian British prime minister, Gladstone, entered the Commons study of John Morley, his minister with responsibility for Ireland. Inside the chamber waited the Irish leader, Charles Stewart Parnell. There was a handshake, and Gladstone sat down beside Parnell, separating the Irishman and Morley. The three men began work almost immediately, haggling over some of the critical financial details of the Home Rule Bill which had been so recently published. The discussion ended at midnight, with Gladstone lamenting that 'I fear I must go: I cannot sit late as I used to.' Morley ushered the Prime Minister out of the room and exchanged a few admiring comments on the talent they had left behind: 'very clever' was Gladstone's verdict on Parnell.

This apparently humdrum meeting signalled the extent and swiftness with which the Irish Home Rule movement had been accommodated by the British political establishment. For much of the preceding six years the Irish leaders had been treated by British ministers as morally untouchable. Parnell, for example, had been imprisoned in 1882, and for long afterwards few Englishmen were prepared to hazard anything approaching serious political negotiation with him. There had certainly been a form of communication between Gladstone and Parnell before 1886, but it had been conducted through intermediaries such as Morley and Mrs Katherine O'Shea. There had been few personal gestures: the handshake between Gladstone and Parnell in Morley's room was as politically charged as the forms of civility between British ministers and the leaders of Sinn Féin in the late 1990s. The social space within the room had a further significance: Gladstone consciously placed himself close to Parnell and did not seek refuge behind a desk or attempt to use Morley as a shield. Parnell, for his part, lounged on the sofa that had once been occupied by one of Morley's predecessors, W. E. Forster.

Forster, Gladstone's Chief Secretary for Ireland between 1880 and

1882, had been a champion of coercion against the Home Rulers, and 'had laid his weary head many a night' on this very piece of furniture after lengthy passages of arms in the Commons chamber. In a grim piece of personal and political symmetry, Forster – who, for the Irishmen, represented marginalisation and suppression – died on the same day that Parnell was debating the details of Irish legislative independence from the vantage point of the Chief Secretary's sofa. In almost every conceivable sense Forster's space had now been annexed by the Home Rule movement.[1]

The first Home Rule movement had been launched by Isaac Butt with the tacit support of the Fenians, and against the background of renewed tenant agitation. It had been an essentially parliamentary initiative taken by a leader who had longstanding (but passive) militant sympathies, and who – though hailed by Catholic Ireland – had been intensely concerned with the role of his fellow Protestants in the future government of the island.

Charles Stewart Parnell, a Wicklow squire, rooted in the lore and rhetoric of the American revolution and in the patriotism of the late-eighteenth-century Irish parliament, would recreate some of Butt's political design at the end of the 1870s.[2] Like Butt, Parnell was essentially a parliamentarian and a social conservative. Like Butt, Parnell was preoccupied with the role of landlords and Protestants in a future Home Rule system. Above all, like Butt and his movement, Parnell was carried along by a popular political tide over which he had at first minimal control. Butt's Home Government Association had benefited from a preceding agrarian agitation and from quiet Fenian endorsement. The distinction between his initiative and the Home Rule movement of the 1880s lay not so much in the two conjunctions of forces as in the differing strengths of these forces. Parnell was able to turn Home Rule into a popular cause not because of infallible political judgement. Indeed, some historians have remarked instead upon his failures in this respect in the early 1880s. Home Rule was popularised because the forces driving it forward – Fenianism in Ireland and America, the agrarian movement – were proportionately stronger in the Parnell era than in that of Isaac Butt. Parnell's success rested above all on his skilful opportunism: Butt's failure rested, not so much on the limits of his imagination or ability, but on the fact that his opportunities were so few and far between.

The rural unrest of the late 1860s had been the result of longstanding complaints about rents and other contractual questions, and pressure on prices from foreign competition in the unprotected United Kingdom marketplace. These issues had been unsuccessfully addressed by

Gladstone's modest land reform of 1870, and had fed into Isaac Butt's Home Rule Association and its campaign in the 1874 election. A more thoroughgoing rural agitation developed speedily in the late 1870s, which was based upon some of the same foundations as its precursor. Donald Jordan has described a rural cash economy in the 1870s where the free growth and operation of the market was (or at least was perceived to be) critically blocked by the landlord system: land could not yet be freely bought and sold by farmers, and rentals could (at least in theory) be set arbitrarily by landlords, and without direct reference to agricultural prices.[3] In practice, the growth of the agrarian economy in the post-famine period meant that rents generally lagged behind prices; but there were always well-publicised and emotive exceptions. And, moreover, after 1877 there was an unfortunate conjunction of low prices, bad weather and poor harvests that effectively increased the burden of the existing rents, and which eventually stimulated a political crisis. The effects were felt throughout rural society, although the levels of distress and the motivation for protest varied. For the largest and wealthiest farmers the crisis was as much one of frustrated expectations as of subsistence; but for the smaller farmers, particularly in the west, there was the immediate threat of real impoverishment. In this context there arose – from within the Fenian movement – an initiative to create a land agitation that would draw upon rural distress and ambition, uniting both distressed and prosperous farmers, and which would simultaneously harness the talents of the constitutional and militant traditions within the national movement.[4]

Two distinct Fenian-dominated initiatives served to create the land campaign, or 'Land War', of 1879–81 and to bind the parliamentarians to an aggressive agrarian policy. At a national level the American Fenian (or Clan na Gael) leader, John Devoy, sought to reach a deal with Parnell, as the most prominent 'advanced' parliamentarian. Several approaches were made which eventually produced the 'New Departure' of June 1879, the informal agreement endorsing full legislative autonomy for Ireland, compulsory land purchase (official compulsion on landlords to sell out to their tenants), and a thoroughly independent Home Rule party at Westminster. In addition, the 'New Departure' asserted the integrity of the Fenian movement and of its armed strategies. Complementing this national initiative was Fenian involvement in the launch of a land campaign in the west of Ireland. This began in County Mayo in 1878-9, and would eventually achieve a national significance. Fenians were active in organising a series of meetings (beginning at Irishtown, Mayo, on 20 April 1879 and Westport on 8 June) which culminated in the creation of the National Land League of Mayo on 16 August. From this provincial initiative came the Irish National Land League, founded in Dublin on 21 October by Michael Davitt, Patrick Egan and Thomas Brennan, all social radicals and IRB members. Hovering uncertainly at the edge of much of this enterprise was Parnell, who had no significant record of agrarian activism, but who saw strategic opportunities both for himself and for the cause of Home Rule.

Parnell was elected President of the Irish National Land League at the time of its formation largely because of his prominence as a parliamentary obstructionist and because he had the confidence of the Fenian movement. He was not, nor was he to become, a thorough-going agrarian radical, but he had influence over other radicals as a successful fund-raiser, gathering some £72,000 in North America in January–March 1880, and as an apparent sympathiser with very advanced nationalist demands. His reported comment in Cincinnati on 20 February 1880 that 'none of us will be satisfied until we have destroyed the last link which keeps England bound to Ireland' won him Irish-American dollars and Fenian plaudits.[5] His importance as a parliamentarian was also growing in keeping with this North American success. At the general election of April 1880 twenty-seven of his supporters were returned, facilitating his nomination in May as the chairman of the Irish parliamentary party. Parnell's American treasure-chest helped to direct the mounting agrarian distress into the channel of the new Land League; and in the autumn of 1880 he toured the country to rouse support for the League, and to define its purpose and strategies. Here perhaps the most significant statement came at Ennis on 19 September 1880, when Parnell outlined the strategy of 'moral Coventry' or, as it was soon dubbed after its most celebrated victim, 'boycotting'.

Yet, the overall strategy of Parnell as land warrior was pacific and parliamentary. The Ennis speech, and others like it, identified parliament as an ultimate source of redress and – while emphasising the need to place pressure on English parliamentarians ('the measure of the land bill of next session will be the measure of your activity and energy this winter') – stressed the importance of non-violent proceedings.[6] An unmistakable account of his priorities was given in a speech at Galway, delivered on 24 October 1880: 'I would not have taken off my coat and gone to work if I had not known that we were laying the foundations by this movement for the recovery of our legislative independence'.[7]

Interpretations of Parnell's wider economic thought at this time and subsequently emphasise its essentially conservative thrust.[8] He was interested in the idea of farmers owning, as opposed to renting, their property. He was interested, too, in the future role of the landed elite in Irish society. But he was also confused and contradictory on the crucial issue

41

of agricultural rent levels. He was a moderate protectionist, but he tended to muffle his views so as not to scare off the free-trade Liberals. Parnell was concerned for the labouring poor of the town and countryside, and saw some relief in terms of industrial development. But, just as he backed away from the more outrageous proposals of the agrarian radicals, such as nationalising land, so he envisaged only a modest role for the state in the wider economic development of the country. It is possible that he was also interested in using agrarian agitation to align Protestant farmers behind the wider national cause. In an early public speech, Parnell was polite about the customary rights of the Ulster farming classes, but keen to emphasise that the rights of southern farmers were much more ancient.[9] On the other hand, some detailed work on south and west Ulster suggests that the Land League had made some progress among the rural Protestant population by 1880–1. Research on the scattered Protestant farming community beyond Ulster is scanty, but there is some ancedotal evidence which suggests that here, too, support for the League was taking root. Henry Kingsmill Moore was a Church of Ireland curate in Fermoy in 1880, and he was surprised to find 'a portrait of Parnell in the place of honour in a Protestant farm-house. "Why do you put him there?". "Doesn't he deserve it, is he not getting us a reduction in our rents?"'[10]

The fact that agrarian crime rose rapidly in the winter of 1880–1, and was linked by the British authorities to the spread of the Land League, should not divert from the substance of Parnell's concerns. Parnell wanted legislative independence, or Home Rule, for Ireland; the land question mattered only in so far as it was a longstanding and unavoidable political issue that all patriots, whether or not they were social radicals, were now compelled to address. Many interpretations of Parnell's approach to the land question have stressed that, while Parnell had some genuine sympathy for rural distress, his principal concern lay as much with landlords as with impoverished farmers: 'Parnell', as Andrew Kettle, a prominent Home Ruler and Dublin farmer, observed, 'was not a democrat'.[11] For Parnell, the social conflict generated by the land issue was the dam that separated the patriotic legacy and political talents of the traditional propertied elite from the wider community. By successfully breaching the land question, Parnell reasoned, the way was open for this old elite to take its rightful place within a new system of Home Rule. Here also was a critical intersection between the thought of Parnell and Gladstone – and an explanation for the Grand Old Man's later and apparently quirky enthusiasm for the Irish leader.

The Land War therefore served, in Parnell's calculation, to force a 'solution' to longstanding agrarian conflict, while also mobilising support behind the Home Rule cause. Equally helpfully, it consolidated his own standing as the national leader. But radicalism was neither an end in itself nor, indeed, for Parnell an end at all: the cohesion of this new national movement, built around the League and his own leadership, was a much more pressing concern. Parnell's own ascendancy to some extent depended upon the conjunction of interest groups within the national movement. With different, countervailing tendencies he could act as supreme arbiter and enforce his will upon the wider cause. At the same time, this form of leadership required a political tight-rope act of considerable dexterity. When one section of the movement achieved pre-eminence, Parnell had to identify himself (at least superficially) with the pre-eminent cause, for fear of looking anything less than 'advanced' or successful. On the other hand, the ascendancy of any one element of the party meant to some extent that Parnell was harnessed to its concerns, and this was an enslavement that he was not prepared to tolerate other than as a temporary expedient.

In the winter of 1880–1 the agrarian radical cause held sway within the movement, with an escalation of rural crime levels and an ever more trenchant statement of the League's demand for compulsory land purchase. Parnell moved with, indeed at the head of, this tendency. But when, in August 1881, the British Liberal government, responding ostensibly to its own two commissions of investigation (under Lord Bessborough and the Duke of Richmond) rather than to the League, passed a sweeping land reform, Parnell and his movement were faced with a dilemma. On the one hand, Gladstone's new Land Act granted the three 'fs' – fair rent, free sale and fixity of tenure – which had been a long-standing rallying cry for Irish tenants. On the other hand, Parnell and the League had not been consulted by Gladstone about the legislation; and, although the League leaders might persuasively claim to the Irish public that the Act was the result of their efforts, it was clear that the measure threatened to defuse the agitation and to undermine both the Home Rule cause and its leader. Gladstone's Land Act brought benefits to the substantial farmers and to northern farmers, but it brought little or nothing to the cottiers and small farmers of the west who had founded the agrarian campaign. Landless labourers, leaseholders and those in arrears of rent were excluded from the provisions of the measure. In addition, though there was a very modest provision for land purchase, the League's demand for compulsory purchase was effectively dismissed. The result of this mosaic of benefit and omission was that the great alliance of substantial farmer, smallholder and cottier which had sustained the League and Parnell's leadership began to collapse, with the beneficiaries of the legislation accepting its terms, and those excluded continuing to seek redress.

Gladstone's Land Act may therefore be seen as a kind of demolition ball, sweeping away the intricate but fragile architecture of the Irish National Land League.

Parnell sought to side-step this blow by avoiding any outright condemnation of the measure, and thus keeping its Irish supporters on-side, and yet by stopping far short of any endorsement. He urged abstention on the second reading of the bill in the House of Commons, and devised a kind of 'wait and see' strategy, whereby local Land League commanders were urged to test the new legislation in the courts. But the challenge created by Gladstone was pressing: he combined a tempting settlement with a number of coercive thrusts designed to divide and then break the national movement. By the late autumn and early winter of 1881, Parnell had been compelled to move away from his initial caution towards a more proactive strategy, designed to rescue both himself and the credibility of the movement over which he presided. It increasingly appeared that Parnell was moving to subvert the new land legislation: certainly his platform allusions to the Act grew more severe in the autumn of 1881. There is a case for arguing that Parnell was courting arrest, in order to acquire a martyr's crown. There may even be a case for arguing that the leaders of the Land League were courting its suppression, applying the same logic at an institutional as at an individual level. Certainly Parnell showed no great dismay when, on 13 October 1881, after a bitter public exchange with Gladstone, he was indeed eventually arrested on suspicion of 'treasonable practices' (as an Irish gentleman he was perhaps affronted by Gladstone's temerity – but this sense of personal slight is to be distinguished from his calculation of political advantage). This, together with other arrests, permitted the League a radical reply and a rallying call. On 18 October, Parnell and his lieutenants issued the 'No-Rent Manifesto', calling for a national rent strike. Two days later the government, having interned the leaders, moved to outlaw the League itself.

The Land Act of 1881 had threatened the national movement and its leader. Parnell, as an ambitious, conservative but thorough-going patriot, was prepared to see the government tame agrarian radicalism provided that this did not subvert either the wider national cause or his own leadership. Imprisonment underlined his national standing and his patriotic sacrifice. It also simultaneously distanced him from the bloody collapse of the League, while confirming his own importance as a leader with some influence over the hawks of the land movement; as a leader (adapting a comment made by Edward Saunderson) controlling 'the throttle-valve of crime'.[12] Imprisonment therefore increased Parnell's stock with both the government and the agrarian radicals, and provided him with leverage over both. It also served to provide a kind of seminar forum for the national leadership, given that they were all incarcerated together in Kilmainham gaol, and had ready access to one another. Andrew Kettle referred, for example, to Parnell and he settling 'the labourers' question one day at exercise'. Comparisons with the political education provided to the veterans of the 1916 rising at Frongoch and other internment camps might be evoked.[13]

But in the end imprisonment had only a limited utility: a temporary disengagement from public leadership might have certain timely benefits, but it could not be allowed to mutate into political abdication. And in April 1882, having made his gesture to radical agrarianism, Parnell moved to strike a deal with the government which would restore him to the public arena. This settlement, the 'Kilmainham Treaty' of 25 April, involved Parnell withdrawing the 'No-Rent Manifesto' and undertaking to move against agrarian crime. In return the government promised to address the two key constituencies excluded from the benefits of the 1881 Land Act – those with rent arrears and leaseholders. In addition, and crucially, Parnell and his imprisoned lieutenants were to be released from gaol.

The Kilmainham Treaty marked a critical turning point in the development of Parnell's leadership and of the wider national cause. It brought Parnell back within the parameters of parliamentary and constitutional politics, and it also suggested that the national movement could do business with the British government. It signalled another shift of direction: Parnell had ridden the storm of agrarian radicalism, but now that this had apparently spent its force, he was anxious to move on. The Kilmainham Treaty was of course unpopular with the radicals; but Parnell was spared the worst of any reaction from this quarter partly because the land war was already flagging, and partly because the treaty was swiftly followed, on 6 May, by one of the most shocking crimes of the late Victorian era, the Phoenix Park murders. The killing of the Chief Secretary for Ireland, Lord Frederick Cavendish, and the Under Secretary, T. H. Burke, by revolutionary nationalists of the bloody but marginal 'Invincibles' sect, inspired a backlash that Parnell was able to put to good use in reconstructing the national movement along new, more conservative lines. As a coda, it may be observed that it is just possible that Parnell, mindful of the continuing challenge of Fenianism and agrarianism, thought it wise to take the IRB oath immediately after his release from Kilmainham: the evidence for this spectacular piece of mistiming, viewed from the perspective of Phoenix Park, is persuasive but not, it should be emphasised, indisputable.[14]

The Kilmainham Treaty evokes a number of parallels. It was Parnell's first effective parley with the government; his most important earlier

45

undertaking had been with the Fenian movement in the 'New Departure' of 1879. But the treaty would also provide a precedent for future deals between advanced nationalism and the British government. In some limited ways it heralded the truce between the Lloyd George administration and Sinn Féin in July 1921, which was accompanied by a suspension (or at least a diminution) of violence, by prisoner releases and by effective political engagement. And, of course, in this sense Kilmainham has a closer, more contemporary resonance – with the Belfast Agreement and the wider peace process in Northern Ireland in the 1990s, when once again radical nationalist leaders pledged to distance themselves from violence in return for a more direct influence over government.

Parnell's careful political diplomacy in 1882 had preserved the national movement from the wreckage of the land campaign, and it heralded the beginning of a reconstruction of the movement and of its strategies. Here Parnell used the opportunity created both by the Phoenix Park killings and by divisions within the land movement to pursue a more directly national as well as a more socially conservative agenda. The Land League had been suppressed, and was in any case internally fracturing. It was replaced in October 1882 by the Irish National League, a body that capitalised upon the achievements of its predecessor (even in terms of its name), but which, differing in its organisation and in its balance of power, was in some ways a tacit repudiation. Much more than the Land League, the Irish National League was hierarchical, indeed even perhaps autocratic in structure, with Parnell wielding immense authority; much more than the Land League, which was heavily infiltrated by Fenianism, the Irish National League harnessed the power of the Catholic Church.

The informal alliance between the new, tightly disciplined National League and the Catholic Church was not the only factor explaining the revitalisation of the Home Rule cause after 1882, but the importance of this alliance was profound. Parnell, a somewhat lax member of the Church of Ireland, had always recognised the importance of keeping the Catholic Church on-side, and he had long cultivated friendly and politically useful connections with individual priests. There had been moments of difficulty, as in 1879, when the influential proprietor of the *Freeman's Journal*, Edmund Dwyer Gray, accused Parnell of referring to some opponents as 'papist rats'.[15] Parnell had also, in 1880, supported the cause of Charles Bradlaugh, the controversial English republican and atheist. This was of a piece with his Fenian politicking at the time, given that Bradlaugh in 1867 and after had been a prominent English sympathiser with the Irish Republican Brotherhood. By 1882–3, however, Parnell's connection with Fenianism was less vivid than hitherto; while his relationship with the hierarchy was beginning to be placed on a new, and more intimate footing.

Although it was condemned by Rome, many Irish priests and bishops were involved with the Parnell tribute, a national fund-raising venture designed to alleviate the leader's financial distress. When the final cheque for £37,000 was presented to a markedly ungracious Parnell in December 1883, forty priests attended the celebration dinner. Changes in the composition and attitudes of the Catholic episcopate at this time helped to nurture harmony with Parnell and his Home Rule party. The marginalisation after 1883 of Cardinal McCabe, an opponent of the Land League, helped matters in this regard, while Archbishop McEvilly of Tuam moved towards the national cause from a position of mild sympathy with the Crown. McEvilly's political migration occurred after a fight with the Dublin Castle authorities over the celebrated Maamtrasna murder case in August 1882, where McEvilly came to believe that a miscarriage of justice had taken place.[16]

But this shuffling episcopal movement was also stimulated by Parnell's own actions and revisions. In the spring of 1883 he reversed his stand on the Bradlaugh question, coming out effectively against the veteran atheist who, despite his Fenian sympathies, was widely disliked in Ireland on account of his godlessness. Challenging godlessness, in fact, was a Parnellite motif in 1883: he spoke against the annual vote of supply for the 'godless' Queen's Colleges, non-denominational institutions which had been a bugbear of the Catholic hierarchy for almost forty years. In July 1884 Parnell, on the prompting of the Irish bishops, moved to take up the cause of the Vatican, whose property was under threat from the secular authorities of the Italian state; only the intervention of Cardinal Manning persuaded Parnell to let the matter rest. The reward for this piety, and perhaps more directly for the growing discipline and influence of the Parnellites, duly came in October 1884, when the Catholic bishops agreed to accept the Irish party as their sole parliamentary agents on the educational issue. This has been seen as the most significant development in the history of Parnell's long relationship with the Catholic Church. It has also been hailed, rather more grandiloquently, as a critical stage in the emergence of Catholicism as the established church of the national movement and of the nascent Irish state (or, for the moment, the Irish state-within-a-state).

The increasingly explicit endorsement of Catholicism was of vital importance to the success of the Home Rule venture, but up to a point this endorsement was earned by Parnell and his supporters. This was not just a matter of Parnell's sensitive handling of traditional Church concerns; it was also a reflection of the extent to which Parnellism was reforming itself, and benefiting from opportunities created by other agencies. The organisational revisions incorporated within the National League have already been mentioned. Like Daniel O'Connell's Catholic Association, the National League worked in close co-operation with the Catholic hierarchy in consolidating its hold over the Irish electorate. Like the Catholic Association, too, or the repeal movement, the National League presented a crisply defined and readily comprehensible goal: legislative independence. There were secondary aims, such as land purchase, but there was also a marked retreat from the radicalism of the Land League, compulsory land purchase being largely set aside as a war-cry.

The elaborate hierarchy of the National League obscured the reality of a carefully policed and highly centralised organisation. The autocratic tenor of the League's structure was now, in 1883–4, replicated within the formerly shambolic Irish parliamentary party. Where once, in the 1870s, the Home Rulers at Westminster had been characterised by schism, disloyalty to the party leader and (beyond the irrepressible obstructionist cohort) idleness, Parnell's party emerged swiftly as a tightly disciplined and, on the whole, energetic body of parliamentarians. The inauguration of the 'party pledge' in 1884 decisively reinforced this tendency: parliamentary candidates undertook to vote with the majority of the party on all occasions when it was judged that a united front was required. This, together with the blessings bestowed upon the Parnellites by the Catholic Church, meant that the kind of dissent that had flourished in the Butt era, emanating not least from Parnell himself, was now virtually impossible to sustain. Parnell increasingly found himself master both of a regimented parliamentary body and a national party machine. And the ultimate end of both, besides sustaining his own pre-eminence, was Home Rule.

In addition to these internal initiatives, the party was aided by political reform originating within the British state and designed principally for British purposes. The Corrupt and Illegal Practices Act (1883) restricted the amount that might be spent on a parliamentary election, and thus curtailed the ability of the very rich (still in Ireland likely to be Protestant and loyalist) to manipulate the democratic process. Parliamentary reform, with the Franchise Act of 1884 and Redistribution Act of 1885, brought the vote to small farmers and agricultural labourers and abolished small borough seats (such as Dungannon, Co. Tyrone, with 279 voters and one MP) where comparatively wealthy Protestants often exercised a disproportionate influence. In total there were now some 738,000 voters, as opposed to 222,000 under the previous electoral law.[17] Whereas old arrangements such as the Irish Franchise Act of 1850 were an important prop to the Home Rule movement, there emerged in 1884–5 a large and more thoroughly Catholic electorate who were likely further to bolster the Home Rule cause.[18]

Parliamentary reform also augmented the forces of nationalism in Britain, as many poorer Irish immigrants were either enfranchised for the first time, or better represented as a result of boundary revisions.[19] Parnell had a longstanding interest in the Irish community in Britain, having ousted Butt from the presidency of the Home Rule Confederation of Great Britain in 1877; and, ever the political opportunitist, he seized the chance created by reform and redistribution to relaunch the British Home Rule movement, and to place it more firmly under his own supervision. Looking ahead somewhat, the results of these reforms and the subsequent reorganisation were first fully seen in the general election of November–December 1885. The Irish parliamentary party increased their total representation from sixty-three seats to eighty-five, and boasted an MP who sat for an English constituency (T. P. O'Connor in the 'Scotland' division of Liverpool).

Having formed this machine, supervised its expansion and shaped its alliances, it might be thought that Parnell was confined to using it to pressure the Liberals. It is true that the Liberals offered the best hope for the fulfilment of the nationalist agenda: Gladstone had shown himself responsive to Irish electoral pressure in the late 1860s, while the Conservative government of 1874–80 had utterly lacked interest in Ireland. But if the Liberals were the best, they were not an only hope. The sympathies of Parnell and of key sections within the National League by no means lay automatically with Gladstonian Liberalism.[20] On some ideological as well as practical grounds the Tories offered almost as much to Parnellism as did the Liberals. The alliance between Liberalism and the Home Rule movement which was formulated in 1886, and which lasted virtually until 1918, was perhaps a likely, but never an automatic denouement to the politicking of the early 1880s; and it was certainly a denouement that – for Parnell – contained many loose ends.

The Tories were not all or always enemies to Irish nationalism, and there is evidence from at least 1880 onwards of a degree of thoughtfulness.[21] Irish Tory peers and landed proprietors had colluded in the passage of the Land Act of 1881, which has been widely interpreted as marking a turning point in the party's attitudes towards the Irish land question.[22] The Tories were held to be more sympathetic to land purchase than the more parsimonious and economically doctrinaire Liberals. *Compulsory* land purchase, the cry of the Land League, was certainly not acceptable to either British party, but then this demand was soon moderated by the leaders of the National League. The Tories, the party of the

Church of England, were also more sympathetic to denominational education than the Liberals; and, given Parnell's closely Catholic line after 1882–3, this meant that the Tories offered the best chance of reform on this key national issue.

Moreover, the National League was socially more conservative than its predecessor, the Land League; and it was dominated by the big farmers and other prosperous types for whom British Toryism, as a party of property and particularly rural property, held some attraction. Andrew Kettle articulated this sympathy in unequivocal language. Writing at the time of the third Home Rule Bill, Kettle affirmed that 'I confess that I felt then [in 1885], and still feel, a greater leaning towards the British Tory Party than I ever could have towards the so-called Liberals'.[23] This leaning was shared by a disparate group of Home Rulers, including T. M. Healy and perhaps Parnell himself, who was much closer on many issues and indeed in political temperament to Tory cynics like Randolph Churchill than to the principled radicals, pious Nonconformists and high-minded Gladstonians who comprised the Liberal front bench.

These affinities were clearly demonstrated when, in June 1885, a minority Conservative government was formed under the premiership of Lord Salisbury. It would, of course, be wrong to read too much into the ingenious efforts of ministers trying to sustain their grip on power; and it would be wrong to neglect the firm evidence indicating that Salisbury was determined not merely to open up communication with the Parnellites but also to mollify Irish loyalism. The Tories, in other words, were playing the political field in 1885, but at the very least this indicates a measure of flexibility in the rules of the parliamentary game. Lord Randolph Churchill, later a much-quoted proponent of Ulster Unionism ('Ulster will fight and Ulster will be right'), held conversations with Parnell, while the Tory whip, Rowland Winn, sounded out his Home Rule counterpart, Richard Power. Churchill and his ally Sir John Gorst made conveniently sneering allusions to Irish loyalists while Salisbury quietly distributed honours and junior offices among the same constituency.[24]

The climax to this flirtation came on 1 August 1885 in 'the spectral ambience' of a vacant mansion in Hill Street, Mayfair, with a confidential meeting between Parnell and the Tory Lord Lieutenant of Ireland, the Earl of Carnarvon.[25] This was interpreted by Parnell to at least one of his followers as the beginning of 'aristocratic home rule' and of 'class conservative government in Ireland', the alternative being a potentially revolutionary alliance between English radicalism and Irish democracy.[26] In fact Parnell seems, uncharacteristically, to have done most of the talking on this occasion; and indeed he seems to have been positively expansive in defining his fundamental (and, in the event, moderate) ambitions. Parnell was keen to remind Carnarvon of his desire for a form of Irish legislative assembly or 'central parliament', but he also accepted the desirability of an incremental approach, with a gradual accretion of powers and the education of the Irish electorate in the atrophied skills of self-government. Land purchase was broached at the Hill Street meeting, with Parnell keen to emphasise both the merits of the strategy and the desirability of settling the land question in advance of Home Rule. In fact the Conservatives passed a land purchase act – the Ashbourne Act – on 14 August, which provided £5 million to fund the sale of holdings to occupying tenants.

Indeed it might well be argued that the Tories at this time were offering (or appearing to offer) Parnell virtually as much as the Liberals on the wider constitutional issue, and were offering more on the vital questions of land purchase and denominational education. The Tories were also much less dangerous for Parnell to deal with than the Liberals: R. Barry O'Brien remarked in 1898 that 'in Ireland the Tory is regarded as an open enemy, the Whig as a treacherous friend. It is the Whigs, not the Tories, who have habitually sapped the integrity of Irish representation'.[27] While many thoughtful, propertied Irish nationalists might have nurtured some quiet fellow feeling with 'the open enemy', there were sections of the national movement who instinctively associated the British Tory Party with Protestant ascendancy: these sections also gave Gladstone credit for disestablishment and tenurial reform. But it was *because* Gladstone maintained a hold over Irish electors that he presented such a danger to Parnell and the national leadership. In 1881 Gladstone had not only conceded a major land reform, but also, simultaneously, wrong-footed Parnell and the Land League; and in 1885 he retained a capacity to throw the national movement into disarray. Concessions from the Tories were never likely to be as subversive as this. At the same time, concessions from the Tories – for the moment, at any rate – were unlikely to be any less complete than the Gladstonian offering. For this reason, and particularly because of Tory sympathy on issues like education, Parnell published a manifesto on 23 November 1885, on the eve of the general election, calling on Irish voters in Great Britain to reject the Liberals.

Was Gladstone forced along new avenues of policy by Irish nationalists, or did he act according to his own convictions? This question is raised by Gladstone's Irish reforms of 1869–70, the Land Act of 1881, and also by the first Home Rule Bill of 1886. Gladstone was certainly not intellectually enslaved to Irish nationalism but he was highly responsive to the national movement at critical moments. Perhaps it was, as Richard

Shannon has suggested, 'incautious and uncritical readiness to take up cues proffered by the Irish'.[28] It is certainly true that, once Gladstone had made up his mind to favour the Irish interest, he could be astonishingly quick to accept supporting evidence for his decision.

Gladstone's response to Fenianism in the late 1860s was typically ambiguous but can, in the end, be pinned down. It has been argued that, though his Irish reforms of 1869–70 appeared to be a direct response to Fenian outrage, 'the fundamental source of Gladstone's interest in Ireland at this time was neither moral conviction, nor fenianism, but [Irish Catholic] votes'.[29] Equally, however, his characteristically hair-splitting observation on the introduction of the Irish Church Bill in 1869 that he had been influenced by 'the *intensity* of Fenianism' appeared to indicate, as the Fenians themselves claimed, that he had been coerced into action.[30] On occasion, as here, it is hard to escape the impression that the subtlety of Gladstone's political intelligence ultimately worked against his favoured ends.

Similar ambiguities are evident with the origins of Gladstone's Land Act of 1881. Although the Act appeared to be a direct response to the agitation of the Land League, and though it certainly served to defuse the League, its immediate roots lay in a veritable 'litter' of official commissions of inquiry. Richard Shannon has noted of the legislation that 'no attempt was made to obtain consent and support in Ireland. The bill was not promoted in Ireland. The Irish MPs were not consulted'.[31] With disestablishment, Irish land and ultimately Home Rule, Gladstone demonstrated an unerring capacity to annex the ideas of others, apparently voluntarily, and to deploy them for his own political ends. Events in Ireland could precipitate action that often had complex origins and a multiplicity of purposes.

Home Rule, like disestablishment and comprehensive land reform, had engaged Gladstone's ever-alert political intelligence for some time before the issue was deemed to be practical politics. Gladstone himself claimed in May 1893 (in what John Morley termed a 'singular self-deception') that 'as to Home Rule he [Gladstone] did not feel that he had much changed. Any time within the last 30 years his mind had been open to it; but the demand had not come in clear constitutional form from Ireland, and in the next place it was tangled and involved with separation, treason and violence'.[32] The gestation of the notion of Home Rule has in fact been rigorously analysed by Gladstone's biographers and other scholars of late Victorian Liberalism. Some emphasis has been laid recently upon the Irish sympathies of those Positivist thinkers who lurked at the fringes of Gladstonian Liberalism, and who had a mild influence over mainstream figures such as Morley himself. It is indeed possible that these Positivist supporters of Irish autonomy might have had an indirect influence over Gladstone, but any connection has yet to be clearly defined.[33]

Notwithstanding Morley's scepticism, some latitude has been detected beneath the apparent steadiness of Gladstone's unionism. In September 1871 Gladstone reminded an audience at Aberdeen that there was 'nothing that Ireland has asked and which this country and this Parliament have refused'.[34] In February 1882 he had prefaced a speech with the observation that he did not think exception should be taken to calls 'for an Irish Legislative Body to deal with Irish affairs', provided that the integrity of the empire was respected. The thrust of his address was, far from being a condemnation of Home Rule, a complaint that the practicalities of the issue had never been satisfactorily explained by the Home Rulers.[35] The speech caused surprise and consternation, but it was defended by Gladstone as merely an expression of his longstanding and principled enthusiasm for local government. Gladstone on this occasion also, privately, expressed a concern that the state itself might be threatened if the demand for Home Rule was pressed by a 'decisive majority' of Irish MPs and then rejected out of hand by the imperial parliament.[36]

A turning point seems to have come 'almost casually' in early March 1885.[37] At a moment when Irish matters were a relatively low priority, and when Gladstone was distracted by more pressing foreign and imperial concerns, he read a speech delivered by the Parnellite lieutenant William O'Brien and realised 'that there was and never could be any moral obligation to the Irish nation in the Act of Union'.[38] Of course this was at one level simply the culmination of long reflection on the issue of Irish local government and it certainly did not signify any desire for immediate movement. Gladstone recognised the significance not merely of personal epiphanies such as this, but also of wider political conjunctions and opportunities, and though Home Rule was now a moral imperative, the time for action was not yet deemed to be at hand.

In the spring of 1885 the Parnellites, though maturing in (for Gladstone) an acceptably moderate form, had not yet been augmented by the reform and redistribution measures of 1884–5 and by the general election results of December 1885: their case, though pressing, was not yet urgent. On the other hand, it seemed possible that a deal might be struck with them which – pleasingly – would fall short of what Gladstone, by March 1885, was prepared to offer. Joseph Chamberlain, the radical MP for Birmingham and President of the Board of Trade in the Liberal administration, was in communication with Parnell at this time, seeking an agreement that would harness the parliamentary power of the Irish party in return for 'the settlement of the Irish difficulty'.[39] The 'settlement' that Chamberlain proposed involved democratic county councils which, in turn, would elect a Central Board for Ireland. There would, in addition, be a softening of the government's special crimes legislation. But the deal was never struck, and the initiative therefore remained with Gladstone. Parnell and Chamberlain had fundamentally different purposes, Parnell seeing the Central Board scheme as a limited and temporary expedient pending the restoration of an Irish parliament, while Chamberlain sought a lasting alternative to full Home Rule. The Board was perhaps a deliberately ambiguous mechanism that was intended (like later fudges in 1916 or indeed in 1998) to circumvent the divisions between the British and Irish positions. In any event, Chamberlain failed to impress his ministerial colleagues and on 9 May 1885, despite Gladstone's support, the Central Board proposal was thrown out by the cabinet. While the Prime Minister wept some crocodile tears for Chamberlain, he now informed selected colleagues that 'the field is open for the consideration of future measures [for Irish autonomy]' and that he was prepared to go 'rather further' than the idea of a Central Board.[40]

The Liberal government fell in June 1885, and Gladstone's calculations henceforth had to take account of an apparently strengthening bond between the Tories and Parnell. This flirtation was perceived by Gladstone as dangerous but potentially useful. There was certainly the prospect that, having been courted by both main parties of the British state, the Irish would inflate their demands. There was also the possibility of a bidding war of sorts between the British parties. In fact Parnell does seem to have firmed up his demands; Gladstone, however, was explicit in rejecting 'any counterbidding of any sort against Lord R. Churchill [perceived as the likely architect of a Tory–Parnellite bond]'.[41] On the other hand, the Tory courtship brought forward the possibility that they might be persuaded to concede something in the nature of Home Rule. This in turn meant that a major threat to the British state would effectively be averted, since the measure could probably pass through the House of Lords. In addition it could probably be treated in the spirit of bipartisanship. There were, of course party advantages. The Tories, having served the national interest by disposing of Parnell, might fracture, leaving the way open for a lengthy Liberal domination of the government: the precedents of 1829 and 1846 were alive in the Gladstonian imagination. Later, when it became clear that the Tories were not in fact prepared to be noble, Gladstone complained in a wonderfully Pecksniffian manner that they 'might have made one of those Party sacrifices which seem now to have gone out of fashion, but which in other days – the days of Sir Robert Peel and the Duke of Wellington – were deemed the highest honour'.[42]

In the highly charged and ambiguous condition of British politics in late 1885 there was still plenty of scope for that most characteristic of Gladstonian vices, wishful thinking. Lord Salisbury's keynote speech at Newport on 7 October 1885 was read by Herbert Gladstone and other Liberals as not entirely 'closing the door' on a settlement with the Irish: 'in the field of Irish autonomy Conservative competition was active and in exasperating contrast to the dull inertness of the Whigs', complained Herbert in 1928, perhaps not without a certain mischievousness.[43] A badly garbled version of the Parnell–Carnarvon interview reached Gladstone in mid-December, and this, in conjunction with the apparent ambiguities of Salisbury's position, sustained hopes that the Tories were prepared to deal. On 15 December Gladstone forced himself upon A. J. Balfour, the Tory President of the Local Government Board and nephew to Salisbury, furiously urging the need for the cabinet to respond to the issue of Irish government. This he deemed to be of paramount importance, given that the Parnellites had triumphed in Ireland in the recent general election, and given the real risk of violence if the demand for Home Rule were resisted. This was followed up by a letter on 20 December promising that, if the Tories were minded to settle the 'whole question of the future Government of Ireland', they would have the full support of the Liberal Party.[44] The approach was, of course, based upon a wilful misreading of Salisbury's subtle and ambiguous gamesmanship in 1885, but it also reflected the extent to which Gladstone was now obsessed with the importance of Home Rule as a social emollient, and the extent to which he was capable of interpreting the wider world in a convenient but ultimately illusory manner.[45]

The general election of 1885 gave Gladstone and the Liberals 335 seats, the Tories 249 and left Parnell and the Home Rulers holding the balance of power with 86 seats. Gladstone's overtures to the outgoing Tory administration are capable of bearing several interpretations, but aside from all else, they indicate a profound sense of urgency at the emerging demands of the parliamentary and Irish political scene. Gladstone had long feared the presence of a disciplined cohort of Home Rulers in an otherwise antagonistic House of Commons. The impact upon parliamentary business and, more important, upon the wider stability of the British state was likely to be highly detrimental. It was the responsibility of the (Tory) government to address this challenge, and not the opposition party: this was one of the fundamental points that Gladstone was seeking to convey to Balfour and to Salisbury (and, indeed, to Parnell).[46] At the same time, Gladstone was simultaneously anxious to resist challenges within his own party, and to maintain charge of the Liberal stand on Ireland. He was also increasingly eager to flag his own sympathies, given the insistent Unionist pressures within Liberalism and given, too, the now urgent dangers of a completely alienated Home Rule party.

In mid-December 1885, Gladstone was receiving rumours from different sources, including Thomas Wemyss Reid, editor of the *Leeds Mercury*, that Chamberlain and his allies were seeking to thwart a Gladstone administration on the grounds that the latter had entered into a diabolical pact with Parnell. At the very least Reid, a Home Ruler, was fearful that even the hint of a Gladstone–Parnell deal would provoke some sections of the Liberal press into premature affirmations of Unionism. Reid was in correspondence with Herbert Gladstone, and it was in an evidently feeble effort to elucidate to the press the studied ambiguity of his father's position that Herbert finally revealed Gladstone's fundamental sympathy with the Home Rule demand.[47] This probably inadvertent revelation, soon to be dubbed the 'Hawarden Kite', was published on 17 December, and it marked an end to the ambiguity in the British parties' dealings with the Irish cause. In January 1886 the dying Tory administration formally rejected Gladstone's offer of a bipartisan initiative on Ireland, and signalled its desire to return to a coercionist approach. Henceforth the distinctions in the parties' approaches would become ever more marked.

The fall of the Tory government and the formation – on 1 February 1886 – of the third Gladstone administration paved the way towards the generous response to Irish demands that the new Prime Minister had promised. But, with the lavish benefits of hindsight, it is possible to distinguish difficulties with Gladstone's manner of proceeding. As late as 6 January 1886 he assured Sir William Harcourt that 'it is for me in forming a government to prepare the terms on which I ask others to join with me: unquestionably they commit no-one to the advocacy of a separate parliament'.[48] When he assumed office he indicated, with equally self-serving precision, that he was merely going 'to examine whether it is or is not practicable to comply with the desire' for limited legislative autonomy.[49] He identified a critical link between the land issue and the wider national question, and indicated the need to address both at the same time.[50] Having given no firm commitment to legislate, but having tied the fate of Home Rule to a land bill, he then proceeded with dangerous speed and secrecy to draft a measure for Irish self-government. Cabinet colleagues were for the most part kept in the dark: Harcourt, now Chancellor of the Exchequer, only received a first detailed intimation of Gladstone's proposals on 7 March; and the wider issue was first raised at cabinet, by Chamberlain, on 13 March.[51] The cabinet discussed a complete draft of the measure only on 26 March, when Chamberlain and G. O. Trevelyan resigned in protest.

The Parnellites, of course, fared little better. Gladstone was anxious to be able to assert that there was no grubby negotiation over terms with the Irish, though there was in fact some indirect communication in the later stages of the drafting procedure: John Morley, a trusted Gladstonian, was the intermediary. In addition, there was a substantive negotiation between Gladstone and Parnell in early April, a few days before the launch of the measure. Parnell fought for a reduction in the Irish contribution to imperial expenditure, and conceded control of customs and excise to the imperial parliament.[52] On 7 April 1886, the day before the introduction of the Home Rule Bill, Parnell was able to assemble his party and inform them of the measure's contents.

The Home Rule Bill of 1886 made provision for a unicameral Irish legislature (the word 'parliament' was avoided), modelled on the general synod of the disestablished Church of Ireland.[53] Controversially, there was to be no Irish representation at Westminster. Instead, there were to be two 'orders' in a new legislature: these might meet and debate together, but if it was so wished, they could meet and vote separately. It was proposed that the first order should have 103 members, comprising the 28 existing representative peers and 75 additional members, elected for ten years on a highly restrictive franchise. The members themselves were to be comparatively wealthy men, possessing either £4000 in capital or property worth £200 a year. The first order, in brief, represented the Irish 'classes', and given the constrained franchise and the presence of the peers, it would have been disproportionately Protestant in composition. The second order was to have either 204 or 206 members, depending on whether the graduates of the Royal University, like those of Trinity College Dublin, were to be enfranchised. Here there were no fancy franchises or restrictions on membership, for the normal (and, after the reforms of 1884–5, relatively expansive) parliamentary franchise applied. The popularly constituted second order was to have preeminence in the proposed Home Rule dispensation. The first order had no right of veto, but merely a delaying power of three years, much like the British House of Lords after 1911. Thereafter legislation might be enacted on the basis of a joint vote of the two orders, a proceeding which – given the size of the second order – underlined the democratic thrust of the proposed chamber.

Who was to govern Ireland? Gladstone seems to have wanted responsible government for the Irish, but at the same time he did not want to offer any clear-cut definitions, perhaps because of the implications for British constitutional practice, and in particular for the royal prerogative. The Lord Lieutenant (who could now be a Catholic) acted for the monarch, and was alone responsible for appointing ministers and summoning or dissolving the legislature. But the Lord Lieutenant was not explicitly required to choose ministers from the majority party, or even from within the wider legislature. Thus, while the shape and composition of the parliament broadly followed Parnell's requirements, the executive fell very far short of the Irish demand, and there are some grounds for suspecting that Gladstone, like the British statesmen of 1782–3, was prepared to concede the lavish trappings of legislative independence, but was deliberately more coy when dealing with executive power. Alan Ward has noted that 'the language of home rule thus provided many opportunities for the British government to interfere in the Irish legislative process through its advice to the Crown, and through the Lord Lieutenant, who was a member of the government'.[54] He has also reasonably inferred that 'this is why Parnell had argued in 1885 that there should be no Lord Lieutenant'.[55]

The Home Rule Bill of 1886 accepted implicitly that the parliament of the United Kingdom remained the supreme legislative authority for Ireland. The new Home Rule legislature was given wide-ranging powers over domestic issues, although Westminster retained in its grasp a list of crucial 'reserved' matters. The Irish were not allowed any legislative control over, among other things, the Crown, declarations of war or the settlement of peace, foreign and imperial affairs, trade and navigation, customs and excise, the coinage and, of course, the Home Rule constitution. The Irish legislature was permitted to take charge of the Dublin Metropolitan Police (DMP) after two years, but control of the Royal Irish Constabulary (RIC) was not immediately conceded. Indeed, given the role of the RIC in suppressing the Fenian Rising of 1867 and in combatting the Land War of the early 1880s, policing was no less sensitive an issue at this time than it would become in the Northern Ireland of the late 1990s. It is also worth observing that the distinction between the DMP and the RIC in the national consciousness was reflected not just in the Home Rule Bill, but also in the different treatment of the two forces at the time of, and shortly after, Irish independence (1921–4).

A number of 'rightful' Irish concerns were flagged: the civil service, the post office (both perennial sources of excitement for those seeking patronage) and the judiciary, although the United Kingdom House of Lords was designated as the Final Court of Appeal for Ireland. Under the terms of the bill, the Irish government was to be responsible for domestic tax charges, although control of Irish customs revenue remained firmly at Westminster. Gladstone had come to believe that any concessions on this issue would precipitate a dissolution of the modified union that he was seeking to preserve. Ireland, it may be noted, was also to bear responsibility for a number of fixed contributions to the Consolidated Fund of the United Kingdom: namely, £1.46 million as the annual Irish share of the National Debt (the Irish share of the debt was calculated to be £48 million), £1.66 million as a contribution to the maintenance of the British army and navy, £1 million to fund the DMP and RIC, and £110,000 to pay for Imperial Civil Service expenditure in Ireland.

Some legislative 'no-go' areas were also mapped out. These mostly involved the ever-controversial question of religion, and were designed to quieten Protestant fears of Rome Rule without giving offence to Catholics. The proposed Irish legislature could not endow any church, restrict religious practice or impose religious tests for public office. The legislature could not require children to receive religious instruction at school: it could not skew the processes of law to favour any denomination.

Debate on the first Home Rule Bill took place at Westminster between 8 April and 7 June 1886. For a short time (16 April to 3 May) there was a parallel debate on a land purchase measure, seen by Gladstone as a complementary part of the wider project to sustain social order in Ireland. The reaction of Parnell and his lieutenants to this twin thrust, Home Rule and land purchase, is revealing. Parnell broadly welcomed the Land Purchase Bill, whereas some of his radical or disaffected colleagues (Davitt, Healy) were more grudging. On the other hand, it was on this issue of purchase that the consonance between Gladstone and Parnell was most marked. Both were concerned that the existing landed elite assume an influence in the new Ireland, with Gladstone affirming that 'even the Irish Nationalists may desire that those marked out by leisure, wealth and station for attention to public duties, and for the exercise of influence, may become in no small degree, the natural and effective and safe leaders of the people'.[56] It may be that Gladstone was alluding to Parnell himself, for whom the future of his own caste was an abiding preoccupation. Already by 3 May, however, it was clear that land purchase was being being suffocated by its companion measure, and on 27 May it was, for the moment, dropped.

The Home Rule Bill raised rather greater difficulties for Parnell than did land purchase. On 30 October 1885 he had directed that an outline constitution be compiled, and this is useful in the context of April–June 1886 in so far as it indicates the disparities between the Parnellite and Gladstonian definitions of Home Rule. The Irish explicitly required the abolition of the office of Lord Lieutenant 'and all other offices in Ireland under the Crown connected with the domestic affairs of that country'. On the other hand, they were prepared to concede that 'no enactment of the [Irish] chamber shall have the force of law until it shall have received the assent of the Crown'.[57] These stipulations, and indeed Gladstone's requirement that the lord lieutenancy be preserved, should probably be seen in the light of the experience of Irish legislative independence at the end of the eighteenth century. At this time the fundamental restraint upon Grattan's parliament rested not with the theoretical rights of the Crown to veto legislation (which were rarely exercised), but rather with the Irish executive, which was appointed in effect by the British government. The Lord Lieutenant, his political influence and powers of patronage were important parts of this restraining mechanism, but other Crown appointments 'connected with the domestic affairs of [Ireland]' equally served often to undermine the patriotic effusions of the newly 'autonomous' parliament in College Green.

The Parnellites also demanded, in October 1885, control over customs duties. Here, again, their logic is not hard to decipher. The overwhelming bulk of Irish revenue was derived from customs receipts, and control of customs was therefore both a practical and a patriotic imperative. It is also conceivable that the Parnellites recalled the formidable power of the late-eighteenth-century revenue commissioners, who were Crown appointees in charge of customs collection, and who, like John Beresford, often used their immense influence in the interests of the British-controlled administration at Dublin Castle. Gladstone was similarly impressed by the significance of the customs issue, perhaps from an Irish historical perspective, but certainly with a view to harnessing the Irish legislature and any separatist impulses that it might contain. Even Harcourt, Chancellor of the Exchequer in the Liberal government and the most reluctant of the Home Rulers within the Liberal leadership, had been taking his Irish history lessons seriously: 'I have been and am studying the question as well as I can. I have found Lecky's book on the period just before Grattan's parliament very instructive'.[58]

In October 1885 the Irish also defined the total contribution of their putative legislature to imperial funds, and registered an explicit claim 'to maintain a police force for the preservation of order and the enforcement of the law'.[59] Gladstone's unwillingness to place the RIC in the hands of the Home Rule parliament has already been noted. But the different definitions of the financial relationship between Ireland and Great Britain require some elucidation. In the manifesto of October 1885 the Irish simultaneously claimed control over a much greater share of Irish revenue than was proposed by Gladstone, and designated a much smaller contribution to the Consolidated Fund. The Irish suggestion was that £1 million be paid 'in lieu of the right of the Crown to levy taxes in Ireland for Imperial purposes'.[60] Moreover, any military expenditure in Ireland undertaken by the Crown would be paid out of the designated £1 million, and if military costs rose above this amount, the British exchequer would be required to foot the bill. It will be recalled that the total Irish contribution suggested in the Home Rule Bill amounted to at least

£3.12 million, even if it assumed that all policing and civil service costs would be borne by the new Dublin administration. In fact the proposed constitution for Ireland of October 1885 makes no mention of any Irish responsibility for the National Debt of the United Kingdom.

Given the disparities between the Parnellite programme of October 1885 and the Gladstonian measure of April 1886, and given the relatively slight consultation between the Prime Minister and the nationalist leaders, it is hardly surprising that the Irish should have greeted the first Home Rule Bill with a measure of caution. Parnell's initial response, on 8 April, was one of guarded welcome, tinctured with complaints about the heavy financial burden that was being proposed for the future Irish exchequer. He also opposed the suggested arrangement whereby the new orders of the proposed legislature might vote separately. On the other hand, he came quickly to recognise that the bill was important less as a specific set of proposals than as a patriotic fillip; and he recognised, too, both the potential of the legislation and the political dangers of further undermining Gladstone. In early May he stayed away from the Commons in order to avoid being pressured into awkward (and probably pointless) negotiations or compromises.[61] By mid-May it was quite clear that the bill was unlikely to succeed and that Parnell and the Irish had nothing to gain by elaborating their qualms. It has been rightly said that, whether or not it was enacted, the Home Rule Bill was a triumph for Parnell: 'its defeat would not impair his standing. Indeed, the more sure the Bill was to fall, the more fully it could be supported'.[62] This assessment is fully borne out by Parnell's remarkable statement on 7 May, hailing the bill as a 'final settlement' of Irish demands.

The Home Rulers' political case concentrated upon the stated democratic will of the Irish people, upon the extent to which the existing arrangement had brought a weakening of social order, and upon the opportunity for a redress of the historic wrongs experienced by the Irish at the hands of British government. Nor were some of the practical benefits ignored by the bill's advocates: Westminster would remain the supreme legislative authority in the United Kingdom, while the Commons would be freed from the congestion of Irish business. The bill, it was claimed, gave adequate recognition to the interests of minorities.

The rival Unionist case, particularly the Irish Unionist case, may also be noted briefly at this stage. Unionists claimed that there was no electoral mandate for the bill, given that it had not been put before voters in November 1885. Unionists also denied that the existing political arrangements had failed, distinguishing instead a failure to work these arrangements. Ireland under Home Rule, it was claimed, would be the haunt of 'Captain Moonlight' (that is to say, agrarian terrorism) and the activists of the National League. Unionists such as the otherwise squabbling W. E. H. Lecky and T. D. Ingram disputed the historical arguments used to bolster the Home Rule case.[63]

Many British and Irish Unionists identified in Ulster a major issue that Gladstone had scarcely deigned to address. Some, particularly British, Unionists canvassed the idea of a form of special status for Ulster, but given the unitary structure of Irish Unionism at this time, and given the general importance of southern Unionism, such notions were not widely held in the north of Ireland or (needless to say) elsewhere on the island.[64] British Unionists were also interested in the impact of Home Rule on the integrity of the empire, where Irish Unionists were alarmed – not so much by the disintegration of Empire – as by the relegation of Ireland from its existing metropolitan status to the drab ranks of the colonies. The North Down MP, Thomas Waring, affirmed on 8 April that 'Irish loyalists were now part of one of the greatest Empires of the world...and were utterly determined that they should not be changed into colonials'.[65] There was also a quirky and recurrent, though admittedly rare, Irish Unionist view that complete independence for Ireland would be a more rational and more desirable option than Home Rule. More perhaps than their British brethren, Irish Unionists complained that the problem with Home Rule was largely the Home Rulers. In May 1886 Colonel Edward Saunderson, MP for North Armagh and leader of the Irish Unionist parliamentary party, identified '85 reasons why this House should not consent to this [Home Rule] Bill. They are not abstract, but concrete reasons – and they are to be found sitting below the gangway, opposite'.[66]

Also peculiar to Irish Unionism was the threat, implied or direct, of physical force. Not all Irish Unionists were prepared to endorse such language, and indeed some endeavoured to distance themselves from their more bellicose colleagues. Still, in 1886 a number of Irish, particularly Ulster, Unionist leaders alluded to the likelihood of armed resistance in the event of the passage of the Home Rule Bill. Of these William Johnston, MP for South Belfast and something of an *ingénu* (despite his fifty-seven years), was perhaps the most direct. On 26 April and 6 May 1886 Johnston announced plans for military preparation at two Unionist meetings in Ulster, while in the House of Commons he warned that resistance would be offered 'at the point of the bayonet'.[67] The respect that such frothings inspired may be gauged by the reaction of Henry Labouchere, who decreed that 'if they judged the intelligence, or the loyalty or the patriotism of these Orangemen by their chosen representative [Johnston], they should have an exceedingly poor opinion of them'.[68] Other Liberals and Home Rulers were perhaps less brutal, but certainly no less dismissive in their mockery.

The vote on the second reading of the Home Rule Bill was taken on 8 June 1886. The result, long foreseen, was the defeat of the measure: 341 MPs voted against the bill, with 311 offering their support. A dissolution of parliament quickly followed, and the country went to the polls in early July. Once again Gladstone's hopes were dashed, for the Conservatives emerged as the largest party and were able – with the help of those Liberals who could not stomach Home Rule – to form a relatively stable government.

Given the lasting nature of the political landscape shaped by these events, and given the subsequent elusiveness of a Home Rule settlement, it is easy to see the defeat of the bill as an inevitable denouement. The antipathy of jingoistic Tories and the hostility of the House of Lords and the English public all seem like constants in the mathematics of Irish legislative independence. Within these contexts, it is also easy to assess Gladstone purely in his own terms – as a conservative visionary, thwarted by the intellectual pygmies within his own party and by the cynicism and narrow-mindedness of the Tories. Yet it is arguable (and some otherwise sympathetic contemporaries like James Bryce did make the case) that Home Rule failed in 1886 not solely because of the limits of Gladstone's opponents or of the British constitution, but partly because of the Grand Old Man's strategic errors.[69] It is clear that Gladstone was driven both by a strong sense of spiritual mission and by a practical fear of the consequences for the British parliament of a strong cohort of disaffected Irish representatives. It is clear, too, that Gladstone had an urgent sense of history, and that in moving forward with Home Rule he had in mind both the injustice of the Act of Union in 1801 and respectful memories of Sir Robert Peel's magnificent personal and party sacrifice with the Corn Laws in 1846.[70] But Gladstone's vision was arguably flawed, and these flaws were compounded by several critical tactical errors in 1885–6.

Perhaps the fundamental problem was that Gladstone was compelling the Home Rule project to bear the weight of too many other political and personal burdens. For all his private (and perhaps formulaic) doubts, Gladstone's political style was charged with an evangelical self-assurance. Home Rule was not simply about the grant of limited legislative autonomy for Ireland; it was a divinely ordained act of political justice that would also serve to provide a meaningful finale to Gladstone's long political career. Home Rule was necessarily tied up with the settlement of social relations in Ireland, and the reconciliation of the landed 'classes' with the tenant 'masses'. Home Rule was also, in one interpretation, bound in with Gladstone's efforts to reassert his control over the Liberal Party, because it was an initiative over which he alone had control: it was about the government and unity of Liberalism.[71] Home Rule, in other words, was about God, Justice and History; and somehow for Gladstone the practical politics of passing a limited measure of self-government were lost within these more heroic contexts.

While the benefits of hindsight are prodigious, and while the wisdom of back-seat political drivers is boundless, it might still be ventured that Gladstone's tactics were problematic. He raised Tory hackles in December 1885 by his clumsy allusions to civil unrest. The Hawarden Kite (December 1885), though perhaps an accident, seemed like a betrayal of political allies and of the voters, coming on the sly, and after the general election had taken place. Thereafter Gladstone did not keep his colleagues, still less the public, informed about his developing thoughts on the Home Rule issue: his infuriatingly legalistic and ambiguous statements often did not accurately reflect his views, and were seemingly designed to mislead. Gladstone's treatment of colleagues was particularly outrageous: cabinet ministers were for the most part kept in the dark about the development of the Home Rule proposal until March 1886, when Gladstone's hand was forced. Able and highly strung figures like Joseph Chamberlain, who had hitherto been one of the most advanced ministerial thinkers on Irish questions, were decisively alienated by Gladstone's mode of proceeding; and it is hard to escape the impression that this was part of the Grand Old Man's intention. The debate on the Home Rule Bill was undermined by the parallel controversy on the land purchase question. And the content of the bill was, arguably, deficient: it went further than was politically necessary, while at the same time containing features that alienated both supporters and opponents. Crucially, no serious effort was made to reconcile the Irish national aspiration with Ulster Unionism, even though there are some grounds for supposing that this might have been slightly easier in 1886 than later. Where he might have mollified colleagues, educated the English public and defused Ulster Unionism, Gladstone – fired by a sense of personal and spiritual mission – drove Home Rule into the political abyss. It has been rightly said that Gladstone's actions demonstrated 'a preoccupation with the probity of social and political actions and a remarkable tendency to undervalue their human or material effects, whether good or bad'.[72]

Parnell had perhaps an easier hand to play, but he did so with consummate shrewdness. He was prepared to treat with all shades of English political opinion, from urban radicals like Chamberlain through to Tory grandees like Lord Carnarvon. He adjusted his demands to the temper of English opinion, showing a willingness to examine Chamberlain's Central Board scheme with Gladstone's second government still in power, while raising his demands at the time of the minority Salisbury administration. He persuaded Gladstone of his essentially conservative instincts, while managing to keep extremist opinion in Ireland within the national alliance. He stamped his will upon murmuring and resentful lieutenants, most spectacularly in February 1886 when he thrust Captain O'Shea, the husband of his mistress, upon the electors of Galway City. He avoided any compromising and superfluous commitments during the protracted debate on the Home Rule Bill, even though he was under pressure. He was able to declare credibly that the bill represented a final Irish demand, even though he had famously told the citizens of Cork in January 1885 that 'no man has the right to fix the boundary to the march of a nation'.[73] He survived the defeat of the bill with his reputation in Ireland and in parliament enhanced rather than diminished; for if he had not yet been able to deliver his people to their promised land, then he could argue with Mosaic conviction that the journey's end was in sight. And he could argue that he had broken the Unionist consensus in British politics, and delivered one of its principal ideologues to the Irish national cause.

But of course the Home Rule débâcle concerned more than the reputations and credibility of Gladstone and Parnell. Traditional interpretations have emphasised the extent to which the Home Rule 'crisis' had a lasting impact upon British and Irish party divisions. After the spring of 1886 the Liberals were divided between Gladstonian loyalists and those 'Liberal Unionists' who, led by Lord Hartington and Joseph Chamberlain, acted increasingly in collusion with the Tories. By the end of 1886 one of the most Whiggish of these Liberal Unionists, G. J. Goschen, had accepted the office of Chancellor of the Exchequer in a Conservative government; after 1895 he was joined by other party colleagues. In 1911 the Conservatives and Liberal Unionists formally amalgamated their respective party machines.

The crisis of 1886 helped to reinforce the parties' loyalties. After some lengthy havering in 1885, the Tories plumped decisively for the Union. The apparent severity of the conflict within Liberalism meant that support for Home Rule was, at least nominally, a touchstone for the party faithful until the radical shifts in Irish politics after 1916. In Ireland the Home Rule crisis of 1886 helped to strengthen organised Unionism and precipitated a shower of loyalist protest bodies. The crisis helped to shape party politics on the island for a generation.

But there are alternative contexts and perspectives. The division between Irish loyalist and nationalist was not created in 1886. The Home Rule movement had developed swiftly from its foundations in 1870, while Irish Unionists (faced with the developing challenge of Parnellism) had been propounding a united loyalist ideology from at least 1883, and had been organising in a formal sense throughout 1885. Moreover, the apparently critical divisions within British Liberalism have been subjected to intense scrutiny, and in particular through the work of W. C. Lubenow. Lubenow has argued that the Liberal schism of 1886 did not occur along any fundamental social or ideological lines, and that 'the crisis in the Liberal Party over Home Rule reflected a crisis in the regime, not in society': 'the great separation...was no yawning chasm involving many matters of policy'.[74] Nor did the split reflect any deeply etched pattern of dissent within Liberal constituencies. The Liberal Unionist defection was, in this view, 'a numerical loss alone'.[75]

The lasting political importance of the first Home Rule 'crisis' cannot be fully denied, but should also not be exaggerated. The striking feature of the episode was not so much turmoil or upheaval as the extent to which the British party system largely and lastingly accommodated the revolutionary challenge of Irish nationalism. There was no revolution in British party politics. Indeed, to quote Lubenow's striking paradox, 'the party system revolutionised the Home Rule issue by domesticating it, by making it a creature of parliamentary politics, and by so containing it for thirty years'.[76]

# CHAPTER 5

# UNITING HEARTS
## 1886–91

The late 1880s is frequently seen as a barren period for the Home Rule idea and movement, and indeed – given the Conservative Party's ascendancy over government from 1886 to 1892 – this perspective is understandable. No major constitutional initiative was forthcoming in these years except a failed effort in 1892 to launch a local government reform for Ireland. There was some relatively modest land legislation, but no sweeping interference in the contractual relationship between landlord and tenant, and no sweeping measure of purchase. Yet some of the materials that had propelled the political advance of the early 1880s were still evident: agricultural prices continued to fall in the late 1880s, leaving those who had had their rents fixed by the new land courts paying over the odds. And indeed, the country remained disturbed, while the electoral support for Home Rule remained undiminished. But the renewal of agrarian agitation with the 'Plan of Campaign' in 1886 precipitated a government clamp-down, and sweeping crimes legislation. There would be no Tory epiphany to mirror that achieved by Gladstone in 1881 and 1885–6, with the Land Act and Home Rule.

There are some superficial problems in deciphering Parnell's strategy in this period. Despite the potential for recreating the political juggernaut of the early 1880s, he remained curiously passive: astonishingly, he did not deign to make a single public speech in Ireland between 1886 and 1890.[1] Even though one of the central features of his early struggle had been the relentless application of both external and internal pressure on the British parliament, the Uncrowned King pursued an apparently more relaxed course after 1886. Even though Parnell had skilfully played off Liberals and Conservatives to the advantage of his cause, notably in 1885, in the late 1880s he settled down in what once might have been seen as an improperly affectionate relationship with the Liberals.

Some of these difficulties are most sharply evident in the divisions within the Home Rule leadership over the renewal of land agitation in the autumn of 1886. In September 1886, Parnell had sought to enact a

Tenants' Relief Bill, designed to extend the operations of Gladstone's measure of 1881, and to make evictions more difficult to execute. He may also have been testing the flexibility of the new Conservative administration, and seeking some means of resolving the threatened agitation in Ireland. In any event, Parnell's measure was thrown out, and the initiative on land swiftly fell into the hands of his more aggressive lieutenants.

Their preferred strategy involved returning to an idea mooted by T. M. Healy in the Land War of the early 1880s – an idea that involved a combination of rent strikes and the creation of war chests from the moneys that would otherwise have been paid to the landlords. The resuscitation of Healy's proposal was carried out by T. C. Harrington in August 1886, and others, such as John Dillon and William O'Brien, fell swiftly into line. A practical scheme was outlined in the Parnellite newspaper *United Ireland* in October: this urged tenants to combine in order to force acceptable levels of rent on to their landlords. If landlords refused to negotiate, the rents would be paid into an estate fund which would be used in turn to pay the maintenance and legal costs of those tenants caught up in the struggle for justice. The resulting agitation, the Plan of Campaign, was carefully orchestrated by the National League, with indebted and therefore vulnerable landlords finding themselves the focus of the assault. It has been argued that the plan was a grander offensive than has generally been assumed, operating in 203 estates throughout the country – including, in a scattered way, Ulster. But, even so, and despite massive publicity for particular controversial evictions or confrontations, only one per cent of the total number of estates was affected by the agitation.[2]

Moreover, the ruthless prosecution of the government and landlord case, combined with the ferocious costs of the tenant enterprise, brought troubles to the organisers of the plan. In March 1887 the temporising Michael Hicks-Beach was replaced as Chief Secretary for Ireland by Arthur James Balfour, who had a reputation as a dilettante, but whose intellectual self-confidence, languid determination and bloody-minded gentility were well known to his intimates. Margaret O'Callaghan has argued that one of Balfour's principal concerns was to undo the constitutional achievement of the Home Rule movement – its movement towards 'respectability'. The strategy by which he pursued this end was the equating of nationalism with criminality.[3] Balfour certainly hastened to enact the Criminal Law and Procedure (Ireland) Bill in July, which enlarged the powers of the government at the expense of 'normal' judicial process, and which facilitated the proclamation of the National League. The creation in July 1888 of a Special Commission to investigate the alleged linkages between the national movement and crime has also been seen as part of this wider strategy of incrimination (the Commission will be examined more fully later in the chapter).[4]

The enactment of this broad vision had other implications. Balfour genially and unwaveringly defended his subordinates, even in controversial circumstances. He stood by the Royal Irish Constabulary after the affray at Mitchelstown, County Cork, on 9 September 1887, when three demonstrators were killed. He backed other sometimes ruthless or over-zealous subordinates, including a youthful crown prosecutor, Edward Carson, who had in fact witnessed the Mitchelstown killings. In addition, Balfour was secretly the guiding genius behind the Ponsonby syndicate, a combination of landlords who were acting to fend off the plan's assault on a vital but also encumbered Cork estate.[5] He tried and failed to find official funds for the Ponsonby enterprise, but proved more adept at raising money for other shady ventures. It has recently been calculated that by 1889 secret service expenditure in Ireland had doubled compared with the average annual outlay under earlier administrations.[6]

But the Plan of Campaign was also, as Parnell quickly grasped, a very expensive proposition for its agents. Sometime in early December 1886, Parnell met one of the protagonists of the agitation, William O'Brien, in a fog-bound rendezvous at the Greenwich Observatory: 'all I propose', he urged O'Brien, 'is that you should set bounds to your operations, or we shall be bankrupt and the Liberals will shake us off'. After their initial exchanges, his concern became more explicit: 'what will you do for money? You will never succeed in collecting your rents a second year'.[7] The preoccupation with bankruptcy and with the Liberal connection is suggestive. The success of the plan hinged upon blunting the threat of eviction by minimising its consequences: while encouraging tenants to resist the demands of their landlords, the strategists of the plan also promised a measure of financial support. By April 1890 the National League was paying out some £32,000 a year for the maintenance of around 800 to 1000 evicted tenants.

In addition, there were some well-publicised and extraordinarily costly initiatives. The most conspicuous of these was unquestionably New Tipperary, an indirect consequence of the Ponsonby business. If Balfour was its secret inspiration, then the public leader of the Ponsonby syndicate was a wealthy Cork landlord, Arthur Smith-Barry, later ennobled as Lord Barrymore. Smith-Barry's tenants, angered by his actions, withheld their rents and were duly evicted. The Smith-Barry estate encompassed the town of Tipperary, and some of the evicted townspeople defiantly created a 'New Tipperary' in order to pursue their livelihoods beyond the reach of the hated former proprietor. William O'Brien, as a leader of the Plan of Campaign, promised the support of the National League for this act of resistance, but it soon became clear that solidarity did not come cheap. By the early summer of 1890 New Tipperary had already cost between £40,000 and £50,000 – impossibly large sums for the national movement to sustain. The significance of these costs has been crisply assessed by F. S. L. Lyons, who has seen New Tipperary as perhaps 'the decisive mistake in their [the Nationalist leadership's] long-running war with the Chief Secretary'.[8] This conflict had been burdened with financial difficulties almost from the time of its inception; and although it burned with a momentary ferocity, by 1890–1 its energies were spent.

The Plan of Campaign also posed wider political difficulties for the Home Rulers, now that part of their strength rested in being a 're-spectable' ally of Gladstonian Liberalism. The cause of Home Rule had few passionate advocates among the Liberals, but it had in Gladstone a ferocious evangelist who compensated for the scores of sullen agnostics in his party. Gladstone's providentialist outlook and his infinite capacity for self-delusion made him – after the strains of the early 1880s – pecu-liarly susceptible to Parnell. If, as Gladstone believed, Home Rule was a divinely ordained enterprise, then Parnell was the somewhat unlikely agent of Providence. Gladstone came increasingly to see Parnell as a sort of Peelite with attitude – an imaginative and perspicacious conservative who was genuinely battling to master the raw political forces under his control. John Morley complained in January 1886 that Gladstone 'regards Parnell far too much as if he were like a serious and responsible party leader of ordinary English style'.[9] Gladstone's admiration graduated in the later 1880s into (what Richard Shannon has called) an 'increasingly blind trust'.[10]

But there were always threats to the connection between the Home Rulers and the Liberals, notwithstanding Gladstone's pious effusions. A few radicals (notably C. A. V. Conybeare, MP for Cornwall North West) were certainly energetic supporters of the Plan of Campaign, but most Liberals were worried and suspicious. Parnell could not – in the aftermath of the land reform of 1881 – simultaneously pose as a social conservative and actively encourage militant agrarianism without threatening Gladstone's faith. The plan, designed as a logical reprise of the Land War, became in this sense a threat to the wider national struggle – 'a parody', as O'Callaghan has it, 'of the confused agrarian conspiracy of 1879–81'.[11] If land had served in the early 1880s as the engine driving Home Rule, then Parnell came to see the Plan of Campaign as (to borrow a Gladstonian metaphor) an obstacle on the line.

It is also perhaps the case that the issue of timing, which Parnell often raised as an objection to the plan, had a wider resonance. Parnell sought justice for Irish tenants, and sought a fair resolution to the historical conflicts in rural Ireland. He was committed to a peasant proprietorship and, in practical terms, interested in the promotion of land purchase. On the other hand, he was also passionately concerned about the future of his own caste within a Home Rule system, and concerned that the Irish gentry should assume a rightful position of influence within any new arrangement. The Land War of 1879–81 had partly been about the resolution of agrarian conflict well in advance of a constitutional settlement, and it had taken place in the context of an apparently secure Unionist consensus in British politics. The Plan of Campaign, aside from its practical difficulties, was launched in the immediate aftermath of the Liberal Home Rule Bill: it involved confrontation not primarily between nationalist farmers and the Crown, but between Irish farmers and, in many cases, vulnerable Irish landlords. The Plan of Campaign involved, like the Land War, the identification of the national movement with a sectional interest, but the crucial distinction was that the national movement was now apparently close to its ultimate victory. In other words, the plan looked like a socially divisive agitation on the eve of legislative independence. And Parnell emphatically did not see Home Rule as the continuation of social warfare by other means.

Parnell's stated objections to the Plan of Campaign related to timing, money and the condition of the Liberal alliance, but there may have been other concerns and motives. He was ill through much of the late 1880s: his health was a recurrent concern at this time, with visits (in disguise) to distinguished doctors, and with acquaintances commenting upon his deathly pallor. It is possibly the case that, since Parnell himself was not up to leading a sustained and successful agrarian campaign, he was not prepared to see his lieutenants take his place. He was also enjoying an increasingly domesticated life, gleefully retreating from the parliamentary grind into the company of his mistress, Mrs Katherine O'Shea. Neither his health nor his domestic inclinations were easily compatible with the task of energising a popular struggle.

Parnell's general response to the Plan of Campaign was therefore cool. The private qualms that he expressed to William O'Brien at Greenwich in December 1886 have already been noted. These doubts were made public in May 1888, when Parnell addressed the Liberal Eighty Club in London, and made clear that he had had nothing to do with the origins of the plan. He stressed that he had intervened to moderate its conduct and to ensure that neither the National League nor the Irish parliamentary party was directly associated with it. He expressed, too, his conviction that the plan would be superseded.[12] In all of this there was no explicit repudiation, but rather an effective combination of bleak diagnosis and personal disavowal. In April 1890 he went further and, speaking in the House of

71

Commons, proposed to Balfour that the plan might be ended if the tenants involved were given the protection of the 1887 Land Act.[13] This was a completely independent parley, which left many Liberals mystified and many of his own lieutenants feeling betrayed and sore. Little wonder, then, that the plan has long been seen as an agent of disunity within the party, and the precursor of the more momentous split of 1890–1.

The 'respectability' of the Home Rule movement – so essential to the Gladstonian project – was being threatened not only by the Plan of Campaign, but also by a series of allegations concerning the relationship between the movement and political violence. Parnell's health and his search for domesticity were certainly distractions at this time, but a greater preoccupation was the personal and political assault launched in 1887 by *The Times*. In March of that year the newspaper began a startling series of reports, 'Parnellism and Crime', which sought to link the leaders of the national movement with the crimes of the Land War. The most shocking of these allegations came on 18 April, when in an article on 'Mr Parnell and the Phoenix Park Murders' the facsimile of what appeared to be a letter from Parnell was printed. The date of the missive was 15 May 1882, and the crucial sentence read 'though I regret the accident of Lord F. Cavendish's death I cannot refuse to admit that Burke got no more than his deserts'.[14]

Parnell, it seems, greeted this report with his habitual calm; and, although he immediately condemned the 'villainous and bare-faced forgery' before the House of Commons, he took no further action for the moment.[15] The allegations did not go away, however. In July 1888 one of Parnell's former colleagues, F. H. O'Donnell, believing himself to have been libelled by *The Times* reports, brought a case against the newspaper. The result was a seeming disaster, for not only did O'Donnell fail, but in the course of the proceedings new evidence was produced by *The Times'* counsel which apparently confirmed the earlier allegations against Parnell. Parnell went on the offensive in the House of Commons, with the result that, on 12 July, the government indicated its willingness to appoint a Special Commission of investigation. Its brief was announced on 17 July, when it became clear that the government was interested not merely in the Parnell 'letters', but also in documenting a wider case.

It has been observed that the Special Commission, once regarded as an expensive mistake for the Conservative government, and as marking the apogee of Parnellism, in fact needs to be examined more critically.[16] The Prime Minister, Lord Salisbury, more than Balfour or any of his colleagues, saw the Commission as an opportunity to demonstrate the equation between Parnell's movement and crime; he was supported in this view by the unlikely combination of Queen Victoria and the influential radical Unionist, Joseph Chamberlain. More than Balfour, Salisbury was prepared to assist *The Times* newspaper and its lawyers to make their case. Astonishingly, he even considered giving the paper financial aid at the end of the Commission hearings.[17]

Between September 1888 and November 1889 the Commission judges sat for 128 days listening to the victims and aggressors of the land war, and to evidence linking (or purporting to link) Irish parliamentarians with the crimes of that conflict. The most celebrated episode of the proceedings came on 22 February 1889, when Parnell's counsel, Sir Charles Russell (Solicitor General in Gladstone's government of 1885-6) demonstrated that the notorious 'Parnell letters' were the handiwork of a Dublin rogue called Richard Pigott. Pigott's guilt had in fact long been surmised, and Russell's skill lay not so much in the discovery as in the effective means by which the discovery was made before the Commission. One of the letters produced by *The Times* in the O'Donnell case purported to contain a plea from Parnell that there should be 'an end to this hesitency [sic]', and at the Commission hearing Pigott was lured by Russell into replicating this spelling mistake.[18] The fact that perhaps a quarter of the population might have made the same error seems to have been overlooked; and Russell's cross-examination was soon entrenched in the Parnell mythology and in the popular nationalist view of the Commission proceedings.

But a number of qualifications to this view have been suggested. Pigott was a complicated figure, who looked like a Pickwickian but was a blackmailer, and who was both a devoted family man and a pornographer. He scavenged on the battlefields of Irish party politics, dealing with all in his quest to turn a profit. His name had long been connected with the letters, although Parnell himself thought that Captain O'Shea, the husband of his mistress, lay behind the skulduggery. Given the involvement of some very senior Irish Unionists in acquiring the letters from Pigott, it is strange that the connection was not more widely known within Conservative circles, and that alarm bells had not rung sooner. In fact, it seems reasonably clear that from the beginning Salisbury and the Tories were sufficiently worried by the letters to avoid any inquiry that dealt with them alone. They had no interest in the vindication of Parnell, but they were sufficiently sure of the broader case made by *The Times* to risk an inquiry. The 'Parnell letters' were the occasion, but emphatically not – from Salisbury's perspective – the object of the Commission.[19]

Salisbury's strategy, and its success, have only recently begun to be appreciated, given the accretion of mythology on the history of the Commission. Margaret O'Callaghan has argued that 'Russell's "skill" in breaking down Pigott, a man already on the point of collapse, appears to have masked his forensic incompetence for the remainder of the [Commission] proceedings'; and that Parnell himself 'was sufficiently shrewd not to be deluded by the significance of his Pigott vindication'.[20] For, while Pigott's collapse was, in theatrical terms, the climax of the Commission hearings, the denouement of the proceedings – certainly for Tories, and possibly for a wider English constituency – was the evidence linking constitutional nationalism and agrarian violence. Aside from the grim detail of the many outrages, there were specific incidents that reflected badly on Parnell or his lieutenants. Parnell's airy admission that once, in January 1881, 'it is possible I was endeavouring to mislead the House' of course did him no harm with advanced nationalism, but it outraged middle England.[21]

If Parnell's great achievement had been to bring some form of order and leadership to the disparate forces of the Land War, and to bring a semi-constitutional movement into the parliamentary mainstream, then this achievement was materially threatened by the Commission hearings, and by its 35-volume report. Parnell had made the transition from inmate of Kilmainham to intimate of Hawarden in a little over seven years, and this progress was now likely to be undone. Gladstone and others may have chosen to focus on the wretched Pigott, and indeed Gladstone led the Commons in giving Parnell a standing ovation after the 'hesitency' episode; but it can be argued that the Tories were the real victors in terms of the wider issue.[22] For, while Parnell was triumphantly vindicated, links between other ostensible constitutionalists and criminality had been firmly established, and a wider relationship between the Home Rule movement and militancy had been posited. The constitutionalist revision of Parnell's approach, which Gladstone so welcomed, had therefore been decisively checked, and there are some grounds for believing that Parnell's return to more militant associations in 1890–1 was not so much an act of desperation as a logical response to this tactical defeat.[23]

The report of the Special Commission was published in February 1890, two months after Captain W. H. O'Shea had filed for divorce, and nine months before the proceedings which found that Parnell and Mrs Katharine O'Shea had committed adultery. Given this chronology, it is impossible to distinguish exactly between the impact of the Commission and that of the divorce scandal upon Parnell's movement. However, it seems fair to assume that, allowing for the damage done by the Commission report and the evident failure of the Plan of Campaign, Parnell might well have had to embark upon a strategic reassessment regardless of the divorce issue. There seems little doubt, on the other hand, that had it not been for the divorce (and setting aside the issue of his health), Parnell would have survived politically.

The O'Shea divorce precipitated a crisis within the parliamentary party which, with peaks and troughs of excitement, was sustained until 1900. The outlines of this fratricidal struggle are familiar, and indeed have assumed an almost mythic quality. Irish nationalists initially rallied around Parnell when news of the divorce case first became known: a demonstration at the Leinster Hall, Dublin, on 20 November 1890 pledged its support. However, British Liberal disquiet swiftly grew, fuelled (like later nationalist anger) as much by the details as by the result of the divorce action. The evidence of Parnell's deceits and apparent poltroonery made a profound impression, particularly upon Nonconformist Liberals. Gladstone's post was so swollen with the effusions of the nonconformist conscience that he soon grasped that action was necessary, if only to secure his own and his party's interests.

On 24 November Gladstone spoke to Parnell's deputy, Justin McCarthy, confiding (in apparently tactful terms) his view of the crisis. A record of the conversation has survived, for McCarthy wrote to a friend, Mrs Praed, recording that Gladstone had argued 'very sadly that [Parnell] remaining in the leadership now means the loss of the next elections and the putting off of Home Rule until a time when he (Gladstone) will no longer be able to bear a hand in the great struggle to which he has devoted the last years of his life'.[24] McCarthy left with the view that Gladstone, though perturbed and disapproving of Parnell, 'would still fight for our cause', and this seems to have been the gloss that he conveyed to his leader on 25 November.[25] But it also seems to be the case that, having spoken to McCarthy, Gladstone hardened his attitude and came to believe that his own leadership of the Liberals was at stake. This is worth stressing because McCarthy, diminutive and honourable and genteel, has often been rendered as the fall-guy of the crisis, either failing to communicate or garbling Gladstone's views. In fact, it seems possible that a mixture of Gladstone's changing mood and his irredeemable opaqueness may have disrupted communication in these crucial hours and days.[26]

In drafting a public letter on the Parnell crisis to his faithful henchman, John Morley, Gladstone initially omitted any reference to his own possible resignation. At Morley's insistence Gladstone devised a second draft that included an allusion to the vulnerability of his own position in the event of Parnell holding on to the nationalist leadership. When, on 25 November, and ignorant of the Liberal attitude, the Irish parliamentary party confirmed Parnell in office, Gladstone struck: the second, revised draft of his Morley letter was published on 26 November. On 29

November, Parnell responded with his great 'Manifesto to the Irish People' wherein, amongst a welter of other accusations, he attacked Gladstone's presumption and repudiated the Liberal alliance. This in turn precipitated a great crisis within the parliamentary party, which in effect was being invited to choose both between Parnell and his political strategies, and between Gladstone's political diagnosis and that of their own leader. The party reconvened on 1 December in Committee Room 15 of the House of Commons, and – after five days of fractious debate – McCarthy led forty-four of his colleagues away from the room and into schism; twenty-eight Irish MPs remained true to their embattled chief. This marked the beginning of a nine-year civil war within the Home Rule movement.

The most ferocious period of conflict occurred between the Committee Room 15 debates in December 1890 and Parnell's death in October 1891. There were two critical focuses of the struggle: the nationalist press and by-elections. The party organ, *United Ireland*, was seized by Parnell after fisticuffs at its offices on 10 December. The anti-Parnellites retaliated by publishing the *Insuppressible* (December 1890–January 1891) and, later, the *National Press* (from March 1891). At the end of July 1891 the proprietor of the influential *Freeman's Journal*, Edmund Dwyer Gray, defected to the anti-Parnellites, carrying the support of his paper with him. The press was of course, the chief medium by which the issues and, much more important, the rhetoric of the contest were conveyed. The editorials and speeches of T. M. Healy plumbed new depths of verbal violence at this time.[27]

Complementing this struggle for the press, and providing a focus for journalistic aggression, were the three by-election contests that coincided with the last desperate months of Parnell's life. These were a crucial test of the mood of the country, and from the beginning it was clear that the anti-Parnellites had the upper hand. At Kilkenny North (22 December 1890), Sligo North (2 April), and Carlow (8 July), anti-Parnellite majorities were recorded. The tightest contest was fought in Sligo, and even here the Parnellite candidate, Valentine Dillon, lost by 768 votes in a total poll of 5,754. When Parnell died, on 6 October, his vacant seat, Cork City, fell to an opponent, Martin Flavin. Only on 23 December 1891 was the first of the Parnellites returned to the Commons after a by-election: this was John Redmond who defeated Michael Davitt in the struggle for Waterford City.

The immediate and long-term significance of the split has, however, generated much greater debate than its main events and chronology. There is a tradition of interpretation, dating back to contemporaries like William O'Brien and Justin McCarthy, which has depicted the confrontation between Parnell and his opponents in essentially personal terms, and which has diagnosed Parnell's actions at this time as exceptional. The grounds for this view are not hard to locate. Parnell's behaviour was often bizarre, reflecting the unique strains with which he was struggling. A number of episodes have attracted attention, including his furious storming of the *United Ireland* building and his last wild, confused speeches. His political strategies at this time have been seen as a reflection not of cool calculation, but rather of despair. Corroboration for this view has been found in Parnell's rejection of the peace deal brokered by William O'Brien and John Dillon during negotiations at Boulogne in January 1891 and in his wider militancy – his 'appeal to the hillsides'.[28]

Against this essentially personal interpretation, which lays stress on unique strains and uncharacteristic actions, Frank Callanan emphasises continuities in Parnell's tactics and the intellectual and strategic issues that were at stake.[29] Parnell's flirtation with Fenianism in 1890–1 was, in this argument, not merely a wild piece of political improvisation, but rather a return to the successful strategies of 1879 and the 'New Departure'.[30] Parnell's heightened interest in the labouring poor and his northern foray (he made a rare trip to Belfast in July 1891) are then not so much pragmatic or desperate acts, as expressions of a deeply rooted social concern and a profound engagement with the Irish Protestant tradition.[31] Parnell's rejection of the offer made at Boulogne to retire gracefully, and probably temporarily, has been seen not so much as an act of supreme folly, the result of horrendous personal pressures, as a logical political judgement. Parnell had hitherto exercised an unbending authority which, even assuming that a comeback were possible, would have been hopelessly compromised by a meekly accepted but effectively enforced retirement.[32]

Thus the view that Parnell acted out of character in 1890–1 reflects a profound misjudgement of his approach. Parnell's rejection of the Liberal alliance in 1890–1, and his growing coolness towards the farmer cause, did not amount to a rejection of what had counted as 'Parnellism', for these were the strategies and not the objects of his movement. It is clear that at the end Parnell saw the increasingly predominant Catholic farming interest as a threat to his vision of an Ireland where industry, the rural poor, indigenous landlords and Protestants would all have a national role. The support of farmers was necessary to the advancement of Home Rule, but Parnell did not want to create a system of government where their concerns suffocated all else. Parnell's vision of Ireland was secular and inclusive; that of his principal opponent, Tim Healy, was chauvinistic and confessional.

Equally, Parnell had little fundamental sympathy for Gladstonian

Liberalism. Liberalism, like Healyite nationalism, had for Parnell a repugnant confessional quality, given its Nonconformist dimension. The Liberals' free-trade and laissez-faire convictions ran contrary to Parnell's protectionist and mildly interventionist impulses.[33] The Liberals, though prepared in 1886 to pursue land purchase, were generally more enthusiastic about tenure reform than about funding the wholescale transfer of property from tenant to landlord. Parnell, on the other hand, was not only committed to land purchase, but also bound to a form of purchase that favoured small residential landlords and small tenants at the expense of the substantial farming interest. In this crucial regard, Parnell was at odds with both his British patron and his so-called supporters in Ireland.[34] Again, there is no paradox here, unless it is assumed that farmers and Liberals were the essence of Parnell's project.

Parnell died in Brighton on 6 October 1891. He was forty-five, and had been married to Katharine O'Shea for barely three and a half months. The intellectual reading of the split, which has been outlined and broadly endorsed above, should not divert from the profound personal and political passions that were raised during the split, and left largely unresolved. Parnell's otherwise acute political intelligence did not wither in November 1890, with the divorce case. His later actions have a remorseless logic, and are often of a piece with what is understood about his broader thought. On the other hand, Parnell evinced a new (or at least a more overt) political passion at this time, and at the end seems to have been all but broken by stress. His last speech, delivered at Creggs, County Roscommon, on 27 September, was described by Dillon as 'incoherent scurrility – sad, sad'.[35] And, at the risk of stating the obvious, the split showed a different, perhaps a more unrestrained or untheatrical Parnell, in so far as he was being forced to enunciate his vision under perhaps the most ferocious and outrageous political bombardment of modern Irish history.

The importance of the split lies largely in the confrontation between two sharply different views of the Home Rule project, and two distinctive political coalitions. It also lies partly in its consequences: the division within the parliamentary party, which lasted until 1900, and W. B. Yeats' argument that the confusion within constitutional politics created space for cultural nationalism. But the split resonates within contemporary consciousness, not primarily because of the intellectual engagement, but rather because of the raw personal emotions that were harnessed. At the end, perhaps the larger political issues may be seen in the personal drama: the combat between the ambitious Catholic peasant, Healy, and Parnell, the mannered representative of a degenerate ascendancy, is an obvious metaphor for the wider social struggle. Perhaps, too, some profound significance may be perceived in Parnell's penultimate words when, lying on his death-bed, he invoked, not Mother Ireland, but rather 'the Conservative party'.[36]

# CHAPTER 6

# FALL AND RISE
# 1892–1910

It is tempting to see the Parnell split as the source of all the subsequent problems that beset the Home Rule movement in the United Kingdom. It is possible, indeed, to argue that the ultimate failure of the movement, and thus of the wider idea of Home Rule, is intimately linked to the warfare between Parnellism and its opponents which was sustained between 1891 and 1900, and which resonated through to the death of the Irish parliamentary party in 1918. This broaches, in turn, the wider issue of the chronology of, and explanations for, the failure of the Home Rule movement in Ireland – an issue that has provoked disagreement among Irish historians over several decades, and which has still not been resolved.

This historiographical debate about the decline of the Home Rule party is paralleled to some extent in the debate about the decline of British Liberalism. Just as with the Liberals, so with Home Rule there is a tension between those historians who enthusiastically supply death certificates for clearly vibrant political parties and those who (after the manner of Monty Python) solemnly identify life in the most resolutely dead political organisms. This chapter seeks to chart the health of the Home Rule movement between 1892 and 1910, and to evaluate the conflicting diagnoses of terminal illness and rude good health which have so far been offered.

The Parnell split unquestionably damaged the Home Rule cause in Britain, and provided opportunities not just for infidel Unionists, but also for doubters within the Liberal Party. The Conservative government of Lord Salisbury fell in June 1892, and the general election held in the following month returned Gladstone and the Liberals to office, albeit with a majority of only forty. Gladstone had been hoping that Providence would supply a margin of 'three figures', but the Almighty did not choose to deliver England, which showed itself as resolutely Unionist.[1] And indeed, while Providence favoured Scotland in 1892 (in so far as Celtic majorities in favour of Home Rule were recorded), Gladstone's own constituency of Midlothian returned him, not with the expected margin of 3000, but only 690 votes ahead of the Tory candidate.

Before the election Gladstone, though chastened by the Parnell débâcle, was relatively confident that his divinely ordained mission in Ireland remained on track. Ireland, and the wrongs inflicted by England on Ireland, remained an inescapable moral burden that induced an intellectual obsessiveness at this time as well as, occasionally, emotional breakdown. After the early election results, when the slimness of the likely Liberal majority began to become apparent, Gladstone swiftly came to accept that Providence had assigned him a more humble role in Ireland than he had hitherto envisaged. Indeed, he may have come to doubt his own reading of the workings of Providence on the issue of Home Rule. Certainly a more briskly pragmatic, not to say resigned, approach is evident. Gladstone entered his last term of office recognising that English (and Scottish) issues were now, in the aftermath of Parnell and of the electors' verdict, of greater political moment than Ireland. Home Rule was a matter of both justice and obligation, but it was a duty that, given the inscrutability of the Almighty and the intractability of parliament, Gladstone accepted with diminished enthusiasm. It was seemingly with difficulty that he was prevailed upon to quit meddling in the realm of foreign affairs in late 1892, and to focus upon the construction of a second Home Rule Bill.[2]

Gladstone's methods and conclusions in 1892–3 did not differ substantially from those of 1886. As in 1886, so in 1892–3 Gladstone kept his cabinet colleagues mostly in the dark about the progress of his thought and of the legislation. Nothing was said about the Home Rule Bill, ostensibly the central plank of the Liberal agenda, in the first cabinet meetings, held in the autumn of 1892. By early November, Gladstone had still not fully turned his mind to the task of drafting a bill.[3] By the end of the month, while he had agreed to form an Irish committee within the cabinet, he purposefully excluded key ministers such as Sir William Harcourt, the Chancellor of the Exchequer. The submissions of outside experts such as Edward Blake, Irish nationalist and former premier of Ontario, and of civil servants like Lord Welby and Alfred Milner, did not fully compensate for the narrow range of reference among the Liberal Party elite.

On 10 February 1893, three days before Gladstone was due to introduce the Home Rule legislation into the Commons, H. H. Asquith wrote to his cabinet colleague, Lord Rosebery, that 'I understand that on Monday [13 February] a Bill (to "amend the provision" for the Government of Ireland), which neither you nor I have seen, is to be introduced into the House of Commons. I send you word of this, as you may possibly like to be present, and hear what Her Majesty's Government have to propose'.[4] The tone was, of course ironic; but the reality conveyed was that, as in 1886, Gladstone had kept the precise details of the Home Rule Bill to himself and to his immediate circle. Again, while it can hardly be said that this divisive proceeding decided the fate of the bill, it is clear that Gladstone's peculiarly personal and providentialist approach to Home Rule ultimately damaged the object that it was designed to sanctify.

In introducing the legislation, Gladstone emphasised that Home Rule was designed to secure Irish control over Irish affairs. It was to be fully compatible with imperial unity, the equality of all of the constituent territories of the United Kingdom, and the security of minorities. In the end, and after some controversy, the preamble to the bill affirmed the supremacy of the Westminster parliament.[5] Home Rule was intended to be a lasting revision of the fraught constitutional relationship between Britain and Ireland. The model for the legislation was the bill of 1886, but there were some notable departures. The Irish executive was to comprise the Lord Lieutenant, but unlike the bill of 1886, it was proposed that he be assisted by an Executive Committee of the Privy Council of Ireland. The Lord Lieutenant had the right, under the legislation, to apply or withhold the royal assent to Irish legislation. He was to be advised by his Executive Committee, but their proceedings were to be subject to instructions from London. A particular Irish nationalist requirement, designed to reduce the risk of veto, was that the Lord Lieutenant had no right to reserve his opinion until London had declared its will. As in 1886, the Lord Lieutenant could be a Catholic; as distinct from the 1886 proposal, he was to hold office for six years.

Unlike the complex mix of one chamber and two orders proposed in 1886, the Irish legislature was now to be bicameral, with the two chambers meeting separately. The upper house (or 'Legislative Council') was to have 48 members elected on a high property franchise, while the lower house (or 'Legislative Assembly') would have 103 members elected on the existing, relatively restricted franchise. The difficult issue of Irish representation at Westminster had been addressed in 1886 by a proposed exclusion, but this had raised the twin spectres of 'taxation without representation' and imperial disintegration. Now, in 1893, it was suggested that Irish representation be retained, albeit at the reduced level of eighty MPs – a number said to be proportionate to the Irish population. A characteristic piece of Gladstonian ingenuity, an 'in and out' arrangement, was devised, whereby these Irish parliamentarians would be excluded from specifically British debates and divisions but admitted to all others. In the end, practicality triumphed when it was conceded that Irish MPs would be free from any constriction. But the 'in and out' proposal was fleetingly reconsidered as late as 1965–6, when Harold Wilson was angrily trying to rid himself of what he considered to be the 'Tory' MPs from Northern Ireland.[6]

The abandonment of the 'in and out' proposal defused one set of criticisms, but stimulated others. The Irish were now to have significant influence over English and Scottish affairs, while enjoying exclusive rights over large areas of their own business. Moreover, other pressing issues, rehearsed in 1886, remained intractable. Gladstone continued to be unmoved by the significance of Ulster Unionism and, as in 1886, he did nothing to address the peculiar concentration of opposition to Home Rule in the north of Ireland. This was clearly an error, although – given the diffuse all-Ireland organisational structures of Unionism – perhaps more understandable than is sometimes allowed. Whether some form of limited partition was practical politics at this stage, and whether it would have facilitated a settlement, are moot points.[7]

Finance was another aspect of this baleful legacy from 1886. Broadly, in 1886 and again in 1893, it was proposed that Ireland pay an 'imperial contribution' as a first charge on its revenue. This 'contribution' was eventually equated with the yield from Ireland's customs duties, which were in any case to be levied by London. The new Irish government's budget was in effect the difference between the customs yield and the island's total revenue. Clearly the solvency of the new administration hinged upon the size of this margin. But the calculations were wrong, a critical error ('to the tune of £360,000') having been committed in Belfast. One wonders whether a mischievous Unionist revenue officer was to blame.[8]

Half-way through the committee stage of the bill, the government was therefore forced, humiliatingly, to revise its proposals. A bright young Treasury official, Alfred Milner, attempted to come to the rescue, proposing that one-third of the total Irish revenue be annexed by London. However, considerable political damage had already been sustained. The financial settlement continued to be pummelled in committee by the Unionists, while a punch-drunk Liberal leadership parried ineffectually. Gladstone was increasingly disengaged; Morley, the Chief Secretary for Ireland, was hampered by other responsibilities; and Harcourt, the Chancellor, showed a huffy detachment, a legacy of his exclusion from the cabinet committee on the legislation.

But, notwithstanding the Unionist onslaught, the Liberal majority in the Commons held, and the bill finally passed its committee stage on 2 September 1893 by a majority of thirty-one votes (307 to 276). It had been a marathon session and a uniquely long debate. This achievement, however, was not reflected in the brisk attitude of the House of Lords, which took four days to decide (by 419 votes to 41) that the bill should be thrown out. Despite Gladstonian murmurings, no attempt was made at a reintroduction. In truth even the Grand Old Man had wearied of the measure, privately appearing to acknowledge its defects, and referring in June to 'that confounded Bill'.[9] Nor was there any dissolution: the electoral risks, not least in Gladstone's own constituency, were too great, and there was other pressing business to transact. There could be no more emphatic portrayal of the government's attitude towards this ostensibly vital aspect of its legislative programme.

The fate of the second Home Rule Bill was always likely to be sealed in the House of Lords, but there were other problems that plagued the measure from its inception. The majority that the Liberals secured in July 1892 was, as Gladstone understood only too well, too small to embark successfully upon a major constitutional revision. This electoral weakness related in turn to the damage done to the Home Rule cause in Britain by Parnell's disgrace and by his contemptuous disavowal of Gladstone through the manifesto of November 1890. Some of these disadvantages might have been offset if Gladstone had spent less time in 1893 fretting over his translation of Horace and more time studying the lessons of his experiences in 1886.[10] But, with the benefit of hindsight, it is easy to see that these lessons were not only missed, but almost consciously avoided. The historical precedents that made sense for Gladstone were to be found in the 1830s and 1840s, and not in the recent past: Melbourne and Peel were more immediate points of reference than Chamberlain and Salisbury. Here too, perhaps, Gladstone's particular providentialist cast of mind limited his effectiveness. In 1893, as in 1886, Gladstone was keen to incorporate powerful independent voices such as Rosebery and Harcourt into his ministry, but having done so, he failed to capitalise on the advantages of their presence. Indeed, as with Chamberlain in 1886, he was resentful of, and sometimes brusque towards, independent-minded senior Liberal ministers. The crucial cabinet committee on Home Rule embraced only a handful of veteran Gladstonian loyalists.

The technical problems of the 1886 legislation – finance, Irish representation at Westminster, Ulster – recurred in 1893, a testimony not only to the intractability of some of these issues, but also to the way in which the experience of 1886 was resolutely ignored. It is astonishing, for example, to read the outburst of Morley in March 1893 that 'Ulster will give us more trouble than we ever had reason to expect': expectations of trouble might well have been stimulated by memories of the riotous summer of 1886 in Belfast.[11]

But if the resonance from the failure of 1886 was faint, then that from the 1893 bill was sonorous and unmistakable. The continuing confusion over critical details of the legislation, the absence of any dissolution after the Lords' vote, the failure to reintroduce the bill or even a supportive resolution – all testified both to the tactical strength of the Unionists and, more alarmingly, to the increasing ambivalence of the Liberals themselves. Little wonder, then, that these events have often been seen as the beginning of the Liberal retreat from Home Rule which occupied the following seventeen years, from 1893 to the constitutional crisis of 1910. With the exception of Henry Campbell-Bannerman, a transitional figure, British Liberalism would be inherited not by the courtiers of Gladstone's cabinet committee on Home Rule, but rather by those who – in Harcourt's words – sat on 'the English bench'.[12] As D. A. Hamer pointed out in 1972, the crashing denouement to the second Home Rule crisis served to highlight the shakiness of the old order in Liberal politics, and to create space for a new, more socially engaged system that was centred less on Ireland.[13] Ireland certainly did not disappear from the pages of the Liberal press, and its importance within the anti-imperialist thought of Edwardian progressivism should not be discounted; but there was no mistaking the diminution that had occurred.[14]

Some aspects of the new order's stand on Home Rule over the following decade may be briefly reviewed at this point. Gladstone's retirement from the Liberal leadership in March 1894 was unquestionably a setback for Home Rule, since he was the chief priest of the cause. Gladstone's successor, Rosebery, immediately set out his convictions in the 'predominant partner' speech of 12 March 1894, so-called because he affirmed that England, as 'predominant partner' in the United Kingdom, would have to be convinced of the justice of Home Rule before any bill on the subject was passed. This signalled the beginning of a disengagement from Home Rule which was continued under the leadership of Sir William Harcourt (1896-8), a confirmed sceptic, and Sir Henry Campbell-Bannerman (1898-1908).

R. B. Haldane, a rising star of the party, and one of an influential clique of young Liberal Imperialists, enunciated a 'step-by-step' formula in December 1896 which won widespread favour and that helped to ease some of the tensions between Gladstonian loyalists like Morley and post-Gladstonians like Asquith and Edward Grey. Haldane's strategy was endorsed by Campbell-Bannerman in a keynote address at Stirling in November 1905, and it characterised the approach of the Liberal government from 1905 until 1910. The intellectual driving force within the party at this time was supplied by the New Liberals, progressives who were concerned to promote a social reforming and anti-imperialist agenda. While the New Liberals' disengagement from Ireland has undoubtedly been exaggerated, their leaders tended to be preoccupied with British welfare issues rather than Home Rule.[15]

The role of the Parnell split and of the 1893 failure was evidently as profound within Irish nationalist politics as within British Liberalism, though the area remains contentious. The death of Parnell and the weakness of the Irish constitutional forces in 1893 were seen by W. B. Yeats as creating the space for a new nationalism, more cultural in orientation and less committed to the old parliamentary nostrum.[16] And, indeed, at least on the surface, there is much to commend this argument. The Parnell split opened up divisions within the Home Rule party which weakened its effectiveness, even after the supposed reunification of the warring elements in 1900. These divisions coincided with a flowering of cultural nationalism and separatist conviction, as evidenced by the foundation of the Gaelic League (in 1893), the Irish Literary Theatre (1899), the Abbey Theatre (1904) and Sinn Féin (1907). In this Yeatsian interpretation, there was a crisp dichotomy between the old and new nationalisms, with the latter inevitably superseding the former. The Irish revolution, in this and other readings, flowed automatically from the deep-seated limitations of the Home Rule movement.

The integrity of this thesis will be evaluated in what follows; but it should be said immediately that a new generation of historians has provided a subtler picture of the Home Rule movement in these years, and a rather more upbeat account of its effectiveness. Scholars such as Patrick Maume and Senia Paseta have outlined a Home Rule movement that was simultaneously more radical than has hitherto been appreciated, and more deeply rooted in key sectors of Irish society.[17]

Still, the case for division and weakness is hard to ignore. The war between the Parnellites (led by John Redmond) and their opponents (led ostensibly by Justin McCarthy, but with John Dillon, T. M. Healy and William O'Brien as the key players) did not end with the Uncrowned King's death in October 1891, or with the comparatively poor showing of Parnell's supporters at the general elections of 1892 and 1895. Indeed, though the anti-Parnellites secured seventy-one seats in 1892, and their opponents only nine, the extent of the victory was greatly magnified by the first-past-the-post electoral system. The Parnellites garnered around one-third of the total nationalist vote, and were thus a much more serious political force than their parliamentary strength suggested. And even with only nine seats, the Parnellites had both outstripped the expectations of their enemies and remained 'politically viable'.[18]

On the other hand, the Home Rule movement was undermined not only by the division between the Parnellites and anti-Parnellites, but also (and perhaps more insidiously) by tensions among the latter. Two distinctive visions of constitutional nationalism were provided by John Dillon and T. M. Healy; and indeed the warfare between Healy and the main anti-Parnellite movement in the mid-1890s was in some ways more eye-catching and therefore more damaging than the almost conventional struggle with the Parnellites. Healy, in the words of Frank Callanan, 'had minted the coin of modern chauvinistic nationalism', annexing parts of the old Parnellite constituency, and in particular the substantial farming interest together with the Catholic Church. He sought to project these fragments of Parnell's support as the whole of a new, ethnic national movement.[19] He had helped to make 'Parnellism', both in an institutional and a mythic sense, but he now re-envisioned the Home Rule movement, defining a local, autonomous organisation, unencumbered by the Liberal alliance. Dillon, in contrast, was perhaps more Parnellite than Parnell himself; he was certainly a more rigid and conventional political thinker than Parnell. Dillon sought to maintain a centralised party machine on the model of the National League; and he remained loyal, too, to the Liberal alliance that Parnell had formulated. While Dillon sought to keep the Catholic Church at arm's length from his political machinery, Healy actively cultivated clerical ties, and his localised movement would, almost by definition, have been strongly influenced by the parish clergy.

The warfare between Healy and Dillon came to a head in 1895. There was a direct confrontation at a party convention in Omagh, County Tyrone, in July 1895, when Healy revealed that the Home Rule leadership was prepared to surrender expensive northern constituencies to the Liberals. In his own unabashed and boastful testimony, Healy 'gave Dillon the devil's scourging, and he [Dillon] was livid with rage, and hadn't a word to reply'.[20] But the gloating was short-lived, for Healy suffered a humiliating setback when a key patron, the entrepreneur William Martin Murphy, was defeated by a Dillonite in the South Kerry by-election of September 1895.

This paved the way for a blitzkrieg assault on Healy's position within the Home Rule party. On 7 November, Healy was voted off the executive committee of the Irish National League of Great Britain; and, as with Isaac Butt in 1877, this body served as a harbinger of more important defeats elsewhere. On 13 November, Healy was removed from the main anti-Parnellite organisation, the National Federation; and on 14 November he was voted off the committee of the Irish parliamentary party. By June 1896, in the aftermath of these jousts, even the lugubrious Dillon was becoming quietly optimistic about the political outlook: 'I am convinced that if the Party abandons squabbles…and does its duty by the country, the country will once more rally to its support'.[21] Further corroboration for this view came in December 1900, when Healy was seen to be electorally vulnerable and was expelled from the party itself.

Healy remained, in the words of his biographer, 'the enemy within' for years to come. He sat for North Louth from 1892 through to his defeat in January 1910, and was reborn in 1911 as the member for North East Cork, sitting until 1918.[22] There was a brief *rapprochement* with the leadership of the Home Rule party in 1908–9, but otherwise the history of Healy's parliamentary career is a history of independent and often vitriolic opposition to his former friends. But Healy was more than an isolated or containable problem for the grandees of the Home Rule party. He was widely acclaimed as one of the most bitterly effective parliamentarians of the time: he was, even for an ostensible ally like John Morley, 'that imp of the devil'.[23] He was formidable because he was ferociously quick-witted, because he was unworried by social or political convention, and because he knew no party discipline. And although his parliamentary following was decimated in 1895 and 1900, Healy retained other resources. A faithful Catholic, he had the support of the Church. He remained rooted in the extended 'Bantry Gang', a highly influential political and commercial nexus based originally in West Cork, which included the business magnate William Martin Murphy. Murphy owned the *Irish Independent* and provided a platform for Healy and other critics of the Irish parliamentary party.

Healy's ruthless and continuing dissection of the failings of the Home Rule leadership helped to damage the popular image and authority of constitutional nationalism. His contribution to the ultimate demise of the Irish parliamentary party should not, of course, be exaggerated or over-dramatised, for there was no single pivotal episode. On the other hand, it is hard to dissent from the measured conclusion that he 'did much to contribute to the slow-burning disillusionment with parliamentary politics which the fall of Parnell had ignited'.[24]

But Healy was not the only internal threat to the Home Rule movement. Like Healy, William O'Brien was a prolific speaker and pamphleteer who, through an avalanche of published work towards the end of his life, helped to mould popular attitudes towards the Home Rule party.[25] O'Brien was the anti-Parnellite leader who was closest in sentiment to the Uncrowned King, and when Parnell died he withdrew for a time from the front line of parliamentary politics. O'Brien was also a tireless agrarian nationalist, who was both genuinely committed to the small farming interest and anxious to further the Home Rule cause through the agency of rural discontent.

O'Brien's political comeback was modelled on his work in the 1880s.

A veteran of the Land War and of the Plan of Campaign, he sought in 1898 to focus the unresolved poverty and resentment of the smallholders of the west of Ireland. His vehicle was the United Irish League (UIL), founded in January 1898. From the beginning it was clear that the cause of the impoverished smallholders was both an end in itself and a means of effecting a reconciliation between the Parnellite and anti-Parnellite traditions. Against the background of the new League's rapid growth, negotiations were opened up between the two rival Home Rule factions, and after some stalling and bickering, this diplomacy produced a deal. On 17 January 1900 the two factions agreed to reunify; and on 6 February 1900 they agreed to accept the Parnellite John Redmond as chairman of the united party.

The contributions of William O'Brien and the United Irish League to this denouement were indirect, but nonetheless substantial. O'Brien (and, indeed, Dillon) had imagined that unity would be imposed from outside the Home Rule party, by the League.[26] In the event, this was not quite the case. Yet, in so far as O'Brien was active in the cause of unity, and in so far as his League did serve to draw members of the two party factions together, he may truly be regarded as an architect of the settlement of 1900. O'Brien's subsequent career would soon illustrate both his own fundamental political limitations and those of the reunified party, and within three years he was threatening to unmake what he had so recently helped to formulate. For the moment, however, optimism reigned: as Jeremiah Jordan, the MP for South Fermanagh, wrote to his former party colleague, John Pinkerton, 'Redmond is making a good leader and as far as I can at all see there is unity and unanimity in the Party... the new Party are much better, very much better, than I expected.'[27]

In 1902-3 there arose one of the most striking and richly complex initiatives in the entire political history of modern Ireland. In June 1902 Lindsay Talbot Crosbie, a landlord of moderate views, wrote to the press, calling for an agreed settlement between representatives of the proprietor and tenant interests. This was followed on 3 September by a second letter, published under the name of Captain John Shawe-Taylor, which set out a proposal for a landlord–tenant conference. Crosbie and Shawe-Taylor were important not because they represented a sea-change of opinion among Irish landlords, for they did not: the Irish Landowners' Convention remained a largely conservative force. They were important because they articulated the desires of a small but highly vocal and influential group of moderate landlords who, in turn, were encouraged by the British administration in Dublin Castle. They were also important because of their timing: this was indeed the centrist moment, with the irreconcilable Dillon in poor health and O'Brien actively seeking a change of direction.

Admittedly, there had been as yet no pacific gesture from the tenants, and indeed both the United Irish League and the northern farmers' organisation had intensified their campaigning in 1901–2. On the other hand, the minority Parnellite tradition, which had been thoroughly bruised in the early 1890s, had a history of searching for conciliation. With John Redmond, the former Parnellite commander, as head of a reunited party, it might have been supposed that the wider Home Rule party would now be relatively open to diplomacy. Moreover, with the end of the protracted and inglorious South African war, political space for centrist endeavour had re-emerged. This was the era not only of the great landlord–tenant *rapprochement* in Ireland, but also of some nervous expeditions, undertaken by the likes of Lord Rosebery, beyond the party divide in Great Britain.

The history of the Shawe-Taylor initiative is well known and need not be rehearsed at length.[28] Blessed by Dublin Castle, by the support of moderate landlords and by Redmond, a conference was held in Dublin between 20 December 1902 and 4 January 1903. This engaged both proprietors and tenants, and eventually issued a report that advocated a massive scheme of voluntary land purchase. The report, in turn, provided the basis for a land act – the Wyndham Act – passed later in the year. It seemed for a fleeting moment both that the historic land dispute had been resolved and that the style of national politics had been recast along new, conciliatory lines. This, indeed, was William O'Brien's view, as he hailed not only the Land Conference Report and the concomitant legislation, but also a new form of Irish politics: 'conference plus business'.[29]

But there was to be no quiet revolution in Irish national politics. Frustratingly, the omens were initially good: the leadership of the United Irish League blessed the Land Conference and the Wyndham Act, as did Redmond and the parliamentary party. But these prospects were soon dashed by John Dillon, who had a record of coolness towards party moderates: 'Dillon keeps very distant', complained Jeremiah Jordan in March 1902, 'but I am only a whig.'[30] Speaking at Swinford, County Mayo, on 25 August 1903, Dillon outlined his objections both to the new legislation and to the form of politics upon which it was based. He pilloried Talbot Crosbie, one of the prophets of centrism, as a greedy and exploitative landlord, on no firmer basis than hearsay. But the crux of Dillon's speech came with the theme of unity, and in particular the urgent need to sustain the loyalty of 'those young men who, although they may be mistaken in the possibility of force, are the salt of any movement they come into, because they are ready for sacrifice'.[31] Dillon was concerned that a conciliatory style would frustrate the young hawks of the Home Rule movement, without effecting any lasting change in the ascendancy caste. It was a characteristically cool performance, but the logic was not unpersuasive. Moreover, the speech tapped into rich veins of suspicion and resentment which were only barely concealed by the centrist overlay. Dillon's call for a 'back to basics' approach – his call for a return to nationalist first principles – was echoed in the Home Rule press, and was in time accepted by the new party leader, Redmond.

Though this episode has been revisited many times by historians, some basic problems of interpretation remain. Was the Land Conference episode an historic opportunity for the Home Rule movement, as William O'Brien claimed? There were undoubtedly some grounds for Dillon's scepticism. Wider landed opinion, certainly as represented by the Irish Landowners' Convention, remained truculently wedded to traditional claims. Wider Unionist opinion, both in Ireland and Britain, appeared to offer little of value: the veteran Irish Unionist leader, Edward Saunderson, refused an invitation to attend the Land Conference, while some of the younger bloods of the party, such as Edward Carson, were resolutely opposed to the initiative. British Unionism continued to harbour not only pragmatic intellectuals like the successive Chief Secretaries, Gerald Balfour (1895–1900) and George Wyndham (1900–5), but also Orange fundamentalists, strong in the north-west of England and Scotland. Even those who took a pragmatic approach were legitimate objects of suspicion, given that their conciliatory thrusts were apparently designed, in Gerald Balfour's tactless phrase, to 'kill Home Rule by kindness'.

This obstinate, but by no means unreasonable, belief in the irreducible qualities of Unionist and landed politics goes some way to explaining Dillon's rejection of the 'conference plus business' approach. But there were other factors. The unhappy result of the attempt to reconcile landlords and tenants was apparently a deal that absolved the landlords of their political and financial problems, and left their tenants with a massive burden of mortgage debt. Moreover, as has been noted, Dillon's abiding concern was the unity of the national movement, and he saw centrism as a threat to the Home Rule state-in-waiting: 'I as you know have all along been opposed to the policy of allowing the initiative on and the direction of the larger Irish question to be taken out of the hands of the Irish Party and handed over to Conferences summoned by outsiders.'[32] It was also an expensive indulgence: he never 'thought it possible to maintain an American organisation alongside of a policy of conciliation in Ireland and the House of Commons'.[33] It was easier to sustain the decidedly shaky unity of the Home Rule movement on familiar, if sometimes unpleasant, territory rather than in an exposed and dangerous political salient. It was also much easier for the new and still vulnerable commander of the Home Rule party, Redmond, to consolidate his leadership on the basis of familiar war-cries rather than complex and ambiguous diplomacy with a traditional and devious enemy. For Dillon, feeble, gradualist reform and the insidious diplomacy of ascendancy lordlings threatened to defuse vital political passions, and to undermine the traditional goals of the Home Rule party. The young bloods of the national movement could not be expected to accept that twenty-five years of heroic struggle had been designed to achieve landlord bonuses and administrative devolution.

Dillon's views are worth elaborating because there is a danger that the counter-arguments, proffered by William O'Brien and Lord Dunraven in a stream of publications, prevail without a contest.[34] Nevertheless, it is possible to question Dillon's case without succumbing completely to the centrists' literary assault. The main theme of his critique was the preservation of his party's unity; yet of course the party leader, the parliamentary party and the United Irish League had all originally united in blessing the conciliationist initiative. In a sense, therefore, the threat to the unity of the Home Rule movement came, not from the centrists, but rather from Dillon himself. It is hard to resist the suspicion that, added to all the ineffably reasonable arguments that he put forward at the time, Dillon was concerned as much with preserving his own influence over the Home Rule movement as with its wider integrity. Dillon was of a highly conspiratorial, not to say paranoid, disposition: he was (in a popular label of the time) 'the melancholy humbug' who had a morbid and begrudging concern for the advance of other, independent talent within the party machine. Moreover, his concern for unity stands a little uneasily with his actions during the reunification debates in 1900, when he was rendered almost motionless with anxiety while different but uniformly unwelcome political alliances took shape around him.

Linked to the theme of unity was the issue, as judged from Dillon's perspective, of landlord perfidy. However, it might well be argued that Dillon, concerned for the unity of his own movement, failed to see the extent to which centrist politics threatened the integrity of the landlord and unionist causes. Although from the perspective of the later Edwardian period, Dillon's bleak faith in the immutability of Unionism might seem to be fully justified, there is a sense in which this perspective is skewed. The political forms of the third Home Rule crisis might well be seen not as automatic creations, but rather as the by-product of decisions pursued at the time of the centrist 'moment'. The Land Conference high-lighted not primarily a division within the Home Rule movement, but rather divisions among Irish Unionists and landlords that were helpful to Dillon. As Dillon correctly averred, Talbot Crosbie and Shawe-Taylor did not represent the interests of Irish landlords, but they did signal a wider division within the landed interest and indeed within southern Unionism.[35] Moreover, one of the key farmer representatives at the Land Conference was the northern radical Unionist, T. W. Russell, and the fleeting success of the centrist experiment was associated with Russell's energetic and damaging assault on the mainstream Ulster Unionist movement.

In other words, centrist politics had the capacity to maim and divide Dillon's loyalist enemies. But he either wilfully neglected this helpful state of affairs, or chose not be impressed. It is difficult to avoid the impression that Dillon's limited and static vision of Home Rule politics blinded him to the possibilities generated within this highly fluid political environ-ment. It is also difficult to avoid the suspicion that his rigid adherence to a traditional political formula would ultimately prove disastrous to both of the issues that he held dear: his personal political influence and the integrity of the Home Rule movement.

This leads naturally to a consideration of the wider impact of the cen-trist failure in 1903–4. At one level, this is a matter of historical report. William O'Brien, distressed and marginalised by Dillon's assault, retired from parliament on 4 November 1903, and embarked upon a lengthy career of independent opposition that was only briefly and unhappily broken, in 1908–9. The supporters of the Land Conference turned them-selves into the Irish Reform Association, led by Lord Dunraven, and pursued their centrist mission by exploring the possibility of a limited devolved government for Ireland. Dunraven and the senior Irish civil servant Sir Antony MacDonnell collaborated in producing two reports on this theme, published on 31 August and 26 September 1904. But the rec-ommendations of the reports quickly became of less significance than the scandalous possibility that the Unionist administration in Dublin Castle (headed by George Wyndham and the Lord Lieutenant, the Earl of Dudley) had 'gone native', and had succumbed to Home Rule.

The devolution crisis of 1904–5 was a wonderfully rich and complex affair, replete with political intrigue and personal drama. To some extent it was a product of Wyndham's political style, which was conspiratorial and oblique. Wyndham and his lieutenants had sought to govern Ireland and to defuse the Home Rule movement through confidential conversa-tions and by encouraging the 'conference plus business' ideal. Wyndham was also keen to incorporate Home Rulers within the process of

93

government by getting them to accept particular pieces of legislation as 'non-controversial' and therefore beyond debate. He and his lieutenants increasingly used the centrists of the Irish Reform Association as a medium through which government thinking might be tested with minimum risk.

It is pretty clear, despite his subsequent denials, that Wyndham tacitly encouraged the debate on devolution in August and September 1904, and it is possible that he and Dudley involved both Tim Healy and some moderate English Unionist backbenchers in an effort to broaden their support base.[36] If so, the effort was to no avail, for the Irish parliamentary party remained largely outside the loop of this centrist conspiracy, while both the Ulster Unionists and mainstream Conservatives sensed political treachery. Wyndham, the key ministerial patron of centrism, fell from office in March 1905, hounded by Ulster Unionist MPs who believed that, in supporting the Reform Association on devolution, he had broken faith with Unionism. Poignantly and predictably, he was helped on his way to political oblivion by a union of angry loyalists and nationalists, inevitably including Dillon. Wyndham and his Irish mentors had been a threat to conventional party politics; and conventional party politicians united in dispatching him.

But there was another long-term resonance from the centrist failure. In fighting for the unity of the Home Rule cause in 1903–5, Dillon had helped to precipitate a schism that lasted for most of what remained of his movement's life. Dillon, of course, can scarcely be blamed for the actions of the leading schismatic, William O'Brien. O'Brien had, in one muted judgement, 'a not always reliable political intelligence', and he was characterised by a manic and uncollegiate political temperament.[37] O'Brien left the party in November 1903, and though he returned in January 1908 to test the strategy of conciliation again, disappointment remained his lot: the parliamentary party had thoroughly regrouped in support of Dillon's policy. If a demonstration were needed, this was provided at the notorious 'Baton Convention' of February 1909, where O'Brien's conciliationist battalion was routed by a well-regimented group of northern heavies under the leadership of Dillon's protégé, Joseph Devlin. O'Brien again left the party and used his political base in Cork to launch a centrist machine, the All for Ireland League. At both the general elections of January and December 1910, the All for Ireland League captured eight seats which, while an irritant rather than a threat to Redmond, was not far off Parnellite parliamentary strength in the 1890s. In a sense, then, Dillon had helped to navigate the Home Rule party into precisely the territory that he claimed he was determined to avoid. The political eruptions of 1903 had created a landscape not altogether dissimilar from that of the 1890s.

The events of 1903 not only helped to shape the divisions of the Home Rule movement, but also helped to determine the substance of Home Rule politics. The Home Rule movement would now be sustained according to Dillon's traditional ideas. It would remain essentially an ethnic national movement, which articulated principally the concerns of a narrow rural constituency. Phillip Bull has argued with passion that a great historical opportunity was lost in 1903-4. He has suggested that the still powerful ex-landed community had much in common with the substantial farmers, and that together they might have provided the foundation for a truly inclusive nationalism.[38] He has also emphasised the shared interests and approaches of northern Presbyterian (and Unionist) farmers and their southern Catholic (and nationalist) counterparts in the years between 1898 and 1903: both co-operated in the Land Conference and both invested in the centrist initiative. Working from these premises, Bull has concluded that 'what happened in 1903-4 was that the political logic of this new economic and class reality was defied, and the primacy of ethnic and sectarian division was asserted to the detriment of both capitalist interest and nationalist potential'.[39] Bull sees the ethnic savagery of the 'Troubles' and the blight of partition as, in part, rooted in the failure of the centrist moment.[40]

The force of some of these observations may be clearly seen with the last great social or agrarian campaign with which the movement was associated – the 'Ranch War', conducted between 1906 and 1909. This was spearheaded by Laurence Ginnell, MP for Westmeath, and launched at Downs, Westmeath, on 14 October 1906.[41] The purpose of the war was to bring relief to the large numbers of landless and smallholders, particularly in the west, who were relatively untouched by the Wyndham Act and by the larger policy of purchase. The strategy that Ginnell pursued was the 'Downs policy', or cattle driving, a proceeding designed to harrass the prosperous grazier interest, whose 'ranches' occupied large, underpopulated and underworked tracts. The 'Downs policy' was also meant to draw public attention to the scandalous inequities that survived in the Irish countryside. The conservatives within the Home Rule leadership were understandably suspicious about the revival of agrarian disturbance, but the mood of the party organisation was hardening in the aftermath of a disappointing devolution bill (May 1907) from the new Liberal government. Given the Liberals' tardiness, it seemed logical for many within the Home Rule movement to turn to the traditional mechanism for reactivating the national question: agrarian agitation.[42]

Ginnell's cattle-drives began to tail off after the summer of 1908, and the agitation was finally dissolved with the passage of a land reform by the Liberal Chief Secretary for Ireland, Augustine Birrell (1907-16). The

Birrell Act was hailed by the national movement as an historic victory, but in reality both the agitation and its legislative conclusion serve to illustrate the increasingly forlorn state of Home Rule politics. The Act was not, in fact, a major legislative achievement for the national movement. The key pressure on Birrell came not from Ginnell's ranch warriors, but rather from the British Treasury, burdened as it was by the costs of the South African War, by the arms race with Germany, and by the Liberal government's welfare legislation. Birrell, indeed, privately viewed Ginnell's challenge with surprising equanimity.[43]

The Treasury was keen to curtail the cost of land purchase, and this the Birrell Act effectively did: it made voluntary land purchase a much less attractive option for landlords than it had been in the past, while it permitted some compulsory purchase in the over-populated or 'congested' districts of the west, where land was poor and cheap. But the details that made life difficult for landlords – the substitution of government stock for cash in the sale, and the watering down of the bonus paid to selling proprietors – also made life difficult for tenants. In the absence of a wholesale measure of compulsion, landlords could, and did, either refuse to sell, or drag their feet. The measure that Dillon and his lieutenants hailed in 1909 was therefore to some extent a sham: it offered little or nothing to the core constituency of the Home Rule movement, and indeed robbed many nationalist farmers of easy access to purchase. The movement greeted the measure not because it helped ordinary farmers, but because it turned the screw on the vestigial landlord interest. It greeted the Act not because it was a measure of class conciliation, but because it fired the embers of social resentment. This above all serves to illustrate the ideological limitations of the Home Rule movement by the end of the Edwardian period.

By 1909–10 the Home Rule movement remained ascendant, certainly in terms of its electoral position. But, as will be increasingly clear, the means by which that control was sustained were highly problematic. Whether or not one interprets the centrist moment in 1903 as a critical turning point, it is indisputable that the decisions taken at that time served to condition the future of constitutional nationalism. It is unclear whether William O'Brien's notion of 'conference plus business' would have worked; it is unclear whether the centrist Unionists and landlords in 1903 could have come to represent anything other than a small ginger group. What is clear is that, however one calculates the possibilities created by the centrist experiment, the Home Rule and Unionist movements swiftly regrouped along fundamentalist lines. The Home Rule movement, influenced very greatly by Dillon, reverted to a narrow, traditional stand that not only stymied any real chance of an inclusive nationalism, but also (and dangerously) failed to incorporate some new interests within Catholic society.

Dillon's Home Rule movement was in effect a confessional or ethnic body. As Phillip Bull has argued, Dillon's ascendancy in the party was now sustained partly through the Ancient Order of Hibernians, an exclusively Catholic and secret fraternity that had spread from Ulster, and which was under the control of the Belfast nationalist Joseph Devlin.[44] It was the Hibernians, or 'Molly Maguires', who policed the United Irish League convention of February 1909 'probably the stormiest meeting ever held by constitutional nationalists' – and assaulted their centrist opponents.[45]

Dillon's Home Rule movement was characterised in effect by permanent class war. Dillon feared that the national struggle would be demoralised by social reconciliation, and he chose to spurn the opportunity created by O'Brien and his colleagues. The alternative was to exploit any remaining agrarian resentments even when – as with the Ranch War – these had little relevance for the core constituency of the movement. Indeed, the Ranch War neatly illustrates the suicidal illogicality of Dillon's strategies, since it was a struggle often pursued by graziers against graziers: it has been observed that 'a remarkably high proportion of the principal leaders of the ranch war either were or became graziers'.[46] The explanations for this striking paradox are not hard to locate. Given that the Ranch War was blessed by party elders like Dillon, and was gathering momentum in 1907–8, the local leaders of the United Irish League, often themselves ranchers, were compelled to join in the hue and cry against their own caste.

Dillon's Home Rule movement was characterised by a failure to satisfy its own constituency. Judged as an issue of social justice, the Ranch War, despite its occasional bloodiness, may be regarded as an honourable enterprise, but it aroused expectations that neither the Home Rule leadership nor the later inheritors of the national tradition chose to satisfy. The Land Act of 1909 was certainly not a definitive solution to western poverty, despite the ebullient rhetoric of the time, while the rulers of independent Ireland did little for the landless of the west. These landless country people, however desperate and needy, were ultimately a means to an end for strategists like Dillon. That end was the national struggle, which could only be sustained through the social resentments of the Irish countryside.

But in truth the plight of the landless was also a marginal concern for the main farming constituency of the Home Rule party, and the Ranch War involved an implosion within sectors of the party, as it threatened to destroy itself in the apparent interests of its own survival. So the war over land continued, even though it seemed that the tenant command did not want victory. The Home Rule leadership did not seek to facilitate the working of the Wyndham Act and it did not address the concerns of those many nationalist farmers who had bought their property through earlier purchase legislation, such as the Ashbourne Act and its successors. The land war continued because Dillon and his like wanted conflict above victory.

In the end, Dillon's strategy was a huge but calculated risk. If British policy, or indeed any secondary policy of the Home Rule movement, achieved a stable, settled Ireland, then the likelihood of devolution diminished and the movement would be destroyed. If the strategies of Conservatives and Unionists looked as if they might stabilise the country, the prospects of Home Rule all but disappeared. The interest of the Home Rule leadership, in this calculation, rested with incomplete reforms and semi-permanent protest, particularly in the traditional agrarian sphere. The risk was that the social and religious resentments which helped to fuel Home Rule would be dissipated before the achievement of the national millennium. But there was also a real threat that, if the Home Rule movement failed to satisfy its supporters, then these would migrate elsewhere. It was fortunate for Redmond and Dillon that, until 1910 and indeed beyond, this risk was minimised – not because they looked after their core support – but because that support had as yet no alternative billet outside of the Home Rule movement.

So far the focus has lingered upon the limitations both of Home Rule, as defined in 1893, and of the Home Rule movement, as defined after 1903 by Dillon and Redmond. The emphasis has been upon the fissile and conservative political culture that arose in part from the Parnell split, and from the failure of the second Home Rule Bill. But a concentration upon division and exclusivism fails to do justice to the movement's hold on the imagination of most Irish people. In a sense the argument so far has been that the Home Rule enterprise survived in spite of itself; and though this is true up to a point, it does not adequately explain the final, glorious flowering of the movement in the years between 1910 and 1914. Fortunately for the cause there was more to Home Rule than the political generosity of John Dillon.

It should be emphasised immediately that there was no real alternative to the Home Rule movement in the period covered by this chapter, and indeed until 1916. Unionism perhaps had a greater political hold than is sometimes allowed – certainly in the sense of a resigned or passive acceptance of the existing link with Britain – but the Unionist movement was becoming increasingly cast as an ethnic or confessional enterprise. By definition this meant the exclusion of most Catholics, and this in turn confirmed that Unionism was a minority phenomenon. Unionism represented a challenge to the Home Rule movement, rather than an alternative; although with the consolidation of a more rigorous northern Unionism after 1904–5, it was a challenge that was becoming ever more coherent and effective.

On the other hand, it is not altogether clear that the forces of the 'new' nationalism – radical separatists and cultural nationalists – represented even as much as a challenge to Home Rule at this stage. There were certainly aspects of the new nationalism that were in formal opposition to the 'old', constitutional, movement. An early and suggestive demonstration of this came in the South Mayo by-election of 1900, when a Home Ruler, John O'Donnell, was opposed by the separatist and pro-Boer, Major John MacBride. O'Donnell represented William O'Brien's revitalised vision of the parliamentary cause, but even this failed to mobilise the new, radical nationalism that had been energised by the South African war. Different scholars have observed the significance of the alignment of forces in South Mayo; and by extension, the contest might be seen as a portent of disaster for the Home Rule movement.[47] As always, however, hindsight invests episodes like this with a charge that they did not always possess at the time (O'Donnell in fact easily defeated his separatist opponent).

Sinn Féin would become, after 1916, the dominant nationalist organisation, clinically dispatching the Irish parliamentary party, but in this period it was scarcely more than an irritant to the Home Rulers. Sinn Féin, 'we ourselves', was a label already in circulation in the 1880s and 1890s, but it was annexed in about 1904 by Arthur Griffith, a separatist activist and polemicist, as a handy description of his own convictions. Griffith launched the newspaper *Sinn Féin* in May 1906; and though he was hostile to the Sinn Féin League, a party launched by rival separatists in April 1907, he helped to reformulate the League as the Sinn Féin organisation in September 1907. There was already in fact a 'Sinn Féin' presence of sorts in local government. Patrick Maume has located the beginnings of a Griffithite influence within Dublin corporation as early as January 1904, and by 1906 Dillon was complaining that 'the Sinn Féin business [in Dublin] is a very serious matter and has been spreading pretty rapidly for the last year'.[48] But only with the official launch of the party in September 1907 was there anything resembling national growth.

Disappointment with the Liberal government's weak Irish Council Bill of 1907 provided one important source of stimulus to the new party, despite Dillon's conviction that 'the explosion of disappointment and anger in the country will have some very wholesome results'. A critical by-election contest provided another, momentary spur.[49] C. J. Dolan, the Home Rule MP for North Leitrim, was won over to the Sinn Féin cause in 1907, and decided to seek the endorsement of his constituents. The ensuing campaign, fought between Dolan and the new Irish Party candidate, F. E. Meehan, was well publicised and aggressive. The Home Rule movement's Belfast stormtroopers were again in evidence, and their brutal tactics seem to have worked, for in the end Meehan triumphed, gaining 73 per cent of the poll. Griffith, of course, trumpeted Dolan's electoral showing of 27 per cent, but the reality was that a familiar, outgoing MP had been unable to mount a serious defence of his own seat – even allowing for the fact that he was given support by Protestants and others beyond the traditional national movement.[50]

Sinn Féin enjoyed some sluggish growth at this time, although by August 1909 there were still only 581 paid-up members in the entire country.[51] And the new party remained a predominantly Dublin phenomenon: 211 of the subscribers were concentrated in the capital, while some areas were barely touched, with County Sligo for example boasting only two Sinn Féin members. According to Michael Laffan, advanced politics in Sligo were represented by a student and a shopkeeper, who could only meet to plan for the millennium whenever the student was given the loan of a bicycle.[52] That the separatist defiance was crushed with such force in 1908 says as much about the febrile defensiveness of the Home Rule movement as it does about the strength of Sinn Féin.

Nor should it be assumed that the massive growth in cultural nationalism at this time represented a challenge or alternative to Home Rule. The narrative of this growth is reasonably familiar. The Gaelic Athletic Association (GAA, founded by Michael Cusack in 1884) and the Gaelic League (founded in 1893 by Douglas Hyde, Eoin MacNeill and Fr. Eugene Downey) fostered interest in Irish games and the Irish language respectively. The Irish Literary Theatre (founded by W. B. Yeats in 1899) was designed to promote an authentically Irish literature, albeit in English. All of these initiatives fed (though not always smoothly) into a wider 'Irish Ireland' enterprise, which appeared to have its roots in the collapse of the Home Rule movement in the 1890s. Certainly the most important (and vicious) philosopher of Irish Irelandism, D. P. Moran, was a frequent critic of the Home Rule party, its fudges and failures.[53]

Indeed one, Yeatsian, view of Irish politics at this time sees the decaying Home Rule tradition as producing cultural growth, and ultimately a flowering of militant separatism. This is problematic in a number of critical respects. Firstly, the notion of an inverse relationship between the health of the Home Rule and cultural nationalist traditions is open to serious question. It is true that the Gaelic League was launched at a time when Home Rule was in the doldrums; it is true, too, that the League retreated somewhat after 1906 and in tandem with the consolidation of the Irish Party. It is also true that the origins of the Irish Literary Theatre predate the reunification of the Home Rule movement, and are located in a time of relative confusion within constitutional nationalism.

But it is not possible to go much further in pressing this thesis. On the contrary, the evidence for a symbiotic, rather than a parasitical relationship between the old nationalism and the new seems overwhelming. Roy Foster has argued with conviction that much cultural nationalist activity was rooted in the early and mid-1880s, when 'new' nationalists were not seeking alternatives to Home Rule, but were in fact planning the cultural life of the emerging Home Rule state. The Gaelic Union (1880) and the GAA (1884) as well as a contemporary literary efflorescence serve to document this view.[54] By extension, the failure of the Home Rule movement in 1891–2 had direct implications for at least some of this activity: the GAA, for example, went into a sharp, if temporary decline in the early and mid-1890s as a result both of the confusion within parliamentary politics and of divisions within the militant Irish Republican Brotherhood. Both the Home Rule movement and the cultural nationalists of the Gaelic League and Literary Revival were helped by the South African war, and the arousal of anti-imperialist and anti-British feeling.

This symmetry in the chronology of the old and new nationalism suggests the existence of other, fertile connections between the two. It is certainly true that there was no absolute dichotomy between Home Rule and the new nationalism; on the contrary, one explanation for the health of the Home Rule movement in this period rests with the connections that it sustained with some new nationalist initiatives. Patrick Maume has pointed out that 'the Irish Party had [not] entirely lost touch with new Irish Ireland movements', and has emphasised the links forged between the two by, for example, the gilded youth of Home Rule, the Young Ireland branch of the party organisation, and the United Irish League.[55] It is possible to trace the reasonably extensive involvement of Home Rule politicians in both the GAA and the language movement. In the end, after 1914, these connections were certainly broken, and both the Gaelic League and the GAA pursued increasingly militant and separatist paths. But until at least 1910 it might well have been argued that cultural nationalism, rather than the avatar of a bloody revolution and national independence, was merely the wayward child of Home Rule.

What was true for the artisans and lower professionals recruited to the Gaelic League and the farmers' sons of the GAA was (as Senia Paseta has demonstrated) all the more emphatically true for other critical areas of Catholic society. Just as cultural nationalism was always to an extent a preparation for the Home Rule state, so the educated and professional elite of Catholic Ireland believed that they were in training for the advent of devolved government – preparing, indeed, to take control of that government.[56] Senia Paseta's examination of the universities and exclusive Catholic schools in the years before 1914 emphasises 'the marginal nature of Gaelicist politics'.[57] Neither aspect of the new nationalism, cultural or separatist, had yet made a serious impression upon this aspect of the Irish Catholic establishment; modernism, whether in a political or cultural form, was also marginal. By extension, the iconic figures of modernist literature or of the 'new' nationalism – James Joyce, Patrick Pearse, Eamon de Valera – were mostly educated with the Catholic elite at University College Dublin, but were also far removed from its intellectual and political focal points. Instead of a conquest of the old by the new, Paseta sees the 'institutionalising' of the Gaelic cultural revival within the Catholic establishment, and argues that the work produced by the revival was tamed and incorporated within an intensely traditional and conservative political framework.[58] The Catholic establishment at this time was interested not so much in creating an Irish Ireland as in colonising Anglo-Irishness: that is to say, they wanted to annex, rather than subvert the existing social, economic and cultural institutions of the country.

Indeed, the decisive political shift within this section of Irish Catholic society came not with any conversion to radical separatism, but rather with the acceptance that Home Rule was now a real prospect. At the turn of the century Home Rule started to have a relevance not just for Fenian wannabees, but also for the rich and socially ambitious. Even so, concern for Crown and Empire (even if one was Protestant and the other British) had a surprisingly long tenure within the pre-war Catholic establishment. The consolidation of nationalist conviction amongst upper-middle-class Catholic students implied reconciling a newly active faith in Home Rule with a respect for British imperialism. 'In retrospect', Paseta concludes, 'we can see the period as one of preparation not for independence, but for Home Rule and a central role in the Empire'.[59]

There are, of course, dangers in pushing these arguments too far, as Paseta clearly recognises. Indeed some suggestive paradoxes are generated by her particular line of reasoning. Her persuasive definition of the views of the young Catholic elite chimes with what has long been known about the convictions of the Home Rule leader, John Redmond. At the same time, however, the Home Rule movement made only half-hearted efforts to engage the young (and indeed other key groups) within its broader constituency. Questions of critical importance to students, such as the long-running controversy over Irish university reform, were of secondary concern to the narrowly focused movement led by Redmond and policed by Dillon. Paseta identifies a series of demonstrations held in 1905 by student radicals against the patriarchs of University College as a defining moment in the inter-relationship between the conservative Home Rule establishment and the educated young.[60] But the tragedy of the Home Rule movement was not that it was fundamentally out of touch with the youthful Catholic elite, but rather that it made so little effort to cultivate this essentially sympathetic constituency. In other words, the Home Rule movement managed to sell its key product to the young, but failed to provide ideological after-care.[61]

This picture of a successful and vibrant, if seriously flawed Home Rule movement is not far removed from that provided in the work of Patrick Maume. There is some apparent tension, in so far as Maume argues that the classes from which Paseta extrapolates her findings have been wrongly equated elsewhere with the movement as a whole. Maume suggests that historical writing on the Home Rule movement has been skewed by an over-emphasis on its conservative and Redmondite aspects, and a simultaneous underplaying of radical influences. In general Maume sees the strength of the movement as resting, in part, with its social and political diversity, and with its cultural engagement.[62]

It is clear from Maume's work that the Home Rule movement was not, in fact, wholly detached from radical nationalist thought in Edwardian Ireland. As was mentioned earlier, he has laid a particular emphasis upon the critical importance of the Young Ireland branch of the United Irish League. These young graduates of University College Dublin helped for a time to connect the party with the different strands of the new nationalism. Maume has constructed an intricate picture of a loose but effective party mechanism, with interlocking clusters of organisation, which centred on several key leaders, their immediate lieutenants and wider retinue.[63] He has shown how, at some cost, the party was able to prove that only with its co-operation could the British peacefully govern Ireland.

But in the end no scholar of the Home Rule movement can fail to be impressed not just by its successes, but by the compromises and paradoxes through which it defied political gravity. The focus of the movement was legislation which, even after two parliamentary trials in 1886 and 1893, and even setting aside the Unionist case, contained unresolved practical problems. The movement itself was broken by the Parnell split, and remained divided even beyond the formal reunification of 1900. It is frequently forgotten that in the general election of January 1910 the Irish parliamentary party won only seventy seats, as opposed to the eighty-five garnered by Parnell in July 1886. The split and the half-hearted nature of the reunification conditioned the form and substance of the leadership:

the united movement was endowed with an able, kindly but highly defensive commander in the shape of Redmond. Redmond was chosen in 1900 as much because of his political weaknesses as because of his strengths, and he for long betrayed this vulnerability in his actions. The split and the ongoing party divisions also touched John Dillon, fostering an ungenerous, narrow and almost masochistic political vision.

This was a movement which, at least as far as Redmond was concerned, was interested in promoting Irish nationality within the British empire, but it was also a movement with a visceral antipathy to the English and their colonies. It was a movement that was often led at a local level by large farmers, yet it was associated with an assault on this class during the Ranch War. The Home Rule cause interested the educated youth of Catholic Ireland, and yet little was done to cultivate and exploit this interest. The cause was led by urban professionals, journalists and dissident landlords, yet it remained cussedly focused on an agrarian battle which, in a sense, it did not want to win. It was a professedly constitutional movement, yet it deployed increasingly aggressive tactics at, for example, North Leitrim and the 'Baton' Convention. It was a movement that in some benign interpretations, was characterised by an overdose of gentility, yet its leaders pursued even mild-mannered opponents with an astonishing verbal violence.

Some of these paradoxes can be explained by the skewed vision of a moderate and right-wing movement that remains in the literature. Others may be illuminated through understanding the political demons that were released during the Parnell split: physical aggression, outrageous rhetoric, organisational and financial chaos, political marginalisation. Some, at least, of these demons tortured the imagination of Dillon, whose narrow focus on the integrity of the party machine is otherwise difficult to explain.

Some of these problems and paradoxes were merely harmless eccentricities of the party machine. Some had little short-term impact. But others were fundamentally dangerous to the survival of the movement. The failure to integrate youth could not, by definition, be borne indefinitely. The curiously ambiguous, sometimes comradely, sometimes bitter, connection with the British Liberal government was ripe with danger. The obsessive commitment to unity occasionally threatened to produce self-mutilation. The imagined Home Rule movement of the leaders, a vision rooted in the 1880s, sometimes jarred with Edwardian realities. The rejection of conciliationist politics in 1903 may have been disastrous, in so far as an accommodation with Unionism – even with only part of southern Unionism – might have defused some of the ethnic and constitutional tensions that later racked the Home Rule enterprise.

Yet, beyond the explanations, there remains the irreducible complexity and diversity of the Edwardian Home Rule movement. The movement was riven with self-contradiction and division: it was maimed by its obsession with Parnell's strategies of the 1880s. It could not always deliver to its diffuse constituency; nor did it deliver even a uniformly generous patriotism. Yet, until 1910 and beyond, the movement worked. And it worked because it had sole rights over that most richly ambiguous and winningly incoherent political concept: Home Rule.

# CHAPTER 7

# THE LEADERSHIP OF REDMOND
# 1910-14

Home Rule reached the pinnacle of its success in Ireland between 1912 and 1914, an ascent which reflected on the very considerable skills of John Redmond as a parliamentary mountaineer. For in these years Redmond had gone much further than any of his predecessors in shaping British politics to the needs of the Irish. He overcame the relative indifference of the new Liberal leadership to Home Rule, and he helped to break the main constitutional obstacles to the Irish cause. He won the introduction and passage of a measure of Home Rule, and there is a case – judged from the perspective of late 1914 – for seeing him as the victor of the struggle with Unionism over the fate of the third Home Rule Bill.

But some nuance has to be introduced into these familiar apologetics. Late Edwardian Liberalism was not, perhaps, as heedless of Ireland as has been frequently assumed. It is true that with the resignation and death of the Prime Minister, Sir Henry Campbell-Bannerman, in 1908, Home Rule lost a Gladstonian stalwart. It is true, too, that the new Liberal leader, Herbert Henry Asquith, and several of his lieutenants had been nurtured in the imperialist wing of the party and were distrusted by the Irish (especially by John Dillon). It is also the case that the key ideologues within the Edwardian party – the New Liberals – were apparently more concerned with British social and welfare issues than with any Irish preoccupation. But while the obstacles that Redmond faced within the Liberal Party should be appreciated, they should not be exaggerated. Recent research by Gary Peatling has stressed the extent to which the New Liberals were in fact preoccupied by the need to grant the Irish some form of legislative autonomy.[1] Moreover, while Asquith certainly lacked the visceral Home Rule commitment of Gladstone or (even) of Campbell-Bannerman, it is not altogether clear that he was distinguished by political passions of any type. The problem that Redmond faced was thus not so much that Asquith had become hostile to Home Rule, but that he needed to be convinced of its political utility. And in 1910-11, given the shifts within British politics, this task of persuasion was becoming markedly easier.

The conflict between David Lloyd George, Asquith's Chancellor of the Exchequer, and the House of Lords over the budget of 1909 has often been narrated and needs little further rendition. Lloyd George's tax-and-spend budget was rejected in the Lords, precipitating a general election in January 1910 and a constitutional impasse. Redmond and the Home Rulers now faced a peculiarly complex political challenge. On the one hand, the House of Lords, with its Unionist majority, had been a formidable obstacle to the enactment of Home Rule: the Lords, it will be recalled, had broken the second Home Rule Bill in 1893. On the other hand, the budget that so upset their Lordships was also unpopular with critical elements of Redmond's support, such as the drink trade and the new Catholic landed interest. Opposing the budget meant, for the Home Rulers, opposing the Liberal Party and endorsing the Unionist Upper House; approving the budget carried with it the threat of electoral humiliation.

In the event Redmond gambled on the Liberal alliance, but reduced the odds by demanding that Asquith renew his commitment to Home Rule. Fearing the defection of the Irish vote, Asquith made the requisite pledge in a speech at the Albert Hall on 10 December 1909. Significantly, however, he would offer no later renewal of his Home Rule vows; and there was also a marked coolness on the subject among other Liberal candidates. For his part, Asquith wanted to keep the Irish on-side while at the same time avoiding a contest on Home Rule, which was an unpopular cause in England. He wanted, too, to keep the electorate focused on the potentially more profitable conflict between the peers and the people. On balance, it may be said that the strategy worked, as the Liberals were returned just ahead of the Tories: the Liberals garnered 275 seats to the Tories' 273, with Labour on 40 seats and the different varieties of Irish nationalist on 82 seats. Asquith and his government survived, but it was the Irish Home Rulers who, holding the balance of power, were the true victors in the contest.

How did Redmond press home his advantage? It should be emphasised immediately that his position was rather more awkward than appearances might at first suggest. A comparison with Parnell's strategic options in 1885–6 is suggestive. After the general election of 1885, Parnell held the balance of power between the Conservatives and Liberals, and because neither party had yet completely fixed its stand on the Union he was able to flirt with each, keeping his options open. It may seem unlikely that the Tories would have plumped for Home Rule, but the ludicrousness of the notion is magnified by hindsight. In contrast, Redmond in 1910 could not play the Liberals off against the Tories because only the Liberals were at all likely to enact Home Rule (at least in its Gladstonian definition). There was little or nothing to be gained by turning out a Liberal administration in order to install a Tory and Unionist successor. After January 1910 Redmond pushed for constitutional change and a reform of the Lords' right of legislative veto. The trade-off was continued Irish support, or at least abstention, on the ongoing question of the budget ('no veto, no budget'). This pressure seemed to be effective, for in March 1910 the government placed three resolutions on the issue of constitutional reform before the House of Commons.

However, while it is important not to exaggerate Redmond's range of choice, or indeed his strength or boldness, it is also important not to overlook the extent to which options were open to the Liberals. The death of King Edward VII in May 1910 and the accession of George V precipitated an interparty conference that excluded the Irish and might well have produced a Liberal–Tory coalition. This was certainly the hope of Lloyd George and certain Tories, all of whom were keen to be liberated from their respective Irish clients, and to push forward towards an agreed scheme of devolution (or 'federalism') for the entire United Kingdom. Some of these Tories would include later Ulster stalwarts like F. E. Smith and even, according to one well-placed source, Andrew Bonar Law.[2] The Unionist editor, J. L. Garvin, gave federalism and coalition his blessing in the pages of the *Observer*. Another Unionist ideologue, F. S. Oliver, pursued a similar course, writing letters to the press under the pen-name 'Pacificus'.[3] On the other hand, Irish and Ulster Unionists were not briefed concerning the progress of the discussions and, in a manner reminiscent of their actions at the time of the Anglo-Irish Agreement of 1985, they succumbed to the wildest suspicions and panic. A few grim letters from Carson to Theresa Lady Londonderry and an hysterical missive from the Ulster Unionist lawyer, William Moore, to Edward Goulding, the grey eminence of late Edwardian Unionism, eloquently document the mood of the time.[4]

In the event there was no liberation of the English from their Irish allies, no coalition government and no devolutionist millennium, but the richness of political opportunity in the summer and autumn of 1910 should not be underestimated. The conference broke up without agreement in November 1910, and an election was called for the following month. The results of this more or less replicated those of the January contest. But the essential difference was that the Liberals had now explored their options, and were at last forced back into the avuncular embrace of Redmond.

The failure of the interparty conference and the marginal Liberal victory in December 1910 permitted Asquith to move ahead with reform of the Lords and thus with Home Rule. A Parliament Act was passed in August 1911, which abolished the absolute veto of the Lords, and which therefore paved the way for the enactment of a Government of Ireland Bill. Even before the last battle on the constitution was fought, Liberal ministers and ideologues were beginning to plan for a Home Rule Bill. In January 1911, fresh from the election contest, the cabinet established a committee on the issue comprising Augustine Birrell, Winston Churchill (as Home Secretary), Lloyd George, Sir Edward Grey (Foreign Secretary), R. B. Haldane (Secretary of State for War), Lord Loreburn (Lord Chancellor) and Herbert Samuel (Postmaster General).

While the outlines of Home Rule finance were, along with federalism, an abiding preoccupation of these ministers, the details of the proposed fiscal arrangements were left to a committee of experts headed by Sir Henry Primrose, a retired chairman of the Board of Inland Revenue. On the whole, both the ministers and Primrose's experts were concerned to curb public expenditure in Ireland. But while Primrose edged towards a settlement that absolved the Treasury by sub-contracting power and responsibility to the new Irish parliament, the ministers wanted to assert the sovereignty of Westminster as much as they wanted to be freed from the expense and bother of Irish government. The result of these conflicting priorities was a numblingly elaborate proposal which, in the end, came not from the wise men of the Primrose Committee, but rather from Herbert Samuel.

All this leads to a detailed consideration of the Home Rule Bill which was at last placed before the Commons in April 1912.[5] The bill owed much to its predecessor of 1893, but there were some new departures. The bill of 1912, like that of 1893, affirmed the supremacy of the parliament at Westminster. The bill of 1893 permitted the retention of eighty Irish members at Westminster; that of 1912 made provision for the retention of only forty-two members. Like the proposal of 1893, the bill of 1912 was constructed around the idea of a bicameral Irish parliament, though there were considerable differences in the detail of the two measures. The new bill proposed the creation of a Senate, comprising forty members, and a House of Commons, comprising 164 members (as opposed to the Legislative Council of 1893, which would have had forty-eight members, and the Legislative Assembly, which would have numbered 103).

Both the second and third Home Rule Bills proposed the creation of an Irish executive, headed by the Lord Lieutenant. The bill of 1912 demanded that ministers should be members of one or other of the houses of the Irish parliament – or at least should become members within six months of their ministerial appointment – and thereby confirmed a provision for responsible government laid down in 1893. The constitutional scholar Alan Ward has emphasised, however, that 'the 1912 Home Rule Bill moved one step forward and two steps back' in so far as the Lord Lieutenant now had the power not only to approve or veto legislation, but also, and more dangerously, to reserve a decision, and thus to postpone legislation indefinitely.[6]

Specific areas were defined in the bill as being beyond the authority of the new administration. These included the Crown, the making of peace or war, all matters pertaining to the army and navy, foreign and colonial relations, honours, the law of treason, and foreign trade and navigation. Military security, the dignity of the Crown and commercial unity were the concerns underlying these restrictions. There were in addition areas, known as the 'reserved services', which were excluded from the prospective Irish government on a provisional basis. These matters included the Land Purchase Acts, the Old Age Pensions Acts (of 1908 and 1911), the National Insurance Act (1911), the Labour Exchanges Act (1909), the collection of taxes, the Royal Irish Constabulary, Post Office Savings Banks, Trustee Savings Banks and Friendly Societies. The proposed fate of these reserved services varied according to the contentiousness of the subject. It was proposed, for example, to transfer control of the Royal Irish Constabulary from the government of the United Kingdom to the new Irish authority after six years. The administration of old age pensions, national insurance and post office savings banks was, of course, less controversial than the police. It was proposed here that control could be passed to Dublin within a year of any joint agreement on the matter between the Irish and British parliaments.

Section 3 of the bill dealt with legislation on religious matters and was designed to allay the fears (or, at any rate, to subvert the arguments) of the Ulster Unionists. They had long complained that Home Rule would represent 'Rome Rule', given the religious demography of the island and the traditional tensions between Irish Protestantism and Catholicism. Section 3 included an expansive prohibition on legislation that would discriminate either in favour of, or against, any form of religious practice. In particular the Irish parliament was prevented from legislating to 'make any religious belief or religious ceremony a condition of the validity of any marriage'. This restriction was a novelty that had not featured in either of the earlier Home Rule Bills, and it was designed to address Protestant fears concerning the Papal decree *Ne Temere*, and its effect on mixed (Protestant–Catholic) marriages. *Ne Temere* was a profoundly contentious topic in the years before 1912. The McCann case – which concerned the bitter break-up of a mixed marriage and the apparent betrayal of a Protestant wife – was a particular source of anger for Irish Unionists and was widely seen as the grim practical reality of the decree. The inclusion of these religious prohibitions was regarded as a humiliation by many Irish nationalists, and in the event it did little to ameliorate Unionist anger.

Some brief observations on the proposed financial settlement may be offered. Under Samuel's elaborate proposal, all Irish revenue was to be paid into the imperial exchequer. Since the administration of Ireland cost more than the yield from Irish taxation, the operating cost of those areas of administration under Irish control – around £6 million – would be returned from London to Ireland as the bulk of a 'Transferred Sum'. In addition, a small surplus of (to begin with) £500,000 would be added to provide a margin of error for the new Irish administration.

The Irish government could levy new taxes, provided that these did not conflict with existing imperial taxation. A Joint Exchequer Board, containing Irish representation but controlled by the British government, would adjudicate on what did or did not constitute 'conflict'. However, the new authority was expressly prohibited from levying new customs duties. The Irish could raise existing taxes, but (in the case of income tax, death duties and customs) by not more than 10 per cent. Part of the levy still raised in Ireland by the imperial government consisted of land purchase annuities, paid by those farmers who had bought their holdings using government credit. Any arrears of these annuities would be charged to the new Irish government through a reduction of the Transferred Sum. As Redmond commented bleakly, 'the whole revenue of Ireland is thus held in pawn for the security of payments under the Land Purchase Acts'.[7] Here was one issue which, in the opinion of contemporaries, held the potential for bitter future controversy between the new Home Rule administration and the imperial parliament.

However, there was no need to wait for controversy. The content of the bill produced a range of immediate dissatisfaction. Irish nationalists were upset by Samuel's niggardly financial proposals and by the suppression of the more generous Primrose scheme. They were also offended by the prohibition on religious legislation. The modesty of the scheme concerned many 'advanced' nationalists: it was in certain respects a more grudging settlement than that proposed by Gladstone, at least in 1886. But the bill was also, to an extent, open-ended, both in its detail and in the more general sense that the ambitions of an Irish parliament, once established, would have been hard to thwart. And many nationalists placed their faith in the dynamics of the legislation, rather than in its immediate, prosaic reality. They would bank in a similar way on the ambiguities of later settlements.

But if the bill failed to meet all nationalist requirements, then it was an even more complete disappointment for British and Irish Unionists. This observation begs the question of whether any formulation of Home Rule in 1912 could have defused Unionist opposition. Here there are two respected, but quite different, views. It is occasionally argued that Asquith missed a magnificent opportunity in April 1912, by failing to incorporate any significant concession to the Ulster Unionists' case into the Home Rule Bill. Patricia Jalland and others have argued that the immediate exclusion of part of the north from the operation of the bill might have defused Unionist opposition and opened the way to the successful enactment of Home Rule.[8] The late Nicholas Mansergh questioned this view, arguing that Ulster Unionists were unlikely to be mollified by the exclusion of, say, four and a half northern counties, and were equally unlikely to be worried by any shift in British Conservative opinion: 'the [Ulster Unionists'] target might have been different, the goal and tactic surely the same'. Any preliminary appeasement of the Unionists would also have 'affronted [Redmond] beyond measure'. The essential problem with Asquith's handling of the Home Rule issue, for Mansergh, was not so much that he got the policy wrong, but rather that he failed to execute it with sufficient rigour.[9]

This is essentially a counter-factual problem, and is thus by definition incapable of decisive settlement. On balance, however, there is more to the Jalland case than Mansergh's critique perhaps allows. It is probably true that any concession on the issue of exclusion in April 1912 would not have completely mollified Ulster Unionists. It is quite true that some form of Ulster Unionist campaign against the Home Rule Bill might have been sustained. It is unquestionably the case that Redmond would have been 'affronted' by any concession smacking of partition. The affronting of Redmond, as the democratically elected leader of the Home Rule movement, would have been a highly serious business. However, at the risk of anticipating arguments later in the chapter, it might be briefly observed that a deal struck in April 1912 – however hard to accept – would have been much less of an affront than the humiliations that Redmond had to endure while Asquith made policy on the hoof in February and March 1914.

If a deal had been struck on exclusion in April 1912, then Ulster Unionists would probably still have sustained some form of opposition to the bill. Some would, indeed, have paid scant regard to any shifts in British Conservative opinion on the issue. But these arguments do not recognise divisions and developments within Ulster Unionism itself; and while Mansergh's case implicitly accepts the notion that the recalcitrant Unionist minority might have had to be coerced, it does not consider how this might have been effected with least pain. Ulster Unionism contained a clear gradation of opinion and fervour, particularly on the issue of militant action. Moreover, in April 1912 militant feeling and preparations within Ulster Unionism were growing, but they were very far from the levels reached in the spring of 1914.

From these observations a number of other points flow. Some form of limited exclusion in April 1912 would have contained the potential to divide Ulster Unionists not just from British Conservatives but also within themselves. Second, a deal in April 1912 would almost certainly have undermined the dangerous growth in Ulster Unionist militancy: Ulster Unionist defiance was as yet largely rhetorical, and a settlement would have been both easier to impose and easier to sustain in April 1912 than at any later date. Third, though some Unionists would indeed have disregarded shifts in Tory opinion in the aftermath of an early settlement, the rupture of the Unionist–Conservative alliance that was such a remarkable feature of the later Home Rule crisis would have rendered Ulster Unionists isolated and vulnerable. Had Asquith's Home Rule Bill contained some form of exclusion as a concession to the Ulster Unionists, then in all probability he would have been spared the later crisis. Such a bill might not have totally silenced Ulster Unionist anger, but it might well have divided Ulster Unionists, separated them from British Tories and subverted the drift to militancy.

The Home Rule Bill of April 1912 contained no concession to the Ulster Unionist case, not because Asquith and all of his senior ministers believed passionately in a unitary settlement, but rather because they did not want to conclude a deal before the haggling took place: this was the logical essence of the much-derided Asquithian maxim, 'wait and see'.[10] There were also some pressures from within the Liberal Party which further confirmed Asquith's tendency to seek refuge in delay. It has been remarked that between 1910 and 1912 the public debate over Home Rule within Liberalism had little to do with Ulster, and focused instead on the rival merits of colonial Home Rule ('dominion status'), advocated by Erskine Childers, and of federal Home Rule (the grant of legislative autonomy within a wider federal constitution), as promoted by the Liberal jurist, J. H. Morgan. It has also been emphasised that sections of the party, and in particular the New Liberals, believed more firmly in a single, united Irish government than has hitherto been allowed. Indeed, it has been cogently argued that 'in retrospect Liberals' "curious" neglect of the Ulster dimension...can be explained by a proper appreciation of the extent of Liberals' ideological commitment to a particular kind of Irish settlement'. 'In these circumstances', it has been said, 'a Liberal Prime Minister would have been remarkably imaginative to propound the policy [of partition] before Asquith did.'[11]

While it is important to include the hitherto neglected issue of New Liberal conviction, it must also be recognised that exclusion, or partition, had been mooted by Liberals, apparently including Asquith himself, from an early stage of the draft legislation. Indeed, it seems clear that some members of the party had been interested in the notion of partition from the time of the first Home Rule Bill. In March 1886 Robert McGeagh, a leading Irish Liberal, argued to James Bryce that 'the only way in which Ulster can hold its own against Munster, Leinster and Connacht is by having a separate parliament of its own'.[12] It is possible that Asquith himself shared these convictions at this time. In 1912 Arthur Gwynne-James forwarded to the Prime Minister a commentary upon the bill of 1886, which it was claimed had been jointly compiled by Sir Henry James, the distinguished Liberal Unionist jurist, and by his legal 'devil', the youthful Asquith. A central principle of this James–Asquith critique was that 'for the purpose of government Ireland [was] to be divided into two provinces to consist (a) of the whole of Ireland except Ulster or a defined portion thereof and (b) of the part so excepted'.[13] It is just conceivable that Gwynne-James's attribution of the document was mistaken. But there is no record of a rebuttal, and the thrust of the document certainly chimes with what is known about Asquith's private sympathies in 1912.

Moreover, if this evidence is not completely certain, the partitionist speculations of some Liberal ministers in 1911–12 are beyond question. On 24 February 1911, Winston Churchill submitted a 'federal' scheme to his ministerial colleagues. When this was elaborated on 1 March, it became clear that Churchill had in mind the division of the United Kingdom into ten constituent territories, including Ulster, each of which he proposed to endow with its own legislature. This was an unwieldy and ambitious undertaking which embodied the paradox favoured by later Unionist devolutionists: namely, that the integrity and coherence of the United Kingdom might best be preserved not by an exceptional grant of devolution to the Irish, but rather by sweeping grants of regional devolution into which the Irish would be subsumed.

Setting aside issues of principle, Churchill's proposal was distrusted by those – like Birrell – who feared that the Irish case might be delayed or spoilt by being incorporated within a larger scheme. But even Birrell, who often acted as the mouthpiece of the Irish nationalists within cabinet, recognised that Ulster Unionism was likely to pose an immense problem. It was Birrell who appears to have been an early advocate of the influential notion of county option – the idea that individual Ulster counties would be permitted to opt out of the Home Rule scheme for a transitional period. On 26 August 1911 he was arguing this case in a letter to Churchill, making the assumption, which was rather alarming in the circumstances, that only Antrim and Down would be likely to withdraw from Home Rule.[14]

Birrell's *ballon d'essai* was taken up by Churchill and Lloyd George, and at a critical meeting of the cabinet on 6 February 1912 county option formed the basis of a plan for Ulster exclusion which they jointly urged on their colleagues. The idea won some favour in the cabinet, but – while it is reasonably clear that the argument could have gone either way – the exclusionists lost out. Asquith, who appears to have shifted ground as the mood of the meeting changed, was not unsympathetic, but seems in the end to have preferred to wait before making concessions.[15] Again it must be emphasised that he did not hold unerringly to the principle of a unitary settlement; and it seems quite clear that the main reason why he did not plump for exclusion in February 1912 had nothing to do with conviction or concern for Irish nationalist sensitivities, and had everything to do with political pragmatism. His report of the cabinet to King George V indicates the tenor of his thought:

> if in the light of such evidence or indication of public opinion, it becomes clear as the Bill proceeds that some special treatment must be provided for the Ulster counties, the Government will be ready to recognise the necessity, either by amendment of the Bill, or by not pressing it on under the provisions of the Parliament Act. In the meantime, careful and confidential inquiry is to be made as to the real extent and character of the Ulster resistance.[16]

The implications of this crisp exposition of the cabinet's thought are surely clear: that the government would act to provide 'special treatment' for the Ulster counties, if the 'extent and character' of their resistance provided justification. Government strategy was thus ultimately dependent upon the ferocity of Unionist resistance.

Before the issue of partition – so central to the political crisis of 1912–14 – is considered more fully, it is perhaps appropriate to comment on the state of Unionism on the eve of the Home Rule crisis. This is all the more necessary in so far as it is often argued that the crisis was profoundly affected by the shifts within British and Irish Unionism occurring at this time. There remains, for example, a view that – in terms of the opposition to Home Rule – a turning point came in 1911, in the months before the launch of the bill.[17] It has been argued since the 1920s that the passage of the Parliament Act in 1911 was the sole cause of the Ulster Unionists' descent into militancy. With the breaking of the Lords' veto, the last secure constitutional obstacle to Home Rule disappeared, and Ulster Unionists were thrust on to their own political resources.

There can be little doubt that the Parliament Act and the British constitutional crisis of 1910–11 had a profound impact upon Ulster Unionist strategies, but a number of wider contextual points must also be made. Some of the mechanisms by which Ulster Unionists sustained their militancy were established in 1910, before the passage of the Parliament Act and before the outcome of the December general election was known. Their governing body, the Ulster Unionist Council, established an arms committee and began the piecemeal importation of weapons in December 1910. Orangemen began drilling and military training in 1910, before and not after the final passage of the Parliament Act. Thus, Ulster Unionists turned to militancy not after the resolution of the British constitutional crisis, but while that crisis was still developing.

They turned to militancy partly perhaps because of the evolving threat to the Lords, but also as a result of their wider relationship with British politics. In the later Edwardian period, Ulster Unionists had a profoundly unsatisfactory bond with British Tories and an even more unprofitable relationship with Birrell's Irish administration. Moreover, throughout the mid- and later Edwardian era, Ulster Unionists were consolidating the local institutions of their movement and were thus becoming more completely ensnared in provincial political passions. Ulster Unionists turned to militancy, therefore, not simply because of the Parliament Act or, indeed, the Home Rule Bill. Anger at the Parliament Act and at the Home Rule Bill unquestionably accelerated the drift into militancy, but the origins of this drift lay elsewhere.

The second apparently decisive shift in Unionism which occurred in 1911 relates to the British party and its leadership. It has been argued that the decision of the British Unionists to elect Andrew Bonar Law as leader (in succession to Arthur Balfour) was 'far more important', in terms of the worsening Home Rule crisis, than 'the timing of Liberal concessions, whether in April 1912 or in March 1914'.[18] In this thesis Bonar Law's strong family connections with Coleraine in the north of Ireland stimulated a ferocious sympathy with Ulster Unionism which, in turn, carried the Conservative Party into an expansive endorsement of loyalist militancy. This argument accepts that Bonar Law was in earnest, rather than bluffing and that he – much more than the Liberals – was responsible for fanning loyalist fury and bringing the United Kingdom to the brink of civil war. Moreover, it is argued that only Bonar Law of the available Conservative leaders could have pursued this dangerous path. It is seen as inconceivable that his rivals for the Tory leadership in 1911 – Walter Long and Austen Chamberlain – would have so fully endorsed Ulster Unionist militancy.

Such arguments are generally rooted in the defence of Asquithian

Liberalism that was offered in the 1930s by sympathetic scholars such as George Dangerfield and R. C. K. Ensor, and they have been communicated to a younger generation by Liberal intellectuals such as Roy Jenkins and Nicholas Mansergh. A general assessment of Tory culpability must wait until the course of the Home Rule crisis is fully reviewed, but some of the details relating to the significance of Bonar Law's election in 1911 may conveniently be assessed here.

Bonar Law had indeed strong family connections with Ulster, and offered ferocious support for the Unionist cause. But this is very far from saying that his loyalist convictions were irreducible, or that his rivals in the Tory leadership would have acted in a much more emollient way than he. Bonar Law came to prominence within Edwardian Toryism as a tariff reformer, not as an advocate of Ulster Unionism, even though there were plenty of parliamentary opportunities to express ultra-loyalist conviction. There is some evidence that he was attracted by Lloyd George's idea of a coalition government in 1910, which is hardly the action of an unreconstructed loyalist.[19] There is no reason whatsoever for assuming that Ulster Unionists wanted him as Tory leader in November 1911. A recent assessment of Bonar Law's strategy over Ulster in 1912–14 emphasises not so much his congenital loyalism, but rather the extent to which he was shrewdly using the crisis to consolidate his own leadership, and to wrest a dissolution and a general election from the Liberals.[20]

Moreover, the notion that Bonar Law's rivals for the leadership in 1911 would have proved more pragmatic than he is highly problematic, to say the least. The main contenders for the leadership were Long and Chamberlain, although Carson's name was also canvassed. Carson did not want the job, but he enjoyed some support and was certainly a credible candidate. It is hard indeed to imagine Austen Chamberlain offering the same kind of commitment to Ulster Unionist militancy as Bonar Law, though Chamberlain's firmness on the issue of Union should not be dismissed. But Walter Long, though unquestionably a highly complex figure, was of a somewhat different mettle to Chamberlain, and it would be a palpable error to discount his credentials as an Ulster militant.

Long was the favoured candidate of the Ulster Unionists in the Tory leadership contest of 1911. He was very closely connected with the financing of loyalist militancy, and he maintained close relations with those running weapons into Ulster in 1913–14: his closest parliamentary lieutenant, Sir William Bull, was actively involved with the gun-running escapades of these years.[21] It is possible that Long acted as an intermediary between the Ulster hawks and Bonar Law: in any event he was much more directly connected with their activities than his party leader. So, the election of Bonar Law in 1911 was ultimately helpful to Ulster Unionism, and may in the end have aided the partitionist cause in Ireland. But his credentials as an Ulster sympathiser were not unalloyed; and there were others within the Tory leadership who – either from personal conviction or political utility – would have ventured as far as he on the path to rebellion.

For a long time, however, the ferocity of the Unionists was comfortably verbal or, at most, gestural. Between 1911 and 1913, while there was a militant undercurrent to Ulster Unionist action, the principal thrusts of their action were constitutional or, to paraphrase a later Irish leader, 'nearly' constitutional. Mass meetings were an important part of this strategy: Craigavon, near Belfast, was a favoured venue, and was used on 23 September 1911 when Carson was introduced to the loyalist crowds as their new leader. For his part, Bonar Law made the acquaintance of popular Ulster Unionism at the Balmoral show-grounds, on the outskirts of Belfast, in April 1912. An important series of meetings was held throughout the north of Ireland in September 1912, which culminated in the signing of a popular protest against Home Rule, the Solemn League and Covenant. The Covenant, which was based on sixteenth- and seventeenth-century Scottish precedents, also signals a strong historical resonance within the Ulster Unionist campaign. Its leaders appealed relentlessly to a popular sense of Protestant tradition, and occasionally used icons from the seventeenth century to underline the message of historical continuity – a flag carried before William III at the Battle of the Boyne was displayed at one of Carson's meetings.[22]

But the Unionists' campaign was also relentlessly modern to the extent that it exploited a wide variety of propaganda media. There was a traditional emphasis on the printed word, with the production of millions of flyers and pamphlets, but there was also, for example, a responsiveness to the press and to the camera.[23] The Ulster Unionist leadership – even at a local level – was sensitive to the usefulness of the moving picture and the photo opportunity. And they were aware, too, of the extent to which modern mass production permitted the spread of political propaganda, not just in terms of print but also with regard to a wide variety of household or personal possessions – badges, rosettes, medals, chinaware, photographic portraits. The Edwardian equivalent of the e-mail message, the halfpenny postcard, was the medium by which thousands of different Unionist images were conveyed – and indeed the extent to which Unionists exploited this device is striking.[24]

But beyond the flamboyance of this public display was a more sombre strategic thrust. From the beginning Unionists seem to have been prepared to countenance both radical political defiance and the use of militant action. In September 1911 plans for the creation of an Ulster

Provisional Government were laid, and exactly two years later this rebel administration was formally launched as the high command of the Unionist movement. As has been noted, gun-running and military manoeuvres, albeit on a comparatively small scale, were being undertaken from as early as December 1910. Weapons filtered into the north of Ireland between 1910 and 1913, but the quantities were small, and a fair proportion of the imports fell into the hands of the authorities. In March 1911 the Ulster Unionists submitted an order worth £1000 to a German arms dealer, but although money changed hands, no rifles were forthcoming and it was believed that the Unionists had been betrayed to the British government.[25] By September 1911 the trickle of weapons coming from continental Europe to the Unionists had been cut off by a series of successful customs raids at the Unionists' entrepôt, Leith in Scotland. A major humiliation came in June 1913 when a consignment of between six and seven thousand Italian rifles (which had been temporarily stored at the Windsor Castle Tavern in King Street, Hammersmith) was seized by the Metropolitan Police. The Hammersmith cache had been the responsibility of a Captain Budden, who was the brother-in-law of Sir William Bull, a senior Tory MP and confidant of Walter Long. There was some mystery at the time about the identity of the police informant, but it was in fact the impecunious Budden who had 'grassed' on the loyalists.[26]

The Hammersmith débâcle and the preceding escapades, though rarely discussed, have considerable resonance. The Leith and Hammersmith affairs indicate that the authorities were prepared to act against the Ulster Unionist militants, and to use a degree of legal ingenuity to achieve their ends. The Hammersmith weapons were seized, not because they were destined for a civil war in Ulster but on the technical grounds that they lacked the appropriate proof mark required under legislation of 1868. The Hammersmith affair, and that of March 1911, also suggest a degree of official penetration of the loyalist enterprise. The £1000 order that went missing was thought by the Unionists to have been part of a secret service ruse. Captain Budden's treachery in 1913 probably alerted the police and government to the strong inter-connection between the Tory leadership and Ulster Unionist militancy. Indeed, the distinguished military historian Ian Beckett has raised the possibility that Tory politicians themselves came under official surveillance.[27] Finally, the Hammersmith débâcle, in combination with the apparent futility of parliamentary debate, persuaded the leading Unionist hawks that a more ambitious smuggling operation was in order; and this in turn paved the way for the Larne gun-running of April 1914, which will be presently discussed.

Complementing the smuggling of weapons was the evolution of a loyalist army. From late 1910 Orangemen and other Unionists had begun to undertake some basic military manoeuvres. Ronald McNeill in his classic account of the Unionist campaign, *Ulster's Stand for Union* (1922), argued that military drilling was first seen at the Craigavon demonstration of September 1911. But, although his account remains highly influential, he was mistaken in this and other telling details. It is perhaps true that the Craigavon demonstration further stimulated the fad for drilling that swept the north in 1911 and into 1912, but the origins of this predated the meeting. This essentially independent activity posed certain dangers to the Unionist political leadership, and at the very end of 1912 the politicians moved to assert their control by creating a formal structure within which this local paramilitary activity might be organised. This new initiative was the Ulster Volunteer Force (UVF), and its success was such that, by the end of 1913, it was claiming a membership of just under 100,000 recruits.

The inspiration for the UVF was the British army, with county-based regiments, separate nursing, transport and special services corps, and a general headquarters. Retired British army officers and men were an important influence in the new force, as were serving reservists. The generalissimo was Sir George Richardson of the Indian army, and he was appointed on the recommendation of no less a commander than Earl Roberts of Kandahar. By 1914 the Ulster Volunteer Force, while hampered still by a variety of strategic and logistical problems, was a formidable force by any reckoning. It served not only as a physical expression of Ulster Unionist intent, but also as a stimulus to the hawks within the nationalist tradition. The UVF was a direct inspiration for the Irish Volunteers, formed in November 1913 by those on the nationalist side who feared that Home Rule had stalled.

All of this broaches the parliamentary and high-political debate on Home Rule, and in particular the evolution of the partition question after 1912: the slow movement of the question from the private into the public arena, and its transformation from a wrecking tactic into a policy goal. Some mention has been made of the debate about partition within the Liberal cabinet in 1911–12, and of the decision not to incorporate any element of exclusion into the bill launched in April 1912. For their part, the Tories had long recognised that Ulster Unionism presented a peculiar difficulty to the proponents of Home Rule; but at first they had refrained from pressing the case for Ulster particularism out of respect for the sensitivities of southern Irish Unionists and out of concern for the wider unity of Unionism. In November 1911 Carson recalled that at the time of the second Home Rule Bill there had been extensive discussions among leading Unionists on the Ulster question, with Joseph Chamberlain particularly keen to pursue a case for exclusion, but in the end the issue was dropped and the concerns of an all-Ireland Unionism prevailed.[28]

In 1910–11 John St Loe Strachey, the editor of the *Spectator*, began lobbying senior Unionists on the issue of Ulster county option and exclusion. Strachey was important in terms of the history of partition, not because he was the very first to moot the idea or had any immediate success as an evangelist, but rather because he was a pioneer, and because he formulated a detailed proposition that he pressed energetically on the Tory leadership. Many of his ideas were swiftly dismissed, but with time they seem to have germinated and to have had an influence on both the Liberal and Conservative front benches. It is possible that Strachey was stimulated into action by J. L. Garvin, the editor of the *Observer*, who on 30 October 1910 sketched a plan for 'a distinct Belfast Assembly for the great Northern conclave' together with an Upper House for all of Ireland: the 'whole of this arrangement will be provisional', argued Garvin, 'after the probationary interval Ulster could decide by referendum whether to continue standing on its local basis … or throw in its lot completely with the Common Irish system'.[29] But, whatever the exact point of departure, it was Strachey who ran with a version of the idea.

In December 1910 Strachey wrote to the Ulster Unionist lawyer William Moore expounding an elaborate system of exclusion whereby individual Irish counties could vote themselves out of the Home Rule scheme, and then be treated for administrative purposes as English counties.[30] Failing that, Strachey argued, Unionists should demand that Home Rule be granted for both the north and south of Ireland. At the heart of Strachey's exposition was the notion that Ireland contained two nations, an Irish and a British, and that partition or exclusion represented a logical and just way of dealing with national and ethnic realities: 'there are two nations in Ireland', he wrote to Bonar Law in November 1911, 'and therefore two national units'.[31]

Strachey is thus of some interest in terms of the history of Irish political ideas. He helped to reinforce a variety of influential notions, including the idea of two Irish nations, county option for the north, and the desirability of a separate parliament for Unionist Ulster. As with other early advocates of exclusion, it is hard to establish whether Strachey was more concerned with wrecking the Home Rule Bill or with devising a workable solution to the problems of Irish government. He was clearly aware that his scheme might have an appeal to those seeking a wrecking device:

I admit that if Ulster could prevent the passage of the Home Rule Bill by refusing separate treatment, she would be right to do this, but as she

121

cannot, and as there is a very good chance that by asking for separate treatment she may prove to the people of England and Scotland the folly of the whole thing and so smash the Home Rule Bill, she ought to use the weapon.[32]

But the tenor of his argument, his faith in the 'two nations', the detail with which he elaborated his ideas, all suggest that (in contrast to the usual pattern of development among Unionist exclusionists) Strachey believed in the intrinsic merits of partition from the start.

It is difficult to assess Strachey's precise impact on political debate at this time. It is possible, for example, that Birrell's early interest in county option was in some way fired by Strachey's thoughts on the subject, but the notion is incapable of proof. The most that may be said is that Strachey was an important Unionist intellectual who corresponded on the issue of exclusion with a number of senior political figures at a very early stage in the evolution of the Home Rule debate. It should also be emphasised that, while his ideas were not dismissed out of hand, senior Unionists were at first unpersuaded by the detail. In 1911 Carson, for example, accepted that 'N.E. Ulster is the key to the situation', but he thought that 'Unionists outside Ulster are prone to be very jealous and suspicious' and that any emphasis on Ulster would thus 'alienate support'. He dismissed Strachey's scheme of county option with rather greater brutality as 'unworkable if not ridiculous'.[33] But from the beginning Carson recognised that it might be necessary to raise the Ulster question, perhaps by an amendment to the Home Rule Bill.

In fact the first amendment along these lines came not from the Unionists, but from a young Liberal backbencher, Thomas Agar-Robartes, who sat for a Cornish constituency with a strong Nonconformist vote. In June 1912 Agar-Robartes proposed to the House that the four most Protestant and Unionist counties of Ulster (Antrim, Armagh, Down and Londonderry) be excluded from the operation of the Home Rule Bill. The intellectual roots of Agar-Robartes' strategy are again incapable of proof, but the amendment was of course foreshadowed by the Strachey scheme, and posed the same sort of problem for the Unionist front bench that Strachey had done. Walter Long was quick to rehearse the traditional case that 'if we waver and try "clever" tactics we shall disgust our friends in the rest of Ireland, and seriously weaken our own position in Great Britain'.[34] But in the end Carson and the Unionists supported the amendment on the clear grounds that it might serve as a means of wrecking the wider bill. This strategy in fact met a wide range of political needs: it kept the Unionists' options open on the issue of Ulster, it temporarily mollified southern Unionist opinion, and it gave the Liberal front bench an argument with which to rally those of their supporters who were sympathetic to Agar-Robartes.

When did the Unionists' support for exclusion graduate into a proactive policy goal, as opposed to a wrecking tactic? This, as with many of the critical interpretative issues arising from the third Home Rule Bill, is ultimately an open-ended question in so far as different Unionists thought in different ways about exclusion. It is reasonably clear that when, in January 1913, Carson proposed to amend the Home Rule Bill by excluding the entire nine-county provice of Ulster, he saw this still as a strategic thrust. He had earlier affirmed that 'the government dare not propose separate treatment [for Ulster] and that Redmond could not accept it', and his exclusion amendment may be seen as a corollary of this insight.[35] But a letter from the Ulster Unionist lawyer and journalist J. R. Fisher (writing to Strachey and giving him notice of the Carson proposal) encapsulates the ambiguity of the Unionists' position on exclusion at this time. Fisher dwelt on strategies for wrecking the Home Rule Bill, but at the same time emphasised that Carson's amendment was 'different' from these, and that it 'must materially affect the situation'.[36]

The amendment was defeated, but it did signal the modification of the traditional political strategies of Unionism. The amendment also thoroughly (and justifiably) alarmed some southern Unionists who saw a compromise in the offing, and who tried to reiterate the traditional wisdom that southern Unionism could still be of 'material assistance' to the north.[37] Only a personal interview with Bonar Law, together with a promise that he would speak in Dublin, served temporarily to dampen the apprehensions of these southern Unionists. But even here all was not well, for there was some confusion over the nature of the promise that Bonar Law had given. The rawness of southern Unionist nerves and the extent of the distrust that was opening up was revealed in a very jittery letter written in July 1913 to the Tory leader on the subject of his forthcoming visit.[38]

There is an argument for seeing the break between southern and Ulster Unionism as dating from the time of Carson's exclusion amendment. But even though the significance of proactive Unionist support for exclusion should not be missed, and even though the deepening of southern Unionist fears should not be discounted, the amendment, like the constitutional conference of 1910, was in a sense an anti-climax: no serious discussions followed, and no compromise was enacted. More significant in terms of the history of partition and the internal dynamics of Irish Unionism was the dialogue that opened up between the Liberals and Tories in the autumn of 1913. Here an independent initiative from a retired Liberal Lord Chancellor, Lord Loreburn, was crucial.

On 11 September 1913 Loreburn, who as a cabinet minister in 1912 had been a stalwart anti-partitionist, issued a public letter calling for a resolution of the Home Rule crisis on the basis of a conference and, by implication, a federal settlement. Loreburn was goaded into action by the high priest of the 'conference plus business' approach to Irish politics, William O'Brien; but he had had no direct contact with his former colleagues in the Liberal cabinet. Scholars, therefore, have tended to argue that the significance of the Loreburn initiative has been over-played. Patricia Jalland has suggested, for example, that it 'was not alone responsible for the opening of negotiations between the leaders, which were inevitable anyway, but it helped to create an atmosphere which allowed conversations to begin sooner than might otherwise have been the case'.[39]

It is difficult to contest Jalland's measured and authoritative verdict, but it might be stressed that the Loreburn letter coincided with a marked change of emphasis in the debate on exclusion. In particular, a shift in Carson's thought should be highlighted. Carson believed, like many others, that Loreburn's letter was written with the knowledge of the government and perhaps the King. While he was wrong on both counts, it is nonetheless true that some ministers, and indeed George V, swiftly came to support the notion of a negotiated settlement. Carson's revised view of exclusion was set out in a letter written on 20 September, in the aftermath of the Loreburn furore. This is a pivotal document in the history of the partition issue, and is therefore worth quoting at some length:

> I am of [the] opinion that on the whole things are shaping towards a desire to settle on the terms of leaving 'Ulster' out. A difficulty arises as to defining Ulster and my own view is that the whole of Ulster should be excluded but the minimum would be the 6 Plantation counties and for that a good case could be made. The South and West would present a difficulty and it might be that *I* could not agree to their abandonment tho' I feel certain it would be the best settlement if Home Rule is inevitable... Of course the ideal thing would be that this should be part of a general scheme for the UK and even if that question is not practical to settle for the moment it could be drafted in such a way as to make it fit in afterwards.[40]

This presents the first clear evidence that Carson had moved away from using exclusion as a wrecking tactic towards embracing it as the means by which the Home Rule crisis might be permanently resolved.

This ideological shift was linked to the growing evidence that exclusion might, after all, be conceded by the Liberals, and it was complemented by a new and growing impatience with southern Unionism. At around the time of the Loreburn letter, Carson met a southern Unionist delegation and, in his characteristically direct and unsentimental court-room style, he urged them towards the admission that logically they should support Ulster exclusion if it were offered by the government.[41] Such forensics did little, however, to improve Carson's standing with the leading defenders of the southern cause, such as the Unionist leader in the Upper House, Lord Lansdowne; nor was Carson's attitude towards these, his own people, improved by such interviews. On the contrary, writing to Lansdowne on 9 October 1913, Carson revealed a new impatience, and even contempt. An additional context for Carson's letter was a new boost to the exclusionist cause, provided on this occasion by Winston Churchill in a speech at Dundee on 8 October, in which the notion of special treatment for north-east Ulster appeared to receive his blessing. '[Southern Unionists] may think', Carson wrote:

> if Ulster obtains separate treatment that they have been betrayed, and although I do not think they have been prepared to run any risks, I should be very sorry if the termination of the contest left them under a sense of betrayal by us. At the same time it is hard to see, if separate treatment was given to Ulster, how I could be justified in asking men to go on preparing for resistance when their only object could be to obtain what had been offered to them. On the other hand, if our friends in the South and West say that they prefer that Ulster should be included in the event of a Bill becoming inevitable, it would mean that we should give up the fight, and I do not think anyone could successfully commend that policy to the Ulster people. It is very difficult to ascertain what the South and West expect us to do, as they only talk in generalities, and I do not think they realise that we have no power to stop the Bill and that even if we refuse the separate treatment of Ulster, the Bill will probably become law all the same.[42]

This letter has a powerful resonance. It incorporated a recognition that, contrary to Carson's expectations in 1911–12, a deal might well be done with the Liberals on the basis of exclusion. It also embodied a much more direct sense of contempt for southern Unionists than had been hitherto apparent in his letters and speeches. Before this he had been concerned that, in advocating the Ulster Unionist cause, he did not trample upon southern sensitivities. This concern was now largely exhausted. Carson's emphasis on the Unionists' inability to stop Home Rule is suggestive, in so far as it underlines his pragmatism and sheds light on the issue of Ulster Unionist bluff in 1913–14. Last, it may be briefly observed that this blunt charting of the limits of what was attainable for the Unionists would be echoed eighty years later by David Trimble, in defending the Belfast Agreement of 1998.[43]

There was no conference in the autumn of 1913, since neither party leadership was prepared to risk compromising itself by issuing a call. Instead there was a series of private and confidential discussions between Asquith and Bonar Law, and later between Asquith and Carson. The sessions with Bonar Law took place on 14 October, 6 November and 10 December 1913, while those with Carson were held on 16 December 1913 and 2 January 1914. The importance of these meetings, in terms of substantive negotiation, should not be exaggerated. Asquith's intentions seem to have been largely tactical. He seems to have been trying to establish for himself the limits of Unionist flexibility, and in particular their bottom line for a deal. He may have been eager to probe the nature of the relationship between Bonar Law and Carson, and possibly to exploit divisions or fire any potential jealousies. He saw the two leaders separately, and the shift of his attention from one to the other came without explanation and with a degree of brusqueness. There is a hint of pique and suspicion in Bonar Law's comment of 22 December 1913 that 'it seems to me a little strange that he [Asquith] should have stopped communication with me, but there is I think some method in it'.[44] Asquith may also have been anxious to buy time: this was certainly the belief of Arthur Balfour, himself a seasoned ditherer, who claimed that 'the government intend to let things slide'.[45] He may have wanted to score points off the Opposition by thrusting them on to the defensive, simultaneously casting them as supplicants seeking terms and burdening them with any responsibility for the failure of negotiation. If so, it is hard to resist the suspicion that he was chasing match points while the constitutional playing field was being enveloped.

No formal proposals were made by Asquith at any of these meetings. However, on 23 December he sent a brief series of 'Suggestions' to Carson which, it is generally accepted, were intended not as a serious offer, but rather as a means of drawing the Opposition into defining their terms.[46] Asquith's 'Suggestions' would have curtailed Home Rule further by removing the post office and customs from the jurisdiction of the proposed Irish government. 'Ulster' was left undefined, but was to occupy a kind of half-way house between Westminster and Dublin, sending representatives to Dublin, but with its policing, educational and local government systems ultimately under the jurisdiction of London. The 'Suggestions' were essentially a blueprint, not for Home Rule within Home Rule, as is occasionally argued, but rather for unitary Home Rule with some regional variation. Carson and Bonar Law's reply to this was profoundly unsatisfactory for Asquith, not so much because they dismissed the 'Suggestions' out of hand (Asquith could not have expected acquiescence), but because they did so with little elaboration.[47]

Asquith was then compelled to request what he had presumably wanted all along – a detailed plan from the Opposition elaborating a scheme for the administration of their excluded 'Ulster'. This was in effect inviting the Opposition to declare their hand, with the risk that the government might use the detail of any plan to divert attention from the debate on the principle of exclusion. And in fact Carson effectively concluded the season of private negotiations with a letter to Asquith which demanded a settlement of the exclusion issue as a preliminary to the consideration of further details.[48] Bonar Law, acting with Asquith's permission, announced in a speech at Bristol on 15 January 1914 that talks had taken place, and had broken down. And, in so far as the failure seemed to have been the fault of the Unionists, Asquith's elaborate diplomacy brought him some slight and temporary political gain.

Asquith had probed the Opposition case, had happily played with ambiguous language and legalistic formulations, but had not substantially advanced towards a settlement of the mounting crisis. He had presented a tough but plausible deal to the Unionists, and had hoped thereby to tempt them into a detailed bargaining process. This had not worked, and the government therefore fell back on a proposal that was more likely to be treated seriously by the Unionists, and which might precipitate a deal.

The scheme in which so much hope was invested had been formulated by Lloyd George in November 1913, but had been set aside while the Prime Minister pursued his more ambiguous and hardline strategies: it was reintroduced in February–March 1914. Lloyd George took the idea of county option and bound it in with a time limit: any Ulster county could vote to be excluded from the operation of Home Rule for an undefined period.[49] Subsequent negotiation with the nationalists (and indeed with Carson) established a three-year moratorium as the 'last word' of the government; but there were in fact two other 'last words', as the government revised the period of exclusion from three to five years, and finally from five to six years. Within four days (2–6 March 1914) Redmond and the nationalists were compelled to accept the principle of temporary exclusion, and then to acquiesce in two redefinitions of what 'temporary' meant.

The final scheme was a characteristic expression of Lloyd George's political genius and, as with other examples of his artifice, its brilliance lay in suggestive ambiguity. It was likely that four counties (Antrim, Armagh, Down and Londonderry – the four counties mentioned by Agar-Robartes) would vote themselves out of the Home Rule scheme, although in the case of Armagh, given the narrow Protestant and Unionist majority, there might have been an element of doubt. But it was not only the territorial limit of exclusion that was undefined: the chronological limits were also, in effect, left open. For nationalists the scheme might be taken to offer an arrangement that was temporary, and which might be sold to voters as a passing irritation. For nationalists, too, the scheme appeared to subvert Unionist militancy, for Lloyd George argued, with some justice, that it would be impossible for the loyalists to sustain their campaign over the six-year exclusion period. For Unionists, on the other hand, there was a good chance that the Liberals might be ousted in one of the two general elections scheduled to take place between 1914 and 1920. Exclusion in these circumstances would be made permanent by an incoming Tory administration. Like later examples of Lloyd George's craft, the ingenuity of this proposal rested essentially on the neatness with which the agreed issues were banked: no less dextrous was the way in which disagreement was left on the backburner in the hope that it would be reduced into more manageable political ingredients.

This seems to have been a real attempt at a settlement, and it created immediate difficulties for the Unionists. Carson had demanded nine-county exclusion in January 1913, but it was clear that he was prepared to settle for six counties. Lloyd George's scheme offered a fair chance that four counties might be permanently excluded from the bill. This was not enough; but, equally, it was not enough for the Unionists to offer any peremptory rejection. The weakest aspect of Carson's demand was his claim over two counties with (albeit narrow) nationalist majorities; and he therefore chose not to question the territorial aspect of Lloyd George's offer, but to concentrate rather on the time limit. This, he said, was a 'sentence of death with a stay of execution for six years'.[50] But there was more to the Unionist case than a memorable quip: without offering any commitment, Carson asked that the four counties should be excluded from Home Rule until Westminster decided otherwise. He was thus seeking to break the six-year deadline, and to render partition more permanent in the eyes of Irish nationalists than the government's offer allowed. For his part, Bonar Law demanded that the whole United Kingdom should decide on the exclusion proposal, and on 19 March he offered to abide by the result of any referendum.

Asquith's reply to this was overtaken by other events, and has frequently therefore been either ignored or misinterpreted in the literature, but it deserves a more prominent place in the history of Irish partition.[51] Around 22 March the Archbishop of Canterbury, Randall Davidson, appears to have acted as an intermediary between Asquith and Bonar Law. Asquith treated Bonar Law's idea of a referendum as a variant of the

Tory demand for a general election, and he may well have feared that, with the tide running against the Liberals in Great Britain, the Lloyd George scheme would have been rejected at the polls. Through the Archbishop (and doubtless without prejudice) he named two alternative strategies, and was now evidently prepared to countenance the partition of the six 'Plantation' counties that had hitherto been singled out by Carson. These six counties would be excluded for a period of years, after which a referendum would be held: 'The Proposal: Have no plebiscite at the outset but let the Bill definitely exclude six counties – i.e. the Protestant four plus Tyrone and Fermanagh – and let these six counties have a plebiscite at the end of [ ] years and abide by it.'[52]

This 'alternative' was named on 22 March 1914, and was rapidly over-taken by events. But its importance should be underlined: for the first time the Liberal government had apparently inched towards accepting Carson's six counties as a unit of political currency. And, given the possibility of Tory electoral success in the course of the six year span, it might be argued that the Liberals were now in effect countenancing an exclusion that was (to apply a favoured Asquithian adjective) 'veiled' but permanent.

The significance of this curious episode was lost as a new dimension to the constitutional crisis was suddenly introduced. The details of the Curragh episode (or, wrongly, 'mutiny') on 20–1 March 1914 need not be rehearsed at length.[53] On 11 March 1914 a subcommittee of the cabinet had been formed to monitor the Ulster question, and its members (Birrell, Lord Crewe, Churchill, J. E. B. Seely and John Simon) seem to have pushed ahead with a plan to strengthen army depots in the north of Ireland. This was evidently a defensive action, designed to prevent military supplies falling into the hands of the UVF. Ministers were clearly aware that the UVF was growing rapidly, and that it had plans to raid official stores. On 14 March the British military commander in Ireland, Sir Arthur Paget, was instructed by telegraph to reinforce arms depots at Armagh, Carrickfergus, Enniskillen and Omagh, all in Ulster; and he attended meetings in London on 18 and 19 March where these instructions were further elaborated. Paget, however, was concerned both that these moves would provoke bloodshed, and that officers with Ulster family connections would be placed in a uniquely impossible situation. Seely, the War Minister, agreed that such men might be allowed to take leave or otherwise opt out of the forces moving north: the broader issue of provocation was discounted. Paget returned to the Curragh and early on 20 March he presented to his officers a garbled version of the London talks and Seely's concession. It seemed from Paget's address that a direct military engagement with the Ulster Unionists was in the offing, and that civil conflict was threatened. In these apocalyptic circumstances, sixty of Paget's officers announced that they would accept dismissal rather than help in the 'initiation of active military operations against Ulster'.[54]

But in a sense this was only the overture to the crisis. In a hastily arranged meeting on 22 March in London, Seely and Sir John French, the Chief of the Imperial General Staff, gave a written undertaking to four of the leading 'mutineers' that the government would not use their right to maintain law and order in Ireland as a pretext for crushing 'political opposition to the policy or principles of the Home Rule Bill'.[55] Moreover, French accepted a coda to this declaration which assured the Curragh officers that the troops under their command would 'not be called upon to enforce the present Home Rule Bill on Ulster'.[56] These, then, were the military events at the heart of the Curragh 'mutiny'.

Was the government seeking to enact Home Rule by force? In addressing this question, the wider issue of ministerial strategy at this time might well be invoked. There is little doubt that the Unionists feared (or in some cases affected to fear) the suppression of Ulster Unionism. Various apparently suspicious official actions, culminating in the Curragh affair, appeared to substantiate this belief. Some Unionists, such as L. S. Amery, passionately believed for the rest of their lives that the government had planned a 'pogrom' against the Unionists of the north.[57] In fact it is reasonably clear that the Liberals had no intention of mounting any coercive assault on Ulster, and that the actions planned for 20 March were of a primarily defensive nature.

It should, however, be emphasised that on the more general issue of military action in Ulster, there was a wide range of opinion within the Liberal cabinet. There is no doubt that some ministers, like Haldane and Birrell, had favoured the idea of an early show of strength in Ulster with a view to undermining the nascent military challenge of the UVF. Coming from a slightly different strategic position, Winston Churchill combined an interest in exclusion with a particularly hardline stand against the Unionists' militancy. On 21 September 1913, he summarised his long-term view when he declared to Asquith that 'I wish it were possible to do two things – (1) treat these Ulstermen fairly and (2) give them a lesson. But I am afraid No. (1) will get in the way of No. (2).'[58]

It is just conceivable that Churchill, who was the leading light of the cabinet subcommittee on Ulster, might have been content if the action planned for 20 March 1914 had created a wider conflagration, and an opportunity for the government to suppress the Ulster militants. It is certainly true that, while the government believed (or affected to believe) that the likelihood of bloodshed was remote, it took elaborate precautions to ensure that, if any conflict developed, it was well prepared. The defensive action of 20 March involved not only the troops of the Curragh, but also a battle squadron of the Royal Navy, a reserve force at Aldershot and the Royal Irish Constabulary in the north. Against this, it should also be said that Asquith was aware of the plans for 20 March; and there is no reason whatsoever to doubt that his inclinations in this, as in other respects, were essentially pacific and emollient.

Some wider comments on Asquith's strategic vision at this time may be offered. It has been argued that in 1912 Asquith postponed dealing with the Ulster Unionists in order to assess the strength of the threat that they represented. It seems clear that this 'masterly inactivity' continued as a central feature of Asquith's strategies; it also seems to be the case that, while he was just occasionally panicked into action (as over the temporary exclusion of the six-county bloc), he retained a faith in the merits of inaction until the very end of the crisis. On the face of it, this might seem a doubtful proceeding whether in moral or political terms, but there was more to Asquith's passivity than met the eye. Asquith had a sharp tactical intelligence, and in the short term he trusted that he could outwit and therefore manage the Opposition. But he also seems to have believed that the Opposition's strategy was fundamentally flawed, and that with time they would either dissipate their energies or stumble into violence that could then be suppressed.

It should be stressed immediately that throughout the crisis Asquith was highly cautious about taking even close colleagues into his confidence. Unlike Lloyd George, he was secretive about his methods, except perhaps to unusually intimate friends like Venetia Stanley. The clues to Asquith's strategic thinking are somewhat scattered, but suggestive nonetheless. On 21 September 1913, at a time when a settlement looked increasingly likely, Churchill wrote that Asquith was 'quite convinced that if events take their course uninterruptedly the upshot will be disastrous for those [Ulster Unionists] who resort to violence or illegality'.[59] Again, in January 1914, Constance Williams, who worked in the household of a junior minister, and who was a Unionist sympathiser, wrote to Carson that members of the government had been overheard discussing their strategies: 'the plan is to procrastinate until the patience of the [loyalist] hooligan element in Belfast is exhausted, and they begin to riot'.[60] Williams reported that troops would be deployed at this point. She also emphasised, however, that Asquith 'still hankers after compromise', and that he was not 'much in favour' of military intervention, but was being overruled on this score.

Asquith's painfully slow and convoluted behaviour in 1913, evinced through his secret talks with the Unionist leadership, tends to confirm this reading of his strategic intentions. His emphasis on the time-limit to exclusion also chimes with this thesis: his shift of position on exclusion in March 1914 indicates that he was less concerned with the territorial extent of exclusion than with the time-limit. His actions also suggest that he was not especially concerned to extend that limit from three to six years: it may be conjectured that he believed that Unionist militancy might be sustained over three, but not over six years. And, despite the momentary panic inspired by the Curragh episode, and the later humiliation supplied by the Unionists at Larne, it seems that Asquith held on to the conviction that time was ultimately on his side. Certainly his otherwise curious actions in June and July 1914, over the Amending Bill and the Buckingham Palace Conference (see below), seem to embody a renewed faith in procrastination.

Although Asquith swiftly repudiated the 'peccant paragraphs' signed by Seely and French, the Curragh more or less eliminated the capacity of the government to pursue a military offensive against the Unionists. On the other hand, this capacity was never more than theoretical. The government had not taken any offensive action when, in 1913, it might have done so with minimal bloodshed; and, despite appearences, it was not intending to coerce Ulster in March 1914. The Curragh was a profound embarrassment, but it did not shake Asquith off course. Equally embarrassing and, in the strategic sense, equally problematic was the Ulster Unionists' gun-running exploit at Larne, County Antrim, on the night of 24–5 April 1914. Here, and in two other small towns on the east coast of Ulster, the Unionists smuggled in some 25,000 rifles and three million rounds of ammunition, defying the authorities and apparently transforming the military capacity of the Ulster Volunteer Force.

This *coup de théâtre* was set in motion in January 1914 against a background of high-political stalemate, some demoralisation among the Volunteers, and a tightening of the law on weapons importation. It marked a victory for the hawks within the Ulster Unionist movement, although this did not mean that support was lacking for the endeavour in other quarters. Indeed, the funding for Larne came partly through the Union Defence League, a primarily British Unionist organisation headed by Walter Long. It seems probable that, despite the present scholarly consensus on the issue, Long and other Conservative leaders knew from the start about the plans to bring in a large cache of weapons. William Bull, Long's parliamentary private secretary, had been a central figure in the main gun-smuggling operation of 1913, which culminated in the seizure of the Hammersmith cache.

The decision to mount the Larne expedition was taken by Carson on or about 21 January 1914 in Belfast. Long was in Ulster at the time, and on 25 January he was writing to Bonar Law requesting an urgent meeting on some important but unspecified business.[61] The protagonist of Larne was the leading Ulster Unionist hawk, Captain F. H. Crawford, who (while his testimony is by no means watertight) stated in his diaries and memoir that he had been interviewed by both Long and, remarkably, Bonar Law before setting off on his Buchanesque adventure. In his manuscript 'Record of the Home Rule Movement', Crawford recalled that sometime in March 1914 James Craig had told him that 'both Bonar Law and Walter Long would like to see me before I went [to buy weapons in Germany], so I saw both these statesmen and they gave me their hand and wished me God speed and a successful issue. They were different men then to what they are today. They were true Unionists then ...'[62] In a separate record, 'Diary of the Gun-Running', Crawford (writing from memory in July 1915) recorded that on 27 March 1914 he

> arrived in London. Called and saw Walter Long, MP. He sent his secretary to see Bonar Law. The latter when introduced to me said, with a twinkle in his eye, 'I have heard of you before, Mr Crawford'. I had a private letter from the Chief, whom I left in Belfast, to him. I had to see W[alter] L[ong] about the finances of the business, and make my final arrangements for paying [a] very large cheque.[63]

These records seem persuasive, but it should be emphasised that Crawford is a not wholly reliable witness, in so far as he had a rather juvenile conspiratorial bent and also an occasional haziness in recording detail: his published memoir, *Guns for Ulster* (1947), is particularly flawed in this respect. But, while historians have rightly treated Crawford's published testimony with some caution, his original records have a greater authority. They are private and near-contemporary documents, which are apparently corroborated by other evidence: for example, Crawford's allusion to delivering a private letter from 'the Chief' on 27 March 1914 seems to be confirmed by a letter dated to 26 March from Carson in the Bonar Law Papers.[64] Crawford's manuscript records have rarely been examined in a comprehensive way; nor has their significance been widely grasped. Some scholars maintain that the Tory leader 'knew nothing beforehand of the operation'.[65] But this view now seems debatable: indeed, it is possible that the Conservative leadership knew about, blessed and (in the case of Walter Long) helped to fund the Larne gun-running coup of April 1914.

What was the significance of the Larne exploit?[66] It shifted the balance of military power in Ulster further to the advantage of the loyalists. It gave an enormous boost to the credibility of the Ulster Volunteer Force, and their political leadership. It was a further political humiliation for the government. But beyond this it would be difficult to venture. The Curragh 'mutiny' had already confirmed the incapacity of the government to mount any serious military offensive against the Unionists. After Larne the Ulster Volunteer Force remained badly armed, to the extent that they had no more than a total of 40,000 weapons for a force numbering around 100,000 men; and these weapons were not of a uniform quality or type. The government was indeed humiliated at Larne, but again the Curragh had been a much more serious proceeding in the sense that it involved accusations of conspiracy, the appeerence of mutiny and a denouement that appeared to involve relatively junior army officers dictating policy to an elected government. Having weathered the Curragh crisis, Asquith's government was unlikely to be nudged off-course by the gun-runners of Larne. And, indeed, Larne may have reinforced Asquith's conviction that in time Unionists would become the victims of their own militant strategies. It certainly seems to have been the case that the government reverted to 'masterly inactivity' for the remaining months of the third Home Rule crisis.

But Larne and the Ulster Volunteers had a further military significance, as an example for militant nationalism. Here, again, it might be argued that Asquith's delaying tactics, though possessing a limited parliamentary logic, proved well-nigh disastrous in Ireland. Redmond was a thorough-going parliamentarian, although recent scholarship has tended to erode the conservative image of his Irish parliamentary party by highlighting the 'striking number' of ex-Fenians and agrarian militants within its ranks.[67] Still, making allowance for some retired revolutionaries, some cattle-drivers and a few hard men within organisations like the Ancient Order of Hibernians, the Edwardian Home Rule movement was an essentially pacific enterprise. The reactivation of the secret militant organisation, the Irish Republican Brotherhood (or Fenians), by Tom Clarke and others after 1907 had no connection with these parliamentarians. Indeed, this lack of contact with a new generation of republican hawks underlined one of the central weaknesses of the Redmondite cause.

The Fenian renaissance would in fact have mattered less, had it not been for the delay in the enactment of Home Rule and the rise of Ulster militancy. Some republicans had been prepared to suspend disbelief when the third Home Rule Bill was introduced into the Commons in April 1912, but by 1913–14, with the apparently interminable parliamentary delays and the growing assertiveness of the Ulster Unionists, suspicions began to re-emerge concerning not only the fate of Home Rule, but also its integrity as a national goal. The literary expression of this frustration may be seen in a work such as Terence MacSwiney's play, 'The

Revolutionist' (1914), which depicts an Ireland where the national spirit is all but crushed by anglicised Home Rulers.[68]

The institutional expression of these militant fears came with the establishment, in November 1913, of the Irish Volunteers, a citizen militia modelled loosely on its Unionist counterpart in the north. The critical political delays of late 1913 and early 1914, while Asquith fenced with Bonar Law and Carson, combined with the threat of the Ulstermen, helped to stimulate the very rapid growth of these new militants; and their leadership was swiftly infiltrated by the re-energised Fenian movement.

There can be little doubt that the humiliating concessions on exclusion prised from Redmond in February 1914 damaged his credibility in Ireland, and not only with hardliners. By June 1914 the threat from the Volunteers had become sufficiently serious to warrant Redmond's intervention: in that month he forced the Provisional Committee of the movement to accept twenty-five new members, the nominees of the Home Rule party. But this was a late and desperate move, for, while Irish Party sympathisers were very well represented in the ranks of the Volunteers (indeed, there were almost 40,000 British army reservists in the movement), its organisational structure was already under the influence of the Irish Republican Brotherhood. The twenty-five Redmondites, middle-aged and uninterested, seem to have cut a poor figure when compared with the active young zealots of the original Volunteer committee. And, even after this board-room coup, Redmond's control of the Irish Volunteers remained tenuous. Moreover, as one of Redmond's lieutenants, Stephen Gwynn, sadly observed, 'few would dispute now that the constitutional party ought either to have dissociated itself completely from the appeal to force, or to have launched and controlled it from the outset'.[69] Compared to Carson's militancy, Redmond's parliamentary thrusts looked feeble; and compared with the Volunteers, the Irish parliamentary party looked enervated and compromised. Even Redmond's belated annexation of the Volunteers looked like weakness, and a panicked reappraisal of his most deeply cherished strategies.

The extent to which the militants remained independent of Redmond is best seen with the the Howth gun-running of July 1914. It was the northern Protestant Home Ruler, Sir Roger Casement, who was the prime mover behind the plan to import weapons for the Volunteers. Early in 1914 he raised £1500 which was later used to buy 1500 Mausers and 45,000 rounds of ammunition from a dealer in Antwerp. On 26 July 1914 these were landed by another Protestant nationalist, Erskine Childers, at Howth, north of Dublin.

The comparisons with the Ulster Unionists' coup at Larne are suggestive. There are obvious differences of scale, although the Howth episode is reminiscent of the earliest Unionist gun-running ventures in terms of cost and the number of weapons landed. While the political leadership of the Ulster Unionist movement was intimately involved with the policy of militancy and with gun-running from the start, Redmond and his lieutenants were unconnected with the foundation of the Volunteers, and knew nothing of the plans for Howth. Similarly, while the Ulster Unionists' Tory allies sanctioned militancy and were almost certainly involved with gun-running, it need hardly be said that there was no Liberal collusion with the gun-runners of Howth. The Larne gun-running was a considerable propaganda success for the Unionists, but it was planned, not overtly as a publicity stunt, but rather as a secret operation to arm the Ulster Volunteers. On the other hand, Bulmer Hobson, who was closely involved with the Howth business, consciously sought to create a propaganda coup. Writing in 1963, he recalled that

> on thinking the matter over I decided that 1,500 rifles would not go very far in solving our problem, but that if we could bring them in a sufficiently spectacular manner we should probably solve our financial problem and the problem of arming the Volunteers as well. With this in mind I decided to land the guns during daylight and as near to Dublin as possible.[70]

The official response to Larne and Howth was ostensibly different: the Ulster Volunteers succeeded in their coup, while the Irish Volunteers were intercepted by the police and army. But it is important to emphasise that these different official reactions say less about official collusion between the authorities and the Unionists than about the different strategies of the rival gun-runners. The Unionists split their weapons into three different caches, organised a decoy vessel to distract the customs and police, and landed their haul under cover of darkness. Hobson wanted to land his small cache in daylight, close to the capital, and under the blaze of publicity: he was consciously seeking to goad the British authorities.

Any discriminatory behaviour on the part of the Crown forces may be detected not in the apparently different reactions to the two landings, but rather in the aftermath of the Howth episode. Returning to their barracks after a humiliating exchange with the Irish Volunteers, some soldiers of the King's Own Scottish Borderers opened fire on an unarmed but hostile crowd at Bachelor's Walk, Dublin: three people were killed and around thirty were injured. English and Irish contemporaries saw a sharp difference in the treatment meted out to hostile nationalists in Dublin, as opposed to the hostile Unionists of Belfast. And, in truth, this perception stands unaltered by the passage of time.

Despite the growing potential for civil war in Ulster, and the reality of bloodshed on the streets of Dublin, Asquith clung to his strategies until the bitter end of the crisis. On 8 May 1914, Bonar Law was told privately that Birrell had begun the task of plotting a boundary between excluded 'Ulster' and Home Rule Ireland. On 23 May the government formally decided to introduce an Amending Bill into the House of Lords in order to give effect to exclusion.[71] But these apparently decisive actions were in fact raddled with Asquithian ambiguity. The Amending Bill was constructed on the basis of county option and six-year exclusion – the same formula that had been comprehensively rejected by the Unionists when it had been originally debated in March 1914. Even George V questioned the purpose of the bill. Moreover, Asquith himself had already seemingly gone further than this towards meeting the Unionist case: he had evidently been prepared to countenance temporary exclusion of the six-county bloc in late March.

So the Amending Bill was not seen as a serious proposition; and the Lords duly altered the legislation to allow for nine-county exclusion, as opposed to county option, and a permanent partition of the island, as opposed to the six-year arrangement. The initiative over the Amending Bill bought Asquith some time, but it produced more or less the same impasse that was evident earlier in the year. Aside from this tactical significance, the bill is also noteworthy as one of the first measures to make provision for a minister for the excluded counties. It may thus be seen as a shadowy precursor to the direct rule arrangements put in place in Northern Ireland after the suspension of Stormont in 1972 (see Chapter 11).[72]

Having for the moment exhausted the possibilities of debate on the issue of the time-limit, Asquith's focus now shifted to the extent of the excluded area. It now seemed that a tactical advantage might be gained by defining exclusion in a politically and demographically more exact manner. Lord Murray of Elibank, the former Liberal Chief Whip, and the press baron Lord Rothermere, undertook an informal and semi-official arbitration in late June and July 1914, and established that both Asquith and the Unionists were willing to make some final territorial concessions. Haggling now began over (for the most part) relatively small areas. Asquith at this stage was apparently willing to exclude the bulk of the four predominantly Protestant counties, but not parts of South Armagh and South Down. The excluded territory would, however, comprise some parishes in Donegal, Cavan and Monaghan, although how these outlying lands were to be effectively administered from the main excluded area was left unresolved.[73]

On 2 July, Murray and Rothermere reported to Redmond that, while Carson and Bonar Law still rejected county option, they were now 'tentatively' prepared to suggest that a plebiscite might be held 'in an area consisting of Antrim, Down, Derry, Tyrone, Northern and Mid Armagh and North Fermanagh, and Derry City'. The Unionist leaders, in other words, were willing to 'concede' nationalist South Armagh and South Fermanagh and also (though this was not precisely defined) the 'Catholic area' of County Down.[74] Redmond summarily dismissed this notion, but Asquith, alert to the possibility that he might 'have to put on the screw to R.', retained an appetite for further bargaining. On 15 July, Asquith asked Murray and Rothermere

> to find out whether C[arson] and his friends would *definitely* treat, if I made them an offer to exclude Antrim, Derry, Down (except the Catholic parts of the South), Armagh (except South), North Fermanagh, with the possibility of a split Tyrone: provision to be made on both sides for the migration at State expense of Protestants and Catholics into and out of the excluded area.[75]

In fact Carson and his 'friends' were not prepared to 'definitely treat' on this basis; and, given that the offer was, in a sense, a modified version of the four-county arrangement, and that it was riven with complications (not least regarding the division of Tyrone), their truculence can hardly have come as a surprise. But the notion of transcending county boundaries and of compensating the displaced would reappear in later debates, and in particular during the negotiations on the Boundary Commission of 1924–5. And it is noteworthy that, despite the sanctified status which the six-county boundary later acquired for Unionists, they were evidently willing to tolerate the 'loss' of South Fermanagh, South Armagh and (possibly) South Down in July 1914.

There remained the possibility that, despite this unpromising context, an interparty conference (an idea which had been mooted for some weeks by, among others, the King) might help to move matters forward. Publicly Asquith professed to feel hope that a settlement might yet be achieved: 'the Prime Minister still thought that there was so much chance of agreement that it would be wrong to risk it for the sake of a few days delay, and he proposed to suggest to H.M. [the King] that he should invite such a conference'.[76] But the central concept in this, Bonar Law's record of a conversation with Asquith on 17 July, was not so much the 'chance of agreement' as 'delay'. Asquith later explained to George V that 'it may be that such a Conference will be unable at the moment to attain a definite settlement, but it will certainly postpone, and may avert dangerous and possibly irreparable action'.[77] Thus Asquith's private assessment of the prospects for a conference chimed more or less with that of the Unionists; and in the event their shared pessimism was fully justified.

The resulting conference, held at Buckingham Palace between 21 and 24 July 1914, achieved little or nothing. There was some hint from the nationalists that the time-limit to exclusion might be abandoned, and this led to a renewed discussion of the territorial question.[78] On 23 July, Asquith suggested that if county option were out of the question, a plebiscite might be held for a bloc consisting of Antrim, Derry, Down, Armagh (excepting South Armagh), North Fermanagh and South Tyrone. He further suggested, in an intriguing and significant premonition of the later Boundary Commission, that 'an arbitrator should be appointed to decide upon the division of County Tyrone'.[79] Otherwise Asquith's proposal was merely a variant of his scheme of 15–16 July and, like this predecessor, it held little attraction for either of the Irish parties.

The only other flicker of understanding between the Unionists and nationalists came, paradoxically, with Carson's favoured nostrum – the exclusion of the entire northern province. His defence of this proposition and the Nationalist leaders' reaction is worth quoting at length:

> in his [Carson's] view the only statesmanlike solution of the problem...
> was that the whole of Ulster should be excluded. He gave it as his
> opinion that if this were done generously, then there would be a likeli-
> hood within a reasonable time of Ulster being willing to come into a
> united Ireland, whereas if any attempt to coerce any part of Ulster were
> made, a united Ireland within the lifetime of any one now living would
> be out of the question.[80]

Viewed with the lavish benefits of hindsight, this was a powerful case, and indeed the nationalist leaders, Redmond and Dillon, broadly con- curred: 'both...admitted that if they were free agents that [nine-county exclusion] is a plan they would adopt, but that if they were to propose it it would mean they would be without a party either in Ireland or any- where else'.[81] Stephen Gwynn, writing in 1919, also shared the convic- tion that nine-county exclusion, while impossible in terms of party politics, had some wider merit:

> as a matter of statesmanship there was much to be said for closing with
> the Ulstermen's original demand that the province should come in or
> out as a whole. It satisfied Ulster sentiment, and lessened the chances of
> crystallising a Protestant block of excluded territory which would tend
> to become less and less Irish.[82]

Such harmony in an otherwise dissonant political chorus deserves to be treated with the utmost seriousness, and it may indeed have been, as contemporaries privately agreed, that the foundations for the creation of a strong national unit in Ireland could only have been laid through the temporary exclusion of the entire northern province from the first taste of self-government. Curiously, despite the apparent deadlock over exclusion, the Buckingham Palace Conference entered the official memory as a worthwhile enterprise, and it was cited as a helpful precedent in April–May 1969 and afterwards when British ministers and civil servants were wrestling with the problems of Northern Ireland.[83]

The Buckingham Palace Conference failed, and while scholars tend to agree that this was entirely predictable, there is some confusion over Asquith's intentions. Patricia Jalland and others argue that the Prime Minister was playing for time, but concede that 'precisely what Asquith hoped to gain by a further delay is not at all clear'.[84] Asquith's secretiveness has already been discussed; and, in the absence of any clear statement for the defence, historians have tended to assume that the Prime Minister was nonchalantly permitting the country to drift into civil war. But Asquith's delaying tactics, however dangerous, had a logic – even if its subtlety is seldom appreciated. Alfred Milner and others contended, with some conviction, that 'the Asquith entourage doesn't believe that Ulster will do anything serious'. Moreover, Milner argued, 'they don't intend, if Ulster does rise, to take any serious steps themselves'.[85] Milner recognised that the Ulster Unionists were threatened with very great difficulties if they postponed decisive action into the parliamentary recess in the late summer of 1914. They would then be forced to sustain their provisional administration for many months 'under great discomfort and in comparative obscurity'.[86] British electors would soon get used to the idea of a defiant Ulster, while the rebellion would be fatal to the business community and Unionist unity: 'in other words', Milner affirmed, 'I don't believe that the Ulster coup will be any coup at all if it is much longer deferred'.[87]

This diagnosis deserves to be treated with the utmost seriousness. Milner declared enigmatically that he had 'rather exceptionally good means of knowing' Asquith's strategic convictions – the Unionists may well have been engaged in some form of political espionage at this time.[88] Milner's view that the Ulster Unionists would probably not act at all chimes with what is known about divisions within the loyalist leadership and the overall thrust of their strategies. And his view that the government did not intend to move against the Ulstermen, but proposed to let them become embroiled in difficulties of their own making, is consistent with other evidence concerning Asquith's strategies.

In other words, it may well have been the case that Asquith was banking on the likelihood that the Unionists were bluffing; and, even if the Ulstermen defied the odds and moved to act, he could still win the game by forcing them to postpone their 'decisive action' until the parliamentary recess had begun. In these circumstances, certainly in the view of one very senior and experienced Unionist strategist, the Ulster rebellion would have been a fiasco and Asquith could have imposed a politically convenient settlement. Even as it was, some slight but suggestive divisions were beginning to open up within the Ulster Unionist leadership by the end of July 1914, particularly between Carson and Craig. In a private meeting with King George V, Craig admitted that there were some differences in strategic judgement between himself and Carson.[89]

In an obvious, short-term sense, Asquith's strategies were a splendid success, for procrastination had brought a broadly favourable solution to the crisis. But the outbreak of war with Germany on 4 August was as much a break for the Unionists as for the Prime Minister, and the alacrity with which they moved to suspend political hostilities and resolve the ambiguities of their position as 'loyal' rebels hints at the complexities underlying their ostensibly simple and obstinate defiance. The outbreak of war also permitted the final revelation of Asquith's delaying strategy, for on 18 September 1914 Home Rule was enacted and simultaneously postponed for the duration of the conflict. The Ulster question was 'solved' in the same way: through the promise of amending legislation which was left undefined. The resolution of the Home Rule crisis precisely matched the manner of its exposition.

Moral indignation pervades the literature on the third Home Rule crisis, and the issue of culpability is never far from the surface of even the calmest interpretations. But a detailed excavation of the crisis tends to deflate the indignant, and to blur the moral certainties. On the other hand, some aspects of the crisis may now be brought into much sharper focus than has formerly been the case. It is, for example, quite clear that the association between the Tory front bench and the illegal smuggling of weapons into Ulster was closer than has generally been allowed. It is reasonably clear, too, that Asquith's handling of the crisis had a much greater logic than has hitherto been assumed. But in the end the great moral questions raised by the crisis are incapable of a definitive resolution. Whether, as Winston Churchill claimed at Bradford in March 1914, there are 'worse things than bloodshed', or whether, as Bonar Law claimed in the Commons in June 1912, 'there are stronger things than parliamentary majorities' are questions for priests and philosophers rather than the historian.[90]

# CHAPTER 8

# THE JAWS OF VICTORY
## 1914–16

A few, perhaps, prayed for the souls of the Home Rule leaders, or placed their portraits beside the household images of the Sacred Heart or of the Virgin. In their day, Redmond, Dillon and Devlin certainly enjoyed widespread respect, but there was never anything approaching a personality cult, and no one looked to them for spiritual blessing. The Irish parliamentary party, which was all too clearly rooted in earthy realities, could never be mistaken for a holy crusade. Yet when the advocates of an Irish republic went to war against the British in Dublin in Easter 1916, their struggle soon acquired an aura of sanctity. The commanders of the rising were popularly seen as men of faith and spirituality, and it became widely known that even the socialist James Connolly had made his peace with the Church.

When the British suppressed the rising and executed its architects, they not only manufactured political victims, they also appeared to create religious martyrs as well. The worldly Home Rule leader, T. P. O'Connor, witnessed a little girl on the streets of Dublin who was denied a new bonnet by her mother, and who invoked 'Saint' Patrick Pearse in a prayer of intercession. The prayer worked, the mother's resistance collapsed, and the (clearly emotionally sophisticated) little girl acquired her hat. Gladstone and perhaps some of the more spiritually minded Irish parliamentary leaders had dared to believe that Home Rule was a divinely ordained proceeding. By the summer of 1916, with the little children praying to 'Saint Pearse', it was no longer certain that God was a Home Ruler.[1]

But the very fact that republicanism acquired a providential dimension meant that Home Rule came to be interpreted as spiritually damned, and materially and electorally exhausted. When war broke out in 1914, Home Rule began (in this popular, fatalistic, reading) its speedy descent into oblivion. The obstinacy of the Unionists, the incompetence and indeed occasional malice of the British authorities, and the cussed honour of Redmond served to maim a party and a principle that had seemed – until so lately – to be on the brink of triumph. After 1914, according to these traditional political narratives, the history of the Home Rule movement was the pathology of a fatally diseased organism, with each humiliating concession, maladroit action or adverse decision being represented as lamentable but irreversible stages in an inevitable decline. In fact, as will become clear, Home Rule and its proponents have been consigned to the charnel house with an often too great alacrity; and the historical pathologists have – until recently – been responsible for a determined misinterpretation of supposedly fatal symptoms.

There is a tendency in the literature to emphasise the difficulties and slights experienced by Redmond and the Home Rulers at this time; and, in so far as any humiliation experienced by the democratically chosen leader of the national tradition was by definition a serious matter, this tendency is understandable.[2] On the other hand, it also seems to be the case that the reverses which Redmond experienced have been elaborated into an accepted narrative of the constitutionalists' failure. There is, for example, a tendency to magnify the weaknesses in, or to misconstrue, Redmond's position during the weeks at the beginning of the war. In fact, judged from the perspective of that time, Redmond had won a form of triumph. On 18 September 1914 he had secured the enactment of Home Rule with the provision that the enforcement of the measure would be delayed 'not later than the end of the present war'.[3] It is frequently argued that Home Rule was thereby postponed until the end of the conflict, but this was not, strictly speaking, the case. Redmond certainly seems at one point to have thought that there might be a delay of around a year.

Moreover, his Unionist opponents were in disarray, wounded by the enactment of Home Rule, and by the absence of any definite arrangement for the exclusion of Ulster. Liberated from the real threat of a political fiasco, and simultaneously trapped by their British patriotism, Unionist politicians could only hint at the complexity of their political emotions by a silent and temporary withdrawal from the House of Commons. These emotions were perhaps rendered more eloquently in Ulster when pictures of George V (who had signed the Home Rule Bill into law) were booed by loyalists, and when there were sporadic protests by loyalists at the singing of the British national anthem.[4]

Two speeches delivered by Redmond in August and September 1914, one to the House of Commons and the other at Woodenbridge, County Wicklow, have also been deemed as critical turning-points in the regress of Home Rule. On 3 August 1914 (and allegedly influenced by Margot Asquith) Redmond told the government that they may tomorrow withdraw every one of their troops from Ireland. I say that the coast of Ireland will be defended from foreign invasion by her armed sons, and for this purpose armed Nationalist Catholics in the South will be only too glad to join arms with the armed Protestant Ulstermen in the North. Is it too much to hope that out of this situation there may spring a result which will be good, not merely for the Empire, but good for the future welfare and integrity of the Irish nation?[5]

The speech was widely seen as a bold, indeed foolhardy, endorsement of the British war effort. In the verdict of some 'advanced' contemporaries and many later critics, Redmond had squandered a unique opportunity to trade Irish support for the immediate enforcement of Home Rule.

But this reading does not allow for the context and rich ambiguities of Redmond's declaration. The widely held assumption at this time was that the European war (like the Franco-Prussian conflict of 1870) would be bloody but short-lived; and in these circumstances, any political horse-trading, particularly in the context of the Ulster Unionists' co-operativeness, might well have been disastrous to Home Rule. Redmond desperately wanted and needed the speedy enactment of the Home Rule Bill, and it is probable that his speech was a means to that end. Certainly on the following day, 4 August, he was writing to Asquith saying that he was 'convinced in the present temper of the Unionist Party after my speech that course could be safely taken [i.e. enactment of the bill], and I am further convinced that before the winter we and Carson would arrive at an agreement'.[6]

At the same time, however, the speech reflected Redmond's ambiguous vision of Ireland's relationship with Britain. Redmond wanted Home Rule and legislative independence, but he saw the new Ireland not as a semi-detached element of a revised United Kingdom, but rather as the effective (if not the legal) equivalent of the great Dominions of the British Commonwealth and Empire. Their support for the British (as friendly but essentially independent nations) justified the support of the Irish. But there were additional complexities. His tone was sentimental and benign, but the content of his remarks did not entirely chime with the emotions of the occasion. In particular his allusion to the Volunteers of the eighteenth century can have given no comfort to students of history on the government benches, in so far as it evoked the image of a disastrous American campaign that denuded Ireland of regular troops while stimulating the rise of a paramilitary threat in the shape of the Irish Volunteers. The Volunteers of the 1770s had helped to exploit the

weakness of the British government, and to lever commercial and constitutional concessions for the Irish parliament. This, then, was a speech rife
with paradox, but it has nonetheless been interpreted as a classic statement of West Britishness. It was in fact an elegant commentary on
Redmond's complex Home Rule convictions, although, in the end, it was
perceived as, and therefore was, detrimental to the national cause.

On Sunday, 20 September 1914, speaking at Woodenbridge, Redmond
reformulated and extended his call to include not only the defence of
Ireland, but also active service 'wherever the firing-line extends, in
defence of right, of freedom and of religion in this war'.[7] Like his speech
of 3 August, this has generally been regarded as a betrayal of Irish nationality, and as a blow to the cause of Home Rule. But, again, such views do
not do justice to the underlying political vision, or to the context. The
Woodenbridge speech was delivered two days after the enactment of
Home Rule, and was in a sense a reply to what Redmond viewed as an
historic act of reparation. Moreover, Redmond saw that the war created
not just the chance for a reconciliation between Ireland and Britain, but
also an opportunity to consolidate the claims of Irish nationality.

This notion was only hazily evoked in the Woodenbridge speech, with
its praise for the Irish military tradition. But it would soon become clear
that, in a striking historical paradox, Redmond believed that the army of
the British King might ultimately serve to further the cause of Home
Rule. Like so much of Redmond's visionary speculation, his ideas were
not given time to germinate. In the long term Redmond might indeed
have been able to smooth the divisions between Ireland and Britain,
while promoting a distinctive Irish military corps. But there was to be no
long-term future for Redmondism. Instead the Woodenbridge declaration
precipitated a division among the Irish Volunteers between Redmond's
sympathisers (the National Volunteers) and a more advanced, 'for Ireland
only', section who retained the original title of the movement.

Nowhere are the misreadings of Redmond's failures more apparent
than with his vision of the Irish in arms. That Redmond was unable to
realise his particular ideals is not in doubt. Stephen Gywnn, who was
both an Irish MP and a captain in the Royal Dublin Fusiliers, catalogued
the problems that Redmond faced in endeavouring to promote recruitment in Ireland.[8] Chief among Gwynn's complaints was the petty-
mindedness of the Secretary of State for War, Lord Kitchener, and of the
department over which he exercised control. Kitchener regarded nationalists as disloyal, and scarcely bothered to conceal his low expectations of
the Irish as a whole. When it was proposed by Colonel Maurice Moore,
the commander of the Irish Volunteers, that both the Irish and Ulster
Volunteers should be trained and used for garrison duty in Ireland,

Kitchener objected – even though Moore's plan was in fact an elaboration of Redmond's much-lauded proposal of 3 August.

Other details rankled with the Irish. Few leading Catholic Home Rulers were chosen by the authorities to serve as recruiting agents; there was instead a marked preference for Protestant Unionists. Officers within Irish units tended to be Protestants, while their men were often Catholic, since it was thought by some diehards that commissioning nationalist officers heightened the risk of Home Rule.[9] Few Irish MPs were permitted to give a lead to the recruitment campaign by being themselves admitted into the army. Enlistment qualifications were, in the opinion of Gwynn, enforced with an elaborate pettiness, with the result that the Irish Party (an ageing and ailing enterprise) seemed to be shirkers, encouraging others to join while cowering safe at home. The major official exponent of this form of pettiness was General Sir Lawrence Parsons, a well-meaning but over-confident squireen, who refused commissions to a number of Irish MPs, including remarkably Redmond's own son.[10]

But the central complaint that Gwynn and other Redmondite Home Rulers had, aside from the War Office's unwillingness to recognise the National Volunteers, was the 'intolerable delay in forming a corps which should appeal definitely to Irish national and Nationalist sentiment'.[11] There still exists a confusion in the literature concerning the dimensions of the slight that had been offered to the Home Rulers on this issue. It is sometimes remarked that Redmond was denied a specifically Irish 'regiment' while the Ulster Volunteers were incorporated into a specifically Ulster 'regiment'.[12] This observation is untrue, although it does reflect an underlying and related grievance.

Redmond wanted a military unit that embodied the National Volunteers, and which had a distinctively Irish national tone. He caused some confusion at the time by resurrecting the historic notion of an 'Irish brigade', which had overtones of Jacobite derring-do, and this confusion has echoed through later interpretations of the issue.[13] Redmond was not, in fact, denied an Irish 'regiment': many ancient regiments that recruited from the south and west of Ireland – the Connaught Rangers, the Royal Dublin Fusiliers, the Leinster Regiment, the Royal Irish Regiment, the Royal Munster Fusiliers – went to war in August 1914. Nor was Redmond denied an Irish division: the 10th (Irish) Division was already in existence at the beginning of the war, although its Irishness was diluted by English drafts; and the 16th (Irish) Division was eventually called into being, although it was officered at first mostly by Englishmen.[14]

Redmond wanted a specifically Irish army corps that united the soldiers of the Ulster and National Volunteers, serving in their respective divisions, and that was in effect a national army for the new Ireland. This would have fought alongside the soldiers of the Canadian, South African and Australian armies and would have reinforced – through the sacrifices of the battlefield – Irish national distinctiveness. And, in so far as Australian nationhood seems to have been strengthened by the blood sacrifice of the Anzac corps at Gallipoli, Redmond's prescription was shrewd.

However, he was denied his vision. The two Irish divisions were not built upon the foundations of the National Volunteers in the same way that the 36th Division reflected the structures of the UVF. Aside from an anti-national prejudice within the War Office, it should also be conceded that the organisation of the National Volunteers was weaker than that of their northern counterparts, and perhaps did not readily permit their transfer into the structures of the British army. But it was also the case that individual Irish divisions were never united into a distinctive national army corps; and Redmond's wishes in other, less crucial, areas of military organisation were treated politely (usually by General Parsons), but as the witterings of a well-intentioned, though interfering, civilian.

Here lay the crux of the matter. Although many aspects of this military issue have been blurred, it is unquestionably the case, as Gwynn argued in 1919, that Redmond 'practically and morally...was the head of Ireland, exactly as Botha was of South Africa'.[15] And yet Redmond's relations with the War Office did not reflect this 'practical' and 'moral' reality. In a sense this was a permutation of a cancerous problem that Redmond faced time and again after the enactment of Home Rule in 1914: he had the responsibilities of national leadership, but little or none of the concomitant power. Before 1914 he had at least the Irish parliamentary party at his command; after 1914, with the Home Rule issue apparently settled, and conventional party hostilities in abeyance, he had not even the the resources of the national movement fully at this command. The 'head' of Ireland had thus scarcely more influence over Irish military matters than any other backbench parliamentarian.

But Redmond not only lacked influence, he also allowed himself – whether culpably or otherwise – to be misled by Asquith on a number of critical military and political issues. He believed that the Liberal government was prepared to recognise and arm the Volunteer movement, and said as much in a speech at Maryborough on 16 August.[16] But his confident predictions came to nothing, and his credibility therefore took a severe knock. Moreover, his persistent pressure for an exclusively Irish military unit was encouraged by Asquith, and indeed the Prime Minister wrote on 30 September 1914 that Kitchener 'will have the announcement made that the War Office has sanctioned the formation of an Irish Army Corps'.[17] But, as has been made clear, no army corps was forthcoming.

These damaging and disappointing episodes were in fact a continuation of similar let-downs that Redmond had experienced during the passage of the Home Rule Bill, and in particular in March 1914 over the time-limit to exclusion. They were also symptomatic of broader problems in the relationship between the Irish leader and Asquith. Asquith took pride in the political effectiveness of his expansive and ambiguous language, and of his emollient manner. But on the whole it may be said that these weapons inflicted slighter damage upon Asquith's political opponents than upon Redmond, for as Denis Gwynn has argued, 'Redmond grasped eagerly at every encouraging sign that he could find. He was absolutely convinced of Asquith's good faith.'[18] And, while there was unquestionably a measure of give-and-take with the Prime Minister, the problem for Redmond was that he never quite knew whether Asquith was 'giving' or 'taking'.

It should also be said that Redmond's grief on military questions reflected, perhaps, not just the ambiguities created by the suspension of Home Rule, but difficulties with the measure itself. Gwynn was surely right in underlining the lofty moral authority that Redmond had earned, and which should have been more widely respected; but under the terms of the suspended Home Rule Act an Irish leader had no direct jurisdiction over military matters. There is little doubt that the Home Rule Act could not – indeed should not – have been a final and complete expression of Irish national aspirations. But the war raises a question about even its short-term viability as a settlement. If Home Rule had been enacted, and Redmond had been Irish Prime Minister in late 1914, then – under the terms of the Home Rule Act – he could have exercised no more authority over the crucial issue of Irish recruitment than he already did as leader of the Irish Party. As Prime Minister of Ireland he might well have had a greater effective influence than as uncrowned national leader, but there is nothing in the Home Rule Bill itself to vindicate this suggestion. It is in fact hard to resist the suspicion that the battles over the Ulster question in 1913–14 diverted attention from very real problems with other aspects of the proposed legislation. It is also hard to resist the suspicion that the Home Rule Act of 1914 could have been no more than a provisional settlement of the historic Anglo-Irish antagonism.

This leads to a further issue, connected with the war, which has traditionally been evoked in the narratives of decline under Redmond: the creation, in May 1915, of the first wartime coalition government, and the recruitment to office of leading Unionists. Here, too, there is occasionally confusion in terms of both details and interpretation. It should be stressed immediately that the creation of the first coalition effectively brought to an end the informal alliance between the Liberals and Home

Rulers which had dominated the politics of the United Kingdom for the preceding five years: the Tories now had a very considerable presence in government. Sir Edward Carson, who had been associated with acts of illegality during the Ulster crisis, was appointed as Attorney-General. Redmond, however, who had pursued a scrupulously constitutional agitation for Home Rule, was not included in the coalition ministry. It is still occasionally said that Redmond was denied office, though Asquith's repeated offers of a ministerial place to him are well documented.[19] The questions arising from this episode have nothing to do, however, with political discrimination; they are connected, instead, with the wisdom of granting office to Carson in the absence of Redmond, and with the merits of Redmond's decision to refuse a place in the ministry.

The appointment of Carson, especially as senior law officer, was in a sense understandable, given his seniority on the Tory front bench, his reputation at the bar and the fact that he had already held office as Solicitor-General (1900–5). But in the immediate aftermath of the Ulster crisis, and in the absence of an Irish nationalist, this was also a highly controversial undertaking which apparently affirmed Ulster militancy while simultaneously slighting Irish constitutionalism. On the other hand, Redmond's refusal of office was also highly questionable, certainly when judged with the benefits of hindsight. One of Redmond's chief difficulties was, as has been noted, that he had no executive authority – that he carried responsibility without power. He would unquestionably have been in a stronger position if the Home Rule administration had been in operation. It is also, arguably, the case that Redmond would have been strengthened by holding office in the coalition government. Had he at least attempted to bargain with Asquith, he might well have extracted concessions, but he decorously resisted any temptation in this direction.[20] As a minister Redmond would unquestionably have been in a position to influence the government of Ireland; he would have been in the 'loop' of policy formulation and administration. He would of course have borne responsibility for the government's mistakes in Ireland, but then he carried this burden anyway. He would also have been in a position to counter some of Carson's ministerial influence. As it was, Redmond had comparatively little communication with ministers in 1914–16, and was rarely consulted even over Irish matters. This represented both a personal political humiliation and a threat to the wider cause that he represented.

Could Redmond have taken office? Irish nationalism had traditionally been deeply opposed to the notion of its commanders accepting ministerial positions under the English Crown. The dire reputation of William Keogh and John Sadleir, who held junior government posts in the early

1850s, served as a warning to later Irish leaders – both committed suicide. But it might have been argued that the war and the (admittedly problematic) enactment of Home Rule had created new political rules of engagement for Redmond's leadership. Indeed, up to a point this was recognised. Traditionally the attitude of the Home Rule party towards the British army had been generally hostile, despite a very substantial Irish presence among the soldiery. For instance, the struggle of even the Calvinist Boers against British imperialism had been warmly applauded on the Irish benches. But Redmond's speech at Woodenbridge and his subsequent recruiting endeavours signalled that new conditions applied and that there should be, if not a redefinition, then a simplification of the traditional nationalist line on the British army. Moreover, with the passage of the Home Rule Bill, the Irish Party was widely seen as a government-in-waiting, and its leaders were beginning to relax traditional stands. Redmond, for example, broke with a sternly held convention and attended an official reception at Viceregal Lodge. The relationship between senior party figures and Dublin Castle was now more intimate than ever, given that the civil servants were having to come to terms with what very much looked like Ireland's new governors.

Attitudes were evidently shifting, and it could be argued that, given Redmond's bold actions on the military question, he might have ventured further and joined the first coalition. He certainly seems to have reflected on the matter. Writing to Asquith on 7 June 1915, he appears to hint at an interest in an Irish office: 'I was offered with great kindness by you a place in the cabinet, some unknown and unnamed English office. I was not offered a place in the government of my own country'.[21] Redmond later told Stephen Gwynn that if he had 'been Asquith, and wished to make it as difficult as possible to refuse, I [Redmond] should have offered a seat in the Cabinet without portfolio and without salary'.[22] The point might have been extended: had Carson been appointed to the government on exactly the same terms, then a form of equality might have been observed and the dangerous anomaly of a Unionist militant as law officer might have been avoided. But no offer of this kind was made to Redmond: Asquith was not given to bold gestures, even with ministerial contracts; and Redmond evidently saw it as beneath his dignity to haggle over terms. This was perhaps a critical missed opportunity. Redmond and the Home Rulers were still blamed for the government's blunders in Ireland and with the war effort, and they might as well have had both power and culpability.

But, aside from missed chances and dangerous gambles, the war generated other, more immediate and personal problems for Redmond and the Home Rule cause. The initial success of Redmond's call to arms meant that it was his most enthusiastic supporters among the Volunteers who went to France and to their deaths. Some of his immediate friends and colleagues fought and fell: Major William Redmond, his brother, died in June 1917 from wounds received during his service with the Royal Irish Regiment; a former member of the parliamentary party, Lieutenant T. M. Kettle, was killed in action with the Royal Dublin Fusiliers in September 1916. Thirty thousand Irishmen were killed in the First World War, and while the casualties sustained by the Ulster Division were indisputably horrific, the sacrifice of Redmond's National Volunteers was probably no less awful, and certainly (until very lately) only inadequately recognised. Exact figures are still wanting, but it might be estimated that a little less than half of the total number of fallen Irishmen were Redmondite Home Rulers. In supporting Irish engagement with the war effort, the Irish Party had embarked upon a career of self-mutilation.

Nor did the military glory begin to compensate for the loss of life. There was much Irish heroism, but the absence of an Irish army corps meant that there was no focus for Irish national pride. Individual soldiers and regiments fought heroically: Sergeant Michael O'Leary of the Irish Guards was awarded the Victoria Cross, and was much celebrated in the early stages of the war; and many other medals were won – Redmond's brother was awarded the Legion of Honour and his son was decorated with a DSO. But there were no great Irish victories to encourage faith in the war effort. There were certainly heroic failures such as Etreux in 1914, where the Royal Munster Fusiliers were in action, and Gallipoli in 1915, where the Royal Dublin Fusiliers fought gallantly and bloodily.[23] But individual or regimental heroism on the edge of the abyss did little to bolster Redmond or his political vision.

In a sense Redmond had imaginatively reinterpreted the historic dictum that 'England's difficulty was Ireland's opportunity', using the challenge of the Great War to promote his particular conception of Irish nationality. But there were others who clung to the traditional interpretation, and who acted accordingly. The history of Redmond's enemies within the Volunteer and wider national movements is only indirectly relevant to this narrative; and the history of the rising that Redmond's opponents launched in Easter Week 1916 is so well known as to need little exposition here. Two strains within advanced separatism existed separately in the year before 1916, and were united in the aftermath of the Rising. The early history of the Sinn Féin party was discussed in Chapter 6. In 1912–15 the party was largely dormant, kept alive only by the very considerable propaganda skills of Arthur Griffith: 'over the years he educated or indoctrinated large numbers of young separatists'.[24] But alongside these constitutional separatists were the Irish Republican

Brotherhood, reformulated after 1907, and the Irish Volunteer Movement.

After the division within the Volunteers in September 1914, there existed a cohort opposed to Redmond's strategy: these men, numbering perhaps 12,000 (out of an original total of around 170,000 Volunteers) were concentrated in Dublin, under the leadership of Eoin MacNeill, an elder within the Gaelic League and Professor of Early Irish History at University College Dublin. There was an overlap between these reformulated Irish Volunteers and the Irish Republican Brotherhood, but it was within the latter organisation that the plans for a rebellion against the British were hatched. Even within the IRB, however, there was no general pressure for military action: the constitution of the Brotherhood required an electoral mandate before any declaration of war against the Saxon oppressor. The conspirators, therefore, were simultaneously subverting the Fenian constitution and the power structures of their own Brotherhood, as well as the more obvious targets of Redmond's leadership and British rule. A newly formed Military Council of the IRB existed beyond the influence of the traditional governing body, the Supreme Council, and it was this new committee that was used by the leading conspirators to forward their plans.

The rebels, as their leader Patrick Pearse later made clear, relied upon the promise of German assistance, and upon a mass mobilisation of MacNeill's Volunteers.[25] But even before the action had begun, these hopes were dashed: a German vessel, the *Aud*, was unable to rendezvous with the rebels, and was captured by the Royal Navy. MacNeill, who had been kept in the dark, discovered the plans for the rising on Holy Thursday, only three days before it was planned to begin. On Good Friday he issued an order cancelling the Volunteer mobilisation which was to have served as an essential preliminary to the insurgency. The thwarted conspirators were forced to delay their action until Easter Monday.

On that day, Patrick Pearse proclaimed the creation of an Irish republic on the steps of the General Post Office in O'Connell Street, Dublin. The other rebel strong-points were the Four Courts, the South Dublin Union, the Mendicity Institution, Jacob's Biscuit Factory, Boland's Mill (where Eamon de Valera was in charge) and, closer to the city centre, St Stephen's Green, where a contingent of the Irish Citizens' Army was led by Michael Mallin and Constance Markievicz. There was virtually no contact with the few scattered rebel centres outside Dublin city: at Ashbourne, in northern County Dublin, where Thomas Ashe and Richard Mulcahy inflicted heavy casualties on a superior force of RIC men; at Athenry, County Galway; and at Enniscorthy, County Wexford. In total perhaps 700 men and women turned out on Easter Monday, while a few more joined the rebel colours as the week wore on. At its peak, the insurgent forces numbered around 1500, although, as Michael Laffan has wryly commented, the numbers of veterans of the rising multiplied as the years passed.[26] Some 450 people died and 2500 were injured in the fighting of Easter week, 1916.

Within six days the rising had been crushed by the British army and navy, and the executions of the leading insurgents had begun. In all sixteen died, fifteen in front of British firing squads in Dublin and Cork, and one (Roger Casement) on the gallows in Pentonville prison. There is a consensus that it was these executions, rather than the rebel action, which nudged public opinion from outright hostility towards a degree of sympathy for the insurgents and their idealism. This is not the place to attempt a comprehensive reassessment of the rising, but given that the rising played a critical part in the fortunes of Home Rule in Ireland and Britain, a number of points have an inescapable significance. It is often argued that Dublin opinion was at first opposed to the rising, but J. J. Lee has suggested that this traditional emphasis is perhaps misplaced, and that latent rebel sympathies should not be overlooked.[27] It is also possibly the case that, in the beginning, the Rising looked like an extremely foolhardy, not to say comic, venture: Pearse's sister, Mary Brigid, arriving at the GPO on Easter Monday, ordered him to 'come home, Pat, and leave all this foolishness'.[28] As the days passed, however, the potentially comic or ludicrous aspect of the rising evaporated, and it was seen to be a serious statement of republican idealism. There is a case for assuming that the staying power of the rebels underlined the dignity of their cause and helped to convert public opinion.

The executions and wholesale arrests – some 3500 were detained, mostly for short periods – were a critical factor in this conversion, but here again some further detail is required. It was widely expected that there would be some executions, but the number and manner of the killings was not foreseen. Even leading Home Rulers assumed that two, possibly three, of the leading insurgents would suffer this fate. The mild response of the British to the risings of 1848 and 1867, and the exceptionally forgiving response of Louis Botha's South African government to the de Wet rising of 1914 (when one conspirator was hanged) encouraged this view. Those executed were often well-known figures in a comparatively small city: the policeman shot in the head at the gates of Dublin Castle by the rebels was a nameless lackey of the English King, but Pearse, Connolly, MacDonagh and many of the other rebel martyrs were familiar and often popular figures in middle-class Dublin society.

The staccato rhythm of the executions (the 'policy of dribbling executions', as Dillon termed it) also enflamed the public, raising and dashing popular expectations of leniency. Even the imperialist ideologue F. S. Oliver believed that 'the method of the execution of two or three a day for several days was one of the most foolish and provocative measures ever adopted. If we had waked up one morning to find that thirteen had been shot all at one go, we should have given a gasp, but there would have been an end of it.'[29] It also seems to have been assumed that when, after eight deaths, Constance Markievicz was reprieved, other commutations would follow.[30] This assumption was without justification and the lurching pattern of executions was swiftly resumed.

Some Home Rule leaders saw the dangers inherent in the actions of the government, and sounded a note of warning. In a letter to Redmond, written on 30 April, Dillon, who had been marooned in his home in North Great George's Street, close to the GPO, advised his leader that he 'should urge strongly on the government the *extreme* unwisdom of any wholesale shootings of prisoners. The wisest course is to execute *no one* for the present. This is *the most urgent* matter for the moment. If there were shootings of prisoners on a large scale the effect on public opinion might be disastrous in the extreme.'[31] But while Redmond, a more conservative and constitutionally minded figure than Dillon, acted on this advice, and while Asquith offered his slippery assurances, the executions began and continued. By 7 May Dillon was being warned by a Capuchin friar that 'ill-feeling amongst the working classes in the city is becoming extremely bitter over the continuance of these executions'.[32]

In a famous speech, delivered in the Commons on 11 May, Dillon passionately denounced the killings, and praised the bravery of the insurgents in provocative terms:

> I say I am proud of their [the rebels'] courage and if you were not so dense or stupid, as some of you English people are, you could have had these men fighting for you, and they are men worth having…it would have been a damned good thing for you if your soldiers were able to put up as good a fight as did these men in Dublin.[33]

F. S. L. Lyons has argued that Dillon's passionate words were 'largely responsible for securing for the parliamentary party the short time for manoeuvre that still was to be left to it'.[34] This is possible, but Dillon's speech might also be seen as a belated and disastrous effort to change tack. In a 'desperate lunge towards neo-Parnellism', he was awkwardly trying to claim the rebels as his own and to annex some of the popular favour that they had won.[35] In a limited sense, as Lyons argues, his claim was comprehensible in so far as he had long sympathised (at least 'instinctively' or 'intuitively') with the rebel tradition.[36] But Dillon was also damning a Liberal-dominated government and this, in turn, was the repudiation of an alliance that he had himself pursued since the death of Parnell. Moreover, his taunting of the British army was in effect the repudiation of a recruiting policy that his party had endorsed since September 1914.

The Easter rebels had exposed the limitations and inconsistencies of the Irish Party's rhetoric and actions – a party that celebrated the achievements of earlier insurgents, and yet which daily compromised the ideals of Irish self-government. The rebels had also exposed the distance that the party had travelled since the death of Parnell – the extent to which his great coalition of militant and constitutionalist had degenerated into a party of tough-talking but sedentary and ageing gentlemen. In the very act of purloining the rebels' sanctity, Dillon underlined the integrity of their case.

And yet, when all this is said, it remains true that the Easter Rising might well have helped to elevate Home Rule and its proponents. Asquith visited Ireland between 11 and 19 May 1916, and gathered opinions from a wide range of sources, from senior civil servants through to some of the republican prisoners in Mountjoy gaol. On his return he moved into action: a cabinet meeting was held on 21 May which resulted in an offer of the Chief Secretaryship to Lloyd George and in a commission to negotiate between the Irish parties. Lloyd George refused the Irish office, but attempted to strike a deal between Redmond and Carson on the basis of six-county exclusion. The initiative stalled because the two Irish leaders had apparently formed very different ideas of the partition proposal, Redmond seeing it as a temporary expedient while Carson viewed it as permanent. Leading Tories and southern Unionists exploited this confusion to register their own protests and thus influence the final shape of the deal, and in the end the bill that was offered to Redmond so completely reflected these Tory fears that he and the nationalists were compelled to turn it down.

This, in brief, is the generally accepted interpretation of the Lloyd George negotiations of 1916. The importance of this episode is inescapable: it was seen by contemporaries, and by later historians, as a critical turning-point in the history of the Home Rule movement, and it therefore requires some detailed exposition.[37] But it is impossible to narrate this episode without acknowledging the ambiguous attitudes of several of the key players, the complexities of the evidence, and conflicts of interpretation. There remains a tendency to explain this episode in terms which do little justice to the rich tactical skills and complex personalities on display.

It should be said immediately that the episode chimes with Asquith's earlier forays into Irish politics. To some extent the apparent double-dealing, lack of candour and trust, and inevitable controversy, while reminiscent of the talks of late 1913 or the Curragh incident, say as much about the limitations of Asquith's enemies as about the Prime Minister himself. There are, however, certain characteristics of the episode that carry the mark of Asquith's diplomacy. It is reasonably clear that, at least before embarking for Ireland, Asquith wanted to use the Easter Rising as a pretext for bringing Home Rule out of suspended animation. On 11 May, the day of his departure, he told the Commons:

> the Government has come to the conclusion that the system under which Ireland has been governed has completely broken down. The only satisfactory alternative, in their judgement, is the creation, at the earliest possible moment, of an Irish Government responsible to the Irish people. The Government has determined, therefore, to address itself forthwith to the task of endeavouring to make such arrangements as will enable it, by agreement between different parties in Ireland, to put the Government of Ireland Act into operation at the earliest practicable moment.[38]

The meaning of this seems clear enough, but at a cabinet meeting held on 21 May, after Asquith's return from Dublin, the Prime Minister placed his apparently considered and private views before his colleagues, which amounted to support for a major reform of the Irish Office together with the conviction that the Home Rule Act could not be put into operation until the end of the European war.[39] However, Asquith was firm about the future only of the Home Rule Act, and not of the wider principle. The meeting did not commission Lloyd George to seek the means by which the Home Rule Act might be brought into immediate operation; nor did it grant Lloyd George the power to conclude any form of deal with the Irish and without reference to ministerial colleagues. Yet Lloyd George wrote to his brother on 22 May that Asquith and Bonar Law had invited him to 'take Ireland with full powers to effect settlement'.[40] Moreover, it was with this grand definition of his commission that Lloyd George set off to negotiate with the Irish leaders.

These conflicts of evidence have a more than antiquarian interest, because they contained the seeds of the later failure of the negotiations, and because they reveal something of Asquith's political style. Comparison may be made with Asquith's handling of the partition issue in 1912–14: here his original leanings were partitionist, but he back-tracked in 1912–13 while sparring with the Unionists and searching for more favourable terms. In May 1916 his sympathies on setting out for Dublin lay towards the immediate enactment of Home Rule, but within ten days he was apparently backtracking, 'veiling' (to use that favoured Asquithian concept) his true views in order to secure his colleagues' agreement, while exploiting the ambiguities of the situation to the full.

It seems at least possible that Asquith used an unclearly framed cabinet decision for his own purposes.[41] His assertion to his cabinet colleagues that the Home Rule Act could not be brought into operation before the end of the war was apparently emphatic, but was in fact a characteristic legal nicety: the Act might not be brought into operation, but this did not rule out the possibility that some provisional form of Home Rule might be set in motion. It seems possible, too, that Asquith sounded out Bonar Law about the potential of the Lloyd George mission (this is certainly one reading of Lloyd George's letter to his brother). Lloyd George's biographer, Bentley Gilbert, has argued that 'the Irish negotiations of 1916 were the product of a private agreement between Lloyd George and the Prime Minister concluded between 22 and 25 May to give Ireland immediate Home Rule'; and there is every reason, judging by Asquith's past form, to support this suggestion.[42]

The structure of the negotiations reflected the experience of the Buckingham Palace Conference of July 1914, when face-to-face talks had rapidly descended into posturing and acrimony. Lloyd George saw the Unionists and nationalists separately, though even this targeted approach was not without unpleasantness: Lloyd George was met by T. P. O'Connor and Dillon on 27 May, when Dillon was so outrageously rude to the two others that he had to write an apology to his party colleague.[43] At first, notwithstanding Dillon's relentless pessimism and suspicion, there were some mild grounds for hope. Redmond had in fact approached Lloyd George before the cabinet of 21 May with a view to securing his involvement, while Walter Long (shortly to emerge as one of the Unionist wreckers) wrote to Lloyd George on 23 May offering his best wishes for the success of the enterprise: 'may I say how earnestly I hope you will go to Ireland'.[44]

A successful meeting was held between Lloyd George and the Ulster Unionists over lunch on 26 May, and the outlines of a settlement were charted. However, the first signs of trouble were also emerging on that day, when the ex-cabinet minister and leading southern Unionist, Viscount Midleton, wrote to Asquith regretting that the Home Rule issue had been reactivated, and hoping that the interests of the Unionists outside Ulster would not be disregarded.[45] Lloyd George, recognising the seriousness of this volley, sought to bind Midleton and his southern Unionist colleagues into the negotiation, but for the moment Midleton resisted the lure, arguing that he and his allies were not yet ready for diplomacy.

The deal that was formulated in late May and early June of 1916 incorporated delicately framed concessions from both the Home Rulers and the Ulster Unionists. In July 1914 the difference between Carson and Redmond had been relatively great, with Carson seeking permanent exclusion for the six north-eastern Ulster counties, and Redmond effectively conceding temporary exclusion for the four most Protestant and Unionist of these counties. In June 1916 Carson accepted the exclusion of the six counties for the duration of the war, when the issue would be reconsidered: that is to say, he accepted a deal which was little different from that offered by Asquith in 1914. Redmond, for his part, still adhered to the principle of temporary exclusion, but conceded that the six counties could be treated as a unit.

In a premonition of the arrangements created in 1972, the new six-county territory was to be administered by a Secretary of State who was to sit in the cabinet.[46] The rest of Ireland was to have a new House of Commons, sitting in Dublin and comprising all of the Irish MPs at Westminster, except those representing seats in the north. Writing to Carson, Lloyd George suggested that there might be in addition twenty or thirty nominated members, representing southern Unionist interests.[47] At the same time, all these MPs would continue to sit in the imperial House of Commons, a feature of the agreement that had a very great symbolic significance. This unwieldy and impractical arrangement was essential to Redmond as proof of the provisional and temporary nature of the deal as a whole and particularly, of course, those aspects relating to partition. Additional provision was made for 'conferences' between MPs from the northern, or excluded, area and those from the rest of Ireland. This foreshadowed various later schemes for cross-border co-operation, formulated in the Government of Ireland Act (1920) and other constitutional revisions through to the Belfast Agreement of 1998.[48]

Partition, or more specifically its future, was the crux in all of this. It was essential for the purposes of agreement that the time-frame for partition should be kept as ambiguous as possible. In the past Lloyd George has frequently been blamed for keeping the two Irish sides in the dark and offering each mutually incompatible promises, but this is surely to interpret the politics of the negotiation in too unforgiving a manner. It is true that Lloyd George's solution to the question of exclusion was absolutely characteristic of his diplomacy, involving clinching a deal where there was agreement, and postponing all difficulties to some indeterminate future date. However, it is hard to believe that the negotiating parties in May–June 1916 did not understand the thrust of Lloyd

George's strategies. There is a letter from A. W. Samuels to Carson, dated 14 June 1916, where Samuels, a leading Unionist lawyer, spells out that 'Asquith and Lloyd George are deep tricksters. For you the exclusion is to be permanent, for Redmond provisional.' It is equally hard to believe that they did not uniformly appreciate the need to keep the partition arrangement as open as the demands of political salesmanship would allow.[49]

There was in fact very little difference in the deal outlined by Lloyd George to both Carson and Redmond. The distinction lay in the fact that Lloyd George affirmed to Carson not that partition was to be permanent, as is frequently stated, but rather that 'at the end of the provisional period Ulster does not, whether she wills it or not, merge in the rest of Ireland'.[50] Only George Boyce has fully recognised the ambiguity with which these apparently reassuring words were charged.[51] Ulster's exclusion from Home Rule would not cease automatically at the end of the 'provisional period', but would depend rather on the action of the London government. This, in turn, hinged upon the result of a general election, and the sympathies of the party in power.

This was little different from the types of time-limit that had been offered by the Liberals in 1914, and Carson was too experienced a parliamentary hand to miss this symmetry. But, while both he and the nationalists had moved from their respective positions in 1914, it was essential that the extent of this movement should be minimised to their followers, and it was here that Lloyd George's richly ambiguous proposal should have offered them assistance. In the event, however, these ambiguities were ripped apart, not by either Carson or Redmond, but by critics outside the negotiation with other interests to defend.

The tragedy of the failure in 1916 is underlined by the very narrow division separating the disputants, and by the fact that a deal was so very nearly concluded. Carson addressed a private meeting of the Ulster Unionist Council (UUC) on 6 June 1916 and, admittedly with some difficulty, secured its support for the continuing diplomacy with Lloyd George and Redmond.[52] Carson's challenge lay not so much with the time-limits of exclusion as with the territorial question. Although in July 1914 he had been prepared to settle for the permanent exclusion of six counties, this had never been fully debated or ratified by his party, which purported to represent the nine-county province of Ulster. His other central problem, related to the territorial issue, was in persuading his audience of earnest northern businessmen and landowners that, by agreeing to the Lloyd George deal, they would not be dishonouring their moral and contractual obligations under the Covenant of 1912 (through signing this document Ulster loyalists had pledged themselves to defeat

Home Rule using 'all means which may be found necessary'). Carson offered to meet with representatives of the three Ulster counties (Donegal, Cavan and Monaghan) not covered by the exclusion plan, for he argued that the negotiations could only justly proceed with their acquiescence. A session was therefore held (on 12 June) at which these 'other' Ulster Unionists effectively agreed to sacrifice themselves for the good of the movement as a whole.[53] Crucially, however, the representatives of southern Unionism – the 200,000 or so Unionists outside the province of Ulster – had no voice in any of these proceedings.

A parallel series of meetings and consultations was held within the Home Rule party. The premise upon which these meetings turned was that partition would be merely temporary. The nationalist leaders had obtained elaborate assurances from Lloyd George on this point, and upon the wider issue of further concessions: Lloyd George said that 'he had placed his life upon the table, and would stand or fall by the agreement come to'.[54]

When the settlement broke down, and recriminations followed, Lloyd George's evident perfidy was highlighted and damned by both the Unionist and Home Rule leadership. But it is likely that the senior figures within both parties were fully aware of the ambiguities and difficulties of the course they were pursuing, and that Lloyd George's strategies merely provided a useful target for blame. Any other interpretation casts the leaders of the Home Rule party and the Unionists as hopelessly ingenuous. Lloyd George himself rated the bargaining skills of the Irish very highly: he once told Lord Riddell that 'the Irish are rare negotiatiors. They bluff so well that you really cannot tell whether they are bluffing or not'.

Given the Home Rulers' lengthy experience in both the Commons and the rough trade of local nationalist politics, their skills did not require Lloyd George's authentication. More specifically, by 1916 the Irish had painful experience of Lloyd George's methods, having been genially conned over the issue of the budget in 1909.[55] When they asked Lloyd George to promise them that no further concessions would be required, they must surely have remembered the series of 'final' concessions that Asquith had extorted from them in February and March 1914. Moreover, although much emphasis was later placed upon Lloyd George's assurances, the Home Rule leaders do not seem to have sought a written version of these pledges. A record of the meeting exists, but it is initialled only by the Home Rulers themselves. One interpretation which this otherwise difficult evidence supports is that the Home Rule leaders accepted that the difference between temporary and permanent exclusion was (for all practical purposes) slight, and that they also tacitly recognised that Lloyd George's assurances were worthless, except as political insurance in the event of failure.

A highly critical and difficult meeting of the Ulster nationalists was held in Belfast on 23 June, and the deal won the approval of a decided majority: 475 supporters as against 265 dissentients. But the figures masked a much more threatening political configuration. Northern nationalists were geographically divided, with the Belfast leader, Joseph Devlin, and his following more supportive than the nationalists of south and west Ulster. Many of the Catholic clergy represented at the meeting of 23 June were antagonistic towards the deal. It took Devlin's very considerable political skills and a threat of resignation from Redmond to clinch the required majority.[56] With the reluctant sanction of the Ulster nationalists, the party organisation as a whole could now signal its approval. On 26 June the National Directory of the party machine, the United Irish League, formally accepted the deal and seemingly opened the way to a final resolution of the Anglo-Irish antagonism: 'you are therefore in a position to proceed with the matter on the basis of your proposals', Devlin proudly reported to Lloyd George.[57]

The agreement of the wider Unionist and nationalist parties had thus been secured, but it had been a difficult business, and the leaders had had to interpret the ambiguities of the deal according to the needs of their respective followers (there is surely a premonition here of the Belfast Agreement of 1998). But, despite partisan interpretations, the settlement was designed and understood to be open-ended, and when in early July the 'headings of a settlement' were finally published, the fate of the proposed exclusion experiment remained unclear. The settlement as a whole, including partition, was to remain in force for the duration of the war and for a year after its conclusion; 'but if Parliament has not by that time made further and permanent provision for the government of Ireland the period for which the Bill is to remain in force is to be extended by Order in Council for such time as may be necessary in order to enable Parliament to make such provision'.[58] It was further understood that an Imperial Conference would be held at the end of the war, which would, amongst other business, examine schemes for a permanent settlement of the government of Ireland.

Carson accepted this persiflage, but understood that the exclusion of Ulster would persist unless parliament decided otherwise: this was his particular definition of 'permanent' exclusion. Redmond was equally accommodating, but he believed that at the end of the alloted span Ulster would be automatically incorporated within a unitary Irish state, unless parliament decided otherwise. Each seems to have been prepared to accept that any settlement would necessarily fudge these points. The ever-astute Devlin remarked, 'as to the apparent difference of opinion between Mr Redmond and Sir Edward Carson whether exclusion is permanent or temporary... [I believe that] this is more apparent than real, that it actually represents two legitimate views of the same proposal, and may easily be cleared up afterwards'.[59] Each leader almost certainly understood that there was a very real possibility that exclusion, however circumscribed, might well achieve an independent momentum and permanence. Neither was ultimately responsible for the failure of the initiative.

This burden lay elsewhere. It was the southern Unionists who, in alliance with Tory malcontents, brought this elaborate diplomacy to an end. Their motives were complex, but their methods were relatively straightforward: with a brutal persistence they declared that they had located treachery in the creative evasions and elaborate ambiguities of the Lloyd George deal. As has been mentioned, the first symptom of southern Unionist unrest came with Viscount Midleton's letter of 26 May to Asquith urging that the interests of southern Unionists be taken into account and fearing that the wider initiative would wreck the party truce.[60] Behind the scenes, Midleton seems to have been orchestrating a chorus of southern Unionist complaint.

On 29 May, Walter Long wrote to Lloyd George warning him that there was an impending split within Irish Unionism, and, in a characteristic thrust, that Carson could not be taken to represent the southern Unionists. On 30 May, Long met Lloyd George and was given an outline of the evolving agreement, which Lloyd George claimed had already been seen by Carson, Craig, Redmond, Dillon, Devlin and, representing the southern Unionists, G. H. Stewart and Lords Midleton and Desart.[61] By early June it had become clear that there were intense divisions among the Unionists in the cabinet, and on 11 June, Long forwarded a devastating memorandum to Lloyd George in which he complained that 'the Unionist Party in Ireland are being driven by the Prime Minister and Minister of Munitions into accepting a situation which they know to be morally wrong and wrong politically'.[62]

On 15 June, Long circulated two memoranda to Unionist cabinet colleagues focusing on some of the elisions and evasions perpetrated by Lloyd George in his search for agreement. He bridled in particular at the report that Lloyd George was telling Unionists that his scheme had the unanimous approval of the cabinet and was 'an imperial necessity'.[63] His own recollection was that 'the task Mr Lloyd George was asked to undertake was to secure some basis of agreement among all Irish Unionists which would lead to the acceptance of Home Rule *at the end of the war*'. With the accuracy of a seasoned political marksman, he targeted the need 'to be quite clear as to what has been told to the various parties' and the need, too, to be precise about the future of partition. For his part, Long was unequivocal that his own continued membership of the government depended upon the satisfactory elucidation of these different issues.

Other leading Unionists were also registering alarm. Lord Salisbury contributed to the flurry of angry memoranda, denouncing the Lloyd George initiative 'even if American support be at stake': 'depend upon it', he affirmed, 'feebleness never pays'.[64] Of the Unionist cabinet ministers, Lords Lansdowne and Selborne felt keenly that Lloyd George had exceeded his brief, and that he was trying to hustle the Unionists into an untimely and dangerous accommodation with Home Rule. Selborne, indeed, was an early casualty of the affair, tendering his resignation on 25 June. Lansdowne and Long, however, both clung on to office, where they were able to do the most damage to Lloyd George.

What motivated the many opponents of Lloyd George's Home Rule scheme? There were certainly profound issues of principle at stake. Many nationalists in southern and western Ulster saw themselves as being cut off from the triumph of self-government in the rest of the island. There was the real possibility that, even though the six counties would remain under the direct jurisdiction of the London government, an aggressive Ulster Unionism would prevail. Given the leakage of support away from the parliamentary party, it was also the case that the deal held little emotional or practical attraction for many Irish nationalists. Indeed, in the context of these ferocious difficulties, the political courage and skill of Devlin shines through as truly extraordinary. Redmond himself, in a rare moment of emotion and informality, was moved to acknowledge that 'Joe's loyalty in all this business has been beyond words. I know what it has cost him to do as he has done.'[65]

On the other hand, many Unionists in the Commons and Lords saw the implementation of Home Rule as a concession to the perceived terrorism and treachery of the Easter Rising, and as an attempt to renege on the suspension arrangement. There were perennial suspicions about the political integrity of Asquith and, particularly, Lloyd George, which were rooted in the duel over the constitutional crisis and the third Home Rule Bill. The extent to which, on the evidence of Unionist ministers, Lloyd George had ranged beyond his cabinet brief compounded these suspicions. In addition, the circumstances of the war, with the costly and inconclusive Battle of Jutland (31 May) and the appallingly bloody Somme offensive (beginning on 1 July), did not encourage an emollient approach. More minor disasters, such as the German bombardment of Lowestoft (25 April), timed to coincide with the rising, and the loss of Lord Kitchener (5 June), compounded this truculence. The opposition was thus not confined to a small circle of ascendancy grandees, but had deep roots in the Unionist parliamentary party. Indeed, On 22 June eighty Unionist MPs met to express their opposition to an immediate grant of Home Rule, and this swiftly gave rise to a more permanent expression of backbench resentment in the shape of the Imperial Unionist Association.

Opposition was also deeply rooted not just among southern peers, but within Ulster Unionism. On 12 June 1916 the Unionists of Cavan, Donegal and Monaghan agreed to abide by the will of the Ulster Unionist Council as a whole, but with the swell of opposition this compliance began to weaken. The Monaghan Unionists remained loyal to Carson and the deal, while the Donegal Unionists reserved their position. But the Cavan men, always markedly suspicious of Belfast, wrote to Carson on 13 July indicating their profound discontent with the progress of the negotiation.[66] Behind this niggling disapproval lay Captain Somerset Saunderson, son of the first leader of the Irish Unionists and a loyal client of Walter Long.

It is hard, however, to resist the suspicion that beyond the understandable fears of those nationalists and Unionists who were adversely affected by the proposed settlement, and beyond the issues of principle, lay a series of more complicated personal issues. It is difficult, for example, to judge whether John Dillon's patriotic scepticism worked to the service of the Home Rule cause, or in fact added to the difficulties that cooler and more pragmatic leaders like Redmond or Devlin faced; it is possible to see Dillon as contributing to the realisation of his own suspicions and fears.[67] It is unquestionably the case that hardline Unionists like Midleton expected that, as in the past, Dillon's extremism would wreck any unpalatable settlement.

It is also difficult to judge whether, among the Unionists, Lord Lansdowne's truculence worked to the service of southern Unionism. As with Dillon, there are some grounds for questioning the soundness of Lansdowne's political judgement. But both Dillon and Lansdowne worked, however controversially, from the purest motives, and each was characterised by an impeccable personal political integrity.

Of the Unionist dissidents, Walter Long was more influential than Lansdowne, and was a much more complex political thinker. The effectiveness of Long as a political operator is still rarely appreciated, for he masked acute sensitivities and jealousies underneath the reassuring garb of the West Country squire.[68] He had carefully constructed a wide and diverse constituency within British Unionism, and the strength of this very nearly won him the leadership in 1911. As it was, he survived at the front rank of party politics while other, ostensibly more brilliant, colleagues fell by the wayside. Balfour thought that Long was 'too discursive, too quick-tempered, and above all too complimentary'; and he certainly moved smartly on 23 May to offer Lloyd George his cloying best wishes for the success of the Irish initiative.[69] But Long was also profoundly defensive and territorial, in the sense that he jealously guarded his own political base including Ireland and, more specifically, Irish Unionism. Long was connected, both through his own family and that of his wife, to the southern Irish gentry, and he served as Chief Secretary in 1905. Moreover, he represented a Dublin constituency in the House of Commons between 1906 and 1910. As was seen in Chapter 7, Long was intimately connected with Ulster Unionist militancy in 1912–14. In May–June 1916, as the nature of the Lloyd George scheme and southern Unionist complaints became clearer, he moved rapidly from a position of support to outright opposition. After mid-June 1916 Long emerged as perhaps the most energetic and influential of Lloyd George's critics.

In a sense, this was an inevitable denouement, given Long's Unionist convictions and his connections with the southern gentry. But the direction of Lloyd George's efforts, and the shape of the proposed settlement, were known to Long by the end of May. He certainly hinted at problems in an otherwise emollient letter on 29 May: 'so far as I can ascertain the progress of your negotiations is all that we could desire, and I hear on all sides the most cheering accounts of your interviews'. But he only moved into an outright attack in the middle of the following month.[70] The formal grounds of complaint at this time were that Lloyd George had exceeded his brief, and had misrepresented the views of the cabinet, but Long also focused on the apparent double-dealing that had been taking place, and the uncertainty about the fate of any partition arrangement. These arguments were vigorously circulated in mid-June and became the staple of the southern Unionist case. Long wrote to Lloyd George along these lines on 11 June, circulated two memoranda to Unionist ministers on 15 June, and between 15 and 19 June bombarded Carson with what Lady Spender called 'reams of fury'.[71] There is a reasonable case for assuming that Long also helped to stimulate Selborne's anxiety: he certainly told Selborne of Lloyd George's grandiose claims, and Selborne in turn emphasised these in his letter of resignation to Asquith.[72]

At the same time Long roused the Unionists of the south and west, and those of Cavan, Donegal and Monaghan. One crucial partner in his campaign was Somerset Saunderson, who was goaded by Long into a sustained attack on Carson. Saunderson, inspired by Long, wrote angrily to Carson on 15 and 17 June, and bearded the Ulster leader at his Belgravia home on 29 June, where Carson was 'abused up hill and down dale'.[73] Saunderson also sought, unsuccessfully, to lead a revolt of the Cavan,

Donegal and Monaghan Unionists who, in his interpretation, had been swindled by Carson at the UUC meetings of early June. This was the first serious criticism that Carson had encountered from within Ulster Unionism, and he was inclined with some justification to interpret it as a more general challenge to his leadership.

There is little doubt that Unionist opponents like Lansdowne and Selborne, however mistakenly, acted from honourable motives, but with Long the picture was more complicated. He looked like a red-neck squire, but in fact had pragmatic instincts, provided always that any pragmatism was of his own making. Despite consistent professions of loyalty, he was, as Austen Chamberlain observed in 1911, 'at the centre of every coterie of grumblers'.[74] He was profoundly jealous of his colleagues, and especially those who occupied political ground which he regarded as his own. He was antagonistic towards George Wyndham, whom he succeeded at the Irish Office, and there are good grounds for assuming that (again, despite protestations of loyalty and affection) he was deeply irked by the ascendancy of Carson, who succeeded him as chairman of the Irish Unionist parliamentary party.

Long's relationship with Carson was thoroughly ambiguous for, while Long was prepared to identify himself as an Ulster militant at a time when Ulster militancy was centre-stage, he effectively undermined Carson on other issues, and there had been some angry confrontations. Lord Balcarres, for example, recorded some menacing words offered by a 'vermilion' Long to a bemused Carson on the issue of the Parliament Bill.[75] 'The worst of Walter Long', Carson observed of his so-called colleague, 'is that he never knows what he wants, but is always intriguing to get it'.[76] On 20 June 1916 Lloyd George reported to Asquith that Carson was 'very angry with Long who has actually been telling his Ulster people to throw Carson over'.[77] On 22 June, F. S. Oliver wrote of the Unionist leadership, doubtless with Long particularly in mind, that they 'didn't mind in the least if they destroyed Carson by taking away the confidence of his followers in him'.[78]

In May–June 1916, with the Lloyd George initiative, there is little doubt that Long delayed, perhaps purposefully, before fully showing his hand. There is no doubt, too, that he orchestrated the opposition to Lloyd George, both at a ministerial level and within southern Unionism. Nor can there be much doubt that this opposition was pitted not just against Lloyd George, but also against those Unionist leaders who had accepted the Lloyd George initiative, namely Carson and Bonar Law. It is possible that Bonar Law had been apprised of Lloyd George's wider ambitions in Ireland from an early stage of the business; he was, in any event, a supporter of the Minister of Munitions. Carson had gone out on a limb to win the approval of the Ulster Unionist Council for the evolving settlement. Lloyd George, who was well qualified to judge, offered a piercing assessment of Long's behaviour and of his performance as an 'English gentleman'. Writing to Dillon, Lloyd George complained:

> Long has behaved in a specially treacherous manner. He has actually been engaged clandestinely in trying to undermine the influence of Carson in Ulster by representing to the Ulster leaders that they were induced to assent to the agreement under false pretences. He told them there was no war urgency, no prospect of trouble in America, and that Carson's reasons for coming to terms were all false. I could not think it possible that any man, least of all one with such pretensions of being an English gentleman, could have acted in such a way.[79]

All of this may indeed have been 'most disingenuous', but the surviving evidence is compatible with Lloyd George's critique, and the allusion to Long's gentility is especially telling as a clue to the effectiveness of his methods.[80]

The negotiation was beginning to unravel from at least 21 June when, at a meeting of the cabinet, four Unionist ministers, including Long, affirmed that they could not accept the Lloyd George scheme. Selborne resigned on 26 June, on the eve of a further cabinet meeting on the Irish settlement. This session revealed the extent of the divisions among the Unionists, with Bonar Law and Balfour largely at odds with Long and Lansdowne.[81] Further resignations were averted by the expedient of a cabinet subcommittee, designed to bolster the proposed agreement in ways that met at least some of the Unionist objections. This was in fact a critical turning point, for the focus of negotiation had now shifted away from addressing Irish qualms (whether nationalist or Unionist) towards calming the nerves of the excited English Unionists, like Long, who were threatening to wreck not just the settlement but, in all likelihood, the entire coalition government. The subcommittee produced an amended settlement that succeeded at least in mollifying Lansdowne; and indeed it looked for a moment as if the two key dissidents might be prised apart. In the event, Long chose to follow Lansdowne's lead, registering continued reservations about the entire initiative, while staying in office.

Asquith believed at this stage that agreement was within reach, and announced the outlines of the settlement to the Commons on 10 July. He did not, however, stress the security arrangements that the Unionists deemed so necessary, and though he affirmed that the reunification of the six and twenty-six counties 'can never be brought about without the free will and assent of the excluded area', some doubt remained in the dissidents' mind about the possible transience of the whole arrange-ment.[82] Lansdowne, therefore, resumed his offensive, and used a speech to the Lords on 11 July as an opportunity to place on record his interpre-tation of the evolving settlement: General Maxwell was doing a good job, existing security arrangements would remain in place and, above all, partition would be 'permanent and enduring'.[83]

This attack was again carried into the cabinet where, on 19 July, minis-ters were persuaded by Lansdowne and Long to underline the perma-nence of exclusion and to reduce Irish representation at Westminster – a move that also served to underline the enduring nature of the partition settlement. Redmond was informed of these changes to the proposed leg-islation on 22 July, and offered an immediate rejection.[84] This was, of course, exactly the outcome that some southern Unionists had hoped for, and which Long and Lansdowne had evidently worked to effect. Asquith and Lloyd George now faced a more or less unified chorus of disapproval, with Unionists and Home Rulers joining in a cacophony of suspicion and disappointment. The great initiative, which had once seemed so close to success, was now formally annulled. Those Unionists (Carson, Bonar Law) who had taken risks for a settlement now courted marginalisation within their party, while the Home Rulers who had gone out on a limb (Redmond, Devlin) also teetered on the edge of oblivion.

Why did Lloyd George fail? Traditional interpretations of the episode lay great emphasis on the Minister of Munitions' guile, or at least the extent to which he exceeded his brief, and also, sometimes, on the naïveté of those with whom he was dealing. Contemporary critics of the proposed settlement complained that, although immediate implementa-tion of the Home Rule Act had been ruled out by Asquith, this was pre-cisely what Lloyd George had set out to achieve. Critics also emphasised that Lloyd George had falsely claimed that the cabinet had unanimously approved his proposed settlement. There was, in addition, anger at the fudging of the partition question.

It is reasonably clear that, while Asquith ruled out the immediate implementation of the Home Rule Act as it stood, he was not ruling out the immediate implementation of Home Rule. It is also reasonably clear that this is how he and others saw the likely shape of a settlement. What else did cabinet colleagues believe would be produced, in commissioning Lloyd George to explore the possibilities of a deal between the Irish parties? Home Rule, as Carson and several other Unionists recognised, had already been enacted. There could be no question of reneging on this, or of negotiating towards an alternative Home Rule settlement to replace that already on the statute books.

It is possible that Asquith and Lloyd George had arranged matters so that the cabinet was given only minimal information. This would have been in keeping with the tenor of their diplomacy, but equally there is no firm evidence to document the suggestion. On the other hand, Lloyd George kept the interested parties reasonably well briefed in late May, and there is a tendency to credit (or debit) him with all the guile and duplicity current in the negotiations. This is surely unrealistic. There is a case for seeing the hand of Asquith in some of the early proceedings. Moreover, certain aspects of Unionist and Home Rule behaviour are difficult to comprehend. There was, for example, a remarkable failure of communication within the Unionist leadership in late May and early June. Carson believed that the cabinet was fully behind the deal placed before the Ulster Unionist Council on 6 June. It would appear, therefore, that there was no communication of any kind between him and Bonar Law in the two-week period between the cabinet of 21 May and the UUC meeting. This again is very hard to credit.

Walter Long, for his part, professed himself happy with the general progress of the initiative on 29 May. He was certainly less happy when he saw Lloyd George on 30 May, but he then kept largely silent for two weeks. What kind of settlement did he and Lansdowne expect Lloyd George to produce? The abolition of the lord lieutenancy was mentioned by Lansdowne on 2 June, as was the reform of the Chief Secretaryship.[85] But this, of course, was open to the criticism that it did not meet the requirements of the Home Rule leadership while it also looked like precisely the concession to the rebels that the Unionist wreckers claimed they opposed.

The other suggestions, posited by Long in early July, were no less astonishing: Long canvassed the name of Dr L. S. Jameson (of the Jameson Raid in the Transvaal) as a possible Chief Secretary for Ireland, and he urged Asquith to take Sir James Campbell (the Attorney-General for Ireland) and Sir Henry Robinson (the Vice-President of the Irish Local Government Board) more completely into the counsels of the government.[86] But Jameson, whatever his subsequent record, was widely identified with aggressive British imperialism, and Robinson, though not unpopular, was viewed as a committed Unionist and as Long's client. Campbell was, rightly or wrongly, seen as the single most contentious Irish Unionist minister: there had been a furious controversy in 1915 when he was suggested as a possible Lord Chancellor of Ireland, and the Home Rulers wanted him out even of the Attorney-Generalship.[87] None of these suggestions was attuned to the need for compromise, and it is probable that none was designed for that end.

The settlement failed because of what were probably deliberate ambiguities in the commission given to Lloyd George, and because ambiguity was essential to the wider negotiation. Carson and the Home Rule leadership seem to have recognised this, and been prepared to take risks; but they also needed to reassert their respective war-cries. The proposed settlement, which was based on partition, was never likely to satisfy southern Unionists, and old divisions between Carson and these southerners, which had first opened up in 1913–14, began to re-emerge. Compounding this critical tension within Irish and British Unionism was the presence in the Unionist leadership of a highly volatile, highly ambitious and relentlessly conspiratorial minister, Walter Long, whose capacity to make trouble was underlined by his connections with southern Unionism. Long's personal feelings (whether interpreted as 'pride and integrity' or as furious ambition) seem to have played a vital role in his decision, taken between 29 May and 11 June, to shift from compliance to opposition.[88] This was perhaps the critical juncture in the whole business. He and Lansdowne then started to demolish the delicate architecture of the compromise, based as it was on creative ambiguity and well-intentioned elision. By relentlessly focusing on the fudges that the agreement embodied, Long and Lansdowne succeeded in mobilising a significant section of Unionist opinion. And this, in turn, meant both that the Unionist moderates (Carson, Bonar Law, F. E. Smith and, for some of the time, Austen Chamberlain) were forced into line, and that the final bill did not adequately reflect the needs of the Home Rule party. Midleton had hoped that Dillon would be responsible for wrecking the Lloyd George initiative; in the end, it was the much more emollient Redmond who could not stomach the proposed deal.

What were the implications of this failure? Southern Unionists had spectacularly missed an opportunity to co-operate with the Home Rule movement at perhaps the last moment when a deal might effectively have been struck. They had sought to undermine Carson, and thus indirectly bolstered the very partitionist impulses within Ulster Unionism that they were seeking to overcome. They had scored off Redmond even though he represented perhaps their securest lifeline in a democratic Ireland. There have been few more spectacular examples of political masochism in the history of modern Irish politics.

Ulster Unionism, on the other hand, had for the first time formally committed itself to six-county exclusion and all that this represented. It need hardly be reiterated that this commitment was to the maintenance of British government within the north, and not to any form of regional parliament. But the UUC meeting of 6 June had also effectively approved the formal separation of Ulster and southern Unionism, and the division of Ulster Unionism itself. The Unionists of Cavan, Donegal and Monaghan, when all the tearful rhetoric had subsided, had been served notice that their brethren in Belfast and eastern Ulster would look after themselves.

In terms of British parliamentary politics, the Lloyd George failure damaged the Asquith coalition and threatened to expose profound divisions within British Conservatism. Long and Lansdowne had at least kept British Toryism together, although Bonar Law had risked the division of his party in order to support the deal. It should also be emphasised, as R. J. Q. Adams has remarked, that 'Bonar Law, Carson and Lloyd George had on this occasion worked in parallel, but not yet as a team'.[89] If Walter Long was right, and Carson and Bonar Law had been hoodwinked by Lloyd George, then the con-trick produced remarkable results. Carson did not in fact berate Lloyd George for jeopardising his leadership in Ulster, but instead was soon working for Lloyd George's succession to the premiership. Carson's anger was reserved for Long himself.

Stephen Gywnn remarked, in a famous lament, that the day on which the Lloyd George initiative effectively collapsed, 22 July 1916, was decisive to the fortunes of the Home Rule movement in Ireland: 'that day really finished the constitutional party and overthrew Redmond's power'.[90] Redmond and the Home Rule leadership had forced unpopular decisions on to their party, they had risked divisions and they had staked their personal authority – all for a deal that in the end was broken by Long and Lansdowne, representatives of a moribund politics. Asquith had urged the negotiators in May–June 1916 to bolster the chances of agreement by refraining from public comment, and while this seemed like reasonable counsel, it effectively silenced the Home Rule leadership at a time when public comment was desperately needed. It has been argued, indeed, that the type of provocative and defiant speech delivered by Dillon in the Commons on 11 May (before the start of the negotiations) might have helped to sustain the credibility of the party when public opinion was shifting in the rebels' favour.[91]

The failure of the negotiations had other consequences. Michael Laffan has argued with some cogency that the débâcle of 22 July left Redmond utterly demoralised, and he has noted the subsequent 'torpor' of both the Home Rule Party and its constituency organisation, the United Irish League.[92] The failure of the Lloyd George initiative also 'gravely damaged' the (always shaky) credibility of emollient or consensual strategies, and left the way open for more radical alternatives to Home Rule. That there was no sudden, avalanche-like collapse reflected not so much the residual strength of the Home Rule movement as the fact that, until mid-1917, there was as yet no well-organised alternative.

However, it might equally be argued that the Home Rule movement was in long-term decline, and that the Lloyd George initiative served simply to catalyse a process that was already well advanced. This view has some grounding in contemporary evidence. For example, the southern Unionists acted as they did in June 1916 partly because they thought that the Home Rule movement was already dead. On the other hand, as already mentioned, a few well-placed supporters of Redmond, like Stephen Gwynn, were inclined to interpret the Lloyd George negotiations as a decisive turning-point in their collective fate. There is also a wide range of evidence which supports the view that the Home Rule movement, though winged, remained in a reasonably healthy condition by the early summer of 1916. Gwynn emphasised that, as late as January 1916, and in the midst of other niggling failures, Redmond secured an important victory in winning Ireland's exclusion from conscription. This underlined Ireland's separate political identity, and represented 'the highwater-line of Redmond's achievement'. Only after the victory on conscription did the constitutional tide begin its relentless ebb.[93]

The evidence of by-election results in the 1914–17 period also broadly supports the view that Home Rule remained a viable creed until at least the Lloyd George failure, and even perhaps in its immediate aftermath. Three scholars – Paul Bew, Patrick Maume and Alan O'Day – have independently worked on this issue, and have broadly united in emphasising the electoral strength of the Home Rule Party until the North Roscommon by-election of February 1917. Bew has argued that the party held on to its traditional rural support, but he has also noted the growing strength of opposition in Dublin, where Eoin MacNeill's Irish Volunteers were concentrated.[94] Maume is inclined to greater caution than this, though he accepts the general case that Home Rule retained a base in the Irish countryside. He quotes the view of Edward MacLysaght, a Sinn Féin sympathiser, that 'unless some opposition came forward more formidable than the motley individuals who contested the [1915–16] by-elections, Redmond would dominate Irish politics for at least two elections after home rule'.[95] Maume also emphasises, however, that this electoral success did not reflect the popularity of the Home Rule movement so much as the absence of any organised or willing opposition. Possible dissidents at this stage either would not offer any opposition (the Irish Volunteers) or could not mount a serious challenge (Sinn Féin and William O'Brien's All for Ireland League). Alan O'Day, by way of contrast, is inclined to stress the Home Rule victories won as late as 1917–18, even after the great reverses experienced in North Roscommon and subsequent contests.[96]

Despite all the difficulties, Home Rule was still viable in the early summer of 1916. Indeed, in a paradoxical sense the vestigial strength of the movement is illustrated by the way in which it was able to cope with

some monumental failures and difficulties. The topsy-turvy world of suspended Home Rule was ridden with difficulties: the Irish leadership had
simultaneously attained and lost their historic goal, and were simultaneously troublesome backbenchers and the masters of a new political
system. In fact the only certainty which the suspension of Home Rule
offered was that the Irish Party could no longer effectively agitate for its
sacred principle. Yet, by the time of the Lloyd George failure, there was
still no coherent opposition to the party.

The war brought petty insult and humiliation. Redmond's speech at
Woodenbridge made sense in the light of his wider ambitions, but as
some of his colleagues felt at the time, it was a grim error of judgement. If
he had contented himself with his Commons statement of 3 August,
then all might have been well; but he felt compelled to go further. Again,
the blame may be laid partly with the ambiguities of the constitutional
position. Redmond believed that the goal of the party had been conceded
by the British, and he was therefore searching for a reciprocal gesture,
which at the same time corresponded with his view of Ireland's role
within the empire. But the Home Rule Act was a chimera, and Redmond
succeeded only in encouraging thousands of his own supporters to march
to their deaths. This close identification with the British war effort also
meant that the panic-stricken blunders of government policy, such as
over the threat of conscription in 1916–18, were blamed on the Home
Rulers. Yet, in 1914–15, Redmond's strategies had still not irreparably
damaged the wider political standing of his movement. The war brought
a measure of agrarian prosperity that seemed for the moment to
compensate for the harvest of human lives at Gallipoli and on the
Western Front.

Even the Easter Rising did not, in itself, overturn the party or its cause.
The total number of insurgents (perhaps 1500) underlines the extent to
which militant separatism was a marginal phenomenon in Irish society;
there were, by way of contrast, over 150,000 men in the Redmondite
National Volunteers. The Home Rulers were initially appalled by the
rising, and were then appalled by the British response. Dillon and others
were confident that both the number and the pattern of the executions
were disastrous in moulding public opinion. There seems little reason to
doubt this view, except to note the possibility that latent sympathies for
the rebels among ostensible Home Rulers might have been more
widespread than Dillon and others assumed.[97] There was some attempt
by the Home Rule leaders to identify themselves with the rebel sacrifice,
but it is impossible to say whether this was regarded as naked opportunism or as a commendable response to patriotic sacrifice. There is some
evidence from the Dillon papers to suggest that the public did not, in

fact, respond with undue cynicism to these efforts.[98] But with the advent of the Lloyd George initiative came the need for restraint, and for two critical months the Home Rule leadership was unable to supply the type of outrageous patriotic rhetoric that was so clearly needed.

The Lloyd George business was, therefore, critical. If a deal had been patched together in June 1916, and if the Home Rulers had been able to cash in on the rebels' achievement, then radical separatism might well have been fatally impeded. It is certainly possible that, as the southern Unionists argued, the swift establishment of a Home Rule parliament would have been accompanied by the continued radicalisation of Irish politics, and either the domination of Sinn Féin or a renewed rebellion. It would indeed be wrong to discount the possibility of a militant separatist rising against a Home Rule administration – this was mooted by the Unionist wreckers in 1916, and was certainly envisaged by separatists like Terence MacSwiney.[99] But it is impossible to offer anything beyond the most hesitant and speculative judgement on such issues. What seems beyond doubt is that the humiliation of the Home Rulers on 22 July 1916, and their subsequent torpor, simultaneously discredited the politics of consent and created the space for radical alternatives. It would, of course, be a gross simplification to blame the fall of Home Rule on the anger-management problems of a rubicund Wiltshire squire, but the temptation is there, nonetheless.

# CHAPTER 9

# CHANGING THE QUESTION
# 1916–20

It does not require a particularly wild leap of imagination to envision the years between 1916 and 1920–1 as a kind of historical consummation, the final resolution of Ireland's 'long' nineteenth century. Many of the half-formulated themes of Home Rule politics and of the wider Anglo-Irish relationship had a forced and vivid flowering in these years at the end of the Union. For some of these political blooms (for the southern Unionists, for the 'conference plus business' ideal, for Redmond-style Home Rule) this was apparently a final effloresence, but the political richness of this period extends beyond the last decadent flourish of the old politics. These years saw new growth in Irish affairs, and not just in the obvious sense that Sinn Féin and a new six-county Ulster Unionism emerged finally as predominant. These years also saw the first sustained and significant lobbying over a devolved or federal United Kingdom and, as a prescient John Kendle remarked in 1989, this 'was a vibrant and important debate of which we have not heard the last'.[1]

Underlying the profound convolutions within Irish politics lay the stimulus of the Great War. Those in Ireland who had encouraged recruiting (particularly the Home Rule leadership) were weakened by the unexpectedly protracted and bloody nature of the conflict. The traditional farmer support of the Home Rule movement was shaken by wartime taxation and by the enforcement of compulsory tillage orders. On the other hand, radical separatism was encouraged by the war, and by the reverses experienced by the British. The Easter Rising is virtually unimaginable without the backdrop of the European conflict, and even assuming that the insurgents had embarked upon a peacetime rebellion, official repression would probably have been less severe and therefore less controversial. The disappearence of opportunities to emigrate during the war created a population of thwarted and economically ambitious young men over whom the threat of conscription periodically loomed. It is frequently argued that radical separatism drew upon the social and economic resentments of young Catholics blocked by the conventions of the old regime in Ireland, and such arguments have an enhanced relevance in the light of wartime constraints.[2]

War had a direct and crucial impact upon the British administration. Senior British ministers were preoccupied by the conflict, and often (as in the case of Asquith, Bonar Law and Long) experienced bitter personal loss. On the other hand, the demands of the war effort, particularly the need to mollify opinion in the Dominions and the United States, underlined the need for action, or at least the appearance of action, when often ministers had little interest in revisiting the complexities of Irish self-government. These countervailing pressures help to explain the otherwise curious politics of the later war years. The all-consuming nature of the conflict tended to mitigate traditional British party convictions on Ireland, and tended to dissipate the pressures within British politics for an Irish settlement. At the same time, external forces underlined the need for action, however symbolic.

The result of these apparently contradictory influences was a period of exceptional political fluidity and fertility when the British government was distracted, certainly, but when it was also relatively uncommitted and open to argument. This was a time when (to adapt F. S. Oliver's label) 'the young men who saw visions' were encouraged in their federalist speculations, and when a wider body of political experience was stimulated into debate and diplomacy.[3] It is certainly possible that this effort was merely a kind of political play-within-a-play, stage-managed by David Lloyd George (now Prime Minister) for the pleasure of President Wilson and the Dominion leaders, and enacted within the wider and crucial drama of the Great War. Yet, whatever the motives for the production, and however short its run, this lesser political piece generated ideas and reactions that had an independent and lasting significance.

The extraordinary volatility of Irish and British politics at this time provides a warning against any overly simplistic analysis of the decline of the Home Rule movement. The Home Rulers were unquestionably demoralised and damaged by the collapse of the Lloyd George negotiations in July 1916. There followed a period of relative passivity, during which radical separatism gained in terms of organisation and electoral credibility. The internment of many separatists in the aftermath of the rising created a more cohesive and discrete revolutionary elite than might otherwise have been the case: the internment camps, with their relatively lax conditions, served as revolutionary academies for a thrusting generation of young radicals. The release of these prisoners in late 1916 augmented the ranks of the separatists, and by early 1917 this strength was being converted into electoral success.

The capture of a succession of safe Home Rule seats – North

Roscommon in February 1917, South Longford in May, East Clare in July, and Kilkenny City in August – were body blows to the punch-drunk Home Rule cause. There was already, in 1917, worrying evidence that local Home Rule institutions and leaders were slipping into the Sinn Féin camp – that what David Fitzpatrick and Patrick Maume have identified as the 'vampirism' of the old Home Rule movement, its tendency to colonise national life, was being subverted by the separatist undead.[4] The reorganisation of advanced nationalism at the Sinn Féin ard-fheis (main conference) of October 1917 meant that the Home Rulers now faced – for the first time – a coherent, nationally organised, opposition.

And yet this pattern of separatist progress might well have been disrupted had Redmond secured a settlement and begun to exercise state power within a Home Rule system. Even during these months of rapid slippage, the Home Rulers retained a considerable following, particularly in Ulster where Joe Devlin was well liked, and where the party machine, the Ancient Order of Hibernians, continued to dominate. There was thus a residual base from which to launch a recovery, were the opportunity to present itself; and, with the British government under pressure to act, opportunities did in fact arise.

On 16 May 1917, Lloyd George wrote to Redmond, offering him a choice between the immediate enactment of Home Rule for the twenty-six counties and a national convention within which to debate the wider future of self-government.[5] The letter came only five days after Joseph McGuinness's narrow victory for Sinn Féin in South Longford, and given the separatist challenge, Redmond evidently did not feel strong enough to settle for Home Rule and an indefinite partition arrangement. He may also have felt that, with the need to recruit American support, the British might have been ready to apply pressure on the Ulster Unionists to acquiesce in a unitary settlement. With the wisdom of hindsight, this call might be seen as questionable: the Ulster Unionists were reluctant to put the demands of the war effort or the empire above their local needs, partition came anyway, and Redmond might conceivably have seized and exercised power in the twenty-six counties to the advantage of his Home Rule cause. Home Rule would not have fully satisfied the separatist aspirations of a growing number of Irish people, but once the Ulster difficulty had been addressed, it might well have provided 'the freedom to achieve freedom'. However, even Redmond's choice of a conference might have produced a deal that secured the future of constitutional nationalism, and halted the progress of the separatist juggernaut.

The conference that was called in July 1917 – the Irish Convention – has a disputed parentage. Its chairman, Sir Horace Plunkett, was inclined to see the origins of the convention in his own Recess Committee, a cross-party body that had met in the parliamentary recess of 1895 to thrash out ideas for the improvement of Irish agriculture.[6] But there were other claimants: F. S. Oliver, writing as 'Pacificus' in 1910, had looked forward to a wide-ranging conference that would address the Irish question and other constitutional problems. In 1913, in *The Alternatives to Civil War*, he reiterated the call for 'some comparatively small body of persons who will meet in private and whose labours are bound to cover some considerable period of time'.[7] In the spring of 1914 Oliver's federalist colleagues were also encouraging the notion of an all-party conference.[8] More recently, in October 1916, a proposal for a conference had been mooted by Joseph Devlin in the House of Commons. In February 1917, L. S. Amery had also called for a representative conference of Irishmen.[9] Denis Gywnn, on the other hand, suggested that the crucial immediate stimulus came from Redmond, and that the Irish leader had floated the idea in conversation with a leading Liberal, Lord Crewe, over dinner on 15 May 1917.[10]

In a wider sense, the convention may be seen as the apogee of the 'conference plus business' approach championed by William O'Brien and other centrists in the early Edwardian period (see Chapter 6). It should be stressed, however, that O'Brien himself eventually repudiated the notion that the convention was rooted in any way in his own ideals and achievement: 'the conference, conciliation and consent child was stolen by gypsy statesmen only to be disfigured to make it pass for their own', he fumed in a characteristically brutal passage published in 1918.[11] The convention, he added, was 'a showy exhibition of puppets for spectacular effect in America'. Setting aside his racist imagery, there is some truth in O'Brien's argument that the conference ideal had been annexed by Lloyd George with a view to mollifying American opinion. It is also true that the classic expression of O'Brienite centrism – the Land Conference of December 1902 – was different from the Irish Convention in certain respects, being smaller and more independent in origin. However, at the time O'Brien welcomed the initiative. Moreover, the convention was like earlier O'Brienite experiments in so far as it was a largely self-selected and generally moderate group of Irishmen who were, for the most part, genuinely interested in a deal. The exceptions to this broad characterisation were the Ulster Unionists, and even here there was some limited flexibility.

The Irish Convention brought together some ninety-five representatives from different parties and interests under the expansive chairmanship of Sir Horace Plunkett.[12] The first meeting was held on 25 July 1917, and the venue was the Regent House, Trinity College Dublin. It has long been recognised that the absence of Sinn Féin and the cussedness of the

Ulster Unionists were the two critical barriers to the convention's success. To this extent, the convention has often been seen as a fore-doomed enterprise. But this judgement reflects the benefits of hindsight. The tractability, or otherwise, of the Unionists will be explored shortly. Sinn Féin did, indeed, boycott the convention, and the sole delegate who had close connections with the party, Edward MacLysaght, left in February 1918 before its proceedings ended. But there were others associated with the enterprise who had some advanced or separatist leanings: the writer G. W. Russell (Æ) was a member of the convention, and Erskine Childers, Cruise O'Brien and Dermot Coffey (all gun-runners for the Irish Volunteers before the war) were employed in the secretariat.[13] Moreover, setting aside any question of political ethics, and judging from a pragmatic Home Rule perspective, it might be argued that the absence of Sinn Féin was not at this stage an impossible barrier to progress.

Sinn Féin was unquestionably gathering momentum, but when the conference was called there had as yet been only two by-election victories for the party, and in one of these, South Longford, McGuinness's majority was only thirty-two in a poll of 2954. Moreover, the party's critical ardfheis occurred only in October. In other words, Sinn Féin was important, but not as important as it would swiftly become. The absence of Sinn Féin was, viewed from the perspective of 1918 and after, disastrous. But in July 1917 it was still possible that the Home Rule party would be re-energised by the results of the convention. That is to say, Redmond might in theory have profited from the absence of Sinn Féin, had a deal been forthcoming and some form of Home Rule swiftly enacted. As it was, the numbingly protracted sessions of the convention meant that the chances of a speedy settlement soon receded. While senior members of the Home Rule delegation orated and bickered and junketed, the Sinn Féin movement consolidated its hold on the Irish electorate. But there was nothing predetermined about this: the Home Rulers were unable to use the convention to force a settlement, and instead came to be suffocated by its proceedings. There was in effect a political vacuum, and this was speedily filled by Sinn Féin.

Nor, as has been hinted, was the undoubted cussedness of the Ulster Unionists an insuperable barrier to a deal. It was indeed likely that the Ulster Unionists would not be budged, but the inevitability of their intransigence should not be assumed. There were certainly structural constraints on the Ulster Unionists' mobility at the convention: their representatives were not in any sense plenipotentiaries, and indeed were specifically instructed to report to Belfast.[14] Other delegates, particularly the southern Unionists under Viscount Midleton, were largely untrammelled by outside authority, and were therefore better able to deal. But, while these organisational problems must be given due attention, there were some more hopeful indications within the Ulster Unionist team. One of the most effective members of the convention was a Belfast solicitor, Sir Alexander McDowell. McDowell, though a government nominee, was close to the northerners and was a moderating influence within their counsels. He had the force of personality and intellectual authority to override even the northern leaders, H. T. Barrie and Lord Londonderry. McDowell's early death may well have scuppered the possibility of a broadly based deal including the Ulstermen. The Home Ruler Stephen Gywnn lamented in 1919 that 'in losing him we lost certainly the strongest will in his group; and it was a will for settlement'.[15]

But McDowell was not the only imaginative political strategist associated with the northerners. Lord Londonderry, like other Unionists at this time, was interested in a sweeping constitutional revision, and on 15 November 1917 he offered to present a federalist proposal to the convention. This notion was swiftly kicked into touch by his party colleagues. Indeed, there is some evidence that Londonderry himself soon got cold feet: He wrote on 26 November that, while he was indeed willing to move towards a federation, he judged that the time was not yet right for such a major change.[16] But the episode simultaneously underlines both the reach of federalism and the existence of a degree of political fertility in the otherwise unpromising territory of the Ulster Unionist delegation.

The delegation's leader, Barrie, also occasionally betrayed an interest in doing a deal.[17] In late 1917, Barrie was beginning to talk privately about the possibility of an all-Ireland parliament and a unitary settlement. In the critical subcommittee of the convention, the clashes between Ulster Unionists and nationalists at this time were occurring not over the issue of partition, but rather over the taxing powers of the proposed Irish parliament. The northerners were apparently increasingly interested in defending the principle of a customs union between Britain and Ireland, rather than in sustaining their partitionist war-cries.

Of course, this seeming readiness to trade may, as the nationalists suspected, have been a feint, designed to promote the image of flexibility and to thrust the responsibility for failure on to others. But there is some evidence to suggest that, despite the truculence of certain Ulster Unionist delegates, and despite the structural restraints within which the entire team worked, there was a fleeting moment during which a deal might have been agreed. Carson, crucially, seems to have been prepared to regard a unitary settlement with a degree of sympathy at this time.[18] Trevor West, the biographer of Plunkett, considers that in January 1918 'the Ulster Unionists, behind the scenes, seem to have been considering some form of compromise'.[19] And Midleton, whose ideas nearly carried the day, recorded that on 3 January, after a junket at the Dublin home of Lord Granard, he was privately assured by Barrie that 'you can count on us [in pursuing a settlement]. We shall certainly not be against you'.[20]

So the Irish Convention was, in the end, more than an elitist talking-shop. The trouble was, so far as the Home Rulers were concerned, that the end was a long time in coming. Yet it is apparent that a kind of consensus was fleetingly attained, and that a deal was very nearly struck. The critical turning-point came on 25 November 1917, when Midleton, the chairman of the Irish Unionist Alliance, announced a dramatic shift in the strategic thinking of some southern Unionists. Midleton proposed that Ireland be given a Home Rule administration with sweeping powers, including the right to levy internal taxes. Customs duties would remain under the jurisdiction of Westminster, although Midleton was later prepared to accept that these might be collected by the new Irish authorities. A variety of safeguards were proposed to protect the position of the Unionists throughout the island. For a brief period – until early January 1918 – it looked as if Midleton's initiative would provide the basis for a political breakthrough.

It is certainly important to be realistic about the origins and limitations of this proposal. In a sense it reflected the plummeting weakness of southern Unionism, and the need to strike terms while there was still some residual strength left in the cause. The initiative also reflected Lord Midleton's unnaturally great freedom of manoeuvre within the convention, and the chasm that had opened up between him and the Ulster Unionists since 1913. The war was taking its toll of the southern Unionist community, in terms both of very high casualty levels at the Front and of rapid political retreat. For southern Unionists the rise of militant separatism was a shocking phenomenon, while their key political patron, Lord Lansdowne, was discredited in November 1917 after publicly advocating a negotiated peace settlement with the Germans. Midleton was thus the effective commander of an increasingly disoriented and weakened community. He had, however, a very considerable (perhaps a deceiving) amount of political autonomy at the convention, with only the most nominal responsibility to the Irish Unionist Alliance.

Midleton had also complained of Ulster Unionist high-handedness from at least April 1914, and the beginning of the convention in July 1917 was marked by what seemed to the southern Unionists like a characteristic piece of northern arrogance.[21] The southerners were summoned to the Dublin headquarters of the Ulster Unionist delegation, were kept waiting for an hour, and were in the end briskly instructed to oppose anybody 'connected with the government of Ireland in the administration of the law' who might be seeking the chairmanship of the Convention. This insult was compounded by the fact that the northern ultimatum was designed to keep a southern Unionist lawyer, J. H. M. Campbell, out of the chair.[22] Midleton's initiative emphatically did not, therefore, reflect any pre-formulated agreement with the Ulster Unionists; indeed, it may be regarded as an expression of division and desperation rather than harmony.

Nor was the plan regarded with any great favour by many nationalists. Control of customs was now widely seen as an essential feature of national self-determination, and many in the convention supported the notion of complete fiscal autonomy. Moreover, even those nationalists who were prepared to settle were worried that, having conceded the principle of fiscal autonomy, they would find that the Midleton deal was whittled down in subsequent negotiation and that they were politically exposed. In this calculation much depended on the attitude of the Ulster Unionists, for if the northerners held out, these nationalist strategists thought that the government would extort further concessions from Redmond. Redmond himself had greater political courage than some of his colleagues, and it is probable, too, that as an old Parnellite he was moved by the prospect of attaining a union between popular national politics and the patriots of the landlord class. But he was not foolhardy, and when the Midleton deal was submitted to the full convention in January 1918, Redmond tabled an amendment which offered support, provided that the government moved to enforce the deal.

It was at this point that an agreement might have been reached. Redmond and the southern Unionists were 'on message', while even the Ulster Unionists were wavering, as was indicated by Barrie's evidently sincere assurances to Midleton on 3 January. Not all Ulster Unionists were going to be satisfied and not all of the nationalists who sought fiscal autonomy were enthusiastic about a deal that reserved the control of Irish customs revenue to Westminster. But while there were serious difficulties, many at the time (including Midleton) thought that a deal was in the offing. Everything hinged upon the timing, and a speedy settlement of the essentials. And at this point the chairman of the convention, Plunkett, intervened.

Rather than clearing the timetable to rush through an agreement, Plunkett chose to assert his authority by initiating a lengthy debate on land purchase and by taking reports from the various committees of the convention. If the advocates of a settlement had indeed achieved any momentum, it was now utterly dissipated. The doubts of the extremists hardened and, given the time lag, could now receive full expression. The supporters of fiscal autonomy, led by Bishop Patrick O'Donnell of Raphoe, gained ground and compelled Redmond to withdraw his support from Midleton. This meant in turn that the Ulster Unionists, who had been under pressure to settle, could regroup around a hardline stand without appearing to be wreckers. The Midleton deal was, in consequence, ruined.

Redmond had long been ill, and he died on 6 March: with his demise an eloquent voice for moderation was silenced. His successor, Dillon, was much less consensual and more sympathetic to the aspirations and strategies of Sinn Féin. Barrie, the Ulster Unionist leader who had once wavered towards a settlement, was now reined in by his advisory committee in Belfast. On 25 February 1918 the Ulster Unionist delegates met with these 'advisers' and jointly reinforced the traditional partitionist demand.[23] Divisions were also opening up within some of the key institutions of Irish Protestantism, such as the General Synod of the Church of Ireland. Hardliners undermined Midleton: a Southern Unionist Committee was formed to represent loyalist opponents of the Midleton deal, and on 4 March a 'Call to Unionists' was published which reinforced a fundamentalist line.[24]

The situation on the Western Front served to eliminate any vestigial hopes of an agreement. The massive German offensive of 21 March for a time swept all before it. It seemed that the Germans, having broken through Hubert Gough's Fifth Army, would reach the Channel coast and turn the Allied lines. There was a manpower crisis: on 28 March the cabinet agreed in principle to extend conscription to include Ireland. It was in this context that the final report of the convention, comprising the main document (which called for Home Rule), two minority reports and five 'notes', arrived at the cabinet table in 10 Downing Street. Though it must have seemed logical to tie the convention's key recommendation to the needs of the war effort, this 'dual policy' of conscription and devolution, which was agreed by ministers on 5 April, signalled the end of a political era. A constitutionalist strategy that was struggling for the oxygen of political support was now connected to, and suffocated by, the military draft.

Why did the Irish Convention fail? Midleton identified some traditional bogeymen – the Ulster Unionists and the Catholic bishops – but he was inclined to place the burden of guilt elsewhere.[25] For him the convention was handicapped from the start by its organisational arrangements, and by the personality of the chairman, Horace Plunkett. Even allowing for Midleton's personal prejudices, there is much to be said for this case. Certainly the convention, which after all comprised only ninety-five members, had an overly baroque structure with a Grand Committee of twenty members, smaller dedicated bodies and eventually a senior subcommittee. There is also much to be said for the case against

Plunkett. Plunkett was a patriot and a philanthropist, who had done much for the improvement and reorganisation of Irish agriculture. He could also be self-important, tactless and lacking in judgement. He was highly pragmatic and fluid in his convictions: the Irish-American judge, D. F. Cohalan, observed that Plunkett was 'always three laps behind' the political pace-setters. He shifted from Liberal Unionism in the 1890s to support for Home Rule before the first World War, and established his own Irish Dominion League in 1919.[26] In 1922 he accepted W. T. Cosgrave's offer of a place in the Senate of the Free State. But this remarkable trek meant that, outside a small cadre of devoted friends and admirers, he was distrusted right across the entire Irish political spectrum. He had, in truth, no talent whatsoever for politics. His most recent biographer, Trevor West, has remarked that 'all his life Plunkett was lured to politics as a moth to the flame with consequences which were as regularly fraught with disaster'. West has also underlined Plunkett's 'unerring capacity for evenhandedly offending both sides'.[27]

This was the man who sought and won, in controversial circumstances, the chairmanship of the Irish Convention on 25 July 1917. Plunkett's tactics and strategies were disastrous from the start. He believed that, by giving delegates a free hand to debate, they would exhaust themselves and succumb to compromise. Thus the convention began with a two-week adjournment to enable its members to prepare their arguments; and this was followed by a two-month 'presentation stage' during which different visions of the future of Irish government were discussed at length. Plunkett told Redmond in August 1917 that 'personally I hope that the Presentation stage will extend over a couple of months...the more we fight over controversial issues under absolutely non-committal conditions, the quicker we shall move in the negotiation stage which must follow'.[28] The result of this was indeed an agreement, though not quite of the type which the chairman might have expected. A cross-party rebellion took place, which resulted in the formation of a senior subcommittee comprising nine leading delegates and excluding Plunkett.

At this point Plunkett, the country's most distinguished centrist politician, reportedly 'said that he was going to attend no matter what happened, he would get in by force if by no other means...he [also] frankly said that he was going to break up the Convention, and was going to make use of his Agricultural Organisations all over the country for this end'.[29] In the event, there was no force and no break-up; and yet it was within this new subcommittee that some limited political progress was made in November and December 1917, and it was here, too, that the groundwork was laid for the Midleton deal. When deadlock occurred over the issue of customs, Plunkett saw a chance to reassert his authority. He intervened (against advice) to impose a form of exam paper on the committee members, requiring nationalists and Unionists to elaborate their views of the Irish economy. But this merely served to harden divisions and resentments.[30]

Otherwise Plunkett took it upon himself to compose sometimes daily reports of convention business to King George V. These documents were misjudged and profoundly unhelpful: they were written in a wry and judgemental vein, but were also condescending and often partial. Although nominally destined for the King, Plunkett desired that they should be widely circulated; it was said that George V alone had left them unread. Inevitably, they fell into the hands of those, such as Carson, whose words and actions were being judged and condemned. The result was, yet again, the generation of at least one monumental row within the convention – and lasting ill-will.[31]

But the nadir of Plunkett's chairmanship came with his decision to postpone the debate and division upon Midleton's Home Rule proposal. Midleton was understandably very bitter about this, and was inclined to believe that Plunkett was exacting a form of revenge for his exclusion from the key subcommittee.[32] Plunkett certainly combined bad judgement with occasional over-confidence and self-assertion: Midleton, therefore, may have been right. It may also have been the case, as Midleton and others certainly believed, that Plunkett's delaying tactics in January 1918 effectively spoilt any chance of a settlement. Of course, the wider significance of this depends upon how great the likelihood of a deal is thought to have been at this time. If the convention is viewed as a massive irrelevance, Plunkett's actions may be discounted. But if the evidence for a possible settlement is accepted, Plunkett's debate on land purchase can be seen as a very costly exercise in self-indulgence. It is just possible that this well-meaning but vain and meddling man may have ruined an historic deal. It is a compelling irony, therefore, that the last effective chance for a peaceful settlement in Ireland may have been wrecked by the country's most prominent centrist.

On 5 April 1918, the convention agreed a report by a majority of forty-four votes to twenty-nine; but given that the dissidents included both the Ulster Unionists and the fiscal autonomists, it could not be claimed with any conviction that the necessary 'substantial agreement' had been reached. Moreover, the fact that the government was prepared to link the implementation of the report with the enactment of conscription immediately ruined both the credibility of the convention and the residual popularity of Home Rule. This signalled the end of Home Rule as a popular cause.

Dillon, as a matter of both strategy and personal sympathy, speedily retreated from the exposed and consensual positions occupied by Redmond, and aligned his party with the Sinn Féin stand. After the official announcement of the dual policy of Home Rule and conscription, Dillon led his men out of the Commons. This seemed to be an obeisance to Sinn Féin's strategy of abstentionism. The Home Rulers united with the separatists in the anti-conscription pledge of 21 April 1918, and in a great one-day general strike held on 23 April. But this radicalisation of the Home Rule movement came too late to stem the electoral tide: Arthur Griffith, the founder of Sinn Féin, defeated J. F. O'Hanlon, a Home Ruler, in East Cavan on 20 June.

The democratic strength of the separatists was further enhanced by the Representation of the People Act, which came into operation in time for the general election of December 1918. The separatist cause was strong among the young and with women, and the Act gave the vote to men aged twenty-one and over and to women aged over thirty. This reform, allied with the disastrous history of Home Rule, meant that Sinn Féin secured a sweeping victory in December, winning seventy-three parliamentary seats, as opposed to the six gained by Dillon and his supporters. There is certainly a case for arguing that Home Rule was stronger than this meagre result suggests, but in the end such arguments are about the extent of the humiliation sustained rather than its reality.[33]

At this point it may be appropriate to consider a variant of the Home Rule creed which had been gaining momentum in 1917–18, at the time of the convention, only to be scuppered by the conscription crisis of April 1918: federalism. The wider history of the federalist cause need only be outlined here. Isaac Butt, it will be recalled, was one of the earliest prominent advocates of a federalist revision of the British constitution, arguing for the establishment of subordinate parliaments and administrations in England, Scotland and Ireland. Butt seems to have wished for a genuinely federal system, with sovereignty divided between the local assemblies and Westminster: the Irish parliament, for example, was to have 'supreme control' in Ireland.[34] In the end, and paradoxically, Butt had perhaps a much greater intellectual influence over Unionists than with the Home Rulers. Many Unionists came to believe that subordinate Irish, Scots and English parliaments would satisfy local aspirations, and also free Westminster for the task of governing the empire. Unlike Butt, however, they were not 'true' federalists, since they took it for granted that Westminster was, and would remain, sovereign.

With the relegation of Home Rule in British politics after 1893, these federal or, strictly speaking, 'devolutionist' speculations faded. But they were revived between 1910 and 1914 in the context of the debates over the powers of the House of Lords, and over the third Home Rule Bill. At this time a group of earnest young Unionist intellectuals, who were often disciples of the 'apostle of Empire', Lord Milner, pressed the case for constitutional reform within the United Kingdom. These efforts were again set aside with the outbreak of the Great War, but after 1916 – when the question of Irish government re-emerged in the British consciousness – the federalists resumed their assault on the political elite.

Leading the cause between 1916 and the end of the war were William Waldegrave Palmer, second Earl of Selborne, and Frederick Scott Oliver.[35] Selborne had been High Commissioner in South Africa between 1905 and 1910, and had been closely associated with the discussions at Pretoria and Cape Town in 1908–9 which had led to the creation of the Union of South Africa. Fred Oliver was a wealthy businessman and polemicist who was deeply interested in the history and operation of federal government in the United States and South Africa. His first major published work, *The Life of Alexander Hamilton: An Essay in American Union* (1906), seems to have been a critical influence on Selborne and other advocates of South African unity. Oliver came back to prominence in and after 1910, through his letters to the press and a series of pamphlets, all propagating the federalist cause. In his 'Pacificus' letters (published originally in *The Times* and collected as *Federalism and Home Rule* in 1910) he drew analogies between the British constitutional impasse and both the Philadephia Conference of 1787 and the South African Conference of 1908. He hoped that the dispute over the British House of Lords would open the way to a broader reform of government in the United Kingdom. During the third Home Rule crisis he confirmed his reputation as a brilliant polemicist (and as an Ulster sceptic) through two other federalist tracts, *The Alternatives to Civil War* (1913) and *What Federalism is Not* (1914).[36]

Perhaps the most striking aspect of the federalist debate in the years 1914–18 is the speed with which the idea colonised the British political elite, and the equal celerity with which retreat and collapse ensued. Federalist ideas had a currency in British politics before 1916, as has been chronicled; but even during the third Home Rule crisis, these ideas had a comparatively slight impact. While some of the key players, such as Carson and Austen Chamberlain, expressed a muted sympathy with Oliver's evangelism in the winter of 1913–14, there is little evidence to suggest that the federalists shaped the course of the Home Rule debate in any serious way. Equally, when Robert Brand, Lionel Curtis, Edward Grigg and Lionel Hichens, members of Milner's circle (or 'kindergarten') and admirers of Oliver, drew up a federalist programme of action in May 1914, they won a sympathetic but limited response from the party leaders whom they approached.[37] Even Lord Milner, the patriarch of the 'kindergarten', commented: 'I don't think it will come to anything.'[38]

However, this situation changed very speedily after 1916, and by May 1918 the government whip, Freddie Guest, calculated that in the Commons there were around 100 federalist sympathisers among the Tories, some 150 among the Official Liberals, twenty-five or so among the Lloyd George Liberals, and around twenty in the Labour parliamentary party.[39] There were at least two fundamental explanations for this turnabout. The failure of the Lloyd George initiative in 1916 simultaneously highlighted the desperate need for progress on the Irish issue and the extent to which traditional approaches were seemingly useless. The war had also served to weaken the sharpness of earlier convictions, and many Tories in particular were no longer true believers in Ulster or, indeed, in an unreformed Union. There was thus a strategic opening for the federalists, a circumstance underlined by the extent to which Oliver was independently establishing his presence at the centre of political debate. The brilliant, if transient, successes of the federalists hinged upon the ruthless and energetic manner in which this opportunity was exploited.

The federalist assault took a variety of forms. It began in the summer of 1916 with two letters, published on 8 and 18 August in the ultra-Tory *Morning Post*, in which Selborne (having considered the alternatives of dominion status and the Union) detailed a scheme of federal government for Ireland and the wider United Kingdom.[40] Public letters of this kind were, by now, a familiar federalist tactic. An equally familiar, but perhaps more distinctive gambit was the pamphlet fusillade: these tracts either appeared in the context of a major political conference, or advocated such a conference, or (very occasionally) did both. Oliver's *Alexander Hamilton* was a key stimulus behind the Pretoria Conference of 1908; the 'Pacificus' letters were issued in October 1910, at the time of the British constitutional talks; Oliver's *The Alternatives to Civil War* recommended a conference as a way out of the Home Rule impasse. In March 1917 Oliver published his *Ireland and the Imperial Conference: Is there a Way to a Settlement?*, in which he argued that the wartime gathering of dominion leaders could set in motion some of the processes by which a permanent settlement of the Irish question could be achieved. Accepting one of the devices used by Lloyd George in the 1916 negotiations, Oliver suggested that a great imperial assembly could meet after the war and be entrusted with the task of defining a system of government for Ireland.[41]

In June 1917 the federalist leaders were again stimulated into action by an impending constitutional conference, the Irish Convention. On this occasion Selborne and Oliver joined forces to produce a tract, *Suggestions for the Better Government of the United Kingdom*. There was much here that was already familiar: once again the alternatives to federalism – a 'centralised union' and 'the independent status of a dominion' – were considered and duly dismissed. The form of federal administration was also familiar: England, Ireland and Scotland would each get a legislature and responsible executive for their 'national' concerns, while the common needs of the three kingdoms would be treated within a supreme parliament. The possibility that a Welsh national assembly might be created was mooted and left open. Under the Selborne–Oliver scheme, the 'national' parliaments would be granted wide-ranging powers, but (as with all the federalist templates) customs and excise were to be specifically reserved for the parliament and government of the United Kingdom. Another article of federalist faith was that each of the constituent nations would be represented within the central, supreme executive and legislature.

Setting aside these two critical issues, Selborne and Oliver were prepared to be generous (indeed, thoroughly radical) in their allotment of powers to the national assemblies. The Irish government, for example, was to have wide authority over taxation, control of the police, old age pensions and national insurance. It was to have virtually complete control over land purchase: the sinking funds created by the Land Purchase Acts were to be handed over to the new regime, which would also control the annual instalments paid by purchasing tenants. As Selborne and Oliver remarked, presciently, 'there is always the danger that…these payments will be represented in a popular agitation as a tribute unjustly exacted from Ireland by "the English".'[42] All remaining leasehold property would be bought out – through compulsory purchase, if need be – and vested with the new Irish administration. Separate national conventions would (in the Selborne–Oliver formula) decide the form and structure of the Irish and other legislatures: 'it is not necessary that there should be uniformity in these constitutions. Their variety will not impair the unity, not threaten the security of the United Kingdom'.[43]

Selborne and Oliver seem to have envisaged that their *Suggestions* would become a key discussion document for the Irish Convention. In this they were profoundly disappointed, and Oliver, for one, laid the blame squarely at the feet of Horace Plunkett.[44] It had been the federalists' hope that their *Suggestions* would be widely circulated among the convention members, but in the event Plunkett, who was prepared to breach etiquette when the dissemination of his own thoughts was at stake, seems to have had qualms about this, and to have sanctioned only a very limited distribution of the manifesto. It is possible that Plunkett did not welcome outside interventions of this kind, but it should also be conceded that even if the document had been put into all the members' hands, it would probably still have failed.

Some of the Ulster Unionists, like Londonderry, certainly had federalist sympathies, but these were stifled by other party elders.[45] Carson had also played with federalist notions, but he did not feel able, given the widespread hostility, to give a lead on the issue: 'one thing is pretty clear', Oliver wrote in March 1918, '*he [Carson] can accept*, but *he cannot himself stand up and propose* a federal settlement. Ergo: someone else must put it forward and Carson must then reluctantly agree.'[46] And even supposing that the *Suggestions* had passed muster with the Unionists, they would have been rejected by the supporters of fiscal autonomy. Bishop O'Donnell and William Martin Murphy would not have sanctioned a document which, despite its expansive definition of national autonomy, was firm on the principle of a customs union. Moreover, at a time when Irish nationalism was embracing the idea of dominion status, the strictures of Selborne and Oliver on this issue were unlikely to have carried much weight.[47]

Blaming Plunkett perhaps made sense for Oliver, in that it protected him from some of the difficult realities of popular Irish sympathies. And, indeed, in so far as the federalists achieved success at this time, it was largely within the realm of high politics, and particularly within the confines of the Unionist elite. Selborne had long been a significant figure in the British political establishment, but Oliver (who was much more of an outsider) was also making progress in this sphere. John Kendle has observed that 'throughout the war [Oliver] had been dining regularly on Monday evenings with Lord Milner, Sir Edward Carson, Waldorf Astor and Geoffrey Dawson', and it is clear from Oliver's letters to his brother that Lloyd George was an occasional (and self-invited) guest at these meals.[48] In November 1917, Oliver was appointed as secretary to the Cabinet Committee on 'the Economic Offensive', and this brought him into even greater contact with ministers and, in particular, the committee chairman, Edward Carson. As Oliver remarked in January 1918, 'having a room within a few yards of several members of the War Cabinet, and their private secretaries, and Cabinet secretary, and all the rest of it, does enable when one has an idea of any sort, to get it considered'.[49]

This social activity and war work was complemented by the relentless pursuit of the federalist ideal. In February 1918, influenced by his admiration for Carson, Oliver cast his arguments in the form of an Ulster Unionist apologetic, *Ulster and a Federal Settlement*. This reframed some familiar material within the equally familiar context of a constitutional conference. The convention was still sitting, and there was a possibility – disastrous from the federalist perspective – that the supporters of fiscal autonomy would win the day and wreck the customs union operating within the British Isles. Oliver argued that a grant of dominion status to

Ireland was out of the question because it would be 'an act of national suicide' for Great Britain. The inauguration of a federal system of government, on the other hand, would safeguard 'the essential substance of Union'.[50] The 'central parliament of the Union' would be the sovereign authority and as such it would be vested with all powers not specifically allotted to the national parliaments. These bodies would all stand in a uniform relationship to each other and to the central legislature. In the long term, Ulster would be protected within the Irish national assembly through having a veto over all legislation affecting the province. In the short term, assuming that the Irish could not wait for the inauguration of a wider federal scheme, 'Ulster' might temporarily opt out of the Dublin legislature. When the wider federation was created, then 'Ulster', properly safeguarded, would take its place in the Irish parliament.

The history of this pamphlet underlines both the strengths and the weaknesses of the federalist enterprise. It was widely circulated amongst opinion formers, and it was reprinted as a series of articles in *The Times*. But its political concept ran counter to what Oliver himself now recognised as the dominant political force in Ireland – separatism. Moreover, even though the piece was chiefly designed to convert the Ulster Unionists, Oliver soon heard 'from various of the Ulster leaders that... [while] they are not prepared to accept my conclusions, they consider the articles to be the best statement of the Ulster case that has yet been made'.[51]

The pamphlet and related articles, nevertheless served to consolidate Oliver's influence over Carson and other figures within the political elite. On 14 February 1918 Carson wrote to Lloyd George urging that a federal settlement be reached, and using the arguments and indeed the language of the Oliver pamphlet.[52] Lloyd George appears to have assumed that this missive signalled some movement within the Ulster Unionist camp, and he in turn wrote to the Ulstermen asking for concessions and hinting that Home Rule for Ireland would be merely the first step in a wider federal reform of British government.[53] This seemed like a victory for the federalists, and indeed it may fairly be regarded as the zenith of their influence. However, the reality was that Carson's letter reflected not so much a sea-change among the Ulster Unionists, as a gap between them and their leader. The federalists had captured the Ulster Unionist commander, but had otherwise made little impression upon the governing counsels of the movement. In a sense, then, this episode highlighted the intrinsic limitations of the federalist strategy no less than the success with which it was applied.

At this juncture the wider context to the federalist debate was completely overhauled. On 21 March 1918 the Germans launched their great offensive, scattering the British Fifth Army, creating a need for troop reinforcements and raising the spectre of conscription in Ireland. It will be recalled that on 28 March the cabinet decided to make provision for a military draft in Ireland, and that on 9 April the simultaneous enactment of Home Rule was approved. On 11 April ministers formed a cabinet committee (with Walter Long as chair) to supervise the drafting of Home Rule legislation, and on 16 April the Military Service (Ireland) Bill passed into law, giving the government the option of conscripting Irishmen into the Crown forces. This dualism certainly signalled the end of Home Rule, but it also marked the beginning of the end of the federalist engagement with Ireland.

For a time, though, the federalists' elitism masked the completeness of their failure at a popular level.[54] On 17 April 1918, Selborne and Oliver reissued their *Suggestions for the Better Government of the United Kingdom* 'with a view to a somewhat wider, though still private, circulation', as compared to the first edition. The document seems to have had a marked influence on Long, Chamberlain and others. Certainly the cabinet committee on Ireland, which numbered Long and Chamberlain among its members, was strongly federalist in its leanings, and the legislation that it drafted clearly reflected the influence of the Selborne and Oliver scheme.

But the sympathies of the committee were not fully shared in the wider cabinet where, when the federalist idea was discussed on 23 April, some of the heavy hitters remained sceptical. Balfour and Lord Curzon were the most thoroughly critical, and argued against any precipitate constitutional change. This remained the view of the cabinet when Ireland was again discussed, on 19 June, and when ministers decided to postpone the implementation of the dual policy. The cabinet's procrastination served to remove some of the urgency from the federalist case, and to underline that the government was not going to be rushed into Home Rule, and still less into a sweeping revision of the British constitution.[55]

There remained one last throw of the dice. An all-party federalist deputation under Lord Brassey was scheduled to meet Lloyd George on 26 June 1918, and the leaders of the cause clung on to the hope that this might wring some meaningful commitment from the Prime Minister. In fact, Lloyd George's attitude had already been determined by the mood of his cabinet, by his own preoccupation with the war effort and by the recognition that, while the federalists had support, their complex and dangerous cause was not yet unstoppable. There would thus be no stampede into a constitutional revolution. Lloyd George, in characteristic form, blessed the federalist enterprise, but told Brassey and the deputation that they would have to wait until they had won the unquestionable support of the English public. As John Kendle has remarked, 'that was obviously the end of federalist hopes in 1918'.[56]

There was, however, a lingering diminuendo to the cause as a whole. There were debates on federalism in the House of Lords, on 5 March 1919, and in the Commons, on 3–4 June 1919. A motion in favour of the federal idea was approved by MPs on 4 June, and this led eventually to the appointment of a parliamentary conference on devolution under the chairmanship of the Speaker, James Lowther. But once again an apparent federalist victory was soon beset with difficulties. Lloyd George remained unconvinced, and indeed the conference might reasonably be seen from his perspective as little more than a delaying tactic – this was certainly the opinion of Lord Brassey.[57] But the Prime Minister's scepticism and procrastination were not the only problems: demoralisation, sickness and death were also beginning to take their toll on the federalist leadership. F. S. Oliver seems to have been wearying after some fifteen years of unremitting struggle. He wrote in August 1918:

> I feel that I have already written enough – probably too much – on the Federal matter. I have found also, during the past three months, that the role of one who writes but does not talk in Parliament is necessarily limited. He finds the gate shut in his face at a certain point, a notice up that only practical statesmen are admitted beyond the barrier.[58]

Walter Long, the federalist champion in the cabinet, was beginning to fail in health by 1919–20. Brassey, who had long been a convinced if somewhat woolly-minded advocate of the cause, died on 13 November 1919 as the result of a car crash.

Nor were these difficulties with the traditional leadership offset by any marked infusion of talent and energy through the Speaker's conference. On the contrary, the political and intellectual quality of the conference membership was thought by contemporaries to be poor.[59] This judgement seems to be borne out in the confused and divided report that was issued at last on 27 April 1920, and which contained arguments for two distinct schemes: for both a transitional and an immediate programme of devolution, and for both regional and national legislatures. These delays and divisions, and the distraction or loss of key advocates, meant that the federalist question was finally divested of any urgency. Lloyd George, ever willing to go through the motions, met a last, forlorn deputation on 16 December 1920. As in June 1918, he proffered his support while regretting that, given the political obstacles, no action could be taken. 'That', it has been remarked, 'was effectively that.'[60]

George Boyce and John Stubbs have argued that federalism failed at this time because the project, defined in terms of both strategies and objectives, was fundamentally misconceived. The federalists' emphasis on high politics, their use of quality newspapers and pamphlets, and their exploitation of exclusive social and political networks meant that, by 1918–19, they had been able to convert at least part of the British political elite.[61] But these same strategies also meant that the federalists remained distant from the tenor of British and Irish popular opinion, a point that Lloyd George, characteristically, was not slow to grasp and to expoit.

Moreover, Boyce and Stubbs have also emphasised that 'federalism to both Oliver and Selborne was, at bottom, an alternative form of unionism': it was conceived as a way of reinventing the United Kingdom, and of preserving it as the imperial heartland.[62] This is substantially true, although it perhaps does not do complete justice to the integrity of the federalist vision. Oliver's quirky convictions for long rendered him an object of suspicion for both 'crusted Unionists' and 'crusted radicals', and his relationship with both parties was often highly fraught.[63] It might be said, therefore, that the problem for the federalists was not so much that they represented 'an alternative form of unionism', as that their creed remained static at a time of profound change – and consequently was often a source not of consensus, but rather of contention. Federalism was conceived originally as a kind of political middle way, but the parameters of the Anglo-Irish relationship changed while federalism remained fixed in place. This meant that a creed which might conceivably have been accepted by Irish nationalists in 1910 looked, by 1918–19, like a crude British survival strategy. Equally, in 1910 federalism was regarded by mainstream Unionists as synonymous with Home Rule, but by the end of the war it was happily accepted by many in the party leadership. Federalism remained largely unaltered: it was the political context that had changed. The integrity and immutability of the federalist faith were in the end its undoing.

A related point might be emphasised. Federalism was based upon the paradox that, by decentralising authority in the United Kingdom, the wider Union might be sustained. Alternatively, it might be said that federalism was a centripetal creed with centrifugal strategies. Either way, federalism seemed to its critics to involve a profound leap of faith – faith that the consolidation of national institutions would in turn consolidate the supranational state. It might be oversimplifying to suggest that a successful businessman like Oliver brought a contractual approach to politics, but arguably his vision of the United Kingdom was utterly dependent upon a binding constitutional agreement. If the Home Rulers had accepted the federalist case in 1914, and subsequently won control of the Irish customs and excise, then Oliver's vision, which depended upon the maintenance of a customs union, would have been completely wrecked. Federalism was at root a tight constitutional contract that permitted no renegotiation of terms.

Federalism sank, therefore, but not completely without trace. In their last fraught efforts to relaunch the cause, the federalists emphasised some ideas which, while not always original, would have a lasting resonance. The rapid evolution of the Irish question and of the war effort in 1918 forced some unpleasant realities into the consciousness of the federalist leaders. By June 1918, given the upsurge of separatist conviction in the south and west of Ireland, even Selborne and Oliver, who had always been relentlessly upbeat, could see that a federal sub-parliament would not be accepted by the Irish people. In this context, Selborne now wondered whether Ulster might be given federal institutions, and the south and west treated as a crown colony until the people came to their senses.[64]

This was also a view accepted by Walter Long, who argued in November 1918 that 'as regards Ireland under a Federal plan, if the three Southern provinces declined to adopt it, the only alternative that I can see would be to include Ulster and govern the other three provinces on some different plan'.[65] This view was confirmed and elaborated by Long after a visit to Ireland in 1919: Belfast and Dublin should each be offered parliaments, and if the south proved recalcitrant it might be governed as a Crown colony. In July 1919, in the aftermath of the successful Commons motion on federalism, *The Times* (which, under the editorship of Geoffrey Dawson, was strongly sympathetic to the federalist cause) advocated the creation of two parliaments in Ireland, united by an All-Ireland Council and bound within a wider constitutional reform.

The Speaker's conference on devolution was created in October 1919, and fumbled its way through a series of sessions in the winter of 1919–20. As has been noted, its report was confused and abortive, but the long-term importance of the conference rests not in its neglected conclusions, but rather in the fact that it kept the federalist debate alive at a crucial juncture in the Anglo-Irish relationship. For, running parallel with the conference was a cabinet committee that would have a lasting impact upon the political landscape of modern Ireland.

With the end of the war in November 1918, the government faced an obligation, under the terms of the Home Rule suspensory measure of 1914, to return to the Irish question. In addition to this statutory responsibility, political pressure was also being applied in Ireland by militant separatists who, in January 1919, began an offensive against the Royal Irish Constabulary and other Crown forces. On 7 October 1919, two weeks before the institution of the Speaker's conference on devolution, a cabinet committee was created to advise on Irish policy and to formulate draft legislation. The new committee, like its predecessor of April 1918, was chaired by the federalist Walter Long, and its terms of reference included the right to consider 'a general Federal Scheme for the United Kingdom'.[66] This brief was a fulfilment of Lloyd George's longstanding, if ambiguous, promise that an attempt would be made to ensure that any Irish settlement was 'consistent' with a wider federal constitution.

In keeping with some of the recent shifts in federalist thought – in particular the *Times* programme of July 1919 – the committee quickly established, by 15 October, that there should be two Irish parliaments, and that this dualism should be compatible with any more sweeping federal reform. In making this recommendation, Long and his colleagues were emphatic that there should be structural mechanisms for the encouragement of Irish unity. There would be a Council of Ireland, consisting of equal representation from southern and northern Ireland, and this could be augmented by the joint agreement of the Dublin and Belfast parliaments.

The committee recommended that the imperial parliament retain permanent control over a wide range of matters (essentially those defined in the Home Rule Act of 1914), but it also suggested that there should be two types of temporarily reserved power. Some matters (agriculture, technical education, transport, pensions, health and unemployment insurance) might be administered by London for one year. The committee proposed that the Council of Ireland could annex these powers on the basis of a joint agreement of the two Irish parliaments. But there would also be temporarily reserved powers over issues such as customs and excise, income tax and the post office. These would be retained indefinitely by London. However, if the two Irish parliaments agreed to combine, then these powers could be transferred to the new unitary parliament. As the committee explicitly stated, it was prepared to grant the two Irish parliaments 'power by agreement to bring about Irish unity on any basis ranging from federation to what is practically Dominion status'.[67] Indeed, the only legal (as opposed to political) obstacle to the attainment of full dominion status lay with the reserved power of defence.

What were the influences on the committee and its proposal?[68] In a general sense, the mixture of security measures and social reform ('coercion and conciliation') pursued by Arthur Balfour as Chief Secretary for Ireland was an influential paradigm for Long and others. For a time, Long believed that Sinn Féin would be swiftly eradicated, and that his report could then be enacted in a gesture of paternalist magnanimity.

The federalist agitation was also an important context for the legislation. Philip Kerr, Private Secretary to Lloyd George, was an imperialist in the style of Milner, and a federalist, and while he was a relatively early convert to the notion of dominion status for Ireland, he also influenced and sponsored the deal that was being honed in 1919–20. Kerr, Long and others hoped that their work would form part of a wide federal reform, and they were keen to ensure that their recommendations did not subvert this grander ambition. However, Long's untrammelled desire to be architect of a lasting settlement outweighed his political or intellectual debt to the federalists. This is clear from his willingness to concede the control of customs and excise to a unitary parliament, which, from the perspective of ideologues like Oliver, was effectively the surrender of an indispensable federalist principle.[69]

Orthodox Unionism was also a critical influence on the Long Committee. The partition of Ireland, which the committee conceded, had been mooted by British Unionist ideologues like J. L. Garvin and John St Loe Strachey in 1910–11, and had been an overt Ulster Unionist goal since 1914. The committee also bore southern Unionist interests in mind, in defining protective electoral and legislative structures.[70] But, at least at the beginning, the Long Committee was more anxious about the survival of Ireland within a redefined Union than about the demands of Ulster or southern Unionists. This is why so much emphasis was laid in the committee report upon the mechanisms for unity.

It was also the case that Long's attitude towards the southern Unionists had dramatically cooled since 1916. In January 1920 he complained about 'the attitude of the Irish Unionists, which consists of crying for the moon and appealing to us here to protect them from their own local enemies. It is a policy which does not appeal to the English people.' The southern Unionists, he continued, 'refuse to face patent facts and continue crying like spoilt children for that which they cannot get'.[71] This outburst is strikingly reminiscent of the language of Carson in October 1913, and indeed it underlines the extent to which Long's approach to Ireland was coloured by his personal jealousies, by bloody-minded last-ditch stands, and ultimately  by annexing policies that he had long opposed. If, to revert to Judge Cohalan's judgement, Plunkett was 'three laps behind' in the marathon of Irish politics, then the distance between Long and the pace-setters was even greater.[72]

Long and his committee (and other influential figures like Garvin) also wanted the partition of the entire province of Ulster from the rest of Ireland, even though this deeply angered James Craig and the Ulster Unionist leadership. A nine-county divide remained the stand of the committee and of the government until 14 February 1920, one day before the first reading of the new Government of Ireland Bill was scheduled to take place. Long himself strongly opposed the Ulster Unionists on this question, although in the end, while the rest of his committee held out, he caved in to their pressure.[73] But, as Nicholas Mansergh has emphasised, the demand for six counties was being endorsed not only by the Ulster Unionists but also in other quarters. James O'Connor, a Lord Justice and a senior figure within the Irish Catholic establishment, was in communication with Lloyd George and Bonar Law and also urged that partition be on the basis of six rather than nine counties.[74] O'Connor was understood by ministers to represent the views not just of the Catholic elite, but of the Church hierarchy, and indeed he explicitly claimed to have been in touch with the bishops concerning the shape of an Irish settlement. Mansergh has argued that O'Connor's views, 'not least [his] expressed preference for the exclusion of six counties', were 'carefully weighed' by the cabinet and by the Long Committee.[75]

Still, the political significance of the Ulster Unionists was very considerable, and they had a marked impact upon the final legislation. It was their pressure, in combination with the influence of O'Connor, which helped to ensure the shape of the new northern and southern Irish territories. The Unionists were also strongly opposed to a single Irish judiciary, and on 18 February 1920 they won a separate court system for the proposed Northern Ireland.[76] Their strength derived largely from the fact that their bloc of some twenty-six votes in the Commons was crucial to the government at a time when the Government of Ireland proposal increasingly hung in the balance. Debates on the legislation, particularly during the committee stage, were often attended by little more than a hundred members; there was a great deal of apathy, and a measure of opposition. Indeed, the government feared that it might lose the bill, and ministers came to the conclusion that the only 'active support' that they were likely to get would be from the Ulster Unionists. Long claimed that in May 1920 he offered the Ulstermen a deal whereby, in return for their votes, the government would guarantee that the borders of the new northern territory would be fixed: 'that the Six Counties...should be theirs for good and all, and there should be no interference with the boundaries or anything else, excepting some slight adjustments'.[77] Lloyd George later disputed that any bargain of this kind had been authorised by the cabinet, but given his support for a Boundary Commission during the Anglo-Irish treaty negotiations of 1921, he could hardly have taken any other line. The evidence, while ambiguous, favours Long's version of events.

The Government of Ireland Act, which received the royal assent on 23 December 1920 and came into effect on 3 May 1921, closely followed the report of Long's committee. The island was to be partitioned into a six-county Northern Ireland and a twenty-six-county Southern Ireland. Each system of government was to have its own parliament and executive (section 1 of the Act). Elections to each House of Commons were to be conducted using proportional representation and multi-member constituencies (section 14), an idea borrowed from the report of the Irish Convention. In a departure from the Long recommendations, each parliament was to be bicameral, although the Northern and Southern arrangements were to be quite different: in the North the Senate was to be elected from the House of Commons, while Southern senators were to represent a wide variety of economic, professional and political interests and were to be nominated (section 13).

As Long had urged, there was to be a Council of Ireland, comprising twenty members from both the North and South. The two parliaments could, by mutual agreement, delegate powers to the Council, and they could also agree to create a single Irish legislature that would replace it (sections 2 and 10). If a union of this kind were achieved, the new Irish administration could apply for the control of customs and excise (section 36). Until this happy consummation, however, the two parliaments would have a comparatively limited range of powers, particularly in the realm of taxation. Aside from customs and excise, the key duties (income tax, excess profits tax and corporation tax) remained in the hands of the United Kingdom parliament (section 22). Westminster retained sovereign authority whether a union of the Irish parliaments was achieved or not (section 75); and certainly in the absence of union it was clear that this sovereignty would have considerable practical force in the two Irish administrations.

Elections to the two Irish parliaments were held in May 1921, and resulted in an overwhelming success for the Unionists in Northern Ireland and for Sinn Féin in the South, underlining the latter's republican mandate. Sinn Féin and the Irish Republican Army, which had been developing their guerrilla war against the British since January 1919, were not going to surrender the national struggle in return for the Government of Ireland Act. The first meeting of the Southern Irish parliament was thus a farce, with only four members in attendance. The Act, in so far as it applied to the twenty-six counties, was still-born. A settlement of sorts for the South was only achieved with the continuation of the guerrilla war into July 1921, and after lengthy and controversial negotiations between the representatives of Sinn Féin and the British in London. The deal that was finally struck on 6 December 1921 – the Anglo-Irish Treaty – swept away the teasing inducements of the Government of Ireland Act and provided dominion status – and, in effect, independence

– to the South. The Government of Ireland Act had offered the faint possibility of a united, autonomous country, but Irish nationalists had long nursed their disappointments, were weary of lures and promises, and now sought instant political gratification.

For their part, the Ulster Unionists had been able to shape the measure in advantageous ways, and the opening of the new Northern parliament on 22 June 1921 was cast as a loyalist triumph and a logical return for years of bitter patriotism and bloody sacrifice. It was particularly fitting that, immediately after the inauguration ceremony, King George V should have held an investiture, distributing honours and titles to the Unionist elite.[78] The paradox that Unionists were rewarded for their years of political struggle with a grant of Home Rule is so well worn as to be a cliché, but there are perhaps some fresh dimensions even to the tired ironies of Northern politics. Unionists had fought to subvert Gladstone's policies, and they were now in control of institutions that had been confined and limited in response to their own arguments. Some Unionists had sought to bind a united Ireland within a federated United Kingdom, but the result was a form of political masochism: the constraints upon the Irish parliaments which were designed to promote Irish unity, and which were a federalist inspiration, hampered only the Unionists of Northern Ireland. As John Kendle has remarked, 'the governing apparatus and powers assigned the six counties under the Government of Ireland Act had not been designed for the operation of devolved government. They had been designed to facilitate the union of Ireland at which time additional powers would have been transferred.'[79] In the end, the paradox is not simply that the Unionists won Home Rule; it is rather that they were burdened by a form of Home Rule that they themselves had subverted. In a very real sense, the Ulster Unionists were the victims of their own success.

Home Rule, therefore, did not die in 1916, with the Easter Rising, or in 1918, with the general election, or in 1921, when the forlorn members of the doomed Southern parliament adjourned their deliberations. It enjoyed a form of after-life in Northern Ireland, where the Unionists struggled with Gladstonian institutions that they themselves had undermined. In the rest of Ireland, Home Rule evinced occasional electoral spasms after 1918. Patrick Maume has identified the 'unexpectedly strong showing of the remnants of the Irish Party' in some urban local government contests in January 1920.[80] He has also drawn attention to the residual Irish Party networks associated with the Ancient Order of Hibernians and other organisations, and the vestigial party structures in Donegal, Louth and Waterford, all of which had a low-grade, right-wing political existence in the new Irish state.[81]

John Redmond's son, Captain William Archer Redmond, tried to resurrect his father's legacy through the short-lived National League (1926–31); John Dillon's son, James, attempted a similar venture in 1932–3 with the Centre Party, an equally forlorn enterprise. However, James Dillon was also a founder of the Fine Gael party and exercised a longstanding influence in its counsels: he was leader of the party between 1959 and 1965.[82] As late as November 1966, during a by-election in Waterford, Garret FitzGerald was told that the Fine Gael candidate, Eddie Collins, would have to be marketed in some areas as 'John Redmond's man'. FitzGerald vividly recalled the response of one elderly lady to his canvass: 'Of course I'll vote for Eddie Collins; haven't I got John Redmond's picture at the top of the stairs, beside the Sacred Heart!'[83]

But the resonance of the Home Rule movement can scarcely be defined by the institutions of government in Northern Ireland, or by the largely futile gestures of William Redmond and James Dillon. Home Rule was always more than Redmondism and the Irish Party; and when these each faded into oblivion, other aspects of this great national alliance lived on. Home Rulers relocated themselves within the two main parties of the new Irish state: Cumann na nGaedheal, later Fine Gael, and Fianna Fáil. The movement bequeathed not only personnel but also an ideological legacy to the two main Irish parties: the economic policies of Cumann na nGaedheal in the 1920s certainly owed more to the Irish Party than to Griffith's Sinn Féin. Home Rule for long commanded the attention and sympathy of liberal and other intellectuals who were disturbed by the challenge of republican and Unionist militancy. The Home Rule movement sustained a patriotic struggle which, in a limited sense, expired in Ireland in 1918; but it also created a constitutional debate that continues to resonate throughout the United Kingdom.

The Home Rule Party collapsed at the polls in December 1918. But there has been an afterlife: the Party's ideological and structural and personal legacies are with us still.

CHAPTER 10

# 'A GRITTY SORT OF PROD BAROQUE'
## 1920–72

A dinner party cleanly exposed some of the fundamental flaws in the political culture of Northern Ireland's devolved, Home Rule, administration. At the beginning of February 1969, in the Scots baronial gloom of Stormont Castle, the Prime Minister of Northern Ireland entertained a number of guests, including a distinguished civil servant from the British Home Office, Robin North. It seems likely that the premier, Terence O'Neill, subjected his guests to a monologue (this would have been quite in character). If so, then he was interrupted only at the end of the meal by the arrival of one of his ministerial colleagues. O'Neill turned from the table to engage the minister, with whom he had a long confidential talk. North, who stayed on until after midnight, had little or no chance for any similar private communion.

Failure of communication was an important, though characteristic, feature of the devolved regime in Belfast, and in particular of O'Neill's premiership. On this occasion, however, the implications were more than usually disastrous. For North had been sent by his masters to Belfast in order to brief certain key individuals concerning the British government's contingency planning. These plans already encompassed, in the context of particular emergencies, the suspension of the Stormont administration and parliament, and the creation of an executive council under the command of the Governor of Northern Ireland, Lord Grey. The foundations of direct rule from London were thus already being laid in these early months of 1969. North and Grey spent an afternoon together reviewing these arrangements; and while they agreed that the issue would not be raised with O'Neill 'unless this were absolutely necessary', Grey clearly expected that the necessity would in fact arise. But through a combination of minor distractions and social quirks, North escaped back to London without having to include O'Neill within the loop of these doom-laden plans.

The dynamics of O'Neill's dinner party have a wider significance. The critical, though perhaps least-noticed, figure was North, who had an influence over the destinies of everyone around the table. O'Neill, who recognised the reality of British sovereignty in Northern Ireland better than many of his colleagues, was still deeply imbued within a political tradition that took the autonomy of Stormont for granted. Even though North had spent half a day with the Governor, the Stormont premier was insufficiently interested or curious to enquire why this should have been so: had he asked, it was expected that North would have had to reveal his hand. O'Neill was instead captivated by the arrival of his minister and by the minutiae and intrigue within the Unionist camp. Even though the sovereignty of London was being quietly and devastatingly exercised, the rulers of the devolved administration remained trapped by their own delusions of ministerial grandeur, and by the parochialism of their culture.[1]

If the general history of Ireland has often been used to point a moral, then the history of Northern Ireland has been applied in an equally didactic manner. This history has been used at different times and by different commentators to make the case both for and against the wider devolution of government in the United Kingdom. It has been used by some commentators as a parable of sin and vengeance, an exploration of Unionist or republican criminality and its consequences. There have been marked curiosities in the literature: in 1936 a liberal of southern Unionist extraction, Nicholas Mansergh, presented an eloquent case for devolution on the basis of a sharp critique of the Northern Ireland regime; while thirty years on, in 1965, R. J. Lawrence, writing with some Unionist sympathies, presented an argument against devolution on the basis of a more generous portrayal of the same administration. More recently and convincingly, the American political scientist, Alan J. Ward, has suggested that Northern Ireland, for all its manifold failings, presents a good general case for devolution, but a bad case for Gladstonian Home Rule.[2]

However, the concern here is not to retell the political history of Northern Ireland under the Stormont government, still less to offer any uncomplicated moral. Northern Ireland was the only part of the island of Ireland to experience the reality of Home Rule, and before the Blair era it was the only part of the United Kingdom to possess a devolved executive and parliament. Northern Ireland is of relevance here, not primarily because of the 'the Ulster question', but because it may be used to illustrate both the strengths and weaknesses of Gladstone's model, and the reality of devolution in a British context. What follows is a practical and theoretical evaluation of the experience of devolution, together with an exploration of the failure of internal reform in the 1960s. The constitution of the new Northern Ireland and its manifold ramifications (financial, territorial and libertarian) represent a logical point of departure.

After 1920 Unionists found themselves corralled in a constitutional compound that they themselves had helped to shape. This was the Government of Ireland Act, and under its terms a six-county Northern Ireland was geographically defined, and endowed with a devolved or Home Rule administration. There would now be a bicameral parliament in Belfast, with a House of Commons elected through proportional representation, and a Senate elected from the Commons. There would also be a Northern Privy Council, from whose ranks would be drawn a team of ministers formally responsible to a Governor, as representative of the Crown. The proposed Northern parliament had the right, along with its Southern counterpart, to send representatives and delegate powers to a Council of Ireland that was designed to function as a machine for the reunification of the island. As a further encouragement the Act provided for the early transfer, in the event of unity, of some of the legislative powers 'reserved' by Westminster. The authority of the new administration was therefore heavily circumscribed, both by Westminster's supremacy and by the system of checks and inducements designed to achieve reunification. But the illusion of autonomy was convincing, and many in the new Northern Ireland came to believe in its reality.

In 1936 Nicholas Mansergh argued that 'the essential weakness of the later Home Rule Bills was that they attempted to solve a problem in political sovereignty by a proposal for better government'.[3] This was apparently the case with the Government of Ireland Act, but given that the Act was quickly superseded in the South by the Anglo-Irish Treaty of 1921, it might be said that the measure in fact exacerbated a dispute over sovereignty in one territory (Northern Ireland) through proposing better government in another (Ireland as a whole). Or, reformulating the Mansergh thesis, it could be argued that the Government of Ireland Act embodied not so much a misreading of the problem, as an honest (if ultimately inadequate) attempt to match the institutions of government in Ireland to the nature of its disputed sovereignty. The Act, therefore, did not reflect a complete failure of British political imagination: its weakness lay, not with the quality of the diagnosis, but with the nature of the proposed cure.

From the beginning Northern Ireland laboured with a constitution that was not designed for its own long-term survival. The Government of Ireland Act looked forward to a unitary Home Rule state, and in a sense the institutions of the Northern administration were seen as transient, and as no more than a means towards an end. Moreover, the Act was also backward-looking to the extent that it propounded a version of Home Rule that was partly intended to address the aspirations and fears of movements (Home Rule nationalism and all-Ireland Unionism) which by 1921 had effectively ceased to matter. The result of these two contradictory thrusts was a constitution that was almost intentionally unstable, and which simultaneously circumscribed the powers of the new Belfast government, while promising greater autonomy within the context of a reunified Irish Home Rule state. In effect, the new Belfast authorities were being encouraged towards unity with a territory that (after the Anglo-Irish Treaty of 1921) did not exist.

Nowhere was this constitutional surrealism more marked than in the financial relationship that bound the new Northern Ireland to the British Treasury.[4] The Northern Ministry of Finance had control over a small range of existing taxes, known as 'transferred' taxes and including death duties and vehicle licence duties, and it had a limited right to levy further taxes. But the bulk of taxation was retained, or 'reserved', by Westminster: this included customs duties, some excise duties, income tax and surtax. These reserved taxes were paid directly into the British Treasury, which deducted the cost of running those aspects of public administration in Northern Ireland that remained under the control of London (the 'reserved services'). Further sums, including an 'Imperial Contribution' (fixed originally at £7.92 million) were deducted from these reserved taxes. Any balance (the 'residuary share of reserved taxes') was paid back into the Northern Irish Ministry of Finance.

But in practice there was never any lasting and coherent formula which governed the financial relationship between Belfast and London. An unelected body, the Joint Exchequer Board, which comprised representatives from both the Exchequer and the Ministry of Finance, exercised an intermittent but extensive control in calculating both the revenue produced by the 'reserved taxes' and the amount to be paid by the Northern Ireland government for the 'reserved services'. After the mid-1920s the Exchequer Board, while continuing to intervene, retreated somewhat – there were no meetings at all between 1935 and 1947. Instead officials of the two governments met regularly to review and tweak the financial relationship between the two territories. Occasionally this ongoing review produced major and lasting change. A committee under Lord Colwyn was appointed in 1923 and determined in 1925 that the Imperial Contribution would cease to be a first and fixed charge on the 'reserved revenue'; instead it would take on a residual and fluctuating (and therefore often minimal) character.[5]

A combination of sustained high levels of unemployment in Northern Ireland and the expansion of British welfare provision gave rise to a succession of deals on the payment of social services. At first, the London government was inclined to take the line that the Government of Ireland Act had bestowed both benefits and liabilities on Northern Ireland, and that some of its problems could not be helped. In May 1922, for example, Lloyd George's Chancellor of the Exchequer, Sir Robert Horne, told Craig that 'I do not see how I can reasonably ask the British taxpayer to provide Northern Ireland with money to make good a deficit on her part of the [Unemployment] Insurance Fund – a liability which she was bound to take over just as in other cases she took over assets.'[6] But by 1926 the two governments had agreed that London would foot the bill for three-quarters of any excess spending from the Northern unemployment fund (the calculations were made on the basis of a comparison of per capita spending in Britain and Northern Ireland across the entire population).

In 1936 this deal was revised along lines more favourable to the Stormont authorities: the basis for calculation was now a comparison of spending across the total insured population in each territory, and because there were comparatively few insured workers in Northern Ireland, its government benefited by the change. In 1938 the British Chancellor of the Exchequer, Sir John Simon (a former Home Ruler and a law officer in Asquith's pre-war administration) agreed in principle that the British should pay to maintain parity in the standard of Northern Ireland's social services; and in May 1945 the Stormont Minister of Finance, Maynard Sinclair, announced that Northern Ireland would keep in step with the future improvement of British welfare services.

A deal was struck in 1946 between the two governments which for-malised some of the earlier precedents and statements of principle. Parity of taxes and services was to be a guiding principle, the Northern budget was to be agreed with the Treasury and submitted to the Joint Exchequer Board, and the Northern Ministry of Finance was to secure the Treasury's approval for any new items of expenditure (other than on maintaining parity) which amounted to £50,000 or more. Subsequent agreements on social services (concluded in 1949 and 1951, but all taking effect from July 1948) provided technical detail to the broad strokes of the deal struck in 1946.

What all of this meant was that Northern Ireland was endowed with a horrendously complex and fluid formula for its income. Mansergh wrote in 1936 of the financial relationship with Britain that 'it is its weakness that in its day to day application it adheres to no clearly-defined princi-ple; and that it carries no conviction of an ability to secure a just distribu-tion of burdens'.[7] Simon's intervention in 1938 and the various post-war agreements established or confirmed a number of governing themes and also, perhaps, led to a more just 'distribution of burdens'. But as late as the early 1960s the formulae under which Northern Ireland received her income remained a mystery even to some senior British officials and ministers.

There are occasional stories in the literature (reminiscent of the legends surrounding the Eastern Question in the nineteenth century) of sudden anomalies in the Northern revenue, coinciding with the death of the single civil servant who had a grasp of the relevant accounting procedures. Patrick Shea's memory of his own botched attempt (as an Assistant Principal Officer in the Stormont Ministry of Finance) to expound the intricacies of the Reinsurance Agreement suggests, however, that even experienced Belfast administrators could fall prey to confusion.[8] Terence O'Neill, looking back in 1972 to his period as Northern Minister of Finance, claimed that 'it was doubtful whether the busy Chancellors ever mastered the incredibly complicated financial arrangements which exist between the two departments [the Exchequer and the Ministry of Finance]'. Puffing his own contribution, O'Neill emphasised that procedures could be subjective or arbitrary: he argued that even in the 1950s and 1960s 'to a large extent Northern Ireland's income rested on attributions of revenue... if you put your case well and establish a good rapport you will get a generous attribution. If, on the other hand, you accept a figure worked out by some junior official in the Customs and Excise department you may get considerably less than your due.'[9] Richard Crossman confirmed this insight: no Chancellor 'knew the formula according to which the Northern Ireland government gets its money. In all these years it has never been revealed to the politicians, and I am longing to see whether now we shall get to the bottom of this very large, expensive secret.'[10]

It was also the case that for much of the early period of its existence the Northern Irish state struggled with a financial system that threatened to suffocate the regime, and over which it had little control. The Colwyn Committee brought relief, but it did not address some of the more fundamental disparities between social conditions in Northern Ireland and the rest of the United Kingdom. Again, the Simon declaration and the subsequent post-war deals on social services helped to address the shortfall in welfare provision within Northern Ireland and to make up leeway. But in the calculation of one eminent Ulster-born economist, Thomas Wilson, it was only after the fall of Stormont in 1972 that Northern Ireland began to receive 'the fiscal support which any other area with the same needs and resources would be entitled to receive from membership of the United Kingdom'.[11]

The Government of Ireland Act not only threatened the financial stability of the Northern regime, but also simultaneously defined and

threatened its wider integrity. For, while the Act determined the geographical span of Northern Ireland and ascribed powers to the new
Belfast administration, it also unequivocally affirmed that executive
power throughout Ireland rested with the King, and (in section 75) 'that
the supreme authority of the Parliament of the United Kingdom shall
remain unaffected and undiminished over all persons, matters, and
things in Ireland and every part thereof'. This was a formula that had
been prominently displayed in the Home Rule Bill of 1912 (section 1.2)
and had been designed to allay Unionist fears. But while in 1912 (in the
context of a determined, united and popular Home Rule administration)
such a declaration might well have proved to be constitutional braggado-
cio, in 1920 (in the context of a vulnerable and disputed Northern
Ireland) it was always likely to carry greater weight.

Thus, while the Act in effect provided for the continuation of
Northern Ireland within the United Kingdom, in practical terms this
meant that Northern Ireland was subordinate to a generally indifferent,
often hostile, but indisputably sovereign London administration. Again,
it is hard to avoid the irony that the Unionist regime was weakened by a
constitutional subordination that they themselves had championed in
the context of earlier Home Rule measures. As L. S. Amery wrote to James
Craig in October 1924:

> the root of all this trouble [over the North–South border] lies in the fact
> that Ulster's status in the matter is weakened as long as she is only a
> province of the United Kingdom…at present your position is anoma-
> lous because on the very issues which affect you most, the legal control
> is at Westminster and you are not an equal partner.[12]

The reality of Westminster's sovereignty became clear almost at once.
In December 1920, with the passage of the Government of Ireland Act,
the London government had defined the territorial limits of Northern
and Southern Ireland; then, on 6 December 1921, with the Anglo-Irish
Treaty, provision was made for a Boundary Commission and the possible
rectification of these frontiers. Again, as Nicholas Mansergh pointed out,
the Commission was simultaneously a threat to the Unionists and a
product of their own political imagination. For, in negotiating the
Government of Ireland Bill in 1919, James Craig, Prime Minister of
Northern Ireland after 1921, had raised the possibility of such a body to
adjust and confirm the territory of Northern and Southern Ireland. 'What
you apparently suggested on December 14 1919', L. S. Amery recalled to
Craig in October 1924, 'was that a Commission should be set up "to
examine the distribution of population along the Boundary of the Six

Counties" and you then went on to suggest that such a Commission might take a vote of the population "on either side of and immediately adjoining the Boundary".'[13]

Much, of course, had changed since Craig made this suggestion in December 1919. Indeed, part of Craig's difficulty as the new political master of Northern Ireland was the disconcerting swiftness with which Anglo-Irish relations developed, not just over two years, but even within a period of as little as two days. Immediately before the Boundary Commission was thrust upon him on 6 December 1921, Craig believed that the protracted peace negotiations between British ministers and Irish revolutionaries were about to break down, and that the military struggle between the Crown forces and the IRA would be resumed. In a revealing (but neglected) letter dated 5 December 1921, C. C. Craig, Ulster Unionist MP for South Antrim, wrote to his brother, James, that he had been sum-moned to No. 10 Downing Street, where Lloyd George was planning for the failure of the talks with the Irish: 'his [Lloyd George's] point is that as the Conference has broken off on the Allegiance question, it is much better that the Ulster side of the question should not be put forward too prominently and that it should go forth to the world that the Conference split on the question of Allegiance'.[14] Having been given this (from the Unionist perspective) happy intelligence, Craig experienced an almost immediate reversal of fortune, with the clinching – in the small hours of 6 December – of the Anglo-Irish Treaty.

Neither Craig nor his lieutenants were involved with the final negotia-tion of the treaty, but they were heavily affected and implicated. The treaty was ostensibly a unitary settlement for the island of Ireland, but the Northern government was still permitted to opt out of its provisions. On the other hand, a pivotal element of the deal was the creation of a Boundary Commission, out of which the Unionists could not 'opt'. The Commission threatened the viability of the Northern state, and it was all the more galling as a notion because, while the Belfast government had not been directly consulted, Lloyd George claimed that 'Carson had approved of the principle'.[15] Much else flowed from these developments. It is possible that Lloyd George's effort to implicate Carson in his diplomacy helps to explain the Unionist leader's subsequent, extraordi-nary anger at the treaty. Lloyd George's treatment of the Belfast govern-ment at this time – its complete subordination to the whims of his diplomacy on 5–6 December – also demonstrates that the affirmation of British sovereignty in 1920, designed as a Unionist gesture, was more than constitutional rhetoric and could well be deployed against the Unionist interest. Here, too, was a portent of threats to come.

At first, as in 1919, Craig was prepared to countenance some minor modifications of the border. In a letter to Austen Chamberlain dated 2 January 1922 (and marked 'withheld') he indicated his willingness to deal on the basis of adequate compensation for those loyalists displaced by any adjustment of the Northern frontier.[16] There was also at this time a degree of pressure on the Unionist government from various quarters. John St Loe Strachey, who had been so important in 1910–11 as a kind of early partitionist, argued to Craig that 'the ultra-Catholic districts of these [outlying] counties were rather a weakness to the Six County area'.[17] Border loyalists, particularly those in West Tyrone, urged Craig to co-operate with the pro-treaty regime in Dublin. Different Unionists from Strabane believed 'that the Griffith party would go far to secure the support of the Northern Unionists', and urged the Belfast government to strike a deal with the new administration in Dublin.[18]

But, as the military campaign of the IRA against Northern Ireland receded in late 1922, so a more bullish attitude took root within Ulster Unionism, and pressure to resist the establishment of the Boundary Commission grew. Still, as late as April 1923, Wilfrid Spender, the secretary to the new Northern cabinet, was writing to a Church of Ireland clergyman in Clones that

> the Prime Minister is most anxious to include in Northern Ireland certain districts of Donegal and Monaghan where there is a splendid type of loyalist population. If, therefore, the Free State would agree to let each County bargain direct with its opposite number across the border regarding the transfer of equal areas and populations there would be great prospect of an amicable settlement being arrived at which would prove to the advantage of the North and South.[19]

Some allowance has to be made for the fact that Spender was indeed addressing these sentiments to 'a splendid type of [border] loyalist', but there is little reason to doubt the sincerity of his view that local and small-scale modifications of the border might well have proved useful.

The election of a Labour government in December 1923 meant that the notion of a Boundary Commission, and of serious territorial change, came back into play. At first Labour ministers, led by J. H. Thomas, the Colonial Secretary, attempted to recondition the machinery for Irish unity. A deal was outlined on 1–2 February 1924 whereby certain services that London administered in Northern Ireland would be vested in a joint North-South ministerial body. Future legislation covering these services would be passed by joint meetings of the Northern parliament and Dáil Éireann. As bait, it was promised that the creation of a Boundary Commission was to be suspended for at least a year. In the event, these proposals came to nothing, though they are worth noting both as evidence of the British government's ongoing commitment to gradual reunification and as a prototype for the kind of North–South mechanism established in 1973, at Sunningdale, and through the Belfast Agreement of 1998.[20]

Further obstacles – Craig's ill-health, the resistance and filibustering of the Belfast government, legal jousting – delayed the activation of the Boundary Commission until October 1924. A veteran supporter of Milner and South African judge, Richard Feetham, was appointed as chairman, while Eoin MacNeill, a Southern cabinet minister and an Ulster Catholic, was appointed by the Dublin government as the representative of the Irish Free State. The Northern Ireland government was divided in its attitude, but came down in favour of non-cooperation. Contrary to some assumptions, Feetham was at first viewed in Belfast with a considerable degree of suspicion. He was seen as the creature of unfriendly elements in the Colonial Office (and in particular Lionel Curtis), and he was the subject of a scathing assessment that Craig received from a South African source.[21] Craig refused to appoint his own representative on the Commission, but it is clear that Joseph R. Fisher, who was named by the British government as an unofficial Northern member, had his tacit approval. It is certainly the case that Fisher had an indirect but effective channel of communication with Craig through the medium of D. D. Reid and his wife. Reid was the Ulster Unionist MP for East Down and chairperson of the Ulster Party at Westminster: he had been a contemporary of Feetham and Curtis at New College, Oxford.[22]

The first meetings of the Boundary Commission were held on 5–6 November 1924, and it gathered evidence until the summer of 1925. Several visits were organised to Northern Ireland, and to the border counties, with the commissioners' movements tracked by the Royal Ulster Constabulary, and thus by the Northern Ireland cabinet. Moreover, through the communication between Fisher and Reid, Craig had a reasonably clear idea of the development of the commissioners' thinking, and he certainly knew the overall shape of their conclusions by September 1925.[23] It is hard to say what, if any, advantage was bestowed by this drip-feed of information. Craig was naturally discreet about his sources, and genially fibbed even to cabinet colleagues like Lord Londonderry. 'No hint has reached me as to Feetham's intentions, and it seems futile to indulge in guess work', he told Londonderry on 24 September 1925, a week after receiving intelligence from Reid.[24] On the other hand, the Unionists knew from Reid's conversations with Fisher (what they might well have been able to surmise anyway) that Newry might be transferred to the Free State, and they were able to focus on this theme throughout the summer of 1925.[25] It is just possible, therefore, that Newry was saved for the Union as a result of Fisher's indiscretion.

The final version of the Commission report was completed by 17 October 1925 and appeared (in an unauthorised form) in the edition of the Tory *Morning Post* published on 7 November. The origin and purpose of the leak are still unclear: Fisher remains a possible culprit, but given that he enthusiastically endorsed the report of the Commission and that the leak helped to scupper its findings, it is equally possible that the guilt lay elsewhere. A number of Fisher's letters from this time have recently come to light, and in one (dated 7 November 1925, the day of the leak) he affirmed to a close friend that the Commission report 'will probably be found to be not very widely different from that in the *Morning Post*'.[26] Whether there is a note of coyness in this remark, or whether Fisher was simply offering a guarded acknowledgement of the truth, is hard to determine. More telling, perhaps, is the record of a conversation that Fisher had with his confidant, D. D. Reid, on the same day, 7 November. As Reid reported to Craig, 'you will see from the *Morning Post* that there has been some leakage in connection with the Boundary Commission...I have seen Fisher, and he says he cannot imagine how it was done, unless some of the map makers have been got at.'[27] This has the ring of authenticity, especially given the frankness of Fisher's relationship with Reid. If Fisher's surmise was correct, then the solution to a minor mystery in recent Irish political history might be found by looking to the mapmakers of the Commission. The chief of these was a Major Boger of the Royal Engineers, and it is just possible that either he or one of his subordinates was the 'guilty man' of 7 November 1925.

In any event, and as both the *Morning Post* story and the official report made clear, Fisher and his fellow commissioners, including MacNeill, had interpreted their function in a minimalist way. They recommended a relatively insignificant adjustment of the border with the transfer of some 130,000 acres and 24,000 people from Northern Ireland to the Irish Free State. They also envisaged a smaller (though, given nationalist expectations, disproportionately shocking) transfer of land and people from the South to the North. The denouement to these proceedings is well known. The *Morning Post* leaks helped to create a fire-storm of rage in Dublin, where there had been high expectations of substantial territorial gains. MacNeill bore the brunt of these disappointed expectations, and was forced into resignation by his baffled cabinet colleagues.[28]

These colleagues moved smartly to limit the political damage, and on 3 December 1925 an agreement was signed between the British, Free State and Northern governments which suppressed the unwanted Commission report and effectively confirmed the existing border.[29] W. T. Cosgrave, the Irish leader, was given some minor financial concessions by the British in order to help him cover his political nakedness, while Craig returned to Belfast with the powers of his administration enhanced and the borders of his territory apparently secured. He had vindicated his battle-cry of 'not an inch', and he had overturned the central legal mechanism for the reunification of the island. As part of the broader deal struck over the Commission, the Council of Ireland (a legal fiction, perhaps, but an unsettling fiction) was finally axed, and the powers that had been reserved for its use were transferred by Westminster to the Belfast administration.

Unionists were more divided about these proceedings than is commonly grasped. There was a strong tendency which opposed any movement on the border question. Craig himself seems to have been reasonably comfortable with the findings of the Commission, although (as Fisher pointed out in November 1925) the Northern premier had 'allowed some of his satellites to write so much nonsense about "not an inch" that it will be difficult for them to claim much credit'.[30] On the other hand, Carson appears to have been informed of the Commission's findings at an early stage, and to have been supportive. He seems to have taken the view that the Commission had more effectively secured the frontiers of his 'Ulster'.[31] And Fisher, naturally enough, saw the final unpublished recommendations of the Commission as a triumph worthy of celebration since 'we have got all that is essential'.[32]

With the benefit of hindsight it might be argued that, even allowing for partisanship, Fisher's arguments had merit. The leaked Commission report was a profound disappointment to political opinion in the Free State, but then (it might equally be said) expectations there were unrealistically high. Moreover, Cosgrave shied away from a deal which, while it would have involved the formal confirmation of partition, was in some practical senses helpful to the national cause. He instead signed an agreement that recognised the existing division of the island. In other words he effectively recognised one form of partition, while denying formal recognition to another, and demonstrably more equitable, variety. For Cosgrave the whole affair was simply an exercise in damage limitation, while, for their part, the Unionists chose to interpret the Boundary Commission as a political triumph. And, indeed, in so far as a ten-year-old political objective (the six-county Unionist 'Ulster') had been successfully defended, this perspective was understandable.

On the other hand, as with Cosgrave, there were alternative viewpoints. Fisher, who was a barrister, argued passionately that the Commission report represented 'a legal and permanent decision by a parliamentary tribunal from which there was no appeal. It could not have been reopened, and Ulster would have occupied an impregnable legal position.'[33] But the makeshift deal struck between the three governments in December 1925 was of a quite different quality: it was a mere 'political compromise' that by its nature was impermanent and susceptible to revision according to the eddies and tides of party politics. In terms of legal security, the Unionists would have done better to have stuck with the original Commission report, but there would also have been some practical advantages. There would have been a shorter and more defensible border, the historic and largely Protestant 'Laggan' region in East Donegal would have become part of the Unionist North, while some 35,000 nationalists ('a burden and a reproach') would have been transferred to the jurisdiction of the Free State. Lest this be misinterpreted as a lurking sensitivity to the national cause, Fisher bluntly emphasised that the lost Catholics 'would not be missed'.[34] But, while allowing for the crudity of his expression, Fisher's general point – that the Commission report gave more Irish people an opportunity to live under the regime of their choice – is persuasive. It is indeed hard to escape the impression that, had the report been enacted, the sum of Irish popular happiness would have been rather greater than in fact was the case.

The Boundary Commission Agreement had the effect of amending the Government of Ireland settlement. In particular, it removed the constitutional machinery for Irish unity. But, while the agreement modified some important details of the settlement of 1920, it did not overturn its central, explicit principles. The Northern Irish government emerged with enhanced powers and with greater political security, but Westminster remained sovereign and the financial dependence of the Belfast administration was intensifying at this time. The image of a ramshackle building (or 'lean-to') has been frequently evoked to depict the Northern administration; and – elaborating this cliché – it might be said that, while with the passage of time the Unionist shack grew ever more extensive, its foundations were weak and, given the financial climate, were steadily being undermined.[35] The autonomy of Northern Ireland appeared to be growing, while British political sovereignty remained unimpaired and British financial dominance was ever more complete.

The British government had acted over the heads of the Belfast ministers in 1921, in making provision for a Boundary Commission, and again in 1924, in activating the relevant section (no. 12) of the Anglo-Irish Treaty. Of course, the Commission report could have been much worse from the Unionist perspective, and in the event it was set aside. But this collapse should not divert from the fact that throughout the affair the British government had exercised its sovereignty by interfering in the territorial integrity of the devolved Northern government. After 1925 the

British government tended to leave the Belfast ministers to their own devices. A convention was formulated that Westminster did not intervene in matters which were the concern of the devolved parliament in Belfast. But this disengagement did not mean that the British were abrogating their political sovereignty. It effectively meant instead that the exercise of this sovereignty was becoming a zero-sum game in which the British either paid little or no attention to Northern Ireland or moved to challenge its very existence.

This is well illustrated by the British attempt to secure Irish support for the Allied war effort in the early summer of 1940. The general relationship between the British government (headed by Neville Chamberlain from May 1937 until May 1940) and the Unionist administration (led by James Craig who had been ennobled in 1927 as Viscount Craigavon) was becoming highly ambiguous. Certain sections of Whitehall, particularly the Dominions Office, were unsettled in the late 1930s by nationalist allegations against the Belfast regime. The Treasury had little time for Stormont. An Anglo-Irish Trade Agreement, signed in 1938, had been highly favourable to the Dublin negotiators and unhelpful to Belfast, but the Unionist ministers had been able to claw back some concessions from the British government.[36] The Treasury was unimpressed, seeing the Belfast ministers' tactics as 'blackmail and bluff (oddly enough called "loyalty")'. The Principal Secretary of the Treasury, Sir Warren Fisher, who had liberal and anti-partitionist sympathies, was a particular and sneering critic of the 'parochial die-hards' in Belfast.[37] Although Belfast's position was strengthened by the retirement of Fisher in 1939 and the deposition of Chamberlain in May 1940, there was an awkward recent history to overcome; and the onset of war served to give real meaning to the contempt and some of the coercive impulses that had been simmering in Whitehall over the preceding years.

In the spring and early summer of 1940 the Germans seemed to be sweeping all before them: in May the Dutch and Belgian forces were overwhelmed, and by 14 June the Germans had reached Paris. The British Expeditionary Force was withdrawn from Dunkirk between 27 May and 4 June. It was against this context, and with the real possibility of an impending invasion of Britain, that a tentative approach was made to Eamon de Valera's Fianna Fáil government in Dublin. Neville Chamberlain, whose relations with the Irish taoiseach were very good, was the 'initiator and "manager" of the initiative'.[38] On 10 May 1940 (the day that Chamberlain was deposed from the premiership) Sir John Maffey, the British representative in Dublin, asked de Valera 'if the Partition question were solved today would you automatically be our active Ally?'.[39] De Valera was not given to uncomplicated affirmation, but the general spirit of his reply was positive, and Maffey duly reported back to his masters in London. This stimulated a British diplomatic initiative that was designed to trade some movement on partition against the qualification of Irish neutrality.

On 17 June the Colonial Secretary, Malcolm MacDonald, met with de Valera and offered a British declaration of support 'in principle' for Irish unity in return for access to defence facilities.[40] A second meeting between MacDonald and de Valera brought some slight movement: the British suggested that a united Ireland be declared in principle (with the practical details of reunification to be worked out in due course); the united Ireland would then enter the war in support of the Allied cause. De Valera thought that the South 'might' indeed enter the war, provided that a constitution for the new Ireland could be agreed.[41]

The British, desperate for a settlement, moved gingerly towards the Irish position. In a document that was shown to de Valera on 26 June, the British outlined a deal that combined their support for the principle of a united Ireland with the immediate establishment of a North–South body charged with the task of sorting out a constitution. A second North–South committee would handle defence matters for the newly united Ireland: the island as a whole would be at war with the Germans. This won a chilly response in Dublin on 27 June, when MacDonald met de Valera, together with his colleagues, Sean Lemass and Frank Aiken. Again, faced with rejection, the British inched a little further to meet the Irish case, firming up their commitment to Irish unity and releasing the South from any formal obligation to act as a belligerent. The British armed forces would still be admitted to the South, and the formal approval of the government of Northern Ireland was also still required for any deal.

Throughout the evolution of this diplomacy the British had insisted that Craigavon's acquiescence was needed before any agreement could be finalised. Indeed, on 4 July 1940, when de Valera formally rejected the plan on behalf of the Irish government, stress was laid upon the Unionist veto. The British, it was claimed, were demanding the immediate abandonment of neutrality and, given the role of the Craigavon government, were offering nothing concrete by way of return. As John Bowman has argued, this emphasis on Northern Ireland carried echoes of the Irish strategy in negotiating the treaty of 1921; and in 1940, as in 1921, it had as much to do with diverting attention from some real difficulties in the Irish position as with the strength of the Ulster Unionist cause.[42] The central problem for de Valera was that his party wanted neutrality *and* Irish unity, and Irish public opinion was not going to endorse a deal that effectively brought the country into the war on behalf of an Allied cause that looked moribund. In other words, there was little attraction in gambling on Irish unity when the odds were so long, and when the cost of failure might well prove to be defeat and conquest.

In reality, though the British paid lip-service to the need for Ulster Unionist acquiescence, they had the legal and practical means to enforce their deal; and there were clear indications that, while the Unionists had some supporters in the cabinet, the British would not let Ulster parochialism stand in the way of the imperial war effort. Craigavon and the Unionist government were intermittently cajoled and ignored through May and June 1940. On 5 June 1940, Craigavon met Chamberlain and was pressed on the issue of partition. Thereafter, although Northern Ireland was never far from the minds of the British ministers, the Stormont government was kept in the dark. On 20 June 1940, Chamberlain warned the British cabinet that 'Craigavon would have to be told that the interests of Northern Ireland could not be allowed to stand against the vital interests of the British Empire'.[43] On 26 June, Chamberlain sent Craigavon a copy of the British proposal that was being submitted to de Valera, and which reflected the earlier discussions between MacDonald and the Irish taoiseach. Craigavon's response was curt but was in fact formulated with great care, and it laid stress (as 'betrayed' Unionists would do in 1972 and 1985) as much on the secretiveness of the British as on the extent of their perfidy: 'Am profoundly shocked and disgusted by your letter making suggestions so far reaching behind my back and without any consultation. To such treachery to loyal Ulster I will never be party.'[44] Indeed, despite the bitterness of his protest, Craigavon remained out of the Anglo-Irish loop until 7 July, by which time de Valera had already firmly rejected the final British proposal.

The Irish expected a German victory, and were distrustful of the British. But the notion of a Unionist veto was largely a red herring. The British had the constitutional right to repeal or amend the Government of Ireland Act and to stifle the Home Rule administration at Stormont, and its six-county domain. There was also the political will in some quarters to effect this end: Chamberlain believed in Irish unity and other Tories, both of an imperialist and 'little England' caste, thought likewise. Churchill, who became Prime Minister on 11 May, consistently urged that 'loyal Ulster' would have to be persuaded, and should not be coerced (he was perhaps mindful of the Curragh débâcle in 1914). But, then, given the financial and constitutional dependence of Stormont on the British government, 'Ulster' might well have found that it had little choice but to acquiesce in the imperial will.

Moreover, there were indications that, while most Unionist ministers shared Craigavon's obduracy, there were some who were amenable to persuasion. It seems clear that Sir Basil Brooke, the Stormont Minister of Agriculture, was more convinced of the menace of Hitler than of de Valera, and would have been willing to negotiate towards the end of Irish unity.[45] Brooke's tractability was noted by Frank MacDermot, a Dublin senator and centrist, who hastened to inform Frank Aiken, the Irish Minister for External Affairs. But the rebuff was memorably emphatic: 'get this into your head, MacDermot, there are *no* conditions under which we would abandon neutrality'.[46]

The prospect of a British-sponsored reunification project withered after July 1940. On 7 December 1941, with Pearl Harbor and the entry of the United States into the war, Churchill famously telegraphed to de Valera that 'now is your chance. Now or never. A Nation once again...'[47] But, although the taoiseach chose to interpret this as a renewed bid to end partition (and indeed this was how Maffey, the British representative, at first interpreted the telegram), in a sense these misreadings reflected nothing so much as the cloistered atmosphere of Dublin politics. Ireland's strategic importance had dropped markedly since the crisis of June 1940, and from Churchill's perspective, American entry into the war made Irish involvement simultaneously easier to procure and less valuable. The telegram was Churchillian bombast, not the opening salvo of a negotiation. The British certainly retained the constitutional right to end Stormont and partition; what was changing after 1940 was that the political will to effect change of this kind was ebbing away.

The contribution of Northern Ireland to the Allied military struggle created a new sense of political obligation at Westminster, and this assumed a particular constitutional importance in the years after 1945. Indeed, at this time the main challenge to the settlement of 1920 came arguably not from within British politics, or even from Dublin's renewed interest in fighting partition, but rather from the support that the notion of dominion status was gaining within the Ulster Unionist elite.[48] This was stimulated in part by the extensive and radical legislative programme of Clement Attlee's Labour government. But when it was grasped in Belfast that ministers like Attlee, Herbert Morrison and James Chuter-Ede were not only socialists but also essentially unionists, and that they were willing to pay for welfare reform within Northern Ireland, much of the support for dominion status cooled.

Indeed, it was Attlee's government that offered Ulster Unionists the firmest legislative endorsement they were ever to receive at Westminster: the Ireland Act of 1949. This measure was passed in the aftermath of the formal inauguration of an Irish republic by the Inter-Party government in Dublin: it was passed with memories of Stormont's wartime co-operation still fresh, and in the context of the intensification of the Cold War, when the strategic importance of Northern Ireland seemed indispensable. Under its terms, which were extensively previewed by the Stormont ministers, no constitutional change in the status of Northern Ireland could be achieved without the authorisation of its parliament: 'it is hereby affirmed that in no event will Northern Ireland or any part thereof cease to be part of His Majesty's dominions and of the United Kingdom without the consent of the Parliament of Northern Ireland'.[49] From the Unionist perspective this was a welcome affirmation, and they were cloyingly appreciative. The Act underpinned the more expansive notions of regional autonomy that characterised the 1950s and 1960s, but it did not change the fundamental character of the 1920 settlement. Westminster had granted this token of its favour, but it had the constitutional right to take away what it had given, and to withdraw its sanction. Stormont now had an apparently greater degree of control over partition, but the supremacy of Westminster and its authority over the Belfast administration remained unimpaired.

Taken as a whole, the experience of the 1940s had underlined the extent to which the Unionists, while they might otherwise deceive themselves, were in reality always subject to the exigencies of British strategy. The British participated in this deception to the extent that it took a very considerable pressure for them to interfere in the workings of the devolved administration in Belfast. Yet the lesson of 1921, and of 1940, was clear: that the constitution of Northern Ireland was ultimately negotiable. And it was a lesson that would reappear on the political curriculum in 1972, when Stormont was prorogued, and again (albeit in a different formulation) in 1985, at the time of the Anglo-Irish Agreement. That there was profound bitterness on each occasion indicated not so much the novelty of 'betrayal', as the extent to which successive generations of Unionists had succumbed to the illusion of local autonomy, and had to relearn the lessons of British sovereignty.

The economist Thomas Wilson has highlighted the apparently paradoxical way in which British sovereignty was exercised in Northern Ireland between 1920 and 1972. His concern has been less the occasional but potentially devastating constitutional initiatives of 1921, 1924–5, 1940 and 1972 than the contrast between the nit-picking micro-management exercised by the British Treasury and the virtually complete neglect of more profound issues. 'Stormont', he has complained, 'has been free from interference in cases where interference might be most justified, but has been unduly restrained by financial control in dealing with certain other matters which should be the core of provincial authority.'[50]

It should be conceded that the vitality of this paradox has not been universally acknowledged: Derek Birrell and Alan Murie, writing in their study of devolved government in Northern Ireland, have argued that the Stormont administration had 'a much wider area of discretion over public expenditure than has often been imagined, while Treasury policy has frequently seemed laissez faire'. They have also suggested that Stormont exercised a substantial influence 'in determining priorities and expenditure levels on nearly all the public services provided in Northern Ireland', while 'it is doubtful whether the Treasury's overall financial power was a significant restriction on Stormont's freedom to distribute its financial resources'.[51] Whatever the final verdict on the effective influence of the Treasury (and there can be no question of its immense theoretical powers), it is clear that financial control mattered more to Westminster than other, evidently more critical issues.

One of these critical issues was civil rights, and specifically the rights of the substantial Ulster Catholic minority. As has been emphasised, the British parliament was sovereign in Northern Ireland, and was the effective guarantor of the Northern constitution, the Government of Ireland Act. Section 5 of the Act contained an expansive prohibition on all forms of legislation that impinged upon religious belief and its expression. The wording of the clause – no law could 'directly or indirectly' promote any sectarian agenda – constituted, in theory, a powerful protection for minority religious interests. Its origins lay with a similar prohibition in the third Home Rule Bill of 1912; and this in turn had been devised as a means of defusing a Unionist argument, that 'Home Rule' would be 'Rome Rule'. In 1912 the proposed ban on sectarian legislation was seen as a slur on the Irish nation, and was deeply resented by John Redmond and the rest of the Home Rule leadership. For their part, Unionists were contemptuous, regarding the clause as ineffective and as a cheap means of buying political consent. But, as with other checks and balances in the topsy-turvy world of Home Rule, this concession to Unionism was eventually incorporated into the constitution of Northern Ireland as a protection against Unionist infringement of Catholic rights. The clause that in 1912 was designed for Unionists, and condemned by them as unworkable, became in 1920 an unworkable guarantee for Ulster Catholics.

The literature on religious discrimination in Northern Ireland is weighty, sombre and occasionally controversial.[52] The concern here is not with the wider aspects of this issue and debate, but rather with the specific interrelationship between discrimination and the Home Rule settlement. Thus the emphasis is not on the pervasive informal discrimination in Ulster society, which often predated partition and devolution. The concern is rather with the evidence of official discrimination undertaken by political leaders, by the ruling Unionist Party and embodied within the law.[53] And, even allowing for this limitation, only the outlines of a highly complex issue can be traced.

What was the state of the Catholic (or nationalist) minority within Northern Ireland in the early 1920s?[54] The community was substantial, totalling around 35 per cent of the Northern population in 1921. Roman Catholicism was the single biggest church denomination, for Ulster Protestantism was, and is, relatively fissile. At first, the Northern Irish administration appeared highly vulnerable: between 1920 and 1922 the Irish Republican Army (IRA) fought hard to overturn the fledgling state, and the Boundary Commission then looked set to accomplish by cartography what the IRA had been unable to do with bullets. Many Northern nationalists in the early 1920s saw no reason to acknowledge a Unionist-dominated regime, and until the collapse of the Boundary Commission in December 1925 many pursued an abstentionist policy. This attitude of non-cooperation was reinforced by the disproportionately heavy casualties that the community had suffered, particularly in Belfast, during the civil unrest of 1920-2. Abstentionism was, in a sense, complemented by the attitude of the Unionist government. Harried by the IRA until 1922, and impressed by republican intelligence successes, Unionists tended to equate Catholicism and militant republicanism and to regard all Catholics as political subversives. This, when combined with Catholic self-denial and the political divisions within nationalism, meant that the minority exercised little effective influence during the critical early years of the Northern state's existence.[55]

The nature of Catholic, or nationalist, disadvantage within Northern Ireland was multifaceted and complex. There was a profound under-representation of Catholics in local government. The Leech Commission on local government boundaries, which sat in 1922-3, was largely boycotted by nationalists and favoured the Unionist cause; subsequent gerrymanders by the Unionist Party created further injustices within local government. Nationalists had little voice within the provincial parliament either: nationalist MPs only took up their seats in the late 1920s, but even then their concerns were generally dismissed. Only one Catholic and moderate nationalist, G. B. Newe, was ever appointed to a Northern Ireland cabinet.[56] There was a marked under-representation of Catholics within the higher ranks of the civil service, and within all ranks of the police. Catholics were much more likely than Protestants to suffer unemployment. In broad terms, there seems to have been an exacerbation of some of these problems with the expansion of Unionist state power in the post-war era. Moreover, nationalists were now better able to articulate their dissatisfaction: the community was growing, was better schooled and, in the context of world-wide civil unrest in the 1960s, was able to exploit an international language of protest.

Catholic dissatisfaction and alienation contributed to the end of the devolved parliament at Stormont in 1972. But to what extent did this unrest not only precipitate the failure of Stormont, but also embody the failures of the Unionist regime and of the Home Rule experiment? It need hardly be stressed that sectarian bitterness in Ulster long pre-dated the establishment of the Belfast parliament. Catholic disadvantage and radical nationalist protest in Ulster pre-dated partition. But it is also emphatically true that the devolved government presided over a remarkable elaboration of inequality and an intensification of protest; and it seems quite clear that the Government of Ireland Act provided little effective protection against the infringement of minority rights.

Three broad areas of controversy seem particularly worthy of attention: electoral arrangements, the issue of policing and special crimes legislation, and the inter-relationship between government ministers and employment discrimination. Local government elections had been held throughout Ireland in 1920, and – benefiting from the new system of proportional representation – nationalists had captured a range of local authorities throughout the south and west of Northern Ireland. These nationalist councils in some cases refused to recognise the authority of the Belfast government, and in 1922 Unionist ministers moved against the 'rebel' authorities by seeking to replace proportional representation with the old first-past-the-post arrangement. In 1929 the Unionist government abolished proportional representation in elections for the Northern Ireland House of Commons, although here the principal victims of change were not the nationalists but rather the proliferation of minor Protestant and Unionist parties.

The franchise qualifications for the devolved parliament remained in line with British practice. But change within the local government franchise lagged behind British reform, with the result that by the 1960s Northern Ireland was burdened with a system that was largely unaltered from the date of its introduction in 1919. In the 1960s there was universal suffrage in parliamentary elections, but at the level of local government there were property and residence qualifications, and multiple votes for businessmen with far-flung property interests. These anomalies gave rise to the 'one man, one vote' cry of the Northern Ireland Civil Rights Association after 1967.

By and large parliamentary electoral boundaries were established with reasonable fairness. But, then again, the Unionist majority within the Northern Ireland House of Commons was so substantial that no cheating was necessary at this level.[57] As with the franchise issue, local government boundaries were a much more hotly contested and controversial issue than parliamentary ones. The Leech commission, which adjusted these boundaries in 1922-3, placed nationalists at an initial disadvantage, and subsequent gerrymanders in Derry, Omagh and Enniskillen further suppressed or disenfranchised local nationalist majorities. These gerrymanders were not the result of some quiet local skulduggery, but instead were embodied in legislation that was formally approved by the Northern Ireland parliament.

How was all of this possible? In a limited technical sense, these actions occurred because they were not expressly prohibited under the terms of the devolution settlement of 1920. Indeed, the Government of Ireland Act not only failed to ban all forms of electoral manipulation, but also specifically empowered the new Northern Ireland parliament to 'alter the qualification and registration of electors, the law relating to elections, and the questioning of elections, the constituencies, and the distribution of members among the constituencies' (section 14.5). This freedom applied to parliamentary elections; but the Government of Ireland Act also provided the Northern administration with the right to interfere in local government electoral matters. Thus the paradoxical situation arose where an otherwise highly constrained local assembly possessed powers to regulate virtually the entire democratic process. Broken and suppressed in matters of finance, in certain respects Stormont had greater constitutional rights than many sovereign parliaments. Here was a pellucid reflection of the nature of British interests.

But, although the Northern Ireland government enjoyed surprisingly wide powers over electoral arrangements, there were certainly some theoretical constraints on its actions. Westminster remained sovereign, and the British cabinet had the effective power (acting through the Crown and the Governor–General of Northern Ireland) to deny assent to any Northern Irish legislation. Moreover, section 5 of the Government of Ireland Act, which prohibited discriminatory legislation, was clearly meant to have a very wide application: the Northern Ireland parliament could not 'make a law so as either directly or indirectly ... to give a preference, privilege, or advantage, or impose any disability or disadvantage on account of religious belief or religious or ecclesiastical status'. In practice, however, this apparently critical aspect of the constitution does not seem to have been widely invoked. The Campaign for Social Justice certainly believed that particular types of discrimination (by local authorities, for example) could not be considered by the courts under the terms of the Act of 1920, but opinions differed sharply. And although British sovereignty was occasionally exercised when the devolution settlement itself hung in the balance, it was hardly ever used to protect human rights.[58]

In this, as in so many other aspects of the Northern Ireland regime, a critical turning-point came in the first months of the state's existence. In 1922, when the Northern Ireland government moved to abolish proportional representation in local government elections, the British cabinet was highly critical and tried to block the measure by denying the royal assent. The Belfast ministers held out, however, and threatened to resign if they did not get their way. This challenge was all the more pointed, given that Northern Ireland was still embroiled in sectarian unrest, and the island as a whole was teetering on the brink of a full-scale civil war. The British government needed Craig in office more than they needed nationalist local councils, and the abolition of proportional representation was therefore confirmed.

This was effectively a test case, and it helped to confirm that British interference in Northern Ireland would be minimal, and that London was not prepared to act either as a policeman for the constitution or as a guardian of minority rights. The British government had powers of interference, but no political will and – after the proportional representation stand-off – no precedents. Future Unionist electoral action (or, indeed, lack of it) would attract no reprimand from London. The abolition of proportional representation in parliamentary elections passed smoothly into law in 1929, while the anomalies in the local government franchise were confirmed as late as 1962 through the Electoral Law Act.

The same broad pattern of partisan action, British disengagement and Catholic upset may be detected in the critical area of policing. The institutions and attitudes of Northern Ireland's security regime were created, again, in the first bitter years of the state's existence. In 1920 the Ulster Special Constabulary (USC) was raised, building upon the structures and personnel of the pre-war Ulster Volunteer Force, but financed in the first place by the British government.[59] With the foundation of the government of Northern Ireland in 1921, responsibility for sustaining the USC passed to Belfast. But Unionist ministers successfully fought for continued British subvention, and moneys were paid from the Treasury, albeit on an *ad hoc* basis, until December 1924. The USC was one of the main weapons deployed by the Northern government during its struggle with the IRA, and it quickly came to be seen by nationalists as an oppressive, and sometimes murderous, force. The episode that defined the USC for many nationalists was the McMahon murders of 23–4 March 1922, when a Catholic publican, three of his sons and an employee were all killed by intruders wearing police uniforms.[60] It seemed that, in the ugly civil war being fought out on the streets of Belfast in the spring of 1922, an armed Protestant militia, responsible to the Unionist junta and paid for by the British, was being deployed against the Catholic people.

The actions of the USC caused some disquiet in London, but this was a particularly bloody period, and the Unionists could point to examples of republican violence. One such episode was the Altnaveigh murders of 17 June 1922, when republicans – one of whom was wearing a police cap – killed six of their Protestant neighbours at Altnaveigh in South Down.[61] Bryan Follis, the historian of the early Northern state, has observed that some imperial officials had severe doubts as to whether the USC, which was nominally an auxiliary police force but which functioned as a paramilitary unit, was in fact constitutional. The Northern Ireland government had no right under the Government of Ireland Act to raise and maintain an 'army'.[62] If the USC was a police force, the argument ran, then it should be deployed as a police force, and its costs should be met by the Belfast government. If, however, it were a military body, then it should not only be paid for by London, but also be fully controlled by the imperial government. The USC, in terms of both its status and its proclivities, raised questions that London ultimately chose not to answer. It retained its military functions, remained directly under the control of the Northern Ireland government and continued, for a time, to be supported by the British taxpayer. Once again the central thrust of British policy was not a sensitive regard for the Government of Ireland Act, but rather disengagement from Ireland. And although direct Treasury support for the USC ended in 1924, and the force was substantially cut back in 1925, it survived as a constitutional anomaly until its disbandment in 1970.

The main police force in Northern Ireland was the Royal Ulster Constabulary (RUC), which was created in 1922 to replace the defunct Royal Irish Constabulary. Here there were fewer constitutional irregularities, though ultimately the RUC came to be disliked by mainstream nationalism as much as its predecessor. The force was originally to have had a strength of 3000, one-third of whom were to have been Catholic. But this proportion was never attained: a peak of 21 per cent Catholic membership was achieved in 1923, and the level of Catholic participation gradually dropped off through the first decades of the state's existence. The RUC was responsible to the Minister for Home Affairs in the Unionist cabinet, and this, together with its strongly Protestant composition, meant that it was generally seen by nationalists as partisan.[63] It was used against republican insurgents during the Second World War and between 1956 and 1962, when seven of its members were killed. In the eyes of its critics, this deployment reinforced the military and political aspects of its role. But a critical turning-point in the Catholic attitude towards the RUC perhaps came only in 1968, with the television footage of heavy-handed police action against civil rights demonstrators.

The third leg of the Unionist security tripod was the Civil Authorities

(Special Powers) Act, which was passed in April 1922 at the height of the civil unrest in the North. The Special Powers Act, as it came to be known, was an adaptation of the Restoration of Order in Ireland Act (1920), which had been passed by an embattled British government at the height of the Anglo-Irish War. The Northern Act granted the Minister of Home Affairs the right 'to take all such steps and issue all such orders as may be necessary for preserving the peace and maintaining order'. An ill-fated effort to hammer out a formula for peace and reconciliation, launched on 31 March 1922 by Craig and Michael Collins, delayed the implementation of the measure, but as the pressure applied by the IRA offensive continued unabated, the Northern government was forced into action.[64]

The specific catalyst was the killing by the IRA of W. J. Twaddell on 22 May 1922. Twaddell was a prominent Belfast loyalist and a member of the Northern Ireland parliament. Although he was only one of fourteen victims of murder on the weekend of 21–2 May, his death created widespread consternation among Unionists, and forced the Northern government into using their newly acquired 'special powers'. A string of decrees followed: the proscription of the IRA, the internment of 500 suspects and a province-wide curfew between 11 p.m. and 5 a.m. Flogging was extensively used as a 'special punishment'. These penalties fell heavily on the nationalist minority within Northern Ireland, and particularly heavily – as with similar legislation in the South – on the republican community. But for the Unionist administration a cowed and demoralised minority was a small price to pay – and a price willingly paid – for the defeat of the IRA within the confines of the new state.

In the context of the turmoil of the early 1920s, and when compared to the legislation enacted by the Cumann na nGaedheal administration in Dublin, the Special Powers Act was unexceptional – a regrettable, but probably inescapable infringement of normal civil liberties. However, the Act outlived the crisis within which it was launched: in 1933 it became a permanent feature of the Northern criminal code, and while in 1949 all but a handful of its provisions were revoked, these were fully restored in 1956 with the onset of an IRA offensive. In the context of more settled conditions in the mid-1920s and after, the Act began to look unusually crude and repressive; and although the measure was rarely activated, its very presence was an affront to normal definitions of civil liberty. Moreover, the fact that the Act had in the past been directed principally against nationalists meant that it seemed to be both a sectarian and a repressive instrument.

In the end, therefore, the Special Powers Act must be judged as a needless provocation to the nationalist minority and an avoidable source of damage to the Unionist regime itself. Given the impact of the measure on

Catholics, the British government might well have invoked section 5 of the Government of Ireland Act to question its legitimacy; given the absence of any organised insurgency in 1933, the British might well have scuppered the Unionist effort to make the Act permanent. But the British once again were not prepared to intervene to protect the interests of the nationalist minority or, indeed, to protect Unionists from the consequences of their own actions. The Unionists, for their part, had effectively won the battle for the six counties by the end of 1925. But the bloodiness of the struggle, and the persistence of its shock-waves, meant that they never developed a magnanimity which might simultaneously have reflected and secured their victory.

There was certainly a conspicuous lack of magnanimity in the Northern job market. Here again was an area where the Government of Ireland Act offered an incomplete and therefore inadequate protection of civil rights. Section 5 of the Act prevented the Northern Ireland parliament from passing legislation that conferred any individual or corporate advantages or liabilities on account of religion. But the Act did not refer to other, non-statutory, forms of religious discrimination, and in particular it did nothing to counter the informal sectarian employment practices that were endemic in Northern society.

In a limited sense, this was a controversy that had been inherited from the era before independence. Then the exclusive employment records of large Protestant-controlled enterprises like the railway companies, the Bank of Ireland and Guinness attracted protests and counter-strategies from radical nationalists such as D. P. Moran. Equally, however, the favouritism displayed by a variety of nationalist-controlled local government authorities led to angry Unionist protests at Westminster and elsewhere.[65] On the whole, and certainly in terms of the Edwardian House of Commons, it was the Unionists who were more energetic and successful in publicising their case (which was, incidentally, another way of expressing Ireland's unfitness for Home Rule). It was ironic, therefore, but in keeping with the paradoxes of devolved government in Northern Ireland, that discrimination by Unionists, particularly in local government, should have emerged as a touchstone for the broader inadequacies of the state, for in a certain sense the issue had been highlighted by the Unionists themselves under the old regime.

The issue of discrimination remains hotly debated. The extent of inequality experienced by Northern Catholics under the Stormont dispensation is beyond question. As has been said, Catholics were much more likely to be unemployed than Protestants, and much less likely to be employed within the top ranks of the police, the judiciary and the civil service. The unfair stranglehold that Unionists possessed over local government until 1973 meant that council patronage – in terms of jobs and housing – fell disproportionately into the hands of Protestants. However, the precise origin of many of these inequalities is less clear – whether, for example, they were created largely through the proactive sectarianism of the Unionist elite and its supporters, or by some other, structural, means. Some of the inequalities in Northern society certainly pre-dated the foundation of the state, and were rooted in wider social and political issues over which Unionist ministers had minimal control. On the other hand, there is no doubt whatsoever that many Unionist leaders – and particularly the generation who had lived through the Irish revolution – automatically equated Catholicism with political subversion, and discriminated accordingly. Nor can there be much doubt that, while popular nationalism harboured some sectarian impulses, the discrimination practised by Unionists had a very much wider importance in the North, if only because it was they who wielded state power.

The complexity of the inequalities within the job market is well illustrated by the career of Patrick Shea, who was a Catholic and (eventually) Permanent Secretary at the Department of Education in Northern Ireland. In his autobiography Shea recalled that his commitment to the Northern Ireland civil service was viewed by some within the Catholic community as at best incomprehensible, and at worst a betrayal.[66] And indeed, it is possible that Catholic applications for some jobs in the public service were disproportionately low because such work was seen as inherently anti-national and demeaning. On the other hand, Shea, who was a high-flyer, was privately told at one stage of his career that because of his Catholicism he would not win a particular promotion.[67] Moreover, there can be no doubt that his experience was not unique, and reflected widely held religious prejudices within the Unionist high command. At the time of his promotion to head up the Department of Education, Shea was only the second Catholic in the history of the state to reach the rank of Permanent Secretary (the other was A. N. Bonaparte-Wyse). But, taken as a whole, Shea's career documents the complex influences within the Northern job market. Political and religious intolerance unquestionably played a dominant role, but its form and relative significance varied.

The Unionist state failed Catholics not least because it offered no serious protection against religious discrimination or defamation, even at the hands of senior government ministers. Craigavon and his lieutenants, who had learnt hard lessons during the Anglo-Irish war, were particularly susceptible to anti-Catholic paranoia. The overarching political concerns of this generation were with the unity of Unionism and republican subversion, which was frequently seen as omnipresent. These men tended to see the shadow of conspiracy wherever they looked: they feared republican penetration of the administration, and they feared, too, that Southern republicans would infiltrate Northern constituencies and overturn often narrow Unionist majorities. In a sense, these men were victims both of the republican intelligence and propaganda coups of 1919–21 and of their own political successes. They were lastingly impressed by the republican infiltration of Dublin Castle. And they spent the rest of their careers defending a territory for which they had long asked, but which it was only just within their capacity to hold.

Successive Unionist leaders either underlined the Protestant character of the Northern state, or pursued the corollary of this by insisting upon sectarian employment practices. Some of these men were not without liberal impulses (or at any rate rhetoric), but the apparent precariousness of the partition settlement in the 1920s and 1930s limited their room for manoeuvre. Craigavon's notorious allusion to a 'Protestant Parliament and a Protestant state' in April 1934 was part of a speech that contained a characteristic mixture of religious chauvinism, political defensiveness and some fragmentary gestures towards inclusiveness:

> I am Prime Minister not of one section of the community, but of all, and that as far as I possibly could I was going to see that fair play was meted out to all classes and creeds without any favour whatever on my part...the Honourable Member must remember that in the South they boasted of a Catholic state. They still boast of Southern Ireland being a Catholic state. All I boast of is that we are a Protestant Parliament and a Protestant state.[68]

The speech defied the spirit, if not the letter, of the Government of Ireland Act, and indeed it illustrates the extent to which the constitution-builders of 1919–20 had defined ideals and mechanisms that were mutually incompatible. But it was also a tragic lost opportunity, for Craigavon might well have used his 'unassailable' political position to define a parliament and a state that belonged to everyone.[69] But the problem was that neither Craigavon nor his successors were ever fully confident that their position was, indeed, unassailable. Occasional and ominous British initiatives, intermittent republican violence and, above all, the demographics of partition served to undermine the confidence necessary for any true and sustained ecumenism. Unionist control of Northern Ireland depended upon maintaining the unity of the majority Protestant population, and since this was concentrated in the east of Northern Ireland, and even there was highly prone to splitting, Stormont ministers faced an unrelenting political challenge. The result of these pressures was an unremitting struggle to maintain the Unionist advantage, and this occasionally produced exceptionally crude sectarian outbursts, such as that offered by Craigavon.

Craigavon's 'Protestant Parliament and Protestant state' boast has been seen as the battle-cry of sectarianism within Northern Ireland. A series of speeches by Sir Basil Brooke in 1933–4, delivered when he was a minister in Craigavon's government, seemed to define the attitude of the Unionist regime towards Catholic employment. On 12 July 1933, speaking at Newtownbutler, Brooke complained:

> a great number of Protestants...employed Roman Catholics...He felt that he could speak freely on this subject as he had not a Roman Catholic about the place...He would point out that the Roman Catholics were endeavouring to get in everywhere and were out with all their force and might to destroy the power and constitution of Ulster. There was a definite plot to overpower the vote of Unionists in the North. He would appeal to loyalists, therefore, wherever possible, to employ Protestant lads and lassies...[Catholics] had got too many appointments for men who were really out to cut their throats if opportunity arose.[70]

These sentiments were not a one-off indiscretion, but were repeated by Brooke at Derry in August 1933, Enniskillen in October, and again at Derry in March 1934. Moreover, when on 20 March 1934 the leading nationalist, Cahir Healy, raised the subject in the Stormont House of Commons, Brooke's sectarianism was endorsed by Craigavon: 'there is not one of my colleagues who does not entirely agree with him, and I would not ask him to withdraw one word'. The equation of Catholicism with disloyalty was automatically accepted, and it was also accepted that 'disloyalty' should be contained or crushed.[71]

As Brooke's biographer has stressed, the context to these outrageous speeches is relevant, providing illumination, though little by way of mitigation.[72] Brooke was from Fermanagh, where Unionism and nationalism were evenly divided; and Fermanagh Unionists widely believed at this time that nationalists were consolidating their hold on the county. Moreover, the unity of Unionism in the area was shaky at the time, for there was an agricultural recession and discontented Protestant farmers were looking to make a protest. Unionists lost control of the district council in Lisnaskea, the main town of Brooke's constituency, and there was talk of a parliamentary challenge from angry farmers. Brooke himself explained these speeches by referring to republican threats to his family, which led him to get 'rid of every man in my place who I thought might betray me'. These threats were made in 1922, and Brooke's call for exclusively Protestant employment was made in 1933; but it is clear that the tensions of the revolutionary period made a lasting and bitter impression.[73] Maurice Hayes' memory of a conversation with Brooke's wife confirms the importance of this personal context.[74] There is evidence to suggest that by the late 1940s Brooke was anxious to strike a more consensual note, and that by the 1960s he was coming to have doubts about his speeches of 1933–4; but there is nothing to show that the general sentiments and values which underpinned them were ever revised or regretted.[75]

Craigavon's 'Protestant Parliament' and Brooke's 'I have not a Roman Catholic about my own place' certainly have to be understood in context, but they were also considered statements by influential leaders, and expressed the values of contemporary Unionism. The harm done, in terms of legitimising discrimination and demoralising and excluding Catholics, was incalculable. Both men were personally more generous than these sentiments might suggest, but given that neither made any retraction, and given that their combined premierships lasted forty years, their contribution to both the reality and the image of sectarianism in Northern Ireland was immense.[76] Viewed from the narrower perpective of Unionist self-interest, these sectarian war-cries brought temporary encouragement to a divided and threatened party, but at the cost of lasting damage to its credibility. Craigavon and Brooke would be regularly invoked in outlining the failure of the Unionist state, and would be cited by opponents anxious to discredit other aspects of Unionist politics. As late as 1999 and 2000, Martin McGuinness of Sinn Féin repeatedly paraphrased Brooke's Newtownbutler speech in condemning Unionist nervousness about sharing executive power with former republican militants.

These speeches, and others like them, illustrate the extent to which the Home Rule constitution of Northern Ireland failed to provide protection for the basic civil rights of all its citizens. They illustrate the extent to which, only twelve years after the passage of the Government of Ireland Act, Britain had abdicated responsibility for the protection of the Northern minority. Brooke, as a Stormont minister, was repeatedly able to encourage sectarian employment practices, yet there was no rebuke from Westminster and no invocation of the Government of Ireland Act by way of sanction. The irony is that this combination of local partisanship and British dereliction had been forecast by the Unionists themselves in 1912. They had foreseen that the protection promised to minorities by the third Home Rule Bill would be inadequate, that it would not stop discrimination, and that it would be silently accepted by the British. Here, again, the Unionists of Northern Ireland were active in fulfilling their own laments concerning Home Rule.

Some stress has been laid upon Craigavon and Brooke in describing the sectarian fears of the Unionist high command, discriminatory employment practices and the limitations of the Northern constitution. But even Terence O'Neill, widely regarded as a secular moderniser, helped to endorse the kind of sectarian employment strategy that Brooke had called for in 1933. As late as November 1959, when O'Neill was the Minister of Finance at Stormont, he advertised in a prominent local newspaper for some domestic help: 'Protestant girl required for housework'.[77] In 1972, when he was keen to defend his reputation as a liberal reformer, O'Neill was asked about this advertisement. He explained ingenuously that he had had 'some trouble' with Catholic staff in the past, and therefore had asked for a Protestant 'to stop Catholics turning up'.[78] This, then, was the Unionist leader who sought to distinguish himself from the Stormont red-necks of an earlier generation, and to bring Brookeborough's Northern Ireland into the 'swinging' 1960s.

By now some of the central weaknesses of the theory and practice of devolution in Northern Ireland will be clear. But a critical aspect of the failure of Home Rule in the province relates not only to the constitutional limitations devised in 1920, the narrowness of Unionist political practice between 1920 and 1960, and the dangers of British minimalism, but also to the attempts by the regime to reform itself in the 1960s. The penultimate section of this chapter looks, therefore, to the modernisation project of Terence O'Neill, Prime Minister of Northern Ireland in the critical years between 1963 and 1969.

Before any assessment of O'Neill's reformism is attempted, it should be said immediately that (contrary to some popular Unionist beliefs) he inherited a challenging political and economic position when he attained the Northern premiership in 1963. Indeed, part of his difficulty was that he only partly understood the extent of his problems. The retreat of key Northern industries (particularly linen and shipbuilding) was accelerating at this time, and unemployment was rising sharply: the unemployment rate rose from 6.7 per cent in 1960 to 7.5 per cent in 1962. Some of the social effects of this were mitigated through the welfare benefits financed by the British state, but there was also political fall-out, and for a time it seemed that the Unionist power base, and therefore the stability of the regime, was under threat. With economic slowdown came a realignment of working-class and other leftist Protestants behind the Northern Ireland Labour Party, which saw its support rise from 37,000 votes at the Stormont general election of 1958 to 77,000 votes (26 per cent of the total cast) at the election of 1962.

In addition to these problems with the economy and the integrity of the Unionist class alliance, there remained the threat posed by republican militants. Mainstream nationalist opinion in the North had eventually accepted the inevitable, and had begun to participate informally in the institutions of the Unionist state. After a period of abstention, nationalist MPs had begun to trickle into the Northern Ireland House of Commons in the late 1920s. But constitutional nationalism in the North for long remained marooned in what Mansergh has called 'the Sargasso Sea of Ulster politics', and indeed the ineffectiveness of its various initiatives (such as the creation of an Anti-Partition League in November 1945) tended to underline the credibility of armed struggle.[79]

The Irish Republican Army had been effectively defeated by the Northern authorities in 1922, but its war against Britain and its lackeys at Stormont was resumed (albeit on an extremely limited scale) after 1939. The successful return of two republican candidates at the Westminster election of 1955 seemed to indicate a growing degree of popular endorsement for the militant position, and after a number of preparatory arms raids an offensive was launched against the Stormont government in December 1956. By the standards of the later 'troubles', this 'Border Campaign' was relatively low-key, though no less painful for those affected: eighteen people (twelve IRA volunteers and six RUC men) were killed, and there were around 600 'incidents', often admittedly of a very minor nature. The campaign was called off in February 1962, partly because Northern Catholics were unimpressed and unsupportive, and partly because both the Belfast and Dublin governments took vigorous action against the insurgents.

But although the struggle was apparently limited, and though the ceasefire was already a year old when O'Neill took office, he had to address a number of important consequences. While the Border Campaign had fizzled out, it had not broken the morale of republicans, who very swiftly embarked upon an intellectual and organisational regrouping. O'Neill, therefore, faced a militant threat which was dormant, rather than extinct. Moreover, the campaign empowered Unionist hardliners: it lent credibility to their fears, while (since it was essentially a failure) it also boosted their morale. O'Neill, anglocentric and aloof, was unable to grasp that the swinging sixties affected Ulster only in so far as the bigots and the gunmen now wore suede shoes and bought the records of The Beatles; modernisation would bring no revision of fundamental loyalties.

How did O'Neill seek to reform the Home Rule administration within

Northern Ireland? The traditional economic substructure of the Unionist regime (the textile, engineering and shipbuilding industries) had been in difficulties virtually since the foundation of the state. Earlier Unionist ministers had sought to bolster these declining industries through subsidies; they had also made some efforts to offset the loss of jobs in traditional sectors by inducing new enterprises to locate in Northern Ireland. O'Neill continued in this vein, using his energetic Minister of Commerce, Brian Faulkner, to sell the commercial wonders of Northern Ireland to international capitalism.

Earlier ministers had also shown some interest in seeking expert advice about Northern Ireland's problems. Brookeborough, for example, had commissioned K. S. Isles and Norman Cuthbert, two academic economists, to undertake and publish *An Economic Survey of Northern Ireland* (1957). Brookeborough also invited Sir Robert Hall to chair a Joint Working Party on the Northern Economy, which reported in 1962. But, much more than his predecessors, O'Neill believed that the economic problems of Northern Ireland were susceptible to rational management and systematic planning. In August 1963, after official recognition of the autonomous Northern Ireland Committee of the Irish Congress of Trades Unions, O'Neill oversaw the creation of an Economic Council, designed to unite trade unionists with industrialists and to provide expert guidance for Stormont ministers. In October 1963 he commissioned a distinguished Ulster-born economist, Professor Tom Wilson of the University of Glasgow, to devise an economic programme along the lines of that already in operation in the South of Ireland. The Wilson Report was ready by late 1964, and resulted in the creation of a Ministry of Development in 1965, headed at first by a close ally of O'Neill, the gifted but unpredictable Bill Craig. Wilson also called for designated areas of urban growth, endorsed an earlier official proposal to create a new city in North Armagh, and outlined other ambitious ideas for the improvement of the economic infrastructure of Northern Ireland: new motorways, and new educational and housing resources. Ancillary reports, by Benson on the railways and by Lockwood on university education, supplied some of the detail that Wilson's broad-brush approach lacked.

These efforts were complemented by a succession of initiatives within the realm of community relations. The pontificate of John XXIII had prepared the way for some mild thawing in the attitude of liberal Unionists towards the Catholic hierarchy, and when Pope John died, in June 1963, the government of Northern Ireland broke from previous practice and sent its condolences to Rome. O'Neill provided his own eulogy of the dead pontiff, an apparently unremarkable but – for an Ulster Unionist leader – an unprecedented gesture. Later rhetoric and (to a lesser extent) actions built upon this tentative diplomacy: in April 1964, O'Neill visited a Catholic school in Ballymoney, County Antrim, the first Prime Minister of Northern Ireland to venture into such an outpost of Babylon. But the most celebrated of these cross-community gestures came in January 1965, with the visit to Stormont of the Irish taoiseach, Seán Lemass. This was the first trip of its kind and, astonishingly, the first official meeting between a Northern and Southern leader since the Boundary Commission affair of 1925.

These actions and gestures, mild and consensual, helped to precipitate a crisis that finally resulted in the collapse of the Home Rule institutions of the Northern state. Despite the generosity of his intentions and the range of expert advice that he enjoyed, it is clear with hindsight that O'Neill got the politics of his reform programme badly wrong. O'Neill for long believed, like the constructive Unionists of the 1890s, that economic and political modernisation progressed hand-in-hand; and he fully expected that with wider prosperity would come a new and more consensual form of politics. But this, as Feargal Cochrane has memorably remarked, was to treat nationalism (to say nothing of popular loyalism) as 'a kind of behavioural problem', susceptible to economic therapy.[80] It was also to ignore the experience of recent Irish history, which tended to indicate that periods of economic dynamism produced social readjustment and often political crisis. And indeed even relatively stable periods of prosperity were sometimes associated with rising social expectations and political radicalism.

In a sense this is what happened as the Wilson and other expert reports – which together embodied the substance of O'Neillism – were gradually implemented in the mid- and late 1960s. Perhaps the role of certain aspects of the O'Neillite project in generating social and political change has been exaggerated: it has long been clear, for example, that the relative internationalisation of the Ulster economy in the 1960s, which O'Neill encouraged, did not in itself destabilise the Unionist regime.[81] However the drive for multinational and other forms of external investment was certainly seen as favouring the eastern part of Northern Ireland, where most of the new businesses were established, and where the Unionist population was concentrated.

Other O'Neillite enterprises can also be linked indirectly to the firing of social unrest: the creation of new dwellings (Wilson's target was 64,000 units in five years) helped to open up longstanding Catholic dissatisfaction with the allocation of public housing, particularly in western Ulster. Debates about the rationalisation of transport (Wilson called for four new motorways) highlighted regional grievances within Northern Ireland, and in particular the anger widely felt in Derry, which was predominantly Catholic, at the axeing of a rail connection to Belfast. Again, the proposal for a new university, allocated by the Lockwood Committee to the predominantly Unionist town of Coleraine, outraged the citizens of Derry, where there was already a long tradition of third-level education based at Magee College. The proposal for a new town invoked similar resentments: the site chosen, in North Armagh, was also in a predominantly Unionist locality, while the name chosen for the new venture – Craigavon – underlined its evidently partisan origins. Finally, the decision by the regime, in 1967, to undertake a review of local government procedures helped to focus attention on one of the most controverial and multifaceted problems within the Unionist state.

Cumulatively these perceived and real injustices represented a new formulation of some traditional sectarian grievances. Moreover, the Catholic community, which was enjoying a degree of educational advancement and social consolidation, was now better able than ever to reframe and articulate its case against the Unionist state.[82] Discrimination within local government housing allocation was the issue that precipitated Catholic mobilisation, and the formation in 1963 of the Homeless Citizens' League in Dungannon, County Tyrone, was an important landmark, in so far as it produced the Campaign for Social Justice (CSJ) in January 1964, which mounted a comprehensive, reasoned and pacific critique of the Stormont regime.

The CSJ united with the labour movement, the Ulster Liberals and the republican Wolfe Tone societies to create a new umbrella grouping, the Northern Ireland Civil Rights Association (NICRA), formed in Belfast on 9 April 1967. NICRA pursued a quietist policy between its foundation and the summer of 1968, after which, adapting the strategies of the civil rights movement in the southern states of the USA, it held a series of high-profile protest marches. These began calmly enough at Dungannon, on 24 August 1968, but a march in Derry, on 5 October, resulted in well-publicised clashes with the police and a massive augmentation of popular sympathy and support. Martyrs were also created when a cross-country trek by the People's Democracy (a radical affiliate of NICRA) was ambushed by loyalist red-necks at Burntollet in January 1969.[83]

O'Neill was caught between popular Catholic mobilisation in 1968–9, loyalist counter-protest and an increasingly impatient and unsympathetic British government. Harold Wilson, elected to the British premiership in 1964, had long been unimpressed by the 'Tories' of Stormont. He had visited Belfast during the Second World War for the Board of Trade, and had been scandalised by the inefficiencies that he had encountered. In addition to this history, there were strong anti-partitionist influences within Wilson's constituency, his back benches and indeed his cabinet.

Some of these back-benchers, briefed by the CSJ, were keen that Wilson should put the squeeze on O'Neill, but he had his own, more immediate and personal, reasons to be angered by the Stormont premier and the Ulster Unionists.

Wilson's experience in 1964–6 of working with a very slight parliamentary majority had convinced him that action was needed to disenfranchise the dozen or so Ulster Unionist MPs who acted, in effect, as an adjunct to the Tory Party. These Unionist MPs had the right to vote on all British and foreign matters before the Commons, and this provided a recurrent grouse for Wilson in his contact with Stormont between 1964 and 1970: he continually, and unavailingly, flagged the issue as one where a deal might be struck. Moreover, Wilson had also been angered by several of O'Neill's political blunders. On 24 August 1965, O'Neill had mocked Wilson's ignorance of Ulster labour leaders at an important function in Belfast. On 1 October 1965, with a general election pending in Britain, O'Neill had introduced Edward Heath, the Tory leader, at a public meeting by saying that 'he hoped it would not be long before they welcomed him [Heath] back to Ulster as the Prime Minister of the United Kingdom'.[84] These episodes were documented at length by Sam Napier of the Northern Ireland Labour Party, and they were clearly taken seriously by Wilson.

This hostility, combined with growing pressure from the Labour back benches, placed O'Neill at an increasing disadvantage. On 8 August 1966, O'Neill met Wilson and James Callaghan, the Home Secretary, at Chequers, and was told to revise the local government franchise in Northern Ireland, and to appoint an ombudsman.[85] For the next two and a half years this pressure for reform was applied with intermittent strength, and with varying degrees of friendliness: O'Neill and his ministers met with their British counterparts on 4 November 1968, when Wilson threatened 'a more radical departure' if reform were not pursued with sufficient alacrity. On this occasion Callaghan had argued that the Stormont ministers should be starved of luncheon, since 'there would be advantages in not appearing so friendly this time'.[86]

O'Neill tried to buy time from his Labour and civil rights critics by offering, on 22 November 1968, a five-point instalment of reform, encompassing the fair allocation of public housing, the appointment of an ombudsman, the reform of local government, the abolition of Londonderry Corporation and the modification of the Special Powers Act. This was followed up on 9 December by his famous 'Ulster at the Crossroads' speech, a broadcast call for moderation.[87] Neither initiative satisfied either the increasingly influential militants within NICRA or the increasingly well-organised loyalist counter-demonstrators – the former intolerant of piecemeal reform, and sensing blood; the latter angry at concessions of any kind, and particularly in response to popular challenge.

O'Neill, in a last gamble, sought electoral endorsement, but it was now a forlorn hope. The Stormont general election of 24 February 1969 produced a divided Ulster Unionist Party, reinforced the apparent directionlessness of the regime, and thus gave added impetus to street protest. O'Neill's inevitable resignation, on 28 April 1969, did little to correct the impression of political melt-down; nor did the choice of his successor, Major James Chichester-Clark, who, gentrified and well meaning, was arguably not up to the job.

O'Neill seems to have thought little about the historic inter-relationship between social and economic upheaval and violent political change in modern Ireland. But he should have been aware of Edmund Burke's dictum which warns that unreformed regimes are at their most vulnerable when they seek to reconstruct themselves. O'Neill's fundamental problem was not that his rhetoric and policies were inappropriate or untimely – far from it – but rather that he lacked the political skills necessary to carry his ideas, or rather those of his immediate circle of advisers, through to a successful conclusion. More than that, it might be said that O'Neill failed because, while he had some reforming impulses, he was too deeply rooted in the limited political culture of Stormont to be an effective moderniser. In other words, the paradox of O'Neillism was that, while it sought to reform Stormont, it was ultimately rooted in, and stymied by, some of the more glaring defects of the regime. There is much truth in the image of O'Neill supplied by Marc Mulholland – that of an ascendancy figure propelled along reformist paths, not so much by his own independent zeal, as by the flattery of liberal subordinates.[88]

O'Neill certainly faced problems that were not fundamentally of his own making, but were rooted partly in the nature of the Unionist state. Moreover, it is impossible to say whether a different type of Unionist reformer could have made a much better job of the Ulster premiership, given the witches' cauldron of political passions which was brewing in the mid-1960s. It is quite clear, however, that O'Neill's leadership contributed to the melt-down in Northern politics that occurred in 1968–9; and it is also quite clear that his political career illuminates some broader, if unflattering, realities about Unionist politics in the Stormont years. How, then, did O'Neill get the politics of his premiership so wrong?

It might be argued that, in terms of his political training, style and aptitudes, O'Neill did not so much embody the limitations of mid-twentieth-century Unionism as those of its late Victorian precursor. He was a dynastic politician, who exploited the residual but still powerful network of squires within Ulster Unionist politics. His father and great uncle had sat at Westminster as utterly undistinguished representatives for Mid Antrim, and it was on the strength of this tradition that he won the Unionist nomination for the Stormont constituency of Bannside in 1946. Once elected, he served as a parliamentary secretary under the tutelage of his aunt, Dehra Parker, the Stormont Minister for Health (1948–57).

In July 1948 he sought nomination as Unionist candidate for the Westminster constituency of South Antrim, recruiting his uncle, Hugh O'Neill (one of the existing County Antrim MPs), to his cause: 'I found', Hugh O'Neill wrote to a rival candidate (Douglas Savory, a veteran Unionist politician who had been displaced from the Queen's University seat), 'that my nephew (now Parliamentary Secretary to the Ministry of Health) was being mentioned as a suitable person to come forward, and I gathered from him that he would certainly consider it with full knowledge that it would mean giving up his present job. In these circumstances I could hardly have put forward your name.'[89]

A cousin, Phelim O'Neill, seems to have been an influence in the tussle over the party leadership in March 1963 which brought Terence to power (without, it need hardly be said, any formal election).[90] Days after his accession O'Neill appointed a distant cousin, James Chichester-Clark, as Assistant Whip. A few months later, in May, Chichester-Clark (who, like O'Neill, was a veteran of Eton and the Irish Guards) was promoted to the strategically crucial office of Chief Whip. O'Neill vigorously campaigned on behalf of Chichester-Clark's wife, who was seeking nomination as Unionist candidate for the Stormont constituency of South Derry.[91] When O'Neill resigned, in April 1969, he encouraged Chichester-Clark to contest the leadership, and in the ensuing ballot he voted for his cousin. All of this gives rise to the suspicion that O'Neill preached meritocracy to his benighted compatriots, but practised a nepotism that they would more readily have understood.

It should be said in fairness that O'Neill's social and family networks were far-flung, giving him metropolitan connections that were beneficial and which recalled the heyday of late Victorian Unionism. This should be placed against the general criticism of devolved politics that they were too insular and too weakly connected with London and the mainstream. Brian Faulkner articulated this view in arguing that, after the war, 'we were too absorbed in our own affairs...this was a mistake, a weakness'.[92] While the accusation of insularity was undoubtedly justified, considering the political culture of the devolved administration as a whole, there are grounds for accepting that Brookeborough and O'Neill (both from old-style landed backgrounds) were able to maintain connections with metropolitan politics that their lieutenants and successors were unable to sustain. Ivan Neill, a Stormont minister in the 1950s and 1960s, has pointed out that Brookeborough enjoyed (through his family ties) good relations with Churchill's Conservative Party.[93] O'Neill was more of a Londoner than an Antrim man, and he was comfortable with the aristocratic Toryism of Harold Macmillan and Alec Douglas-Home. On the other hand, there is a lurking possibility that, despite his distance from Ulster politics and his reforming rhetoric, O'Neill may well still have looked and sounded like the archetypal dead-head Tory squire to the impatient reformers of Harold Wilson's Labour Party.

O'Neill's rise also corroborates some reflections on the political culture of Stormont first put forward by Mansergh in 1936. Mansergh then remarked upon the 'stagnation of political life in Northern Ireland', on the scarcity of political talent, and on the relative ease with which it was possible to win ministerial position.[94] Mansergh believed that the abolition of proportional representation had encouraged political atrophy; and he also accepted that the multiple layering of representative institutions (Westminster, Stormont, county councils, district councils) exhausted the political talent in a polity of only one and half million citizens. He noted that, at the time of his writing, 27 per cent of Stormont MPs received official (often ministerial) salaries. This compared with 10 per cent of deputies in Dáil Éireann and eight per cent of members in the British House of Commons. Some Stormont ministerial salaries were fully equal to those of their Westminster counterparts, despite the considerable disparity in workload, to say nothing of prestige and importance.[95]

O'Neill's career provides documentation for this critique. He had no political experience whatsoever at the time of his election to Stormont, in 1946. In addition, he had no third-level education and no professional success – or, indeed, sustained business or professional experience of any kind. After his schooling and a year abroad, he recalled that 'I tried my hand at various jobs ending up in the Stock Exchange' and that an aunt (inevitably) 'got me a job as civilian ADC to the Governor of South Australia'.[96] He had war service as a junior officer in the Irish Guards, but won no recognition for gallantry or distinguished service, whereas Brookeborough, for example, had received the Military Cross in the First World War. O'Neill was an Intelligence Officer in Brigade Headquarters, and in September 1944 was wounded on the sciatic nerve – 'caught in his truck at lunchtime', as the official historian of the Guards laconically noted.[97] O'Neill used his modest military title (Captain) until his ennoblement in 1970. He had family roots in Antrim, but no direct, personal connection with the county and no particular ties with his constituency of Bannside. He was an indifferent, sometimes a highly awkward, speaker; and while he devoured newspapers, 'he was not a reader of files', as Sir Kenneth Bloomfield remembered.[98] And yet, in the uncompetitive environment of Stormont, O'Neill found himself a junior minister at the age of thirty-four, a senior cabinet minister at the age of forty-two, and prime minister while still aged only forty-eight.

But the main problem with devolution which the O'Neill years illustrate was foreseen not by liberals like Mansergh, but by the Unionists themselves. Home Rule was originally envisioned as a means both of maintaining the unity of the United Kingdom and of persuading the Irish that they had effective legislative independence. Unionists, of course, refused to believe that this constitutional high-wire act could be sustained. They complained that a grant of Home Rule would serve only to whet Irish national ambitions, and stimulate further claims. The Government of Ireland Act conformed to the pattern of earlier Home Rule Bills in so far as it was an attempt to buy off Irish national feeling at a bargain basement price, but it also, paradoxically, led to the development of Unionist political ambition.

The Home Rule parliament at Stormont was a rigidly constrained institution, but Unionists came increasingly to treat it as a sovereign authority in precisely the way that they warned nationalists would do in an all-Ireland polity. The realities of British power were largely obscured from the Northern public, who instead saw, and were persuaded by, the trappings of local parliamentary dignity and ministerial authority. Successive Unionist ministers were sometimes tempted by the prospect of dominion status for Northern Ireland (as O'Neill was, briefly) or even (in the case of Bill Craig) independence. Faulkner saw that 'politicians in Northern Ireland [were led] into illusions of self-sufficiency, of taking part in a sovereign parliament', and that 'unspoken separatist tendencies' had emerged.[99] Ultimately these Unionist visionaries could not evade the reality of the North's financial dependence upon the British. Nonetheless, successive ministers, and pre-eminently O'Neill, sought to exploit fully the powers and paraphernalia of the Northern state.

Ivan Neill observed that 'the little understood limitations of devolved government confronted us from time to time as expectations, indeed calls, for greater effort were being pressed upon us'.[100] While this was undoubtedly true, there was a clear sense in which Unionist ministers created these same expectations. They wanted to play-act as ministers of an autonomous state, and yet they also wanted the benefits of Westminster as a sovereign authority. O'Neill certainly sought to expand the possibilities of devolution, both through extensive economic and social planning initiatives at home, and through acting as a national leader on the world stage. 'O'Neill was fond of overseas travel', it has been observed, because it 'gave him a chance to meet foreign leaders who, on the thesis that one prime minister is much like another, often accorded him the courtesy and respect appropriate to some significant sovereign government.'[101]

But Northern Ireland was not, of course, a sovereign government. Thus O'Neill's extravagant definition of Home Rule created popular expectations which – particularly when the crisis came, in 1968–9 – he was unable to satisfy. In his 'Ulster at the Crossroads' address of December 1968, he underlined the reality of British sovereignty; but this warning was issued when London's interference was already upon him and his people.[102] There can be little doubt that O'Neill inadvertently helped to make the humiliation of British intervention all the more glaring; there can be little doubt, too, that he thereby limited his own and his successors' room for manoeuvre. To this extent, his ambitions (and indeed those of earlier Unionists) helped to make the entire devolution experiment untenable.

O'Neill's career not only illustrates some of the generic problems with the political culture of the devolved parliament; it also reveals some more personal limitations. He had ideas, but bad judgement – some members of his extended family thought him dim.[103] Marc Mulholland has recorded one splendid proposal by O'Neill, as Minister of Finance, to solve the endemic local unemployment problem by draining Lough Neagh, the biggest inland lake in the British Isles and a feature of outstanding natural and cultural significance.[104] O'Neill was a peculiarly introverted player within an introverted political culture. He had a tendency towards monologue or harangue. He was painfully shy, but monumentally insensitive: as a 42-year-old, untried Minister of Finance, he addressed peremptory memoranda to his Permanent Secretary, Sir Douglas Harkness, using only the distinguished official's surname.[105] He 'cut' (or failed to recognise) his own backbenchers: Lady Brookeborough once explained her son's hostility to O'Neill by saying that 'John is a backbencher, a member of the [Unionist] party, a supporter of the government. He meets the PM [O'Neill] in the corridor at Stormont, who walks past him without speaking. Then he comes home and turns on the television and there is the prime minister announcing some other great initiative which his backbenchers haven't heard of.'[106] The Governor of Northern Ireland, Lord Grey, complained in 1969 that 'it is plain to me that it is lack of openness with his cabinet that has brought some of his principal troubles on him'.[107] A. J. Langdon, a senior official at the Home Office, believed that 'Captain O'Neill's downfall was brought about as much by his personal unpopularity as by his policies'.[108]

These traits reflected a wider unhappiness in dealing with his peers or indeed with any mildly competitive or combative relationship. On the other hand, he felt comfortable with, even affectionate towards, junior or unchallenging figures. There is an unsettling vignette in the official history of the Irish Guards recording that O'Neill 'kept a pet Mongol youth [a prisoner of war] for a week, to dig trenches and carry his kit and maps'.[109] O'Neill would later establish warm ties with other, less vulnerable subordinates, such as middle-ranking civil servants.

There is no evidence to suggest that, for all his pretensions, O'Neill forged any meaningful friendship with the world statesmen whom he nervously courted. Some mention has been made of O'Neill's political errors with Wilson. But O'Neill's contact with Wilson also underlined his profound personal limitations and lack of judgement. His defensive self-aggrandisement permeates their relationship: in January 1965 he unblushingly told Wilson that 'I have been praised by a Labour member of parliament at Stormont for being a prime minister who works "really hard"'; in January 1967 he laboriously explained to Wilson's Private Secretary that he might appear 'a little less "overtly" liberal' when next they met, but that any hardline performance would be purely for the benefit of his accompanying Stormont colleagues.[110] On 4 November 1968, during a meeting of British and Northern Ireland ministers, while Brian Faulkner presented an unsentimental, if somewhat tricky, defence of the Unionist record, O'Neill alluded embarrassingly to his own 'Kennedy-like' reception in nationalist towns such as Newry.[111] His very mode of address betrayed a profound lack of self-confidence: he could not decide, in writing to Wilson, whether 'Dear Harold', 'Dear Prime Minister' or 'Dear PM' was appropriate, or whether to sign off, in his curiously child-like print, as 'Terence', 'Terence (O'Neill)' or 'Terence O'Neill'.

His personal insensitivity frequently veered into political incorrectness, even by the standards of the 1960s and 1970s. By his own lights he was a genuine reformer, yet he was capable of grating condescension. His auto-biography provides the most lurid examples of this: here he recounts, with evident glee, a grim 'joke' concerning a schoolboy suicide.[112] Here too, despite the ongoing feminist revolution, he patronises the recently widowed Jacqueline Kennedy, who had correctly identified one of his awkward historical allusions: 'I wonder how many English girls would have been as quick on the draw?'[113] His vision of class relations was painfully Edwardian. In January 1969 he boasted to the *Washington Post* that 'I have been succeeding, first with the professional class, and gradually with the artisans'.[114] His profound condescension sometimes bordered on sectarianism: his advertisement for a Protestant housemaid has already been mentioned. His account in his autobiography of the Malvern Street

Murders (sectarian killings committed in West Belfast in 1966) suggests that he was less concerned for the Catholic victims than for the upset that they had inadvertently caused to his high-flown social plans.[115] A notoriously ugly example of this crudity occurred after his resignation when, in explaining his social engineering to a journalist, he remarked that 'if you treat Roman Catholics with due consideration and kindness, they will live like Protestants in spite of the authoritative nature of their Church'.[116]

It might be thought that sentiments such as these would have propelled O'Neill into the embrace of even his most diehard Orange ministerial colleagues. Indeed, O'Neill shared some of the convictions and prejudices of his cabinet, and he was no radical. Ken Bloomfield, who as deputy secretary to the Stormont cabinet was close to O'Neill, was confident that the Prime Minister had 'no grand plan for community relations'; nor is it likely that he had any cabalistic scheme for Irish unity, although there is a highly ambiguous reminiscence from Kathleen Lemass, widow of the Irish taoiseach, which suggests the reverse.[117] The fact that he failed to carry some of his cabinet colleagues reflects as much on his own painful managerial failings as on their undoubted cussedness.

It seems clear that O'Neill handled his senior ministers with deplorable crudity. He was a weak manager of the cabinet, whose meetings could become 'helplessly sunk in disagreement about trivia'. It is admittedly just possible that this was a calculated strategy, for the real influences on O'Neill's thinking were not his ministers but the staff of the cabinet office.[118] His intolerance of questioning or criticism led to a sometimes disastrous secretiveness: the Lemass visit in January 1965 was planned in an excessively underhand way, and some Unionist ministers were only informed (by the still relatively junior Ken Bloomfield) after the taoiseach had actually arrived at Stormont.[119] No ministerial colleague had been taken into O'Neill's confidence, and the result was that the whole episode appeared conspiratorial and shady, and generated unnecessary personal distrust. O'Neill's disastrous handling of his colleagues indicates that he was never prepared to be *primus inter pares*: he was always the Captain Mainwaring of his ministerial platoon.

Bloomfield was convinced, too, that the coolness between O'Neill and his most able colleague and rival, Brian Faulkner (Minister for Commerce) was 'not about policy'.[120] Faulkner and John L. Andrews were widely canvassed as contenders for the party leadership when O'Neill was appointed in 1963, and it seems that O'Neill moved initially to neutralise any residual threat that these men might pose. In 1964 he removed Andrews from the Ministry of Finance, and at the same time he threatened Faulkner at Commerce by the creation of a new high-powered Ministry of Development under the control of Bill Craig, widely regarded as a king-maker in 1963. Faulkner was only told of these developments after they had taken place, and when he was on holiday in Majorca.[121] Marc Mulholland regards O'Neill's secretive planning of the Lemass visit in 1965 as a bid to 'upstage' Faulkner, who had already been consolidating informal cross-border linkages.[122] Faced with mounting party unrest, O'Neill offered Faulkner the Deputy Premiership in 1966, but this was not so much the beginning of an intimate and effective partnership as merely a brief truce in their war of attrition.

O'Neill complained in his autobiography of Faulkner's unremitting disloyalty, and there can be little doubt that the Minister for Commerce was restless: 'everyone knew', Bloomfield recalled, 'that [Faulkner] was clever, energetic and ambitious. Some thought he was shallow, devious and unprincipled.'[123] In the light of this judgement, Faulkner's testimony must be treated with caution, but there is a ring of truth in his characterisation of O'Neill as an elusive and inconsistent man who alternately blew hot and cold over his friendships. Moreover, Bloomfield, who was professedly 'in the prime minister's camp' and who recognised Faulkner's complexities, believed that O'Neill had both mishandled his Minister for Commerce and regressed towards paranoia.[124] On balance, then, Faulkner's apparently pained memory that 'Terence spent a lot of his time manoeuvering politically, and one constantly felt the need to tread warily' may be accepted as accurate.[125]

When Faulkner resigned from the Stormont cabinet in January 1969, over the premier's handling of the civil rights crisis, the end of O'Neill was in sight. Yet this was not an inevitable outcome. The balance of the evidence suggests that if O'Neill had overcome his own weaknesses, and had retained the confidence of this and other crucial lieutenants, then the reform project might have been strengthened and sustained. But here, as in so much else, O'Neill spoilt a good reformist case by combining some of the worst features of the old Unionist regime with a range of debilitating personal traits. He improved upon his predecessors only in so far as he brought a personal rather than a sectarian paranoia into Stormont Castle.[126]

Before O'Neill is set aside, it should be recognised that, for all his limitations, he caught the imagination of some Ulster Catholics, who indeed still remain sympathetic to his memory: Marianne Elliott's *Catholics of Ulster* (2000) illustrates the continued vigour of this loyalty.[127] In a sense this is not hard to understand, given the friendly gestures that he made towards the improvement of community relations. But, on the other hand, O'Neill's approach was always gestural rather than substantive – a triumph of public relations rather than policy – and underlying the stage-management were some highly archaic attitudes that might easily be seen as passive sectarianism. Catholic sympathy for O'Neill illustrates the conservative impulses within the community and the extent to which it had been starved of even the basic forms of official affirmation. Yet in a sense this response was paradoxical, since the central reforms of the O'Neill years inadvertently helped to underline the extent of the minority's disadvantage. Catholic sympathy did not, in any case, extend to significant electoral endorsement in February 1969: O'Neill was to find, like other crusading 'centrists', that winning cross-community plaudits was easier than cross-community votes.

The devolved administration was badly (and perhaps fatally) damaged by the time that O'Neill bequeathed his 'damnosa hereditas' to Chichester-Clark in April 1969.[128] The apparently unstoppable civil unrest created pressures for the Unionist administration, and was an ongoing humiliation. The deployment of troops on 14 August 1969, after severe rioting in Belfast and Derry, underlined the extent to which the popular revolt had challenged the regime's capacities, to say nothing of its credibility. The use of the army weakened Stormont's control over the maintenance of law and order; it also signalled the vulnerability of Northern ministers, and marked the beginning of a dangerous and reluctant British re-engagement with Ulster. The troops were followed into Northern Ireland by senior British civil servants, Oliver Wright and Alex Baker, who were meant to liaise between Stormont and Whitehall, but who came to be seen as an alternative means of political access beyond the devolved administration.[129] Wright can have done little to dispel Stormont's apprehensions when, in an interview, he denied that he was playing 'Big Brother' to the devolved administration: 'Good gracious no. Nothing like that. Big Brother's little brother, perhaps.'[130]

The crescendos of violence in 1969 stimulated increasing, if belated, British ministerial interest in the problems of the devolved government; but in time this came to mean that Stormont was being over-ruled or sidetracked or otherwise discredited. O'Neill, contemptuous of the provincials around his own cabinet table, had meekly succumbed to the pressure of British ministers; Chichester-Clark was more thoroughly helpless in the face of unremitting and humiliating British intervention. It is clear that the new Northern premier enjoyed a good personal relationship with the ebullient British Home Secretary, James Callaghan, but it is equally clear that Callaghan exploited this connection to impose his will.[131] This applied to little issues as well as big: the unsuitable Sir Arthur Young, who had made his name in Malaya and Kenya, was foisted upon Chichester-Clark as head of the RUC; but the rambling Ulster premier was also brow-beaten by Callaghan into delivering an important television address without a script, and with disastrous results.[132]

However, it was Harold Wilson, the British Prime Minister and an unforgiving critic of the Stormont 'Tories', who inevitably delivered the most thorough humiliation to Chichester-Clark and the devolved government. On 19 August 1969 – after a meeting between the Belfast and London ministers, and after an agreed statement (the 'Downing Street Communiqué') had been issued – Wilson went on television and unilaterally announced that the Ulster Special Constabulary, the pride-and-joy of traditional Unionism, would be 'phased out'. In general, the reforms that London was imposing had been quietly adopted as a face-saving mechanism by the Northern ministers, but here was a case where the Northerners had been wrong-footed, and the brutal novelty of their political subservience had been exposed.

O'Neill had bequeathed not only a deteriorating pattern of street violence, but also a welter of half-formulated, but far-reaching reform proposals. The most recent assessments of Chichester-Clark's two-year premiership stress the extent to which he had to grapple not only with sustained civil unrest, but also with a series of important, but necessarily unsettling reform recommendations.[133] The Cameron Commission, which investigated the violence of October 1968 to April 1969, reported in September 1969 with criticisms of the police. The Scarman tribunal, which examined the unrest of April to August 1969, reported later with broadly similar conclusions. The Hunt Report, which dealt with police reform, was published in October 1969, recommending a substantial restructuring of the RUC and (true to Harold Wilson's predictions) the abolition of the USC. The Macrory Report, which was published in May 1970, contained a blueprint for sweeping reform of local government. The implementation of these four reports, together with the package of measures outlined by O'Neill in November 1968, was a formidable undertaking; and yet considerable progress was made towards this end under the apparently somnambulant leadership of Chichester-Clark. By 1971 it was already clear that some of the key institutions of the devolved administration were being subjected to comprehensive scrutiny and revision.

But it was equally clear that these quick-fire changes, in the context of unremitting violence, suggested a regime in crisis, and arguably helped to fracture the political substructure of Northern Ireland. The reforms certainly coincided with a massive realignment of constitutional and militant forces which gave rise to the Alliance Party (April 1970), the Social Democratic and Labour Party (August 1970), the Democratic Unionist Party (September 1971), the Provisional IRA (January 1970) and the Ulster Defence Association (September 1971). Moreover, the reform programme served to provoke a loyalist reaction, while simultaneously enflaming republican ambition. Loyalists protested at the very notion of reform, while militant nationalists were increasingly looking beyond the structures of the devolved administration for inspiration and redress. Ken Bloomfield has referred to Unionist ministers at this time trying 'unsuccessfully to buy reform at last year's prices'. At the risk of stretching the image, it might be said that popular Unionism did not want to make the purchase at all, while republican militants were interested in selling a quite different commodity.[134]

And yet, even as late as March 1971, when the security situation remained bleak and Chichester-Clark left office, it is just possible (with effort) to imagine that Stormont might have been successfully re-launched. Chichester-Clark was honourable and decent, and certainly by the end of his tenure he understood the fundamental challenge of his office – the extent to which Stormont was caught between popular expectations in Ulster and the whims of British political opinion. But he was not a proactive political thinker, still less a popular communicator, and he left office (as he said to Basil McIvor, a Unionist MP) with 'great relief'. The record of a telephone call to Edward Heath on 19 March 1971, in which Chichester-Clark threatens resignation, confirms the extent of his intellectual and emotional exhaustion.[135]

His successor, Brian Faulkner, more than made up for these deficiencies, and it is just conceivable that, with luck and time, he might have been able to pull the devolved administration out of the conflagration. Faulkner's brief premiership, remembered primarily for the tragedies of internment and Bloody Sunday, provides some evidence of both a high-voltage political imagination and a willingness to tackle the central structural weaknesses of the devolution settlement. But in the end he, like Chichester-Clark, had to confront the unpalatable realities of ongoing violence, and of British sovereign power.

As early as 1936 Nicholas Mansergh identified the overweening might of the Stormont executive as one of the central flaws of the Northern constitution.[136] Later scholars bemoaned the weakness of the committee structure within the devolved parliament, and the resulting lack of public scrutiny and accountability.[137] Nationalist politicians incorporated these detailed points within a more general indictment of Stormont as a one-party regime, but many fundamentalist Unionists were unwilling to compromise the classic, 'British' model of majoritarian government. It was to this broad theoretical and practical challenge that Faulkner turned after his accession to the premiership.

His solution, published in June 1971, was the creation of three new powerful parliamentary committees which would join the existing Public Accounts Committee as a check on government. The committees would be empowered to consider policy formulation, to review legislation and to monitor the performance of the executive; two of the four would be chaired, as of right, by members of the Stormont Opposition. This blueprint was accompanied by an invitation, addressed to all interested parties, to informal talks. Henry Kelly (then Northern editor of the *Irish Times*) and other contemporary sceptics were inclined to see this initiative as 'a trick' and 'a gimmick', but its significance should not be dismissed. As Ken Bloomfield has observed, 'for the first time a Northern Ireland prime minister [had] openly acknowledged weaknesses in a system that had operated for fifty years'.[138]

Faulkner also sought to address the widespread and damaging recognition that Stormont was a one-party regime. On the formation of his government in March 1971, he appointed David Bleakley, leader of the Northern Ireland Labour Party, to the cabinet as Minister for Community Relations. Bleakley was not a member of the Stormont parliament, but the Government of Ireland Act made provision for the short-term appointment of ministers in his position. This was a brave initiative, but perhaps less bold and more subtle than is sometimes claimed. Hitherto there had been only one minister, Harry Midgley, who had not been a member of the Unionist Party: Midgley had been appointed during the war, in 1943, and soon took the Unionist whip.[139] Bleakley had been an acerbic critic of earlier Unionist governments, and in this sense might have been seen as a daring appointment. But his party, the NILP, was formally anti-partitionist, and Bleakley himself was a prominent Protestant liberal. Moreover, the influential Catholic moderate Maurice Hayes, who was Chairman of the Community Relations Council, was unenthusiastic about Bleakley's advancement 'both because of the personality and because it still further diluted the effectiveness of the office to have a nonpolitician in it'.[140] In these senses, therefore, Bleakley's appointment, while still a risk, was a very shrewdly calculated risk.

When Bleakley resigned in September 1971, Faulkner furthered his experimental ecumenism by appointing a prominent lay Catholic, Dr G. B. Newe, to be Minister of State in the Cabinet Office. Newe was the only Catholic ever to serve under the Unionist regime as a Stormont minister. Again this was a carefully assessed gamble: Newe, like Bleakley, was not an MP, and therefore challenged parliamentary sensitivities; by virtue of his Catholicism he was likely to be an object of suspicion for some Unionist backbenchers. But he was also non-political, and had a distinguished record of community service. As with O'Neill's cross-community gestures, it was a particular, safe and passive, form of Catholicism that Faulkner was keen to recruit. As with O'Neill's gestures, however, the elements of boldness and ingenuity should not be completely discounted.

In earlier, more peaceful times, the appointment of non-Unionists as ministers might have been more meaningful, but, Midgley aside, such appointments did not occur. As it was, the deteriorating security situation in 1971 and 1972 tended to distract attention from Faulkner's constitutional and ministerial initiatives, and to divest them of significance. Before July 1971 the situation was not so desperate that Faulkner's hand was exhausted, and that the options for the devolved administration were completely spent. Indeed, the constitutional initiative of June 1971 was regarded with cautious interest by the members of the new nationalist grouping at Stormont, the SDLP. The first inter-party talks session, held on 7 July, was a modest success and seemed to presage better things to come. But once again, as in 1969–70, it became clear that the initiative could only be grasped by constitutional politicians in the fleeting intervals between the pulses of violence. On 9 July, two young Catholic men were shot dead by the army in Derry, and this triggered an intensification of bombings and rioting over the remainder of the summer. The Faulkner gambit was lost: the SDLP, which had a strong base in the north-west, demanded a public inquiry into the Derry killings, and when this was not forthcoming they withdrew from Stormont. As Maurice Hayes has commented, 'not for the last time in the SDLP did Derry issues and the Derry view of things overwhelm all others'.[141]

The acceleration of violence also increased the political pressure on Faulkner. Although he had previously hesitated, by early August 1971 he was arguing to the British government that the internment of terrorist suspects was now a military and political necessity.[142] The British had, in fact, already incorporated this notion into their contingency planning: in May 1971, Peter Carrington, Heath's Minister of Defence, had agreed to fund the construction of a prison camp at Long Kesh, and the relevant structures were thus in place when, on 9 August, the first men were 'lifted'.[143] But these arrests were made on the basis of faulty and outdated intelligence: the first internees were exclusively Catholic and were sometimes ill-treated. Internment, therefore, decisively weakened any residual chance of a political deal within the structures of the devolved administration. Faulkner, indeed, was well aware of this: Heath privately warned him at this time that 'if internment failed...the next step and the only remaining step would be direct rule'.[144]

Stormont by now had seemingly entered an ominous pattern of decline. There were plummeting falls in the health of the institution, linked to surges of violence, then brief respites, accompanied perhaps by forlorn political initiatives, followed swiftly by further rapid deterioration and the rattle of death. Faulkner gathered his constitutional ideas for the reform of Stormont into a green paper, or discussion document, 'The

Future Development of the Parliament and Government of Northern Ireland', published in October 1971. This again recognised that the British democratic system was a profoundly inadequate model for a society with the cultural and political divisions of Northern Ireland, and it looked forward to cross-community participation in the Stormont executive. The basis for this power sharing was to be the reformed committee structure that Faulkner had outlined in June. Bloomfield, who helped to draft the green paper, thought that it was 'the first document produced by any Northern Ireland government to approach the heart of the matter'; but, in the light of internment, this ministerial revelation mattered little.[145] It was now clear that nationalists, who in July had seemed interested in the reform of Stormont, had come to believe that the institution could be overturned, and that nothing less would serve their interests.

Another ominous development for Stormont was the extent to which both Edward Heath's Conservative government and the Labour Opposition were moving to include the Dublin administration in their diplomacy. Heath had hitherto brusquely swatted the claims of the Dublin government to intervene in Northern politics, but on 6–7 September 1971, in the wake of internment, he hosted a session at Chequers with Jack Lynch who, well fortified with 'Paddy' whiskey, agreed to return on 27 September in order to meet Faulkner. Heath calls this summit of 27–8 September 'one of the historic events of my premiership', but in fact little was achieved, and Faulkner and Lynch already knew and had the measure of each other.[146]

At the same time as Heath was choreographing 'historic' North–South meetings, the British Labour leadership was making policy on the hoof, throwing out various proposals to reshape the government of Northern Ireland in a manner that conceded greater influence to Dublin ministers. Wilson's 'Fifteen Point Plan' of November 1971 was a particularly painful intervention, in so far as it laid out a programme for the reunification of Ireland, and thereby simultaneously encouraged the IRA and destabilised hardline loyalism. For the Unionists, the configuration of political forces and threats was beginning very much to resemble those of 1921–2 and 1940. The main and, in the event, the crucial distinction was that in these earlier years the devolved government had overcome all local challengers and was therefore secure at home.

This was emphatically not the case in 1971–2, and if further proof were needed then it came on Sunday, 30 January 1972, when British soldiers shot dead thirteen Catholic demonstrators in Derry. The killings of 'Bloody Sunday' undoubtedly precipitated the final demise of Stormont. Jack Lynch was now pressing for this, and Heath, fearing 'complete anarchy' in Northern Ireland and a spill-over into Britain, was inclined to accept that 'direct rule' was the only way forward.[147] Heath had also just (on 24 January) signed the Treaty of British Accession to the European Economic Community, and was more than usually sensitive to the clamour of international opinion. Faulkner and Bloomfield, from the Stormont perspective, knew that a possible shift in British strategy was being planned after January 1972. Bloomfield picked up warning signs from the British government representative at Stormont, Howard Smith, and Faulkner was aware – on the basis of a meeting with Heath on 4 February – that British ministers were 'casting around for a new line'.[148] But the Stormont regime was reassured by a telegram from Heath, as late as 3 March, affirming that press reports about the threat of direct rule were 'pure speculation'.[149]

Given Heath's emollient, if admittedly 'elastic', words, Faulkner was able to calm the nerves of his colleagues at a Unionist Party meeting, also on 3 March.[150] Faulkner meanwhile continued to work on his own reform proposals, honing the ideas contained in 'The Future Development of the Parliament and Government of Northern Ireland' into a white paper, the publication of which, as it transpired, was to be the last act of his administration. On 22 March, when the Stormont ministers next met Heath and his lieutenants, it was clear that the Faulkner programme was not the radical departure that the British had in mind. The Unionists were instead presented with a demand that they surrender their powers over law and order. They were also pressed to agree to the scaling down of internment and the appointment of a Secretary of State for Northern Ireland. After it had been established that the British were not bluffing, and were not merely making an opening bid, the Unionists were aghast. Faulkner argued that the annexation of security would be an intolerable humiliation, and would destroy the credibility and purpose of any surviving devolved administration. His plea made no impression: Heath was adamant, the Unionist ministers resigned, and the Stormont parliament was immediately prorogued. In this anti-climactic manner, fifty years of devolved government came to an end.[151]

The demise of Stormont illustrates some wider points about the history of devolved government, and it also raises some questions about the long-term gestation of direct rule. When did the British first start to plan seriously for the end of the devolved administration? The objective of British policy towards Northern Ireland in the late 1960s remained the effecting of reform through the agency of a pliant Stormont. However, the British recognised that a diehard regime might well be installed in Belfast through which they would be unable to work; they also realised that, in the context of extreme civil unrest, the Unionist regime might break down completely. Each of these seemed like a very real threat in 1969–71, and there arose the need for a carefully planned fall-back position.

At first the idea was that, with the projected failure of Stormont, the functions of government should be vested in the Governor of Northern Ireland acting through a council of senior officials (there is a faint echo here of the Dublin Castle regime). Lord Grey, the Governor of Northern Ireland (1968–73), was in fact brought into the planning loop as early as February 1969 at a time when the Unionist ministers, including O'Neill, remained firmly excluded.[152] Secret drafts of an Emergency Provisions Bill were placed on file in February 1969 which incorporated precisely this form of administration.

These plans were periodically 'dusted down' and revised over the following three years, as the political and military crisis ebbed and flowed. By late 1969, however, opinion was shifting in favour of appointing a resident minister in Belfast who would bear the responsibility for the government of Northern Ireland. In September 1969 Oliver Wright was envisaging 'a UK minister with full powers to take up residence and direct Northern Ireland affairs from Stormont Castle'.[153] By early 1970 this notion was finding favour elsewhere: A. J. Langdon of the Home Office wrote that 'as I see it there would be no alternative but to establish a Northern Ireland department in the United Kingdom government with its own cabinet minister…although the establishment of a Northern Ireland department on the lines of the Scots office goes beyond immediate contingency planning, it is a clear consequence of a Westminster takeover'.[154] The debate over the replacement institutions for Stormont was effectively resolved in May 1970 when James Callaghan unequivocally decided in favour of a 'resident Minister of State in Belfast'.[155]

Edward Heath's Conservative government inherited and, on the whole, accepted these contingency arrangements. In March 1971, when Chichester-Clark resigned, the threat of a hardline successor re-emerged and the Emergency Provisions Bill was taken from the files and amended to provide for a 'Secretary for Northern Ireland'. In September 1971, after internment, Heath's Central Policy Review Staff outlined three radical strategies for the future of Northern Ireland: repartition, power sharing and joint Irish–British sovereignty.[156] This, together with the Lynch visits, seems to have stimulated wider talk than hitherto about 'direct rule'. The possibility was discussed at the Tory Party conference in October, and found its way into the *Irish Times* and to the ears of the radical loyalist cleric, Ian Paisley.[157]

It is also clear that in February 1972, stimulated by the Central Policy Review Staff, the Tories were preparing to change tack over a variety of issues, including both incomes policy and Northern Ireland. After 'Bloody Sunday', Heath certainly wanted to assume control of all security matters in Northern Ireland, but the tenor of his memoir suggests that he equated this with 'direct rule'.[158] He also recounts an (undated) cabinet meeting at which the prorogation of Stormont was evidently debated and accepted. He then describes the meeting with Faulkner on 22 March at which the British proposals were discussed: 'to begin phasing out intern-ment; to hold a first plebiscite in Northern Ireland on the border issue; and to assume direct control of security in the province. All other aspects of government would remain in the hands of Faulkner and his Cabinet.'[159] Heath was clearly unhappy that Faulkner declined to co-operate with his schemes at the meeting of 22 March: 'nor was he [Faulkner] politically sound in refusing to carry on the rest of the func-tions of government in Northern Ireland after we had taken over com-plete responsibility for security there'.[160] He seems to have had a carefully formulated vision of Stormont emerging 'as eventually something along the lines of a county council or the Greater London Council'.[161] But these sentiments do not altogether chime with the earlier decision of the British cabinet to prorogue Stormont, unless this decision was taken purely on the basis of contingency.

Given the evidence at present available, it is clear that Heath hoped, perhaps even expected, that Faulkner and the Unionists would relinquish their security powers and muddle on in a diminished form. It is also clear, however, that the suspension of Stormont was a carefully formu-lated fall-back plan, which had its roots in the crisis of early 1969, and which had been put on red alert as late as March 1971. Perhaps, then, the final end of Stormont reflected not so much the fundamental priorities of British policy as its vagaries and contingencies, and the desire to resist embroilment for as long as possible. The fact of Stormont's demise reflected the completeness of British sovereignty in Northern Ireland; the manner of its end reflected the realities of this sovereignty and the extent to which Stormont ministers could be commanded (or ignored or humiliated) by their British masters.

Why did Faulkner reject Heath's offer of a diminished Stormont? Faulkner, who seems to have been regarded as a serious player by the British, was still kept in the dark about the development of British policy, and indeed was politically exposed by Heath's apparent assurances of 3 March. Having already been wrong-footed by Heath, he believed that he could not survive a second humiliation on the issue of security: he was much influenced in this calculation by the memory of Chichester-Clark's treatment at the hands of Harold Wilson over the USC. Heath's Home Secretary, Reggie Maudling, eventually came to accept this prognosis, but at the time it seems that he and the other Tory ministers thought that Faulkner was merely posturing: 'I wonder if Brian is bluffing?'[162] Faulkner also probably believed that, in the absence of Stormont, the British would falter, and so he may well have thought that the Unionist ministers' day was not yet done. As he said to Basil McIvor, in a few handwritten lines appended to his final official letter to his ministerial colleagues, 'we are not yet finished!'.[163]

Was Faulkner right to resign, and thus to bring down the Stormont edifice? By this stage, from the republican and nationalist perspective, the crushing of the devolved government was a triumph, even if it was achieved through the agency of a Tory government. Viewed from the perspective of an integrationist, or Westminster-oriented, Unionism, direct rule made more sense than the sham autonomy of Stormont. Judged within the more limited guage of the devolution settlement, Faulkner might perhaps have hesitated longer. It made sense for security policy to be directed and co-ordinated by one government. For three years responsibility had been divided unhelpfully between Stormont, which had authority over the RUC and (until 1970) the USC, and London, which had ultimate responsibility for the army. Moreover, this question of security co-ordination had been in the open for some time. The Chichester-Clark analogy was therefore only partly relevant, for Heath was not making policy in front of the television cameras and behind the backs of the Stormont ministers. The practical autonomy of Stormont over security matters after the introduction of troops in August 1969 was also highly questionable. In a sense, Heath was only proposing to formalise and streamline supervisory structures that were already in place. As the constitutional lawyer, Brigid Hadfield, has remarked, the troop deployment 'effectively meant that the Westminster government assumed full responsibility for security in Northern Ireland'.[164] And, freed from these highly controversial matters, Faulkner might have been able to make progress with his reform agenda. A repetition of the SDLP action after the Derry killings of July 1971 would have been less likely, if the Stormont government had been divested of all policing responsibilities.

Faulkner argued that Heath made a profound mistake over the suspension of Stormont. Writing in April 1972, he complained that 'Heath's decision is not only unjust, but is politically wrong. If I believed that his "initiative" would solve the problem or even greatly mitigate it at the expense of the Unionist Party and Government, I would feel less depressed...'[165] Faulkner also argued that Heath's action was in defiance of the Government of Ireland Act, which empowered Stormont 'to make laws for the peace, order and good government' of Northern Ireland. But the same Act prohibited the Northern government from 'the making of peace or war, or matters arising from a state of war' and from exercising any influence over the armed forces.[166] Moreover, the very clause that Faulkner quoted was arguably as much a legislative constraint on Stormont as a grant of authority, in the sense that Stormont legislation which did not effect the 'peace, order and good government' of Northern Ireland was likely to be judged unlawful. The humiliation threatened by Heath in March 1972 arose not so much because he was overturning the constitution of Northern Ireland; it arose because Unionists had created a grandiloquent form of devolution which bore little relation to constitutional realities. Earlier Unionist leaders had punched beyond their constitutional weight in the national and international arena, and in March 1972 Faulkner paid the price.

Henry Kelly has said that 'the downfall of the parliament and government of Northern Ireland is inextricably bound up in the style, the personality, and the political career and beliefs of Brian Faulkner'.[167] In an obvious sense this is true, in so far as Faulkner's resistance on 22 March precipitated the end of his administration and the prorogation of his parliament. But, as with O'Neill, it is possible to argue that Faulkner's career illustrates both some resonant personal issues and some generic problems with the wider political culture of Stormont. It should be stressed again, as with O'Neill, that Faulkner faced a series of formidable political challenges – continued Catholic mobilisation, loyalist counter-pressure, unpredictable British intervention – which would have been difficult in any circumstances to resist. But it is also true that Faulkner, for all his gifts and pragmatism, had certain critical limitations that impacted upon the developing crisis of 1971–2.

Like many Unionists before and since, Faulkner had a background in the right wing of his party, before settling comfortably into the centre-ground. This meant that, even more than most of his colleagues, he was distrusted by Catholics: 'the trouble with Brian Faulkner', Austin Currie of the SDLP once pronounced, 'is that if the Catholics asked him to stand on his head for them and he agreed they would still say "rat"'.[168] Even G. B. Newe, a Catholic and a loyal supporter of Faulkner, was occasionally alarmed by the Unionist leader's political excursions, and particularly in the early summer of 1972 when Faulkner had to respond to pressure from right-wingers on the verges of his party: 'I am very concerned over the fact that BF seems "hell bent" upon committing political suicide.'[169]

Distrust of Faulkner did not simply spring from his Orange ancestry; his very strengths – intellectual fluency, political responsiveness and pragmatism – were very widely distrusted in the fundamentalist political cultures of Ulster. The historian J. C. Beckett privately thought that Faulkner was 'ambitious, unscrupulous and above all able – the only really able politician in the whole Stormont set-up – the only member of the House (on either side) whom one could possibly think of as reaching cabinet rank in Britain'.[170] His slipperiness of language and even the slanted set of his mouth were held against him. His irrepressible self-confidence and breeziness were frequently interpreted as arrogance; and indeed, like O'Neill, he was not overly endowed with humility.

Faulkner also pursued an ambitious and high-risk strategy through his premiership. Like Arthur Balfour in the 1880s, Faulkner combined coercion with conciliation – he linked structural reform of Stormont with an aggressive stance on security. His first statement as premier, in March 1971, dwelt largely on the security issue.[171] In May 1971 he endorsed a toughening up of the army's policy on firing at terrorist suspects. He was also a longstanding proponent of internment. This 'carrot and stick' approach to political dissent won favour with Heath, and it was only when internment had demonstrably failed – both in political and in military terms – that the British Prime Minister began to lose confidence in his Belfast counterpart, and to consider other options.

It has indeed been said that Faulkner blundered, partly because he placed too great a reliance upon his longstanding friendship with Heath.[172] This illustrates a wider, though apparently inconsistent, indictment of the political culture of Stormont. As has been mentioned, many critics of Stormont (and indeed Unionist insiders) recognised that the insularity of the devolved administration helped to cut it off from communication with the sovereign British power.[173] On the other hand, it has also been observed that Stormont possessed some good contacts, particularly with the Tory Party, but these often served simply to lull Unionist leaders into a false sense of security. Carson, for example, ultimately felt betrayed by his former friends and allies in the Tory high command. Craigavon seems to have felt that his good personal relations with Neville and Anne Chamberlain counted for nothing in June 1940, when the British were courting Eamon de Valera. James Molyneaux's apparently warm relationship with the Thatcher government did not prevent the humiliation, for Unionists, of the Anglo-Irish Agreement of 1985. And Faulkner's connection with Heath, while it worked for a time, did not avert the 'betrayal' of March 1972.

Stormont was indeed insular and self-regarding, but it would be wrong to ignore the personal networks binding Ulster and British politics. Often these were thought to have produced only disappointment and treachery, but arguably this perception reflects not so much on the quality of these relationships as on the nature of Stormont politics. The political culture of Stormont was intimate and clientilist and contractual; and the ministers of the devolved administration expected that their wider networks would operate on the same terms as those within Ulster politics. Stormont's insularity was not defined by the absence of links with British politics; it was defined, rather, by the essentially parochial way in which these links were expected to operate.

The devolved administration survived for fifty years in spite of, rather than because of, its constitution. As the constitutional lawyer, Brigid Hadfield, has argued, the Government of Ireland Act 'left the country with a form of government created for a situation other than that prevailing within its own borders'.[174] The Act, treated reverently by Unionists as a foundation charter, was a burden from the start. It was devised not for a small, culturally divided country, but for a constitutional never-never land – an Ireland containing two symmetrical Home Rule administrations, with a mutual enthusiasm for reunification. The financial provisions of the Act were unworkable, the statutory protection for minorities was derisory, and the authority that it granted over internal security was unclear. The rigidly majoritarian structures created by the Act were a barrier to the effective representation of a divided community, although it should be said that, had the Unionists been more magnanimous and less fixated on their own unity, these structures need not have been an insuperable barrier. The measure as a whole was cobbled together from earlier Home Rule Bills, which themselves had been drafted quickly to meet political deadlines. It mixed colonial and federal elements in a richly, if dangerously, unstable compound. As a result, the bill fostered a highly ornate, ambiguous and vulnerable political culture: Northern Ireland, a poor and financially dependent corner of the United Kingdom, had some of the trappings of a fully fledged dominion, and produced ministers who felt that it was their right to strut on the world stage.

Stormont worked for Unionists in so far as it helped, as they expected, to preserve Northern Ireland within the United Kingdom. It worked for a broader section of the community in so far as its ministers were able to tailor policy, and to address local issues and local needs in a more direct way than would have been possible at Westminster. It failed nationalists, not because there were batteries of oppressive legislation (there were not), or because of sustained 'misrule', but because of the lost opportunities for magnanimity, and because of relentless, pin-pricking humiliation. It failed, not because it was proactively oppressive, but because it did not try until it was too late to put its own house in order.[175]

But this democratic deficit, combined with the pretensions of the devolved administration, meant that Stormont not only failed to represent its citizens, but also fostered a belief in its own omnipotence. This meant that when the British chose to flex their constitutional muscles, the humiliation visited upon Stormont was disproportionately great.

There is little doubt that, had popular expectations been more realistic, the shock of British intervention (or sometimes inactivity) between 1969 and 1972 might have been more tolerable. Both Chichester-Clark and Faulkner fell because they could not reconcile their followers' high expectations with the actions of the British: Chichester-Clark explicitly conceded this in his resignation statement of 20 March 1971.[176] They fell because they were increasingly expected, not to govern, but to mediate between Unionist popular opinion and Westminster; and they were ultimately unable to accommodate themselves to this diminished and dangerous role.

But there was another, critical, dimension to Stormont's grandeur. For most of the lifetime of the devolved parliament its ministers affected the status of national leaders: they were paid comparable salaries to their British counterparts, enjoyed similar perquisites, and did half the work. There were abundant opportunities for the bestowal of patronage or for personal self-aggrandisement. The most striking illustration of the incestuousness that could be achieved is Walter Topping, Minister of Home Affairs (1956–9), who was rumoured to have appointed himself as Recorder of Belfast.[177] In the end, Stormont worked principally to flatter the egos and line the pockets of a small, parochial elite within the Unionist community. In so doing, it very nearly destroyed the credibility of devolution itself.

There are dangers in creating an administration where the rewards are perceived to be out of proportion to the responsibilities, and where the trappings of the institution are held to be grander than its authority. It is too early to say whether the evolving culture of the new 'Stormont' is simply a politically variegated version of the old, or represents a genuine new beginning. The errors of the old regime were manifold, and it would be tragic if any successor were to correct only some of these, while allowing others to poison democratic hopes and expectations.[178]

# CHAPTER 11

# REIMAGINING DEVOLUTION
# AND THE UNION, 1972–2000

The Belfast Agreement of April 1998, through which a devolved legislature was restored at Stormont, may or may not provide a lasting settlement to the constitutional wrangles and civil unrest within Northern
Ireland. It is certainly too early to view the agreement as the triumphant
consummation of the narrative of Home Rule in these islands; it would
also be an over-simplification to treat it as the natural finale to this
history. But, while the agreement should be seen as a fragile deal rooted
in a particular political configuration, it may also be placed in the context
of a much longer history of constitutional ingenuity and experimentation. The parties to the agreement were, in many cases, veteran players in
the arena of Northern politics (Trimble, Hume, Taylor, Mallon); in some
cases they were closely interested in the history of the North (Trimble
and Hume, again, are cases in point).[1] Thus, while the temptations of an
overly Whiggish reading have to be acknowledged, it is also true that the
agreement reflects not only the political exigencies of the late 1990s but
also a deeper historical memory and experience. The constitutional
lineage of the agreement is striking and important, though frequently
underplayed.

The agreement is sometimes compared with the deal struck at
Sunningdale in December 1973, but while such comparisons are illumi-
nating, it might also be said that the fall of Stormont in March 1972
stimulated an intensely fertile period of constitutional thought, of which
Sunningdale was only the most prominent expression. The intensification of violence – 1972 was the bloodiest year of the 'Troubles' by far –
also concentrated minds, and helps to explain some of the more exotic
constitutional formulations as well as the ferocity of opposition to
change. A supposedly temporary official carapace was provided by the
Northern Ireland (Temporary Provisions) Act of 1972. This created the
office of Secretary of State for Northern Ireland (a post first envisioned in
the abortive Lloyd George deal of 1916) as well as an Advisory
Commission of local notables (a device that was worryingly reminiscent

of the Viceregal Advisory Council, formed by Lord French in 1918 as a last effort to connect the Dublin Castle administration with popular realities).[2] But beyond these apparently transient official arrangements there was a widespread and fertile debate about the reinvention of the Northern constitution.

In early 1972 Bill Craig, the architect of the Vanguard pressure group within Unionism, resurrected the notion of dominion status for an autonomous 'Ulster'; and indeed he went further, toying with the notion of a Rhodesian-style unilateral declaration of independence. Craig was responding to the disruption of Stormont and the threat of British withdrawal by excavating a minor theme within Unionist thought which dated back at least to the mid-1920s. The possibility of dominion status for Northern Ireland had been raised originally by James Craig and was occasionally revisited by his successors, for example in the years following the Second World War.[3] But dominion status, still less independence, was never likely to be a popular option within the Unionist elite: the system of Home Rule practised at Stormont had equipped these patriarchs with the trappings (and some of the reality) of state power, while ensuring that the British taxpayer would bolster the standard of living of the rest of the Northern population.

Dominion status and independence were generally deployed, therefore, only as crisis options, and though Craig's proposals chimed with the apocalyptic mood of Unionism in 1972, even then they won comparatively few converts. An Ulster Dominion Group was formed in 1975, becoming the British Ulster Dominion Party in 1977. The leader of the party was the colourful and volatile Professor Kennedy Lindsay, but it had little electoral impact: Lindsay could not even make it into Newtownabbey district council in the local government elections of 1977.[4] Still, at other moments of crisis or reappraisal for Unionism, the notions of dominion status and independence have re-emerged, and it is striking that David Trimble has periodically flirted with these strategies: for example, after the Ulster Workers' Strike of 1974 and again after the Anglo-Irish Agreement of 1985.[5]

Trimble, however, also bitterly opposed a scarcely less flamboyant loyalist effort to reinvent the Stormont regime. In late 1971, Ian Paisley who, with the barrister Desmond Boal, had recently founded the Democratic Unionist Party believed that a British withdrawal was impending, and evidently began to consider the fate of Unionism after the end of the Union. Paddy Devlin claims in his autobiography that at this time he and John Hume journeyed to St John's Point in County Down, where they met Paisley and Boal and where the conversation centred on a federal Ireland – the possible reconstitution of a devolved Stormont parliament within the context of an Irish state. According to Devlin, 'Boal and Paisley were clearly motivated to seek ways of protecting unionist rights and governance, as they had serious doubts about the British commitment to keep Northern Ireland within the United Kingdom.'[6]

News of this conversation somehow leaked out and Paisley quickly got off-side, but the episode is not without significance. At a personal level it perhaps suggests that Paisley has more political imagination and less political dogmatism than is sometimes thought. At the same time, the inspiration for the federal idea clearly came not from Paisley, but from Boal, who later made his thoughts public. He, in turn, may have been influenced by some of the ideas thrown up during debate on the third Home Rule Bill, or by the unitary mechanisms contained in the Government of Ireland Act. Boal was arguably more concerned to protect Unionists than the Union – more concerned with community than with constitutional type. To this extent he prefigured the advocacy of Conor Cruise O'Brien, who as a Unionist sympathiser argued in 1998 that pacific Northern Protestants could do worse than throw in their lot with like-minded Southerners, creating a society divided by religion but united by a civic morality.[7]

Boal's prescription, whatever its logical and moral standing, served only to confirm the political marginalisation of its author. One of the most painstaking critics was the thirty-year-old David Trimble, who supplied a scathing repudiation – 'Independence may be the only alternative to Direct Rule' – in a Belfast newspaper.[8] But the final collapse of 'Home Rule' in 1972 stimulated other radical speculations that would have a rather greater political purchase. In April 1972, speaking at a meeting of the Conservative Bow Group, Brian Faulkner raised the possibility that 'if there was not to be a worthwhile devolved parliament restored then Unionists would demand full integration on the Scottish model as their second choice'.[9] Writing on 16 April 1972 to Sir Patrick Macrory, Faulkner elaborated this thought: 'as you may have seen, the policy which I am advocating is that we should go all-out for either the restoration of a worthwhile regional parliament or – a poor second best – full integration on the Scottish pattern'.[10]

Integration was not Unionist Party policy, and Faulkner later conceded that 'in a sense I was kite-flying to test reaction among Unionists and in Britain'.[11] For the moment, the 'reaction among Unionists' was decidedly cool; but nevertheless the speech gave prominence to an idea which, as with the Boal initiative, had deep roots in the history of the Home Rule debate. When Unionists originally mooted the idea of partition in 1913–14, it was with a view to maintaining the northern counties under the direct rule of Westminster and with no thought of an Ulster parliament. The establishment of a devolved assembly in 1921, and its survival until 1972, all but extinguished enthusiasm among Ulster Unionists for full integration. But, with the prorogation of Stormont, and with the Tory government mooting the idea of an emasculated 'GLC-type' Northern Assembly, Faulkner was anxious to chart the range of acceptable constitutional options.

Given the extent of opposition to his 'kite', Faulkner quickly set the notion of integration aside to focus on the campaign to restore a meaningful devolved assembly. The influential Ulster Unionist manifesto, *Towards the Future*, published in September 1972, affirmed that 'if Northern Ireland were governed entirely from London, a significant minority of the population would remain totally opposed to the administration…the basic tension and division of the community can only be resolved inside a parliament of Northern Ireland'.[12] But the idea of 'full integration' had deep roots and, in the context of the prolonged constitutional impasse in the 1970s and early 1980s, it achieved a fuller flowering than hitherto. Indeed, for a time, under the leadership of James Molyneaux (1979–95), it seemed that the Ulster Unionist Party itself might be won for the integrationist cause.

Nationalists and republicans also responded to the challenge of Stormont's demise. In March 1972 Provisional Sinn Féin (the political party linked to the Provisional IRA) inaugurated its 'Éire Nua' policy, which envisioned a federal Ireland with regional parliaments in each of the four provinces. The proposed Ulster assembly, Dáil Uladh, was designed as a concession to Unionists, although it was also intended to serve the nine counties of the historic province rather than the six counties of the partition statelet. The programme was a step back from the traditional republican goal of a unitary Irish state, and it contained the very faint resonance of ideas that had been mooted by Unionists. The notion of a parliament for the nine counties of Ulster had been urged by British Unionists in 1919–20, during the preparation of the Government of Ireland Bill. Carson had always privately favoured the treatment of Ulster on the basis of nine counties. Moreover, as has been noted, some isolated and radical Unionist ideologues were considering the possibility of a federal Ireland on the basis of the retention of Stormont and a six-county 'Ulster'.

But a nine-county Dáil Uladh was a very different proposition to that mooted even by the most radical or isolated Unionist. The Catholic and Protestant populations of a nine-county Ulster would have been more or less evenly divided, and the prospect of maintaining Unionist culture and identity, still less political ascendancy, within such a system would have been remote. The pay-off for accepting the end of the British connection and a unitary Irish state was therefore too feeble to be worth a second glance. Needless to say, even if the 'Éire Nua' strategy had held out more, its authors were too hateful to Unionists, particularly in the circumstances of 1972, for the latter to be capable of persuasion. As it was, Sinn Féin abandoned the modest consensuality of 'Éire Nua' in the early 1980s, when a new generation of Northern hardliners took over the party and its policies.

A more lasting and influential nationalist by-product of the ferment of 1972 was the idea of a condominium, or joint British–Irish sovereignty in Northern Ireland. In September 1972 the new constitutional nationalist party, the SDLP, held a conclave at Gweedore, County Donegal, at which the idea of joint sovereignty was debated. This was the inspiration of the journalist Desmond Fennell and a Belfast surgeon, Paddy Lane. The notion was taken seriously by the leaders of the new party, and incorporated into its influential policy statement *Towards a New Ireland*, the final draft of which was the work of John Hume.[13] In this Hume and his colleagues proposed that Britain and Ireland negotiate a treaty through which – as 'an interim system of Government' pending full reunification – responsibility for the government of Northern Ireland be shared.[14]

Provision was made for both a unicameral assembly, elected by proportional representation, and a fifteen–strong executive, elected by proportional representation from the assembly. Two commissioners, representing the British and Irish governments, were to function effectively as joint heads of state, signing the assembly's bills into law, and judging the constitutionality of proposed legislation. Their work was to be complemented by a constitutional court, comprising the 'Chief Justice' of Northern Ireland and two additional judges, one appointed by each of the commissioners. The assembly, together with Dáil Éireann, would send equal numbers of representatives to a new National Senate of Ireland, whose function would be 'to plan the integration of the whole island by preparing the harmonisation of the structures, laws and services of both parts of Ireland and to agree on an acceptable constitution for a new Ireland and its relationships with Britain'.[15] The flags of the two sovereign states, Britain and Ireland, were to have equal status within the new condominium of Northern Ireland.

In the light of the subsequent constitutional history of Northern Ireland, and particularly of the Good Friday Agreement, some of these proposals look highly ambitious. *Towards a New Ireland* was in fact an expression of constitutional nationalist confidence rooted in the rapid retreat of Unionist power after 1968, and in the summary dispatch of Stormont in March 1972. It reflected, too, the prevalent belief that the British could be levered out of Northern Ireland.

Some of the manifesto's central features have re-emerged in periods of general confidence within the wider nationalist community, such as the mid-1980s through to the very early 1990s. The New Ireland Forum of 1983–4, which was heavily influenced by the SDLP, embraced the notion of joint sovereignty, and this in turn was fed into the Anglo-Irish Agreement of 1985. The agreement, indeed, might be interpreted as an anodyne version of the joint sovereignty treaty envisaged by the SDLP in 1972. The SDLP and the Irish certainly saw it in this light, but the British seem to have been much more interested in sharing responsibility for Northern Ireland than in sharing power or sovereignty. In 1991 the SDLP returned to another feature of the *Towards a New Ireland* project when it proposed that the government of Northern Ireland be vested with a panel of six commissioners (one a British appointee, one Irish, one appointed by the European Union, and three elected locally).

*Towards a New Ireland* was thus a major long-term influence on constitutional nationalists in the North and upon those in the South, like Garret FitzGerald, who were closest to John Hume and the SDLP leadership. But, with regard to its immediate impact, the most that might be said is that the manifesto helped to underline the consensus of approval in the North for the restoration of some form of unicameral legislature, elected by proportional representation. It also, significantly, prefigured the type of executive power sharing that was built into the Sunningdale Agreement of December 1973. It might also be observed that the proposal for a National Senate had an influence over the Council of Ireland arrangements that were put in place at Sunningdale.

What of mainstream Unionist thought on devolution at this time? Mention has already been made of Brian Faulkner's ill-fated 'kite' on integration. By September 1972 Faulkner and his Unionists had largely resisted the temptations of any of the more extreme options that had been mooted at the time of the fall of their parliament. G. B. Newe, a Catholic and a former Stormont minister, appears to have been an important moderating influence on the development of Faulkner's thought at this time.[16] The party had instead opted for an evolutionary approach, taking Faulkner's 1971 plans for the reform of Stormont as a starting-point. In the manifesto, *Towards the Future* (September 1972), the Ulster Unionists explicitly abandoned the notion of integration and instead outlined a plan for a reformed local parliament.

As with the SDLP's *Towards a New Ireland*, the Unionists proposed to create a unicameral assembly. Indeed, they conceded that 'any shortcomings in the Northern Ireland Parliamentary system hitherto have been due to too slavish an imitation of the Westminster model in circumstances which that model was not evolved to meet'.[17] But at this time the

Unionists' abandonment of the 'Westminster model' did not encompass the notion of proportional representation either in the planned assembly or still less in its executive. Minority influence was to be ensured not through power sharing, but through an elaborate system of parliamentary committees: 'the kernel of our proposals for a new Regional Parliament'.[18] There were to be six committees, which would have considerable powers of scrutiny over legislation, and at least three were to be chaired by 'members of opposition parties'. The committees would, in effect, act as a counterweight to the power of the executive. The concerns of the Northern minority were further addressed through a proposed Bill of Rights and through 'a joint Irish Inter-Governmental Council'. This was to have an equal number of Northern and Southern members, and would be empowered 'to discuss matters of mutual interest, particularly in the economic and social field'.[19]

Viewed in the light of the SDLP's maximalism, the Unionist vision of devolved government looked decidedly unappealing. The essence of the Unionist proposal was Faulkner's effort to reform the majoritarian regime at Stormont in 1971, and the idea of the Inter-Governmental Council seems to have been rooted in the ill-fated proposal for a Council of Ireland contained in the Government of Ireland Act. From the point of view of the SDLP, *Towards the Future* preserved an exclusively Unionist executive and a simple first-past-the-post electoral system. Committee chairmen, though likely to be influential, would be appointed by the Prime Minister, who would inevitably be a Unionist, and they would preside over Unionist-dominated committees. The Inter-Governmental Council, though superficially attractive and certainly a remarkable Unionist inspiration, would be simply a consultative body, a talking shop. Otherwise – from the SDLP perspective – *Towards the Future* embodied no visionary ambition, no leap of the political and constitutional imagination.

Indeed, *Towards the Future* reflects the strengths and weaknesses of Faulkner himself, who supplied and signed the foreword to the manifesto. It was essentially a pragmatic work, a carefully calculated and defensible bargaining position. It combined a reasonable response to some traditional and non-partisan criticisms of Stormont, while dealing with the nationalist critique in a subtle, not to say disingenuous, manner. The proposed legislative assembly was to be expanded in number in order to allow for greater minority representation, while the executive was to be reduced from its Stormont dimensions. This revised relationship between government and back benches was designed to answer the criticism, made by academic commentators like Nicholas Mansergh as early as the 1930s, that the Northern government was too large and overweening for the size of the legislature.[20]

On the other hand, the Unionists were not yet prepared to endorse compulsory power sharing at executive level; nor were they prepared to accept formal proportional representation. The elaborate committee structure – which, despite the commentary on 'slavish' imitation of Westminster, echoed the select committee system of the British parliament – was doubtless included partly because the SDLP had reacted favourably when the idea was originally mooted – in June 1971. But the Unionist position had waned since then, and the committees could now be seen not as a thorough-going reform, but as a means of relaunching Stormont. It has been said that the Anglo-Irish Agreement of 1985 provided the SDLP with a 'banker position' from which it would not be budged, and in a sense the suspension of Stormont supplied the party with an initial 'banker position' that Faulkner's committee system could not dislodge.[21]

It was the task of the British government to try to reduce these evidently divergent Unionist and nationalist proposals into an agreed constitution. A cross-party conference was held at the Europa Lodge Hotel, Darlington, at the end of September 1972, where representatives of the Ulster Unionists, the Alliance Party and the moribund Northern Ireland Labour Party aired their proposals; the SDLP, the Democratic Unionists and Vanguard chose to stay away. In the circumstances, Faulkner and his colleagues dominated the proceedings and the resultant green paper, *The Future of Northern Ireland*, while striving to steer a path between the rival demands, probably erred more towards the Unionist position than might otherwise have been the case (Faulkner nevertheless deemed the green paper to be 'comprehensive and extremely fair').[22]

However, the more formal statement of official intent – the white paper, *Northern Ireland Constitutional Proposals* of March 1973 – caused greater problems for Faulkner within his party, and opposition raged over the issue of executive power sharing and the powers of the proposed new assembly. The terminology of the white paper ('Assembly', 'Executive' and 'Measures' as opposed to 'Parliament', 'Government' and 'Acts') wounded Unionist sensitivities, and the paper contained a much-needed official critique, both explicit and implied, of the Stormont regime. Faulkner, pragmatic as ever, was prepared to work to shape the emerging deal, but the extreme Vanguard wing of his party was unable to follow him, and at this point broke away to form a separate organisation.

The *Constitutional Proposals* were duly given legislative force as the Northern Ireland Constitution Act (1973). This made provision for a unicameral legislative assembly, as both the Unionists and SDLP had urged. The Assembly was to be elected by proportional representation, as the

SDLP had sought, and was to be associated with a power-sharing executive, again reflecting the wishes of the SDLP. Elections for the new legislature were held on 28 June 1973 and resulted in an overall majority in favour of the white paper, but also left Faulkner with only a minority of the Unionist vote, albeit a substantial minority. Faulkner was undoubtedly bloodied by this contest, but in talks at Stormont Castle in November 1973 he was still able to strike a deal with the SDLP and Alliance on the formation of the Executive.[23]

As with the Government of Ireland Act the constitution of 1973 outlined the 'transferred' powers to be enjoyed by this new administration, and the 'excepted' powers to be retained by Westminster; some 'reserved' powers, as with the Act of 1920, would be wielded for a time by London. Brigid Hadfield has observed that the number of 'excepted' matters was greater than ever, a reflection of British unwillingness to restore powers that the old Stormont regime had allegedly misused.[24] As with the Government of Ireland Act, provision was made in the measure of 1973 for a Council of Ireland, the form of which was to be decided after future negotiation between the Northern Irish parties and the British and Irish governments. This was the trigger for the Sunningdale Conference of December 1973, where the relationship between Belfast and Dublin was defined in greater (and, in the event, fatal) detail.

Hadfield also observed, writing in 1989, that the assertion of British sovereignty in the Government of Ireland Act (section 75) was carried over into section 4.4 of the Act of 1973.[25] But she affirmed that neither instrument was in itself the guarantee of Northern Ireland's constitutional position within the Union: this lay instead with Article 1 of the Act of Union itself.[26] This argument would assume very great importance at the time of the Belfast Agreement when the British and Irish governments were seeking to trade off constitutional concessions.

The ultimate fate of the arrangements established by the Northern Ireland Constitution Act and the Sunningdale Conference is well known: the power-sharing Executive created under the terms of the Act fell on 28 May 1974 after a two-week protest strike by loyalists organised as the Ulster Workers' Council (UWC). The fundamental interpretative problem of this débâcle, as with so many other aspects of modern Irish political history, remains the issue of causation and blame: why did the power-sharing Executive fall, and who carried the responsibility? Supporters of the constitutional arrangements of 1973–4 tend to see the Executive and Assembly as a disastrous lost opportunity, and to apportion blame with a corresponding bitterness.[27] The workers' strike is seen from this perspective as an act of political blackmail, organised by loyalist paramilitaries and a handful of privileged workers, and bolstered by the collusion of the Protestant middle classes: Maurice Hayes, a civil servant at the time, recalls his concern at the queues of besuited supplicants at the UWC headquarters in East Belfast.[28] By not acting to suppress these forces, it is argued, the British government displayed a culpable weakness. Opponents of the 1973–4 constitution included entrenched Unionists and republicans, and both (in different ways) indicted the Irish government and the SDLP. Unionists also blamed Faulkner for weakness and trimming, while republicans blamed the British for (as in 1921) ensnaring ingenuous constitutional nationalists.

Even at this distance, it is not always possible to separate sentiment from logic in approaching the fall of the Executive. Perhaps the feat is *especially* difficult at this remove, given the parallels that are frequently made between Sunningdale and the Belfast Agreement. Still, while acknowledging the difficulties, some aspects of the politics of 1973–4 seem to require emphasis. These years – 1972–4 – were among the very worst of the 'Troubles': republicans killed 566 people in 1972–4, loyalists killed 342, and the security forces killed 135. Some of these deaths occurred after the fall of the Executive in May 1974; but the statistics are still chilling enough, and they underline the challenge and difficulties of making political concessions and achieving compromise.

There were, however, some positive aspects. Constitutional nationalism was broadly satisfied with the government's *Northern Ireland Constitutional Proposals* and the subsequent Northern Ireland Constitution Act. Though a majority of Unionists voted against the government's proposals in June 1973, Faulkner was able to sustain the (admittedly tenuous) support of his following for a power-sharing executive until December 1973. On 23 October 1973, the governing committee of the Unionist Party voted to support a power-sharing government, and on 20 November a wider party forum, the Ulster Unionist Council, refused to condemn power sharing.[29] It has been said that these votes 'mark the high water mark of genuine consensus'.[30] They indicate the shakiness of consensual feeling and they do not, of course, take account of the attitudes of loyalist hardliners beyond the ranks of the Unionist Party. But the votes illustrate that, while there were clearly significant constitutional or sectarian fears, the main Unionist party was prepared to abandon its traditional support for majority rule, and to share executive power with nationalists. On this basis, Faulkner and his lieutenants were able to enter the Executive on 22 November 1973.[31]

Viewed from this perspective, it is just conceivable that the power-sharing experiment was sustainable. But power sharing was only one element of the constitutional settlement: the government white paper and legislation envisaged a significant cross-border dimension ('the government favours, and is prepared to facilitate, the establishment of institutional arrangements for consultation and co-operation between Northern Ireland and the Republic of Ireland'). It was the task of the Sunningdale Conference, which met between 6 and 9 December 1973, to hammer these aspirations into a detailed agreement; and it was Sunningdale which seems to have marked a turning-point in the fortunes of the power-sharing enterprise. After the publication of the Sunningdale communiqué, which summarised the deal that had been struck, Faulkner's faltering command over Unionist opinion collapsed, and this meant that the whole constitutional settlement, including those aspects for which tentative support had already been won, was put at risk.

The commentators on Sunningdale tend to part company in apportioning exclusive blame either to the loyalist bully-boys and British poltroons of May 1974, or to the nationalist buccaneers of December 1973, who smelt blood and who ruthlessly sought to maximise their gains. There can be little doubt that Sunningdale was a highly problematic episode, whether in terms of the timing of the conference, its composition or the resultant deal. With the benefit of hindsight it might have been better to bank the achievement of a power-sharing executive and postpone the adjustment of cross-border relations until the new consensual government in the North was more securely rooted. This was the view of the liberal Unionist negotiator, Basil McIvor. The distinguished Catholic civil servant Maurice Hayes went further, arguing that the whole enterprise – both the Executive and Sunningdale – was launched too quickly, and that the political dust should have been allowed to settle after the fall of Stormont.[32]

On the other hand, it was felt among the SDLP that, if the cross-border aspects of the agreement were allowed to slip at this juncture, then the Unionists could never be cajoled back to the negotiating table. (Interestingly, this apprehension re-emerged in 1998, when nationalists wanted the simultaneous establishment of the new assembly and cross-border institutions for the same reasons.) The SDLP's position seems to have reflected a perception that the configuration of forces in Britain and Ireland was helpful to the nationalist cause, and that Sunningdale presented an opportunity to maximise political gains. Hayes has called this emphasis on the cross-border dimension 'an odd inversion of values and a retreat from reality'; and indeed it is comprehensible only in terms of the long-term strategic vision and hard-nosed instincts of some of the SDLP leadership.[33] Thus the SDLP and their Irish ministerial allies wanted a speedy and comprehensive agreement, and for his part, Edward Heath, the British Tory Prime Minister, saw an Ulster settlement as a major policy goal of his increasingly embattled administration.[34] None of these key parties would have been content with an open-ended or incomplete deal: Sunningdale was too important to too many players to be postponed.

Turning to the disposition of forces at Sunningdale, it should be stressed that Faulkner did not represent a clear majority of Unionists – and yet the Democratic Unionists and Vanguard leaders were not invited to participate at the conference.[35] In a sense this was quite understandable: Paisley and Craig had not hitherto shown themselves to be co-operative, and they were always likely to be barriers to a deal. On the other hand, as Garret FitzGerald argued at the time, there was a chance that the participation of opponents might have defused some of their hostility.[36]

There were other problems in terms of the representation at the conference. William Whitelaw, the Secretary of State for Northern Ireland, was naturally well informed about the background to the talks and was, in the verdict of Ken Bloomfield, 'infinitely cunning'. But he had been replaced by Francis Pym, a figure with no ministerial experience, and with little previous knowledge of the Ulster imbroglio.[37] And it was Pym who attended Sunningdale, albeit as an entirely marginal presence: FitzGerald recounts that 'Pym was like a fish out of water at Sunningdale, tending to buttonhole other participants to ask anxiously: "What's happening?"'[38] Addressing one of the Unionist negotiators, Basil McIvor, Pym betrayed a hint of his own feelings: 'I am writing to say how much I benefited from the opportunity which the [Sunningdale] conference gave me to work with you. It was a great experience for me, especially in my early days as Secretary of State, and I was most grateful for all the help and understanding which you showed.'[39]

It is possible (though by no means probable) that if Whitelaw had been present, he might have acted as a restraining influence upon Heath who, in his determination to force a deal, compounded the difficulties faced by the already beleaguered Faulknerites. In one well-documented episode at the conference, Heath (who – according to Woodrow Wyatt – wanted 'to be feared') descended on the Unionist delegation in an effort to browbeat them into what they considered an unsellable agreement on policing. The Prime Minister began by staring at each of the negotiators, and then threatened to blame them for any breakdown of the talks. He argued angrily with several of those present, then withdrew into another prolonged silence before suddenly leaving the room.[40] Whether Whitelaw could have moderated such antics is an open question – Ken Bloomfield has noted that even the normally ebullient Secretary of State was cowed by his master – but in any event he could have done no worse than Pym.[41]

Heath's performance, given the harmony between the Irish government and the SDLP, meant that the Unionists were largely outgunned at Sunningdale, and it is generally agreed that they got the worst of the deal. At Sunningdale it was accepted that the cross-border institutions would embrace a Council of Ministers equipped 'with executive and harmonising functions and a consultative role' as well as a Consultative Assembly 'with advisory and review functions'.[42] In addition there was to be a permanent Secretariat (Paddy Devlin jokingly suggested that this elite and cosmopolitan enterprise be based in the hamlet of Ahoghill, County Antrim).[43] The Council of Ministers, with its 'executive and harmonising functions', comprised seven ministers from each of the two Irish jurisdictions, and decisions could only be made on the basis of a unanimous vote. The Consultative Assembly was to comprise sixty members, also drawn equally from North and South. FitzGerald saw this balance as 'a significant concession', given that the Republic had twice the population of Northern Ireland.[44] Taken together, the Council of Ministers and the Consultative Assembly formed a Council of Ireland.

Agreement was also reached on the 'areas of common interest' where the Council of Ministers could exercise its executive powers. The promise of cross-border security co-operation was reaffirmed, and the prospect of changes in the law of extradition was raised. The Unionists' greatest gains were held to have been on the issues of constitutional status and policing. Reform of the RUC, mooted by the SDLP, was effectively buried by the Sunningdale deal, while in Article 5 the Irish government accepted that there would be no change in 'the status' of Northern Ireland until a majority of its people so desired.

What were the problems with this deal? Faulkner had himself proposed the creation of an Irish Inter-Governmental Council in the manifesto, *Towards the Future*. But it is clear that he saw this both as a consultative body and as a way of improving cross-border co-operation on security. He did not want the Council to have executive powers, and he did not want either a parliamentary body or an established Council secretariat. But the arrangements that were eventually formulated went far beyond this modest vision, even though Faulkner gamely sought to emphasise that the Council was originally a Unionist inspiration and that much of the agreed construct was 'necessary nonsense' which meant 'nothing in practice'.[45]

To the extent that the key Council of Ministers required total unanimity before action could be achieved, Faulkner had a case. Moreover, the construction of the Consultative Assembly ensured that the Unionists, though a minority, would have had a substantial representation, and indeed might have been able to work informally with one or other of the Southern parties. But, whatever the checks and balances, the Council of Ireland was designed to be an impressive step towards reunification, and

Faulkner seems to have failed to grasp that the elaborate symbolism of the Council would scare his electorate: 'I felt confident that Unionists, being basically practical people, would judge our final agreement on a practical rather than symbolic level'.[46]

In retrospect it seems likely that Faulkner was pressed too hard on the issue of the Council of Ireland; and it is suggestive that, with the negotiation of the Anglo-Irish Agreement, the same relentless pressure on the cross-border question does not seem to have been applied to David Trimble. At the time, however, influential elements within the SDLP, and thus within the Irish government, seem to have been concerned more with quickly securing the mechanisms for national reunification than with a workable internal settlement in the North. The moderate Eddie McGrady remarked to Hayes that 'the SDLP had only assented to power-sharing in order to get the Council of Ireland'.[47] John Hume and Garret FitzGerald, who were good friends, were earnest advocates of the Council; and according to the admittedly unsympathetic Conor Cruise O'Brien, FitzGerald, influenced by Hume, persuaded his cabinet colleagues that 'the Protestant population would accept the Council of Ireland without any difficulty'.[48] If this is true, it is possible that the reference to an Inter-Governmental Council in Faulkner's *Towards the Future* encouraged false hopes among the Irish; it is also possible that the SDLP and the Dublin government, having witnessed the relative calm that greeted the fall of Stormont, were banking upon the acquiescence or demoralisation of the Unionist middle classes.

Either way, it seems clear that FitzGerald and Hume pushed the Council idea with vigour. FitzGerald recalls that he encountered difficulties with both his own civil servants, who were reluctant to relax their administrative grip, and with Paddy Devlin of the SDLP, who was poised to take charge of Health and Social Services in the Northern Executive, over the list of areas where the putative Council of Ministers might exercise its authority.[49] There are two versions of a key exchange between FitzGerald and Devlin. In his autobiography FitzGerald recalls that Devlin, having read the proposed list of executive functions, said that 'he was not going to have his friends [the Unionists]...hung from the lamp-posts on their return to Belfast, as they assuredly would be if the list of executive functions we had agreed were published': the list was accordingly reduced in number.[50] In the memoirs of Ken Bloomfield, the same confrontation is rendered rather differently: 'as [Devlin] came into the meeting room, Garret FitzGerald was well launched upon a characteristically visionary exposition of a potential Council of Ireland with wide-ranging executive responsibilities for this and that. "Garret", said Paddy, not even bothering to sit down, "you can keep your hands off my f—ing ambulances for a start".'[51]

It is reasonably clear that, in terms of the Council of Ireland, FitzGerald and Hume were not only out of step with Northern Protestant opinion, but also in advance of sections of their own support. Faulkner wanted the trade-off for the Council of Ireland to come in the area of security and constitutional recognition. But no deal could be achieved on the controversial issue of extradition, a political necessity for the Unionists but an electoral and constitutional minefield for the Irish government. Basil McIvor, who was partly responsible for presenting the Unionist case on this issue, recalled that he could muster 'no adequate support from the British side'.[52] It was agreed to disagree, and – in a fudge worthy of Lloyd George – this issue, along with the possibility of a common law enforcement area in Ireland, was relegated for the future consideration of a legal commission. In terms of the status of Northern Ireland, it was effectively accepted that any change in articles 2 and 3 of the Irish constitution, where a territorial claim to the North was set out, was too politically fraught to be worth pursuing. Faulkner had wanted such a change, but even Conor Cruise O'Brien, with whom he had established a rapport, argued that this was not likely to be passed by the necessary referendum.[53]

It was finally settled that the British and Irish governments would make parallel declarations affirming the right of the people of the North to self-determination. But the Irish declaration was necessarily ambiguous, given the constraints of their 1937 Constitution: 'The Irish Government fully accepted and solemnly declared that there could be no change in the status of Northern Ireland until a majority of the people of Northern Ireland desired a change in that status.'[54] The 'status' of Northern Ireland was thus left undefined, and in the event even this well-intentioned ambiguity did not go without challenge.

At the end it seemed that policing was the issue that would make or break the deal; and, again, it is perhaps significant that in 1998 this was a matter which the negotiators of the Good Friday Agreement sub-contracted to a special commission. At Sunningdale the SDLP and the Irish ministers wanted sweeping reform of the RUC, and in particular they wanted it to be directly responsible to the new Council of Ireland. Faulkner, on the other hand, wanted control of the police to be vested exclusively with the Executive. The deadlock on this issue seems to have aggravated the Unionists' despair, and by Sunday 9 December 1973 they were preparing to return home.

At this point FitzGerald, for one, seems to have grasped the magnitude of the political difficulties that the Unionists were facing, as well as the extent to which they had so far been worsted in the negotiations.[55] It was agreed, accordingly, that the British would undertake to consider returning control of the police to the Executive, once conditions permitted; and it was also accepted that the key supervisory body, the Northern Ireland Police Authority, would be appointed not by the Council of Ireland, but by the British government, acting on the advice of the Executive, which in turn would consult with the Ministerial Council. Faulkner was content with these concessions, and this permitted his Unionists to swallow the pill of the wider deal.

How did contemporaries assess the balance of the Sunningdale agreement? Writing to G. B. Newe in February 1974, Faulkner argued that 'far from representing loss or gain to one side or the other, "Sunningdale" provides a unique opportunity for all sections of the community to work together for the good of Northern Ireland. Certainly there are unique features in the new institutions which could easily become established practice in other democracies.'[56] Later, writing in his autobiography, Faulkner shifted ground somewhat, breezily claiming that, with the deal on policing secured, 'all of us in the Unionist deputation were convinced that we had come off best... We felt elated and expected our success to be recognised. One member of our delegation remarked that Sunningdale would go down in history as a Unionist victory.'[57] There is a premonition here of some of the determinedly upbeat language used by some Unionist defenders of the Good Friday Agreement.

Basil McIvor, the only other member of the Unionist negotiating team to have published a memoir, presents a less detailed, but also a more despairing and rebarbative assessment: 'Unionists could see the futility of it all. We had gained nothing.'[58] McIvor, relatively liberal and consensual, is severe in his criticism of John Hume, whose 'part in the Sunningdale Agreement [in pushing for a powerful Council of Ireland] spelt disaster for the survival of powersharing'.[59] Hume, for his part, is convinced that the Executive fell solely because of the workers' strike, and because of the 'political cowardice of the government': 'the British served to underwrite the maintenance of sectarian solidarity and negativism as the basic method of Unionist politics'.[60]

Only Paddy Devlin among the SDLP team has recorded his memories of Sunningdale at length; and, while avoiding any specific assessment of the winners and losers at the conference, his concern for Faulkner's difficulties and his willingness to retreat from some of the more advanced SDLP and Dublin positions are very clear.[61] Maurice Hayes, who was a senior official in the secretariat of the Executive, was close to SDLP leaders like Gerry Fitt, and accepts that 'Faulkner was saddled with a load that he could not carry, and which eventually brought him down, and with him the whole power-sharing experiment'. Hayes has also suggested that 'the SDLP got more, probably, than it bargained for at Sunningdale'.[62]

Of the other participants, Edward Heath's memoir of Sunningdale offers little by way of critical assessment, in terms either of his own role or of the overall deal. There is, however, a perceptible trace of the anger that he felt at the Unionist stand on policing, and there is also a clear allusion to the personal importance that he ascribed to a deal: 'this historic accord was one of the proudest moments of my premiership'.[63] Conor Cruise O'Brien predictably – given his good relations with Faulkner – was sensitive to the possibility that the Unionists had been driven 'too hard' and that the 'Faulkner Unionists were in real and serious danger, and therefore so was the whole Sunningdale deal'.[64]

Garret FitzGerald unambiguously felt that the Unionists were worsted during the negotiations, certainly before their gains on the policing issue. In an informal test conducted among members of the Irish team, the SDLP was awarded 1580 marks out of a possible 3200 for its achievement at the conference, while the Unionists lagged behind with 1205.[65] He has in fact argued that too much time was probably devoted to the policing issue, and not enough to the matter of Northern Ireland's status. He has also argued that, on balance, the possibility of a referendum on articles 2 and 3 should have been explored with greater vigour.[66]

The fall-out from Sunningdale seems clear enough. Faulkner had secured the support of a bare majority in his party in October–November 1973, and less than a month after the conference this critical margin of support had disintegrated. On 4 January 1974 he lost a key party vote on 'the proposed all-Ireland Council settlement' by fifty-three votes.[67] There is a view that Sunningdale and the Council of Ireland were essentially feints, and that it was popular Unionist distaste for sharing power with Catholics that finally brought down the Executive. It would be wrong, certainly, to exaggerate Ulster Unionist support for the power-sharing Executive before Sunningdale; it would also be quite wrong to overlook anti-Catholic or, at least, anti-nationalist feeling among sections of the Unionist electorate. But the evidence seems to suggest that before Sunningdale Faulkner might well have carried off the power-sharing experiment, and that afterwards the odds turned against him. In the aftermath of the conference it is quite clear that Unionists were impressed and fearful of the reality of a Council of Ireland endowed with 'executive and harmonising' powers, and they were unpersuaded by the trophies of article 5 (on Northern self-determination) and articles 10 and 15 (on security). If, as FitzGerald has pretty much conceded, the Irish team underestimated the sophistication of their own electorate, then it is clear that Faulkner gambled on the discernment of Unionist voters, and lost.[68]

And, in truth, it would have required an unusually high level of sophistication to have been unmoved by the discrediting of Faulkner's gains. The SDLP was clearly delighted by the Council of Ireland and the deal as a whole. To judge by the evidence of Paddy Devlin's memoirs, they were evidently conscious of the need to avoid any gloating or triumphalist tone in subsequent media interviews.[69] But restraint was not always possible: on 16 December Austin Currie claimed on RTE radio that the Sunningdale deal 'fulfilled Wolfe Tone's desires to break the connection with England and substitute the common name of Irishman for Catholic, Protestant and dissenter'.[70] On 17 January 1974, Hugh Logue, an SDLP Assemblyman, described the Council of Ireland as 'the vehicle that would trundle unionists into a united Ireland'.[71] Even more significant than this bragging was the developing controversy in Dublin over the status of Northern Ireland. An interview with the taoiseach, Liam Cosgrave, appeared on 16 December 1973 in which he reiterated the formula that the Irish ministers had signed at Sunningdale: 'there could be no change in the status of Northern Ireland until a majority of the people of Northern Ireland desired a change'. But he also confirmed that there would be no alteration of the constitution and no repudiation of the territorial claim on the North.

This distinction between the practical and the legal positions of Northern Ireland was central to the Irish strategy at Sunningdale. It enabled them to withstand a damaging legal challenge from a former Fianna Fáil minister, Kevin Boland, who was a republican opponent of Sunningdale and who claimed that the Irish government had acted unconstitutionally over the status issue. Government lawyers were able to argue that the Sunningdale deal was not an intergovernmental agreement (as distinct from a communiqué), and that the Irish declaration in no way limited Dublin's claim over the North, or its right to exercise jurisdiction there. This defence was successful both at the original hearing and, when Boland appealed, in the Supreme Court. But it was a pyrrhic victory, for the political impact was disastrous. The elusive nature of the original Irish declaration had protected the government from legal challenge, but this very quality had unsettled many Unionists who, contractually minded, had scrutinised the communiqué for some unambiguous evidence of Irish goodwill. Cosgrave's press interview, which was raised in the Assembly by Ian Paisley, and the subsequent ministerial defence against Boland effectively demolished Faulkner's claim to have wrested a meaningful concession from the Irish.

As has been noted, Faulkner had already lost a key vote in the Ulster Unionist Council, on 4 January, and had resigned from the leadership of his party. However, he retained a sizeable following within the Assembly, and this, together with the support of the SDLP and Alliance Party, meant that he could claim a democratic mandate to continue in office. It is just possible, if unlikely, that Faulkner might have overcome the setbacks supplied by the Boland case if the mood of the Unionist electorate had been given a chance to cool. But here, again, the ill-luck that dogged the Sunningdale enterprise intervened: Heath, broken by widespread industrial action, called a general election for 28 February, and inadvertently provided Faulkner's opponents with an opportunity to test their strength.

This opposition was massed in a body called the United Ulster Unionist Coalition (UUUC). Although the result did not directly affect Faulkner's position in the Assembly, the UUUC secured a startling 51 per cent of the votes cast, capturing eleven of the twelve Westminster seats in Northern Ireland. Faulkner and his supporter could only amass 13 per cent of the total poll, and were unable to retain any of their former seats. The political scientist Gordon Gillespie has pointed out that, under the terms of the Northern Ireland Constitution Act (1973), there was a requirement that the Executive 'be widely accepted throughout the community'.[72] However regrettable from a consensual perspective, it was clear from the results of the February election that neither Faulkner's supporters nor the Executive as a whole now enjoyed the widespread acceptance called for by the Act. The disposition of forces in the Assembly allowed Faulkner to struggle on, but the rapid movement of Northern Protestant opinion after Sunningdale meant that both he and the institutions that he had helped to shape were becoming dangerously isolated.

It was this perception of a democratic deficit which, ironically perhaps, helped to stimulate strike action against Sunningdale and the Executive. On 14 May 1974 the Assembly finally voted on a motion (originally tabled by the UUUC representative, John Laird, in March) which called for a renegotiation of Sunningdale. Laird's call was easily rejected, but it had a dramatic outcome. The vote was finalised by seven minutes past six on 14 May; one minute later the leader of the newly formed Ulster Workers' Council announced that electricity production would be dramatically cut back because Faulkner 'and his friends are ignoring the wishes of 400,000 people who voted against them in the General Election'.[73] By the following day industrial action, rooted originally in the power and fuel supply industries, had begun in earnest; and within perhaps seventy-two hours this had been ratcheted up into something approaching a general strike.[74] While the British remained broadly passive, Faulkner desperately struggled to claw back support through delaying the implementation of the Council of Ireland. By 22 May he had secured a deal with the SDLP on the staggered activation of the Council. But, while this might have impressed some wavering hardliners earlier in the year, in the midst of the UWC action it cut little ice. On 28 May, with his civil servants predicting social collapse, Faulkner resigned: falling, he took both Sunningdale and the power-sharing Executive with him.[75]

As has been said, the explanations for this end are still heavily tinctured by the political positions that were assumed in 1973–4. Supporters of Sunningdale lay stress upon the strike and upon the ugliness within Unionist political culture that was thereby exposed; opponents of Sunningdale tend to look to the limitations of the agreement itself. In a sense, however, this divergence reflects not only political differences, but also differences of chronology: some interpretations of the fall of the Executive emphasise the immediate causes of its failure, while others emphasise the mid-term or long-term perspective.

There can be little doubt that the immediate crisis generated by the strike brought the Executive down. A variety of issues are generally highlighted: the high level of intimidation by loyalist paramilitaries is frequently stressed, as is the 'collusion' (or, at best, passivity) of the Protestant middle classes.[76] The response of the British government is often seen as problematic, in so far as little was done to mitigate the effects of the strike action. Emphasis is frequently laid (for example by the SDLP) upon the failure to use the army to break the strike: Paddy Devlin stresses what he sees as the malign influence of Sir Frank Cooper, Permanent Secretary at the Northern Ireland Office, and General Frank King, the General Officer Commanding in Northern Ireland, in allegedly resisting the deployment of the army.[77] It is sometimes claimed that the British government was wary of opening up a 'second front' against the loyalists; it is also sometimes suggested that ministers were fearful that military orders would be disobeyed – here there is surely a lingering memory of the Curragh incident of 1914.

On the other hand, the political intervention of Harold Wilson served to complicate and inflame an already difficult situation. On 13 May, the day before the crucial Assembly vote on Laird's motion, Wilson announced that the army had uncovered a PIRA doomsday plan to annex parts of Belfast. Having stimulated widespread fear, Wilson then – on 25 May – characterised the organisers of the strike as 'spending their lives sponging on Westminster', and thereby hardened their anger and resolve.

For their part, Hume and the SDLP have also been criticised for insisting upon the integrity of the Council of Ireland while the wider deal sank beneath their feet.[78] Other aspects of the Executive's action have been found wanting. Not only was it slow in sorting out the Council of Ireland issue, it was also tardy in establishing a co-ordinated response to the

279

strikers. Only on 23 May was a Joint Ministerial Steering Group (a sort of government High Command) established in a belated effort to manage official action.[79] The failure of the Executive's publicity and public relations has also been stressed, G. B. Newe arguing that Faulkner and his colleagues 'were all concerned too much to work out a theology of "Sunningdale", and not enough concerned with the reality which was community government'.[80] Other, ostensibly lesser issues, feature in reminiscences of the period. A junior civil servant, the Information Officer at the Electricity Board, seems to have loomed large in the lives of ministers and high officials: the luckless official is widely blamed for encouraging pessimism through his regular, sepulchral reports of the state of the power supply.[81] More senior civil servants are blamed for persuading the normally unflappable Faulkner that a social melt-down was impending.

Some of these arguments have greater weight than others. But even if one suspends disbelief and accepts that the army and police could, and should, have been used quickly to suppress the strike, this does not preclude the likelihood that Faulkner and the Executive might only have been spared for a few more lingering weeks. It is entirely probable that the combination of heavy-handed official action and the apparent flouting of the February election results would have brought the downfall of the Executive anyway. And it is just possible that in these circumstances, with perhaps the martyring of some of the strikers, the traditionally passive Protestant middle classes might have shifted towards a more militant political stand. It is thus by no means clear how the crushing of the strike, even assuming it were possible, would have saved the Executive and Sunningdale.

Faulkner had a case: Sunningdale need not have operated as a threat to Unionists, given the unanimity required on the proposed Council of Ministers. But the reality was that he was unable to get this argument across to his own party and the wider Unionist constituency: G. B. Newe argued to Faulkner in April 1974 that 'perhaps a major weakness on the pro-Executive side has been a failure to make the Sunningdale "package" properly understood in simple terms'.[82] Moreover, in return for the deal on the Council, he sought concessions from the Irish government which (because of the 1937 Constitution) were not in their gift: Faulkner swopped the immediate reality of a Council of Ministers, Joint Parliament and Secretariat in addition to the promise of a United Ireland for a well-intentioned but constitutionally meaningless Irish declaration on the status issue. It is a striking testimony to the relative insignificance of Ulster Unionism within British and Irish priorities that such a deal should have been foisted upon Faulkner, and it is a reflection on the overwhelming forces lined up against him that he should have been pre-pared to sign. Sunningdale might have worked if the 'winners' in the deal had not 'overplayed their hand'; it might also have worked if the 'losers' had accepted that the odds were against them, and had acted with the passivity that was evidently expected in London and Dublin.[83]

The legacy of Sunningdale is rich and complex, and may be only briefly summarised here. The basic constituents of the settlement of 1973–4 – a power-sharing executive, a unicameral legislature elected through proportional representation, and some form of institutionalised cross-border dimension – have remained relevant to many of the planned initiatives since then. It is sometimes said that, in negotiating the Good Friday Agreement, Trimble was determined to avoid the mistakes com-mitted by Faulkner a generation before. Indeed, it has been said that he has taken this determination to extremes.[84] But there is a case for arguing that, while Trimble and Faulkner had slightly different emphases, and were operating within quite distinct political contexts, both shared the same broad negotiating goals. Faulkner insisted that at Sunningale 'all our efforts were directed towards ensuring that, however many tiers and secretaries the Council of Ireland might have, it remained essentially pro-paganda and in no way impinged on the powers of the Northern Ireland Assembly'.[85] Trimble shared this determination that full authority would remain with the devolved legislature, and that any Council of Ireland would be 'essentially propaganda'. But Faulkner's tolerance was stretched to include the possibility that the Council of Ireland might have 'execu-tive and harmonising' functions, while Trimble was adamant that, in its 1998 reformulation, the Ministerial Council was to be a largely consultative body.

Trimble's victories on these constitutional questions were bought at a price. Policing, for example, re-emerged in 1998 in the important role that it had occupied at Sunningdale. Garret FitzGerald believed that too much time had been spent on the issue in 1973, given that it 'never seemed to feature in the heated debates within Unionism that followed Sunningdale'; but in a sense, its absence in the ensuing crisis vindicated Faulkner's concern to get the issue right.[86] In terms of his loyalist con-stituency, Faulkner got a tolerable deal on the police but miscalculated on the Council; it is just possible that Trimble may have negotiated a sell-able deal on constitutional issues, and miscalculated on policing. It would be grimly ironic if Trimble ultimately lost out by focusing on Faulkner's strategic failure at the expense of his tactical successes.

As in 1972, the failure of devolution in 1974 brought the activation of direct rule. As in 1972, the failure of devolution apparently reopened a wide range of constitutional possibilities. The collapse of the Executive stimulated, for a time, a loyalist maximalism, which was not altogether discouraged by the British government. Merlyn Rees and Stan Orme, Minister of State at the Northern Ireland Office, were inclined to interpret the strike as a manifestation of a new type of popular loyalist political consciousness, or 'Ulster nationalism'. Both seem to have been impressed by the stress laid by strike leaders such as Glenn Barr on the limits and contractual nature of their Britishness.[87] This was linked to a renewed interest among some loyalist hardliners in the possibility of independence.

The Ulster Loyalist Coordinating Committee was an alliance of Protestant paramilitaries which in early 1975 was ruminating on the feasibility of an independent Ulster. David Trimble was approached, and contributed to *Your Future: Can Ulster Survive Unfettered?*, a discussion paper that made the case for Ulster as an independent republic within the British Commonwealth. Trimble's biographer, Henry McDonald, has pointed out that this manifesto incorporated the notion of executive power sharing, 'cross-border cooperation on matters of mutual interest' and the possibility of 'some community of the British Isles'. In other words, and in a telling irony, *Your Future* represented the first airing of a political vision that would be partly incorporated into the settlement of 1998.[88]

The British view that loyalist politics were in transition encouraged them – notwithstanding the collapse of the Assembly – to sponsor a new white paper on the government of Northern Ireland, and a new constitutional forum in the shape of the Convention. This embodied a recognition that Faulkner had outlived his political usefulness, a fact which he seems to have recognised himself: 'I am not at all happy about the White Paper. I think it could be a gift to Paisley and Co. They could tell the public "all options are open. Send us to the Convention and we'll dictate terms."'[89] More importantly, these initiatives also reflected a localist thrust within British strategy – the view that, given the failure of what was essentially an externally imposed settlement, the main parties in the North would instead be able to forge a workable internal deal. On the face of it, this might seem impossibly optimistic, but given that the focus of the opposition to Faulkner had been the Council of Ireland, and given that radical loyalist thinkers were beginning to envisage sharing power with nationalists in an independent Ulster, the British calculations appear less fantastic.

Elections for the new Convention were held on 1 May 1975, and its proceedings began a week later. By August it seemed as if, against all the odds, some form of *rapprochement* was emerging between the SDLP and the wreckers of Sunningdale. Three representatives of the UUUC – Bill

Craig of Vanguard, the Revd William Beattie of the Democratic Unionists, and Captain Austin Ardill of the Official Unionists – met with the SDLP leaders to explore the opportunities for political progress. This dialogue was associated with Craig's Voluntary Coalition idea, which encompassed a plan for power sharing in the context of the emergency that beset the country.

This notion, though sponsored by the Vanguard leader, may have originated with his lieutenant, David Trimble.[90] There is an understandable tendency in some quarters to identify and stress the consensual theme throughout Trimble's extremely complex political evolution; there is a countervailing tendency among Trimble's loyalist critics to identify his handiwork in every conceivable piece of political 'treachery' since the fall of Stormont. In any event both apologists and critics unite to ascribe 'voluntary coalition' to Trimble. In truth, this idea does bear some of Trimble's intellectual hallmarks: it placed a highly characteristic emphasis on historical precedent, citing the wartime coalitions in Britain as an argument for treating with the SDLP in the context of the terrorist warfare of the 1970s. Trimble would later seek historical vindication for some of his more difficult strategic decisions as leader of the Ulster Unionists. The episode also seems consistent with certain other features of Trimble's political style and strategies. He has been prepared to be emollient, but often only from a position of relative strength achieved through toughness. He has been prepared to be conciliatory, but often only when the proposal for conciliation was his own. Finally, the seemingly unconsidered way in which the Vanguard proposal was launched perhaps hints at a weakness for solo initiatives or political risk-taking.

The 'voluntary coalition' kite is of interest in terms of Trimble's political evolution, and in so far as it precipitated a division within Vanguard which effectively spelt the end of the movement and the marginalisation of its leaders. 'Voluntary coalition', in other words, very nearly did for Trimble what Sunningdale had done for Faulkner; and it is just possible that Trimble's subsequent actions, particularly at the time of the Belfast Agreement, have been at some level influenced by this failure in 1975. 'Voluntary coalition' also marked the opening of a period in which mainstream Unionism sought to maximise its demands. The expulsion of the 'voluntary coalitionists' from the UUUC meant that this key body emerged as a much more uncompromising enterprise.

The UUUC dominated the remaining proceedings of the Convention, and its majoritarian and devolutionist preferences were infused into the final Convention report, which was issued in January 1976. This document, which effectively demanded the restoration of Stormont, was almost immediately shelved by the government. The UUUC thereupon formed an Action Council in order to push for the implementation of the Convention report. At the same time, in March 1976, one of the UUUC leaders, Ernest Baird, launched an aggressive campaign to end direct rule and to achieve improvements on the security front. This culminated in May 1977 with an effort to reprise the industrial action that had over-turned the Executive; but the 'United Unionists' of the UUUC were split, the crucial power workers were unsympathetic, and the strike swiftly petered out. With the benefit of hindsight, it is arguable that this marked the high water mark of the effort to restore the Unionist ascendancy.

What were the wider implications of this Unionist thrust? It is unques-tionable that the failure of the 1977 action discredited the use of strikes as a loyalist political tool, and the failure also possibly undermined the threat of all future loyalist protest action. More specifically, the divisions over the strike suggested that sections of the Unionist elite were disturbed by expressions of loyalist working-class power. These divisions also indi-cated some of the political boundaries beyond which propertied Unionism was not going to venture, even (perhaps especially) in the context of substantial civil unrest: 367 people died at the hands of repub-licans between 1975 and 1977, while 276 fell victim to loyalist killers in the same period. The Ulster Workers' Strike of 1974 seemed to suggest that the Unionist middle-classes had some militant potential, but in reality middle-class 'collusion' with the strikers probably only reflected a desire to get on-side with what looked like the new regime (Maurice Hayes has pointedly suggested that these actions were reminiscent of the Weimar elite's accommodation with National Socialism).[91] It is likely that these misreadings of 1974 were corrected by the fiasco of the 1977 strike. The quiescence of the Unionist middle classes, which seems to have been assumed in the negotiations at Sunningdale, was apparently confirmed; and it is possible that this, in turn, had a bearing on British policy in the run-up to the Anglo-Irish Agreement of 1985.

The failure of the strike, and the subsequent electoral marginalisation of those such as Harry West and Ernest Baird who sought to maximise Unionist goals, opened the way to a revision of Unionist strategies. The election of James Molyneaux as Ulster Unionist leader in 1979 marked the onset of a temporary retreat from a full-blooded devolutionist stand.[92] Molyneaux had already, in December 1976, set out a case for a limited form of 'rolling devolution', with the creation at first of a regional body with administrative powers, and the future promise of a highly constrained legislature. This scheme is not without interest, in terms of both the history of the devolution idea and the internal politics of Ulster Unionism. Molyneaux's thoughts were heavily influenced by Enoch Powell, and they carried echoes of the Edwardian debates on administrative devolution and federalism. It will be recalled that administrative devolution had been mooted by some advanced Unionists in 1904; a glorified form of local government had been pushed by the Liberals in the Irish Councils scheme of 1907.

Like some of the Edwardian reformers, Molyneaux seems to have believed that a grant of administrative authority (in this case to Northern Ireland) would simultaneously stifle calls for more sweeping autonomy and improve the quality of local government. Like the Edwardian Tories who toyed with reform of the Union, Molyneaux evidently believed that the restoration of full-scale devolution outside of a wider federal system created a constitutional anomaly in Ireland, and weakened the Union. This was an argument that would have been familiar to, and readily appreciated by, a Tory federalist like F. S. Oliver or a federalist sympathiser like Carson. And in a sense, this hints at the weakness of the proposal, and indeed the weakness within Molyneaux's wider position.

Garret FitzGerald has talked of the 'Redmondite' quality of Molyneaux's politics, by which is meant the excessively metropolitan and parliamentary emphasis.[93] Molyneaux's thoughts certainly chimed with opinion at Westminster: although his mentor, Powell, was in some senses a marginal figure, their shared views of devolution seem to have been more widely acceptable. The concept of rolling devolution, which was implicit in the Molyneaux scheme, was taken up by Roy Mason, the new Secretary of State for Northern Ireland, in 1977. Molyneaux's notion of a provincial administrative body chimed with the GLC-type assembly favoured by Ted Heath in the early 1970s, and was therefore welcomed by the former Tory leader. This idea of a regional administrative council was also embraced by the new Tory spokesperson on Northern Ireland, Airey Neave, and was incorporated into the party's election manifesto of 1979.

The integrationists' goal of assimilating Northern Ireland within the structure of British government was furthered by James Callaghan's Labour government as a whole. In return for Ulster Unionist support in the lobbies, Callaghan increased the number of Northern MPs from twelve to seventeen, a reform that was complete by the 1983 general election. Because of Stormont, and following Gladstone's compromise on the issue of representation, Northern Ireland had a relatively small number of MPs at Westminster. The Callaghan government's offer, though apparently modest enough, was in fact a reversal of the traditional Home Rule formula, and implied that a devolved assembly would be a long time in coming.

Molyneaux's problem was thus not that, like some Unionists, he was incomprehensible to the British political elite; his difficulty was rather that he was in danger of losing touch with the strong particularist tradition in the grass roots of his own party. By the early 1980s, as David Hume has observed, the Unionist Party had swung in favour of Molyneaux's constitutional ideas; but the tensions over devolution had not gone away, and to some extent this swing depended upon Molyneaux's political credibility and upon his capacity to deliver.[94]

Unionist maximalism also impacted upon nationalist and republican thought. The failure of informal negotiations with the Unionists in 1975 and again in early 1976, combined with the apparent hardening of Unionist attitudes in 1976-7, reduced the confidence of the SDLP in the possibilities of a settlement. There was a parallel hardening of attitudes in the party, with an increasing emphasis on its nationalist and Catholic priorities, and a waning stress on its social democratic origins. The SDLP had previously rejected the idea of an immediate British withdrawal from Northern Ireland on the pragmatic grounds that anarchy might well ensue. But at the party conference of November 1978 it was moved that an eventual British withdrawal was 'desirable and inevitable'.[95]

Those members with roots in the labour movement, or in old-style secular republicanism, were now marginalised: Paddy Devlin was expelled from the party in 1977 after an acrimonious dispute with its executive, and Gerry Fitt (the leader) resigned in disillusion in 1979. The handful of Protestants in the party, such as Ivan Cooper, mostly left at this time. John Hume, who succeeded Fitt as leader, inherited most of these changes; and the party's centre of gravity moved to the north-west and Hume's power-base in Derry. The SDLP increasingly embodied his strategic vision, with a more emphatic social democratic ethos, and with a stress on the strengthening of connections in Washington, Dublin and Brussels. This, again, reflected the prevailing austerity of political relationships both within Northern Ireland and between the SDLP and London.

For their part, republicans maintained their commitment throughout the 1970s and beyond to the 'armed struggle', though they were inevitably affected by the demands of British policy and, if only indirectly, by Unionist action. The localist strategy of the British in 1974-5 was designed not only to probe the apparent new turn within loyalist thought, but also to tempt militant republicans into the constitutional process. In 1974 the ban on Sinn Féin was lifted with a view to encouraging its participation in the forthcoming Convention. Leaders of the party were involved in renewed talks with the British in early 1975, and when on 9 February the Provisionals called a temporary ceasefire, public money was used to fund seven incident centres which were run by Sinn Féin officials, and which were in contact with government.

However, the effort to lure republicans into the political process failed: communication with the government waned, the ceasefire ended and in 1976–7, with Roy Mason now the Secretary of State, the British campaign against the Provisionals grew more aggressive. The hardening of attitudes that affected the Unionists and the SDLP in the later 1970s was also perceptible within republican politics. A new tough-minded cadre of northern activists took over the party leadership in the early 1980s, and the old (and, in republican terms, conciliatory) federalist programme, 'Éire Nua', was summarily dropped. The hunger strikes of 1980–1, the culmination of republican prisoners' campaign for political status, were associated with a massive recruitment of support for militancy and with mounting violence.

On the other hand, there were signs that republicans would participate in the political process, albeit not quite on the terms envisaged by the British in 1974–5. The emergence of Gerry Adams as a decisive influence within the leadership of Sinn Féin was accompanied by a greater emphasis on electoral politics, though this did not by any means signify a retreat from the 'armed struggle'. On the contrary, Adams understood that the Provisionals' campaign was unlikely in itself to bring a comprehensive victory, and it had to be correlated with constitutional action in order to maximise the likely political dividends.[96] Democratic action, in a sense, was a way of liquidating the otherwise unrecoverable political capital amassed by the gunmen.

Adams was a major influence on the hunger strikes of 1981, and electoral politics were central to republican strategy from this time on. In April 1981 republicans ran Bobby Sands, the leader of the hunger strikers, as a candidate in the Fermanagh–South Tyrone by-election; and (in a turnout of 86.9 per cent) Sands was returned with a majority of 1446 over the veteran Ulster Unionist, Harry West. When Sands died in May, another by-election was required; and on 20 August, Owen Carron, standing on behalf of the remaining hunger strikers, was returned with a slightly increased majority (2230) over his nearest rival, the Unionist Ken Maginnis. At the 1982 elections for the new Northern Ireland Assembly, Sinn Féin captured over 10 per cent of the total poll, and emerged as the fourth most successful party: at the general election in the following year, Adams captured West Belfast from the veteran socialist Gerry Fitt.

As has been said, these electoral victories were designed as a complement, and not as an alternative, to the 'armed struggle'. Danny Morrison, the Sinn Féin Director of Publicity, famously defined this synergy in 1981, saying 'will anyone here object if, with an Armalite in one hand, and a ballot paper in the other, we will take power in Ireland?' In 1982 it was affirmed at an ard fheis that all Sinn Féin electoral candidates had to pledge their unambivalent support for the Provisionals' campaign. Thus, while in the mid-1970s the British hoped that republican militants could be stifled within the democratic process, by the early 1980s it looked as if democracy could be suborned for the 'armed struggle'. This threat soon became a major determinant of British and Irish constitutional strategy.

In terms of republican strategy, a turning-point can arguably be identified in 1980, with the launch of the first hunger strikes and the growing interest in electoral politics. It is in fact possible to suggest that the events of 1980 had a strategic significance that went beyond the republican movement, and to view 1980 as presenting the last chance of an internal accommodation on devolution between the main Northern Irish constitutional parties.[97]

On 7 January 1980 the new Tory Secretary of State for Northern Ireland, Humphrey Atkins, opened a conference at Stormont which was designed as yet another effort to secure an internal agreement for a devolved assembly. The government's objectives remained broadly as they had been throughout the 1970s, although there was slight evidence of a retreat from executive 'power sharing'. The SDLP, Alliance and DUP participated in the Atkins initiative, but the Ulster Unionists stood apart, purportedly because they divined that the whole endeavour would prove nothing more than a 'time-wasting exercise' on the part of the government.

The problem for the Ulster Unionists was that the integrationist sympathies of their leadership were not truly compatible with a negotiation designed to lead to an agreed form of devolution. Moreover, Molyneaux also seems to have felt aggrieved that the Tories' manifesto commitment to a regional council for Ulster – an idea that chimed with his own convictions – had been so brutally sidelined. But with the divisions on devolution unresolved, with Molyneaux facing in one direction and others (like the rising star, Edgar Graham) facing the opposite way, remaining aloof from the Atkins talks may have been a necessary strategy to preserve party unity.

However, given the failure of the talks, and the subsequent shift of direction in government thinking, it is sometimes argued that Molyneaux's refusal to engage with Atkins was a colossal strategic error. Criticism has come from some unsurprising quarters: Jim Allister, once of the DUP, has said that 'from anticipating an internal form of solution based on a form of majority rule, the Government in record time performed a U-turn of monumental proportions in which it opened negotiations with the Haughey government in Dublin'.[98] David McNarry, a prominent Ulster Unionist supporter of devolution in the 1980s, has lamented that 'we spurned a real chance to cut a new deal with the SDLP at the Atkins talks before the rise of Sinn Féin'.[99] Henry McDonald, the biographer of the First Minister, has observed that 'Trimble shares this analysis that Atkins, like the Voluntary Coalition, was a wasted opportunity, and helped pave the way for the rise of Sinn Féin in the 1980s'.[100]

Such criticisms perhaps say more about personal and party rivalries than about the extent of the opportunity present in 1980. It is certainly true that the government of Margaret Thatcher, at the beginning of its tenure, was relatively sympathetic to the Unionist case; but at the same time as Thatcher's accession, a new and evidently more republican taoiseach, Charles Haughey, had taken office in Dublin. It is not altogether clear why the SDLP would have cut a deal on the basis of 'a form of majority rule' in these circumstances. In terms of changes within the SDLP itself, there is little to suggest that an unfavourable settlement would now be swallowed. On the contrary, as has been said, the party had toughened its stand in the late 1970s, and a number of relatively consensual figures, such as Paddy Devlin, had left its ranks. On the other hand, there is no evidence that Ian Paisley of the DUP was significantly more consensual in 1980 than he had been in 1975, when he had rejected Craig's 'voluntary coalition' idea. In other words the view that a deal was possible in 1980 is based on little more than the perception of relative British sympathy. It reflects not a striking political opportunity, but later Unionist recrimination and nostalgia.

The missing feature from the Atkins negotiation was the cross-border dimension and it was not yet clear whether the government had consciously decided to remove this issue from the hands of the local parties, or was prepared to set it aside. The failure of Atkins certainly coincided with the beginnings of a *rapprochement* between the British and Irish governments, and the first tentative steps towards the formalisation of their particular 'special relationship'. Thatcher and Haughey met in May 1980 and again in December and these sessions produced some suggestive documents concerning the likely future shape of British–Irish institutions: pre-eminently, *Anglo-Irish Joint Studies: Joint Reports and Studies*. It also led to the creation of an Anglo-Irish Intergovernmental Council.

To some extent, attention was distracted from the significance of these developments by the Falklands War in 1982, and by the unfriendly Irish attitude towards the British campaign against the Argentinians. The focus of debate on Northern Ireland also shifted, momentarily, to a renewed effort to secure local agreement – through an assembly, for which elections were held in October 1982. But, as it became clear that the Assembly was not going to produce a breakthrough, and as Sinn Féin consolidated its hold on the Northern electorate, the Anglo-Irish *détente* was reactivated. Another critical influence on this resurrection was the partial success of FitzGerald and Hume in producing broadly based nationalist agreement on the goals of the national movement. This was done through the agency of the New Ireland Forum (1983–4), which will be examined in greater detail presently.

On 7 November 1983 the first meeting of the British–Irish Inter-governmental Council was held. A second session of the Council was held on 19 and 20 November 1984, but in the background senior civil servants and politicians from each country were meeting more fre-quently and informally, and defining the extent of their agreement. Garret FitzGerald's memoir is at present the main authority for these negotiations, and it may be opportune to record the gentle, if defensive, warning that Sir David Goodall (one of the British promoters of the Anglo-Irish *détente*) has issued concerning this volume: '[the memoir] is written from a strictly Irish point of view; and in any negotiation the par-ticipants tend to see and hear what they are listening for and to miss or misinterpret what they are not'.[101] Accepting this caveat, FitzGerald's chronology suggests that some advance was made in the discussions between May and September 1984, followed by retreat in October and December, and (after a reappraisal by the British) renewed progress between January and June 1985. By June 1985 it would seem that the outline of a deal was in place.

On the way towards this end there were some near-disasters, however; and even in June there was a major confrontation between Thatcher and FitzGerald on the periphery of a European Council meeting at Milan.[102] Earlier, on 19 November 1984, Thatcher famously and curtly dismissed the strategic objectives of constitutional nationalism, as defined in the report of the New Ireland Forum. While some of the tensions within the Irish side had been resolved through the Forum, there were significant and potentially fatal differences of approach among the British. The ini-tiative was encouraged by the Cabinet Office and Foreign Office, while the mandarins of the Northern Ireland Office and Northern Ireland Civil Service were either more sceptical or kept outside the loop.

FitzGerald claims that the introduction of some NIO involvement after the end of September 1984 had a detrimental effect on the negotia-tions.[103] He has also documented the apparently distinctive approach favoured by the British Foreign Secretary, Sir Geoffrey Howe. Howe, it seems, sincerely believed that the embryonic deal in June 1985 was 'the start of an evolving situation of historic significance'.[104] On 6 November 1985, at a meeting of four British and Irish ministers, Howe sided point-edly with the Irish against a last-ditch effort by Tom King to water down the arrangements for the proposed Anglo-Irish Secretariat (King was the newly appointed Secretary of State for Northern Ireland, and he had taken some informal soundings about the proposed deal).[105] Howe later encouraged the Irish government to seek European money unilaterally for Northern Ireland, at a time when the Thatcher government found it unhelpful to press the Ulster case: 'this', as FitzGerald has reasonably commented, 'seemed a somewhat inconsistent position to be taken up by a British government that was insistent on the maintenance of its sovereignty over Northern Ireland'.[106]

But these inconsistencies permeated the British stand. The implication from FitzGerald's memoir would seem to be that (to put it mildly) Howe had a much more relaxed attitude towards Irish unity than his cabinet colleagues. And, indeed, this is apparently confirmed by Howe's own autobiography, in which he claims that he 'had ceased thinking of [British sovereignty in Northern Ireland] as a commodity which could or should be measured and upheld in so many vertically designated packages. I was more concerned to provide for the interpenetration of influence between the several communities that have to share the British Isles together.'[107]

Although Belfast civil servants and the Unionists were by and large excluded from this diplomacy, Northern constitutional nationalists did have an indirect avenue of influence. In early 1983, when Anglo-Irish relations were still relatively cool, John Hume and Garret FitzGerald co-operated in establishing the New Ireland Forum, a conference designed to establish agreement across the constitutional national tradition on political strategies and goals.[108] The particular electoral impetus behind the Forum (as, indeed, behind so much of the political movement of the early 1980s) was the consolidation of the Sinn Féin vote in the North, and the threatened eradication of the constitutional approach. Aside from rescuing the SDLP, Hume and FitzGerald's particular objective seems to have been to insinuate the notion of joint British–Irish authority over Northern Ireland into the 'mission statement' of Irish constitutional nationalism.

After eleven months of negotiation at Dublin Castle, after over 100 sessions ('including over 50 leaders' meetings'), a form of agreement was reached. This proposed three acceptable models of government: a unitary state, a confederal arrangement within Ireland, and joint authority. There was a slight emphasis on the unitary ideal: this was 'the particular structure of political unity which the Forum wish to see established'.[109] The Forum expressed its openness to other views, however, and accepted (after lengthy bickering) that unification could only be achieved, having been 'agreed to by the people of the North and by the people of the South'.[110] A strongly green-tinted rendering of Irish history was included at the behest of Fianna Fáil, as part of the final report.

It is difficult to gauge the overall value of the Forum. It may be seen as consolidating some of the (already strong) personal ties between leading members of the SDLP and the Dublin political establishment, and in particular the bond between Hume and FitzGerald. This was occurring at a time when FitzGerald was preparing to deal with the British. FitzGerald also saw the Forum as providing a crucial mandate for his negotiating position. Joint authority was one of the forms of government approved at the Forum, and this then formed a central objective for the Irish negotiators in 1984–5.[111] The Forum was also seemingly designed to freeze out militant republicans and to put a brake on their political progress in the North; and in so far as Sinn Fein's initial electoral surge (some 13.4 per cent of the vote in 1983–4) was contained by the time of the local council elections in June 1985 (when the party's vote was down to 11.8 per cent), some temporary success on this front may be acknowledged.

On the other hand, it was also hoped, certainly by FitzGerald, that the Forum would send out friendly signals to Ulster Unionists, and indeed some markedly liberal Northern Protestants (such as the historian David Harkness) gave evidence during its sittings. But although the issue of political consent was flagged, this was counterbalanced by the highly tendentious historical sections of the report, and by Charles Haughey's republican spin on its recommendations.[112] Moreover, neither the three constitutional proposals nor the sight of the massing of constitutional nationalism can have done much to allay Ulster Unionist anxieties. Neither they nor their sensitivities were in fact a major priority for the members of the Forum; nor were they central to the British–Irish diplomacy that ensued.

The fruit of this diplomacy was the Anglo-Irish Agreement, signed at Hillsborough Castle on 15 November 1985. This was a document of thirteen articles, covering the status of Northern Ireland, the creation of an Anglo-Irish Intergovernmental Conference, and the definition of the Conference's remit and powers.[113] Through the agreement the two governments affirmed that any constitutional change in Northern Ireland would only occur with the consent of a majority there. The 'present wish' of the people for no change was explicitly recognised, although account was also clearly taken of possible shifts in the popular mood.

The Anglo-Irish Conference was designed to afford the Irish an opportunity to 'put forward views and proposals' (article 2b) on a wide range of matters relating to the administration of Northern Ireland, with the exception of any issue that might eventually be ceded to a devolved assembly. The issues that fell within the remit of the Conference expressly included a wide range of political and security matters (sections C and D), and an equally wide range of legal and judicial concerns together with 'cross-border cooperation on economic social and cultural matters' (sections E and F). Both governments affirmed their commitment to the restoration of a devolved government 'on a basis which would secure widespread acceptance throughout the community' (article 4b). It was agreed that the Conference would act as a medium by which the Irish government would put forward 'views and proposals on the modalities of bringing about devolution in Northern Ireland in so far as they relate to the interests of the minority community'. Though there was explicitly no lessening of British (or Irish) sovereignty (article 2b), the Irish interpreted the agreement as affording them rather more than a consultative role, while admittedly somewhat less than executive power: the British chose to stress that the Conference was not an executive body.

Each party had brought very different expectations to the agreement (to say nothing of those excluded from the negotiations); and it was perhaps inevitable that disappointment should swiftly have set in. The British seem to have been divided in their counsel, with some (Thatcher in particular) seeing the negotiation and agreement as being primarily a means of improving security arrangements. An early British overture to the Irish, in March 1984, had involved creating a joint security corridor along the border and also, more remarkably, in West Belfast.[114] Some elements within the British leadership (Howe, for example) seem to have explicitly accepted the inevitability, if not the desirability, of Irish unity, and to have handled some aspects of the talks with this in mind.[115] Of the senior British administrators, the views of Goodall are best known: he seems to have cherished a neo-Gladstonian conviction that the Union could be strengthened by ceding the Irish some limited but institutionalised political influence in Ulster. Following on from this, Goodall has emphasised what he sees as Garret FitzGerald's concern to reconcile Northern Catholics to the Union.[116]

For FitzGerald, however, the security of the Irish state was an overriding priority: republican militancy threatened not only the North, but also the Republic; and the causes of this militancy, which FitzGerald defined broadly as Northern Catholic 'alienation', were a significant target of his diplomacy. The agreement sought to embody these different emphases: the British seem to have been willing, in the words of Goodall, to concede 'a role, and hence a share of responsibility, to the Republic in the affairs of the North': that is to say, the British were happy to share responsibility for Ulster, but not authority. The Irish, for their part, seem to have accepted what they saw as power with the vestiges of joint responsibility.[117]

In the event, judged by these various expectations, there was disappointment. In the short term, Thatcher was clearly shocked by the extent of Unionist protest. In the longer term, she was unpersuaded that there had been significant security dividends.[118] Others within her cabinet were also perturbed: Nigel Lawson, for example, has recorded his profound scepticism concerning the value of the agreement.[119] For his part, FitzGerald was keen to emphasise some of the important reforms (for example, on the issue of flags and emblems) which had been achieved through the aegis of the Conference. He, too, was taken aback by Unionist protest, although he was also concerned that the Unionist reaction had overly impressed the British and had overshadowed the progress that had been achieved.[120] In this way, he rationalised, the agreement had had a much less decisive impact on hardline Northern nationalist opinion than might otherwise have been the case. As will be shown, the sustained violence of the mid- and late 1980s, together with Sinn Féin's steady electoral performance, suggest that FitzGerald had got his original political calculations badly wrong.

In terms of the wider reaction in Ireland, republicans within Sinn Féin (and some within Fianna Fáil) clung to their theological certitudes and pronounced the agreement as unsound. It is possible, as Conor Cruise O'Brien alleges, that this public anathematising of the agreement was complemented by a degree of private satisfaction at the routing of Unionism.[121] On the other hand, John Hume and the SDLP unequivocally recognised that gains had been made, and for long treated the agreement as what Feargal Cochrane has called 'a banker position' from which they would not be tempted.[122]

The corollary of this was, as has already been outlined, massive Unionist opposition. Unionists saw the agreement as a significant step towards joint British–Irish sovereignty, and thus towards the end of the Union; and they reacted with appropriate bitterness. Their protest drew heavily upon the example of their forebears' protest against the third Home Rule Bill in 1912–14. A strategic brinkmanship was attempted in 1985 and after, as in 1912–14: militancy was widely threatened, but never thoroughly embraced. A massive demonstration was held at Belfast City Hall on 23 November 1985 (echoing 'Covenant Day' in September 1912), at which a united Unionist leadership proclaimed its undying opposition to the deal. The 'Unionist Clubs' movement, originating at the time of the second Home Rule Bill, and reactivated in 1911, was launched in 1985 as a popular protest organisation.

Unionist MPs resigned their seats in order to demonstrate the extent of their popular mandate: the by-elections were held on 23 January 1986, and 418,000 votes were recorded for anti-agreement candidates. A day of strike action followed on 3 March 1986. Opposition to the agreement was also pursued within the arena of local government and through other forms of civil disobedience. This campaign continued, sometimes in a highly piecemeal fashion, through to late 1988, by which time it was clear that the effort needed reappraisal. With the exhaustion of the constitutional endeavour, and the apparent humiliation and ineffectiveness of the Unionist political leadership, the initiative slipped into the hands of the loyalist gunmen for a time.

What, then, can be said to have gone wrong with the agreement? It need hardly be repeated that, from the point of view of the SDLP, the agreement represented a major advance, and despite some initial qualms it was soon regarded as canonical. Yet there were still (perhaps inescapable) problems both with the structure of the negotiations and with the architecture of the final deal. While the British were seized by the need for quite extraordinary secrecy, the Irish maintained very close communication throughout the negotiations of 1984–5 with the SDLP. It seems reasonably clear, on the basis of his memoir, that FitzGerald was consistently well briefed on the condition of the Northern minority either directly or indirectly by the SDLP leadership, and that he was able to present a highly effective case to apparently less well-informed British politicians. In addition he had an extremely shrewd grasp of the personalities and power structures with which he was engaging; there is no evidence as yet of an equal competence on the British side. The point of the secrecy that the British maintained was presumably to preserve their room for manoeuvre, and to prevent opponents killing off any embryonic deal. But in the end, the cloak-and-dagger aspect was self-defeating in so far as it undermined their effort to present a coherent response to the Irish, and certainly brought the exclusion of an unusually wide range of interested parties.

Most British ministers were not in the know: Nigel Lawson has described the extent to which he and his cabinet colleagues were ignorant of the negotiation until a deal was finally presented for their approval.[123] Given that senior figures like Lawson were kept in the dark, it is scarcely surprising that a lowly parliamentary private secretary like Brian Mawhinney (an Ulsterman) should have known little of the talks.[124] A further quirk was added to the British ministerial scene in September 1985 when, at a very late stage of the talks, the Secretary of State for Northern Ireland, Douglas Hurd, was promoted to the Home Office, and was replaced by Tom King. This was almost a replay of Sunningdale when the veteran Willie Whitelaw was superseded a few days before the conference by Francis Pym. This combination of exclusivity and lack of ministerial continuity can have done little to bolster the political coherence of the British case. The cabalistic look to the negotiations, and to the eventual Anglo-Irish Agreement, signed on 15 November 1985, would prove a serious liability.

Informed civil servants were also kept outside the diplomatic loop. It is admittedly difficult to define a 'norm' for a negotiation of this type, but it seems likely that a very small coterie of senior British civil servants, led by Sir Robert Armstrong and Sir David Goodall of the Cabinet Office, had an unusually great influence. The corollary of this, however, was the exclusion not just of senior politicians, but also of other senior bureaucrats, many with more relevant experience than the principals (this, indeed, may have been partly the point of their exclusion). It is reasonably clear, for example, that neither Ewart Bell nor Kenneth Bloomfield, successive heads of the Northern Ireland Civil Service, was aware of the speed of progress, still less of the details of the deal that was emerging – at least in the case of Bloomfield (who succeeded Bell in 1984) until a very late stage indeed.[125]

But it is the exclusion of the Unionists from the talks which has received most attention, and which was probably most damaging. A sceptical reading might suggest that the Assembly, which ran from 1982 to 1986 and which (in the light of the SDLP boycott) was effectively a Unionist body, was a useful means of diverting and occupying a number of potentially disruptive and destructive political forces. This is probably too cynical an analysis. But it is certainly the case that the different Unionist leaders were largely kept in the dark as the Anglo-Irish diplomacy progressed, while the SDLP was informally briefed by the Irish government. In the early summer of 1985 the veteran Bill Craig seems to have got wind of the impending Anglo-Irish deal, and he, aided by David Trimble, wrote to warn the Unionist Party leader, James Molyneaux.[126] Molyneaux seems in addition to have received a sketchy briefing at one point, and not to have been unduly perturbed by its content. As a point of comparison, it may be noted that the Chief Constable of the RUC, Sir John Hermon, has also referred to 'a rather superficial [official] briefing' that he had received, and he has recorded that as late as 12 November 1985 'my knowledge of the intergovernmental talks and their outcome was limited'.[127] It was certainly only at a very late stage that Molyneaux and Paisley finally grasped the scale of the disaster that was overtaking them.

It is all too easy to find explanations for Molyneaux's failure: the issue impinges on the personal and ideological struggles within Unionism as well as upon the subtleties and failings of British and Irish strategy. Trimble and others have been inclined to argue that 'the Unionists did not work hard enough and did not have their finger on the pulse of the British government to an adequate extent'.[128] The rout has been blamed by devolutionists on the particular kind of political integration supported by Molyneaux. It has been blamed on Molyneaux's over-dependence upon close, but necessarily informal, relations with the British political elite (just as Faulkner was criticised for depending upon Heath, and – looking ahead – as Trimble himself would be upbraided for his faith in Tony Blair). FitzGerald has argued that 'in retrospect it came clear that we both [the British and Irish] overestimated the extent of the briefing that had been provided by the British to Molyneaux personally and underestimated his unwillingness to face realities'.[129] Summarising these arguments, it may be said that Unionist supporters of devolution have used the débâcle of 1985 to punish their integrationist rivals, while the Irish have blamed Molyneaux's confusion partly on the British, and partly on his own detachment from reality.

The convenience of these cases does not eliminate the possibility that they have merit. On the other hand, while Molyneaux's lassitude seems indisputable, it is also reasonably clear that the Unionists' humiliation was not entirely of their own making. FitzGerald alludes to contact that the Irish government had with politicians from both the Ulster Unionists and the DUP. Each of these sources, combined with public statements from Molyneaux and Peter Robinson (Deputy Leader of the DUP), made it clear what their likely reaction would be to a deal that ceded a substantial role in the North to Dublin. Given this contact, it is unclear why the Irish could not have set up a channel of communication with Molyneaux. FitzGerald suggests that 'we were inhibited from such a contact by concern about the possible British reaction; but I doubt whether Molyneaux for his part would have welcomed an approach from us at that time'.[130]

It is reasonable to assume from this that the Irish simply did not try to communicate with Molyneaux. FitzGerald chose to place greater faith in unnamed 'serious observers' and 'middle class moderate unionists with whom we had been in touch', who told him what he wanted to hear: namely, that Unionists would accept power sharing and a role for Dublin 'if the result were to be peace in Northern Ireland'.[131] FitzGerald thought that some form of loyalist paramilitary backlash was possible, but because the loyalist paramilitaries 'lacked the resources for a sustained military campaign' he was not inclined to be persuaded by this threat, in the way that he was clearly moved by the threat of militant republicanism.[132]

Some elements within the British team also seem to have calculated that the Unionists would take the deal quietly. Thatcher's surprise at the Unionist political backlash strongly suggests that she had been persuaded of the likely passivity of the Unionists. Geoffrey Howe was inclined to discount the possibility of serious unrest: when, on 6 November 1985, Tom King sketched out the possibility that loyalists might besiege the new Anglo-Irish Secretariat, 'Howe demurred at this picture, saying that this involved making assumptions with regard to the scale of protests that might not be justified'.[133] It is reasonably clear that the British, banking upon this ultimate quiescence, saw no value in alerting Molyneaux and Paisley to what lay ahead.

Other issues arise not from the talks, but from the agreement itself. The British co-authors of the agreement clearly believed that it promised, in Goodall's formula, 'full and formal Irish acceptance of the Union' and that it embodied, in Thatcher's words, 'a major [constitutional] concession by the Irish'.[134] And indeed article 1(a) of the agreement contains a joint affirmation that 'any change in the status of Northern Ireland would only come about with the consent of a majority of the people of Northern Ireland'. But, as the constitutional lawyer, Brigid Hadfield, has argued, there was no precise definition of this 'status', and the article (particularly paragraph c) effectively emphasised the possibilities for change.[135]

Moreover, there were two versions of the Agreement: the British version mentioned the 'Government of the United Kingdom of Great Britain and Northern Ireland' and the 'Government of the Republic of Ireland', while the Irish version mentioned simply 'the United Kingdom' and 'Ireland'. These ambiguities reflected the Irish need to remain within the bounds set by their constitution; and indeed a subsequent constitutional challenge, launched by two Unionists in 1988, failed thanks to the care of the Irish draftsmen and signatories in this respect. On the other hand, this legal action looked like (and was designed to be) a replay of the Boland case of 1974 which had so effectively undermined Sunningdale. Here again an Irish judge decided that an Irish government had simply recognised the 'factual' position, or 'the situation on the ground in Northern Ireland'. Once again, an Irish government had shown a measure of political goodwill, but had conceded nothing of substance in terms of the moral, legal or constitutional aspects of the case. Given this reprise of Sunningdale, it was hardly to be expected that the Unionists would be impressed.

Its authors also intended that the agreement should act as a catalyst which would eventually produce an acceptable form of devolution. The agreement endowed the Irish government with the right to forward its 'views and proposals' only 'in so far as those matters are not the responsibility of a devolved administration in Northern Ireland' (article 2(b)). However, Brigid Hadfield has pointed out that the likely powers of a devolved administration (as judged by the Northern Ireland Acts of 1973 and 1982) would not include a range of issues that the agreement expressly placed within the remit of the Conference.[136] Moreover, Hadfield has also drawn attention to article 10(c) of the agreement,

which further limited the powers of any devolved assembly: 'if responsibility is devolved in respect of certain matters in the economic, social or
cultural areas...machinery will need to be established by the responsible
authorities in the North and South for practical cooperation in respect of
cross-border aspects of these issues'.[137] In other words the central thrust
of the agreement, in Hadfield's view, was defective: it offered no real
inducement to the Unionists, while the SDLP had no reason to become
embroiled in a devolved assembly when their existing gains were already
so marked.

On the whole, it seems that both the British and Irish cherry-picked
those lessons from Sunningdale which they felt they could stomach,
while leaving other unpalatable truths untouched. Care seems to have
been taken in 1985 to create a deal that would withstand the type of
Unionist challenge offered in 1974. Beyond the Anglo-Irish Secretariat
(housed at Maryfield, County Down), there was no tangible institution
that the Unionists could topple. Sunningdale had been dependent upon
the survival of the devolved administration, and when the power-sharing
regime fell, so did the cross-border institutions. In the deal of 1985,
however, the Irish dimension could be sustained without devolution,
and indeed the Conference was designed to encourage rather than
undermine the devolution of power.

In other respects, the progress of negotiations in 1973 and 1985 was
similar. As in 1973, the British and Irish negotiators evidently felt that
they could achieve a lasting settlement on the basis of excluding either a
significant section of Unionist opinion or Unionism *en bloc*. Both sets of
negotiators in 1973 and 1985 seem to have had an unshakeable faith in
the passivity (if not the reasonableness) of the Unionist middle class;
both seem to have dismissed the idea that loyalist paramilitaries could
inflict sustained damage. Both sets of negotiators seem to have assumed
that the ambiguous formula on constitutional status which had been
tried in 1973 could be refurbished for the agreement of 1985. As in 1973,
the British believed in 1985 that they could maintain a coherent negotiating strategy while replacing the responsible minister immediately
before concluding a deal.

Even at this distance in time, it is hard to be precise about the results
of the agreement. The ongoing secrecy surrounding the Conference,
combined with the reticence of the British and Irish governments, has
made it difficult to trace the origins of specific reforms. The chief architect of the agreement, Garret FitzGerald, has catalogued its benefits on a
number of occasions, and although he is an interested party, his assessment remains virtually all that there is to go on. FitzGerald, both in a
letter to *The Times* in October 1987 and in his autobiography, has

chronicled how the agreement has helped to stem nationalist alienation through a wide variety of reform initiatives. These have included improvements in housing provision, the abolition of the Flags and Emblems Act (1954), a stronger line on fair employment, and reforms in a wide variety of policing and judicial matters.

There are reasonable grounds for accepting that FitzGerald's illustrations were, in fact, rooted in the agreement and the Conference. But his assertion that the Anglo-Irish Agreement 'was clearly sufficient to consolidate the drop in IRA support that had begun while it was under negotiation' seems more problematic, if the level of Catholic alienation is judged through the electoral strength of Sinn Féin and through the level of republican violence.[138]

Taking local council results as an indicator, Sinn Féin won 11.8 per cent of the poll in May 1985, 11.2 per cent in 1989 and 12.4 per cent in 1993. In terms of the casualty levels, an average of sixty-six people were killed by republicans in each of the five years (1981–5) preceding the agreement, whereas the average annual republican total for 1986–90 was fifty-nine deaths. It is conceivable that this diminution in the murder rate is attributable to the the agreement, but it is impossible to be certain; and, while every life spared is clearly important, the difference between the two averages is obviously very slight. On the whole, it seems reasonable to conclude that the agreement was much less significant for republicans than, say, their entry into electoral politics in the early 1980s.

It is also hard to be precise about the direct impact of the agreement on Unionists.[139] Molyneaux was certainly damaged by the completeness of the Unionist rout in November 1985; and his integrationist vision of the Union also suffered in consequence. The agreement, therefore, indirectly encouraged the re-emergence of a strong devolutionist Unionism, as expressed within bodies such as the Charter Group and the Campaign for a Devolved Parliament; a cross-party Unionist think-tank, the Task Force, formed in July 1987, devised a strongly devolutionist programme, *An End to Drift*. But though the Unionists talked privately with the SDLP and Northern Ireland Office in the autumn of 1987, and with the SDLP and Alliance parties at Duisburg, Germany, in October 1988, they were unable to win the suspension or modification of the agreement. This tended to underline the apparent irrelevance of constitutional Unionism; and there is evidence of a drift towards militarism in the late 1980s and early 1990s.

Judging by the evidence of contemporary paramilitary publications, there was a growing contempt among loyalist hawks for the mainstream political leadership. In February 1987 the Ulster Defence Association's journal, *Ulster*, predicted that 'students of history will contrast and compare the snivelling wrecks of manhood who masquerade as political leaders in the 1980s with the giants of Ulster'.[140] There was certainly a marked fall in the vote garnered by the hardline (but constitutional) DUP at the general elections of 1987 and 1992; and there was no corresponding gain by the Ulster Unionists. Indeed, there is some evidence to suggest that even Ulster Unionists were seeking notably radical solutions at this time: in August 1989 David Trimble was calling for the creation of a new loyalist private army 'in certain extreme circumstances', and returning to a Vanguard-style demand for dominion status.[141]

There was also a sharp rise in loyalist violence in the late 1980s and, particularly, the early 1990s. In the five years before the agreement (1981–5) loyalists killed an average of eleven people each year, while in the five-year period 1986–90 they killed on average twenty people annually. If the timespan is widened to include the nine years from the agreement to the loyalist ceasefires (1986–94), then the average annual number of killings perpetrated by loyalists comes out at twenty-nine. The early 1990s were a particularly bloody period, with (in 1993 and 1994) the number of loyalist killings exceeding those committed by republicans for the first time in the grisly history of the 'Long War'. The extent to which this relative militarisation can be explained by the failure of constitutional Unionism and thus, indirectly, by the agreement is open to debate, but there is clearly a case for making the connection.

While constitutional Unionism struggled to reinvent itself, the leadership of the SDLP was content to use the agreement as a basis for further political gains. The confusion within Unionism, and some discreet cross-party conversations in the autumn of 1987, made it clear that no satisfactory deal could be struck across the sectarian and constitutional divide. This impasse was reinforced by the unwillingness of the British to goad Unionism further, and thereby threaten further civil unrest. In these circumstances John Hume seized upon an interview that Gerry Adams, the president of Sinn Féin, had given to a Dublin magazine in November 1987. In this Adams affirmed that he would 'be prepared to consider an alternative, unarmed struggle to attain Irish independence' and that 'there can only be a political solution [to the Northern conflict]'.[142]

Hume, Adams and their respective lieutenants met in January 1988, but the sessions served only to highlight the extent of their divisions. As Tom Hennessey has recorded, 'there were fundamental lines of departure between the SDLP and Sinn Féin on the issue of self-determination, Britain's role in Ireland and the question of violence'. In particular Adams continued to insist that the origins of the conflict in the North lay with the British and their strategic, economic and political interests, while Hume believed that the British were now 'neutral' on the Union, and only fought because they could not permit the triumph of others' violence.[143] This was a significant point of fracture, and one that the British themselves would shortly address. In the short term, therefore, the Hume–Adams dialogue failed; but it highlighted several suggestive issues, and it began a process whereby constitutional and militant nationalism came into gradually closer communion. For this reason the sessions of January 1988 have been seen as the advent of a second New Departure – a reinvention of the deal between parliamentarians and militarists which had been struck originally in 1879.[144]

It may be appropriate at this point to consider the configuration of forces that were in place by the late 1980s and early 1990s, and to reflect on their significance for the 'peace process' (as it came to be called) and the Belfast Agreement of 1998. The Hume–Adams dialogue, though initially fruitless, was clearly a starting-point for the dynamic through which Sinn Féin was brought into the political mainstream. On the other hand, Hume's overture was (at least in one reading) a response to signals that Adams was sending out; and this in turn was linked to the strategic retooling that had taken place within the republican movement in the early 1980s. The potential for future progress was undoubtedly helped by the fact that Adams and his colleague Martin McGuinness, unlike others within the republican leadership, were essentially political, and unlike some anti-clericalists within the republican tradition, were Mass-going Catholics in common with SDLP leaders like Hume: a vital intermediary for Adams was the Belfast Redemptorist, Father Alec Reid. In other words, Adams as an unusually shrewd and pragmatic republican was arguably as important to the early evolution of the peace process as Hume. Adams was clearly keen to consider the use of electoral politics to advance the republican cause, although it should be emphasised that Hume was prepared to facilitate this 'journey' of exploration, even at the risk of sacrificing his own brand of constitutional politics to that devised by the Sinn Féin leader.

The Anglo–Irish Agreement allowed Hume to argue that the British were 'neutral' over Northern Ireland, and this served to convince some key republicans that their cause could be advanced through the ballot box rather than by deploying the Armalite. In this sense, therefore, the agreement might be seen as aiding the peace process. However, it should also be said that, while proponents of the agreement believed that it would protect the SDLP, in fact, partly because of the sacrificial way in which Hume used his party's gains, it ultimately led to the electoral advance and transformation of Sinn Féin.

It might also be argued that the agreement facilitated the peace process by educating the Unionists in the extent of their weakness, and by creating an unpopular structure that they would have to work to replace. But here, again, some caution is necessary. The agreement certainly stimulated a difficult and prolonged internal debate within Unionism, but it also encouraged the expectations of nationalists and created a search for maximum gains among the leaders of the SDLP.[145] Moreover, as has been said, the way in which the Agreement was passed served to undermine the constitutional Unionist parties, particularly the DUP, and to inflame loyalist paramilitarism.

Thus, it may eventually be seen that, whether directly or indirectly, the Anglo-Irish Agreement served to assist those at the extremes of Northern politics, and to reduce the chances of a deal struck between the traditional constitutionalists. Perhaps the most that may be said of the agreement, in terms of its contribution to the later peace process, is that – paradoxically – it served ultimately to underline the extent to which the hard men were central to a lasting settlement.

The Anglo-Irish Agreement was an influence on the peace process of the 1990s, but its impact was often indirect and unpredictable, and it certainly has to be read in the context of a much longer history of political arbitration. Peter Brooke, the Secretary of State for Northern Ireland between 1989 and 1992, was well briefed by John Hume on the possibilities opening up within republicanism, but then Brooke and his predecessor, Tom King, also alledgedly had lines of communication, through Father Reid and others, with Gerry Adams. Hume was a critically important facilitator, but creative political intelligence and leadership were also supplied by Adams, and there was a history of covert dialogue between the establishment and the Provisionals dating back to the early 1970s. Brooke emphasised in his Whitbread speech of November 1990 that the British had 'no selfish or strategic interest' in Northern Ireland, a declaration that was disproportionately important to the republicans, and to which they had been given advance access. He also underlined that he could not foresee the military defeat of the Provisionals.[146] Brooke was therefore significant in sending some pacific signals to republicans; and he was also important in defining the broad structures that the constitutional parties (and, much later, the militants) would use to shape their dialogue.

The Brooke Talks, which lasted from March through to July 1991, were organised into three 'strands', involving political relationships within Northern Ireland (Strand One), between North and South (Strand Two), and between Britain and Ireland (Strand Three). These talks failed, but the policy markers that had been laid down under Brooke remained in place when in April 1992 he was succeeded as Secretary of State by Sir Patrick Mayhew. As with Brooke, so with Mayhew, a keynote speech was addressed and pre-circulated to republicans. Mayhew spoke at Coleraine in December 1992, emphasing that the British would present no obstacle to a united Ireland, were the citizens of Northern Ireland to support such an eventuality. As with Brooke, so with Mayhew, a halting communication with the republican leadership was sustained, at least until November 1993. As with Brooke, so with Mayhew, talks between the constitutional parties were organised, and developed within the 'three strand' structure between April and November 1992.

It has been argued that these two thrusts – the diplomacy sponsored by the British (and Irish) governments, and the Hume–Adams dialogue – provided a vital context for the deal that was struck in 1998.[147] Eventually these two quite distinct political processes melded, but it is impossible to resist the suspicion that for a time they were almost mutually self-defeating. The stalled Hume–Adams dialogue of 1988 provided the basis for later meetings between the two nationalist leaders; and in early 1992 they agreed upon a declaration that they wanted the British government to make, and which embodied a daunting republican-nationalist wish-list.

In April 1993 the two men published a joint statement in which they laid down a number of shared principles: 'the Irish people as a whole have a right to national self-determination … the exercise of self-determination is a matter for agreement between the people of Ireland. It is the search for that agreement and the means of achieving it on which we will be concentrating.'[148] But Hume–Adams (as the SDLP–Sinn Féin *détente* came to be called) was simultaneously a complement and a threat to the initiatives sponsored by the British government, which was also in contact with republicans.

It is possible that the goal of tempting Sinn Féin into constitutionalism, with all the blessings and challenges that such an achievement would bring, was more significant in John Hume's calculations than the task of reaching an agreement with the bruised and contumacious Unionists. Certainly the history of modern Ireland, of which Hume was a keen student, was littered with the remains of constitutional nationalists who had attempted to strike deals with Unionism either in advance of their own hard men or of republican militants: the political scalps of William O'Brien, John Redmond and W. T. Cosgrave had taken a long time to moulder. Moreover, a reading of modern Irish history also tended to suggest that those constitutionalists, like Parnell and Eamon de Valera, who could command the hard men might achieve formidable advances for the national cause. It seems likely, then, that with the real gains won through the Anglo-Irish Agreement, and the potential offered by a second 'New Departure', there was no real enthusiasm among the SDLP for a deal with the Unionists in 1991 or 1992.

On the other hand, the logic of Hume–Adams was that, by achieving peace and a widely based national consensus, the British government would be pressured into becoming 'persuaders for unity', a phrase that Hume had hit upon in the early 1980s. But the British Prime Minister, John Major, was unremittingly critical of the Hume–Adams document, and even the taoiseach, Albert Reynolds (who was to an extent in the confidence of Hume) seems to have been unconvinced.[149] The Hume–Adams enterprise was about peace – about giving republicans conditions upon which they could lay down their weapons; and it was about harnessing the formidable political influence of the international community of Irish patriots and their sympathisers. The dialogue was not concerned with the practicalities of British politics, and still less with the sensitivities of the Unionists: it seems pretty clear that even Reynolds understood these profound limitations.[150] It is also likely that both Major and Reynolds were unsettled by the emergence of a new initiative that had dramatic potential and which was more or less beyond their direct control.

Accordingly, when (against the backdrop of the Provisionals' Shankill Road bomb on 23 October 1993) Hume–Adams seemed likely to stall, the two governments seized the initiative from Northern nationalism, and put in place their own statement of shared principles. This was the Downing Street Declaration, enunciated by Major and Reynolds on 15 December 1993. While the form and style of the declaration owed something to the Hume–Adams document, its content was quite distinct and, indeed, senior Ulster Unionists were consulted by its drafters.[151]

Major reiterated that the British had no 'selfish strategic or economic interest in Northern Ireland' (the absence of the comma between 'selfish' and 'strategic' concerned some republican textual analyists). He also affirmed that the British wanted 'peace, stability and reconciliation established by agreement among all the people who inhabit the island', and that they would strive for an agreement founded upon 'full respect for the rights and identities of both traditions in Ireland'.[152] But the British were not prepared to become, in the language of Hume, 'persuaders for unity'; and while they recognised the right of the Irish people to self-determination, and to achieve a united Ireland, the exercise of this right would occur on the basis of the structures of the partition settlement.

For his part, Reynolds renounced the imposition of a united Ireland in the absence of majority support in the North. He undertook on behalf of his government to examine the political institutions of the South with a view to eliminating any elements that might be regarded as incompatible with a pluralist society. He also promised that, in the context of a wider settlement, the Irish government would change the 1937 Constitution in order to accommodate northern apprehensions. Both Major and Reynolds accepted that political parties with a democratic mandate, which were bound to 'exclusively peaceful methods and which have shown that they abide by the democratic process, are free to participate fully in democratic politics and to join in dialogue in due course between the governments and the political parties on the way ahead'.[153]

In a sense, the Downing Street Declaration provided a starting-point and a constitution for the subsequent peace process. The declaration provided a reality check for republicans, and indeed for Hume, in so far as it was clear that the Northern majority would not be side-stepped by the two governments, or brow-beaten by the British. The Unionists were also assured of the possibility of some satisfactory changes within southern politics and society. But the declaration was charged with ambiguity and with loose definitions: it sought to woo Unionists in the language of nationalism and to disarm republicans (in every sense) by lecturing them on the limits of the possible. It was essentially an elaborate invitation addressed to Sinn Féin, beckoning them in from the cold of the 'armed struggle' but on exacting terms.

Sinn Féin devoted a very lengthy consideration to the document, and eventually came to a decision at Letterkenny, County Donegal, in July 1994. With characteristic elusiveness, the republican leadership formally rejected the declaration but shortly afterwards accepted the invitation and challenge that it contained. On 31 August 1994 the Provisionals declared a 'complete cessation of military operations' in order 'to enhance the democratic peace process'.[154] On 13 October the Unionist paramilitaries, organised within the Combined Loyalist Military Command, followed this lead.

At the very least this 'cessation' marked the end of the main thrust of the 'Long War', but it also signalled the beginning of the battle over the peace settlement. The British position was that a permanent renunciation of violence, accompanied by the decommissioning of terrorist weapons, would secure Sinn Féin a place at the conference table; a programme for disarmament was spelt out by Mayhew at Washington on 7 March 1995. Republicans, on the other hand, emphasised the significance of the silent weapons, and claimed their seat at the talks on the basis of a democratic mandate. There was clearly a danger that this impasse would wreck whatever limited progress had been recorded, and it was seemingly with a view to re-energising the peace process, and demonstrating to Sinn Féin the rewards of compliance, that the British and Irish governments outlined proposals for the future government of Northern Ireland. These joint proposals were embodied within two 'Frameworks Documents', and were published in February 1995.

If the Downing Street Declaration had represented the skeleton of a deal, then the Frameworks Documents showed how flesh might be applied to these bones.[155] The result was, for the Unionists, an unlovely construction, which nevertheless (or perhaps therefore) held some attractions for the republicans. The first part of the Frameworks proposed a unicameral assembly, dominated by all-party departmental committees and a three-person managerial panel. This certainly chimed with aspects of earlier Unionist proposals: Faulkner had attempted in 1971-2 to create a strong committee structure within the Stormont House of Commons. It also side-stepped the issue of ministerial power-sharing by subcontracting executive responsibility to the committees. Of course, Sinn Féin did not want to see anything resembling the restoration of Stormont, and indeed this aspect of the Frameworks was certainly far removed from the old government and parliament of Northern Ireland. But the lure for republicans came not so much with the new Northern Assembly, as in the proposals for co-operation between Belfast and Dublin.

Part Two of the Frameworks corresponded to 'Strand Two' of the earlier talks, and addressed the issue of cross-border institutions. This envisioned a North–South body, created by special legislation, which would discharge a variety of 'consultative', 'harmonising' and 'executive' functions. The language was a reprise of the Sunningdale formula; the Sunningdale Council of Ministers was to possess 'executive and harmonising functions'. Indeed, for Unionists this section of the Document combined some of the worst features of the deal of 1973 and the later Anglo-Irish Agreement. Like Sunningdale, the Frameworks Documents envisaged a free-standing cross-border body with wide-ranging executive authority. Like Sunningdale (certainly in the Unionist imagination), the Frameworks were proposing to lay the foundations for an all-Ireland government. Like the Anglo-Irish Agreement, there were aspects of the Frameworks (in particular the controversial paragraph 47) which hinted at the possibility of joint British–Irish authority over Northern Ireland.

With the benefit of even a little hindsight, it can now be judged that the Frameworks Documents represented a green-tinged corrective to the Downing Street Declaration. It may also be seen that, in the context of the impasse over weapons decommissioning, the Frameworks were meant – at least in part – as a lure for republicans. But in the event they failed to mollify the Provisionals who, angered by what they saw as continued stalling on the part of the British, ended their ceasefire in February 1996 with the bomb at Canary Wharf in London's Docklands.

At the same time, the Frameworks Documents also seriously desta-bilised Unionism, in terms of both its leadership and popular loyalist mil-itancy. James Molyneaux, who as Ulster Unionist leader had pursued an integrationist vision, and who (despite the humiliation of the Anglo-Irish Agreement) remained confident that he had the ear of the British estab-lishment, was largely unprepared for the shock of the Frameworks: in August 1995 he announced his resignation. It seems likely that some of the anger that urged him towards retirement fed into the mounting dispute over the issue of public marches, and in particular into the unrest arising from the Drumcree parade. The violence associated with Drumcree spiralled bloodily in July 1995, and evoked memories of the Ulster Workers' Strike of 1974. Indeed, it is just conceivable that, for some Unionist ideologues, Drumcree mattered less as a marching issue than as a means of reminding the British and Irish governments that the acquiescence of popular loyalism could not be taken for granted.

Perhaps the most significant aspect of the political fallout from the Frameworks, and indeed from Drumcree, was the election on 8 September 1995 of David Trimble as the new leader of Ulster Unionism. There is a natural tendency in political biography towards what Roy Foster has called 'the pious imputation of consistency', and there has also been an entirely understandable tendency to emphasise the consensual elements in the careers of Ulster's peacemakers, whether Trimble, Gerry Adams or, more conventionally, John Hume.[156] This is not the place to offer a lengthy reconstruction of Trimble's career; on the other hand, his profound political significance needs little emphasis, and his biography presents a number of important interpretative challenges that demand to be addressed.[157]

In September 1995, when he became leader, Trimble looked like a hardliner: he had been a supporter of the Drumcree protest, and he had alienated nationalists when – after the Orange parade had been forced through – he had joined hands with Ian Paisley in a euphoric gesture that was interpreted as triumphalism. But there were important consensual efforts in Trimble's earlier career: he was a proponent of 'voluntary coali-tion' between Unionists and the SDLP in the aftermath of the Ulster Workers' Strike, and advocated sharing executive power during the national emergency represented by the paramilitary onslaught of the mid-1970s. He also believed that the Ulster Unionists should have used the opportunity presented by the Atkins Talks in early 1980 to strike a deal with constitutional nationalism, in advance of the political chal-lenge mounted by Sinn Féin. Against this, Trimble (though rooted in the quiet suburbs of North Down) was an early recruit to the Orange Order. He was an influential opponent of Sunningdale in 1973–4, and in the late

1980s he had proposed radical action against the Anglo-Irish Agreement. In the 1970s and 1980s he had occasionally offered political advice to those connected with loyalist paramilitarism.

Can these apparent inconsistencies be reconciled? A number of aspects of Trimble's career seem to require emphasis. According to his biographer, Henry McDonald, Trimble's paternal family were Presbyterian farmers from County Cavan, who moved into the newly created Northern Ireland with the partition settlement of 1920–1; his mother's people were from the west bank of Derry City.[158] Trimble's father was a civil servant who settled in the relatively tranquil and prosperous Unionist haven of Bangor. It need hardly be stressed that location is frequently a striking influence within Irish, and Northern Irish, politics. On the whole, the Unionists of the border and the South, whose experience of revolutionary nationalism was often bloody and acute, tended to be militant influences within the Northern state. They were also, in a sense, marginal to a Unionism that was increasingly grounded in eastern Ulster. Trimble's Cavan and Derry ancestry may be viewed as a militant and embittering influence on his background. His immediate roots within the comfortable Unionism of North Down may perhaps be seen as helping to modulate these influences and as providing more emotional room for manoeuvre.

Indeed, a combination of marginality and manoeuvrability appear to be hallmarks of Trimble's political career. Another constant seems to be his strong sense of historical precedent: his vision of politics and its possibilities seems to be shaped by his reading of the past. Trimble's roots were far removed, both socially and geographically, from the networks that traditionally upheld Ulster Unionism. Located in the lower middle classes, and in Derry and Cavan, Trimble was in every sense distant from the substantial farmers and businessmen, from what Maurice Hayes has called the 'presbyterian meritocracy' of Inst and Campbell College, who ran the Ulster Unionist Party and the government of Northern Ireland in the 1960s.[159] Reportedly a shy and awkward man, Trimble also seems to have been temperamentally at a distance from his Unionist colleagues. He has attracted intellectual respect, but there seems little evidence of much personal devotion or (beyond his family) of longstanding intimates or confidants. Like Terence O'Neill, it would seem that Trimble is more comfortable with courtiers than with equals; like O'Neill, he has a political vision that he has so far failed to communicate.

These qualities are surely linked to the unconventionality of his political intelligence and imagination. He has certainly been a highly resourceful player throughout his career, continually searching for political options even in the apparently most barren of circumstances. It is this ability to keep options open, or indeed to create options, which has marked him out as the most gifted tactician that Unionism has produced since the foundation of the Northern Irish state. The pattern of Trimble's career tends to suggest that he has regularly sought to build a constituency within the radical right of Ulster Unionism, which he then seeks to deploy in creative ways: he flirted with the hard men of loyalism in 1974, and then – having constructed a position of strength – sought to negotiate.

The voluntary coalition plan of 1975 is arguably much less important as evidence of 'moderation' than of Trimble's desire to be proactive, to create initiatives and to shape events. After the Anglo-Irish Agreement he flirted with notions of dominion status and loyalist armies. When the Unionist candidature for the Upper Bann constituency was up for grabs in the spring of 1990, he was prominently associated with protest action in Belfast against the visiting Irish taoiseach, C. J. Haughey. These actions almost certainly helped to secure his election to the House of Commons on 18 May 1990. But at the same time that he was pursuing these hardline strategies, Trimble was also probing the limits of Unionist flexibility on the issue of cross-border bodies, examining successful precedents such as the Great Northern Railways Board and the Foyle Fisheries Commission.

It is likely that Trimble's identification with the Drumcree dispute in 1995 was linked to his ambitions for the leadership of Ulster Unionism. Certainly his accession in September 1995 owed much to his high profile over Drumcree, and to the energies of a group of young right-wing activists who believed, in the aftermath of the disputed march, that they had found an Orange messiah. It need hardly be stressed that his career since 1995 again underlines the extent to which, having utilised the resources of the right wing, he is not prepared to be held in thrall. He seems determined to escape from the safe, predictable, emotional and reactive Unionism of the recent past.

It is reported that Trimble has been much influenced by Karl Popper's *Poverty of Historicism*, but it is not the least of the rich ambiguities in the Ulster Unionist leader's political thought that, while he evidently rejects the notion that there are general laws of historical development, he also instinctively looks to the past to help unravel the pattern of the present.[160] He has been fascinated by the Home Rule and revolutionary eras in modern Irish history, and has contributed two short, skilful and polemical volumes on the 1916 rising and on the foundation of the Northern Irish state. He is an admirer of James Craig, the first Prime Minister of Northern Ireland and a dextrous and pragmatic statesman: Henry McDonald has gone so far as to suggest that 'Trimble sought to resurrect Craig as the true champion of unionism to the detriment of Sir

Edward Carson' and that, in the Trimble analysis, 'Craig demonstrated a grasp of new realities which Carson never did'. Asked whether he identified most with Carson or Craig, Trimble replied that 'I would say Craig actually because he did the dirty work. He did the deal with Collins – he went to Dublin to negotiate while Carson lapsed into manic depression'.[161] Craig, the uncharismatic man of business, the arch-partitionist who treated with Collins and de Valera in 1921–2, and who released IRA prisoners – Craig, who was even prepared to adjust the northern border – has provided an invaluable set of precedents to his successor. It is just possible that Trimble has carried the analogies with 1921–2 even further: it is conceivable that, in clinching the Belfast Agreement in April 1998, Trimble may have half expected republicanism to fracture and implode in the way that it had done after the Anglo-Irish Treaty of December 1921.

Henry McDonald has laid some stress upon another relevant historical episode, which has evidently impressed Trimble – the transformation of the Official IRA and Official Sinn Féin after 1970 into constructive constitutional enterprises that have developed some understanding of the nature and condition of Ulster Unionism.[162] Whether Trimble was more influenced by 1921 than 1970 in Easter Week of 1998 is perhaps less important than the cast of mind which these references illustrate. Trimble evidently thinks in terms of historical precedents and parallels, and he deploys history creatively to defend the positions that he assumes. It would indeed be ironic if, in the end, he were to be misled by the historicism that he repudiates.

Where, then, is the real Mr Trimble? He has certainly been a consistent devolutionist, even when (in the 1980s) such convictions were profoundly unfashionable within Unionism. It is possible to detect a slight anglophobic or 'little Ulster' mentality in his political make-up. Though he has used and abused the right wing of his party, it seems pretty clear that this is where his own fundamental sympathies are to be located. As will be explored later, he began to outline a vision of an inclusive and consensual Unionism in key speeches delivered at Malone House in May 1998 and at Oslo in December 1998. This clearly picks up on earlier themes within his career, but it must be conceded that if he were now to call for an independent Ulster then this could also be said to make sense in terms of his earlier convictions.[163] It is too early to judge whether Trimble's pluralist Unionism is an electoral strategy or a profound ideal. It is also too early to say whether Trimble's advocacy of Edmund Burke is less a matter of intellectual conviction than part of an unattractive contest with Conor Cruise O'Brien and Robert McCartney (both also professed Burkeans) for the moral high ground within Unionism.

Perhaps a judgement does not have to be made on these binary terms. But the central reality of Trimble's leadership is that he has charge of a movement which has been in retreat since at least 1972, and arguably (in terms of its geographical spread and relative economic strength) since before the First World War. He has fundamentalist instincts, but – in the context both of this decline and the apparently inexorable consolidation of nationalism – he has consistently treated politics as the art of the possible: 'you can't start from an imagined or idealised position', he told a youthful audience in Belfast in October 1998, 'you have to start from where you are, in terms of reality…the only sensible thing is to be seriously engaged in the situation that you are in'.[164] This principled pragmatism, tinctured with an inevitable personal ambition, is perhaps the bottom line of Trimble's politics.

The wider 'reality' of the peace process was changing rapidly in 1996–7. The British and Irish governments at last agreed to sub-contract the problem of decommissioning to an international panel headed by the former United States Senate majority leader, George Mitchell.[165] His report, published in January 1996, recognised that the paramilitaries were not in fact going to disarm before the beginning of any talks. Mitchell did, however, recommend that some decommissioning should take place in parallel with negotiations, and he outlined six principles to which all those involved in talks should subscribe: these included the total and verifiable disarmament of the paramilitaries. All of this was some way removed from the British position, as defined by Patrick Mayhew at Washington in March 1995. Nevertheless the British accepted the Mitchell Report, and thus by implication agreed to retreat from their 'guns before talks' demand of the previous year. Mitchell had also taken up an idea floated by David Trimble – that the election of a democratic forum might help at this point to build community confidence and energise debate; and the British also expressed an interest in following up this suggestion. But the Provisionals chose to downplay the movement on decommissioning and to interpret the proposal for elections as a means of delaying the start of all-party talks. This was the context for the end of their ceasefire, and for the detonation of the bomb at Canary Wharf on 9 February 1996.

The resumption of the 'war' seems to have had a grim political usefulness, in so far as it apparently energised the British and Irish governments, and permitted them to fix a date for all-party talks: 10 June 1996. Stalling on the question of the Provisionals' sincerity no longer had any point, since the ceasefire was now broken and Sinn Féin was not likely to be present at the start of any discussions. The Canary Wharf bomb was thus, in a sense, a pyrrhic victory for republicans. The unseemly scramble on the part of the British to be seen to be proactive must have been grati-fying; the speedy fixing of a date for all-party talks, after the earlier pro-crastination, must also have seemed to vindicate the republican offensive. On the other hand, when the talks began on 10 June, Sinn Féin was still excluded, and this effectively meant that in the vital first months of negotiations the republican position was not directly represented. Moreover, though the British had indeed moved in early 1996 to meet some aspects of their case, John Major remained an object of republican distrust. The slow erosion of Major's parliamentary majority, and his increasing dependence on Ulster Unionist votes, only served to confirm this viewpoint. Nor was there much consolation in Dublin, where a Fine Gael-led coalition government had been in power since December 1994, and where the taoiseach, John Bruton, was held by republicans to be so soft on Unionism as to be a 'national disgrace'. Only in Washington was some encouragement to be gleaned, and even here, while President Clinton had granted Gerry Adams an entry visa and had made other pacific gestures, there was a lingering suspicion that Irish republicans had taken the administration for 'suckers'.

This configuration of power and political sympathy seemed to change dramatically in May and June of 1997. In May, Tony Blair and the Labour Party were returned to office in Britain on the back of a massive parlia-mentary majority; in the Irish general election of June, a Fianna Fáil–Progressive Democrat coalition was elected, with Bertie Ahern (who was held to be close to republican sensibilities) as taoiseach. Clinton, meanwhile, had been re-elected in December 1996 for a second term as President of the United States. The survival of Clinton, and the ousting of Bruton and Major, were thought by republican strategists to signify an important augmentation of their likely negotiating position, and this analysis, combined with the softening British line on decommissioning, led to the Provisionals calling a second ceasefire on 20 July 1997.

The official prevarication that had occurred in 1994–5 was now set aside, and events moved with startling rapidity. Having subscribed to the Mitchell principles, Sinn Féin was speedily inducted into the process, and was ushered into Castle Buildings, the venue for the talks, on 10 September 1997. On 11 December, Adams was welcomed into 10 Downing Street by Blair. There was a momentary rattling of nerves on 20 February 1998, when (after two IRA killings) Sinn Féin was suspended from the talks, but on 23 March the party resumed its place in Castle Buildings, and on the doorstep of state power.

The intricate negotiations that produced the Belfast Agreement of April 1998 have been the subject of two highly detailed studies and need not be disinterred once again.[166] In terms of the highlights, it should be stressed that the accession of Sinn Féin to the talks precipitated the departure of the Democratic Unionists, led by Ian Paisley, and the United Kingdom Unionists, led by Robert McCartney. It is difficult to judge the precise impact of these moves, but weighing the not inconsiderable abilities of McCartney and some of Paisley's lieutenants against the weakness of their combined relationship with Trimble, it is probable that their exit significantly increased the likelihood of an agreement, albeit one of a slightly greener hue than might otherwise have been the case. But even with the departure of these Unionists, the talks were an unwieldy enterprise, with seven parties and two governments represented, together with an army of civil servants, aides and advisers.

On 3 December 1997, Mitchell persuaded the different delegates to opt for a more streamlined approach, which placed greater responsibility on the party leaders. With an efficient negotiating structure in place, a discussion document, *Propositions on Heads of Agreement*, the work of the two governments, was placed before the parties on 12 January 1998. This, with some considerable modifications, formed the basis for the deal that was eventually struck.[167] Mitchell, who throughout had fought to maintain the focus of the delegates, in the end tried to establish 9 April as the 'ne plus ultra' of the talks. There was some minor slippage after a peculiarly intense diplomatic onslaught during Easter Week, but a deal was finally done on Good Friday, 10 April 1998.

The Belfast Agreement brought the restoration of devolved government to Northern Ireland after an absence of twenty-four years. Under its terms there was to be an assembly of 108 members, and an executive committee with ten ministers. These institutions were to 'exercise full legislative and executive authority in respect of those matters currently within the responsibility of the six Northern Ireland Government Departments'; there was the possibility of a further extension of their powers.[168] Ministers were to be shadowed by committees of the Assembly, replete with chairpersons and their deputies. Certain 'key decisions' of the Assembly would only be operative either if majorities were recorded within both main traditions or if 60 per cent of members, including at least 40 per cent of the Unionist and nationalist groupings, voted in a particular way.

There was to be a North–South Ministerial Council (or NSMC), established by separate British and Irish legislation, and the operation of this was to be a statutory responsibility of the new Northern ministers. The Council was intended to 'take decisions by agreement on policies for implementation separately in each jurisdiction' and 'to take decisions by agreement on policies and action at an all-island and cross-border level'. Complementing the North–South enterprise was a British–Irish Council

(BIC) designed to bring together ministers from the different governments contained within 'these islands'. It was intended that 'the BIC will exchange information, discuss, consult and use best endeavours to reach agreement on cooperation on matters of mutual interest'. As part of a constitutional swap, the Irish undertook to amend articles 2 and 3 of Bunreacht na hÉireann, while the British agreed to repeal the Government of Ireland Act of 1920. Human rights, and economic, social and cultural issues were all addressed as part of the overarching deal. Provision was made for a review of the policing and criminal justice systems in Northern Ireland. Mechanisms were also put in place 'for an accelerated programme for the release of prisoners...convicted of scheduled offences'.

The Belfast Agreement stood at the confluence of a number of political streams. In an obvious sense it was the product of a diplomacy that began with (depending on emphasis and political preference) either the Brooke–Mayhew talks of the early 1990s, or the Hume–Adams dialogue of the late 1980s, or earlier shifts within republican strategy. The agreement was also, to an extent, shaped by the concerns, skills and strength of the different negotiators at Castle Buildings between September 1997 and April 1998. The republican and loyalist emphasis on the prisoner issue was clearly reflected in the final deal. Republican disquiet on decommissioning is also clearly perceptible in the ambiguity and 'wriggle room' that the Agreement contains on this issue.

Nationalists wanted a power-sharing executive and cross-border bodies established by separate legislation, whereas Unionists wanted a devolved legislature, limited cross-border institutions and fundamental constitutional change in the Republic. On the whole, the shape of the final deal reflects Trimble's successful emphasis on Strand Two, with a highly constrained range of cross-border enterprises and with the North–South Ministerial Council (despite its separate legislative existence) ultimately dependent upon the Assembly. It has been argued that the shape of the final deal reflects Trimble's over-emphasis on the cross-border question and his comparative disregard for the internal aspects of the settlement and other highly charged questions of substance and symbolism. It would also appear that the Unionist team was run in an autocratic manner particularly in the last days of the negotiation. To this extent the deal – from the Unionist perspective – reflects the strengths and weaknesses, the preoccupations and lapses, of Trimble himself.

But of course the agreement was imbued with the influences of a longer history. Many of the positions assumed in 1997–8 and many aspects of the deal struck on Good Friday, 1998, were rooted in a much deeper substratum of Irish politics. The legislative instrument that had defined the original partition settlement was the Government of Ireland Act (1920); and though this was repealed under the terms of the Belfast Agreement, its influence could not be lightly expunged. The six-county territory defined in 1920–1 remained in place, and Northern Ireland retained a devolved executive and legislature. Certain of the structures of the parliament created in 1920–1 are perceptible within the new Assembly: just as former Unionist governments sought to copper-fasten the loyalty of back-benchers through an array of ministerial and other jobs, so in the Assembly the assimilation of members is encouraged by a comparatively large number of salaried executive and committee positions. The crucial distinction, of course, between Stormont and the Assembly is that all the parties now have access to official patronage.

As was made clear in Chapter 9, the Act of 1920 made provision for a Council of Ireland, a body that was intended to unite the Northern and Southern parliaments and to promote the political unity of the island; a faint trace of this is perceptible in the Council of Ireland defined at Sunningdale in 1973, and in the NSMC of 1998. It is clear that Trimble was heavily influenced by Brian Faulkner's inability to prevent the Council of 1973 being endowed with executive powers; and to some extent Trimble's entire strategy in 1998 has to be viewed in the light of the Sunningdale débâcle. The cross-party acceptance of a unicameral parliament (as opposed to the bicameral Stormont) may also be dated back to 1972–3, while the nationalist emphasis on executive power-sharing and the Unionist interest in parliamentary committees are also both to be rooted in the politics of the early 1970s. There is a case for arguing that the British–Irish Council of 1998, which was Trimble's particular hobby-horse (and which represents a good example of his ability to create potentially fruitful political options), is connected – through the Anglo-Irish Intergovernmental Council of 1981 – with ideas thrown up by the federalist debate on the government of the British Isles in the Edwardian era, and revived in the era of Terence O'Neill.[169]

Equally, the proposed revision of articles 2 and 3 of Bunreacht na hÉireann together with the repeal of the Government of Ireland Act had a resonance that carried far beyond Castle Buildings. Unionists had sought the repeal of articles 2 and 3 virtually since the promulgation of the Irish constitution in 1937. The issue was raised at Sunningdale, only to be fudged because even sympathetic Irish ministers like Conor Cruise O'Brien did not believe that it could successfully be put to a referendum.[170] The repeal of the Government of Ireland Act represented a gesture towards the longstanding republican struggle against the partition settlement, but it was also a highly complex and controversial proceeding.

Tom Hennessey, who was a Unionist adviser at Castle Buildings in 1997-8, argues strongly that, in demanding the repeal of the Government of Ireland Act (and specifically section 75, which asserted the sovereignty of Westminster in Northern Ireland), the Irish made a serious tactical error: 'the whole basis of the Irish government's policy towards constitutional issues was based on a fundamental misinterpretation of British constitutional law'.[171] Hennessey's argument is that the Irish believed that the repeal of section 75 would 'end Britain's territorial claim to Northern Ireland', where in legal reality that claim was founded in the Act of Union of 1801: 'the new regional unit of Northern Ireland was part of the United Kingdom since 1801 because of the Act of Union, not the Government of Ireland Act in 1920'.[172] This last point was of course not a discovery unique to the Unionist negotiating team in 1997-8, but had been underlined in classic legal texts such as Brigid Hadfield's *The Constitution of Northern Ireland* (1989).[173] Martin Mansergh, speaking for the Irish negotiators, has naturally enough disputed Hennessey's interpretation; and indeed it does seem unlikely that the Irish would have so conspicuously failed to do their constitutional homework.

But in a sense this persiflage diverts attention from an equally important aspect of the Government of Ireland Act. From the foundation of the Northern Ireland state, Unionists found the Act to be a profound burden in so far as it defined institutions and relationships that were either unwieldy or impossible to work. Yet the measure itself came to be charged with such a symbolic significance that serious amendment was out of the question, and the Act survived on the statute books largely because of a series of administrative wheezes and dodges that circumvented its more arcane provisions. Repealing the Government of Ireland Act, even in 1998, was perhaps a more emotionally charged event than Trimble and his lieutenants would have conceded, but it is still hard to resist the thought that – in terms, at least, of administrative ease and efficiency – its demise would not have been much regretted even in the heyday of the Stormont regime.

The repeal of the Government of Ireland Act was part of wider endeavour, on the part of Northern republicans and the Irish government, to overturn the constitutional settlement of 1920-1. Yet, though republicans expressly committed themselves to undoing Lloyd George's handiwork, it might be said that the agreement to which they subscribed bore some of the influences of his statecraft: in a sense, his legacy in Ireland was as much a matter of diplomatic style as substance. For, as in Lloyd George's proposed settlement of 1916, and the Anglo-Irish Treaty of 1921, the agreement of 1998 was riven with conscious ambiguity, fudging and procrastination. It united an impossibly wide range of opinion partly because so many of the controversial issues – policing, decommissioning, criminal justice – were addressed, only to be effectively set aside for another day. Just as the criticial issue of the RUC was handed over in 1998 to Chris Patten, so in 1921 the final shape of the North–South boundary was left to a commission. Just as in 1916 Lloyd George very nearly secured a deal between Carson and Redmond on the basis of an ambiguous definition of partition, so in 1998 agreement was facilitated by ambiguous language concerning decommissioning. In 1998 even the very definition of 'agreement', at least in terms of the operations of the NSMC, was treated ambiguously: 'all Council decisions to be by agreement between the two sides'.

But there was also a more fundamental paradox within the republican attitude towards the settlement of 1920–1. For, while the official spin emphasised the extent to which Ahern and Adams were striving to overturn the injustices of the early 1920s, it might well be argued that the Belfast Agreement signified an effective reconciliation between northern republicans and the Anglo–Irish Treaty of 1921. The treaty had for long been reviled by republican fundamentalists because it was seen as an insidious kind of instant political gratification. It had involved a series of difficult compromises and concessions by its revolutionist signatories. Leaders like Michael Collins fought for a republic, but accepted dominion status, an oath of allegiance to the British King and, in effect, partition. Adams and the Sinn Féin leadership, who had been schooled to abhor the 'traitors' of 1921 and to fight for nothing less than a 32-county Irish republic, chose in 1998 to 'renegotiate the Union', and to work for the time being within the context of partition.[174] It is frequently implied that the agreement is Sunningdale for slow-learning Unionists; but it is also, in a sense, the Treaty for slow-learning republicans.

But to conclude by emphasising the ancestry of the agreement, while logical enough in terms of the themes of this book, would be to obscure the extent to which it is a forward-looking document. In a general sense, it is clear that the agreement is primarily concerned with the provision of agreed institutions and relationships which are designed to ensure a peaceful future for the much-troubled people of Northern Ireland. But it is also the case that the agreement has been used as a shared starting-point for two radically different visions of the future of 'the North'. For Gerry Adams and Sinn Féin, the agreement is evidently an interim settlement, wherein republicans can exercise power and enjoy 'parity of esteem', pending reunification. It is clear that republicans, banking on the electoral consolidation of Sinn Féin and the related issue of Catholic demographic advance, are envisioning a time when they are more than a 'significant minority' within the Assembly. Indeed, it is possible that the institutions of partition, as defined in the agreement, will come to suit Northern republicans more than the traditional goal of a unitary Irish state.

For David Trimble and his supporters, the agreement has an altogether different logic. One of the fundamental political quirks of the party that he leads is its combination of devolutionist and integrationist sympathies. James Molyneaux sought to resolve these inconsistencies by moving towards a more thoroughly integrationist stand, but the loyalties of the Stormont years could not be so easily put to rest. Using the agreement, Trimble has been able to create the conditions under which Northern Ireland can enjoy devolution and at the same time be more smoothly integrated within the Union than at any time since partition. He has been able to make a virtue of the paradoxes of Unionism by linking the Northern Ireland settlement to Tony Blair's broader devolution project of 1997. Viewed from this perspective, the new Assembly and Executive Committee in Belfast apparently serve to underline not the oddness of Northern Ireland, but rather its closeness to the 'variable geometry' of the Blairite model of the United Kingdom. Indeed, Trimble has sought to go much further than this, by outlining a secular and inclusive Ulster Unionism, which transcends traditional ethnic and religious loyalties, and which chimes with the diversity of the modernised British state.

But, in the end, the freshness of the Belfast Agreement and the rawness of the issues involved mean that even the immediate future remains occluded. It will be for long unclear whether Adams' vision of the agreement as 'the freedom to achieve freedom' or Trimble's ideal of a flexible and inclusive Union comes to be realised. It will be for long uncertain whether the agreement marks 'the end of Irish history', or whether it has only served to underline the efficacy of violent protest for future generations.[175] The agreement could be a lasting beacon for those committed to peace and justice; but it just might, in the baleful light of episodes such as the Omagh bomb, be the spark for a future bloody endgame. Who yet can say?

# CHAPTER 12

# HOME RULE AND IRISH HISTORY

On 4 September 1969, in the city of Armagh, Oliver Wright, the senior British official in Northern Ireland, met Cardinal William Conway, the Catholic primate, for the first of what would become a series of private briefing sessions. Wright had been chosen by James Callaghan to be (in the nicest possible sense) a troubleshooter within the crumbling Ulster of 1969–70, and he soon came to provide a direct channel of communication to London for those, like Conway, who were the dispossessed of the Stormont regime. The appointment had come out of the blue: Wright had been at home on furlough, painting his house and 'repairing the depredations of three years of tenants', when the summons from Whitehall arrived.

A decorated war hero, Wright was charming and voluble – he favoured extended sporting and naval metaphors in his speech and prose; he was also fair-minded, frank and sympathetic. He half-convinced even those, like the Cardinal, who were not otherwise disposed by tradition or temperament to trust chummy representatives of the British establishment. But he was, as he told Conway, 'unprejudiced by knowledge so far as Northern Ireland was concerned', and the Cardinal understood that he had history to learn. Conway's parting gift was not, therefore, a devotional work, a volume of prayers or reflections. Instead Wright left Armagh with a copy of Thomas Jones's recently published *Whitehall Diary*, a work that chronicled the making of devolution and partition between 1918 and 1920. Conway had provided a handbook to the settlement that Wright and his masters were now seemingly poised to dismantle: he had connected Wright, one of the key players in the fate of the devolved government, with the history of Home Rule.[1]

Home Rule is often seen as a discrete moment in modern Irish history, the heyday of Parnell and Redmond; but it is, in fact, a much more extended and complex theme than convention allows. Politicians, civil servants and ideologues, through their actions and allusions, have certainly recognised that the story of Home Rule has been protracted and resonant; but historians have been rather slower on the uptake, and keener to emphasise the crises of 1886, 1912 and 1920 than the continuities and linkages binding these years with the decades that lay ahead. They have tended to stress the perceived fractures and turning-points in Irish politics, and to treat the histories of nationalism and Unionism as altogether distinct. But, as Oliver Wright discovered, Home Rule has had a continuous relevance for all Irish people, nationalists and Unionists, from the time of Gladstone's first bill, and before, to the era of the Troubles.

Throughout this book, emphasis has been laid upon the ways in which Home Rule and the Home Rulers have provided a lasting inspiration for later generations; upon the various constitutional motifs that recur throughout Irish political history from the age of Gladstone and Parnell. Isaac Butt, whose lieutenants stressed their debt to Daniel O'Connell, provided a federalist programme that would be revisited by a later generation of English constitutional reformers. Federalism was invoked by Terence O'Neill in 1969, and has provided an inspiration for some of the unionist signatories to the Belfast Agreement. Parnell's strategies and achievements, equally, have had a lasting resonance, whether in terms of the 'New Departure' of 1879 and the broadly based nationalist coalition that he thereby created, or his harnessing of social grievances and American support for the national cause. All of these features have had a lasting resonance: the New Departure, for example, has been seen as the forerunner for the *détente* between John Hume and Gerry Adams in the late 1980s.

The authors of the first Home Rule Bill in 1886 provided a template and a political agenda that would be revisited with the measures of 1893, 1912 and, to a lesser extent, 1920. Debate on an exclusion from Home Rule began (albeit quietly) at least as early as 1886, became more focused in 1910–11 and was rehearsed in parliament for the first time in 1912. The first serious proposal to exclude the six counties of the North came in 1914, and was revived in 1916 and 1920. But the territorial limits of 'Northern Ireland' have been variously and vigorously debated for a century, with the British proffering nine counties in 1919, and the Ulster Unionists digging into 'their' six counties in 1920 and after. W. T. Cosgrave may have suggested a nine-county deal in 1924, and republicans certainly sought a federal arrangement and a nine-county 'historic' Ulster in 1972.[2] The office of Secretary of State for the six counties of Northern Ireland was first envisioned in 1916, and revived in 1972. The cross-border mechanisms of the Government of Ireland Act (1920) provided a precedent for similar devices within the Sunningdale Agreement of 1972 and the Belfast Agreement of 1998. As was suggested in Chapter

11, much of the style and substance of the Belfast Agreement is rooted more deeply in the constitutional history of modern Ireland than has generally been allowed. And indeed, in a sense the Belfast Agreement is just as much a direct descendant of the Act of 1920 as of Sunningdale. It certainly has the arrangements for cross-border co-operation and for the effective protection of minorities which the measure of 1920 promised, but so conspicuously failed to deliver.

Other issues and episodes that preoccupied politicians in the Home Rule era would re-emerge in the 1960s and after. Gladstone's complex proposal of 1893 for the voting rights of Irish MPs was reviewed in 1965, when Harold Wilson was seeking to rid himself of the troublesome Ulster Tories at Westminster. The Curragh incident of 1914 seems to have infected British concerns in 1969, when contingency planning for direct rule began, and when the loyalty of the army, police and civil service was being assessed. The Buckingham Palace Conference of July 1914 was cited several times in 1969–70 as a useful precedent for an all-party brainstorming session on the problems of Northern Ireland.[3]

These overlaps and resonances have not been accidental. This book has documented the ways in which legislators and civil servants have worked within a historical framework, being historically literate or careful readers of precedent or politically active over many decades. Republicans have long regarded the Anglo-Irish settlement of 1920–2 as an offence, and they directed much of their political effort in the mid- and late 1990s towards a repeal of the Government of Ireland Act. Constitutional nationalists have been no less historically aware, with Seamus Mallon, John Hume's lieutenant, famously defining the Belfast Agreement in terms of Sunningdale. For his part, Hume has charged Ulster Unionists with bringing the gun into Irish politics, an indictment based upon his assessment of their militant stand against the third Home Rule Bill.

The Ulster Unionists have been equally keen to revisit the history of the Home Rule era, and defined their stand against the Anglo-Irish Agreement of 1985 in terms of their forebears' opposition to Home Rule in 1912–14. David Trimble, an energetic student of this period, has emphasised his respect for James Craig, who reinvented Home Rule as an Ulster Unionist shibboleth in and after 1920. Ian Paisley's interest in the Home Rule era has been well-documented, and he has used Edward Carson both as a political model and as a means of political legitimisation: Paisley's deputy, Peter Robinson, is the co-author of a short work on Carson. Sir Kenneth Bloomfield is a good example of a civil servant who, as an Oxford history graduate, has been aware of the significance of the past, and who for long influenced the efforts to reform and revise the constitution of the Unionist 'Home Rule' state. Northern politicians and bureaucrats have clearly been well-grounded in the history of Home Rule, and it is evident that the personalities and issues of this period have thereby been invested with a real contemporary significance.

It is also the case that the story of Home Rule illustrates some of the ways in which political and personal histories may be manipulated for contemporary effect. It is not just the case that (for example) Gladstone read, shaped and applied a particular version of Irish history; his commitment to Home Rule became so complete that he began to reinvent his own personal history, and argued in 1893 (against all the evidence) that 'any time within the last 30 years his mind had been open to [the idea]'.[4] It might also be suggested that, in an imposition of consistency, the personal histories of some of the authors of the 1998 agreement have been modified.

An extended treatment of the theme of 'Home Rule' also helps to highlight what might be broadly defined as a 'centrist' tradition in modern Irish political history – a tradition that has sought to accommodate Irish nationalism within the British state, and which has also sought to reconcile Irish nationalism and Irish Unionism within the structures of a devolved parliament and government. Again, though the notions of peace and reconciliation have been part of the vocabulary of Anglo-Irish relations for over a century, there has been little sustained effort to define Irish 'peacemakers' and 'reconcilers' as an historical theme. Hitherto, writers have tended to emphasise the militants or fundamentalists within both nationalist and Unionist traditions, and it is only comparatively lately that due attention has been paid to a centrist like William O'Brien and his political legacy. William O'Brien did not invent the peace conference, but he did promote the notion that 'conference plus business' might alleviate historic social and political animosities. And it is arguable that later efforts to negotiate a centre-ground owed something to O'Brien's political achievement: indeed, it might even be tentatively suggested that the Belfast talks of 1997–8 had a distant ancestor in the Land Conference of 1902.

At the same time, if there is indeed a centrist political 'tradition', then it has not been of a uniformly emollient quality. On the contrary, it might be argued that part of the problem with the centrist tradition in modern Ireland has been the centrists themselves. Men like William O'Brien, Horace Plunkett, T. W. Russell and, looking to the late twentieth century, Terence O'Neill, have all been unusually intense, angular or volatile personalities.

A related, equally neglected motif within the story of Home Rule is the reconciliation between Irish Protestantism and the new Catholic order –

an order based upon political enfranchisement and growing commercial and agricultural prosperity in the nineteenth century. In several definitions this reconciliation of traditions is the essence of Home Rule. Parnell's political vision embraced a settlement on the agrarian question as a necessary prelude to the emergence of Irish landed gentlemen as significant influences within a Home Rule administration. Gladstone saw Home Rule in similar terms, as a means of closing the distance between the Protestant landed elite and the Catholic democracy, and of permitting this elite to assume a legitimate place of honour within a new Ireland. Ulster Unionists defined their version of Home Rule for Northern Ireland as a means of avoiding, or at least of postponing, the new order; and subsequent constitutional experiments (in 1973–4, for example) failed because most Unionists were not yet sufficiently impressed that their interests lay in squaring up to, and accommodating, the strength of Catholic Ireland. It is arguable that the institutions created by the Belfast Agreement of 1998 embody the first adequate recognition by Northern Protestants of the political and economic influence of their Catholic compatriots. It is also arguable that these institutions, with their complex array of safeguards and checks and balances, reflect a Protestant wish to create a form of devolution that will offer protection and continuity in the event of the Catholic order prevailing. There are perhaps some broad parallels between the outlook of some of the cooler Unionist supporters of the agreement and those southern Unionists who, in 1917–18, after years of opposition to Home Rule, began to seek a belated accommodation with Redmond's policy.

Both Irish Protestants and Catholics unite in agreeing that the perfidy of the British has had a significant role to play in the story of Home Rule. Indeed, it is curious that both nationalists and Unionists have looked to British villainy as an explanation for the failure of their respective versions of Home Rule. Gladstone's public letter of 26 November 1890, which referred to his own vulnerability in the event of Parnell retaining the command of the Irish Party, has been seen as an act of betrayal and a critical moment in the Irish leader's descent. Redmond's failure is partly ascribed to Asquith, who dithered and extracted concessions, but who ultimately did not deliver an Irish parliament. Lloyd George is also commonly blamed for the failure of Redmondism, in so far as the critical negotiations of 1916 are seen as an example of the Welshman's double-dealing character. Indeed, this broad interpretation is also applied to the Anglo-Irish Treaty negotiations of 1921, where Lloyd George is seen as duplicitous and histrionic, and altogether too wily a bird for the honest Irish negotiators.

But, although the point is rarely made, the same type of interpretation is applied by Unionists. Carson denounced the perfidy of the Tory Party in a famous outburst during debate on the Anglo-Irish Treaty. James Chichester-Clark is seen as having been critically undermined by Harold Wilson in 1970. Faulkner's downfall in 1972 is sometimes partly blamed on his misplaced trust in Edward Heath, and upon the alleged disingenuousness of the British Prime Minister in March 1972. James Molyneaux's humiliation over the Anglo-Irish Agreement in 1985 is explained in terms of his over-reliance upon ministerial friendships and other high-political contacts. David Trimble's difficulties are partly blamed upon the alleged duplicity of Tony Blair, particularly when selling the Belfast Agreement to Ulster Unionist voters in 1998. British treachery is, of course, a familiar trope in the writing of Irish history, but it is a particularly striking element within interpretations of Home Rule under Parnell and Redmond, and of the Unionist variant. And, indeed, the formulaic nature of some of these accusations does not rule out the possibility that they may, in fact, have merit.

Turning to the British themselves, guilt and a sense of history have been important influences on those politicians who, since the 1880s, have sought to devolve power to an Irish or Northern Irish legislature. Gladstone's commitment to Home Rule was underpinned by his research into eighteenth-century Ireland; but it is striking that his ministerial colleagues, such as Harcourt and Morley, should also have found time either to work up their Irish history or, in the case of Bryce, to become actively involved in its production. Given the intellectual nature of his attachment to Home Rule, it is scarcely surprising that Gladstone should have invested so much effort into winning not just the political campaign for Irish self-government, but also the battle over the historical record.

Tony Blair is a less cerebral figure than his perceived historical model, Gladstone, but like Gladstone and other British liberals, he seems to accept that the British record in Ireland has been inglorious, and he evidently has some sense of the broader historical resonance of his actions. One of Blair's earliest acts as Prime Minister was to offer the Irish an expression of regret over the Great Famine of 1845. In his personal interventions to salvage the peace process, he has referred to the 'hand of history'. There is some (admittedly flawed) evidence to suggest that Blair has read into contemporary Irish history.[5] But Blair, like Gladstone, is also a highly religious and spiritual individual. And, just as Home Rule for Gladstone was largely a personal spiritual enterprise, so the Belfast Agreement and the restoration of a devolved government in Belfast are, it might be argued, an expression of Blair's religiosity.

This spiritual investment partly helps to explain the moral ascendancy that Home Rule and devolution occasionally seem to have acquired.

Gladstone believed until 1892–3, that Home Rule was divinely ordained, and he acted accordingly. Later devolutionists like Terence O'Neill and Brian Faulkner – both active church-goers – believed that the parliamentary institutions of Northern Ireland would serve as a model and exemplar for others. O'Neill thought that regional parliaments such as Stormont would eventually spread throughout Britain, while Faulkner came to believe in what G. B. Newe called 'a theology of "Sunningdale"' – that there were 'unique features in the new institutions [created through the agreement of 1973] which could easily become established practice in other democracies'.[6] Defenders of the Belfast Agreement and its concomitant institutions have frequently represented this deal as an essentially moral enterprise.

Not all British ministers have carried the burden of evangelical guilt in relation to Home Rule. For some, like Asquith and Lloyd George, Ireland was not so much a spiritual as a tactical challenge. Asquith's words and actions in 1912–14, though frequently underestimated, carry nothing of the moral urgency that pervades, say, the Gladstone diaries. Nor, despite his sentimental attachment to Welsh Nonconformity, is there overt evidence to suggest that Lloyd George was driven by any sense of spiritual challenge. However, it is quite clear that his negotiating style has had an influence (however indirect) on the resolution of later Irish disputes, and perhaps even on the Belfast Agreement itself. The fruits of his diplomacy – the settlement of 1920–2 – have, of course had a lasting significance as a central element of the modern Irish political landscape.

Through the history of Home Rule the British have regularly oscillated between policies of criminalisation and accommodation – between outlawing Home Rulers and later nationalists, and then seeking to win their allegiance. Indeed, Gladstone himself moved from the proclamation of the Land League, the motor force of the Home Rule movement, to the creation of a 'union of hearts' between the Liberals and the Irish parliamentary party in 1886 and after. Arthur Balfour and the Tories shifted from a vigorous pursuit of the national movement, in the shape of the Plan of Campaign, towards the more emollient strategies of 'constructive Unionism'. Lloyd George pursued his bloody war against the IRA in 1919–21, only to seek an accommodation with the representatives of the Dáil government through the truce and the negotiations for the Anglo-Irish Treaty. After detonating Unionist 'Home Rule' in 1972, the British moved uncertainly between criminalising the leadership of the IRA and earnestly negotiating with them. Ultimately, in the latest instalment of 'Home Rule', the British have helped to devolve the vestiges of state power upon those who at one time condoned armed struggle.

One of the most striking examples of a militant British response to the Home Rule movement came in 1912–14, with the alliance between Andrew Bonar Law's Conservative party and the hawks of Ulster Unionism. It is well known that senior Tories publicly endorsed Ulster Unionist paramilitarism at this time. It has also been long understood that numerous Conservative politicians were actively associated with Ulster Unionist gun-running. But until now little or no attention has been paid to the evidence that links Bonar Law himself to the most cussed of the Unionist gun-runners, F. H. Crawford, and the most spectacular of the gun-running coups, at Larne. There is, at the very least, a strong likelihood that Bonar Law knew about, and blessed, the enterprise that culminated in the landing of weapons at Larne, Bangor and Donaghadee on the night of 24–5 April 1914.

This point might be extended to suggest that the lines of demarcation between constitutional and militant politics within the extended history of Home Rule have not been as sharp as some comforting observers would have us believe. Successive generations of constitutional – or perhaps in some cases, to borrow Sean Lemass's designation, 'slightly constitutional' – politicians have sought to harness the influence and support of the militants within their tradition. Parnell, himself perhaps a Fenian, reached a political accommodation with the Irish Republican Brotherhood which lasted until his death. Carson helped to create the Ulster Volunteer Force at least partly in order to indicate the seriousness of Unionist protest against the third Home Rule Bill and to ratchet up the pressure on Asquith. Ian Paisley and David Trimble have each, at different points in their careers, been associated with loyalist hardliners. John Hume, to the chagrin of many of his SDLP colleagues, opened up a dialogue with Gerry Adams which matured into the Hume–Adams political offensive of the early 1990s.

It would doubtless be wrong to over-simplify the strategic insights of those who have entered into debate with the hard men of their respective traditions. Friendly interpretations tend to stress that constitutional politicians have taken risks for peace, and have served to guide their militants into more peaceful ways. Unfriendly interpretations tend to see the links between constitutionalists and the militants as evidence of moral danger. It is, of course, hard to decipher private motives. But it is arguable that, on the whole, successive generations of constitutional politicians have been augmented through their association with the hard men, while those squeamish few who have resisted such associations have generally suffered in consequence.

But to emphasise the continuities within the long history of Home Rule is perhaps to imply that there is a fundamental symmetry between late

Victorian and late-twentieth-century Irish politics. It is striking that the ends of the eighteenth, the nineteenth and the twentieth centuries have all been characterised by profound political and constitutional change in Ireland. Some of the parallels between the Ireland of the 1790s and of the 1990s have been discussed elsewhere, but there is an obvious case for comparing the social and political conditions that generated Home Rule in 1886 with those which spawned the devolution settlement of 1998.[7] Rising Catholic power and prosperity could not be contained within the rigid structures of the old British regime in the nineteenth century. Equally, rising Catholic expectations in the late twentieth century could not be contained within the rigid structures of the Unionist state. The effort to incorporate Irish people within a British imperial identity failed in the nineteenth century, while the Unionist state's piecemeal efforts to construct an 'Ulster' identity did not effectively embrace Northern Catholics.[8]

This combination of Catholic social and economic consolidation, together with the existing political and cultural failure of the state, created the space in both 1886 and 1998 for some constitutional experimentation. Home Rule was designed by Gladstone at least partly as an effort to accommodate the nationalist challenge within the British connection – and on bargain-basement terms. The Belfast Agreement has evidently been regarded by Tony Blair and David Trimble as an effort to accommodate the Northern nationalist challenge within the British connection at a necessarily higher price. Gladstone failed because he faced an economically powerful and culturally self-confident Unionism. It remains to be seen whether the war-weary, culturally disoriented and economically fragile Unionist middle classes will accept the new Home Rule.

# NOTES

## Chapter 1 Shared Histories

1. F. S. L. Lyons, *John Dillon: A Biography* (London, 1968), pp. 368–72.
2. Brian Faulkner, *Memoirs of a Statesman* (London, 1978), pp. 157–9.
3. See also Alan O'Day, *Irish Home Rule, 1867–1921* (Manchester, 1998) and Alan Ward, *The Irish Constitutional Tradition: Responsible Government and Modern Ireland, 1782–1992* (Dublin, 1992). For a general political history of modern Ireland, see Alvin Jackson, *Ireland, 1798–1998: Politics and War* (Oxford, 1999).
4. For excellent interpretations of the Agreement and the politics of Northern Ireland in the 1980s and 1990s see Deaglán de Bréadún, *The Far Side of Revenge: Making Peace in Northern Ireland* (Cork, 2001), Thomas Hennessey, *The Northern Ireland Peace Process: Ending the Troubles?* (Dublin, 2001) and Ed Moloney, *A Secret History of the IRA* (London, 2002).

## Chapter 2. The Evolution of an Idea

1. See, for example, T. M. Kettle, *The Day's Burden: Studies, Literary and Political* (Dublin, 1910), p. 30. See also Alan O'Day, *The English Face of Irish Nationalism: Parnellite Involvement in British Politics, 1880–1886* (Dublin, 1977).
2. See Joseph Spence, 'Isaac Butt, Nationality and Irish Toryism, 1833–52', *Bullán*, 2, 1 (summer 1995), pp. 45–60.
3. See James Kelly, 'The Origins of the Act of Union: An Examination of Unionist Opinion in Britain and Ireland, 1650–1800', *Irish Historical Studies*, xxv, 99 (May, 1987), pp. 236–63; Jim Smyth, 'An Anglo-Irish Unionist Discourse, c.1656–1707: From Harrington to Fletcher', *Bullán*, 2, 1 (summer 1995), pp. 17–34.
4. This theme is explored by Roy Foster in 'The Story of Ireland', *The Irish Story: Telling Tales and Making it Up in Ireland* (London, 2001), pp. 1–22. See also Donal McCartney, 'The Writing of History in Ireland, 1800–1830', *Irish Historical Studies*, x, 40 (September 1957).
5. P. J. Corish, *The Catholic Community in the 17th and 18th Centuries* (Dublin, 1981); Marianne Elliott, *The Catholics of Ulster: A History* (London, 2000), pp. 213–19.
6. For a survey of recent arguments on the Union see Alvin Jackson, 'The Irish Act of Union', *History Today*, vol. 51(1), January 2001, pp. 19–25. Important recent research on the Union includes Patrick Geoghegan, *The Irish Act of Union* (Dublin, 1999) and 'British-Irish Union of 1801', *Transactions of the Royal Historical Society*, 6th Series, vol. 10 (2000), pp. 167–408.
7. See Oliver MacDonagh, *O'Connell: The Life of Daniel O'Connell, 1775–1847* (London, 1991).

8. See Gearóid Ó Tuathaigh, 'The Folk Hero and Tradition' in Donal McCartney (ed.), *The World of Daniel O'Connell* (Dublin, 1980), p. 34, for the folklore on O'Connell's sexual prowess.
9. MacDonagh, *O'Connell*, pp. 102–3.
10. MacDonagh, *O'Connell*, p. 459.
11. MacDonagh, *O'Connell*, pp. 515–16.
12. B. A. Kennedy, 'Sharman Crawford's Federal Scheme for Ireland', in H. A. Cronne, T. W. Moody and D. B. Quinn (eds), *Essays in British and Irish History in Honour of James Eadie Todd* (London, 1949); J. G. V. Porter, *Ireland* (Dublin, 1844). See also John Kendle, *Ireland and the Federal Solution: The Debate over the United Kingdom Constitution, 1870–1921* (Kingston and Montreal, 1989), pp. 8–31.
13. See Richard Davis, *The Young Ireland Movement* (Dublin, 1987).
14. John Whyte, *The Independent Irish Party, 1850–59* (Oxford, 1958); Steven R. Knowlton, *Popular Politics and the Irish Catholic Church: The Rise and Fall of the Independent Irish Party, 1850–1859* (New York and London, 1991).
15. Patrick Maume, 'Parnell and the IRB Oath', *Irish Historical Studies*, xxix, 115 (May 1995).
16. F. S. L. Lyons, *John Dillon: A Biography* (London, 1968), pp. 1–10 for the family connections.
17. K. T. Hoppen, *Elections, Politics and Society in Ireland, 1832–1885* (Oxford, 1984), pp. 278–332.
18. See Spence, 'Butt'.
19. Spence, 'Butt', p. 46.
20. Spence, 'Butt', p. 47; Alvin Jackson, *The Ulster Party: Irish Unionists in the House of Commons, 1884–1911* (Oxford, 1989), pp. 122–3.
21. An important letter book for the Home Government Association is preserved in PRONI. There are also some fragmentary Edward King-Harman papers in this repository.
22. Alvin Jackson, *The Ulster Party: Irish Unionists in the House of Commons, 1884–1911* (Oxford, 1989), pp. 40–1; Alvin Jackson, *Colonel Edward Saunderson: Land and Loyalty in Victorian Ireland* (Oxford, 1995), pp. 55–6, 71.
23. This is one of the arguments offered by John Hutchinson, *The Dynamics of Cultural Nationalism: The Gaelic Revival and the Creation of the Irish Nation State* (London, 1987).
24. Hoppen, *Elections*, pp. 17–18.
25. See James Loughlin, 'Constructing the Spectacle: Parnell, the Press and National Leadership, 1879–86', in D. George Boyce and Alan O'Day (eds), *Parnell in Perspective* (London, 1991), pp. 221–41.
26. William O'Brien, *Recollections* (London, 1905), pp. 347–8. I am grateful to Patrick Maume for this reference.

### Chapter 3 All But a Nation: Home Rule, 1870–79

1. A. M. Sullivan, *Old Ireland: The Reminiscences of an Irish KC* (London, 1928), pp. 20–1.
2. R. Barry O'Brien, *Life of Charles Stewart Parnell*, 2 vols (London, 1898), i, p. 229; ii, p. 61. F. S. L. Lyons, *Charles Stewart Parnell* (London, 1977). The standard assessment of Butt remains David Thornley, *Isaac Butt and Home Rule* (London, 1964).
3. The letter book of the Home Rule League is accessible at PRONI (D.213).

4. Quoted in Joseph Spence, 'Isaac Butt, Nationality and Irish Toryism, 1833–1852', *Bullán*, 2, 1 (summer 1995), p. 47.

5. Thornley, *Butt*, pp. 16–17.

6. K. T. Hoppen, *Elections, Politics and Society in Ireland, 1832–1885* (Oxford, 1984), pp. 464–79.

7. Isaac Butt, *Land Tenure in Ireland: A Plea for the Celtic Race* (Dublin, 1866).

8. Thomas Macknight, *Ulster as it is: Twenty-eight Years' Experience as an Irish Editor*, 2 vols (London, 1896), i, p. 227.

9. Thornley, *Butt*, pp. 92–3.

10. Thornley, *Butt*, p. 96.

11. Butt's classic work on his constitutional views was *Home Government for Ireland, Irish Federalism: Its Meanings, Its Objects and Its Hopes* (Dublin, 1874). Curiously the HRL allowed the work to go out of print in 1874, despite sustained demand: HRL Letter Book, D.213: McAlister to Butt, 19 September 1874. The work is discussed in John Kendle, *Ireland and the Federal Solution: The Debate over the United Kingdom Constitution, 1870–1921* (Kingston and Montreal, 1989), pp. 12–15.

12. HRL Letter Book, D.213: pp. 74–5, John Martin to William Markin, 17 February 1874 (defining Butt's vision of Home Rule); pp. 99–102, John Martin to E. Murphy, 11 December 1874 (outlining the distinctions – as opposed to differences – between O'Connell and Butt).

13. Kendle, *Ireland and the Federal Solution*, pp. 11–19.

14. HRL Letter Book, D.213, gives details of the frantic preparations for the general election of 1874.

15. Desmond Bowen, *Paul Cullen and the Shaping of Modern Irish Catholicism* (Dublin, 1983), pp. 272–81, for the Cardinal's reactions to the new Home Rule movement.

16. R. V. Comerford, *The Fenians in Context: Irish Politics and Society, 1848–1882* (Dublin, 1985).

17. Thornley, *Butt*, p. 96.

18. HRL Letter Book, D.213, gives details of the organisation's electoral machinery in 1873–4. For the League's recurrent financial problems see HRL Letter Book p. 88, Alfred Webb to J. Dunne; p. 329, McAlister to James Collins, 20 July 1878; pp. 332–3, McAlister to the Council of the League, 22 July 1878.

19. Thornley, *Butt*, p. 176.

20. Hoppen, *Elections*, p. 274.

21. Thornley, *Butt*, p. 213.

22. HRL Letter Book, D.213: pp. 105–8, John Martin to 'Rev. Dear Sir', 11 January 1875 (where Martin indicates his suspicions of Westminster, and his sympathy for an absentionist policy).

23. T. P. O'Connor, *Memoirs of an Old Parliamentarian*, 2 vols (London, 1929), i, p. 33.

24. T. M. Healy, *Letters and Leaders of My Day*, 2 vols (London, 1928), i, p. 63. Laurence J. Kettle, *Material for Victory: The Memoirs of Andrew J. Kettle, Right Hand Man to Charles S. Parnell* (Dublin, 1958), p. 66.

25. O'Connor, *Memoirs of an Old Parliamentarian*, i, p. 33.

26. Kettle, *Material for Victory*, p. 55.

27. Thornley, *Butt*, pp. 65–6. There is a small collection of Joseph Biggar papers in PRONI (D.3905).

28. Macknight, *Ulster as it is*, i, p. 228.

29. Macknight, *Ulster as it is*, i, pp. 327–8.

30. HRL Letter Book, D.213: pp.130–4, J. A. Galbraith to E. Murphy, 19 August 1875. See also F. H. O'Donnell, *History of the Irish Parliamentary Party*, 2 vols (London, 1910), i, pp.134–5.
31. Thornley, *Butt*, pp.384–5.
32. Healy, *Letters and Leaders*, i, p.55.
33. William O'Brien and Desmond Ryan (eds), *John Devoy's Post Bag*, 2 vols (Dublin, 1948–53), i, p.76.
34. O'Brien and Ryan (eds), *Devoy's Post Bag*, i, p.395.
35. O'Brien and Ryan (eds), *Devoy's Post Bag*, i, p.395.
36. Thornley, *Butt*, p.167.
37. Thornley, *Butt*, p.255.
38. O'Donnell, *Irish Parliamentary Party*, i, p.108.
39. HRL Letter Book, D.213: pp.130–4, J. A. Galbraith to E. Murphy, 19 August 1875.
40. O'Brien and Ryan (eds), *Devoy's Post Bag*, i, p.396.
41. Lyons, *Parnell*, p.60.
42. Butt was not so far gone in late 1877 that he was uable to identify, and move to subvert, a Parnellite challenge to undermine his authority. See HRL Letter Book, D.213: pp.268–9, J. McAlister to Richard O'Shaughnessy, 20 November 1877.
43. Sullivan, *Old Ireland*, pp.20–1.
44. The literature on the New Departure is extensive. An invaluable starting point remains T. W. Moody, 'The New Departure in Irish Politics, 1878–9' in H. A. Cronne, T. W. Moody and D. B. Quinn (eds), *Essays in British and Irish History in Honour of James Eadie Todd* (London, 1949), pp.303–34.
45. O'Brien and Ryan (eds), *Devoy's Post Bag*, ii, p.379.

**Chapter 4  Forster's Sofa: The Advance of Parnell, 1879–86**

1. John Morley Diary, 5 April 1886.
2. R. F. Foster, *Charles Stewart Parnell: The Man and His Family* (Hassocks, 1976).
3. Donald Jordan, *Land and Popular Politics in Ireland: County Mayo from the Plantation to the Land War* (Cambridge, 1994).
4. See Paul Bew, *Land and the National Question in Ireland, 1858–1882* (Dublin, 1978).
5. F. S. L. Lyons, *Charles Stewart Parnell* (London, 1977), p.111.
6. R. Barry O'Brien, *Life of Charles Stewart Parnell*, 2 vols (London, 1898), i, p.236.
7. Lyons, *Parnell*, p.138.
8. For Parnell's economic thought, see Liam Kennedy, 'The Economic Thought of the Nation's Lost Leader: Charles Stewart Parnell', in D. G. Boyce and Alan O'Day (eds), *Parnell in Perspective* (London, 1991), pp.171–200.
9. Thomas Macknight, *Ulster as it is: Twenty-eight Years' Experience as an Irish Editor* (London, 1896), i, pp.315–16.
10. H. Kingsmill Moore, *Reminiscences and Reflections from Some Sixty Years of Life in Ireland* (London, 1930), p.41.
11. See Paul Bew, *C. S. Parnell* (Dublin, 1980). See also Laurence J. Kettle, *Material for Victory: The Memoirs of Andrew J. Kettle, Right-hand Man to Charles Stewart Parnell* (Dublin, 1958), pp.34, 58.
12. Alvin Jackson, *Colonel Edward Saunderson: Land and Loyalty in Victorian Ireland* (Oxford, 1995), p.97.
13. Kettle, *Material for Victory*, p.57.
14. See Patrick Maume, 'Parnell and the IRB Oath', *Irish Historical Studies*, xxix, 115 (May 1995).

15. Lyons, *Parnell*, pp. 93–5.
16. See, for example, Thomas J. Morrissey SJ, *William J. Walsh, Archbishop of Dublin, 1841–1921: No Uncertain Voice* (Dublin, 2000), pp. 67–143.
17. K. T. Hoppen, *Elections, Politics and Society in Ireland, 1832–1885* (Oxford, 1984), pp. 87–8. See also Brian M. Walker, 'The Irish Electorate, 1868–1915', *Irish Historical Studies*, xviii, 71 (March 1973), pp. 359–71.
18. Hoppen, *Elections*, pp. 32–3.
19. Alan O'Day, *Irish Home Rule, 1867–1921* (Manchester, 1998), p. 93.
20. Kettle, *Material for Victory*, p. 69.
21. Alan O'Day, *The English Face of Irish Nationalism: Parnellite Involvement in British Politics, 1880–86* (Dublin, 1977), pp. 93–107.
22. O'Day, *Irish Home Rule*, p. 71.
23. Kettle, *Material for Victory*, p. 69.
24. Alvin Jackson, *The Ulster Party: Irish Unionists in the House of Commons, 1884–1911* (Oxford, 1989), pp. 34–5.
25. Jackson, *Ulster Party*, p. 37; Lyons, *Parnell*, pp. 285–8. See also Andrew Roberts, *Salisbury: Victorian Titan* (London, 1999), p. 349.
26. Kettle, *Material for Victory*, pp. 63–4.
27. O'Brien, *Parnell*, i, p. 90.
28. Richard Shannon, *Gladstone: Heroic Minister, 1865–1898* (London, 1999), pp. 372–3.
29. R. V. Comerford in W. E. Vaughan (ed.), *A New History of Ireland V: Ireland under the Union I: 1800–1870* (Oxford, 1989), p. 441.
30. R.V. Comerford, *The Fenians in Context: Irish Politics and Society, 1848–1882* (Dublin, 1985). My italics.
31. Shannon, *Gladstone*, p. 270.
32. John Morley Diary, 2 May 1893.
33. G. K. Peatling, *British Opinion and Irish Self-government, 1865–1925: From Unionism to Liberal Commonwealth* (Dublin, 2001), pp. 34–46.
34. Shannon, *Gladstone*, p. 357.
35. Shannon, *Gladstone*, pp. 288–9.
36. Shannon, *Gladstone*, p. 290.
37. Shannon, *Gladstone*, p. 352.
38. Shannon, *Gladstone*, p. 356.
39. Peter Marsh, *Joseph Chamberlain: Entrepreneur in Politics* (New Haven and London, 1994), pp. 192–7.
40. Shannon, *Gladstone*, p. 360.
41. Gladstone Papers, Add.Ms. 44269, f. 225: Gladstone to Mrs O'Shea, 8 August 1885.
42. Shannon, *Gladstone*, p. 396.
43. Viscount Gladstone, *After Thirty Years* (London, 1928), p. 283.
44. Shannon, *Gladstone*, p. 395.
45. Roberts, *Salisbury*, p. 364: 'it is not impossible that Salisbury deliberately led MacColl [acting as an intermediary with Gladstone] into thinking that he was more willing seriously to consider the issue than he in fact was in order to lure Gladstone into flying the Hawarden Kite'.
46. Gladstone Papers, Add.Ms. 44269, f. 234: Gladstone to Mrs O'Shea, 3 November 1885.

47. Gladstone, *After Thirty Years*, pp. 306–14.
48. Harcourt Papers, dep. 10, f. 2: Gladstone to Harcourt, 6 January 1886.
49. Shannon, *Gladstone*, p. 412.
50. Gladstone Papers, Add.Ms. 44200, f. 44: Gladstone to Harcourt, 12 February 1886.
51. Gladstone Papers, Add.Ms. 44200, f. 82: Harcourt to Gladstone, 7 March 1886.
52. John Morley Diary, 5 April 1886.
53. Alan Ward, *The Irish Constitutional Tradition: Responsible Government in Modern Ireland, 1782–1992* (Dublin, 1992), p. 65
54. Ward, *Irish Constitutional Tradition*, p. 63.
55. Ward, *Irish Constitutional Tradition*, p. 63.
56. Alan O'Day, *Parnell and the First Home Rule Episode, 1884–87* (Dublin, 1986), p. 185.
57. O'Day, *Irish Home Rule*, p. 318
58. The historicist approach of Gladstone has been examined in James Loughlin, *Gladstone, Home Rule and the Ulster Question, 1882–93* (Dublin, 1986). Gladstone Papers, Add.Ms. 44200, f. 1: Harcourt to Gladstone, 4 January 1886.
59. O'Day, *Irish Home Rule*, p. 318.
60. O'Day, *Irish Home Rule*, p. 318.
61. Gladstone Papers, Add.Ms. 44255, f. 86: Morley to Gladstone, 8 May 1886 ('have you seen our friend [Parnell]?').
62. O'Day, *Parnell and the First Home Rule Episode*, p. 199.
63. Loughlin, *Gladstone, Home Rule and the Ulster Question*, p. 193.
64. Though see, for example, Bryce Papers, dep. 213, f. 90: R. McGeagh to Bryce, 13 March 1886.
65. Jackson, *Ulster Party*, pp. 120–1.
66. Jackson, *Ulster Party*, p. 123.
67. Jackson, *Ulster Party*, pp. 124–5.
68. Jackson, *Ulster Party*, p. 126.
69. O'Day, *Irish Home Rule*, p. 116.
70. Discussed by Loughlin in *Gladstone, Home Rule and the Ulster Question*, pp. 57–9.
71. See, for example, the thesis of A. B. Cooke and John Vincent, *The Governing Passion: Cabinet Government and Party Politics in Britain, 1885–6* (Brighton, 1974), pp. 15–18. See also D. A. Hamer, *Liberal Politics in the Age of Gladstone and Rosebery: A Study in Leadership and Policy* (Oxford, 1972), pp. 124–5. See the critique supplied by W. C. Lubenow, *Parliamentary Politics and the Home Rule Crisis: The British House of Commons in 1886* (Oxford, 1988), p. 255.
72. Loughlin, *Gladstone, Home Rule and the Ulster Question*, p. 288.
73. Lyons, *Parnell*, pp. 260–1.
74. Lubenow, *Parliamentary Politics*, pp. 205, 264.
75. Lubenow, *Parliamentary Politics*, p. 286.
76. Lubenow, *Parliamentary Politics*, p. 285.

## Chapter 5 Uniting Hearts, 1886–91

1. Alan O'Day, 'Parnell as Orator and Speaker', in D. G. Boyce and Alan O'Day (eds), *Parnell in Perspective* (London, 1991), p. 212.
2. Laurence Geary, *The Plan of Campaign, 1886–91* (Cork, 1986), p. 141.
3. Margaret O'Callaghan, *British High Politics and Nationalist Ireland: Criminality, Land and the Law under Forster and Balfour* (Cork, 1994), pp. 118, 120.

4. O'Callaghan, *British High Politics*, pp. 105, 112.
5. L. P. Curtis, *Coercion and Conciliation in Ireland, 1880–1892: A Study in Conservative Unionism* (Oxford, 1963), pp. 248–52.
6. Andrew Roberts, *Salisbury: Victorian Titan* (London, 1999), p. 451.
7. F. S. L. Lyons, *Charles Stewart Parnell* (London, 1977), pp. 364–7.
8. Lyons, *Parnell*, p. 435.
9. John Morley Diary, 15 January 1886.
10. Richard Shannon, *Gladstone: Heroic Minister, 1865–1898* (London, 1999), p. 472.
11. O'Callaghan, *British High Politics*, p. 118.
12. Lyons, *Parnell*, p. 384.
13. Lyons, *Parnell*, p. 437.
14. Lyons, *Parnell*, pp. 374–5.
15. Lyons, *Parnell*, p. 377.
16. O'Callaghan, *British High Politics*, p. 112.
17. Roberts, *Salisbury*, p. 455.
18. Lyons, *Parnell*, p. 390.
19. Roberts, *Salisbury*, pp. 452–3.
20. O'Callaghan, *British High Politics*, p. 112.
21. Lyons, *Parnell*, p. 427.
22. O'Callaghan, *British High Politics*, pp. 112–13, 119.
23. Frank Callanan, *The Parnell Split, 1890–91* (Cork, 1992), pp. 238–56.
24. Eugene Doyle, *Justin McCarthy* (Dublin, 1996), p. 37. See also Justin McCarthy and Mrs Campbell Praed, *Our Book of Memories* (London, 1912).
25. Doyle, *McCarthy*, p. 37.
26. Doyle, *McCarthy*, pp. 36–7.
27. Frank Callanan, *T. M. Healy* (Cork, 1996), pp. 257–9.
28. Callanan, *Parnell Split*, pp. 86, 156.
29. See Callanan, *Parnell Split*. See also Philip Bull's important 'The Fall of Parnell: The Political Context of His Intransigence' in Boyce and O'Day (eds), *Parnell in Perspective*, pp. 129–50.
30. Callanan, *Parnell Split*, pp. 238–56.
31. Callanan, *Parnell Split*, p. 267; Paul Bew, *C. S. Parnell* (Dublin, 1980), p. 127. See also Thomas Macknight, *Ulster as it is: Twenty-eight Years' Experience as an Irish Editor* (London, 1896), ii, p. 267, which emphasises his residual support among Belfast nationalists.
32. Callanan, *Parnell Split*, pp. 80–109.
33. Liam Kennedy, 'The Economic Thought of the Nation's Lost Leader: Charles Stewart Parnell' in D.G. Boyce and Alan O'Day (eds), *Parnell in Perspective* (London, 1991), pp. 171–200.
34. Callanan, *Healy*, p. 219
35. Callanan, *Parnell Split*, pp. 154, 180; Lyons, *Parnell*, pp. 599–600.
36. Lyons, *Parnell*, p. 601.

### Chapter 6  Fall and Rise, 1892–1910

1. Richard Shannon, *Gladstone: Heroic Minister, 1865–1898* (London, 1999), p. 514.
2. Shannon, *Gladstone*, p. 534.
3. Gladstone Papers, Add.Ms. 44257, f. 29: Gladstone to Morley (copy), 'Heads of the Home Rule Bill', 11 November 1893.

4. Shannon, *Gladstone*, p. 539.
5. This issue, which was the focus for a Unionist assault, would later cause some frustration for the government. See Morley Diary, 16 May 1893. See also Alan Ward, *The Irish Constitutional Tradition: Responsible Government and Modern Ireland, 1782–1992* (Dublin, 1992), pp. 65–6, 67–70, 73–4, 76–7.
6. See, for example, PREM.13/1663: Harold Wilson to Lord President of the Council, 31 January 1966.
7. James Loughlin, *Gladstone, Home Rule and the Ulster Question, 1882–1893* (Dublin, 1986), pp. 278–9.
8. Morley Diary, 15 May 1893: 'Mr G very low ... I fancy the secret of his depression was the discovery which he announced to me that the collector at Belfast had made a mistake to the tune of £360,000 in the amount of excise on goods consumed in Engl[an]d'. See also Harcourt Papers, dep. 13, f. 53: Gladstone to Harcourt, 21 January 1892 ('it is annoying in the matters of Irish finance that the figures shift as in a kaleidoscope ...')
9. Shannon, *Gladstone*, p. 544.
10. Shannon, *Gladstone*, pp. 520, 536.
11. Shannon, *Gladstone*, p. 541.
12. Shannon, *Gladstone*, pp. 535–6.
13. D. A. Hamer, *Liberal Politics in the Age of Gladstone and Rosebery: A Study in Leadership and Policy* (Oxford, 1972), p. 184.
14. G. K. Peatling, *British Opinion and Irish Self-government, 1865–1925: From Unionism to Liberal Commonwealth* (Dublin, 2001), pp. 53–65.
15. Peatling, *British Opinion*, pp. 53–65.
16. See R. F. Foster, *W. B. Yeats: A Life. I: The Apprentice Mage* (Oxford, 1997).
17. Patrick Maume, *The Long Gestation: Irish Nationalist Life, 1891–1918* (Dublin, 1999); Senia Paseta, *Before the Revolution: Nationalism, Social Change and Ireland's Catholic Elite, 1879–1922* (Cork, 1999).
18. Frank Callanan, *T. M. Healy* (Cork, 1996), p. 415.
19. Callanan, *Healy*, pp. 258–9.
20. T. M. Healy, *Letters and Leaders of My Day*, 2 vols (London, 1928), ii, p. 422. See also Callanan, *Healy*, p. 424, and F. S. L. Lyons, *The Irish Parliamentary Party, 1890–1910* (London, 1951), pp. 51–2.
21. John Pinkerton Papers, D.1078/P/66: Dillon to Pinkerton, 21 June 1896.
22. Callanan, *Healy*, p. 426.
23. John Morley Diary, 7 June 1893.
24. Callanan, *Healy*, p. 426.
25. See for example William O'Brien, *The Downfall of Parliamentarianism: A Retrospect for the Accounting Day* (Dublin, 1918). See Philip Bull, *Land, Politics and Nationalism: A Study of the Irish Land Question* (Dublin, 1996) for a persuasive assessment of William O'Brien. See also Sally Warwick-Haller, *William O'Brien and the Irish Land War* (Dublin, 1990).
26. Redmond Papers, 15182/2: Dillon to Redmond, 26 July 1899.
27. Pinkerton Papers, D.1078/1/70: Jeremiah Jordan to Pinkerton, 23 April 1901.
28. For assessments of the land conference (1902), the Irish Reform Association, and the devolution affair of 1904–5 see (*inter alia*): Earl of Dunraven, *The Crisis in Ireland: An Account of the Present Condition of Ireland and Suggestions Towards Reform* (Dublin, 1905); Earl of Dunraven, *The Outlook in Ireland: The Case for*

*Devolution and Conciliation* (Dublin, 1907); William O'Brien, *An Olive Branch in Ireland and the History of its Undoing* (London, 1910); F. S. L. Lyons, 'The Irish Unionist Party and the Devolution Crisis, 1904–5', *Irish Historical Studies*, 6, 21 (March 1948); Andrew Gailey, *Ireland and the Death of Kindness: The Experience of Constructive Unionism, 1890–1905* (Cork, 1987); Alvin Jackson, *The Ulster Party: Irish Unionists in the House of Commons, 1884–1911* (Oxford, 1989).

29. Bull, *Land, Politics and Nationalism*, pp. 163–4. See O'Brien, *Olive Branch*.
30. Pinkerton Papers, D.1078/P/71: Jeremiah Jordan to Pinkerton, 1 March 1902.
31. F. S. L. Lyons, *John Dillon: A Biography*, pp. 239–40.
32. Redmond Papers, 15182/5: Dillon to Redmond, 2 October 1903.
33. Redmond Papers, 15182/6: Dillon to Redmond, 24 January 1904.
34. See n. 28 for some of the relevant literature by Dunraven and O'Brien.
35. Warwick-Haller, *William O'Brien*, p. 224.
36. Jackson, *Ulster Party*, pp. 243–83.
37. Paul Bew, *Conflict and Conciliation in Ireland, 1890–1910: Parnellites and Radical Agrarians* (Oxford, 1987), p. 45.
38. Bull, *Land, Politics and Nationalism*, pp. 176–92.
39. Bull, *Land, Politics and Nationalism*, p. 190.
40. Bull, *Land, Politics and Nationalism*, pp. 191–2.
41. Bew, *Conflict and Conciliation*, p. 140.
42. R. R. Cherry Papers, D.2166/3/1/10: Birrell to Cherry, n.d. ('Ginnell seems coming to the front … Redmond seems losing himself in verbiage').
43. Cherry Papers, D.2166/3/1/10: Birrell to Cherry, n.d.
44. Bull, *Land, Politics and Nationalism*, pp. 171–2.
45. Bew, *Conflict and Conciliation*, p. 186.
46. Bew, *Conflict and Conciliation*, p. 207.
47. Warwick-Haller, *William O'Brien*, p. 201.
48. Maume, *Long Gestation*, p. 58. See also Redmond Papers, 15182/12: Dillon to Redmond, 29 September 1906.
49. Redmond Papers, 15182/14: Dillon to Redmond, 11 May 1907.
50. Michael Laffan, *The Resurrection of Ireland: The Sinn Féin Party, 1916–23* (Cambridge, 1999), pp. 25–9.
51. Laffan, *Resurrection of Ireland*, p. 30.
52. Laffan, *Resurrection of Ireland*, p. 30.
53. For a calm and persuasive view of Moran see Patrick Maume, *D. P. Moran* (Dublin, 1995).
54. Foster, *W. B. Yeats*, p. 41.
55. Maume, *Long Gestation*, pp. 63–5.
56. Paseta, *Before the Revolution*, p. 75.
57. Paseta, *Before the Revolution*, p. 150.
58. Paseta, *Before the Revolution*, pp. 49, 150.
59. Paseta, *Before the Revolution*, p. 153.
60. Paseta, *Before the Revolution*, p. 71–2.
61. Stephen Gwynn, *John Redmond's Last Years* (London, 1919), p. 60. See also Paseta, *Before the Revolution*, p. 62.
62. Maume, *Long Gestation*, pp. 215, 220.
63. Maume, *Long Gestation*, p. 77.

## Chapter 7 The Leadership of Redmond, 1910–14

1. See G.K. Peatling, *British Opinion and Irish Self-government, 1865–1925: From Unionism to Liberal Commonwealth* (Dublin, 2001), pp. 53–107.
2. Austen Chamberlain, *Politics from Inside: An Epistolary Chronicle, 1906–14* (London, 1936), p. 193. See also A. M. Gollin, *The Observer and J. L. Garvin, 1908–1914: A Study in a Great Editorship* (Oxford, 1960), pp. 222, 229.
3. There were later collected as a single volume, *Federalism and Home Rule* (London, 1910).
4. Theresa Londonderry Papers, D.2846/1/1/55: Carson to Lady Londonderry, 27 October 1910. See also Goulding Papers, A/3/2: William Moore to Goulding, 25 October 1910 and 28 October 1910.
5. For a useful summary of the bill, see Alan O'Day, *Irish Home Rule, 1867–1921* (Manchester, 1998), pp. 247–50.
6. Alan Ward, *The Irish Constitutional Tradition: Responsible Government and Modern Ireland, 1782–1992* (Dublin, 1992), p. 65.
7. John Redmond, *The Home Rule Bill* (London, 1912), p. 23.
8. Patricia Jalland, *The Liberals and Ireland: The Ulster Question in British Politics to 1914* (Brighton, 1980), pp. 49, 56.
9. Nicholas Mansergh, *The Unresolved Question: The Anglo-Irish Settlement and its Undoing, 1912–72* (New Haven, 1991), p. 50.
10. H. H. Asquith Papers, Ms.Asquith 6, f. 95: Asquith to George V, 7 February 1912.
11. Peatling, *British Opinion*, pp. 69, 81.
12. James Bryce Papers, Ms.Bryce, 213 f. 90: Robert McGeagh to Bryce, 13 March 1886. See also Ms.Bryce, 213 f. 92: McGeagh to Bryce, 13 March 1886.
13. Asquith Papers, Ms.Asquith 36, f. 22: A. Gwynne-James to Asquith.
14. Jalland, *Liberals and Ireland*, pp. 58–9.
15. Asquith Papers, Ms Asquith 6, f. 95: Asquith to George V, 7 February 1912.
16. Asquith Papers, Ms Asquith 6, f. 95: Asquith to George V, 7 February 1912.
17. Alvin Jackson, *The Ulster Party: Irish Unionists in the House of Commons, 1884–1911* (Oxford, 1989), pp. 284–5.
18. Mansergh, *Unresolved Question*, pp. 77–8.
19. Chamberlain, *Politics from Inside*, p. 193.
20. See Jeremy Smith, *The Tories and Ireland, 1910–1914: Conservative Party Politics and the Home Rule Crisis* (Dublin, 2002).
21. See John Kendle, *Walter Long, Ireland and the Union, 1905–20* (Dublin, 1992). See also Churchill College, Cambridge, William Bull Papers, and PRONI, Bull's annotated copy of Ronald McNeill's *Ulster's Stand for Union* (London, 1922), D.3813 (which contains much correspondence relating to gun-running).
22. Additional James Craig Papers, T.3775/3/5: Charles Beresford, 1 September 1912. See also T.3775/3/7: Beresford to Craig, 10 September 1912.
23. Additional James Craig Papers, T.3775/2/1: Carson to Craig, 29 July 1911 ('as far as possible we ought also to be sure of our press').
24. Alvin Jackson, 'Unionist Myths, 1912–1985', *Past & Present*, 136 (August 1992), p. 172.
25. Jackson, *Ulster Party*, p. 316.
26. Crawford Papers, D.1700/8/17–18, f. 73: 'Record of the Home Rule Movement'.
27. Ian Beckett, 'A Note on Government Surveillance during the Curragh Incident, March 1914', *Intelligence and National Security*, 1, 3 (September 1983), pp. 435–8. It is likely that the Unionists attempted some counter-espionage.

28. Bonar Law Papers, 24/3/57: Carson, Memorandum on Strachey Proposal, 18 November 1911.
29. Gollin, *The Observer*, p. 227; Peatling, *British Opinion*, p. 129.
30. Strachey Papers, 21/1/6: Strachey to Moore, 29 October 1910.
31. Andrew Bonar Law Papers, 24/3/50: Strachey to Bonar Law, 17 November 1911.
32. Strachey Papers, 21/1/6: Strachey to Moore, 29 December 1910.
33. Bonar Law Papers, 24/3/57: Carson, Memorandum on Strachey Proposal, 18 November 1911.
34. Bonar Law Papers, 26/4/12: Long to Bonar Law, 7 June 1912.
35. Bonar Law Papers, 24/3/57: Carson, Memorandum on Strachey Proposal, 18 November 1911.
36. Strachey Papers, 2/1/12: Fisher to Strachey, 15 December 1912.
37. Bonar Law Papers, 29/2/19: G. Stewart to Bonar Law, 13 March 1913.
38. Bonar Law Papers, 29/6/27: G. Stewart to Bonar Law, 21 July 1913.
39. Jalland, *Liberals and Ireland*, p. 128.
40. Bonar Law Papers, 30/2/15: Carson to Bonar Law, 20 September 1913.
41. Bonar Law Papers, 30/3/23: Carson to Lansdowne, 11 October 1913.
42. Bonar Law Papers, 30/3/23: Carson to Lansdowne, 11 October 1913.
43. See, for example, Deaglán de Bréadún, *The Far Side of Revenge: Making Peace in Northern Ireland* (Cork, 2001), pp. 188–9. Trimble (unlike other Unionist leaders) has otherwise distanced himself from Carson's legacies.
44. Bonar Law Papers, 33/6/115: Bonar Law to Lansdowne, 22 December 1913.
45. Bonar Law Papers, 31/1/41: Balfour to Bonar Law, 18 December 1913.
46. Jalland, *Liberals and Ireland*, p. 185, where she lays a somewhat different emphasis on Asquith's motives.
47. Jalland, *Liberals and Ireland*, p. 184.
48. Jalland, *Liberals and Ireland*, p. 186.
49. Carson had clearly been in some limited negotiation with Lloyd George at this time: Additional Craig Papers, T.3775/2/6: Carson to Craig, 5 March 1914 ('I am very anxious about Monday and all you say has been very fully talked over (for hours) between Ll.G. and myself … it looks as if some kind of exclusion could be offered').
50. Jalland, *Liberals and Ireland*, p. 203.
51. Jalland, *Liberals and Ireland*, p. 205.
52. Asquith Papers, Ms.Asquith 39, f. 92: memorandum, 22 March 1914 (on the notepaper of the Archbishop of Canterbury). J. S. Sandars Papers, Ms.Eng.Hist.c766, f. 94: memorandum, 25 March 1914 (signed by Sandars) ('Bonar Law had a conversation with the Archbishop of Canterbury on the political crisis. In the result BL said … he would agree to the exclusion of the six Ulster counties *only* …'). See Jalland, *Liberals and Ireland*, p. 205, and R. J. Q Adams, *Bonar Law* (London, 1999), pp. 153, 159, for different interpretations of this episode.
53. See Ian Beckett, *The Army and the Curragh Incident, 1914* (London, 1986).
54. Beckett, *Curragh Incident*, p. 14.
55. Beckett, *Curragh Incident*, p. 218.
56. Beckett, *Curragh Incident*, p. 218.
57. L. S. Amery, *My Political Life, Volume One: England Before the Storm, 1896–1914* (London, 1953), p. 445. See also L. S. Amery, 'The Plot Against Ulster' ('Private and Confidential') (London, 1914).

58. Jalland, *The Liberals and Ireland*, p.146. See also Michael and Eleanor Brock (eds), *H. H. Asquith: Letters to Venetia Stanley* (Oxford, 1982), p.60, letter 51 (Asquith to Venetia Stanley, 23 March 1914).

59. Bonar Law Papers, 30/2/18: Churchill to Bonar Law, 21 September 1913.

60. Edward Carson Papers, D.1507/A/5/3: Constance Williams to Carson, 14 January 1914.

61. Bonar Law Papers, 31/2/58: Long to Bonar Law, 25 January 1914.

62. Fred Crawford Papers, D.1700/2/17–18, ff.96–7: 'Record of the Home Rule Movement'. See also, however, f.61 where (in describing the details of the various minor gun-running escapades) Crawford concedes the limits of his memory: 'it is very hard to keep writing consecutively as to when each event happened after the lapse of eight or nine years [he was evidently writing in *c.*1920–1]. These days were so covered with excitements and incidents that I can only remember some of them and not always in the order in which they happened.'

63. Crawford Papers, D.1700/5/17/2: 'Diary of the Gunrunning', 27 March 1914.

64. Bonar Law Papers, 32/1/65: Carson to Bonar Law, 26 March 1914. Carson used other messengers at this time: see Bonar Law Papers, 32/1/54: Carson to Bonar Law, 23 March 1914 ('if you have any message Mr Young, who brings this, will take it to me').

65. Adams, *Bonar Law*, p.160.

66. See Alvin Jackson, 'The Larne Gunrunners', in *History Ireland*, 1, 1 (1993).

67. Paul Bew, *Ideology and the Irish Question: Ulster Unionism and Irish Nationalism, 1912–1916* (Oxford, 1994), pp.13–14. Patrick Maume, *The Long Gestation: Irish Nationalist Life, 1890–1918* (Dublin, 1999), pp.215, 218.

68. Terence MacSwiney, 'The Revolutionist' (Dublin, 1914). See Francis J. Costello, *Enduring the Most: The Life and Death of Terence MacSwiney* (Dingle, 1995).

69. Stephen Gwynn, *John Redmond's Last Years* (London, 1919), p.92.

70. See *Report of the Royal Commission into the Circumstances connected with the Landing of Arms at Howth on 26 July 1914*, Cd.7631 (London, 1914); see also F. X. Martin (ed.), *The Irish Volunteers, 1913–15* (Dublin, 1963), p.33.

71. Bonar Law Papers, 32/3/17: Wicks to Bonar Law, 8 May 1914.

72. Asquith Papers, Ms.Asquith 7, f.131: Asquith to George V, 18 June 1914 ('it was agreed that the excluded area should be in the hands of an imperial minister responsible to the Crown and the Imperial Parliament').

73. Adams, *Bonar Law*, pp.163–4.

74. Denis Gwynn, *The Life of John Redmond* (London, 1932), pp.330, 332.

75. Brock (ed.), *Asquith Letters*, p.105, letter 97 (Asquith to Venetia Stanley, 15 July 1914).

76. Bonar Law Papers, 39/4/43: Memorandum of a Discussion with Murray and Asquith, 17 July 1914.

77. Asquith Papers, Ms.Asquith 7, f.143: Asquith to George V, 17 July 1914.

78. Bonar Law Papers, 39/4/44: 'Conference at Buckingham Palace', 21 July 1914.

79. Gwynn, *Life of John Redmond*, p.341.

80. Bonar Law Papers, 39/4/44: 'Conference at Buckingham Palace', 21 July 1914.

81. Bonar Law Papers, 39/4/44: 'Conference at Buckingham Palace', 21 July 1914.

82. Gwynn, *John Redmond's Last Years*, p.101.

83. CJ/3/1: 'Memorandum by Secretary of State on Round Table Conference', April 1969.

84. Jalland, *The Liberals and Ireland*, p. 254.

85. Bonar Law Papers, 33/1/28: Milner to Bonar Law, 15 July 1914.

86. Bonar Law Papers, 33/1/28: Milner to Bonar Law, 15 July 1914.

87. Bonar Law Papers, 33/1/28: Milner to Bonar Law, 15 July 1914.

88. Bonar Law Papers, 33/1/28: Milner to Bonar Law, 15 July 1914. The evidence for Unionist 'espionage' is inconclusive, but see, for example, Milner Papers, dep. 13, f. 59: Milner to Oliver, 30 November 1913 ('what is wanted is some good hard but very unobtrusive "mole" work, like the late J. H. Hofmeyr's'). For other possible evidence of 'mole' work, see Carson Papers, D.1507/A/5/3: Constance Williams to Carson, 14 January 1914.

89. Additional Craig Papers, T.3775/10/5: Memorandum of a Conversation between King George V and James Craig, 14 July 1914.

90. Jalland, *The Liberals and Ireland*, p. 219; Adams, *Bonar Law*, p. 113.

## Chapter 8 The Jaws of Victory, 1914–16

1. Lloyd George Papers, 14/2/35: T. P. O'Connor, 'Memorandum', 13 June 1916.

2. See Maume's discussion of the predominant themes within the literature on Redmondism: Patrick Maume, *The Long Gestation: Irish Nationalist Life, 1891–1918* (Dublin, 1999), pp. 215–18.

3. Nicholas Mansergh, *The Unresolved Question: The Anglo-Irish Settlement and Its Undoing, 1912–72* (New Haven and London, 1991), p. 85.

4. CO.904/94: Inspector Generals' Monthly Report for September 1914: 'After the King had given his assent to the [Home Rule] Bill, His Majesty's picture was greeted with disrespect at the picture houses and music halls at Belfast, and at several Protestant churches members of the congregation walked out during Divine Service when the National Anthem was played.' Compare CAB 6/77: Lord FitzAlan to Craig, 14 December 1921, referring to a Unionist public dinner in Belfast where local dignitaries snubbed the loyal toast. George V 'was a good deal moved by it – and agitated'.

5. Stephen Gwynn, *John Redmond's Last Years* (London, 1919), pp. 133–4; Denis Gwynn, *The Life of John Redmond* (London, 1932), pp. 356–7.

6. See, for example, Redmond's own assessment: Asquith Papers, Ms.Asquith, 36, f. 62: Redmond to Asquith, 4 August 1914.

7. Gwynn, *Redmond's Last Years*, pp. 154–5; Gwynn, *Life of Redmond*, pp. 391–2.

8. Gwynn, *Redmond's Last Years*, pp. 162ff. See also Asquith Papers, Ms.Asquith, 36 f. 73: Redmond to Asquith, 8 August 1914. Ms.Asquith, 36, f. 89: Redmond to Asquith, 7 June 1915. Ms.Asquith 41, f. 172: Redmond to Asquith, 12 November 1914, enclosing a memorandum (f. 173) on recruiting. Ms.Asquith 41, f. 185: Redmond to Asquith, 11 February 1915, enclosing a memorandum (f. 186) on the possible recruitment of the National Volunteers for home defence.

9. Redmond Papers, 15215/2: T. P. O'Connor to Redmond, 27 February 1915.

10. Asquith Papers, Ms.Asquith 36, f. 89: Redmond to Asquith, 7 June 1915. Gwynn, *Redmond's Last Years*, p. 168; Gwynn, *Life of Redmond*, pp. 410–11.

11. Asquith Papers, Ms.Asquith 36, f. 73: Redmond to Asquith, 8 August 1914. Gwynn, *Redmond's Last Years*, p. 168.

12. Michael Laffan, *The Partition of Ireland, 1911–1925* (Dundalk, 1983); Gwynn, *Life of Redmond*, p. 385.

13. Asquith Papers, Ms.Asquith 41, f. 172: Redmond to Asquith, 12 November 1914. Gwynn, *Redmond's Last Years*, p. 169.

14. Asquith Papers, Ms.Asquith 36, f.89: Redmond to Asquith, 7 June 1915.

15. Gwynn, *Redmond's Last Years*, p.172. See also Lloyd George Papers, D.14/1/3: T. P. Gill to Asquith (copy), 20 May 1916.

16. Gwynn, *Life of Redmond*, pp.369–70.

17. Gwynn, *Life of Redmond*, p.394. Redmond Papers, 15165/4: Asquith to Redmond, 30 September 1914.

18. Gwynn, *Life of Redmond*, p.394.

19. Redmond Papers, 15165/5: Nathan to Redmond, 18 May 1915, Asquith to Redmond, 24 May 1915.

20. Asquith Papers, Ms.Asquith 36, f.89: Redmond to Asquith, 7 June 1915.

21. Though see Asquith Papers, Ms.Asquith 36, f.89: Redmond to Asquith, 7 June 1915.

22. Gwynn, *John Redmond's Last Years*, p.192.

23. See, *inter alia*, Henry Hanna, *The Pals at Suvla Bay, Being a Record of 'D' Company, 7th Royal Dublin Fusiliers* (Dublin, 1916).

24. Michael Laffan, *The Resurrection of Ireland: The Sinn Fein Party, 1916–23* (Cambridge, 1999), p.33.

25. See Asquith Papers, Ms.Asquith 43, f.149: P. H. Pearse to Margaret Pearse, 1 May 1916 (copy): 'I understand that the German expedition, which I was counting on, set sail but was defeated by the British ...'.

26. Laffan, *Resurrection of Ireland*, p.44.

27. J. J. Lee, *Ireland 1912–1985: Politics and Society* (Cambridge, 1989), p.36.

28. Ruth Dudley Edwards, *Patrick Pearse: The Triumph of Failure* (London, 1977), p.277.

29. F. S. L. Lyons, *John Dillon: A Biography* (London, 1968), p.379; Stephen Gwynn (ed.), *The Anvil of War: Letters between F. S. Oliver and his Brother, 1914–1918* (London, 1936), p.145. Oliver believed (p.143) that the suppression of the rising had strong implications for labour unrest in Britain: 'In many ways the incident, regrettable as it is, has been beneficial. The miners of South Wales and the workmen on the Clyde, who have remained in a state of chronic mutiny ever since the beginning of the war and have been levying blackmail on the whole community, have always banked upon the belief that no British government would ever order the shooting down wholesale of any British citizens. This pleasant idea has been entirely dispelled by the events in Dublin.'

30. Gwynn, *Life of Redmond*, p.490.

31. Lyons, *Dillon*, p.373. Redmond Papers, 15182/22: Dillon to Redmond, 30 April 1916.

32. Redmond Papers, 15182/22: Dillon to Redmond, 7 May 1916.

33. Lyons, *Dillon*, pp.381–2.

34. Lyons, *Dillon*, p.383.

35. D. G. Boyce, *Nationalism in Ireland*, 2nd edition (London, 1991), p.288.

36. Lyons, *Dillon*, p.383.

37. Strong treatments of the episode are to be found in D. G. Boyce, 'British Conservative Opinion, the Ulster Question and the Partition of Ireland, 1912–21', *Irish Historical Studies*, xvii (1970); D. G. Boyce, 'How to Settle the Irish Question: Lloyd George and Ireland, 1916–21' in A. J. P. Taylor (ed.), *Lloyd George: Twelve Essays* (London, 1971); D. G. Boyce, 'British Opinion, Ireland and the War, 1916–18', *Historical Journal*, 17, 3 (1974); Bentley Gilbert, *David Lloyd George, A*

*Political Life: Organiser of Victory, 1912–16* (London, 1992); John Kendle, *Ireland and the Federal Solution: The Debate over the United Kingdom Constitution, 1870–1921* (Kingston and Montreal, 1989); John Kendle, *Walter Long, Ireland and the Union, 1905–1920* (Dublin, 1992).

38. Gwynn, *Life of Redmond*, p. 493.
39. Asquith Papers, Ms.Asquith 16, f. 207: Austen Chamberlain to Asquith, 23 June 1916. Asquith Papers, Ms.Asquith 37, f. 60: Austen Chamberlain to Asquith, 22 June 1916.
40. Boyce, 'How to Settle the Irish Question', pp. 137–8.
41. Asquith Papers, Ms.Asquith 37, f. 60: Austen Chamberlain to Asquith, 22 June 1916.
42. Gilbert, *Lloyd George*, p. 322.
43. Lyons, *Dillon*, p. 386; Laffan, *Resurrection of Ireland*, p. 58.
44. Gilbert, *Lloyd George*, p. 322. Lloyd George Papers, D.14/1/9: Long to Lloyd George, 23 May 1916.
45. Gilbert, *Lloyd George*, p. 322–4. Lloyd George Papers, D.14/1/26: Midleton to Asquith (copy), 26 May 1916.
46. Asquith Papers, Ms.Asquith 39, f. 258: 'Headings of a Settlement as to the Government of Ireland', n.d. (but May–June, 1916).
47. Edward Carson Papers, D.1507/A/17/7: Lloyd George to Carson, 3 June 1916.
48. Carson Papers, D.1507/A/17/4: Draft Amendments to the Government of Ireland Act [June 1916?]. Gwynn, *Life of Redmond*, p. 517.
49. Carson Papers, D.1507/A/17/13: A. W. Samuels to Carson, 14 June 1916.
50. There is a copy of this note in CAB 9Z/5/1: Lloyd George to Carson, 29 May 1916.
51. Boyce, 'British Opinion, Ireland and the War', p. 580.
52. Patrick Buckland, *Irish Unionism II: Ulster Unionism and the Origins of Northern Ireland, 1886–1922* (Dublin, 1973), p. 106.
53. Buckland, *Irish Unionism II*, pp. 106–7.
54. Lyons, *Dillon*, p. 393.
55. Redmond Papers, 15165/2: Redmond to Asquith, 2 October 1909 (copy).
56. Eamon Phoenix, *Northern Nationalism: Nationalist Politics, Partition, and the Catholic Minority in Northern Ireland, 1890–1940* (Belfast, 1994), p. 33. Redmond Papers, 15181/3: Devlin to Redmond, 3 June 1916.
57. Lloyd George Papers, 14/3/39: Devlin to Lloyd George, 26 June 1916.
58. Gwynn, *Life of Redmond*, p. 517.
59. Boyce, 'British Opinion, Ireland and the War', p. 581.
60. Kendle, *Walter Long*, p. 99.
61. Kendle, *Walter Long*, pp. 102–3.
62. Kendle, *Walter Long*, p. 109; Gilbert, *Lloyd George*, pp. 328–9. See also Asquith Papers, Ms.Asquith 16, f. 185: Long to Asquith, 8 June 1916; f. 191: Long to Asquith, 12 June 1916; f. 193: Long to Asquith, 13 June 1916; f. 195: Long to Asquith, 11 June 1916. Lloyd George Papers, 14/2/28: Long to Lloyd George, 11 June 1916.
63. Kendle, *Walter Long*, p. 111. See also, for example, George Cave Papers, Add.Ms. 62461: Walter Long, Memoranda 'A' and 'B', 15 June 1916.
64. Selborne Papers, dep. 6, f. 163: Lord Salisbury, 'Memorandum on Ireland for the Unionist Members of the Cabinet'.
65. Gwynn, *Redmond's Last Years*, p. 235.

66. Carson Papers, D.1507/A/18/13: W. Martin to Carson, 13 July 1916. Carson Papers, D.1507/A/18/15: Secretary, Cavan Unionists, to Carson, 13 July 1916. See also Alvin Jackson, *Colonel Edward Saunderson: Land and Loyalty in Victorian Ireland* (Oxford, 1995), pp. 228–31.
67. Lyons, *Dillon*, pp. 402–3.
68. Richard Murphy and John Kendle have persuasively sought to provide a counter-argument: Murphy, 'Walter Long and the Making of the Government of Ireland Act, 1920', *Irish Historical Studies*, xxv, 97 (May 1986); Kendle, *Walter Long*. See also Alvin Jackson, 'Walter Long, 1st Viscount Long of Wraxall' in the *New Dictionary of National Biography* (Oxford, forthcoming).
69. John Vincent (ed.), *The Crawford Papers: The Journals of David Lindsay, 27th Earl of Crawford and 10th Earl of Balcarres, 1871–1940* (Manchester, 1984), p. 225.
70. Lloyd George Papers, 14/1/37: Long to Lloyd George, 29 May 1916.
71. Wilfrid Spender Papers, D.1295/17/2: Lady Spender Diary, 19 June 1916.
72. Asquith Papers, Ms.Asquith 16, f. 198: Selborne to Asquith, 16 June 1916.
73. Spender Papers, D.1295/17/2: Lady Spender Diary, 29 June 1916.
74. Austen Chamberlain, *Politics from Inside: An Epistolary Chronicle, 1906–14* (London, 1936), p. 387.
75. Vincent, *Crawford Papers*, p. 214.
76. Kendle, *Ireland and the Federal Solution*, p. 192.
77. Lloyd George Papers, 14/3/21: Lloyd George to Asquith, 20 June 1916 (copy).
78. Gwynn (ed.), *Anvil of War*, p. 149.
79. Kendle, *Walter Long*, p. 115.
80. Kendle, *Walter Long*, p. 115.
81. Asquith Papers, Ms.Asquith 8, f. 171: Asquith to George V, 27 June 1916.
82. Kendle, *Walter Long*, p. 125.
83. Kendle, *Walter Long*, pp. 125–6.
84. Asquith Papers, Ms.Asquith 37, f. 107: Redmond to Asquith, 23 July 1916.
85. Kendle, *Walter Long*, p. 105.
86. Kendle, *Walter Long*, pp. 127–9.
87. See Asquith Papers, Ms.Asquith 36, f. 89: Redmond to Asquith, 7 June 1915. See also Ms.Asquith 36, f. 103: Redmond to Asquith, 10 June 1915.
88. Kendle, *Walter Long*, p. 130.
89. R. J. Q. Adams, *Bonar Law* (London, 1999), p. 219.
90. Gwynn, *Redmond's Last Years*, p. 234.
91. Lyons, *Dillon*, pp. 380–2.
92. Laffan, *Resurrection of Ireland*, p. 61.
93. Gwynn, *Redmond's Last Years*, p. 212.
94. Paul Bew, *Ideology and the Irish Question: Ulster Unionism and Irish Nationalism, 1912–16* (Oxford, 1994), pp. 144–52.
95. Maume, *The Long Gestation*, p. 171.
96. Alan O'Day, *Irish Home Rule, 1867–1921* (Manchester, 1998), pp. 281, 283.
97. Lee, *Ireland, 1912–1985*, p. 36.
98. Lyons, *Dillon*, p. 383.
99. Terence MacSwiney, *The Revolutionist* (Dublin, 1914).

**Chapter 9 Changing the Question, 1916–20**

1. John Kendle, *Ireland and the Federal Constitution: The Debate over the United Kingdom Constitution, 1870–1921* (Kingston and Montreal, 1989), p. 238.

2. See John Hutchinson, *The Dynamics of Cultural Nationalism: The Gaelic Revival and the Creation of the Irish Nation State* (London, 1989).

3. 'Pacificus' [F. S. Oliver], *Federalism and Home Rule* (London, 1910), dedication.

4. Patrick Maume, *The Long Gestation: Irish Nationalist Life, 1891–1918* (Dublin, 1999), p. 153.

5. Denis Gywnn, *The Life of John Redmond* (London, 1932), pp. 547–9.

6. Trevor West, *Horace Plunkett, Cooperation and Politics: An Irish Life* (Gerrard's Cross, 1986), p. 158.

7. F. S. Oliver, *The Alternatives to Civil War* (London, 1913), p. 58.

8. Asquith Papers, Ms.Asquith 39, f. 155, 'Suggestions for a Settlement of the Irish Question, 6 April 1914'.

9. L. S. Amery, *My Political Life, Volume Two: War and Peace, 1914–1929* (London, 1953), pp. 112–13.

10. Gwynn, *Life of Redmond*, pp. 546–7. See also Asquith Papers, Ms.Asquith, 37, f. 140: Crewe to Asquith, 16 May 1917.

11. William O'Brien, *The Downfall of Parliamentarianism: A Retrospect for the Accounting Day* (Dublin, 1918), p. 48.

12. See R. B. McDowell, *The Irish Convention, 1917–18* (London, 1970).

13. The Unionists were also given the right to nominate one of the Assistant Secretaries to the convention, and chose Thomas Moles: UUC Papers, D.1327/2/17: Minute Book of the Ulster Unionist Delegation to the Convention, 26 July 1917, 20 August 1918. McDowell, *Irish Convention*, pp. 104–5.

14. McDowell, *Irish Convention*, pp. 80–2.

15. Stephen Gwynn, *John Redmond's Last Years* (London, 1919), p. 308.

16. For the history of this proposal, and for Londonderry's relations with the southern Unionist delegation, see Lord Londonderry Papers, D.3077/2/7/14: Midleton to Londonderry, 25 October 1917. See also D.3099/2/7/15, Londonderry to Fingall (copy), 26 November 1917; D.3099/2/7/16, Fingall to Londonderry, 28 November 1917; D.3099/2/7/18, Midleton to Londonderry, 19 December 1917; D.3099/2/7/28, Londonderry to Lloyd George, 13 August 1918: 'Home Rule on the lines of what is known as federalism can be given to Ireland as a portion of a much larger system… dominion Home Rule cannot be granted for obvious reasons.'

17. Earl of Midleton, *Records and Reactions, 1856–1939* (London, 1939), p. 242.

18. Stephen Gwynn (ed.), *The Anvil of War: Letters Between F. S. Oliver and His Brother, 1914–1918* (London, 1936), pp. 297–8. McDowell, *Irish Convention*, p. 72.

19. West, *Horace Plunkett*, p. 170.

20. Midleton, *Records and Reactions*, p. 242. See also the views of Lord Granard, as reported privately to Asquith: Ms.Asquith, 37, f. 145, Granard to Asquith, 2 October 1917: Ulster Unionists 'are prepared to accept an Irish Parliament of King, Lords or Senate, and Commons'.

21. Bonar Law Papers, 32/3/31: Midleton to Bonar Law, 13 April 1914.

22. McDowell, *Irish Convention*, p. 103. The Ulster Unionists opposed not 'any person connected with the government of Ireland, or the administration of the law there', but rather any 'person… who is connected with the government of Ireland in the administration of the law' (UUC Papers, D.1327/2/17: Minute Book of the Ulster Unionist Delegation to the Convention, 24 July 1917).

23. McDowell, *Irish Convention*, pp. 163–4.

24. Patrick Buckland, *Irish Unionism I: The Anglo-Irish and the New Ireland, 1885–1922* (Dublin, 1973), p. 150.
25. Midleton, *Records and Reactions*, pp. 244–5.
26. West, *Horace Plunkett*, p. 202.
27. West, *Horace Plunkett*, p. 180.
28. Redmond Papers, 15221: Plunkett to Redmond, 25 August 1917.
29. Asquith Papers, Ms.Asquith 37, f. 151: Granard to Asquith, 20 October 1917.
30. Asquith Papers, Ms.Asquith 37, f. 169: Granard to Asquith, 23 November 1917.
31. West, *Horace Plunkett*, p. 167. See also Asquith Papers, Ms.Asquith, 37, f. 161: Granard to Asquith, 14 November 1917, describing a row over these letters and remarking that 'if we arrive at a settlement it will be a great achievement, but it will be entirely owing to Hopwood and not to the Chairman'. Plunkett's letters may be read in several archives, but see, for example, Bryce Papers, Mss.Bryce 216, ff. 38, 48, 51, 52, 67: Plunkett to Bryce, different dates from 21 November 1917 to 13 June 1918.
32. Midleton, *Records and Reactions*, p. 242.
33. Maume, *The Long Gestation*, pp. 215ff.
34. See Chapter 2.
35. See, for example, John Kendle, *Ireland and the Federal Solution: The Debate over the United Kingdom Constitution, 1870–1921* (Kingston and Montreal, 1989); D. G. Boyce and J. O. Stubbs, 'F. S. Oliver, Lord Selborne and Federalism', *Journal of Imperial and Commonwealth History*, 5, 1 (October 1976); John Kendle, 'Federalism and the Irish Problem in 1918', *History*, 56, 187 (June 1971).
36. Bonar Law Papers, 27/1/47: F. S. Oliver, Memorandum on the Home Rule Bill [*c*.August 1912].
37. For a copy of this see Asquith Papers, Ms.Asquith 39, f. 155: 'Suggestions for a Settlement of the Irish Question'. For Redmond's reaction, see Ms.Asquith 39, f. 167: Redmond to Asquith, 5 May 1914: 'the proposals in this document are absolutely unacceptable by us, and would make the Home Rule Bill intolerable to our people'. Bonar Law Papers, 32/2/26: Carson to Bonar Law, 7 April 1914. Bonar Law Papers, 32/3/9: Grigg to Bonar Law, 4 May 1914.
38. Milner Papers, dep. 84: diary for 11 May 1914.
39. Kendle, *Ireland and the Federal Solution*, pp. 201–2.
40. Kendle, *Ireland and the Federal Solution*, pp. 179–81.
41. F. S. Oliver, *Ireland and the Imperial Conference: Is there a Way to a Settlement?* (London, 1917), pp. 8–10.
42. Lord Selborne and F. S. Oliver, *Suggestions for the Better Government of the United Kingdom* (London, 1917), p. 26.
43. Selborne and Oliver, *Suggestions*, p. 18.
44. Boyce and Stubbs, 'F. S. Oliver, Lord Selborne and Federalism', p. 70. West, *Plunkett*, p. 124.
45. McDowell, *Irish Convention*, p. 126.
46. Kendle, *Ireland and the Federal Solution*, p. 192.
47. Selborne and Oliver, *Suggestions*, pp. 5–6.
48. Kendle, *Ireland and the Federal Solution*, p. 189; Gwynn (ed.), *Anvil of War*, p. 202 (for example).
49. Gwynn (ed.), *Anvil of War*, p. 298.
50. F. S. Oliver, *Ulster and a Federal Settlement* (1918), pp. 14, 19.

51. Gwynn (ed.), *Anvil of War*, pp. 318–19.
52. Kendle, *Ireland and the Federal Solution*, p. 191.
53. Kendle, *Ireland and the Federal Solution*, pp. 191–2.
54. Boyce and Stubbs, 'F. S. Oliver, Lord Selborne and Federalism', pp. 75–6.
55. Kendle, *Ireland and the Federal Solution*, pp. 200–1.
56. Kendle, *Ireland and the Federal Solution*, p. 207.
57. Kendle, *Ireland and the Federal Solution*, p. 218.
58. Boyce and Stubbs, 'F. S. Oliver, Lord Selborne and Federalism', p. 76.
59. Kendle, *Ireland and the Federal Solution*, pp. 217–18.
60. Kendle, *Ireland and the Federal Solution*, p. 224.
61. Boyce and Stubbs, 'F. S. Oliver, Lord Selborne and Federalism', pp. 75–6.
62. Boyce and Stubbs, 'F. S. Oliver, Lord Selborne and Federalism', p. 75.
63. Boyce and Stubbs, 'F. S. Oliver, Lord Selborne and Federalism', p. 67.
64. Boyce and Stubbs, 'F. S. Oliver, Lord Selborne and Federalism', p. 73.
65. Kendle, *Ireland and the Federal Solution*, pp. 211–12.
66. John Kendle, *Walter Long, Ireland and the Union, 1905–20* (Dublin, 1992), p. 226. Nicholas Mansergh, *The Unresolved Question: The Anglo-Irish Settlement and Its Undoing, 1912–72* (New Haven and London, 1991), pp. 122ff.
67. Kendle, *Ireland and the Federal Solution*, p. 229.
68. See Gary Peatling, *British Opinion and Irish Self-government, 1865–1925* (Dublin, 2001), pp. 152–5.
69. For a pioneering assessment of Long's pragmatism see Richard Murphy, 'Walter Long and the Making of the Government of Ireland Act, 1919–20', *Irish Historical Studies*, xxv, 97 (May 1986).
70. Peatling, *British Opinion*, p. 154.
71. Kendle, *Walter Long*, p. 186.
72. West, *Horace Plunkett*, p. 202.
73. Kendle, *Walter Long*, p. 185.
74. Mansergh, *The Unresolved Question*, p. 128.
75. Mansergh, *The Unresolved Question*, p. 128.
76. Kendle, *Walter Long*, p. 188.
77. Kendle, *Walter Long*, p. 191.
78. For the early institutional consolidation of the Northern Ireland state, see Bryan Follis, *A State under Siege: The Establishment of Northern Ireland, 1920–25* (Oxford, 1995).
79. Kendle, *Ireland and the Federal Solution*, p. 233.
80. Maume, *Long Gestation*, pp. 216–17.
81. Maume, *Long Gestation*, pp. 218–19.
82. Maurice Manning, *James Dillon: A Biography* (Dublin, 1999).
83. Garret FitzGerald, *All in a Life: An Autobiography* (Dublin, 1992), p. 77.

## Chapter 10 'A Gritty Sort of Prod Baroque', 1920–72

The title of the chapter is taken from Tom Paulin, 'Off the Back of a Lorry', *Liberty Tree* (London, 1983).

1. CJ 3/39: Lord Grey to James Callaghan, 2 February 1969.
2. Nicholas Mansergh, *The Government of Northern Ireland: A Study in Devolution* (London, 1936), pp. 321–2; R. J. Lawrence, *The Government of Northern Ireland: Public Finance and Public Services, 1921–64* (Oxford, 1965), p. 183. See also Alan J.

Ward, *The Irish Constitutional Tradition: Responsible Government and Modern Ireland, 1782–1992* (Dublin, 1992), p. 133.

3. Mansergh, *Government of Northern Ireland*, p. 16.
4. The early development of this financial relationship may be explored in a number of works including Bryan Follis, *A State under Siege: The Establishment of Northern Ireland, 1920–1925* (Oxford, 1995); Patrick Buckland, *The Factory of Grievances: Devolved Government in Northern Ireland, 1921–39* (Dublin, 1979); Derek Birrell and Alan Murie, *Policy and Government in Northern Ireland: Lessons of Devolution* (Dublin, 1980); Lawrence, *Government of Northern Ireland*.
5. For Colwyn, see the papers in CAB 6/83 and Follis, *State under Siege*, pp. 135–47. See also CAB 6/92: Baldwin to Craig, 22 November 1922.
6. CAB 6/92: Horne to Craig, 29 May 1922.
7. Mansergh, *Government of Northern Ireland*, p. 222.
8. Patrick Shea, *Voices and the Sound of Drums: An Irish Autobiography* (Belfast, 1981), pp. 152–3.
9. Terence O'Neill, *The Autobiography of Terence O'Neill, Prime Minister of Northern Ireland 1963–1969* (London, 1972), pp. 38–9.
10. Quoted in Patrick Buckland, *A History of Northern Ireland* (Dublin, 1981), p. 23.
11. Thomas Wilson, *Ulster: Conflict and Consent* (Oxford, 1989), p. 86.
12. See CAB 9Z/3/2: L. S. Amery to Craig, 8 October 1924.
13. Nicholas Mansergh, *The Unresolved Question: The Anglo-Irish Settlement and its Undoing, 1912–72* (New Haven and London, 1991), p. 130. See also CAB 9Z/3/2: L. S. Amery to Craig, 4 October 1924.
14. CAB 9Z/3/1: C. C. Craig to James Craig, 5 December 1921.
15. CAB 9Z/1/1: Wilfrid Spender to General Ricardo, 24 December 1921.
16. CAB 9Z/3/1: James Craig to Austen Chamberlain, 2 January 1922 ('Withheld').
17. CAB 9Z/1/1: Strachey to Craig, 2 November 1921.
18. CAB 9Z/1/1: J. F. A. Simms to Craig, 14 January 1922; T. Elliott to Craig, 14 January 1922.
19. CAB 9Z/1/1: Spender to Revd J. R. Mearn, 5 April 1923.
20. CAB 9Z/6: Richard Best, Memorandum of Boundary Conference, 1–2 February 1924.
21. CAB 9Z/11/1: D. D. Reid to Craig, 5 June 1924. See also CAB 6/97: Memorandum on Mr Justice Richard Feetham, September 1924.
22. CAB 9Z/11/1: D. D. Reid to Craig, 5 June 1924.
23. CAB 9Z/2/2: D. D. Reid to Craig, 16 September 1925.
24. CAB 9Z/2/2: Craig to Lord Londonderry, 24 September 1925.
25. CAB 9Z/2/2: D. D. Reid to Craig, 7 July 1925.
26. R. J. Lynn Papers, D.3480/59/58: Fisher to Lynn, 7 November 1925.
27. CAB 9Z/2/2: D. D. Reid to Craig, 7 November 1925.
28. CAB 6/109: 'Summary of Statements Made at Meetings between the Prime Minister and Representatives of the Governments of the Irish Free State and Northern Ireland at Chequers on the Morning of Sunday, 29 November 1925'. On this occasion Kevin O'Higgins complained that 'Professor MacNeill's attitude of giving agreement in the abstract and yet fighting his colleagues section by section was incomprehensible to his colleague on the Executive Council.'
29. There is an original copy of the agreement in CAB 9Z/11/4 (Articles of Agreement for a Treaty, 3 December 1925).

30. Lynn Papers, D.3480/59/58: Fisher to Lynn, 7 November 1925.
31. Lynn Papers, D.3480/59/58: Fisher to Lynn, 7 November 1925.
32. Lynn Papers, D.3480/59/58: Fisher to Lynn, 11 November 1925.
33. Lynn Papers, D.3480/59/58: Fisher to Lynn, 8 December 1925.
34. Lynn Papers, D.3480/59/58: Fisher to Lynn, 8 December 1925. See also CAB 9Z/11/4: Fisher to Craig, 8 December 1925.
35. Lawrence, *Government of Northern Ireland*, p.61.
36. It was widely believed in the Unionist establishment that Chamberlain had caved in too quickly to de Valera, and that de Valera would have been content to see two of the 'Treaty Ports' of 1921 remain in British hands. See Douglas Savory Papers, D.3015/1A/7/5/2: Spender to Savory, 16 February 1941, 21 February 1941 and 1 March 1941.
37. Deirdre McMahon, *Republicans and Imperialists: Anglo-Irish Relations in the 1930s* (New Haven, 1984), pp.278–9.
38. John Bowman, *De Valera and the Ulster Question, 1917–1973* (Oxford, 1982), p.228.
39. Bowman, *De Valera*, p.220.
40. Bowman, *De Valera*, p.227.
41. Bowman, *De Valera*, p.228.
42. Bowman, *De Valera*, p.229.
43. Bowman, *De Valera*, p.228.
44. Additional Craig Papers, T.3775/20/6: Craig to Chamberlain, 27 June 1940 (draft telegram). It is clear from this that the well-known wording of Craig's outburst was not spontaneous, but was in fact very carefully calculated.
45. Brian Barton, *Brookeborough: The Making of a Prime Minister* (Belfast, 1988), p.161.
46. Bowman, *De Valera*, p.237.
47. Bowman, *De Valera*, pp.246–7.
48. The debate within the Ulster Unionist Party on the issue of dominion status may be followed in CAB 9J/53/2.
49. See CAB 9B/267/3, especially C. R. Attlee to Brooke, 21 March 1949: 'the information I have given you about the contents of the proposed Ireland Bill is of course confidential and you will appreciate how awkward it would be if any question of privilege were to be raised in Parliament'. See also CAB 9B/267/6, J. Chuter-Ede to Brooke, 25 April 1949, enclosing a copy of the draft Ireland Bill, and Brooke to Attlee and other cabinet ministers and Tory leaders, 3 June 1949, offering thanks for support over the bill. See also C. R. Attlee Papers, Mss.Attlee dep.82, for evidence of the extent to which the Stormont government was influencing the briefing papers that Labour ministers were receiving on the Ireland Bill: see f.150, NSM to Helsby, 6 May 1949; f.182, Ministerial briefing notes on the Ireland Bill; ff.256–8, 'Ireland Bill: Partition Question'; f.311, J. Chuter-Ede to Attlee, 9 May 1949.
50. Wilson, *Ulster: Conflict and Consent*, p.65.
51. Birrell and Murie, *Policy and Government*, p.22.
52. For a starting point, see John Whyte, 'How Much Discrimination was There under the Unionist Regime, 1921–68?', in Tom Gallagher and James O'Connell (eds), *Contemporary Irish Studies* (Manchester, 1983). See also the valuable, if inevitably dated, *Interpreting Northern Ireland* (Oxford 1990) by the same author.
53. Denis P. Barritt and Charles Carter, *The Northern Ireland Problem: A Study in Group Relations* (Oxford, 1962), pp.93–108.

54. For more detailed studies of the Catholic community in Northern Ireland see Marianne Elliott, *The Catholics of Ulster: A History* (London, 2000); Brendan Lynn, *Holding the Ground: The Nationalist Party in Northern Ireland, 1945–72* (Aldershot, 1997); Eamon Phoenix, *Northern Nationalism: Nationalist Politics, Partition and the Catholic Minority in Northern Ireland, 1890–1940* (Belfast, 1994); Oliver Rafferty, *Catholicism in Ulster, 1603–1983: An Interpretative History* (Dublin, 1994).

55. Phoenix, *Northern Nationalism*, pp. 390–99.

56. G. B. Newe's important archive is preserved in PRONI as their D.3687.

57. Though see the stimulating argument offered by Marc Mulholland, *The Longest War: Northern Ireland's Troubled History* (Oxford, 2002), pp. 41–45.

58. Conn McCluskey, *Up off their Knees* (Galway, 1989), p. 44. PREM 13/2847: Position Paper, October 1968.

59. See Follis, *A State under Siege*. See also Michael Farrell, *Arming the Protestants: The Formation of the Ulster Special Constabulary and the Royal Ulster Constabulary, 1920–27* (London, 1983).

60. Phoenix, *Northern Nationalism*, pp. 392–3, 397.

61. For this episode see, for example, Toby Harnden, *'Bandit Country': The IRA and South Armagh* (London, 1999), pp. 99–101.

62. Follis, *A State under Siege*, pp. 122–3.

63. It is generally accepted that a particular problem arose from the personality of the first Minister of Home Affairs, the limited and partisan R. Dawson Bates. Even a strongly Unionist figure like Sir Henry Wilson was critical: see Additional Craig Papers, T.3775/17/2: Henry Wilson to Craig, 19 March 1922.

64. See Additional Craig Papers, T.3775/15/4, for an original copy of the first Craig–Collins pact, 21 January 1922. See CAB 6/109 for drafts of 'Heads of Agreement Between the Provisional Government and the Government of Northern Ireland, 30 March 1922', where it is clear that the striking and resonant opening sentence 'Peace is today declared' was only arrived at after some effort (the original version, 'Peace between Southern and Northern Ireland is today ratified', lacked the impact of the revision).

65. Alvin Jackson, *The Ulster Party: Irish Unionists in the House of Commons, 1884–1911* (Oxford, 1989), pp. 248–53.

66. Shea, *Voices and the Sound of Drums*, pp. 112–13.

67. Shea, *Voices and the Sound of Drums*, p. 142.

68. Wilson, *Ulster: Conflict and Consent*, p. 73.

69. Wilson, *Ulster: Conflict and Consent*, p. 74.

70. Barton, *Brookeborough*, p. 78.

71. Barton, *Brookeborough*, p. 80.

72. Barton, *Brookeborough*, pp. 81–9.

73. Barton, *Brookeborough*, p. 87.

74. Maurice Hayes, *Minority Verdict: Experiences of a Catholic Public Servant* (Belfast, 1995), p. 64.

75. Barton, *Brookeborough*, p. 89. See also Henry Patterson, 'Party versus Order: Ulster Unionism and the Flags and Emblems Act', *Contemporary British History*, 13, 4 (Winter 1999), p. 122.

76. See Newe Papers, D.3687/1/7/8: Newe to Bishop A. H. Butler, 3 September 1973: '[Brooke] was everything you said about him – a man of essential charm, undoubted courage and firm, almost too firm, conviction, but of limited political

vision ... [in 1958] we urged him to enlarge his political vision then and reach out to involve the minority more and more in running the show. He claimed he was very ready to do just that but wanted the Catholic leadership ... to publicly accept and recognise the constitution of Northern Ireland, and wanted us to persuade the then Dublin government to do just that. I always felt that Basil could have done quietly and effectively over his long years as Prime Minister all that Terence O'Neill tried to do so quickly and ineffectively in five or six years. Of course "our side" would have had to be ready to "play ball" and that wasn't evident.'

77. Marc Mulholland, *Northern Ireland at the Crossroads: Ulster Unionism in the O'Neill Years, 1960–69* (London, 2000), p. 14.

78. Mulholland, *Northern Ireland at the Crossroads*, p. 14.

79. Mansergh, *Government of Northern Ireland*, p. 248.

80. Feargal Cochrane, '"Meddling at the Crossroad": The Decline and Fall of Terence O'Neill within the Unionist Community', in Richard English and Graham Walker (eds), *Unionism in Modern Ireland: New Perspectives on Politics and Culture* (Dublin, 1996), p. 148.

81. This is argued by Paul Bew, Peter Gibbon and Henry Patterson in *Northern Ireland, 1921–94: Political Forces and Social Classes* (London, 1995).

82. See Bob Purdie, *Politics in the Streets: The Origins of the Civil Rights Movement in Northern Ireland* (Belfast, 1990).

83. See Paul Arthur, *The People's Democracy, 1968–73* (Belfast, 1974).

84. PREM 13/456: Sam Napier to Sara Barker, 19 November 1965.

85. PREM 13/2266: 'Note for the Record', 8 August 1966 (Wilson–O'Neill Meeting of 5 August 1966).

86. PREM 13/2847: Le Cheminant to Wilson, 18 October 1968.

87. The speech is reprinted in Terence O'Neill, *Ulster at the Crossroads* (London, 1969), p. 140.

88. Mulholland, *Northern Ireland at the Crossroads*, p. 203.

89. Douglas Savory Papers, D.3015/1A/7/4: Hugh O'Neill to Savory, 26 July 1948.

90. Brian Faulkner, *Memoirs of a Statesman* (London, 1978), p. 27.

91. David Hume, *The Ulster Unionist Party, 1972–92: A Political Movement in an Era of Conflict and Change* (Belfast, 1996), p. 141.

92. Faulkner, *Memoirs of a Statesman*, p. 26.

93. Ivan Neill, *Church and State* (Dunmurry, 1995), p. 58. Neill's argument would appear to be confirmed by the official records of the Northern Ireland government in the Brooke era, which on the whole suggest good personal relations between the Northern Ireland Prime Minister and both the Labour and Conservative leaderships.

94. Mansergh, *Government of Northern Ireland*, p. 138.

95. Mansergh, *Government of Northern Ireland*, pp. 176, 179.

96. Terence O'Neill, *The Autobiography of Terence O'Neill, Prime Minister of Northern Ireland, 1963–69* (London, 1972), p. 18.

97. Major D. J. L. FitzGerald, *History of the Irish Guards in the Second World War* (Aldershot, 1952), p. 512.

98. Kenneth Bloomfield, *Stormont in Crisis: A Memoir* (Belfast, 1994), p. 75.

99. Faulkner, *Memoirs of a Statesman*, p. 26. O'Neill was originally attracted to the idea of dominion status, but swiftly retreated: see CAB 9J/53/2, O'Neill to Brooke, 23 November 1947.

100. Neill, *Church and State*, p. 54.
101. David Gordon, *The O'Neill Years: Unionist Politics, 1963–69* (Belfast, 1989), p. 11.
102. O'Neill, *Ulster at the Crossroads*, pp. 142–3.
103. Private information.
104. Mulholland, *Northern Ireland at the Crossroads*, p. 18.
105. Mulholland, *Northern Ireland at the Crossroads*, p. 19; Bloomfield, *Stormont in Crisis*, p. 27.
106. Hayes, *Minority Verdict*, p. 65.
107. CJ 3/39: Lord Grey to Callaghan, 2 February 1969.
108. CJ 3/9: Langdon to North, 27 October 1970.
109. FitzGerald, *Irish Guards in the Second World War*, p. 426. Despite the generally eulogistic tone of such histories, FitzGerald seems oddly contemptuous of Captain O'Neill.
110. PREM 13/983: O'Neill to Wilson, 19 January 1965. PREM 13/2266: Le Cheminant to Wilson, 10 January 1967.
111. PREM 13/2847: Cabinet Office Minute of Wilson–O'Neill Meeting, 4 November 1968.
112. O'Neill, *Autobiography*, p. 60.
113. O'Neill, *Autobiography*, pp. 57–8.
114. Mulholland, *Northern Ireland at the Crossroads*, p. 185.
115. O'Neill, *Autobiography*, pp. 80–2.
116. Mulholland, *Northern Ireland at the Crossroads*, p. 1.
117. Bloomfield, *Stormont in Crisis*, p. 76. But see Mulholland, *The Longest War*, pp. 43–4.
118. Bloomfield, *Stormont in Crisis*, p. 88.
119. Bloomfield, *Stormont in Crisis*, pp. 80–2. See also Faulkner, *Memoirs of a Statesman*, p. 39.
120. Bloomfield, *Stormont in Crisis*, p. 85.
121. Faulkner, *Memoirs of a Statesman*, p. 38.
122. Mulholland, *Northern Ireland at the Crossroads*, p. 82.
123. Bloomfield, *Stormont in Crisis*, p. 138.
124. Bloomfield, *Stormont in Crisis*, p. 103.
125. Faulkner, *Memoirs of a Statesman*, p. 40. This is borne out by some of the Stormont cabinet minutes: see, for example, CAB 4/1427, Minutes of Cabinet Meeting on 15 January 1969, for a good example of O'Neill's convoluted and defensive strategies.
126. Passage adapted from Alvin Jackson, *Ireland 1798–1998: Politics and War* (Oxford, 1999), p. 359.
127. Marianne Elliott, *The Catholics of Ulster: A History* (London, 2000), p. xxxvii. See also Mulholland, *The Longest War*, pp. 60–1.
128. Bloomfield, *Stormont in Crisis*, p. 136.
129. Bloomfield, *Stormont in Crisis*, pp. 117–18; Hayes, *Minority Verdict*, p. 108.
130. Hayes, *Minority Verdict*, p. 108.
131. Bloomfield, *Stormont in Crisis*, pp. 120, 124. Clive Scoular, *James Chichester-Clark, Prime Minister of Northern Ireland* (Killyleagh, 2000), p. 91. See also James Callaghan, *A House Divided: The Dilemma of Northern Ireland* (London, 1973).
132. Bloomfield, *Stormont in Crisis*, p. 124.
133. Scoular, *Chichester-Clark*, pp. 161–5.

134. Bloomfield, *Stormont in Crisis*, p. 100.

135. Basil McIvor Papers, D.2962/1/5/2: Chichester-Clark to McIvor, 30 March 1971. See also PREM 15/476: Record of the telephone conversation between Heath and Chichester Clark at 5 p.m., 19 March 1971.

136. Mansergh, *Government of Northern Ireland*, pp. 176ff.

137. Birrell and Murie, *Policy and Government in Northern Ireland*, pp. 57, 60–2.

138. Henry Kelly, *How Stormont Fell* (Dublin, 1972), p. 37; Bloomfield, *Stormont in Crisis*, p. 143.

139. For Midgley's career, see Graham Walker, *The Politics of Frustration: Harry Midgley and the Failure of Labour in Northern Ireland* (Manchester, 1985).

140. Hayes, *Minority Verdict*, p. 124.

141. Hayes, *Minority Verdict*, p. 126.

142. PREM 15/477: Note of a Meeting held at No. 10 Downing Street on Thursday 1 April at 4 p.m. (5 April 1971).

143. PREM 15/477: Carrington to Heath, 21 May 1971.

144. PREM 15/477: Burke Trend to R. T. Armstrong, 6 August 1971.

145. Bloomfield, *Stormont in Crisis*, p. 153.

146. Edward Heath, *The Autobiography of Edward Heath: The Course of My Life* (London, 1998), pp. 431–2.

147. Heath, *Autobiography*, p. 436.

148. Bloomfield, *Stormont in Crisis*, p. 160. Faulkner, *Memoirs of a Statesman*, pp. 142–4.

149. Faulkner, *Memoirs of a Statesman*, p. 149.

150. Faulkner, *Memoirs of a Statesman*, p. 149; Bloomfield, *Stormont in Crisis*, p. 161.

151. See the varied accounts by Bloomfield, *Stormont in Crisis*, pp. 160–7; Faulkner, *Memoirs of a Statesman*, pp. 139–60; Heath, *Autobiography*, pp. 436–7; Kelly, *How Stormont Fell*, pp. 130–42; Basil McIvor, *Hope Deferred: Experiences of an Irish Unionist* (Belfast, 1998), pp. 83–4.

152. CJ 3/39: Grey to Callaghan, 2 February 1969.

153. CJ 3/46: Oliver Wright to J. H. Waddell, 16 September 1969.

154. CJ 3/46: Langdon to Neill, 12 February 1970.

155. CJ 3/46: Langdon to Cairncross, 6 May 1970, covering 'Northern Ireland: Contingency Planning'.

156. Heath, *Autobiography*, p. 430.

157. Kelly, *How Stormont Fell*, p. 113.

158. Heath, *Autobiography*, p. 436.

159. Heath, *Autobiography*, p. 436.

160. Heath, *Autobiography*, p. 437.

161. Faulkner, *Memoirs of a Statesman*, p. 153; Heath, *Autobiography*, pp. 436–7.

162. Bloomfield, *Stormont in Crisis*, p. 163, Faulkner, *Memoirs of a Statesman*, p. 152.

163. Basil McIvor Papers, D.2962/1/7/8: Faulkner to McIvor, 28 March 1972. See also Wilson, *Ulster: Conflict and Consent*, p. 172.

164. Brigid Hadfield, *The Constitution of Northern Ireland* (Belfast, 1989), p. 9.

165. Patrick Macrory Papers, D.4025/6: Faulkner to Macrory, 18 April 1972.

166. Faulkner, *Memoirs of a Statesman*, p. 152. See also Basil McIvor Papers, D.2962/7/6: Faulkner and his ministerial collleagues to Heath, 23 March 1972 (copy).

167. Kelly, *How Stormont Fell*, p. 28.

168. Kelly, *How Stormont Fell*, p. 27.

169. G. B. Newe Papers, D.3687/1/16/1: Newe to Ken Bloomfield, 10 June 1972.

170. J. C. Beckett Papers, D.4126: Diary for 23 March 1971.
171. Faulkner, *Memoirs of a Statesman*, pp. 78–9.
172. Kelly, *How Stormont Fell*, pp. 138–9.
173. Faulkner, *Memoirs of a Statesman*, p. 26.
174. Hadfield, *Constitution of Northern Ireland*, p. 45.
175. Hayes, *Minority Verdict*, p. 319.
176. Kelly, *How Stormont Fell*, p. 13; Scoular, *Chichester-Clark*, p. 130.
177. Paul Bew, Peter Gibbon and Henry Patterson, *Northern Ireland, 1921–94: Political Forces and Social Classes* (London, 1995), p. 179.
178. See, for example, Eric Waugh, 'Ulster Suffers while MLAs Twiddle their Thumbs', *Belfast Telegraph*, 30 January 2002, for an example of growing unrest with the perceived self-indulgence of the new Legislative Assembly.

## Chapter 11 Reimagining Devolution and the Union, 1972–2000

1. See for example Henry McDonald, *Trimble* (London, 2000), pp. 87–90. For the importance of Irish history within John Hume's career see Barry White, *John Hume: Statesman of the Troubles* (Belfast, 1984), pp. 29, 175, 282.
2. Eunan O'Halpin, *The Decline of the Union: British Government in Ireland, 1892–1920* (Dublin, 1987), pp. 165–6.
3. See the lengthy official reflections on the issue by Stormont ministers between 1946 and 1951 in CAB 9J/53/1, 2, 3/1 and 3/2.
4. See the Kennedy Lindsay Papers, D.4175.
5. McDonald, *Trimble*, pp. 62, 99.
6. Paddy Devlin, *Straight Left: An Autobiography* (Belfast, 1993), p. 259.
7. Conor Cruise O'Brien, *Memoir: My Life and Themes* (Dublin, 1998), pp. 439–42.
8. McDonald, *Trimble*, p. 48.
9. Brian Faulkner, *Memoirs of a Statesman* (London, 1978), p. 161.
10. Patrick Macrory Papers, D.4025/6: Faulkner to Macrory, 16 April 1972. See also G. B. Newe Papers, D.3687/1/10/1: Newe to Faulkner, 24 May 1972: 'I am quite sure our right objective is a strong regional parliament but there will be many obstacles in the way.'
11. Faulkner, *Memoirs of a Statesman*, p. 161.
12. *Towards the Future: A Unionist Blueprint* (Belfast, 1972), p. 8.
13. Devlin, *Straight Left*, p. 185.
14. *Towards a New Ireland* (Belfast, 1972), reprinted in Northern Ireland Office, *The Future of Northern Ireland: A Paper for Discussion* (London, 1972), pp. 74–5. See also Ian McAllister, *The Northern Ireland Social Democratic and Labour Party: Political Opposition in a Divided Society* (London, 1977), pp. 56–8.
15. *Future of Northern Ireland*, p. 76.
16. The rapid evolution of Faulkner's thought in the months after the suspension of Stormont is an important and neglected theme. The Brian Faulkner Papers (D.3591) are largely (though not completely) closed to researchers, but an excellent insight into Faulkner's views may be obtained in the G. B. Newe Papers, where there are numerous letters to and from Faulkner. Newe was a moderating influence on Faulkner, urging him (D.3687/1/10/1: Newe to Faulkner, 22 May 1972) to meet Paddy Harte TD and the political scientists R. J. Lawrence and J. H. Whyte, and sounding out Ken Bloomfield and Ken Whitaker. See also, for example, Newe Papers, D.3687/1/16/1, Newe to Bloomfield, 16 June 1972: 'I

recognise that Brian must be under big pressures [from Bill Craig and the right] but he must be helped to get his thinking right'; Newe Papers, D.3687/1/10/1, Newe to Lawrence, 20 June 1972: 'I fear that he is in danger of finding himself a "prisoner" of his extremists and non-thinkers. Brian is a "loner". He lacks real vision, and so, in my view, needs guidance in formulating a modern realistic Unionist policy which, of course, he would have to "sell" to his Party'; and Newe Papers, D.3687/1/36/1, Newe to Ken Whitaker, 26 June 1972: 'I have deemed it my duty to keep in touch with him [Faulkner], and I have at last persuaded him to take the advice, or at least listen to the advice of a couple of good political scientists here…I am pressing for a quiet break with the Orange Order – a suggestion which I floated months ago, and which Brian accepted.'

17. *Towards the Future*, p. 9.
18. *Towards the Future*, p. 10.
19. *Towards the Future*, p. 20. See the critique of this document in the Newe Papers, D.3687/1/10/1: Newe to Faulkner, 9 June 1972.
20. Nicholas Mansergh, *The Government of Northern Ireland: A Study in Devolution* (London, 1936), p. 176.
21. Feargal Cochrane, *Unionist Politics and the Politics of Unionism since the Anglo-Irish Agreement* (Cork, 1997), p. 271.
22. Faulkner, *Memoirs of a Statesman*, p. 181.
23. Newe Papers, D.3687/1/10/1: Faulkner to Newe, 27 November 1973.
24. Brigid Hadfield, *The Constitution of Northern Ireland* (Belfast, 1989), p. 107.
25. Hadfield, *Constitution of Northern Ireland*, p. 108.
26. Hadfield, *Constitution of Northern Ireland*, p. 105.
27. See, for example, John Hume, *Personal Views: Politics, Peace and Reconciliation in Ireland* (Dublin, 1996), pp. 38–9.
28. Maurice Hayes, *Minority Verdict: Experiences of a Catholic Public Servant* (Belfast, 1995), p. 198.
29. See Sir George Clark Papers, D.4234/A/1/17, Faulkner to Clark, 23 September 1973, for a flavour of internal Unionist debates at this time, albeit in Faulkner's characteristically upbeat interpretation.
30. Gordon Gillespie, 'The Sunningdale Agreement: Lost Opportunity or an Agreement Too Far?', *Irish Political Studies*, 13 (1998), p. 103.
31. Newe Papers, D.3687/1/10/1: Newe to Faulkner, 27 November 1973. Even the normally unflappable Faulkner found that 'the past week in particular was trying and was something of a strain on the nerves'.
32. Basil McIvor, *Hope Deferred: Experiences of an Irish Unionist* (Belfast 1998), p. 104. Hayes, *Minority Verdict*, p. 202.
33. Hayes, *Minority Verdict*, p. 180.
34. Edward Heath, *The Autobiography of Edward Heath: The Course of My Life* (London, 1998), p. 421.
35. Gillespie, 'The Sunningdale Agreement', p. 104.
36. Garret FitzGerald, *All in a Life: An Autobiography* (Dublin, 1992), p. 210.
37. Kenneth Bloomfield, *Stormont in Crisis: A Memoir* (Belfast, 1995), p. 173.
38. FitzGerald, *All in a Life*, p. 216.
39. Basil McIvor Papers, D.2962/1/12/5: Pym to McIvor, 11 December 1973.
40. Heath, *Autobiography*, p. 444. McIvor, *Hope Deferred*, pp. 100–1. See also Sarah Curtis (ed.), *The Journals of Woodrow Wyatt*, vol. 1, paperback edition (London, 1999), p. 440.

41. Bloomfield, *Stormont in Crisis*, p. 187.
42. See the discussion on the agreement in Hadfield, *The Constitution of Northern Ireland*, pp. 110–17.
43. Faulkner, *Memoirs of a Statesman*, p. 229.
44. FitzGerald, *All in a Life*, p. 212.
45. Faulkner, *Memoirs of a Statesman*, p. 237.
46. Faulkner, *Memoirs of a Statesman*, p. 229.
47. Hayes, *Minority Verdict*, p. 180.
48. O'Brien, *Memoir*, p. 349.
49. FitzGerald, *All in a Life*, p. 203.
50. FitzGerald, *All in a Life*, p. 215.
51. Bloomfield, *Stormont in Crisis*, p. 191.
52. McIvor, *Hope Deferred*, p. 101.
53. O'Brien, *Memoir*, p. 351.
54. Quoted in Hadfield, *Constitution of Northern Ireland*, p. 113.
55. FitzGerald, *All in a Life*, p. 220.
56. Newe Papers, D.3687/1/10/1: Faulkner to Newe, 11 February 1974. See also Faulkner to Newe, 14 December 1973: 'without relinquishing principles, we have achieved a settlement whereby there will be considerable cooperation between the governments in Belfast, London and Dublin towards ending violence and promoting good relations in Ireland. I am certain that as people realise just what this means there will be widespread support for it.'
57. Faulkner, *Memoirs of a Statesman*, p. 236.
58. McIvor, *Hope Deferred*, p. 102.
59. McIvor, *Hope Deferred*, p. 104.
60. Hume, *Personal Views*, pp. 38–9.
61. Devlin, *Straight Left*, pp. 202–12.
62. Hayes, *Minority Verdict*, pp. 167, 203.
63. Heath, *Autobiography*, p. 444.
64. O'Brien, *Memoir*, p. 351.
65. FitzGerald, *All in a Life*, p. 219. See also the determinedly upbeat letter that he sent to Basil McIvor in the McIvor Papers, D.2962/1/11/24: FitzGerald to McIvor, 13 December 1973.
66. FitzGerald, *All in a Life*, p. 224.
67. Gillespie, 'Sunningdale Agreement', p. 108.
68. FitzGerald, *All in a Life*, p. 224.
69. Devlin, *Straight Left*, p. 210.
70. Quoted in Gillespie, 'Sunningdale Agreement', p. 107.
71. Quoted in Gillespie, 'Sunningdale Agreement', p. 107.
72. Gillespie, 'Sunningdale Agreement', p. 110.
73. Gillespie, 'Sunningdale Agreement', p. 112.
74. For the strike see, for example, Robert Fisk, *The Point of No Return* (London, 1975); Don Anderson, *Fourteen May Days: The Inside Story of the Loyalist Strike of 1974* (Dublin, 1994) and Merlyn Rees, *Northern Ireland: A Personal Perspective* (London, 1985), pp. 65–90.
75. Faulkner, *Memoirs of a Statesman*, pp. 276–7; Hayes, *Minority Verdict*, pp. 200–1.
76. Hayes, *Minority Verdict*, p. 198.
77. Devlin, *Straight Left*, p. 242.

78. Hayes, *Minority Verdict*, p. 180.

79. Devlin, *Straight Left*, pp. 240–1; Bloomfield, *Stormont in Crisis*, p. 218.

80. Newe Papers, D.3687/1/10/1: Newe to Faulkner, 10 July 1974.

81. Hayes, *Minority Verdict*, p. 200; Bloomfield, *Stormont in Crisis*, pp. 216–17.

82. Newe Papers, D.3687/1/10/1: Newe to Faulkner, 15 April 1974.

83. This phrase was used by Whitelaw in referring to the preliminary negotiations: Rees, *Northern Ireland*, p. 31.

84. McDonald, *Trimble*, pp. 213–14.

85. Faulkner, *Memoirs of a Statesman*, p. 229.

86. FitzGerald, *All in a Life*, p. 222.

87. Rees, *Northern Ireland*, pp. 90–1.

88. McDonald, *Trimble*, p. 62.

89. Newe Papers, D.3687/1/10/1: Faulkner to Newe, 23 July 1974.

90. McDonald, *Trimble*, p. 60.

91. Hayes, *Minority Verdict*, p. 198.

92. For James Molyneaux's career see Ann Purdy, *Molyneaux: The Long View* (Antrim, 1989).

93. Cochrane, *Unionist Politics*, p. 98.

94. David Hume, *The Ulster Unionist Party, 1972–92: A Political Movement in an Era of Conflict and Change* (Belfast, 1996), p. 82.

95. Gerard Murray, *John Hume and the SDLP: Impact and Survival in Northern Ireland* (Dublin, 1998), p. 74. Devlin, *Straight Left*, pp. 277–8.

96. On Adams see David Sharrock and Mark Devenport, *Man of War, Man of Peace? The Unauthorised Biography of Gerry Adams* (London, 1997). See also Peter Taylor, *Provos: The IRA and Sinn Féin* (London, 1997).

97. Hume, *Ulster Unionist Party*, p. 65; McDonald, *Trimble*, p. 83.

98. Hume, *Ulster Unionist Party*, p. 65.

99. McDonald, *Trimble*, p. 83.

100. McDonald, *Trimble*, p. 83.

101. David Goodall, 'A Prime Minister of Ireland to do Business with', *The Tablet*, 1 February 1992, pp. 142–3. See also Conor Cruise O'Brien's verdict that FitzGerald 'lived in the sunny confidence that he was invariably acting for the common good which, by a happy coincidence, often coincided with his own good' (*Memoirs*, pp. 347–8).

102. FitzGerald, *All in a Life*, pp. 544–50.

103. FitzGerald, *All in a Life*, p. 510.

104. FitzGerald, *All in a Life*, p. 542.

105. FitzGerald, *All in a Life*, p. 559.

106. FitzGerald, *All in a Life*, p. 569.

107. Geoffrey Howe, *Conflict of Loyalty* (London, 1995), pp. 426–7.

108. For the SDLP and the New Ireland Forum, see Murray, *John Hume and the SDLP*, pp. 123–42. FitzGerald, *All in a Life*, pp. 462–93.

109. FitzGerald, *All in a Life*, p. 489.

110. FitzGerald, *All in a Life*, p. 490.

111. FitzGerald, *All in a Life*, pp. 490, 493.

112. FitzGerald, *All in a Life*, pp. 491–2.

113. The text has been widely reprinted. See, for example, Hadfield, *Constitution of Northern Ireland*, pp. 261–8.

114. FitzGerald, *All in a Life*, pp. 494–6.
115. Howe, *Conflict of Loyalty*, pp. 426–7.
116. David Goodall, 'The Irish Question: Headmaster's Lecture Given at Ampleforth College, November 1992', *Ampleforth Journal*, 48, 1 (January 1993), p. 130.
117. Goodall, 'A Prime Minister of Ireland to do Business with', p. 143.
118. Margaret Thatcher, *The Downing Street Years* (London, 1993), p. 415; FitzGerald, *All in a Life*, p. 569.
119. Nigel Lawson, *The View from No.11* (London, 1992), p. 669.
120. FitzGerald, *All in a Life*, p. 514.
121. O'Brien, *Memoir*, p. 418.
122. Murray, *John Hume and the SDLP*, pp. 143–58. Cochrane, *Unionist Politics*, p. 271.
123. Lawson, *View from No.11*, p. 669.
124. Brian Mawhinney, *In the Firing Line: Politics, Faith, Power and Forgiveness* (London, 1999), pp. 81–2.
125. Bloomfield, *Stormont in Crisis*, pp. 253–6; Mawhinney, *In the Firing Line*, p. 82.
126. McDonald, *Trimble*, pp. 91–2.
127. Sir John Hermon, *Holding the Line: An Autobiography* (Dublin, 1997), p. 179.
128. Cochrane, *Unionist Politics*, p. 129.
129. FitzGerald, *All in a Life*, p. 565.
130. FitzGerald, *All in a Life*, p. 565.
131. FitzGerald, *All in a Life*, p. 564.
132. FitzGerald, *All in a Life*, p. 564.
133. FitzGerald, *All in a Life*, p. 559.
134. Goodall, 'The Irish Question', p. 120.
135. Hadfield, *Constitution of Northern Ireland*, pp. 192–3.
136. Hadfield, *Constitution of Northern Ireland*, pp. 196–7.
137. Hadfield, *Constitution of Northern Ireland*, pp. 197–8.
138. FitzGerald, *All in a Life*, pp. 572–5.
139. See Arthur Aughey, *Under Siege: Ulster Unionism and the Anglo-Irish Agreement* (Belfast, 1989), and Aughey's 'Unionism, Conservatism and the Anglo-Irish Agreement' in D. G. Boyce and Alan O'Day (eds), *Defenders of the Union: A Survey of British and Irish Unionism since 1801* (London, 2001), pp. 294–315. See also Cochrane, *Unionist Politics, passim*, and Hume, *Ulster Unionist Party*, pp. 106–36.
140. Alvin Jackson, 'Unionist Myths, 1912–85', *Past and Present*, 136 (August 1992), p. 177.
141. McDonald, *Trimble*, p. 102.
142. Thomas Hennessey, *The Northern Ireland Peace Process: Ending the Troubles?* (Dublin, 2000), p. 39. For a striking new interpretation of the origins of this dialogue see Ed Moloney, *A Secret History of the IRA* (London, 2002), pp. 277–9.
143. Hennessey, *Northern Ireland Peace Process*, p. 47.
144. Deaglán de Bréadún, *The Far Side of Revenge: Making Peace in Northern Ireland* (Cork, 2001), p. 5.
145. Cochrane, *Unionist Politics*, pp. 280–1.
146. Hennessey, *Northern Ireland Peace Process*, pp. 67–70. A new interpretation emphasises the importance of the indirect communication between Gerry Adams and Tom King: see Molony, *Secret History*, pp. 248–9.
147. Hennessey, *Northern Ireland Peace Process*.
148. For the ongoing Hume–Adams dialogue and its significance see Murray, *John*

*Hume and the SDLP*, pp. 187–206. See also Hennessey, *Northern Ireland Peace Process*, p. 77.

149. John Major, *The Autobiography* (London, 1999), p. 448.

150. Hennessey, *Northern Ireland Peace Process*, pp. 76–77.

151. The text of the declaration has been reprinted in Michael Cox, Adrian Guelke and Fiona Stephen (eds), *A Farewell to Arms? From 'Long War' to Long Peace in Northern Ireland* (Manchester, 2000), p. 327. See also Hennessey, *Northern Ireland Peace Process*, p. 92, McDonald, *Trimble*, pp. 130–1; and Cochrane, *Unionist Politics*, pp. 317–21.

152. The declaration is discussed in Major, *Autobiography*, p. 454.

153. Cox, Guelke and Stephen (eds), *Farewell to Arms?*, p. 330.

154. Hennessey, *Northern Ireland Peace Process*, p. 84.

155. A substantial portion of the Frameworks Documents in reprinted in Cox, Guelke and Stephen (eds), *Farewell to Arms?*, p. 330.

156. R. F. Foster, *Lord Randolph Churchill: A Political Life* (Oxford, 1981), p. 1.

157. McDonald, *Trimble*, is valuable, probing and sympathetic. Dean Godson, a journalist on the *Daily Telegraph* who is opposed to the Belfast Agreement, has embarked upon what will evidently be a detailed and substantial biography of Trimble.

158. McDonald, *Trimble*, pp. 8–13.

159. Hayes, *Minority Verdict*, p. 219.

160. McDonald, *Trimble*, pp. 35, 252, 269, 305.

161. McDonald, *Trimble*, p. 90.

162. McDonald, *Trimble*, pp. 45, 157–8.

163. McDonald, *Trimble*, pp. 247, 277.

164. De Bréadún, *Far Side of Revenge*, pp. 188–9.

165. Mitchell has published a record of his work: Senator George Mitchell, *Making Peace: The Inside Story of the Making of the Good Friday Agreement* (London, 1999).

166. Hennessey, *Northern Ireland Peace Process*; de Bréadún, *Far Side of Revenge*.

167. The 'Propositions' are reprinted in Cox, Guelke and Stephen (eds), *Farewell to Arms?*, p. 344.

168. The Belfast Agreement is widely reprinted. See, for example, Cox, Guelke and Stephen (eds), *Farewell to Arms?*, pp. 301–25.

169. Marc Mulholland, *The Longest War: Northern Ireland's Troubled History* (Oxford, 2002), p. 44.

170. O'Brien, *Memoir*, p. 351.

171. Hennessey, *Northern Ireland Peace Process*, p. 141.

172. Hennessey, *Northern Ireland Peace Process*, p. 141.

173. Hadfield, *Constitution of Northern Ireland*, p. 5.

174. De Bréadún, *Far Side of Revenge*, p. 56, for the notion of 'renegotiating' the Union.

175. See the concluding section of Alvin Jackson, *Ireland, 1798–1998: Politics and War* (Oxford, 1999), pp. 415–17.

## Chapter 12 Home Rule and Irish History

1. CJ 3/18: Oliver Wright, 'Record of Conversation with Cardinal Conway', 4 September 1969.

2. CAB 9Z/8: Spender to Londonderry, 22 August 1924, reporting on a conversation with Wickham Stead, editor of the *Review of Reviews*.

3. See, for example, CJ 3/1: Memorandum by the Secretary of State on a Round Table Conference, April 1969.
4. John Morley Diary, 2 May 1893.
5. Henry McDonald, *Trimble* (London, 2000), p. 197.
6. Newe Papers, D.3687/1/10/1: Faulkner to Newe, 11 February 1974.
7. Alvin Jackson, *Ireland 1798–1998: Politics and War* (Oxford, 1999), pp. 1–2.
8. See G. V. McIntosh, *The Force of Culture: Unionist Identities in Twentieth Century Ireland* (Cork, 1999).

# CHRONOLOGY

| | | |
|---|---|---|
| **1782** | 27 July | Amendment of Poynings' Law through Yelverton's Act ('legislative independence'). |
| **1783** | 17 April | Renunciation Act passed by the British parliament ('legislative independence'). |
| **1798** | 23–4 May | Beginning of the Rebellion in Leinster. |
| | 6–13 June | Rebellion in Ulster. |
| **1800** | 21 May | Introduction of the Bill for Union into the Dublin parliament. |
| | 1 August | Act of Union receives the royal assent. |
| | 2 August | Last meeting of the Irish parliament. |
| **1801** | 1 January | Act of Union effective. |
| **1823** | 12 May | Foundation of the Catholic Association. |
| **1824** | 24 January | Catholic Association inaugurates 'Catholic Rent'. |
| **1826** | 19–29 June | Waterford election: defeat of Lord George Beresford by emancipationist candidate, Henry Villiers Stuart. |
| **1828** | 5 July | Clare election: return of Daniel O'Connell. |
| **1829** | 13 April | Passage of the Catholic Emancipation Act. |
| **1830** | 4 February | O'Connell takes his seat in the House of Commons. |
| **1831** | 3 March | Start of the tithe war in the midlands. |
| | 9 September | Establishment of the National primary school system. |
| **1833** | 14 August | Irish Church Temporalities Act |
| **1834** | 22 April | O'Connell introduces a parliamentary debate on repeal. |
| **1835** | January | General election, United Kingdom. |
| | 18 February | Lichfield House Compact: informal alliance between Whigs, Radicals and O'Connell's followers affirmed. |
| **1838** | 31 July | Irish Poor Law enacted. |
| | 15 August | Tithe Rent Charge Act passed. |
| **1840** | 15 April | Establishment of the National Association by O'Connell. |

| | 13 July | National Association relaunched as the Loyal National Repeal Association. |
| | 10 August | Irish Municipal Reform Act. |
| 1842 | 15 October | *Nation* appears for the first time. |
| 1843 | 15 August | 'Monster' repeal meeting held at Tara, County Meath: perhaps 750,000 attend. |
| | 7 October | Repeal meeting at Clontarf (planned for 8 October) cancelled. |
| 1844 | 10 February | O'Connell convicted of sedition. |
| 1845 | 9 September | Potato blight first reported in Ireland. |
| | 16 September | Death of Thomas Davis. |
| 1846 | 26 June | Repeal of the Corn Laws. |
| | 30 June | Peel and the Tory government ousted by the Whigs: Lord John Russell heads the new administration. |
| | 28 July | O'Connellite movement splits over the use of physical force. |
| 1847 | 10 April | Peak of fever epidemic. |
| | 15 May | Death of Daniel O'Connell. |
| 1848 | 29 July | Rising in Ballingarry, County Tipperary. |
| 1850 | 9 August | Establishment of the Irish Tenant League. |
| | 14 August | Passage of the Irish Reform Act: county electorate trebled. |
| 1851 | 30 March | Census taken: population recorded as 6,552,385. |
| 1852 | July | General election, United Kingdom. |
| | 8–9 September | Tenant League conference in Dublin. |
| 1854 | 28 March | Outbreak of the Crimean War. |
| 1857 | March–April | General election, United Kingdom. |
| 1858 | 17 March | Foundation of the Irish Republican Brotherhood (the Fenian movement) in Dublin. |
| 1859 | April | Foundation of the Fenian Brotherhood in the USA. |
| | May | General election, United Kingdom. |
| 1861 | 7 April | Census taken: population recorded as 5,798,967. |
| 1864 | 29 December | National Association of Ireland founded. |
| 1865 | July | General election, United Kingdom. |
| 1867 | 5 March | Fenian rising: rapidly suppressed. |
| | 20 June | Clan na Gael founded (New York). |
| | 23 November | Execution of the 'Manchester Martyrs'. |
| | 13 December | Fenian bomb at Clerkenwell, London: 12 killed. |
| 1868 | 13 July | Irish Reform Act. |
| | 3 August | Foundation of the Amnesty campaign for the Fenian prisoners. |
| | November | General election, United Kingdom. |

**1869** 26 July       Passage of the Irish Church Act: disestablishment of the Church of Ireland.

**1870** 19 May       Home Rule movement formed by Isaac Butt.
       1 August       Gladstone's first Irish land act.
       1 September       First meeting of the Home Government Association.

**1871** 2 April       Census taken: population recorded as 5,412,377.

**1872** 18 July       Ballot Act establishes secrecy during voting.

**1873** 8 January       Formation of the Home Rule Confederation of Great Britain.
       12 March       Defeat of Gladstone's Irish University Bill.
       18–21 November Formation of the Home Rule League (Dublin).

**1874** February       General election: 60 Home Rulers returned.
       3 March       Home Rule parliamentary party created.
       30 July       Obstruction campaign begins in parliament.

**1875** 22 April       Charles Stewart Parnell enters House of Commons (MP for Meath).

**1876** 20 August       IRB Supreme Council withdraws support from the Home Rule movement.
       29 December       Society for the Preservation of the Irish Language established.

**1877** 31 July       Acceleration of obstructionist strategy by militant Home Rule MPs (including Parnell).
       28 August       Charles Stewart Parnell elected President of the Home Rule Confederation of Great Britain.

**1878** 24 October       John Devoy (Clan na Gael) first proposes 'new departure' to the Parnellites.

**1879** 20 April       Launch of the land agitation at Irishtown, Co. Mayo.
       5 May       Death of Isaac Butt, founder of the Home Rule movement.
       16 August       National Land League of Mayo formed.
       21 October       Irish National Land League formed.

**1880** March–April       General election, United Kingdom.
       17 May       Parnell elected Chairman of the Irish Parliamentary Party.
       19 September       Parnell launches the boycott campaign against those defying the Land League (Ennis, County Clare).

**1881** 31 January       Ladies' Land League launched in Ireland.
       3 April       Census taken: population recorded as 5,174,836.
       22 August       Gladstone's second land act: legalisation of the 'three Fs'.
       15–17 September Parnell advises Land League to test the new act.
       13 October       Arrest of Parnell.
       18 October       Land League leaders' 'no rent' manifesto.
       20 October       Proscription of the Land League.

| 1882 | 2 May | Parnell released after the Kilmainham 'treaty' with Gladstone. |
| | 6 May | Phoenix Park: the assassinations of Lord Frederick Cavendish and T. H. Burke. |
| | 17 October | Irish National League formed. |
| 1883 | 11 December | Parnell National Tribute handed over (£38,000 raised). |
| 1884 | 1 October | Agreement between the Catholic hierarchy and the Irish Party over the representation of Catholic educational claims. |
| | 1 November | Foundation of the Gaelic Athletic Association. |
| | 6 December | Representation of the People Act: Irish electorate increased from 224,000 to 738,000. |
| 1885 | 21 January | Parnell's 'ne plus ultra' speech. |
| | 1 May | Irish Loyal and Patriotic Union founded. |
| | 25 June | Redistribution of Seats Act reforms constituency divisions. |
| | 14 August | Ashbourne Act: land purchase extended. |
| | 24 November–9 December | General election: Liberal victory, with Parnellites holding 86 seats. |
| | 17 December | Reports of Gladstone's conversion to Home Rule published. |
| 1886 | 8 April | Introduction of the first Home Rule Bill. |
| | 8 June | Defeat of Gladstone's Home Rule Bill. |
| | 1–17 July | General election: Conservative victory. |
| | 23 October | Launch of the Plan of Campaign (agrarian agitation). |
| 1887 | 7 March | Arthur Balfour appointed as Chief Secretary for Ireland. |
| | 18 April | 'Parnellism and Crime': article and letter published in *The Times* linking Parnell to the Phoenix Park murders. |
| | 19 July | Criminal Law and Procedure (Ireland) Act. |
| | 9 September | 'Mitchelstown Massacre': three demonstrators killed by RIC. |
| 1888 | 17 September–22 November 1889 | Special Commission of enquiry into the allegations published in *The Times*. |
| 1889 | 20–22 February | Pigott exposed as the forger of *The Times* letter. |
| | 24 December | O'Shea divorce petition lodged, citing Parnell. |
| 1890 | 15–17 November | O'Shea divorce hearing. |
| | 24 November | Gladstone reports to Justin McCarthy that Liberal support for Home Rule is threatened by Parnell's continued leadership of the Irish Party. |
| | 25 November | Parnell re-elected as chairman of the Irish Party. |
| | 28 November | Parnell's Manifesto to the Irish People: he denounces the Liberal alliance. |
| | 1–6 December | Debate within the Irish Party: the majority come down in opposition to Parnell. |
| 1891 | 3 February | Final breakdown of the effort for agreement within the Irish Party. |
| | 5 April | Census taken: population recorded as 4,704,750. |
| | 6 October | Death of Parnell (Brighton). |
| | 28 December | Irish Literary Society founded in London by W. B. Yeats and others. |

1892  17 June          Ulster Unionist Convention, Belfast.

4–18 July       General election: Liberal victory.

16 August      Foundation of the National Literary Society.

25 November   Douglas Hyde speaks on 'The Necessity for De-Anglicising Ireland'.

1893  13 February   Introduction of the second Home Rule Bill.

31 July        Formation of the Gaelic League.

9 September   Rejection of the second Home Rule Bill by the Lords.

1894  27–8 April    Foundation of the Irish Trades Union Congress.

1895  12–26 July    General election: Conservative victory.

1896  14 August     Gerald Balfour's Land Act.

1898  23 January    Foundation of the United Irish League.

12 August      Local Government Act.

1899  4 March        *United Irishman* launched by Arthur Griffith.

8 May         First production of the Irish Literary Theatre.

9 August      Agriculture and Technical Instruction Act.

11 October    Outbreak of the South African war.

1900  30 January    Reunification of the Irish Parliamentary Party

6 February     John Redmond elected leader of the IPP.

29 September–12 October  General election: Conservative victory.

30 September  Foundation of Cumann na nGeadheal by Arthur Griffith.

9 November    George Wyndham appointed Chief Secretary.

1901  31 March       Census taken: population recorded as 4,458,775.

1902  31 May         Treaty of Vereeniging marks end of South African war.

20 December   Land Conference brings together landlords and tenants.

1903  14 August     Land Act: comprehensive scheme of land purchase launched.

1904  2 January     Arthur Griffith begins 'The Resurrection of Hungary' articles in the *United Irishman.*

26 August      Irish Reform Association (centrist) launched: promotes private discussion of the possibility of devolution for Ireland.

2 December    Ulster Unionist conference calls for the creation of an Ulster Unionist Council.

27 December   Opening of the Abbey Theatre.

1905  3 March        Ulster Unionist Council launched (Belfast).

6 March        Resignation of George Wyndham.

8 March        Formation of the Dungannon Clubs (Belfast).

28 November   Griffith proposes the Sinn Féin policy to the National Council.

1906  13–27 January  General election: Liberal victory.

14 October    Laurence Ginnell advocates cattle driving (Downs, County Westmeath).

21 October    Death of Colonel Edward Saunderson, Unionist leader.

1907    28–30 January    Riots at the premiere of the 'Playboy of the Western World'.
        29 January       Augustine Birrell appointed as Chief Secretary.
        21 April         Sinn Féin League formed from Cumann na nGaedheal and
                         Dungannon Clubs.
        21 May           Irish Party conference declares against Irish Council Bill.
        2 August         Pius X issues the Ne Temere decree on mixed marriages.
        5 September      Sinn Féin formed from the union of the National Council
                         with the Sinn Féin League.
        December         Return of Tom Clarke, veteran Fenian, to Dublin.

1908    21 February      North Leitrim by-election: first parliamentary outing for Sinn
                         Féin.
        1 August         Irish Universities Act passed: formation of the National
                         University of Ireland and Queen's University, Belfast.
        11 November      Irish Women's Franchise League established.
        29 December      Proposal for Irish Transport Workers' Union.

1909    4 January        James Larkin founds the ITGWU.
        9–10 February    'Baton' Convention of the United Irish League.
        30 November      House of Lords rejects the 'People's Budget': precipitates
                         constitutional crisis.
        3 December       Passage of the Birrell Land Act.

1910    15–28 January    General election: Liberals retain power under Asquith.
        21 February      Edward Carson elected as leader of the Irish Unionist
                         Parliamentary Party.
        June–November    Constitutional conference, London, fails.
        December         General election: Liberals retain power.

1911    2 April          Census taken: population recorded as 4,381,951.
        18 August        Parliament Act (abolishes absolute veto of the Lords).
        21 August        Formation of the Irish Women's Suffrage Federation.
        23 September      Ulster Unionist demonstration at Craigavon, Belfast.
        13 November      Andrew Bonar Law elected Conservative leader.

1912    9 April          Andrew Bonar Law (British Conservative leader) pledges
                         unconditional support for Ulster Unionist resistance to Home
                         Rule (Balmoral, Belfast).
        11 April         Introduction of the third Home Rule Bill.
        11 June          Agar-Robartes exclusion amendment to the Home Rule Bill.
        28 June          Irish Labour Party founded.
        28 September      Ulster Solemn League and Covenant (of opposition to Home
                         Rule) signed by Unionists.

1913    1 January        Carson's exclusion amendment to the Home Rule Bill.
        31 January       Formation of the Ulster Volunteer Force.
        26 August        Start of the ITGWU strike in Dublin.
        24 September      Provisional Government of Ulster launched by the UUC,
                         Belfast.
        19 November      Formation of the Irish Citizen Army.
        25 November      Foundation of the Irish Volunteers under Eoin MacNeill.

| 1914 | 20 March | Curragh Incident. |
| | 2 April | Foundation of Cumann na mBan. |
| | 24–5 April | Larne gun-running. |
| | 23 June | Government of Ireland (Amendment) Bill proposes exclusion through county option in Ulster. |
| | 21–4 July | Buckingham Palace Conference fails to reach an agreement on Ulster exclusion from Home Rule. |
| | 26 July | Howth gun-running: four killed at Bachelor's Walk, Dublin, in a confrontation between the army and protestors. |
| | 3 August | Outbreak of war between Germany and France: Redmond pledges the support of the Irish Volunteers for the defence of Ireland. |
| | 4 August | Outbreak of war between Britain and Germany. |
| | 15 September | Home Rule suspensory measure passed. |
| | 18 September | Home Rule enacted but suspended. |
| | 20 September | Redmond at Woodenbridge, County Wicklow: he commits the Irish Volunteers to serving outside Ireland. |
| | 24 September | Split opens up within the Volunteers between supporters and opponents of Redmond's position. |
| 1915 | 25 May | Coalition government formed under Asquith. |
| | May | Foundation of the Military Committee of the IRB Supreme Council. |
| 1916 | 19–22 January | Military Council of the IRB agree on a rising no later than Easter. |
| | 3 April | Plans published for Irish Volunteer 'manoeuvres' on 23 April (Easter Sunday). |
| | 20–1 April | German arms shipment intercepted by the Royal Navy: the *Aud* captured and scuttled. |
| | 21 April | Roger Casement arrives from Germany and is arrested. |
| | 22 April | Eoin MacNeill countermands the order for manoeuvres. |
| | 23 April | MacNeill's countermanding order published. Military Council of the IRB agrees to proceed with its plans for rebellion. |
| | 24 April | Initial military operations of the rebels: key buildings (including the GPO) seized and reinforced. |
| | 29 April | The unconditional surrender of the insurgents. |
| | 3–12 May | The leaders of the Rising executed. |
| | May–July | Lloyd George attempts to negotiate a deal between the Irish Party and the Ulster Unionists on the basis of exclusion. |
| | 1 July | Opening of the Somme offensive. |
| | 7 December | Lloyd George replaces Asquith as PM. |
| | 22–3 December | The first of those interned after the Rising return to Ireland. |
| 1917 | 5 February | Roscommon by-election: Count Plunkett returned for Sinn Féin. The first of a series of decisive by-election victories for the Party. |
| | 9 May | Longford South by-election: Joseph McGuinness (Sinn Féin) victorious. |
| | 16 May | Proposal for an Irish Convention launched. |

| | | |
|---|---|---|
| | 10 July | Clare East by-election: Eamon de Valera (Sinn Féin) victorious. |
| | 25 July | First meeting of the Convention: it survives until 5 April 1918. |
| | 25–6 October | Sinn Féin ard-fheis: Eamon de Valera elected president of the Party; the constitution of the Party is modified. |
| | 27 October | De Valera elected President of the Irish Volunteers. |
| 1918 | 6 February | Representation of the People and Redistribution of Seats Acts. |
| | 6 March | Death of John Redmond. |
| | 18 April | Military Service Act raises the possibility of conscription in Ireland: Mansion House conference of nationalist protestors. |
| | 21 April | Anti-conscription pledge signed by nationalists. |
| | 17–18 May | Arrest of Sinn Féin leadership. |
| | 11 November | Armistice. |
| | 14–28 December | General election: Sinn Féin wins 73 seats to the six captured by the nationalists. The Unionists win 26 seats. |
| 1919 | 21 January | Soloheadbeg ambush, County Tipperary: two RIC men shot. First meeting of Dáil Éireann and opening of Anglo-Irish War. |
| | 3 June | Local Government (Ireland) Act. |
| | 28 June | Treaty of Versailles signed. |
| | 4 July | Sinn Féin and IRA proscribed. |
| | 12 September | Dáil Éireann proscribed. |
| 1920 | 15 January | Local elections: sweeping Sinn Féin victories. |
| | 25 February | Government of Ireland Bill introduced into the Commons. |
| | 20 March | UUC, Belfast, accepts the Government of Ireland Bill. |
| | 23 December | Government of Ireland measure enacted: devolved administration launched in Northern Ireland. |
| 1921 | 4 February | James Craig succeeds Carson as Ulster Unionist leader. |
| | 5 May | Craig and de Valera meet in Dublin. |
| | 24 May | General election, Northern Ireland: Ulster Unionists win 40 out of 52 seats. |
| | 22 June | Opening of the Northern Ireland parliament, Belfast: George V makes a conciliatory address. |
| | 9 July | Truce proclaimed between the crown forces and the IRA. |
| | 16 August | Second Dáil formed. |
| | 11 October | Negotiations launched between representatives of the British government and that of the Dáil. |
| | 6 December | Anglo-Irish Treaty signed. |
| | 14 December | Debate on the Treaty within Dáil Éireann begins. |
| 1922 | 7 January | Dáil accepts the Treaty. |
| | 9 January | Arthur Griffith elected as President, following the resignation of de Valera. |
| | 14 January | Formation of the Provisional Government of Ireland. |
| | 16 January | Hand-over of power: the end of the Castle administration. |
| | 26–27 March | Anti-Treaty IRA repudiate the authority of the Dáil. |
| | 30 March | Craig-Collins pact signed in an effort to ease sectarian confrontation in Northern Ireland. |

| | | |
|---|---|---|
| | 14 April | Republican forces opposed to the Treaty seize the Four Courts. |
| | 16 June | General election in the Irish Free State: electorate endorses the Treaty. |
| | 28 June | Irish Free State forces move to dislodge irregulars from the Four Courts: effective beginning of the civil war. |
| | 12 August | Death of Arthur Griffith. |
| | 22 August | Michael Collins shot dead in the Béal na mBláth ambush. |
| | 9 September | Third Dáil: W. T. Cosgrave elected as president. |
| | 11 September | Abolition of proportional representation for local elections in Northern Ireland. |
| | 25 October | Passage of the Irish Free State constitution through the Dáil. |
| | 15 November | General election, United Kingdom. |
| | 6 December | Irish Free State formally established. |
| 1923 | 24 May | Republican military campaign ended. |
| | 27 August | General election, Free State: Cumann na nGaedheal victory. |
| | 6 December | General election, United Kingdom. |
| 1924 | 29 October | General election, United Kingdom. |
| | 6 November | First meeting of the Boundary Commission. |
| 1925 | 3 April | General election in Northern Ireland. |
| | 7 November | Boundary Commission proposals leaked to the press. |
| | 3 December | Tripartite Agreement. |
| 1926 | 18 April | Census taken, Irish Free State and Northern Ireland: population recorded as 2,971,992 (IFS) and 1,256,561 (NI). |
| | 16 May | Foundation of Fianna Fáil. |
| 1927 | 9 June | General election, Irish Free State. |
| | 10 July | Assassination of Kevin O'Higgins. |
| | 4 August | Death of John Dillon. |
| | 12 August | Fianna Fáil deputies take their seats in Dáil. |
| | 15 September | General election, Irish Free State. |
| 1928 | 25 February | Death of William O'Brien. |
| | May | Joseph Devlin forms the National League of the North. |
| 1929 | 16 April | PR abolished for parliamentary contests in Northern Ireland. |
| | 22 May | General election, Northern Ireland. |
| | 30 June | General election, United Kingdom. |
| | 29 October | Wall Street Crash. |
| 1931 | 27 October | General election, United Kingdom. |
| | 11 December | Statute of Westminster. |
| 1932 | 16 February | General election: Fianna Fáil victory. |
| | 9 March | First Fianna Fáil government formed. |
| | 4–13 October | Unemployed riot in Belfast. |
| | 16 November | Opening of the Stormont parliament building. |
| 1933 | 24 January | General election, Irish Free State. |
| | 3 May | Oath of allegiance removed from the Free State constitution. |

| | 2 September | United Ireland (Fine Gael) formed from Cumann na nGeadheal, National Guard and the Centre Party. |
|---|---|---|
| | 2 November | Legislation curtails power of the governor general of the Free State. |
| | 16 November | Legislation restricting right of appeal from the Irish Free State to the Privy Council. |
| | 30 November | General election, Northern Ireland. |
| 1934 | 18 January | Death of Joseph Devlin. |
| 1935 | 6–9 May | Rioting in Belfast during celebrations of George V's Jubilee. |
| | 12–21 July | Rioting in Belfast after Orange demonstrations. |
| | 22 October | Death of Edward Carson. |
| | 14 November | General election, United Kingdom. |
| 1936 | 26 April | Census taken, IFS: population recorded as 2,968,420. |
| | 29 May | Irish Free State Senate abolished. |
| | 10 December | Abdication of King Edward VIII. |
| | 11 December | Amending Act removes references to the Crown from the Free State constitution. |
| | 12 December | External Relations Act (IFS). |
| 1937 | 28 February | Census taken, Northern Ireland: population recorded as 1,279,745. |
| | 14 June | De Valera's new constitution approved by the Dáil. |
| | 1 July | General election and constitutional referendum, Irish Free State. |
| 1938 | 9 February | General election, Northern Ireland. |
| | 25 April | Anglo-Irish Agreement: settlement of the economic war; return of the Treaty ports. |
| | 17 June | General election, Éire: Fianna Fáil victory. |
| | 25 June | Douglas Hyde inaugurated as first president of Ireland. |
| 1939 | 16 January | IRA launches bombing campaign in England. |
| | 25 August | IRA bomb, Coventry: five killed. |
| | 3 September | Beginning of the Second World War. |
| 1940 | 24 November | Death of James Craig. |
| | 25 November | John M. Andrews succeeds as Prime Minister of Northern Ireland. |
| 1941 | April-May | German air-raids on Belfast: raid of 15–16 April kills 745. |
| | 7 December | Japan attacks US naval base at Pearl Harbor, Hawaii. |
| 1943 | 28 April | John Andrews resigns as Prime Minister of Northern Ireland, and as Ulster Unionist leader. |
| | 1 May | Basil Brooke appointed Prime Minister of Northern Ireland. |
| | 22 June | General election, Éire: Fianna Fáil victory. |
| 1944 | 30 May | General election, Éire: Fianna Fáil victory. |
| | 6 June | D Day: Allied invasion of France. |

| | | |
|---|---|---|
| **1945** | 2 May | De Valera offers condolences on the death of Hitler. |
| | 8 May | Victory in Europe Day. |
| | 14 June | General election, Northern Ireland. |
| | 5 July | General election, United Kingdom. |
| | 14 August | Surrender of Japan. |
| **1946** | 19 February | National Insurance (Northern Ireland) Act passed. |
| | 12 May | Census taken, Éire: population recorded as 2,955,107. |
| **1947** | 27 March | Education Act (Northern Ireland) passed. |
| **1948** | 4 February | General election, Éire: first inter-party government takes office under John A. Costello. |
| | 7 September | Costello announces the Irish intention to declare a republic. |
| | 21 December | Republic of Ireland Act passed by the Dáil. |
| **1949** | 10 February | General election, Northern Ireland. |
| | 18 April | Ireland becomes a republic and leaves the commonwealth. |
| | 2 June | Ireland Act passed by the British parliament. |
| **1950** | 23 February | General election, United Kingdom. |
| **1951** | 8 April | Census taken, Republic of Ireland and Northern Ireland: population recorded as 2,960,593 (ROI) and 1,370,921 (NI). |
| | 30 May | General election, Republic of Ireland: Fianna Fáil victory. |
| | 25 October | General election, United Kingdom. |
| **1953** | 22 October | General election, Northern Ireland. |
| **1954** | 6 April | Flags and Emblems Act passed in Northern Ireland. |
| | 18 May | General election, Republic of Ireland: second inter-party government formed. |
| **1955** | 26 May | General election, United Kingdom. |
| **1956** | 8 April | Census taken, Republic of Ireland: population recorded as 2,898,264. |
| | 12 December | IRA launches its Border Campaign. |
| **1957** | 5 March | General election: Fianna Fáil returned to power. |
| **1958** | 20 March | General election, Northern Ireland. |
| **1959** | 17 June | De Valera elected President. |
| | 23 June | Seán Lemass succeeds as taoiseach. |
| | 8 October | General election, United Kingdom. |
| **1961** | 9 April | Census taken, Republic of Ireland: population recorded as 2,818,341. |
| | 23 April | Census taken, Northern Ireland: population recorded as 1,425,042. |
| | 4 October | General election, Republic of Ireland: Fianna Fáil victory. |
| **1962** | 26 February | IRA calls off its Border Campaign. |
| | 31 May | General election, Northern Ireland. |

**1963** 25 March      Terence O'Neill appointed Prime Minister of Northern Ireland.

       26–29 June      President John F. Kennedy visits Ireland.

**1964** January      Campaign for Social Justice founded in Dungannon, County Tyrone.

       2 June      Eddie McAteer elected leader of the Nationalists, Stormont.

       15 October      General election, United Kingdom.

**1965** 14 January      Lemass and O'Neill meet at Stormont.

       7 April      General election, Republic of Ireland: Fianna Fáil returned.

       16 November      Death of William T. Cosgrave.

       25 November      General election, Northern Ireland.

       14 December      Anglo-Irish Free Trade Agreement signed by Lemass and Harold Wilson.

**1966** 31 March      General election, United Kingdom.

       10–17 April      Commemorations of the fiftieth anniversary of the Easter Rising.

       17 April      Census taken, Republic of Ireland: population recorded as 2,884,002.

       26 June      Malvern Street Murders by the UVF.

       9 October      Census taken, Northern Ireland: population recorded as 1,484,775.

       10 November      Lemass resigns: replaced by Jack Lynch.

**1967** 1 February      Formation of the Northern Ireland Civil Rights Association.

**1968** 24 August      NICRA lead march from Coalisland to Dungannon, County Tyrone.

       5 October      Civil rights march, Derry: RUC conflict with marchers.

       9 October      Evolution of the People's Democracy, Belfast; Derry Citizens' Action Committee formed.

       22 November      O'Neill announces five-point programme of reform.

       30 November      Civil rights march in Armagh.

       9 December      O'Neill delivers 'Ulster at the Crossroads' speech on television.

**1969** 1–4 January      PD march from Belfast to Derry: Burntollet clash.

       11 January      PD demonstration, Newry, County Down.

       24 February      General election, Northern Ireland: Unionists divided over O'Neill's leadership.

       28 April      Resignation of O'Neill: James Chichester-Clark succeeds as Prime Minister of Northern Ireland.

       18 June      General election, Republic of Ireland: Fianna Fáil victory.

       14 July      First death of the 'Troubles': Dungiven, County Londonderry.

       August      Rioting in Derry and Belfast: introduction of British troops onto the streets.

       12 September      Cameron Commission report (into disturbances of 1968) published.

       10 October      Hunt Committee report into N. Ireland policing published.

**1970** 11 January      Split within the IRA: formation of the Provisional IRA.

| | | |
|---|---|---|
| | March–April | Phased disbandment of the B Specials in N. Ireland. |
| | 21 April | Foundation of the Alliance Party in N. Ireland. |
| | May–June | Arms controversy, Dublin: Haughey and Blaney sacked from the Lynch government and arrested. |
| | 29 May | Macrory report on local government in Northern Ireland published. |
| | 18 June | General election, United Kingdom. |
| | 21 August | Social Democratic and Labour Party formed. |
| 1971 | 6 February | First British soldier killed by PIRA. |
| | 20 March | Resignation of Chichester-Clark as prime minister, Northern Ireland. |
| | 23 March | Brian Faulkner succeeds Chichester-Clark as Prime Minister of Northern Ireland. |
| | 18 April | Census taken, Republic of Ireland: population recorded as 2,978,248. |
| | 20 April | Census taken, Northern Ireland: population recorded as 1,536,065. |
| | 11 May | Death of Seán Lemass. |
| | 16 July | SDLP withdraw from the Northern Ireland parliament. |
| | 9–10 August | Internment introduced in Northern Ireland. |
| | 14 September | Formation of the Democratic Unionist Party. |
| | 4 December | Loyalist bomb attack on McGurk's pub, Belfast: 15 killed. |
| 1972 | 22 January | Republic signs the treaty of accession to the EEC. |
| | 30 January | Bloody Sunday, Derry: 13 demonstrators shot by soldiers. |
| | 24 March | Stormont prorogued: introduction of direct rule. |
| | 19 April | Widgery Tribunal (on Bloody Sunday) reports. |
| | 7 July | Willie Whitelaw (Secretary of State, NI) meets PIRA leaders. |
| | 21 July | Bloody Friday, Belfast: 11 killed by PIRA bombs. |
| | 7 December | Special position of the Roman Catholic church removed from the Irish constitution after a popular referendum. |
| | 20 December | Diplock Commission (on judicial procedure) reports. |
| 1973 | 1 January | Republic's membership of the EEC formalised. |
| | 28 February | General election, Republic: Fine Gael-Labour coalition formed. |
| | 20 March | Northern Ireland Constitutional Proposals published. |
| | 30 May | Local elections, Northern Ireland: first contest conducted under proportional representation since 1920. |
| | 28 June | Northern Ireland Assembly elections. |
| | 18 July | Northern Ireland Constitution Act formally abolishes local parliament. |
| | 31 July | First meeting of Northern Ireland Assembly. |
| | 18 August | Death of Viscount Brookeborough (Basil Brooke). |
| | 6–9 December | Conference on the future government of Northern Ireland (Sunningdale, Berkshire). |
| 1974 | 1 January | Power-sharing executive takes office in Northern Ireland. |
| | 4 February | PIRA bomb, Catterick: 11 killed. |
| | 28 February | General election, United Kingdom. |

| | | |
|---|---|---|
| | 14 May | Start of the Ulster Workers' Council strike. |
| | 17 May | Loyalist bombs in Dublin and Monaghan: 31 killed. |
| | 28 May | Resignation of Faulkner and the fall of the Executive. |
| | 29 May | Direct rule resumed: UWC strike called off. |
| | 10 October | General election, United Kingdom. |
| | 21 November | Birmingham pub bombings: 21 killed. |
| 1975 | 1 May | Elections to Northern Ireland Constitutional Convention |
| | 29 August | Death of Eamon de Valera. |
| 1976 | 4–5 January | 15 killed (10 Protestants and five Catholics) in sectarian onslaughts in County Armagh. |
| | 5 January | Death of John A. Costello. |
| | 21 July | Assassination of Christopher Ewart-Biggs, British ambassador to Ireland. |
| | 30 November | Mairead Corrigan and Betty Williams share Nobel Prize for Peace. |
| 1977 | 3 March | Death of Brian Faulkner. |
| | 16 June | General election, Republic: Fianna Fáil victory. |
| 1978 | 17 February | La Mon Hotel bomb: 16 killed. |
| 1979 | 3 May | General election, United Kingdom: Margaret Thatcher and the Conservatives returned to power. |
| | 27 August | Assassination of Earl Mountbatten and three others at Mullaghmore, County Sligo. IRA ambush, Warrenpoint, County Down: 18 soldiers killed. |
| | 29 September | First papal visit to Ireland. |
| | 28 November | John Hume succeeds Gerry Fitt as leader of the SDLP. |
| | 7 December | Charles Haughey elected leader of Fianna Fáil and subsequently as taoiseach. |
| | December | Census, Republic of Ireland: population recorded as 3,364,881. |
| 1980 | 21 May | Margaret Thatcher and Charles Haughey meet in London. |
| 1981 | 1 March | Hunger strike at the Maze Prison begins, led by Bobby Sands. |
| | 9 April | Sands elected as MP for Fermanagh and South Tyrone. |
| | 5 May | Death of Sands on hunger strike. |
| | May–August | Deaths of ten hunger-striking prisoners. |
| | 11 June | General election, Republic: Fine Gael-Labour coalition formed. |
| | 14 November | Assassination of Revd Robert Bradford, MP for South Belfast. |
| | December | Census, Northern Ireland: population recorded as 1,481,959. |
| 1982 | 18 February | General election, Republic: Fianna Fáil victory. |
| | 20 July | IRA attack on Household Cavalry, London: 8 killed. |
| | 20 October | Northern Ireland Assembly elections. |
| | 24 November | General election, Republic: Fine Gael-Labour coalition in power. |
| | 6 December | INLA bomb, Droppin' Well bar, Ballykelly, Co. Londonderry: 17 killed. |

| 1983 | 30 May | First meeting of the New Ireland Forum, Dublin Castle. |
| | 9 June | General election, UK: Conservative victory. Gerry Adams returned for West Belfast. |
| | 7 November | First meeting of the Anglo-Irish Intergovernmental Council. |
| 1984 | 2 May | New Ireland Forum report published. |
| | 12 October | PIRA bomb, Grand Hotel, Brighton, during the Conservtaive Party conference: five killed. |
| 1985 | 28 February | PIRA attack on Newry police station: nine killed. |
| | 15 November | Hillsborough Agreement signed. |
| | 11 December | First meeting of the Anglo-Irish Intergovernmental Conference. |
| | 21 December | Foundation of the Progressive Democrats. |
| 1986 | 23 January | By-elections held in Northern Ireland (caused by Unionist protest resignations). |
| | 26 June | Divorce referendum in the Republic: prospect of divorce rejected. |
| | December | Census, Republic of Ireland: population recorded as 3,537,195. |
| 1987 | 14 February | General election, Republic: Fianna Fáil victory. |
| | 11 March | Garret FitzGerald retires from the leadership of Fine Gael. |
| | 8 May | Loughgall, County Armagh: eight PIRA members shot dead by security forces. |
| | 26 May | Single European Act approved in Irish referendum. |
| | 8 November | Enniskillen, County Fermanagh: 11 die in PIRA bomb during Remembrance Day commemorations. |
| | 22 December | Assassination of UDA leader, John McMichael. |
| 1988 | 11 January | John Hume and Gerry Adams meet in Belfast for talks. |
| | 6 March | Three PIRA members shot dead in Gibraltar. |
| | March–July | Intermittent SDLP-Sinn Féin talks. |
| | 20 August | PIRA bomb at Ballygawley, County Tyrone: 8 soldiers killed. |
| 1989 | 15 June | General election, Republic: inconclusive result. |
| | 12 July | Fianna Fáil-Progressive Democrat coalition formed. |
| | 22 September | PIRA bomb at Royal Marine barracks, Deal, Kent: 10 killed. |
| 1990 | 18 May | David Trimble elected MP, Upper Bann constituency. |
| | 13 June | Terence O'Neill (Lord O'Neill of the Maine) dies. |
| | 30 July | Ian Gow (Conservative MP and prominent Unionist) killed. |
| | 24 October | PIRA detonates human bombs: seven die. |
| | 9 November | Mary Robinson elected President of Ireland. |
| | 27 November | John Major succeeds to the Conservative leadership after the deposition of Mrs Thatcher. |
| 1991 | 7 February | IRA mortar bomb attack on 10 Downing Street. |
| | 14 March | Birmingham Six freed. |
| | 21 March | Census taken, Northern Ireland: population recorded as 1,577,836. |

| 26 June | Maguire Seven cleared. |
| 3 July | End of the cross-party talks sponsored by Peter Brooke (Secretary of State, N. Ireland). |

| **1992** | 17 January | Teebane, Co. Tyrone: eight Protestants killed. |
| | 5 February | Sean Graham's bookmakers, Ormeau Road, Belfast: five Catholics killed. |
| | 6 February | Albert Reynolds elected as leader of Fianna Fáil. |
| | 9 April | General election, United Kingdom. |
| | 10 August | UDA proscribed. |
| | 10 November | Final collapse of the Brooke-Mayhew inter-party talks. |
| | 25 November | General election, Republic of Ireland; abortion referendum. |

| **1993** | 12 January | Fianna Fáil-Labour coalition government formed in Dublin. |
| | 24 April | Hume–Adams statement on the future of Northern Ireland. |
| | 25 September | Hume–Adams agreement. |
| | 23 October | PIRA bomb a fish shop, Shankill Road, Belfast: 10 killed. |
| | 30 October | UFF attack on the Rising Sun bar, Greysteel, Co. Londonderry: seven killed. |
| | 20 November | Hume–Adams joint statement. |
| | 15 December | John Major and Albert Reynolds issue their Joint Declaration on Northern Ireland. |

| **1994** | 9 March | Select Committee on Northern Ireland Affairs established in the House of Commons. |
| | 2 June | RAF helicopter crashes, Mull of Kintyre: 25 British anti-terrorist experts killed. |
| | 18 June | UVF attack on The Heights bar, Loughinisland, Co. Down: six killed. |
| | 31 August | PIRA announces 'a complete cessation of hostilities'. |
| | 13 October | The Combined Loyalist Military Command announces that it will 'universally end all operational hostilities'. |
| | 16 November | Labour ministers resign from the Irish coalition government. |
| | 17 November | Resignation of Albert Reynolds as taoiseach. |
| | 19 November | Bertie Ahern elected leader of Fianna Fáil. |
| | 15 December | John Bruton is elected taoiseach at the head of a coalition government containing Fine Gael, Labour and Democratic Left. |

| **1995** | 22 February | Frameworks for the Future document published by the British and Irish governments. |
| | 9 July | The RUC prevent Orangemen from marching along the nationalist Garvaghy Road, Portadown, after a church service at Drumcree: a stand-off and loyalist violence ensues. |
| | 11 July | The Drumcree stand-off ends: 500 Orangemen, without bands, march down the Garvaghy Road. |
| | 28 August | James Molyneaux resigns from the Ulster Unionist leadership. |
| | 8 September | David Trimble elected as leader of the Ulster Unionists. |
| | 28 November | Launch of the twin-track British-Irish strategy to reactivate inter-party talks, and to establish an 'international body' to examine the decommissioning question. |
| | 30 November–1 December | President Clinton in Northern Ireland. |

| | | |
|---|---|---|
| **1996** | 9 February | Canary Wharf bomb, and the end of the IRA ceasefire. |
| | 28 February | British and Irish governments attempt to restart the talks process: all-party talks planned for 10 June. |
| | 30 May | Elections held for the Northern Ireland Forum. |
| | 10 June | Talks begin at Stormont. |
| | 14 June | First meeting of the Northern Ireland Forum. |
| | 7 July | Stand-off develops between Orangemen and police at Drumcree, County Armagh: loyalist violence escalates. |
| | 11 July | RUC backs down over the Drumcree march in the face of loyalist pressure: the banned march proceeds. |
| | 13 July | SDLP withdraws from the Forum. |
| **1997** | 5 March | Adjournment of the (stalled) multi-party talks. |
| | 1 May | General election, United Kingdom: Labour victory. |
| | 16 May | Tony Blair delivers a keynote, pro-union address in Belfast. |
| | 2 June | Alban Maginness (SDLP) is elected the first nationalist Lord Mayor of Belfast. |
| | 3 June | Multi-party talks resume at Stormont. |
| | 6 June | General election, Republic of Ireland: Fianna Fáil-Progressive Democrat coalition returned to power under Bertie Ahern. |
| | 19 July | The IRA announces a resumption of their ceasefire, offering 'a complete cessation of miitary operations'. |
| | 9 September | Sinn Féin joins the multi-party talks process. |
| | 15 September | All-party talks formally begin. |
| | 24 September | The international panel on decommissioning (headed by General de Chastelain) begins its work. |
| | 31 October | Mary McAleese elected president of Ireland. |
| | 10 December | A Sinn Féin delegation meets Tony Blair in Downing Street. |
| **1998** | 20 February | Temporary expulsion of Sinn Féin from talks process because of recent republican killings. |
| | 7 April | Tony Blair flies to Belfast in order to support the endangered talks process at Stormont. |
| | 10 April | The signing of the Good Friday Agreement. |
| | 11 April | The executive of the Ulster Unionist Party endorses the deal. |
| | 18 April | The Ulster Unionist Council endorses the Agreement. |
| | 6 May | Tony Blair and John Major jointly visit Belfast to support the Agreement. |
| | 10 May | Sinn Féin ard fheis endorses the Agreement. |
| | 22 May | Referenda in Northern Ireland and the Republic of Ireland: the Good Friday Agreement is endorsed by 71 per cent of the Northern Irish electorate. The Agreement and proposed changes to Articles 2 and 3 of the Irish Constitution are approved by 94 per cent of the Southern electorate. |
| | 3 June | Independent commission on policing in Northern Ireland named. |
| | 25 June | Elections to the Northern Ireland Assembly. |

| | |
|---|---|
| 12 July | Three Catholic brothers – Jason Quinn (aged 9), Mark (10) and Richard (11) are killed by a fire-bomb thrown into their home in Ballymoney, Co. Antrim. |
| 8 August | Last remaining loyalist belligerents, the LVF, announce ceasefire. |
| 15 August | The Omagh car-bomb: 29 people killed by dissident republicans in the Real IRA. |
| 22 August | INLA ceasefire announced. |
| 8 September | Real IRA ceasefire. |
| 16 October | John Hume and David Trimble awarded the Nobel Peace Prize. |

Adapted from the chronology in Alvin Jackson, *Ireland 1798–1998: Politics and War* (Oxford, 1999). Other sources: Paul Bew and Gordon Gillespie (eds), *Northern Ireland: A Chronology of the Troubles, 1968–1993* (Dublin, 1993); Paul Bew and Gordon Gillespie (eds), *The Northern Ireland Peace Process, 1993–1996: A Chronology* (London, 1996); J. E. Doherty and D. J. Hickey, *A Chronology of Irish History since 1500* (Dublin, 1989); T. W. Moody, F. X. Martin and F. J. Byrne (eds), *A New History of Ireland VIII: A Chronology of Irish History to 1976* (Oxford, 1982). I am grateful to Gordon Gillespie for permitting me to use material from his ongoing chronicle of Northern Ireland politics.

# SELECT BIBLIOGRAPHY

**Primary Sources**
*1. Individual Manuscript Sources*

H. H. Asquith (1st Earl of Oxford and Asquith) Papers, Bodleian Library, Oxford.
Clement Attlee (1st Earl Attlee) Papers, Bodleian Library, Oxford.
Arthur Balfour (1st Earl Balfour) Papers, British Library, London.
James Camlin Beckett Papers, Public Record Office of Northern Ireland, Belfast.
Roy Bradford Papers, Public Record Office of Northern Ireland, Belfast.
James Bryce (1st Viscount Bryce) Papers, Bodleian Library, Oxford.
Sir William Bull Papers, Churchill College, Cambridge.
Edward Carson (Lord Carson) Papers, Public Record Office of Northern Ireland, Belfast.
George Cave (1st Viscount Cave) Papers, British Library, Oxford.
Richard R. Cherry Papers, Public Record Office of Northern Ireland, Belfast.
George Anthony Clark Papers, Public Record Office of Northern Ireland.
James Craig (1st Viscount Craigavon) Papers, Public Record Office of Northern Ireland, Belfast.
Additional James Craig Papers, Public Record Office of Northern Ireland, Belfast (T/3775).
Frederick H. Crawford Papers, Public Record Office of Northern Ireland, Belfast.
Joseph Devlin Papers, Public Record Office of Northern Ireland.
Brian Faulkner (Lord Faulkner of Downpatrick) Papers, Public Record Office of Northern Ireland.
Richard Feetham Papers, Rhodes House Library, Oxford.
W. E. Gladstone Papers, British Library, London.
Edward Goulding (Lord Wargrave) Papers, House of Lords Record Office, London.
H. A. Gwynne Papers, Bodleian Library, Oxford.
Sir William Harcourt Papers, Bodleian Library, Oxford.
Jeremiah Jordan Papers, Public Record Office of Northern Ireland.
Sir James Kilfedder Papers, Public Record Office of Northern Ireland.
Edward King-Harman Papers, Public Record Office of Northern Ireland.
Andrew Bonar Law Papers, House of Lords Record Office, London.
Kennedy Lindsay Papers, Public Record Office of Northern Ireland.
David Lloyd George (1st Earl Lloyd George of Dwyfor) Papers, House of Lords Record Office, London.
Walter Long (1st Viscount Long) Papers, British Library, London, and Wiltshire Record Office, Trowbridge.

Antony MacDonnell (1st Baron MacDonnell of Swinford) Papers, Bodleian Library, Oxford.
Basil McIvor Papers, Public Record Office of Northern Ireland.
Sir Patrick Macrory Papers, Public Record Office of Northern Ireland.
St John Brodrick, Viscount Midleton (1st Earl of Midleton) Papers, Public Record Office, Kew.
Alfred Milner (1st Viscount Milner) Papers, Bodleian Library, Oxford.
John Morley (1st Viscount Morley of Blackburn) Papers, Bodleian Library, Oxford.
Gerard Benedict Newe Papers, Public Record Office of Northern Ireland.
John Pinkerton Papers, Public Record Office of Northern Ireland.
Sir Horace Plunkett Papers, consulted in the Plunkett House, Oxford.
John Redmond Papers, National Library of Ireland, Dublin.
Herbert Samuel (1st Viscount Samuel) Papers, House of Lords Record Office, London.
J. S. Sandars Papers, Bodleian Library, Oxford.
William Waldegrave Palmer (2nd Earl of Selborne) Papers, Bodleian Library, Oxford.
Wilfrid Spender Papers, Public Record Office of Northern Ireland.
Charles Stewart Vane-Tempest-Stewart (6th Marquess of Londonderry) Papers, Public Record Office of Northern Ireland.
Charles Stewart Henry Vane-Tempest-Stewart (7th Marquess of Londonderry) Papers, Public Record Office of Northern Ireland.
Theresa Vane-Tempest-Stewart (Marchioness of Londonderry) Papers, Public Record Office of Northern Ireland, Belfast.
John St Loe Strachey Papers, House of Lords Record Office, London.

## 2. Institutional Manuscript Sources

Anti-Partition League (Unionist) Papers, Public Record Office of Northern Ireland.
Cabinet Office Papers (Northern Ireland), Public Record Office of Northern Ireland.
Cabinet Papers (Great Britain), Public Record Office, Kew.
Campaign for Democracy in Ulster Papers, Public Record Office of Northern Ireland.
Defence Ministry Papers, Public Record Office, Kew.
Foreign and Commonwealth Office Papers, Public Record Office, Kew.
Home Office Papers, Public Record Office, Kew.
Home Rule League Papers, Public Record Office of Northern Ireland.
Northern Ireland Office Papers, Public Record Office, Kew (CJ series).
Prime Ministers' Papers, Public Record Office, Kew.
Ulster Unionist Council Papers, Public Record Office of Northern Ireland.

## 3. Government Printed Papers

The Agreement: Agreement Reached in the Multi-Party Negotiations (n.d., n.p.).
Cameron, Lord (et al.), Disturbances in Northern Ireland: Report of the Commission appointed by the Governor of Northern Ireland, Cmd. 532 (Belfast, 1969).
Electoral Law Act (Northern Ireland), 1962 [1962, Ch. 14].
Electoral Law Act (Northern Ireland), 1968 [1968, Ch. 20].
The Future of Northern Ireland: A Paper for Discussion (London, 1972).
Government of Ireland Act, 1920 [10 & 11 Geo.5, Ch. 67].
Hunt, John (Baron) (et al.), Report of the Advisory Committee on Police in Northern Ireland, Cmd. 535 (Belfast, 1969).

Isles, K. S., and Cuthbert, Norman, *An Economic Survey of Northern Ireland* (Belfast, 1957).

Kilbrandon, Lord (et al.), *Report of the Royal Commission on the Constitution, 1969–73*, Cmd. 5460 (London, 1973).

Macrory, Patrick A. (Chairman), *Review Body on Local Government in Northern Ireland, 1970*, Cmd. 546 (Belfast, 1970).

*Northern Ireland Constitutional Proposals*, Cmd. 5259 (London, 1973).

Plunkett, Sir Horace (et al.), *Report of the Proceedings of the Irish Convention, 1918*, Cd. 9019 (London, 1918).

*Royal Commission into the Circumstances Connected with the Landing of Arms at Howth on 26 July 1914*, Cd. 7631 (London, 1914).

*Royal Commission on the Rebellion in Ireland: Report of Commission*, Cd. 8279 (London, 1916).

*Royal Commission on the Rebellion in Ireland: Minutes of Evidence and Appendix of Documents*, Cd. 8311 (London, 1916).

Wilson, Thomas (et al.), *Economic Development in Northern Ireland: Including the Report of the Economic Consultant, Professor Thomas Wilson*, Cmd. 479 (Belfast, 1965).

## Other Printed Primary Sources

Æ (G. W. Russell), *The National Being: Some Thoughts on an Irish Policy* (Dublin, 1916).

Æ (G. W. Russell), *Thoughts for a Convention: Memorandum on the State of Ireland* (Dublin, 1917).

Amery, L.S ., *My Political Life*, 3 vols (London, 1953–5).

Bloomfield, Kenneth, *Stormont in Crisis: A Memoir* (Belfast, 1994).

Brassey, Earl, *The Case for Devolution and a Settlement of the Rule Question by Consent* (London, 1913).

Brock, Michael and Eleanor (eds), *H. H. Asquith: Letters to Venetia Stanley* (Oxford, 1982).

Butt, Isaac, *Home Government for Ireland, Irish Federalism: Its Meaning, Its Objectives and Its Hopes*, 3rd edn (Dublin, 1874).

Callaghan, James, *A House Divided: The Dilemma of Northern Ireland* (London, 1973).

Chamberlain, Austen, *Politics from Inside: An Epistolary Chronicle, 1906–14* (London, 1936).

Childers, Erskine, *The Framework of Home Rule* (London, 1911).

Crawford, Fred H., *Guns for Ulster* (Belfast, 1947).

Curtis, Sarah (ed.), *The Journals of Woodrow Wyatt*, paperback edition, vol. 1 (London, 1999).

Devlin, Paddy, *Straight Left: An Autobiography* (Belfast, 1993).

Dicey, A. V., *England's Case against Home Rule* (London, 1887).

Dicey, A. V., *A Leap in the Dark: A Criticism of the Principles of Home Rule as Illustrated by the Bill of 1893* (London, 1911).

Dicey, A. V., *A Fool's Paradise: Being a Constitutionalist's Criticisms of the Home Rule Bill of 1912* (London, 1913).

Dunraven, Lord, *The Legacy of Past Years: A Study of Irish History* (London, 1912).

Faulkner, Brian, *Memoirs of a Statesman* (London, 1978).

Ferguson, Lady, *Sir Samuel Ferguson and the Ireland of His Day*, 2 vols (London, 1896).

FitzGerald, Garret, *All in a Life: An Autobiography* (Dublin, 1992).

Gailey, Andrew (ed.), *Crying in the Wilderness: Jack Sayers, a Liberal Editor in Ulster* (Belfast, 1995).

Gwynn, Stephen (ed.), *What Home Rule Means* (Dublin, n.d. [c.1910]).

Gwynn, Stephen, *The Case for Home Rule* (Dublin, n.d. [c.1910]).

Gwynn, Stephen, *John Redmond's Last Years* (London, 1919).

Gwynn, Stephen (ed.), *The Anvil of War: Letters Between F. S. Oliver and His Brother, 1914–1918* (London, 1936).

Hayes, Maurice, *Minority Verdict: Experiences of a Catholic Public Servant* (Belfast, 1995).

Healy, T. M., *Letters and Leaders of My Day*, 2 vols (London, 1928).

Heath, Edward, *The Autobiography of Edward Heath: The Course of My Life* (London, 1998).

Hermon, Sir John, *Holding the Line: An Autobiography* (Dublin, 1997).

Howe, Geoffrey, *Conflict of Loyalty* (London, 1995).

Kettle, Laurence J. (ed.), *Material for Victory: The Memoirs of Andrew J. Kettle, Right Hand Man to Charles S. Parnell* (Dublin, 1958).

Kettle, T. M., *Home Rule Finance: An Experiment in Justice* (Dublin, 1911).

Lawson, Nigel, *The View from No. 11* (London, 1992).

McCarthy, Justin, and Mrs Campbell Praed, *Our Book of Memories* (London, 1912).

McCluskey, Conn, *Up off their Knees* (Galway, 1989).

Macdonagh, Michael, *The Home Rule Movement* (Dublin, 1920).

McIvor, Basil, *Hope Deferred: Experiences of an Irish Unionist* (Belfast, 1998).

MacKnight, Thomas, *Ulster as it is: Twenty-eight Years' Experience as an Irish Editor* (London, 1896).

McNeill, Ronald, *Ulster's Stand for Union* (London, 1922).

Major, John, *The Autobiography* (London, 1999).

Martin, F. X. (ed.), *The Irish Volunteers, 1913–1915: Recollections and Documents* (Dublin, 1963).

Mawhinney, Brian, *In the Firing Line: Politics, Faith, Power and Forgiveness* (London, 1999).

Midleton, Earl of, *Records and Reactions, 1856–1939* (London, 1939).

Mitchell, George, *Making Peace* (London, 1999).

Monypenny, W. F., *The Two Irish Nations: An Essay on Home Rule* (London, 1913).

Morgan, J. H. (ed.), *The New Irish Constitution: An Exposition and Some Arguments* (London, 1912).

Murray, Robert H., *Archbishop Bernard: Professor, Prelate and Provost* (London, 1931).

Needham, Richard, *Battling for Peace* (Belfast, 1998).

Neill, Ivan, *Church and State* (Dunmurry, 1995).

O'Brien, Conor Cruise, *Memoir: My Life and Times* (Dublin, 1998).

O'Brien, William, *Recollections* (London, 1905).

O'Brien, William, *An Olive Branch in Ireland and Its History* (London, 1910).

O'Brien, William, *The Downfall of Parliamentarianism: A Retrospect for the Accounting Day* (Dublin, 1918).

O'Connor, T. P., *Memoirs of an Old Parliamentarian*, 2 vols (London, 1929).

Oliver, F. S., *The Alternatives to Civil War* (London, 1913).

Oliver, F. S., *What Federalism is Not* (London, 1914).

Oliver, F. S., *Ireland and the Imperial Conference* (London, 1919).

Oliver, F. S., 'Ulster and a Federal Settlement' (private memorandum, 1918).

O'Neill, Terence, *Ulster at the Crossroads* (London, 1969).

O'Neill, Terence (Lord O'Neill of the Maine), *The Autobiography of Terence O'Neill: Prime Minister of Northern Ireland, 1963–1969* (London, 1972).

Pacificus (F. S. Oliver), *Federalism and Home Rule* (London, 1910).

Plunkett, Sir Horace, *Ireland in the New Century* (London, 1904).

Plunkett, Sir Horace, *Noblesse Oblige: An Irish Rendering* (Dublin, 1908).

Plunkett, Sir Horace, *A Better Way: A Plea to Ulster Not to Desert Ireland* (London, 1914).

Plunkett, Sir Horace, *A Defence of the Convention* (Dublin, 1917).

Plunkett, Sir Horace, *Home Rule and Conscription* (Dublin, 1918).

Plunkett, Sir Horace, *The Irish Convention: Confidential Report to H. M. the King by the Chairman* (n.p., 1918).

Porter, J. G. V., *Ireland* (Dublin, 1844).

Redmond, John, *The Home Rule Bill* (London, 1912).

Rees, Merlyn, *Northern Ireland: A Personal Perspective* (London, 1985).

Rosenbaum, S. (ed.), *Against Home Rule: The Case for the Union* (London, 1912).

Samuel, A. W., *Home Rule: What is it?* (Dublin, 1911).

Samuel, Herbert, *Irish Self-Government: A Speech Delivered by the Rt. Hon. Herbert L. Samuel (Postmaster General) at Belfast on Friday, 6 October 1911* (Belfast, 1911).

Selborne, Lord, and Oliver, F. S., 'Suggestions for the Better Government of the United Kingdom' (private memorandum, 1918).

Shaw, G. B., *How to Settle the Irish Question* (Dublin, 1917).

Shea, Patrick, *Voices and the Sound of Drums: An Irish Autobiography* (Belfast, 1981).

Sullivan, A. M., *Old Ireland: Reminiscences of an Irish KC* (London, 1928).

Sullivan, A. M., *The Last Serjeant: The Memoirs of Serjeant A. M. Sullivan, QC* (London, 1952).

Thatcher, Margaret, *The Downing Street Years* (London, 1993).

*Towards the Future: A Unionist Blueprint* (Belfast, 1972).

*Who's Who in Northern Ireland* (Belfast, 1938).

Wicks, Pembroke, *The Truth about Home Rule* (London, 1913).

## Secondary Sources

Adams, R. J. Q., *Bonar Law* (London, 1999).

Aughey, Arthur, *Under Siege: Ulster Unionism and the Anglo-Irish Agreement* (Belfast, 1989).

Barritt, Denis P., and Carter, Charles, *The Northern Ireland Problem: A Study in Group Relations* (Oxford, 1962).

Barton, Brian, *Brookeborough: The Making of a Prime Minister* (Belfast, 1988).

Beckett, Ian, 'A Note on Government Surveillance during the Curragh Incident, March 1914', *Intelligence and National Security*, 1, 3 (September 1983).

Beckett, Ian (ed.), *The Army and the Curragh Incident, 1914* (London, 1986).

Beckett, Ian, 'Some Further Correspondence Relating to the Curragh Incident of March 1914', *Journal of the Society for Army Historical Research*, lxix, 278 (Summer 1991).

Beckett, Ian, and Jeffery, Keith, 'The Royal Navy and the Curragh Incident', *Bulletin of the Institute of Historical Research*, 62, 147 (1989).

Bew, Paul, *Land and the National Question in Ireland, 1858–1882* (Dublin, 1979).

Bew, Paul, *C. S. Parnell* (Dublin, 1980).

Bew, Paul, *Conflict and Conciliation in Ireland, 1890–1910: Parnellites and Radical Agrarians* (Oxford, 1987).

Bew, Paul, *Ideology and the Irish Question: Ulster Unionism and Irish Nationalism, 1912–1916* (Oxford, 1994).

Bew, Paul, *John Redmond* (Dublin, 1996).

Bew, Paul, *The Parnell Lecture, 1996: Why Did the Northern Irish Peace Process Collapse?* (Cambridge, 1997).

Bew, Paul, Gibbon, Peter, and Patterson, Henry, *Northern Ireland, 1921–1994: Political Forces and Social Classes* (London, 1995).

Bew, Paul, Patterson, Henry, and Teague, Paul, *Northern Ireland: Between War and Peace: The Political Future of Northern Ireland* (London, 1997).

Birrell, Derek, and Murie, Alan, *Policy and Government in Northern Ireland: Lessons of Devolution* (Dublin, 1980).

Blake, Robert, *The Unknown Prime Minister: The Life and Times of Andrew Bonar Law, 1858–1923* (London, 1955).

Bogdanor, Vernon, *Devolution* (Oxford, 1979).

Bowman, John, *De Valera and the Ulster Question, 1917–1973* (Oxford, 1982).

Boyce, D. G., 'British Conservative Opinion, the Ulster Question, and the Partition of Ireland, 1912–21', *Irish Historical Studies*, 17 (1970).

Boyce, D. G., 'How to Settle the Irish Question: Lloyd George and Ireland, 1916–21' in A. J. P. Taylor (ed.), *Lloyd George: Twelve Essays* (London, 1971).

Boyce, D. G., 'British Opinion, Ireland and the War, 1916–18', *Historical Journal*, 17, 3 (1974).

Boyce, D. G. (ed.), *The Revolution in Ireland, 1879–1923* (London, 1988).

Boyce, D. G., *Nationalism in Ireland*, 2nd edn (London, 1991).

Boyce, D. G., and Hazlehurst, Cameron, 'The Unknown Chief Secretary: H. E. Duke and Ireland, 1916–18', *Irish Historical Studies*, 20, 79 (1977).

Boyce, D. G., and O'Day, Alan (eds), *Parnell in Perspective* (London, 1991).

Boyce, D. G., and O'Day, Alan (eds), *Defenders of the Union: A Survey of British and Irish Unionism since 1801* (London, 2000).

Boyce, D. G., and Stubbs, J. O., 'F. S. Oliver, Lord Selborne and Federalism', *Journal of Imperial and Commonwealth History*, 5, 1 (October 1976).

Brockington, William S., 'The Unionist Party and Irish Home Rule: Andrew Bonar Law and the Irish Home Rule Crisis, 1912–14', (Ph.D. thesis).

Bruce, Steve, *God Save Ulster! The Religion and Politics of Paisleyism* (Oxford, 1986).

Bruce, Steve, *The Red Hand: Protestant Paramilitaries in Northern Ireland* (Oxford, 1992).

Bruce, Steve, *The Edge of the Union: The Ulster Loyalist Political Vision* (Oxford, 1994).

Buckland, Patrick, *Irish Unionism I: The Anglo-Irish and the New Ireland, 1885–1922* (Dublin, 1972).

Buckland, Patrick, *Irish Unionism II: Ulster Unionism and the Origins of Northern Ireland, 1886–1922* (Dublin, 1973).

Buckland, Patrick, *The Factory of Grievances: Devolved Government in Northern Ireland, 1921–1939* (Dublin, 1979).

Buckland, Patrick, *A History of Northern Ireland* (Dublin, 1981).

Bull, Philip, *Land, Politics and Nationalism: A Study of the Irish Land Question* (Dublin, 1996).

Callanan, Frank, *T. M. Healy* (Cork, 1996).

Catterall, Peter, and McDougall, Sean (eds), *The Northern Ireland Question in British Politics* (London, 1996).

Chambers, Ian, 'Winston Churchill and Irish Home Rule, 1899–1914', *Parliamentary History*, 19, 3 (2000).

Chauvin, Guy, 'The Parliamentary Party and the Revolutionary Movement in Ireland, 1912–1918', Ph.D. thesis (Trinity College, Dublin, 1976).

Cochrane, Feargal, *Unionist Politics, and the Politics of Unionism since the Anglo-Irish Agreement* (Cork, 1997).

Collins, Peter (ed.), *Nationalism and Unionism: Conflict in Ireland, 1885–1921* (Belfast, 1994).

Collins, Stephen, *The Cosgrave Legacy* (Dublin, 1997).

Cox, Michael, Guelke, Adrian, and Stephen, Fiona (eds), *A Farewell to Arms? From 'Long War' to Long Peace in Northern Ireland* (Manchester, 2000).

Davis, Richard, *The Young Ireland Movement* (Dublin, 1987).

De Bréadún, Deaglán, *The Far Side of Revenge: Making Peace in Northern Ireland* (Cork, 2001).

Digby, Margaret, *Horace Plunkett: An Anglo-American Irishman* (Oxford, 1949).

Doyle, Eugene, *Justin McCarthy* (Dublin, 1996).

Dutton, David, *Austen Chamberlain: Gentleman in Politics* (Bolton, 1985).

Elliott, Marianne, *The Catholics of Ulster: A History* (London, 2000).

Elliott, Sydney, and Flackes, W. D., *Northern Ireland: A Political Directory, 1968–1999* (Belfast, 1999).

English, Richard, and Walker, Graham (eds), *Unionism in Modern Ireland: New Perspectives on Politics and Culture* (London, 1996).

Fair, John D., 'The King, the Constitution and Ulster: Interparty Negotiations of 1913 and 1914', *Éire-Ireland*, 6, 1 (spring 1971).

Fair, John D., *British Inter-party Conferences: A Study of the Procedure of Conciliation in British Politics, 1867–1921* (Oxford, 1980).

Fanning, Ronan, 'The Unionist Party and Ireland, 1906–10', *Irish Historical Studies*, 16, 58 (September 1966).

Fanning, Ronan, 'The Irish Policy of Asquith's Government and the Cabinet Crisis of 1910', in Art Cosgrove and Donal McCartney (eds), *Studies in Irish History Presented to R. Dudley Edwards* (Dublin, 1979).

Fanning, Ronan, 'Playing It Cool: The Response of the British and Irish Governments to the Crisis in Northern Ireland, 1968–9', *Irish Studies in International Affairs*, 12, (2001).

Ferguson, Niall (ed.), *Virtual History: Alternatives and Counterfactuals* (London, 1999).

Finlay, Richard J., *A Partnership for Good? Scottish Politics and the Union since 1800* (Edinburgh, 1997).

Fisk, Robert, *The Point of No Return* (London, 1975).

Fitzgerald, D. J. L., *History of the Irish Guards in the Second World War* (Aldershot, 1952).

Follis, Bryan, *A State under Siege: The Establishment of Northern Ireland, 1920–1925* (Oxford, 1995).

Foster, R. F., *Charles Stewart Parnell: The Man and His Family* (Brighton, 1976).

Garvin, Tom, *The Evolution of Irish Nationalist Politics* (Dublin, 1981).

Garvin, Tom, *Nationalist Revolutionaries in Ireland, 1858–1923* (Oxford, 1987).

Gilbert, Bentley Brinkerhoff, *David Lloyd George, A Political Life: Organiser of Victory, 1912–16* (London, 1992).

Gleeson, Ellen, 'The Campaign for Social Justice and the Demise of the Convention of Non-interference by the United Kingdom in the Affairs of Northern Ireland', BA dissertation (University College Dublin, 2001).

Gollin, A. M., *The Observer and J. L. Garvin, 1908–1914: A Study in a Great Editorship* (Oxford, 1960).

Gordon, David, *The O'Neill Years: Unionist Politics, 1963–69* (Belfast, 1989).

Grigg, John, *Lloyd George: From Peace to War, 1912–16* (London, 1985).

Gwynn, Denis, *The Life of John Redmond* (London, 1932).

Gywnn, Stephen, *John Redmond's Last Years* (London, 1919).

Hadfield, Brigid, *The Constitution of Northern Ireland* (Belfast, 1989).

Hadfield, Brigid (ed.), *Northern Ireland: Politics and the Constitution* (Buckingham, 1992).

Hamer, D. A., *Liberal Politics in the Age of Gladstone and Rosebery: A Study in Leadership and Policy* (Oxford, 1972).

Hand, Geoffrey J., 'The Parliament Contemplated by the Irish Home Rule Act of 1914', in *Studies Presented to the International Commission for the History of Representative and Parliamentary Institutions* (London, 1968).

Hennessey, Thomas, *A History of Northern Ireland, 1920–1996* (Dublin, 1997).

Hennessey, Thomas, *Dividing Ireland: World War One and Partition* (London, 1998).

Hennessey, Thomas, *The Northern Ireland Peace Process: Ending the Troubles?* (Dublin, 2000).

Hepburn, A. C., 'The Irish Council Bill and the Fall of Sir Antony MacDonnell', *Irish Historical Studies*, xvii, 68 (September 1971).

Hill, Jacqueline, *From Patriots to Unionists: Dublin Civic Politics and Irish Protestant Patriotism, 1660–1840* (Oxford, 1997).

Hume, David, *The Ulster Unionist Party, 1972–92: A Political Movement in an Era of Conflict and Change* (Belfast, 1996).

Hutchinson, John, *The Dynamics of Cultural Nationalism: The Gaelic Revival and the Creation of the Irish Nation State* (London, 1987).

Hyde, H. Montgomery, *Carson: The Life of Sir Edward Carson, Lord Carson of Duncairn* (London, 1953).

Jackson, Alvin, 'Irish Unionism and the Russellite Threat, 1894–1906', *Irish Historical Studies*, xxv, 100 (November 1987).

Jackson, Alvin, 'The Failure of Unionism in Dublin, 1900', *Irish Historical Studies*, xxvi, 104 (November 1989).

Jackson, Alvin, *The Ulster Party: Irish Unionists in the House of Commons, 1884–1911* (Oxford, 1989).

Jackson, Alvin, 'Unionist Politics and Protestant Society in Edwardian Ireland', *Historical Journal*, 33, 4 (1990).

Jackson, Alvin, 'Unionist Myths, 1912–1985', *Past & Present*, 136 (August 1992).

Jackson, Alvin, *Sir Edward Carson* (Dublin, 1993).

Jackson, Alvin, *Colonel Edward Saunderson: Land and Loyalty in Victorian Ireland* (Oxford, 1995).

Jackson, Alvin, *Ireland, 1798–1998: Politics and War* (Oxford, 1999).

Jackson, Alvin, 'The Irish Act of Union, 1801–2001', *History Today*, 51, 1 (January 2001).

Jackson, Alvin, 'Walter Hume Long, 1st Viscount Long of Wraxall', *New Dictionary of National Biography* (Oxford, forthcoming).

Jalland, Patricia, 'A Liberal Chief Secretary and the Irish Question: Augustine Birrell, 1907–1914', *Historical Journal*, 19, 2 (1976).

Jalland, Patricia, 'United Kingdom Devolution, 1910–14: Political Panacea or Tactical Diversion?', *English Historical Review*, 94, 373 (October 1979).

Jalland, Patricia, *The Liberals and Ireland: The Ulster Question in British Politics to 1914* (Brighton, 1980).

Jalland, Patricia, 'Irish Home Rule Finance: A Neglected Dimension of the Irish Question, 1910–14', *Irish Historical Studies*, 23, 91 (May 1983).

Jalland, Patricia, and Stubbs, John, 'The Irish Question after the Outbreak of War in 1914: Some Unfinished Party Business', *English Historical Review*, vol.96, no.381 (October 1981).

Jordan, Donald E., *Land and Popular Politics in Ireland: County Mayo from the Plantation to the Land War* (Cambridge, 1994).

Kelly, Henry, *How Stormont Fell* (Dublin, 1972).

Kelly, James, 'The Origins of the Act of Union: An Examination of Unionist Opinion in Britain and Ireland, 1650–1800', *Irish Historical Studies*, 99 (1987).

Kendle, John, 'The Round Table Movement and "Home Rule All Round"', *Historical Journal*, 9, 2 (July 1968).

Kendle, John, 'Federalism and the Irish Problem in 1918', *History*, 56 (1971).

Kendle, John, *The Round Table Movement and Imperial Union* (Toronto, 1975).

Kendle, John, *Ireland and the Federal Solution: The Debate over the United Kingdom Constitution, 1870–1921* (Kingston and Montreal, 1989).

Kendle, John, *Walter Long, Ireland and the Union, 1905–20* (Dublin, 1992).

Kennedy, B. A., 'Sharman Crawford's Federal Scheme for Ireland', in H. A. Cronne, T. W. Moody and D. B. Quinn (eds), *Essays in British and Irish History in Honour of James Eadie Todd* (London, 1949).

Laffan, Michael, *The Partition of Ireland, 1911–25* (Dundalk, 1983).

Laffan, Michael, *The Resurrection of Ireland: The Sinn Féin Party, 1916–23* (Cambridge, 1999).

Lawlor, Sheila, *Britain and Ireland, 1914–23* (Dublin, 1983).

Lawrence, R. J., *The Government of Northern Ireland: Public Finance and Public Services, 1921–64* (Oxford, 1965).

Leersen, J. T., *Mere Irish and Fior-Ghael: Studies in the Idea of Irish Nationality, its Development and Literary Expression Prior to the Nineteenth Century* (Amsterdam and Philadelphia, 1986).

Loughlin, James, *Gladstone, Home Rule and the Ulster Question, 1882–1893* (Dublin, 1986).

Lubenow, W. C., *Parliamentary Politics and the Home Rule Crisis: The British House of Commons in 1886* (Oxford, 1988).

Lynn, Brendan, *Holding the Ground: The Nationalist Party in Northern Ireland, 1945–72* (Aldershot, 1997).

Lyons, F. S. L., *The Irish Parliamentary Party, 1890–1910* (London, 1951).

Lyons, F. S. L., *John Dillon: A Biography* (London, 1968).

Lyons, F. S. L., *Charles Stewart Parnell* (London, 1977).

McAllister, Ian, *The Northern Ireland Social Democratic and Labour Party: Political Opposition in a Divided Society* (London, 1977).

McBride, Lawrence, *The Greening of Dublin Castle: The Transformation of Bureaucratic and Judicial Personnel in Ireland, 1892–1922* (Washington, 1991).

McCartney, Donal (ed.), *Parnell: The Politics of Power* (Dublin, 1991).

MacDonagh, Michael, *The Home Rule Movement* (Dublin, 1920).

McDonald, Henry, *Trimble* (London, 2000).

McDowell, R. B., *The Irish Convention, 1917–18* (London, 1970).

McGarry, John, and O'Leary, Brendan, *Explaining Northern Ireland: Broken Images* (Oxford, 1995).

McKittrick, David, Kelters, Seamus, Feeney, Brian, and Thornton, Chris, *Lost Lives: The*

*Stories of the Men, Women and Children who died as a Result of the Northern Ireland Troubles* (Edinburgh and London, 1999).

McMahon, Deirdre, *Republicans and Imperialists: Anglo-Irish Relations in the 1930s* (New Haven, 1984).

Mallie, Eamon, and McKittrick, David, *The Fight for Peace: The Secret Story behind the Irish Peace Process* (London, 1996).

Manning, Maurice, *James Dillon: A Biography* (Dublin, 1999).

Mansergh, Nicholas, *The Government of Northern Ireland: A Study in Devolution* (London, 1936).

Mansergh, Nicholas, *The Unresolved Question: The Anglo–Irish Settlement and its Undoing, 1912–72* (New Haven and London, 1991).

Matthews, Kevin, 'Stanley Baldwin's "Irish Question"', *Historical Journal*, 43, 4 (2000).

Maume, Patrick, *The Long Gestation: Irish Nationalist Life, 1891–1918* (Dublin, 1999).

Moloney, Ed, *A Secret History of the IRA* (London, 2002).

Morgan, K. O., *Rebirth of a Nation: Wales, 1880–1980* (Oxford, 1982).

Muenger, Elizabeth, *The British Military Dilemma in Ireland: Occupation Politics, 1886–1914* (Dublin, 1991).

Mulholland, Marc, *Northern Ireland at the Crossroads: Ulster Unionism in the O'Neill Years, 1960–9* (London, 2000).

Mulholland, Marc, *The Longest War: Northern Ireland's Troubled History* (Oxford, 2002).

Murphy, Richard, 'Faction in the Conservative Party and the Home Rule Crisis, 1912–14', *History* (1986).

Murphy, Richard, 'Walter Long and the Making of the Government of Ireland Act, 1919–20', *Irish Historical Studies*, xxv, 97 (May 1986).

Murray, Gerard, *John Hume and the SDLP: Impact and Survival in Northern Ireland* (Dublin, 1998).

Neill, D. G. (ed.), *Devolution of Government: The Experiment in Northern Ireland* (London, 1953).

O'Brien, Conor Cruise, *Parnell and his Party, 1880–90* (Oxford, 1957).

O'Callaghan, Margaret, 'The Boundary Commission of 1925 and the Copperfastening of the Irish Border', *Bullán* (Spring 2000).

O'Day, Alan, *The English Face of Irish Nationalism: Parnellite Involvement in British Politics, 1880–86* (Dublin, 1977).

O'Day, Alan, *Parnell and the First Home Rule Episode, 1884–87* (Dublin, 1986).

O'Day, Alan, *Irish Home Rule, 1867–1921* (Manchester, 1998).

O'Day, Alan, *Charles Stewart Parnell* (Dublin, 1998).

O'Halpin, Eunan, *The Decline of the Union: British Government in Ireland, 1892–1920* (Dublin, 1987).

O'Leary, Brendan, and McGarry, John, *The Politics of Antagonism: Understanding Northern Ireland* (London, 1993).

Paseta, Senia, *Before the Revolution: Nationalism, Social Change and Ireland's Catholic Elite, 1879–1922* (Cork, 1999).

Patterson, Henry, 'Party versus Order: Ulster Unionism and the Flags and Emblems Act', *Contemporary British History*, 13, 4 (winter 1999).

Pearce, Edward, *Lines of Most Resistance: The Lords, the Tories and Ireland, 1886–1914* (London, 1999).

Peatling, G. K., 'The Last Defence of the Union? The Round Table and Ireland, 1910–25', in A. Bosco and A. May (eds), *The Round Table, The Empire/Commonwealth and British Foreign Policy* (London, 1997).

Peatling, G. K., 'New Liberalism, J.L. Hammond and the Irish Question, 1897–1949', *Historical Research*, lxxiii (2000).

Peatling, G. K., *British Opinion and Irish Self-government, 1865–1925: From Unionism to Liberal Commonwealth* (Dublin, 2001).

Phoenix, Eamon, *Northern Nationalism: Nationalist Politics, Partition and the Catholic Minority in Northern Ireland, 1890–1940* (Belfast, 1994).

Purdie, Bob, *Politics in the Streets: The Origins of the Civil Rights Movement in Northern Ireland* (Belfast, 1990).

Purdy, Ann, *Molyneaux: The Long View* (Antrim, 1989).

Quinn, Dermot, *Understanding Northern Ireland* (Manchester, 1993).

Rafferty, Oliver, *Catholicism in Ulster, 1603–1983: An Interpretative History* (Dublin, 1994).

Roberts, Andrew, *Salisbury: Victorian Titan* (London, 1999).

Rodner, W. S., 'Leaguers, Covenanters, Moderates: British Support for Ulster, 1913–14', *Eire-Ireland*, 17, 3 (1982).

Rodner, W. S., 'Conservatism, Resistance and Lord Hugh Cecil', *History of Political Thought*, 9, 3 (winter 1988).

Rose, Richard, *Governing without Consensus: An Irish Perspective* (London, 1971).

Rose, Richard, *Northern Ireland: A Time of Choice* (London, 1976).

Savage, David, 'The Attempted Home Rule Settlement of 1916', *Éire-Ireland*, 2, 3 (autumn 1967).

Scoular, Clive, *James Chichester-Clark: Prime Minister of Northern Ireland* (Killyleagh, 2000).

Shannon, Catherine B., *Arthur J. Balfour and Ireland, 1874–1922* (Washington, 1988).

Shannon, Richard, *Gladstone: Heroic Minister, 1865–1898* (London, 1999).

Sharrock, David, and Devenport, Mark, *Man of War, Man of Peace: The Unauthorised Biography of Gerry Adams* (London, 1997).

Smith, Jeremy, 'Bluff, Bluster and Brinkmanship: Andrew Bonar Law and the Third Home Rule Bill', *Historical Journal*, 36, 1 (1993).

Smith, Jeremy, *The Tories and Ireland, 1910–1914: Conservative Party Politics and the Home Rule Crisis* (Dublin, 2002).

Smyth, Jim, 'Anglo-Irish Unionist Discourse, c.1656–1707: From Harrington to Fletcher', *Bullán*, 2, 1 (summer 1995).

Spence, Joseph, 'Isaac Butt, Nationality and Irish Toryism, 1833–1852', *Bullán*, 2, 1 (summer 1995).

Steele, David, *Lord Salisbury: A Political Biography* (London, 1999).

Stewart, A. T. Q., *The Ulster Crisis* (London, 1967).

Stubbs, John O., 'The Unionists and Ireland, 1914–18', *Historical Journal*, 33, 3 (1990) .

Thornley, David, *Isaac Butt and Home Rule* (London, 1964).

Turner, John, *British Politics and the Great War: Coalition and Conflict, 1915–18* (New Haven, 1992).

Walker, Graham, *The Politics of Frustration: Harry Midgley and the Failure of Labour in Northern Ireland* (Manchester, 1985).

Walsh, Pat, *From Civil Rights to National War: Northern Ireland Catholic Politics, 1964–1974* (Belfast, 1989).

Ward, Alan, *The Irish Constitutional Tradition: Responsible Government and Modern Ireland, 1782–1992* (Dublin, 1992).

West, Trevor, *Horace Plunkett, Cooperation and Politics: An Irish Biography* (Gerrard's Cross, 1986).

Wheatley, Michael, 'John Redmond and Federalism in 1910', *Irish Historical Studies*, xxxii, 127 (May 2001).

Whyte, John, 'How much Discrimination was there under the Unionist Regime, 1921–68', in Tom Gallagher and James O'Connell (eds), *Contemporary Irish Studies* (Manchester, 1983).

Whyte, John, *Interpreting Northern Ireland* (Oxford, 1990).

Wichert, Sabine, *Northern Ireland since 1945*, 2nd edn (London, 1999).

Wilford, Rick (ed.), *Aspects of the Belfast Agreement* (Oxford, 2001).

Wilson, Thomas (ed.), *Ulster under Home Rule: A Study of the Political and Economic Problems of Northern Ireland* (Oxford, 1955).

Wilson, Thomas, *Ulster: Conflict and Consent* (Oxford, 1989).

# INDEX